Warships of the Civil War Navies

PAUL H. SILVERSTONE

WARSHIPS OF THE CIVIL WAR NAVIES

NAVAL INSTITUTE PRESS

ANNAPOLIS, MARYLAND

Library of Congress Cataloging-in-Publication Data

Silverstone, Paul H.
    Warships of the Civil War navies / by Paul H. Silverstone.
        p.   cm.
    Bibliography: p.
    Includes index.
    ISBN 0-87021-783-6
    1. United States. Navy—Lists of vessels.   2. United States.
Navy—History—Civil War, 1861–1865.   3. Confederate States of
America. Navy—Lists of vessels.   4. Confederate States of America.
Navy—History.   5. Warships—United States.   6. Warships—
Confederate States of America. I. Title.
VA61.S573   1989
359.3′2′0973—dc20   89-3341
                                                                            CIP

Designed by Moira M. Megargee

Printed in the United States of America

9 8 7 6 5 4 3 2

First printing

A special word of thanks to
Martin E. Holbrook
who helped initiate this project, and whose
knowledge and assistance in locating,
identifying, and selecting many of the
photographs used in this book has been of
inestimable help.

CONTENTS

INTRODUCTION

As the drums of war sounded in North America in 1861, a great technological change was taking place in the realm of naval warfare. The introduction of the armored warship was only one aspect of this revolution at sea. Steam was well on its way to supplanting sail as the motive power for ships, and the first armored warships were already at sea. Larger and more powerful cannons were being developed using shells instead of solid shot. These developments changed not only the outward appearance of ships but also their capabilities and use as well as tactics at sea.

The United States Navy grew in size with the onset of war and continued to expand throughout the conflict. Prior to 1861 the duties of the navy were restricted to protecting American interests abroad, a task that was handled by the forty-two ships in commission in March. Now it was called upon to provide ships to blockade the entire coast of the southern states from Hampton Roads to the Rio Grande as well as to protect American shipping abroad from Confederate commerce destroyers. It quickly became apparent that the strength of the navy was totally inadequate for the new and varied duties imposed by the war.

The navy suffered its first losses with the withdrawal of many experienced southern naval officers and the loss of valuable ships, equipment, and facilities at its largest navy yard at Norfolk. Gideon Welles was appointed secretary of the navy by President Lincoln.

The United States Navy was the possessor of some fine new propeller-driven warships, such as the frigates of the *Merrimack* class and the *Lancaster*-class sloops which, although having machinery problems, were greatly admired in naval circles.

Many vessels were required to enforce the blockade. Southern privateers and later raiders started to make war on American commerce on the high seas, and fast ships with high endurance were needed to protect merchant ships abroad.

As war loomed, many new ships were ordered, including such revolutionary designs as the ironclad vessels *Monitor* and *New Ironsides*. Whole classes of new sloops and monitors were built; 90-day gun boats, double-enders, and others rapidly enlarged the fleet. Numerous merchant vessels were requisitioned for use in the blockade to cover the long coastline and the major southern ports. To our eyes these quaint-looking vessels seem quite inadequate to have performed the arduous tasks they were assigned, yet they gave good service and won the day for the Union.

In addition, a fleet was created to fight on and take control of the inland rivers, such as the Mississippi, the Cumberland, and the Tennessee. Here, too, ironclad ships were built and others converted; the strange shapes of these vessels belied their deadly strength. Initially it was the army that built and converted river steamers to fighting vessels, but the navy soon inherited this fleet, to which were added many sternwheel river steamers, lightly armored and fitted with guns to become known as tinclads.

By 1863 the navy had seized control of the major waterways. Using the rivers as highways into the interior of the South, the navy and army cooperated in expeditions and campaigns up the rivers, culminating in the capture of Vicksburg. The other major expedition was the Red River Campaign of 1864.

The Confederate Navy obviously did not exist and had to make do with makeshift designs and conversions. Greatly hampered by lack of industrial capacity, it was unable to match the shipbuilding program of the North and tried by various devices to raise a fleet. Of great interest were the several ships built and purchased in Great Britain and France, only a few of which ever sailed under the Confederate flag. Some, however, such as the *Alabama* and *Shenandoah*, were responsible for a great deal of activity by the Union navy and many celebrated incidents of the war.

The expansion of the United States Navy during the war was great. Construction of over 200 vessels was started, and 418 vessels were purchased. A roster of 7,600 men in service in 1861 increased to over 51,000 in 1865.

The blockade of southern ports ordered by President Lincoln in

1861 required a huge investment in resources of ships and men. Endless hours lengthened into days and months and years for the blockaders patrolling off the major ports, such as Charleston and Wilmington.

In September 1861, the fleet was divided into four major commands. The Atlantic coast from Virginia to Key West was covered by the North and South Atlantic Blockading Squadrons. The East and West Gulf Blockading Squadrons covered the Gulf of Mexico coast from Key West to Brownsville, Texas. The success of the blockade can be seen by the numbers of ships captured and destroyed as reported in the Annual Report of the Secretary of the Navy for 1865.

	Captured	*Destroyed*
Steamers	210	85
Schooners	569	114
Sloops	139	32
Ships	13	2
Brigs	29	2
Barks	25	4
Yachts	2	—
Small boats	139	96
Rams	6	5
Gunboats	10	11
Others	7	—
Total	1,149	351

The demobilization of the navy swiftly followed the end of hostilities. Most of the purchased vessels and many of those built by the navy were sold out of service by 1869, including practically all the river steamers. The merchant vessels had inferior machinery unsuitable for warships and went quickly. The Potomac Flotilla was disbanded on July 31 and the Mississippi Squadron on 14 August, 1865. At the end of June 1865 the North and South Atlantic Squadrons were merged as were the East and West Gulf Squadrons. The navy went back to its peacetime dispositions with squadrons in Europe, the Far East, and South America.

The purpose of this book is to provide a single comprehensive source of definitive information on Civil War navy vessels with ships' details and brief war records. Despite the intense and continuing interest in the Civil War, the naval vessels of that conflict have not been as well described as those of other eras.

A major problem is that despite the variety of sources, there is much conflicting information. Systems of measuring ships, both tonnage and dimensions, varied so that the numbers given differ from source to source. One has no assurance that these figures are right or wrong or are only reporting different measurements. Some judgment has been required to choose which of these various measurements should be used.

Similarly, it has been difficult to identify some acquired ships as to their prior identity, name of builder, or even date of construction. This is particularly true of the Confederate ships, for which records are few and sparse or even nonexistent.

In the matter of pictures, Martin Holbrook and I have tried to illustrate the book with photographs only. For this period in which photography was still in its infancy, surprising gaps appear and some famous ships are unavailable in photographs. For instance, although images are known of the crew of the *Alabama* taken in South Africa, no photograph of the famous ship has yet been found. The *Merrimack*, later *Virginia*, it appears, was never photographed either before or after her conversion. Nevertheless, search has been crowned with success in finding photographs of some ships of which no photograph was previously known. In a few cases we have been forced to use contemporary drawings to depict a ship's appearance.

Appreciation is extended to the following for assistance in obtaining information and photographs: William Gladstone, Ian Grant, Charles R. Haberlein, Rowan M. B. H. Hackman, Charles Lawesson, Rear Admiral Lauren S. McCready, Dr. Charles Peery, and William Rau.

EXPLANATION OF DATA

In order to make it easier to use this book and to identify the Navy's ships, the various types of vessels have been divided into categories based on mode of propulsion and size, as well as duties.

Navy-built ships are listed first, followed by those merchant ships acquired during the war for temporary service. The categories are arbitrary, and some may disagree with the placement of any particular ship. Each category is subdivided into separate sections for side-wheel and propeller steamers, which, it is felt, will be helpful to the reader, as is separating steam and sailing ships.

The larger acquired vessels were used as distant blockaders and as cruisers to search for Confederate raiders. Medium-sized ships acted as close blockaders, while the smaller vessels operated in coastal waters and the rivers and inlets of the southern Atlantic coast. As a distinct type, the former ferryboats are listed in one section. Ships that served principally in service roles are listed as auxiliaries in a separate section, as are tugs. The ships of the inland navy are listed in another section, navy-built vessels first, followed by those acquired and armed.

For Confederate ships the task is much more difficult, inasmuch as much information and many records are lacking. The Confederate Navy was not able to operate as a unified force, and ships, except in unusual cases, did not move from one area to another. The bulk of the ships are therefore listed geographically by area of operation. To help the reader, exception is made to this order by listing some ships together as distinct types, such as armored vessels, ocean cruisers, torpedo boats, and government-operated blockade runners rather than by their areas of operation. Most blockade runners were privately owned and therefore are not within the scope of this work; their listing must await another book.

The Confederate section is necessarily sparse as to information, both in the particulars and the service records of ships. Many ships turn up in the records only once or on a few occasions and then disappear. Often the vessel's antecedents or later history are unclear or unknown.

Because many Confederate ships remained in their own local area, sections are provided for each locality. These are: Louisiana, Texas, the Gulf Coast (Alabama, Mississippi, and the west coast of Florida), the Atlantic Coast (North and South Carolina, Georgia, and the east coast of Florida), Virginia, and inland rivers.

In many cases, for both North and South and particularly with regard to acquired vessels, it has proved difficult to obtain details. Authoritative sources often differ as to such details; these variations may occur as a result of differences in methods of measurement. Reputable sources, as often as not, do not agree. Too often, basic information has been found lacking altogether.

Particulars are given for each ship as follows: For certain types of ships, such as sailing vessels and lesser Confederate vessels, these are given in a single line without explanation.

Name: Navy name as launched, with former names given below. Further changes of name, if any, are indicated in the Service Record with new navy names in *bold* type.

Builder: Name of the builder of the hull followed by the maker of the machinery in parentheses. If hull and machinery were built by the same firm, the builder's name is followed by (bldr). If the builder's name is not known, the place of construction appears in parentheses, followed by the maker of the machinery in other parentheses, if known.

Construction Dates: For navy-built ships dates given are for laying down of keel, launching, and commissioning. For acquired vessels, dates given are date of launching, acquisition by navy, and commissioning.

Tonnage: This figure is taken from various sources, many of which do not explain what formula of measurement was used. A merchant ship's measurement was usually expressed in "tons burden," a measurement of the carrying capacity of the ship, giving little guide to its size, and the rules for calculating this measurement varied widely. In 1864 a new uniform system of measurement was started that led to a more accurate figure and could serve as a better guide to relative size.

D = displacement, B = tons burden (old measurement), n/r = new measurement 1864, GRT = British gross registered tonnage.

Dimensions: Standard dimensions given in feet and inches are length × beam × draft (or depth of hull, prefixed with "d").

Here, too, figures varied widely and were often published without explanation of the measurement method. Where known, length is specified as (oa) overall, (bp) between foreside of stem and aftside of rudder post, (dk) on deck, & (wl) on the waterline. On occasion an authoritative source has given a measurement of length without specific explanation. To guide the user of this book as to a possible discrepancy, it has been felt useful to provide this information followed by empty parentheses (). Where used with beam, (oa) refers to width, including the paddle boxes.

Machinery: Showing the mode of propulsion, propeller (screw) or side/stern wheels, number, type, and size of engines and number of boilers where known, horsepower and speed. Occasionally no indication as to type has been found, and none is given. Propeller-driven ships generally, but not always, had direct-acting engines, while side wheelers had beam engines. The diameter of the cylinder(s) and the length of the stroke of the piston are shown in feet and inches following the type of engine, thus (50″ × 2′). The symbol # indicates a disagreement in sources as to the mode of propulsion, particularly whether a river steamer had stern or side wheels.

Complement: Normal figure for officers and crew. For many ships, where sources vary, a range (50/75) is given.

Armament: Original number and type of guns is given first. Later significant changes made during the war are given with date, either by listing the entire complement of guns (total), or by indicating modifications as additions, subtractions or replacements to the previous armament shown. The date reflects the date of survey rather than when changes were actually made. Minor variations are not necessarily given. Guns were described by caliber (inches) or weight (pdr/pounder) of projectile. R = muzzle-loading rifle, SB = smoothbore, H = howitzer, M = mortar. The entry 4 32-pdr/42 refers to four smoothbore guns of 42 cwt, a reference to the size of the cannon, firing 32-pound projectiles.

Armor: (Armored vessels only) Maximum or a range of thickness of the armor only is given.

Notes: Additional information pertaining to design, construction, or later modifications, acquisition or earlier historical notes of interest, not included in other categories.

Service Record: A capsule history of each ship's naval service, showing assignment by station or squadron and war service, including participation in engagements, major damage to vessel, or loss. Changes in navy names are given here. Also, final disposition by the navy, loss, sale, or transfer to another agency.

Prizes: Names and dates of ships captured or sunk, principally blockade runners for USN ships. Some prizes were credited to several ships acting together and so appear more than once. Ships named are sailing vessels unless indicated as steamers ("str"). Those ships destroyed are marked *.

Later History: Brief details of the ship's career after leaving naval service, including later merchant names, service in other government departments, or in foreign navies. Ultimate fate is given where known, or the year the ship disappeared from shipping registers (RR) or was sold to foreign buyers. Occasionally a date is given for the last published reference (SE = still existing).

ABBREVIATIONS

*	destroyed (as to prizes taken)
#	sources disagree as to type of propulsion
B	burden (tonnage) (old measurement)
bldr	builder
BLR	breach-loading rifle
bp	length between perpendiculars
BU	broken up
comm	commissioned
CSN	Confederate States Navy
CSS	Confederate States Ship
D	displacement (tonnage)
decomm	decommissioned
dk	length on deck
EGulfBS	East Gulf Blockading Squadron
FFU	further fate unknown
GRT	gross registered tonnage (British)
H	howitzer
HP	horsepower
IHP	indicated horsepower
L	launched
M	mortar
mph	miles per hour
NAtlBS	North Atlantic Blockading Squadron
NHP	normal horsepower
n/r	new register (tonnage) (1864 rules)
NYd	Navy Yard
oa	length overall
R	muzzle-loading rifle
recomm	recommissioned
RR	removed from shipping registers
SAtlBS	South Atlantic Blockading Squadron
SB	smoothbore gun
SE	still existing
sqn	squadron
stn	station
str	steamer
(U)	unknown
USAT	United States Army Transport
USCS	United States Coast Survey
USRC	United States Revenue Cutter
USLHS	United States Light House Service
USS	United States Ship
WGF	Western Gunboat Flotilla
WGulfBS	West Gulf Blockading Squadron
wl	length on waterline

Warships of the Civil War Navies

PART I
U.S. Navy Warships

Overleaf: The monitors *Miantonomoh* and *Terror* at Portland, Maine, January 1870. Their flags are at half-mast for the arrival of the funeral fleet carrying the body of George M. Peabody, the noted merchant and philanthropist. (Peabody Museum of Salem)

Right: The start of the famous competition held in New York harbor on 13 February 1866 to test the respective merits of the engines of the double-enders *Winooski* and *Algonquin*. The *Winooski*, whose engines were designed by Chief Engineer Benjamin F. Isherwood, was the undoubted winner. E. N. Dickerson, the designer of *Algonquin*'s engines, also designed those of the *Pensacola* and *Idaho*. The navy board then condemned the *Algonquin* as "totally unfit for naval service." (U.S. Naval Historical Center)

ARMORED VESSELS

By 1861, the first ironclad warships had been developed in France and Britain; the *Gloire* and *Warrior* were already afloat. Earlier, Robert L. Stevens had started construction of his giant unnamed ironclad warship, known to history as the *Stevens Battery*. This revolutionary design was modified from time to time, but the navy refused further funds to complete this vessel and it was never finished.

The navy ordered construction of three experimental ironclads of radically different design in 1861. The first of these revolutionized naval warfare. A low-draft ship without superstructure or rigging, it had only a revolving turret on a flush deck and was aptly described as "the cheesebox on a raft." Designed by John Ericsson and named *Monitor*, it presented a very small target area by eliminating all tophamper and having an extremely low freeboard. The ship was built extremely quickly, being launched within 101 days of the keel laying.

Following the *Monitor*'s stunning success in standing off the Confederate *Virginia* at Hampton Roads in March 1862, the navy ordered many additional vessels of this type. The *Passaic* and *Canonicus* classes were basically modified repeat *Monitor*s. Ericsson also designed the larger *Dictator* and the twin-turreted *Puritan*.

Other twin-turret monitors, *Onondaga* and the four near sisters of the *Miantonomoh* class, were designed by others. Construction of the larger oceangoing *Kalamazoo* class was suspended at the end of the war and never resumed, as was the similar-sized *Puritan*. Many of these ships were built with poorly seasoned timber that quickly deteriorated.

The *Puritan* and the four *Miantonomoh*-class ships remained on the Navy List for many years by the subterfuge of "repairing" the old hulls while actually building new ones. As appropriations did not cover the cost of new monitors, old ships were turned over to the contractors as payment.

Not all the monitor designs were successful. A need for low-draft monitors for river operations led to the disastrous *Casco* class of 20 ships. Because of poor planning and erroneous calculations, they floated with their decks barely above water before fitting the turrets and other heavy gear. A few served as torpedo boats without turrets, but most were never used, and all were scrapped within about ten years.

The second experimental ironclad ordered in 1861, the *New Ironsides*, was a more conventional armored broadside vessel. Speed was not considered important for the ship, but she suffered practically no damage from enemy fire although hit numerous times. The third vessel was the smaller *Galena*, whose armor proved inadequate against shore batteries and she was quickly converted to an unarmored corvette.

Another curious vessel produced at this time was the *Keokuk*, whose defense against shellfire was so poor that she sank the day after her first day under fire. The monster ironclad ram *Dunderberg*, a broadside vessel similar in design to the Confederate ironclads, was so delayed in construction that she was rejected by the navy in 1865 and eventually sold to France. The screw frigate *Roanoke* was cut down to the gun deck, armored, and three turrets were mounted on the low hull. The conversion was not successful, as the weight of the turrets was too great for the wooden hull.

Of all the new designs, only the monitors seemed to be successful. At Charleston they proved their worth against land batteries; at Mobile Bay they led the fleet into battle. After the war they were laid up and kept as America's ace against foreign attack. Never the equal of foreign oceangoing ironclad warships, their continued existence led to a sense of false security. Some were recommissioned during the 1873 war scare caused by the *Virginius* Affair, and in 1898 those remaining were again commissioned to defend the East Coast against the threat of the Spanish fleet.

Despite many attempts to provide for modern warships, Congress remembered their successes decades earlier and preferred to rely on the inadequate and obsolete monitors. When the first true American battleships were built, the *Indiana* class of 1890, they were described as coast defense battleships and had a monitor-like low freeboard.

On deck on the *Monitor*, July 1862. Notice dents in the turret from hits sustained during her epic fight with the *Virginia*. No full-length views of this ship exist.

MONITORS

MONITOR

Name	Bldr	Laid down	L	Comm
Monitor	Continental (Delamater)	25 Oct 1861	30 Jan 1862	25 Feb 1862

Tonnage:	987 tons D; 776 tons B
Dimensions:	179′ (oa) × 41′6″ × 10′6″
Machinery:	1 screw, 2 Ericsson vibrating-lever engines (36″ × 2′2″); IHP 320 = 9 knots
Complement:	49
Armament:	2 11″ SB guns
Armor:	8″ turret, 4.5″ sides, 2″ deck, 9″ pilothouse

NOTES: The first ironclad warship built without rigging or sails. One of three experimental ironclads ordered in 1861. Designed by John Ericsson. Spindle-type turret built by Novelty Iron Works on iron hull (126′ × 34′) with overhanging armored deck. Hurried to completion and towed to Hampton Roads with workmen still on board.
SERVICE RECORD: Engaged CSS *Virginia* at Hampton Roads in first action between ironclads, Battle of Hampton Roads, Va., 9 Mar 1862. Engaged battery at Sewells Point, Va., 8 May and at Drewry's Bluff, Va., 15 May 1862. Engagement with CSS *Teaser* in James River, Va., 4 Jul 1862. Foundered in gale off Cape Hatteras while under tow of USS *Rhode Island*, 31 Dec 1862.

ROANOKE

Name	Converted by	L	Recommissioned
Roanoke	Novelty	13 Dec 1855	29 Jun 1863

Tonnage:	6,300 tons
Dimensions:	278′ (oa) × 52′6″ × 24′3″
Machinery:	1 screw, 2 horizontal direct-acting engines (79.5″ × 3′), 4 boilers; IHP 997 = 6 knots
Complement:	350
Armament:	(forward) 1 15″ SB, 1 150-pdr. R. (middle) 1 15″ SB, 1 11″ SB. (aft) 1 11″ SB, 1 150-pdr R.
Armor:	11″ turrets, 4.5″ sides, 3″ ends, 2.25″ deck, 9″ pilothouse

NOTES: Converted from screw frigate, cut down to gundeck and armor plated. Ram bow. The only monitor with three turrets; originally planned with four turrets but weight created too great a draft. Weight of turrets caused ship to roll excessively; wooden hull was not strong enough for their weight. Draft was too great for inshore operations, but freeboard was too small for ocean cruising. The first ship with more than two turrets on centerline. The guns were arranged in the turrets as indicated above.
SERVICE RECORD: NAtlBS. Harbor defense ship, Hampton Roads 1863–65. Decomm 20 June 1865. Sold 27 Sep 1883 and BU at Chester, Pa.

PURITAN

Name	Bldr	Laid down	L	Comm
Puritan	Continental (Allaire)	1863	2 Jul 1864	never

Tonnage:	4,912 tons D; 3,265 tons B
Dimensions:	340′ (oa) × 50′ × 20′
Machinery:	2 screws, 2 Ericsson vibrating-lever engines (100″ × 4′), 6 boilers; 15 knots (designed)
Armament:	2 20″ SB guns (designed)
Armor:	15″ turret, 6″ sides, 12″ pilothouse

NOTES: The largest of Ericsson's monitors. Originally designed with two turrets, redesigned by Ericsson with one. Never completed, armament was never mounted. Officially "rebuilt" as a new ship after 1874 (BM 1).
SERVICE RECORD: Construction suspended 1865.

DICTATOR

Name	Bldr	Laid down	L	Comm
Dictator	Delamater (bldr)	16 Aug 1862	26 Dec 1863	11 Nov 1864

Tonnage:	4,438 tons D; 3,033 tons B
Dimensions:	312′ (bp) × 50′ × 20′6″
Machinery:	1 screw, 2 Ericsson vibrating-lever engines (100″ × 4′); IHP 3,500 = 9 knots
Complement:	174
Armament:	2 15″ SB guns
Armor:	15″ turret, 6″ sides, 1.5″ deck, 12″ pilothouse

NOTES: Single turret. Forward overhang of upper hull omitted. Supports for main shaft were inadequate, requiring new fittings

The converted frigate *Roanoke* at the Brooklyn Navy Yard after being decommissioned in 1865. Notice the different size gunports in the turrets for the different caliber guns. At left is the receiving ship *Vermont*. (U.S. Naval Historical Center)

before ship could go into active service. Excellent sea boat but had low speed and endurance. Designed by Ericsson as *Protector*.

SERVICE RECORD: NAtlBS 1864–65. Decomm 5 Sep 1865. N. Atlantic Sqn 1869–71, 1874–77. Decomm 1 Jun 1877. Sold 27 Sep 1883 and BU.

A deck view of the monitor *Dictator* looking forward, 1870s. Notice the muzzle of a 15-inch gun in the turret and the elevated pilothouse at left. (Silverstone collection) (U.S. Naval Historical Center)

Another deck view of *Dictator* looking aft with turret in foreground. Compare this picture with the view at left, taken at the same time.

The double-turret monitor *Onondaga* in the James River during the war. Despite her very low freeboard this vessel crossed the Atlantic and served for many years in the French Navy.

ONONDAGA

Name	Bldr	Laid down	L	Comm
Onondaga	Continental (Morgan)	1862	29 Jul 1863	24 Mar 1864

Tonnage:	2,592 tons D; 1,250 tons B
Dimensions:	226′ (oa) × 49′3″ × 12′10″
Machinery:	2 screws, 4 horizontal back-acting engines, 4 boilers; IHP 642 = 7 knots
Complement:	130
Armament:	2 8″ R, 2-15″ SB. Feb 64 total: 2 15″ SB, 2 150-pdr R.
Armor:	11.75″ turrets, 5.5″ sides, 1″ deck

NOTES: Built under contract by her designer G. W. Quintard. Iron hull with two turrets. Returned to Quintard 1867.
SERVICE RECORD: James River flotilla 1864–65. Engagements at Howletts, Trents Reach, Va., 21 Jun and at Dutch Gap, Va., 13 Aug 1864 and 16–18 Aug 1864. Engaged battery at Howletts Farm, Va., 5–6 Dec 1864. Engagement at Trents Reach, 24 Jan 1865. Decomm 8 Jun 1865. Sold to France 2 Mar 1867.
Later history: French *Onondaga*. BU 1903.

MONADNOCK CLASS

Name	Bldr	Laid down	L	Comm
Agamenticus	Portsmouth (Morris)	1862	19 Mar 1863	5 May 1865
Monadnock	Boston (Morris)	1862	23 Mar 1864	4 Oct 1864

Tonnage:	3,295 tons D; 1,564 tons B
Dimensions:	250′ (oa) × 53′8″ × 12′3″
Machinery:	2 screws, 2 Ericsson vibrating-lever engines (32″ × 1′8″), 4 boilers; IHP 1,400 = 9 knots
Complement:	167
Armament:	4 15″ SB guns
Armor:	11″ turrets, 4.5″ sides, 1.5″ deck, 8″ pilothouse

NOTES: Double-turret monitors designed by Lenthall, with wooden hulls that deteriorated rapidly; "rebuilt" 1874. *Agamenticus* had hurricane deck added between turrets prior to completion. Good sea boats.

SERVICE RECORDS:
Agamenticus—Decomm 30 Sep 1865. Renamed **Terror**, 15 May 1869. Recomm 27 May 1869. N. Atlantic fleet 1870–72. Decomm 10 Jun 1872. BU 1874. (Officially rebuilt as BM 4.)
Monadnock—NAtlBS 1864–65. Unsuccessful attack on Ft. Fisher, NC, 24–25 Dec 1864. Second attack on Ft. Fisher, 13–15 Jan 1865. Supported final assault on Richmond, Apr 1865. Voyaged to Pacific coast, rounding Cape Horn, 1865–66. Decomm 30 Jun 1866. BU 1874. (Officially rebuilt as BM 3.)
Prize: 18 Feb 1865: str *Deer*.

MIANTONOMOH

Name	Bldr	Laid down	L	Comm
Miantonomoh	Brooklyn (Novelty)	1862	15 Aug 1863	18 Sep 1865

Tonnage:	3,401 tons D; 1,564 tons B
Dimensions:	250′ (oa) × 50′ × 14′9″
Machinery:	2 screws, 2 horizontal back-acting engines (30″ × 2′3″), 4 boilers; NHP 800 = 9 knots
Complement:	150
Armament:	4 15″ SB guns
Armor:	11″ turrets, 4.5″ sides, 1.5″ deck, 8″ pilothouse

NOTES: Twin-turret monitor designed by Lenthall, engines by Isherwood. Excellent sea boat.
SERVICE RECORD: N. Atlantic Sqn 1865. Cruise to European waters 1866–67. Recomm 15 Nov 1869. Sank schooner *Sarah* in collision at New York, 4 Dec 1869. Sank tug USS *Maria* in collision off Martha's Vineyard, 4 Jan 1870. Decomm 28 Jul 1870. BU 1874. (Officially rebuilt as BM 5.)

The monitor *Camanche* in dry dock at Mare Island Navy Yard. (U.S. Naval Historical Center)

The twin-turret monitor *Terror* with the hurricane deck, which was added in 1865, between the turrets. (U.S. Naval Historical Center)

The double-turret monitor *Miantonomoh* during her European voyage in 1866.

TONAWANDA

Name	Bldr	Laid down	L	Comm
Tonawanda	Philadelphia (Merrick)	1863	6 May 1864	12 Oct 1865

Tonnage:	3,400 tons D; 1,564 tons B
Dimensions:	259′6″ (oa) × 52′10″ × 13′5″
Machinery:	2 screws, 2 inclined back-acting engines (30″ × 1′9″), 4 boilers
Complement:	150
Armament:	4 15″ SB guns
Armor:	11″ turrets, 4.5″ sides, 1.5″ deck, 8″ pilothouse

NOTES: Hull designed by Lenthall, engines by Isherwood.
SERVICE RECORD: Training ship, Annapolis, 1866–72. Renamed **Amphitrite**, 15 May 1869. BU 1874 at Wilmington, Del. (Officially rebuilt as BM 2.)

The monitor *Tonawanda* at Annapolis in 1870. Her turrets were closer together than others of the class. (U.S. Naval Historical Center)

The monitor *Camanche* in commission in San Francisco Bay about 1898. The low freeboard of these ships is clearly apparent in this view. (U.S. Naval Historical Center)

PASSAIC CLASS

Name	Bldr	Laid down	L	Comm
Camanche	Donahue (Colwell)	1862	14 Nov 1864	24 May 1865
Catskill	Continental (Delamater)	1862	16 Dec 1862	24 Feb 1863
Lehigh	Reaney (Morris Towne)	1862	17 Jan 1863	15 Apr 1863
Montauk	Continental (Delamater)	1862	9 Oct 1862	17 Dec 1862
Nahant	City Point (bldr)	1862	7 Oct 1862	29 Dec 1862
Nantucket	Atlantic (bldr)	1862	6 Dec 1862	26 Feb 1863
Passaic	Continental (Delamater)	1862	30 Aug 1862	25 Nov 1862
Patapsco	Harlan (bldr)	1862	27 Sep 1862	2 Jan 1863
Sangamon (ex-*Conestoga*: 9 Sep 1862)	Reaney (Morris Towne)	1862	27 Oct 1862	9 Feb 1863
Weehawken	Secor (Colwell)	17 Jun 1862	5 Nov 1862	18 Jan 1863

Tonnage:	1,335 tons D; 844 tons B
Dimensions:	200' (bp) × 46' × 11'6"
Machinery:	1 screw, 2 Ericsson vibrating-lever engines (40" × 1'10"), 4 boilers; IHP 340 = 7 knots
Complement:	67/88
Armament:	1 15" SB, 1 11" SB guns, except *Camanche*: 2 15" SB. *Catskill, Montauk, Nahant*: Jan 65: add 2 12-pdr R. 1873 total: all, 2 15" SB.
Armor:	11" turret, 5" sides, 1" deck, 8" pilothouse

NOTES: Highly successful class designed by Ericsson, who wanted to name the first six *Impenetrable, Penetrator, Paradox, Gauntlet, Palladium,* and *Agitator*. Improved *Monitor* with pilothouse located on top of turret and a permanent smokepipe. 15" gun did not project from the turret. Surviving units rebuilt 1871–75.

SERVICE RECORDS:

Camanche—Built by Secor in Jersey City, then shipped in parts to San Francisco aboard ship *Aquila*, which sank there at her pier 14 Nov 1863. Reassembled by Union Iron Works. Training ship 1896–97. Sold 22 Mar 1899.

Catskill—SAtlBS 1863–65. Bombardment of Charleston forts, 7 Apr; of Ft. Wagner, Charleston, 10-11 Jul and 18 Jul–8 Sep 1863. Hit by enemy fire, captain killed, 17 Aug 1863. Decomm 26 Jul 1865. Renamed **Goliath**, 15 Jun 1869. Renamed **Catskill** 10 Aug 1869. N. Atlantic Sqn 1876–77. Recomm 1898. Sold 4 Dec 1901.

Prizes: 9 Aug 1864: str *Prince Albert*; 18 Feb 1865: strs *Celt & Deer*.

Lehigh—NAtlBS 1863. Expedition up James River, Va., 6–20 Jul 1863. SAtlBS Aug 1863. Bombardment of Charleston forts, 1–8 Sep 1863, hit many times, and of Ft. Sumter, 26 Oct–4 Nov 1863. Expedition up Stono River, SC, 5 Jul 1864 and up Stono & Folly Rivers, 9–14 Feb 1865. James River, Mar 1865. Decomm 9 Jun

The monitor *Catskill* during the 1890s. The deckhouse and boats were added after the Civil War. (Martin Holbrook Collection) (Mariners Museum)

The monitor *Lehigh* in 1864. Monitors in the James River area were differentiated by the bands on the turret.

Another view of the *Lehigh* in the James River shortly after her completion. Notice the field gun on deck forward. (National Archives)

The monitor *Jason* late in her career, possibly in 1898. This vessel served in the Civil War as *Sangamon*. The flying deck and other deck clutter were added after the war. (U.S. Naval Historical Center)

1865. Practice ship, Naval Academy 1875–76. N. Atlantic Stn 1876–79. Recomm 1898. Sold 14 Apr 1904.

Prize: 2 Feb 1864: str *Presto*.

Montauk—SAtlBS Jan 1863. Engaged battery at Ft. McAllister, Ga. (hit 14 times), 27 Jan and 1 Feb (hit 48 times), 1863. Bombardment of Ft. McAllister, damaged by torpedo during engagement with CSS *Nashville*, 28 Feb 1863. Bombardment of Charleston forts, 7 Apr and of Ft. Wagner, Charleston, 10 Jul–4 Aug 1863. Expedition up Stono River, SC, 5 Jul 1864. Bombardment of Ft. Anderson, Cape Fear River, 11–21 Feb 1865. Decomm 1865. Sold 14 Apr 1904.

Nahant—SAtlBS 1863. Bombardment of Ft. McAllister, Ga., 3 Mar 1863. Bombardment of Charleston forts, 7 Apr 1863, hit 36 times. Engagement with CSS *Atlanta*, Wassaw Sound, Ga., 17 Jun 1863. Bombardment of Ft. Wagner, Charleston, Jul–Aug 1863. Decomm 11 Aug 1865. Renamed **Atlas**, 15 Jun 1869. Renamed **Nahant**, 10 Aug 1869. Recomm 1898. Sold 16 Apr 1904.

Prize: 2 Feb 1864: str *Presto*.

Nantucket—SAtlBS 1863. Bombardment of Charleston forts (hit 51 times), 7 Apr, and of Ft. Wagner, Charleston, 18 Jul–8 Sep 1863. Decomm 24 Jun 1865. Renamed **Medusa**, 15 Jun 1869. Renamed **Nantucket**, 10 Aug 1869. Recomm 1882 and 1884. Sold 14 Nov 1900.

Prize: 13 Sep 1863: str *Jupiter*.

Passaic—NAtlBS 1863. Bombardment of Ft. McAllister, Ga., 3 Mar 1863. Damaged during bombardment of Charleston forts, 7 Apr 1863. Bombardment of New Smyrna, Fla., 28 Jul 1863. Bombardment of Charleston forts, Aug–Sep 1863. Decomm 16 Jun 1865. Recomm 1876. Receiving ship, Washington, 1878–82, Annapolis 1883–92, and Boston 1893–94. Recomm 1898. Sold 10 Oct 1899.

Prizes: 23 Feb 1863: *Glide*; 2 Feb 1864: str *Presto*.

Patapsco—NAtlBS 1863. Bombardment of Ft. McAllister, Ga., 3 Mar 1863. Bombardment of Charleston forts, 7 Apr, and of Ft. Wagner and Charleston forts, Jul–Oct 1863. Hit a torpedo (mine) and sank in Charleston River 16 Jan 1865.

Prizes: 9 Feb 1864: *Swift*.

Sangamon—NAtlBS 1863. James River flotilla 1863. Expeditions up James River, 6–20 Jul and 4–7 Aug 1863. SAtlBS 1864. Decomm mid-1865. Renamed **Jason**, 15 Jun 1869. Recomm 1898. Sold 16 Apr 1904.

Weehawken—SAtlBS 1863. Bombardment of Charleston forts (hit 53 times), 7 Apr 1863. Engagement with CSS *Atlanta*, Wassaw Sound, Ga., 17 Jun 1863. Bombardment of Ft. Wagner and Charleston forts, Jul–Oct 1863. Went aground under fire at Charleston, 8 Sep 1863. Foundered off Morris Island, Charleston, 6 Dec 1863.

CANONICUS CLASS

Name	Bldr	Laid down	L	Comm
Canonicus	City Point (bldr)	1862	1 Aug 1863	16 Apr 1864
Catawba	Swift (Niles)	1862	13 Apr 1864	10 Jun 1865*
Mahopac	Secor (Colwell)	1862	17 May 1864	22 Sep 1864
Manayunk	Snowden & Mason (bldr)	1862	18 Dec 1864	27 Sep 1865*
Manhattan	Perine (Colwell)	1862	14 Oct 1863	6 Jun 1864
Oneota	Swift (Niles)	1862	21 May 1864	10 Jun 1865*
Saugus	Harlan (bldr)	1862	16 Dec 1863	7 Apr 1864
Tecumseh	Secor (Colwell)	1862	12 Sep 1863	19 Apr 1864
Tippecanoe	Greenwood (bldr)	22 Sep 1862	22 Dec 1864	15 Feb 1866*

*delivered

Tonnage:	2,100 tons D; 1,034 tons B
Dimensions:	235′ (oa) × 43′8″ × 13′6″, except *Catawba* and *Oneota* 225′ × 43′3″; *Tippecanoe* 224′ × 43′ × 11′6″; *Mahopac*, *Manhattan*, *Tecumseh* 223′ × 43′4″
Machinery:	1 screw, 2 Ericsson vibrating-lever engines (48″ × 2′), 2 boilers; IHP 320 = 8 knots
Complement:	85
Armament:	2 15″ SB guns. *Canonicus* 1865: add 2 12-pdr.
Armor:	11″ turret, 5″ sides, 1.5″ deck

NOTES: Enlarged *Passaic* class. *Catawba* and *Oneota* were never commissioned. *Canonicus* and *Tippecanoe* rebuilt 1872–74.

SERVICE RECORDS:

Canonicus—James River flotilla 1864. Engagement at Howletts, Trents Reach, Va., 21 Jun; at Dutch Gap, Va., 16–18 Aug; and at Howletts Farm, Va., 5–6 Dec 1864. NAtlBS Dec 1864. Unsuccessful attack on Ft. Fisher, NC, 24–25 Dec 1864. Second attack on Ft. Fisher, 13–15 Jan 1865, hit 36 times. SAtlBS Feb 1865 off Charleston. Decomm 30 Jun 1865. Renamed **Scylla**, 15 June 1869. Renamed **Canonicus**, 10 Aug 1869. Atlantic coast cruises, 1872–77. Decomm 1877. Sold 19 Feb 1908.

Prize: 18 Feb 1865: str *Deer*.

Catawba—No active service. Sold to Peru, 2 Apr 1868.

Later history: Peruvian *Atahualpa*. Scuttled at Callao to prevent capture by Chile, 16 Jan 1880. Probably refloated & hulked.

Mahopac—SAtlBS 1864–65. Engaged battery at Howletts Farm, Va., 5–6 Dec 1864. Unsuccessful attack on Ft. Fisher, NC, 24–25 Dec 1864. Second attack on Ft. Fisher, 13–15 Jan 1865. Advance on Richmond, Apr 1865. Decomm Jun 1865. Recomm 1866–72. Renamed **Castor**, 15 Jun 1869. Renamed **Mahopac**, 10 Aug 1869. Sold 25 Mar 1902.

Manayunk—Laid up at Mound City, Ill., until 1867, then New Orleans. Renamed **Ajax**, 15 Jun 1869. First comm 1 Jan 1871. N. Atlantic Sqn 1871, 1874–76. Decomm 1 Sep 1898. Sold 10 Oct 1899.

Manhattan—GulfBS 1864. Battle of Mobile Bay, 5 Aug 1864. Bombardment of Ft. Morgan, Mobile Bay, 9–23 Aug 1864. Laid up Aug 1865. Renamed **Neptune**, 15 Jun 1869. Renamed **Manhattan**, 10 Aug 1869. Recomm 1873–77. Sold 24 Mar 1902.

Oneota—No active service. Sold to Peru, 2 Apr 1868.

Later history: Peruvian *Manco Capac*. Blown up at Arica to prevent capture by Chile, 7 Jun 1880.

The monitor *Canonicus* as she appeared at the Jamestown Exposition Naval Review held at Hampton Roads in 1907. (U.S. Naval Historical Center)

The monitor *Wyandotte* with crew mustering on deck, probably in 1898. Notice the deckhouse aft and name on the turret. Built as the *Tippecanoe*, she was first commissioned only in 1876. (U.S. Naval Historical Center)

Saugus—NAtlBS 1864. James River flotilla. Engagement at Howletts, Trents Reach, Va., 21 Jun; at Dutch Gap, Va., 13 Aug; and at Howletts Farm, Va., 5–6 Dec 1864. Unsuccessful attack on Ft. Fisher, NC, 24–25 Dec 1864. Damaged by bursting of 15-inch gun and several enemy hits at second attack on Ft. Fisher, 13–15 Jan 1865. Decomm 13 Jun 1865. Recomm 30 Apr 1869. Renamed **Centaur**, 15 Jun 1869. Renamed **Saugus**, 10 Aug 1869. Decomm 31 Dec 1870. Recomm 1872–76. Decomm 8 Oct 1877. Sold 15 Mar 1891.

Tecumseh—NAtlBS 1864. James River flotilla. Engagement at Howletts, Trents Reach, Va., 21 Jun 1864. WGulfBS Jul 1864. Struck by torpedo (mine) and sank during Battle of Mobile Bay, 5 Aug 1864.

Tippecanoe—Laid up at New Orleans. Renamed **Vesuvius**, 15 Jun 1869. Renamed **Wyandotte**, 10 Aug 1869. First comm 24 Jan 1876. N. Atlantic Sqn 1876–79. Station ship, Washington, D.C. 1879–85. Recomm 1898. Sold 17 Jan 1899.

KALAMAZOO CLASS

Name	Bldr	Laid down	L	Comm
Kalamazoo	Brooklyn (Delamater)	1863	never	never
Passaconaway	Portsmouth (Delamater)	18 Nov 1863	never	never
Quinsigamond	Boston (Atlantic)	15 Apr 1864	never	never
Shackamaxon	Philadelphia (Pusey)	1863	never	never

Tonnage:	5,660 tons D; 3,200 tons B
Dimensions:	345′5″ (oa) 332′6″ (bp) × 56′8″ × 17′6″
Machinery:	2 screws, 4 horizontal direct-acting engines (46.5″ × 4′2″), 8 boilers; 10 knots (designed)
Armament:	4 15″ SB guns
Armor:	10″ turrets, 6″ sides, 3″ deck

NOTES: Double-turret monitors, hull designed by Benjamin F. Delano and machinery by John Baird, adapted for ocean cruising. None was ever launched; hulls built of poorly seasoned wood that rotted on the stocks.

A sketch of a *Kalamazoo*-class double-turret monitor. This is the only illustration extant of this class, none of which was ever launched.

SERVICE RECORD:

Kalamazoo—Construction suspended 17 Nov 1865. Renamed **Colossus** 15 Jun 1869. BU on the stocks 1884.

Passaconaway—Construction suspended 17 Nov 1865. Renamed **Thunderer**, 15 Jun 1869. Renamed **Massachusetts**, 10 Aug 1869. BU on the stocks 1884.

Quinsigamond—Construction suspended 17 Nov 1865. Renamed **Hercules**, 15 Jun 1869. Renamed **Oregon**, 10 Aug 1869. BU on the stocks 1884.

Shackamaxon—Construction suspended 17 Nov 1865, with armor and machinery in place. Renamed **Hecla**, 15 Jun 1869. Renamed **Nebraska**, 10 Aug 1869. BU on the stocks 1874.

CASCO CLASS

Name	Bldr	Laid down	L	Comm
Casco	Atlantic (bldr)	1863	7 May 1864	4 Dec 1864
Chimo	Adams (bldr)	1863	5 May 1864	20 Jan 1865
Cohoes	Continental (Hews)	1863	31 May 1865	19 Jan 1866*
Etlah	McCord (bldr)	1863	3 Jul 1865	12 Mar 1866*
Klamath	Swift (Moore)	1863	20 Apr 1865	6 May 1866*
Koka	Wilcox (bldr)	1863	18 May 1865	28 Nov 1865*
Modoc	Underhill (bldr)	1863	21 Mar 1865	23 Jun 1865†
Napa	Harlan (bldr)	1863	26 Nov 1864	4 May 1865†
Naubuc	Perine (Dolan)	1863	19 Oct 1864	27 Mar 1865
Nausett	McKay (bldr)	1863	26 Apr 1865	10 Aug 1865
Shawnee	Curtis & Tilden (bldr)	1863	13 Mar 1865	18 Aug 1865
Shiloh	McCord (bldr)	1863	14 Jul 1865	12 Mar 1866*
Squando	McKay (bldr)	1863	31 Dec 1864	6 Jun 1865
Suncook	Globe (bldr)	1863	1 Feb 1865	27 Jul 1865
Tunxis	Reaney (bldr)	1863	4 Jun 1864	12 Jul 1864
Umpqua	Snowden & Mason (bldr)	1863	12 Dec 1865	7 May 1866†
Wassuc	Lawrence (bldr)	1863	25 Jul 1865	28 Oct 1865†
Waxsaw	Denmead (bldr)	1863	4 May 1865	21 Oct 1865†
Yazoo	Cramp (Merrick)	1863	8 May 1865	15 Dec 1865†
Yuma	Swift (Moore)	1863	30 May 1865	6 May 1866*

*delivered
†completed

Tonnage:	1,175 tons D; 614 tons B, except *Squando*: 1,618 tons D; *Nausett*: 1,487 tons D
Dimensions:	225' × 45' × 9'
Machinery:	2 screws, 2 inclined direct-acting engines (22" × 2'6"); IHP 600 = 9 knots
Complement:	69
Armament:	1 11" SB gun, except *Cohoes, Shawnee, Squando, Wassuc*: 2 11" SB. *Tunxis*: 1 11" SB, 1 150-pdr R. *Casco, Napa, Naubuc*: 1 11" SB, 1 spar torpedo. *Chimo*: 1 150-pdr R, 1 spar torpedo. *Modoc*: 1 spar torpedo.
Armor:	8" turret, 3" deck, 10" pilothouse

NOTES: Single-turret monitors with turtleback deck, designed by Stimers with light draft to operate in shallow rivers. Design changes caused errors resulting in only 3" of freeboard without turret and stores, and the deck was raised 22" before completion. *Tunxis* almost foundered on maiden voyage. Modifications caused delay in completion; most were delivered after war's end and laid up with no active service. *Casco, Chimo, Modoc, Napa,* and *Naubuc* were completed without built-up deck or turrets and armed with spar torpedoes.

SERVICE RECORD:

Casco—James River 1865. Decomm 10 Jun 1865. Renamed **Hero**, 15 Jun 1869. BU Apr 1875 at Washington.

Chimo—Station ship, Point Lookout, NC, 1865. Decomm 24 Jun 1865. Renamed **Orion**, 15 Jun 1869. Renamed **Piscataqua**, 10 Aug 1869. Sold 1874 & BU.

Cohoes—Laid up 1867. Renamed **Charybdis**, 15 Jun 1869. Renamed **Cohoes**, 10 Aug 1869. Sold Jul 1874.

The *Casco*, a shallow-draft monitor converted to a torpedo boat. Her turret was never fitted to save weight.

Monitors laid up at Washington Navy Yard shortly after the war's end. The ship in the center is either *Casco* or *Chimo* with no turret fitted. At left (left to right) are *Mahopac*, *Saugus*, and probably *Montauk*. (Silverstone Collection) (U.S. Naval Historical Center)

The monitors *Chimo* and *Tonawanda* anchored at Washington Navy Yard about 1865–66. The former Confederate ironclad *Stonewall* can be seen behind. (Martin Holbrook Collection) (U.S. Naval Historical Center)

The low-draft monitors *Shawnee* and *Wassuc* laid up at Boston 1871–72. These *Casco*-class monitors were never in active commission. At right is the housed-over monitor *Miantonomoh*. (Martin Holbrook Collection) (U.S. Naval Historical Center)

Etlah—Laid up 1866. Renamed **Hecate**, 15 Jun 1869. Renamed **Etlah**, 10 Aug 1869. Sold 12 Sep 1874.

Klamath—Laid up 1866. Renamed **Harpy**, 15 Jun 1869. Renamed **Klamath**, 10 Aug 1869. Sold 12 Sep 1874.

Koka—Construction suspended 17 Jun 1865 and laid up. Renamed **Argos**, 15 Jun 1869. Renamed **Koka**, 10 Aug 1869. BU Oct 1874.

Modoc—Laid up on completion. Renamed **Achilles**, 15 Jun 1869. Renamed **Modoc**, 10 Aug 1869. Sold and BU Aug 1875.

Napa—Laid up on completion 1865. Renamed **Nemesis**, 15 Jun 1869. Renamed **Napa**, 10 Aug 1869. BU 1875.

Naubuc—Decomm 27 Jun 1865. Renamed **Gorgon**, 15 Jun 1869. Renamed **Minnetonka**, 10 Aug 1869. BU 1875.

Nausett—Decomm 24 Aug 1865. Renamed **Aetna**, 15 Jun 1869. Renamed **Nausett**, 10 Aug 1869. BU Aug 1875.

Shawnee—Laid up Nov 1865. Renamed **Eolus**, 15 Jun 1869. Renamed **Shawnee**, 10 Aug 1869. Sold 9 Sep 1875 & BU.

Shiloh—Construction suspended 17 Jun 1865. Laid up 1866. Renamed **Iris**, 15 Jun 1869. In comm 1874. Sold 1874.

Squando—N. Atlantic Sqn 1865–66. Decomm 26 May 1866. Renamed **Erebus**, 15 Jun 1869. Renamed **Algoma**, 10 Aug 1869. Sold 1 Jul 1874 and BU.

Suncook—Laid up on completion. Renamed **Spitfire**, 15 Jun 1869. Renamed **Suncook**, 10 Aug 1869. Sold Jul 1874 and BU.

Tunxis—Rebuilt by Cramp 1864–66 and laid up 1866. Renamed **Hydra**, 15 Jun 1869. Renamed **Otsego**, 10 Aug 1869. BU 1874.

Umpqua—Laid up on completion. Renamed **Fury**, 15 Jun 1869. Renamed **Umpqua**, 10 Aug 1869. Sold 12 Sep 1874.

Wassuc—Laid up on completion. Renamed **Stromboli**, 15 Jun 1869. Renamed **Wassuc**, 10 Aug 1869. Sold 9 Sep 1875 and BU.

Waxsaw—Laid up on delivery. Renamed **Niobe**, 15 Jun 1869. Sold 25 Aug 1875 and BU.

Yazoo—Laid up on delivery. Renamed **Tartar**, 15 Jun 1869. Renamed **Yazoo**, 10 Aug 1869. Sold 5 Sep 1874.

Yuma—Laid up on delivery. Renamed **Tempest**, 15 Jun 1869. Renamed **Yuma**, 10 Aug 1869. Sold 12 Sep 1874.

The broadside ironclad *New Ironsides* in a somewhat retouched photograph. The gunports are open; her rigging was later removed. (Smithsonian Institution)

IRONCLADS

"STEVENS BATTERY"

Name	Bldr	Laid down	L	Comm
(*unnamed*)	Stevens (Delamater)	1854	never	never

Tonnage:	4,683 tons
Dimensions:	420' × 53' × 20'6"
Machinery:	2 screws, 8 vertical overhead-beam engines, 10 boilers; IHP 8,624
Armament:	5 15" Rodman R, 2 10" R (proposed)
Armor:	6.75"

NOTES: Designed by Robert L. Stevens and laid down by him but never completed or named. Offer to complete vessel rejected by the Navy 1861. After the Civil War title passed to others, and the design was modified as a ram with an Ericsson turret, new machinery and boilers. But Congress refused to appropriate funds, and the vessel was finally broken up on the stocks.
SERVICE RECORD: BU on stocks 1874–75.

NEW IRONSIDES

Name	Bldr	Laid down	L	Comm
New Ironsides	Cramp (Merrick)	1862	10 May 1862	21 Aug 1862

Tonnage:	4,120 tons D; 3,486 tons B
Dimensions:	232' (oa) × 57'6" × 15'8"
Machinery:	1 screw, 2 horizontal direct-acting engines (50" × 2'6"), 4 boilers; HP 700 = 6 knots
Complement:	460
Armament:	2 150-pdr R, 2 50-pdr R, 14 11" SB, 1 12-pdr R, 1 12-pdr SB. Oct 64: 2 50-pdr R replaced by 2 60-pdr R.
Armor:	3 to 4.5" sides, 1" deck, 10" conning tower

NOTES: One of three experimental ironclads ordered in 1861. Casemate ironclad with ram bow designed by Merrick. Too slow for sea duty but was practically invulnerable to enemy fire. Originally had bark rig but masts were removed & replaced with light poles before going into action.
SERVICE RECORD: SAtlBS Jan 1863. Bombardment of Charleston forts (hit 50 times), 7 Apr, and of Ft. Wagner, Charleston, 18 Jul–8 Sep 1863. Slightly damaged by spar torpedo explosion of torpedo boat CSS *David*, 5 Oct 1863. Unsuccessful attack on Ft. Fisher, NC, 24–25 Dec 1864. Second attack on Ft. Fisher, 13–15 Jan 1865. Decomm 6 Apr 1865. Destroyed by fire at League Island, 16 Dec 1866.

The *New Ironsides* with her masts and rigging removed for action and funnel cut down. Her commander complained she was very difficult to handle at sea in this condition. The ladder amidships accentuates the pronounced tumblehome of the ship's sides. A newly discovered picture of the most powerful ship of the Navy. (Dr. Charles L. Peery)

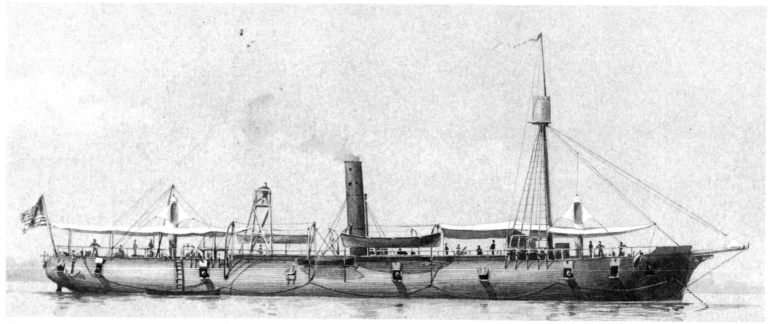

The ironclad steamer *Galena* as she appeared before being rebuilt in 1863. Sketch by R.G. Skerrett. (U.S. Naval Historical Center)

GALENA

Name	Bldr	Laid down	L	Comm
Galena	Maxson Fish (Delamater)	1861	14 Feb 1862	21 Apr 1862

Tonnage:	950 tons D, 738 tons B
Dimensions:	210′ (oa) 180′ (bp) × 36′ × 11′, d 12′8″
Machinery:	1 screw, 2 Ericsson vibrating-lever engines (48″ × 3′), 2 boilers; HP 800 = 8 knots
Complement:	150
Armament:	2 100-pdr R, 4 9″ SB. Apr 64 total: 1 100-pdr R, 1 30-pdr R, 8 9″ SB, 1 12-pdr H. Apr 65: 1 100-pdr R replaced by 1 60-pdr R.
Armor:	3.25″ sides

NOTES: Third of three experimental ironclads authorized in 1861. Designed by S. H. Pook for C. H. Bushnell & Co. Ironclad corvette with tumblehome sides and armor of interlocking iron bars; 2-mast schooner rig. Armor and engines installed at Greenpoint, NY. Armor was considered unsuccessful when hit by plunging fire at almost right angles and was removed in 1863. Converted to unarmored screw sloop with 3-mast ship rig.

SERVICE RECORD: NAtlBS 1862. Severely damaged during engagement at Drewry's Bluff, Va., 15 May 1862. Undergoing conversion 1863–64, recomm 15 Feb 1864. WGulfBS May 1864. Battle of Mobile Bay, 5 Aug 1864. Bombardment of Ft. Morgan, Mobile Bay, 9–23 Aug 1864. EGulfBS Apr–Nov 1864. NAtlBS Apr 1865. Decomm 17 Jun 1865. BU 1872. "Repaired" as new ship.

A view of the port side of the ironclad *Galena* looking forward. The unusual shape of the hull is clearly visible.

The casemate ironclad *Dunderberg* prior to her completion, at Brooklyn Navy Yard in 1865. The funnel and masts have not yet been fitted, but the sloping ram bow is prominent.

The *Dunderberg* as the French *Rochambeau* in dry dock at a French dockyard. (Marius Bar)

DUNDERBERG

Name	Bldr	Laid down	L	Comm
Dunderberg	Webb (Etna)	4 Oct 1862	22 Jul 1865	never

Tonnage:	7,060 tons D; 5,090 tons B
Dimensions:	377'4" (oa) 358'8" (bp) × 72'9" × 21'
Machinery:	1 screw, 2 horizontal back-acting engines (100" × 3'9"), 6 boilers; IHP 4,500 = 11.5 knots
Armament:	4 15" SB, 8 11" SB guns (designed)
Armor:	3.5" sides, 4.5" casemates

NOTES: Ironclad frigate ram designed by Lenthall as a reproduction of CSS *Virginia*, with sloping armored casemate sides and a 50-foot ram. Had double-bottom and collision bulkheads. The longest wooden ship ever built. Not accepted by the Navy and returned to builder, Sep 1866. Purchased by France to prevent Prussia buying the vessel.

Later history: Sold to France, Jul 1867. Renamed *Rochambeau*. Rebuilt and rearmed 1867. BU 1874.

The ironclad ram *Dunderberg* as she appeared running trials in New York Bay in April 1867.

KEOKUK

Name	Bldr	Laid down	L	Comm
Keokuk (ex-*Moodna*)	Underhill (bldr)	19 Apr 1862	6 Dec 1862	Mar 1863

Tonnage:	677 tons B
Dimensions:	159'6" (oa) × 36' × 8'6"
Machinery:	2 screws, 2 horizontal direct-acting condensing engines (23" × 1'8"); 9 knots
Complement:	92
Armament:	2 11" SB
Armor:	4" hull

NOTES: Designed by Charles W. Whitney with guns mounted in two stationary cylindrical towers each with 3 gunports. Armor of horizontal layers of timber and iron bars was unsuccessful.
SERVICE RECORD: SAtlBS 1863. Bombardment of Charleston forts (hit over 90 times), 7 Apr 1863. Foundered next day off Morris Island, 8 Apr 1863.

Confederate ironclads *Atlanta* and *Tennessee* were commissioned after being captured and served actively during the war.

SPAR TORPEDO BOATS

Tugs *Alpha*, *Belle*, *Delta*, *Gamma*, *Hoyt*, and *Martin* were armed with spar torpedoes in 1864–65. In addition *Fortune* and *Triana* were converted to experimental spar torpedo boats in 1871.

SPUYTEN DUYVIL

Name	Bldr	Laid down	Built	Comm
Stromboli	Pook (Mystic)	1864	1864	Oct 1864

Tonnage:	207 tons D; 116 tons B
Dimensions:	84'2" (oa) 73'11" (bp) × 20'8" × 7'5"
Machinery:	1 screw, 1 HP engine; 5 knots
Complement:	23
Armament:	1 spar torpedo
Armor:	5" sides, 3" deck, 5" pilothouse

NOTES: Designed by William W. W. Wood. Wood, low-freeboard flush-deck vessel with funnel and conning tower. Increase in draft used as protection. Retractable spar torpedo in bow but too slow and unwieldy.
SERVICE RECORD: Renamed **Spuyten Duyvil**, 19 Nov 1864. James River 1865. Engagement at Trents Reach, James River, Va., 24 Jan 1865. Used as experimental vessel. Sold 1880.

Bow view of the torpedo boat *Spuyten Duyvil* laid up at Brooklyn Navy Yard about 1870. The bow rudder has been removed.

INTREPID

Name	Bldr	Laid down	L	Comm
Intrepid	Boston (Morgan)	1873	5 Mar 1874	31 Jul 1874

Tonnage:	1,150 tons D, 438 tons B
Dimensions:	170'3" (wl) × 35' × 12'
Machinery:	2 screws, 2 compound engines, 6 boilers; IHP 1,800 = 10.6 knots
Complement:	(U)
Armament:	4 24-pdr H, 5 spar torpedoes

NOTES: Designed by Isaiah Hanscom as an experimental torpedo ram. Conversion to light-draft gunboat 1882 for China service canceled 1889, planned armament 2 8" guns. Too slow to be effective.
SERVICE RECORD: Sold 9 May 1892.

ALARM

Name	Bldr	Laid down	L	Comm
Alarm	Brooklyn (Morgan)	1873	13 Nov 1873	1874

Tonnage:	800 tons D
Dimensions:	173' (oa) 158'6" (bp) × 28' × 10'6"
Machinery:	Fowler wheel, 2 compound engines, 4 boilers; IHP 600 = 10 knots
Complement:	25
Armament:	1 15" SB, 3 spar torpedoes

NOTES: No rudder. Fowler feathering paddle wheel turning horizontally was used for both propulsion & steering, later replaced by a steering propeller. 32-foot ram bow with spar torpedoes on bow and on each beam.
SERVICE RECORD: Experimental vessel. Decomm 1885. Sold 28 Feb 1898.

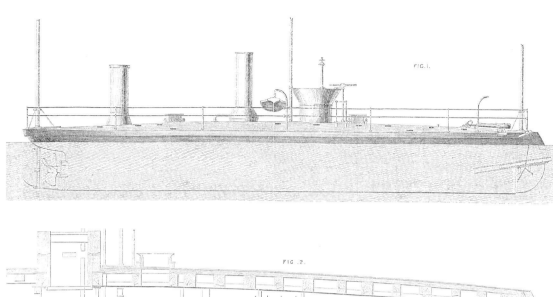

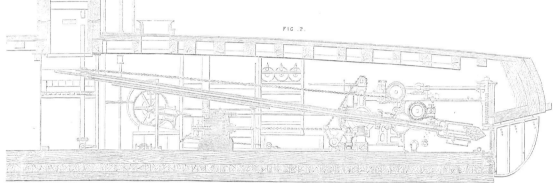

A drawing of the torpedo boat *Spuyten Duyvil* showing placement of the torpedo tube and forward rudder.

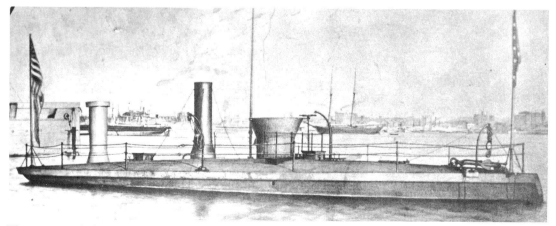

The spar torpedo boat *Spuyten Duyvil*. A retouched photograph of this unusual vessel at Brooklyn Navy Yard. (U.S. Naval Historical Center)

The torpedo boat *Alarm* in dry dock. Notice her long ram bow.

HAND-PROPELLED SUBMARINE

Name	Bldr	Laid down	L	Comm
Alligator	Neafie	1862	30 Apr 1862	Jun 1862

Dimensions:	47′ × 4′6″ × d6′
Complement:	17
Armament:	2 spar torpedoes

SERVICE RECORD: Disappeared at sea when cut adrift from tow in storm off North Carolina, 2 Apr 1863.

PICKET BOATS

Names	Bldr
No. 1–3	Lewis Hoagland, New Brunswick, NJ
No. 4–6	Sylvanus Smith, Boston

NOTES: They were 45′ × 9′6″, had double-piston reciprocating Root engines, 1 12-pdr H, and a complement of 7.

UNARMORED STEAM VESSELS

The first steam warships were driven by paddle wheels, but screw-propelled ships were much more efficient for naval purposes. In particular, the large paddle boxes interfered with the placement of the guns, which were traditionally sited along the ship's broadside. Development of low-pressure and more powerful engines enabled propeller-driven ships to move faster. In addition, the engines could be placed below the waterline for better protection against enemy gunfire.

The Navy built several side-wheel warships, and among the earliest were the frigates *Missouri* and *Mississippi* of 1840. Although the *Missouri* was soon destroyed by fire, succeeding vessels, notably the *Susquehanna* and *Powhatan*, were especially successful and efficient ships. In 1847 the paddle wheeler *Saranac* and propeller *San Jacinto* were built as competitive sisters. In all tests between paddle-wheel and propeller-driven ships, the propeller won, and it soon permanently displaced the earlier system.

In 1854 six large screw frigates were built, the five ships of the *Merrimack* type and the *Niagara*. On her first cruise to Europe, the *Merrimack* created a sensation in naval circles with battery and steaming endurance greater than contemporary European frigates. The *Hartford* class of steam sloops in 1858 again combined superior firepower with high endurance on a smaller hull.

A large number of sturdy steam sloops were built during the war. In addition, smaller warships known as double-enders and 90-day gunboats were produced in large numbers and served throughout the war. Hastily built, they wore out quickly.

A series of new vessels was ordered towards the end of the war that sought to utilize the lessons learned during the war. Unfortunately, most of these were built with unseasoned timber, and the hulls deteriorated very quickly. These included the swift cruisers of the *Ammonoosuc* class, the frigates of the *Java* class, and the sloops of the *Contoocook* and *Algoma* classes. Only a few were actually completed, and all soon disappeared from the Navy list.

Of the cruisers, designed for high speed, the *Wampanoag* attained a sustained speed of 17 knots on her trials, a speed unequalled by steam vessels to that time. Nevertheless, the ships were never put into service and were the subject of some controversy. It was said the engines were too powerful for the frame, and fuel consumption was so great that the space required for coal left no room for sufficient ammunition.

The majority of the ships of these classes were broken up on the stocks, and those that were completed had very short careers.

Most of the ships of the *Swatara* and *Adams* classes were built under the guise of "repairing" older ships, as this was the only way to obtain authorization of funds. Only the frigate *Trenton*, laid down in 1875, was built as a new ship.

SIDE-WHEEL FRIGATES

MISSISSIPPI CLASS

Name	Bldr	Laid down	L	Comm
Mississippi	Philadelphia (Merrick & Towne)	10 Aug 1839	5 May 1841	22 Dec 1841
Missouri	Brooklyn (West Point)	1839	7 Jan 1841	early 1842

Tonnage:	3,200 tons D, 1,732 tons B
Dimensions:	229' (oa) × 40' × 21'9" (66'6" oa beam)
Machinery:	Side wheels, *Mississippi*: 2 side-lever engines (75" × 7'), 3 boilers; HP 650 = 11 knots; *Missouri*: 2 inclined direct-acting condensing engines (65.5" × 10'); HP 515 = 11 knots
Complement:	257
Armament:	2 10" SB, 8 8" SB guns *Mississippi*: May 61 total: 1 9" SB, 10 8"/63, 1 12-pdr; Nov 62 total: 1 10" SB, 19 8" SB/63, 1 20-pdr R

NOTES: Wood hull, bark rig. Hulls designed by Lenthall, Hartt & Humphreys; engines by Copeland. Machinery differed to test long- and short-stroke engines. Very successful and good steamers.

SERVICE RECORDS:

Mississippi—Flagship of Commodore Matthew Perry during the Mexican War and the first expedition to Japan in 1853. Far East 1857–60. Blockading operations off Key West, Jun 1861. Passage past

The *Mississippi*, a side-wheel frigate built in 1841, drying sails at Baton Rouge shortly before her loss in 1863. Notice that the line of gunports is interrupted by the paddle box. Her mast tops have been removed. (Martin Holbrook Collection) (U.S. Naval Historical Center)

New Orleans forts and engagement with CSN vessels, 24 Apr 1862. Went aground during attempt to pass Port Hudson, was burned to prevent capture; later, magazines blew up, 14 Mar 1863.

Prizes: 13 Jun 1861: *Forest King*; 26 Nov: *Empress*.

Missouri—Caught fire and blew up at Gibraltar, 15 Aug 1843.

SARANAC

Name	Bldr	Laid down	L	Comm
Saranac	Portsmouth (Coney)	May 1847	14 Nov 1848	12 Oct 1850

Tonnage:	2,100 tons D; 1,446 tons B
Dimensions:	216′ (oa) 210′ (bp) × 37′9″ × 16′6″ (60′ oa beam)
Machinery:	Side wheels, 2 inclined direct-acting condensing engines (60″ × 9′), 3 boilers; HP 795 = 13.5 knots
Complement:	228
Armament:	6 8″ SB guns. 1862 total: 1 8″ SB, 8 8″/57, 2 20-pdr R, 2 12-pdr SB. Jan 64: 1 8″ SB replaced by 1 11″ SB. Mar 65 total: 1 11″ SB, 8 8″/55, 2 30-pdr R, 2 12-pdr.

NOTES: Bark rig. Hull designed by Hartt; engines by Copeland. Reboilered 1857.

SERVICE RECORD: Stationed on Pacific coast. Wrecked in Seymour Narrows off Vancouver Island, 18 Jun 1875.

Above: The side-wheel frigate *Saranac*. An undated picture taken on the Pacific coast. (Martin Holbrook Collection) (Mariners Museum) *Opposite top*: Mare Island Navy Yard in the 1870s. Tied up nearest camera at left is side-wheel steamer *Saranac*, wrecked in 1875, and receiving ship *Independence* in center. The sloops anchored in midstream are *California* (left) and probably *Pensacola*. At right is the wooden floating dry dock. (U.S. Naval Historical Center)

The side-wheel frigate *Susquehanna* at New York Navy Yard after the war. (Martin Holbrook Collection) (U.S. Naval Historical Center)

SUSQUEHANNA

Name	Bldr	Laid down	L	Comm
Susquehanna	Philadelphia (Murray)	8 Sep 1847	5 Apr 1850	24 Dec 1850

Tonnage:	3,824 tons D; 2,450 tons B
Dimensions:	257′ (bp) × 45′ × 19′6″, d26′6″ (69′ oa beam)
Machinery:	Side wheels, 2 inclined direct-acting condensing engines (70″ × 10′), 4 boilers; HP 795 = 12 knots
Complement:	300
Armament:	3 8″ SB, 6 32-pdr R. 1861 total: 15 8″ SB, 2 12-pdr H, 1 24-pdr H. Jun 63 total: 2 150-pdr R, 12 9″ SB, 1 12-pdr R. 1865 total: 2 100-pdr R, 12 9″ SB, 1 30-pdr R, 1 12-pdr R.

NOTES: Hull designed by Lenthall; engines by Copeland. Engines were very reliable, but machinery was removed after Civil War; conversion to screw propulsion never completed.

SERVICE RECORD: East India Sqn 1851–55. Mediterranean Sqn 1856–58, 1860–61. AtlBS 1861. Capture of Hatteras Inlet, 28–29 Aug 1861. Bombardment and occupation of Port Royal, SC, 7 Nov 1861. NAtlBS Apr 1862–63. Engagement with batteries at Sewells Point, Va., 8 May 1862. Out of commission, May 1863–Jul 1864. NAtlBS, 1864–65. Unsuccessful attack on Ft. Fisher, NC, 24–25 Dec 1864. 150-pdr rifle burst during second attack on Ft. Fisher, 13–15 Jan 1865. Decomm 14 Jan 1868. Sold 27 Sep 1883 and BU.

Prizes: 9 Sep 1861: *Prince Alfred*; 13 Sep: *Argonaut*; 28 Sep: *San Juan*; 29 Sep: *Baltimore*; 3 Apr 1862: *Coquette*; 11 Jun: *Princeton*; 29 Jun: str *Ann*; 18 Apr 1863: *Alabama*

POWHATAN

Name	Bldr	Laid down	L	Comm
Powhatan	Norfolk (Mehaffy)	14 Jul 1847	14 Feb 1850	2 Sep 1852

Tonnage:	3,765 tons D; 2,415 tons B
Dimensions:	276′6″ (oa) 250′ (bp) × 45′ × 20′9″ (69′6″ oa beam)
Machinery:	Side wheels, 2 inclined direct-acting engines (70″ × 10′), 4 boilers; IHP 1,100 = 11 knots
Complement:	300
Armament:	3 8″ SB, 6 32-pdr R. Nov 61 total: 1 11″ SB, 10 9″ SB, 5 12-pdr. Oct 63 total: 3 100-pdr R, 1 11″ SB, 14 9″ SB. Jan 65: add 2 9″ SB, 4 12-pdr SB.

NOTES: Hull designed by Grice; engines by Haswell. Bark rig. Similar to *Susquehanna*, but engines of a different design. Engines most reliable, a fast steamer even in old age.
SERVICE RECORD: East India Sqn 1853–56. Blockade of Mobile 1861. Operated off Charleston 1862–63. West Indies Sqn 1863–64. Unsuccessful attack on Ft. Fisher, NC, 24–25 Dec 1864. Second attack on Ft. Fisher, 13–15 Jan 1865. South Pacific Sqn 1866–69. Home Sqn 1869–86. Decomm 2 Jun 1886. Sold 30 Jul 1887 and BU.
Prizes: 29 May 1861: *Mary Clinton*; 13 Aug: *Abby Bradford*; 19 Apr 1863: *Major E. Willis*; 16 May 1863: *C. Routereau*

SIDE-WHEEL SLOOPS

ALLEGHENY

Name	Bldr	Laid down	L	Comm
Allegheny	Tomlinson (bldr)	1844	22 Feb 1847	Apr 1847

Tonnage:	1,020 tons D; 989 tons B
Dimensions:	185′ (dk) × 33′4″ × 14′8″
Machinery:	Hunter wheels, 2 horizontal condensing engines; NHP 243 = 6 knots
Complement:	190
Armament:	4 8″ SB. May 63 total: 4 32-pdr/33, 2 32-pdr/27

NOTES: Iron hull. Hull and machinery designed by Hunter. A failure on trials and laid up. Rebuilt 1852 by Mehaffy & Co. at Portsmouth, Va. as a screw steamer using original engines as converted by Isherwood.
SERVICE RECORD: Brazilian Station and Mediterranean 1848. Gulf of Mexico 1849. Receiving ship, Baltimore, 1856–68. Sold 15 May 1869.

FULTON

Name	Bldr	Laid down	L	Comm
Fulton	Brooklyn (Dunham)	1851	30 Aug 1851	25 Jan 1852

Tonnage:	1,200 tons D; 750 tons B
Dimensions:	181′6″ (bp) × 34′10″ × 10′6″
Machinery:	Side wheels, inclined condensing engine (50″ × 4′10″), 2 boilers; HP 500 = 11 knots
Complement:	79
Armament:	4 8″ SB, 4 32-pdr SB. 1858 total: 2 9″ SB.

NOTES: Hull designed by Humphreys and engines by Charles B. Stuart. Original vessel launched 18 May 1837, laid up 1842 and rebuilt 1851 with new engines. Schooner rig.
SERVICE RECORD: Home Sqn 1852–58. Paraguay Expedition 1859. Anti-slave trade patrol off Florida 1859 until stranded near Pensacola. While undergoing refit captured by Confederates at Pensacola NYd, 12 Jan 1861, and destroyed by them, 10 May 1862.

WATER WITCH

Name	Bldr	Laid down	Built	Comm
Water Witch	Washington (Ellis)	1852	1852	8 Feb 1853

Tonnage:	378 tons B
Dimensions:	150′ (dk) × 23′ × 9′
Machinery:	Side wheels, 1 inclined condensing engine (37½″ × 6′), 2 boilers; HP 180 = 11.5 knots
Complement:	55
Armament:	1 32-pdr. 1862 total: 4 32-pdr SB, 1 24-pdr H. 1864 total: 1 30-pdr R, 1 12-pdr R, 2 12-pdr SB.

NOTES: Hull designed by Lenthall; engine by Isherwood. Machinery taken from the previous *Water Witch* built in 1845. Schooner rig.
SERVICE RECORD: Surveyed rivers of South America 1853–56. Paraguay Expedition 1859. GulfBS May 1861. Engagement with CSN squadron near Head of Passes, Miss., 12 Oct 1861. EGulfBS 1862. SAtlBS Sep 1862. Joint expedition to St. Johns Bluff, Fla., 1–12 Oct and to Pocotaligo, SC, 21–23 Oct 1862. Despatch vessel. Assault on Jacksonville, Fla., 22 Feb–16 Apr 1864. Captured by Confederate boarders in Ossabaw Sound, Ga., 3 Jun 1864 and taken into service.
Prizes: 13 Nov 1861: *Cornucopia*; 5 Mar 1862: *William Mallory*.

SAGINAW

Name	Bldr	Laid down	L	Comm
Saginaw (ex-*Toucey*)	Mare Island (Union IW)	16 Sep 1858	3 Mar 1859	5 Jan 1860

Tonnage:	508 tons (U); 453 tons B
Dimensions:	155′ × (U) × 4′5″ light
Machinery:	Side wheels, 2 inclined oscillating engines (39″ × 4′); 9 knots
Complement:	59
Armament:	1 50-pdr R, 1 32-pdr/42, 2 24-pdr R

SERVICE RECORD: East India Sqn 1860–62. Pacific Sqn 1863–66. Wrecked on Ocean Island, east of Midway, 29 Oct 1870.

SIDE-WHEEL GUNBOAT (LAKE)

Name	Bldr	Laid down	L	Comm
Michigan	Stackhouse (bldr)	1842	5 Dec 1843	29 Sep 1844

Tonnage:	685 tons D; 582 tons B
Dimensions:	163′3″ (bp) × 27′2″, 45′10″ (oa) × 9′
Machinery:	Side wheels, 2 inclined direct-acting condensing engines (36″ × 8′), 2 boilers; HP 365 = 10.5 knots
Complement:	85
Armament:	2 8″ SB, 4 32-pdr SB

NOTES: First iron-hulled vessel in the Navy. Built in Pittsburgh and reassembled at Erie, Pa.; remained on the Great Lakes during her entire service. Hull designed by Hartt; engines by Copeland.
SERVICE RECORD: Lake Erie. Renamed **Wolverine**, 17 Jun 1905. Transferred to City of Erie, Pa., as a relic, 1927. BU 1949.

The side-wheel sloop *Water Witch*, built in 1852 using machinery taken from a previous *Water Witch*. (Peabody Museum of Salem)

A rare view of the side-wheel sloop *Saginaw*, which was wrecked near Midway Island in 1870. (U.S. Naval Historical Center)

SCREW FRIGATES

SAN JACINTO

Name	Bldr	Laid down	L	Comm
San Jacinto	Brooklyn (Merrick)	Aug 1847	16 Apr 1850	30 Mar 1852

Tonnage: 2,150 tons D; 1,446 tons B
Dimensions: 237′ (oa) 210′ (wl) × 37′9″ × 17′3″
Machinery: 1 screw, 2 horizontal condensing engines (62.5″ × 4′2″), 3 boilers; HP 500 = 11 knots
Complement: 235
Armament: 6 8″ SB guns. 1862 total: 1 11″ SB, 10 9″ SB, 1 12-pdr R. Dec 63 total: 1 100-pdr R, 10 9″ SB, 1 20-pdr R.

NOTES: Hull designed by Hartt; engines by Haswell. Competitive sister with paddle frigate *Saranac*. Propeller shaft was off center. Engines were inadequate and unreliable. Re-engined 1853–54.
SERVICE RECORD: Far East 1855–58. Africa Sqn 1859–60. Captured brig *Storm King* with 619 slaves off Congo River, 8 Aug 1860. In collision with French brig *Jules et Marie* off Cuba, 3 Nov 1861. Under command of Captain Charles Wilkes, stopped British str *Trent* east of Havana and removed Confederate envoys Mason & Slidell, 8 Nov 1861. NAtlBS Mar 1862. Engaged batteries at Sewells Point, Va., 8 May 1862. EGulfBS Jun–Aug 1862. Search for CSS *Alabama* Nov 1862–Jan 1863. Blockade off Mobile Sep 1863. Search for CSS *Tallahassee* in N. Atlantic, Aug 1864. Wrecked on Great Abaco Island, Bahamas, 1 Jan 1865.
Prizes: 7 Aug 1863: *Buckshot*; 16 Sep: str *Lizzie Davis*; 7 Jan 1864: *Roebuck*; 11 Mar: *Lealtad*.

FRANKLIN

Name	Bldr	Laid down	L	Comm
Franklin	Portsmouth (Atlantic)	May 1854	17 Sep 1864	3 Jun 1867

Tonnage: 5,170 tons D; 3,173 tons B
Dimensions: 265′ (wl) × 53′8″ × 24′3″
Machinery: 1 screw, 2 horizontal back-acting condensing engines (68″ × 3′6″), 4 boilers; IHP 2,065 = 10 knots
Armament: 4 100-pdr R, 1 11″ SB, 34 9″ SB
Complement: 228

NOTES: Officially considered to be the rebuilt 74-gun ship-of-the-line of 1814, authorized 1853. Ship rig. Engines designed by Isherwood ordered 1863.
SERVICE RECORD: European Sqn 1867–71. N. Atlantic 1873. European Sqn 1874–76. Receiving ship, Norfolk 1877. Stricken and sold, 26 Oct 1915.

Another view of the *Franklin* in a European port in 1870 with her funnel lowered. This ship was laid down in 1854 but launched only in 1864. Notice guns protruding from the gunports. (Martin Holbrook Collection) (U.S. Naval Historical Center)

The steam frigate *Franklin* at Boston Navy Yard. (U.S. Naval Historical Center)

The screw frigate *Wabash* lying in Port Royal harbor, 1863. This slightly retouched photograph was taken from the monitor *Weehawken*. (U.S. Naval Historical Center)

MERRIMACK

Name	Bldr	Laid down	L	Comm
Merrimack	Boston (West Point)	11 Jul 1854	15 Jun 1855	20 Feb 1856

Tonnage:	4,636 tons D; 3,200 tons B
Dimensions:	300′ (oa) 275′ (bp) 257′9″ (wl) × 51′4″ × 24′3″
Machinery:	1 screw, 2 horizontal double piston-rod condensing engines (72″ × 3′), 4 boilers; IHP 869 = 10.5 knots
Complement:	519
Armament:	14 8″ SB/63, 2 10″ SB, 24 9″ SB

NOTES: *Merrimack*, *Wabash*, *Minnesota*, *Colorado*, and *Roanoke* were sisters designed by Lenthall with differing machinery. Very fine warships, considered on completion to be superior to any warship in the world. They were good sailers, the engines being auxiliary only. *Merrimack*'s engines were too weak and unreliable and were being refitted in 1861.
SERVICE RECORD: European cruise 1856–57. Pacific Sqn 1857–60. Burned to prevent capture while out of commission at Norfolk NYd, 20 Apr 1861. Salved and rebuilt by CSN as ironclad *Virginia*.

WABASH

Name	Bldr	Laid down	L	Comm
Wabash	Philadelphia (Merrick)	16 May 1854	24 Oct 1855	18 Aug 1856

Tonnage:	4,650 tons D; 3,200 tons B
Dimensions:	301′6″ (oa) 262′6″ (bp) × 51′4″ × 23′
Machinery:	1 screw, 2 horizontal direct-acting steeple condensing engines (72″ × 3′), 4 boilers; IHP 950 = 10 knots
Complement:	642
Armament:	1861: 2 10″ SB, 28 9″ SB, 14 8″ SB/63, 2 12-pdr SB. Jul 62: 8″ replaced by 9″ SB. 1863 total: 1 150-pdr R, 2 100-pdr R, 1 10″ SB, 42 9″ SB, 1 30-pdr R, 1 12-pdr H. 1865 total: 1 150-pdr R, 1 10″ SB, 42 9″ SB, 4 32-pdr SB, 1 30-pdr R.

SERVICE RECORD: Home Sqn 1856–58. Mediterranean Sqn 1858–59. AtlBS 1861. Capture of Hatteras Inlet, 28–29 Aug 1861. SAtlBS Oct 1861–Jan 1865. Occupation of Port Royal, SC, 7 Nov 1861. Blockade of Charleston. Attacked by torpedo boat CSS *David*, 18 Apr 1864. Unsuccessful attack on Ft. Fisher, NC, 24–25 Dec 1864. Second attack on Ft. Fisher, 13–15 Jan 1865. Decomm 14 Feb 1865. Mediterranean Sqn 1871–74. Decomm 25 Apr 1874. Receiving ship, Boston, and housed over, 1875. Stricken 15 Nov 1912, sold and BU.
Prizes: 18 Jun 1861: *Amelia*; Jul: *Hannah Balch*; 3 Aug: *Sarah Starr*, *Mary Alice*; 15 May 1863: *Wonder*

The screw frigate *Minnesota* as she appeared in 1871. Notice the trim, compact lines, the guns in open gunports. (National Archives)

MINNESOTA

Name	Bldr	Laid down	L	Comm
Minnesota	Washington (bldr)	May 1854	1 Dec 1855	21 May 1857

Tonnage: 4,833 tons D; 3,200 tons B
Dimensions: 264′9″ (wl) × 51′4″ × 23′10″
Machinery: 1 screw, 2 horizontal trunk engines (79.5″ × 3′), 4 boilers;
             IHP 973 = 12.5 knots
Complement: 646
Armament: May 61 total: 1 10″ SB, 28 9″ SB, 14 8″ SB/63, 2 24-pdr SB,
             2 12-pdr SB. Dec 62 total: 1 200-pdr R, 1 11″ SB, 4 100-
             pdr R, 36 9″ SB. Jul 63 total: 1 150-pdr R, 1 11″ SB, 4
             100-pdr R, 38 9″ SB, 2 12-pdr RH, 2 12-pdr HSB. Oct 63:
             add 4 9″ SB.

NOTES: Ship rig. Machinery designed by Daniel B. Martin.

SERVICE RECORD: East India Sqn 1857–59. AtlBS May 1861 (flag). Capture of Hatteras Inlet, 28–29 Aug 1861. Battle of Hampton Roads, went aground and damaged by gunfire of CSS *Virginia*, 8–9 Mar 1862. NAtlBS 1862–65 (flag). Not damaged when attacked by Confederate torpedo boat *Squib* while anchored off Newport News, 9 Apr 1864. Unsuccessful attack on Ft. Fisher, NC, 24–25 Dec 1864. Second attack on Ft. Fisher, 13–15 Jan 1865. Decomm Jan 1868. Gunnery training ship, New York, 1875. Stricken 12 Jul 1901, sold and burned.
Prizes: 14 May 1861: *Mary Willis, North Carolina*; 15 May: *J. H. Ethridge, William Henry, William & John, Mary, Industry, Belle Conway*; 17 May: *Star, Crenshaw, Almira Ann*; 20 May: *Hiawatha, Tropic Wind*; 22 May: *Arcola*; 25 May: *Pioneer*; 27 May: *Iris, Catherine*; 26 Jun: *Sally Magee*; 1 Jul: *Sally Mears*; 10 Jul: *Amy Warwick*; 11 Jan 1864: str *Vesta* and *Ranger*.

COLORADO CLASS

Name	Bldr	Laid down	L	Comm
Colorado	Norfolk (Tredegar)	May 1854	19 Jun 1856	13 Mar 1858
Roanoke	Norfolk (Tredegar)	May 1854	13 Dec 1855	4 May 1857

Tonnage:	4,772 tons D; 3,400 tons B
Dimensions:	268'6" (wl) × 52'6" × 23'9"
Machinery:	1 screw, 2 horizontal direct-acting trunk engines (79.5" × 3'), 4 boilers; IHP 997 = 11 knots
Complement:	674
Armament:	2 10" SB, 28 9" SB, 14 8" R/63 (*Roanoke* also: 2 12-pdr SB H). *Colorado*: 1864 total: 1 150-pdr R, 1 11" SB, 46 9" SB, 4 12-pdr H. 1871 total: 2 100-pdr R, 1 11" SB, 42 9" SB, 2 20-pdr H, 6 12-pdr H.

NOTES: Ship rig.

SERVICE RECORDS:

Colorado—GulfBS Jun 1861–Jun 1862. Boat party destroyed Confederate privateer *Judith* outfitting at Pensacola, 14 Sep 1861. NAtlBS Oct 1864–Jan 1865. Unsuccessful attack on Ft. Fisher, NC, 24–25 Dec 1864. Second attack on Ft. Fisher, 13–15 Jan 1865. European Sqn 1865–67. Asiatic Stn 1870–73. Korean Expedition, 1871. North Atlantic Sqn 1873–75. Receiving Ship, New York, 1876–84. Sold 14 Feb 1885.

Prizes: 13 Sep 1861: *Judith; 6 May 1862: str *Lewis Whitemore*.

Roanoke—Home Sqn, 1858–60. N. Atlantic Sqn 1861. Present at Hampton Roads, 8 Mar 1862. Decomm 25 Mar 1862 for conversion to ironclad (q.v.).

Prizes: 13 Jul 1861: *Mary; 16 Aug: *Albion*; 6 Oct: *Alert*; 15 Oct: *Thomas Watson*.

The screw frigate *Colorado* anchored at a European port. (INRO) *Below*: Another view of the *Colorado* at Port Mahon, Minorca, about 1866. (U.S. Naval Historical Center)

NIAGARA

Name	Bldr	Laid down	L	Comm
Niagara	Brooklyn (Fulton)	Oct 1854	23 Feb 1856	6 Apr 1857

Tonnage:	5,540 tons D; 4,580 tons B
Dimensions:	345′ (oa) 328′10″ (bp) × 55′3″ × 24′8″
Machinery:	1 screw, 3 horizontal direct-acting engines (72″ × 3′), 5 boilers; IHP 1955 = 14.5 knots
Complement:	657
Armament:	4 32-pdr guns. Apr 61 total: 12 9″ SB. Jun 62 total: 1 80-pdr R, 11 11″ SB. Oct 63 total: 12 150-pdr R, 20 11″ SB, 1 24-pdr H, 2 12-pdr R.

NOTES: Hull designed by George Steers. The largest vessel built in the United States at the time; actually a large sloop with single gun deck. Ship rig, two funnels. Re-engined 1862. Rearmed 1863, but additional guns caused excessive weight. Modifications started in 1870 canceled because of cost. Was to receive new machinery, armor plating, and changes in gun & berth decks.

SERVICE RECORD: Laid first transatlantic cable, 1857–58. Made cruise to Japan 1860–61. Blockade of Charleston, May 1861. EGulfBS Jul 1861–62. Bombardment of defenses of Pensacola, Fla., 22–23 Nov 1861. Refitting Jun 1862–Oct 1863. European Sqn 1864–65. Unable to prevent escape of Confederate ironclad *Stonewall* from Ferrol, Spain, Mar 1865. Decomm 28 Sep 1865. Sold 6 May 1885.

Prizes: 12 May 1861: *General Parkhill*; 5 Jun: *Aid*; 15 Aug 1864: str *Georgia*.

JAVA CLASS

Name	Bldr	Laid down	L	Comm
Antietam	Philadelphia (Morris Towne)	1864	13 Nov 1875	1876
Guerriere	Boston (Globe)	1864	9 Sep 1865	21 May 1867
Illinois	Portsmouth (Corliss)	1864	never	never
Java	Brooklyn (Etna)	1864	never	never
Kewaydin	Boston (Loring)	1864	never	never
Minnetonka	Portsmouth (Woodruff)	1864	3 Jul 1867	12 Dec 1870
Ontario	Brooklyn (Etna)	1864	never	never
Piscataqua	Portsmouth (Woodruff)	1864	11 Jun 1866	21 Oct 1867

Tonnage:	3,954 tons D; 3,177 tons B
Dimensions:	336′6″ (oa) 312′6″ (bp) × 46′ × 21′5″
Machinery:	1 screw, 2 horizontal back-acting engines (60″ × 3′), 4 boilers (*Ontario* 6); IHP 1,780 = 12 knots
Complement:	325
Armament:	2 100-pdr R, 1 60-pdr R, 2 20-pdr R, 16 9″ SB guns

NOTES: Hulls designed by Delano and engines by Isherwood. Built of unseasoned wood with diagonal iron bracing and decayed quickly. Construction of *Ontario* and others suspended 27 Nov 1865. Ship rig with two funnels.

SERVICE RECORDS:

Antietam—Machinery never installed, unarmed. Used as store hulk. Sold 8 Sep 1888.

Guerriere—S. Atlantic Sqn 1867–69. Went aground on Nantucket I., 29 Sep 1870. Mediterranean Sqn 1871–72. Badly damaged when stranded near Leghorn, 26 Jul 1871. Repaired for return to U.S. and decomm 22 Mar 1872. Sold 12 Dec 1872.

Illinois—BU on stocks, Feb 1872.

Java—BU on stocks, 1884.

Kewaydin—Renamed **Pennsylvania**, 15 May 1869. BU on stocks 1884.

Minnetonka—Renamed **California**, 15 May 1869. Pacific Sqn (flag) 1871–73. Decomm 3 Jul 1873. Sold May 1875.

Ontario—Renamed **New York**, 15 May 1869. BU on stocks, 1888.

Piscataqua—Asiatic Sqn 1867–70. Renamed **Delaware**, 15 May 1869. Decomm 5 Dec 1870. Foundered at wharf, New York, Feb 1877. Sold 1877 and BU.

The frigate *Niagara*, anchored off Boston in 1863, clearly identified by her distinctive two tall funnels. She was the largest ship launched in the United States when built. (Martin Holbrook Collection) (U.S. Naval Historical Center)

The frigate *Guerriere*, which remained in service less than five years. Only three ships of the *Java* class were completed. She was named after a British ship captured by the USS *Constitution* in a famous action in 1812. (INRO) (U.S. Naval Historical Center)

The *California*, a frigate of the *Java* class, was launched as *Minnetonka*. Her two telescopic funnels have been lowered. (Martin Holbrook Collection)

The *Java*-class frigate *Delaware*, originally named *Piscataqua*, at Shanghai in 1869 with her funnels lowered. (Martin Holbrook Collection) (U.S. Naval Historical Center)

HASSALO CLASS

Name	Bldr	Laid down	L	Comm
Hassalo	(unknown)	never	never	never
Watauga	(unknown)	never	never	never

Tonnage:	3,365 tons

NOTES: Modified *Java* class. Projected, never built. Other details unknown.

TRENTON

Name	Bldr	Laid down	L	Comm
Trenton	Brooklyn (Morgan)	Dec 1873	1 Jan 1876	14 Feb 1877

Tonnage:	3,900 tons D
Dimensions:	271'6" (oa) 253' (bp) × 48' × 20'6"
Machinery:	1 screw, horizontal back-acting compound engines, 8 boilers; IHP 3,500 = 13 knots
Complement:	477
Armament:	11 8" R, 2 20-pdr BLR

NOTES: Wood hull. Ship rig with single funnel and ram bow. First warship fitted with electric lighting 1883.
SERVICE RECORD: European Stn 1877–81. Asiatic Stn 1883–86. South America 1887. Pacific 1888–89. Wrecked in hurricane at Apia, Samoa, 16 Mar 1889.

SCREW CRUISERS

Fast cruisers designed to attack British shipping and ports in the event of war. Hulls unusually long compared to width. *Wampanoag* and *Madawaska* were competitive sisters as to machinery, with similar hulls and boilers. Machinery took up too much space, leaving inadequate room for crew and stores. The hull was too narrow forward to mount bow guns.

AMMONOOSUC CLASS

Name	Bldr	Laid down	L	Comm
Ammonoosuc	Boston (Corliss)	1863	21 Jul 1864	15 Jun 1868
Neshaminy	Philadelphia (Etna)	1863	5 Oct 1865	never

Tonnage:	3,850 tons D; 3,213 tons B
Dimensions:	335' × 44'4" × 16'6"
Machinery:	1 screw, 2 horizontal geared direct-acting engines (100" × 4'), 8 boilers (*Neshaminy* 12); IHP 4,480 = 17 knots
Armament:	10 9" SB, 3 60-pdr R, 2 24-pdr SB

NOTES: Hulls designed by Delano; engines by Isherwood.
Ammonoosuc never used although average speed on trials was 16.8 knots. *Neshaminy* not completed because hull was "twisted" 1869.
SERVICE RECORDS:
Ammonoosuc—Laid up after trials. Renamed **Iowa**, 15 May 1869. Sold 27 Sep 1883.
Neshaminy—Renamed **Arizona**, 15 May 1869. Renamed **Nevada**, 10 Aug 1869. Sold incomplete Jun 1874 and BU.

WAMPANOAG

Name	Bldr	Laid down	L	Comm
Wampanoag	Brooklyn (Novelty)	3 Aug 1863	15 Dec 1864	17 Sep 1867

Tonnage:	4,215 tons D; 3,281 tons B
Dimensions:	355' × 45'2" × 19'10"
Machinery:	1 screw, 2 horizontal geared direct-acting engines (100" × 4'), 8 boilers; IHP 4,049 = 17.5 knots
Complement:	375
Armament:	10 9" SB, 3 60-pdr R guns. 1874 total: 2 100-pdr R, 10 9" SB.

NOTES: Hull designed by Delano, engines by Isherwood. Exceeded designed speed on trials, averaging 16.75 knots. The fastest ship afloat when completed.
SERVICE RECORD: N. Atlantic Fleet 1868. Decomm 5 May 1868. Renamed **Florida**, 15 May 1869. Receiving ship, New London, 1874. Sold 27 Feb 1885 and BU.

MADAWASKA

Name	Bldr	Laid down	L	Comm
Madawaska	Brooklyn (Allaire)	1863	8 Jul 1865	27 Jun 1866

Tonnage:	4,170 tons D; 3,281 tons B; 1871: 4,840 tons D
Dimensions:	355' (bp) × 45'2" × 21'8"
Machinery:	1 screw, 2 vibrating-lever engines (100" × 4'); IHP 2,143 = 11 knots; 1871: 2 horizontal back-acting compound engines, 10 boilers; IHP 3,200 = 13 knots
Complement:	480
Armament:	10 9" SB, 3 60-pdr R. 1871 total: 2 100-pdr R, 2 8" R, 18 9" SB. 1880 total: 2 11" SB, 16 9" SB, 2 100-pdr R, 1 60-pdr R.

NOTES: Hull designed by Delano, engines by Ericsson. Engines were unsuitable, and the ship failed her designed speed on trials by 2 knots, making only 12.7 knots. 1869–71 converted to gun-deck frigate with new machinery (Morgan), 2 funnels, clipper bow and ship rig; again failed contract speed by 4 knots.
SERVICE RECORD: Renamed **Tennessee**, 15 May 1869. Asiatic Sqn 1872. N. Atlantic Sqn 1879. Sold 15 Sep 1886.

POMPANOOSUC

Name	Bldr	Laid down	L	Comm
Pompanoosuc	Boston (Corliss)	2 Jan 1864	never	never

Tonnage:	4,446 tons D; 3,713 tons B
Dimensions:	335' × 48' × (U)
Machinery:	1 screw, 2 horizontal geared direct-acting engines (100" × 4'), 12 boilers
Armament:	2 100-pdr R, 2 60-pdr R, 12 9" SB guns (projected)

NOTES: Hull designed by Lenthall, engines by Isherwood
SERVICE RECORD: Renamed **Connecticut**, 15 May 1869. BU on stocks 1885.

Vampanoag, laid up in dry dock at Brooklyn Navy Yard in 1874, before proceeding to New London as receiving funnels were distinctive of this class. (U.S. Naval Historical Center)

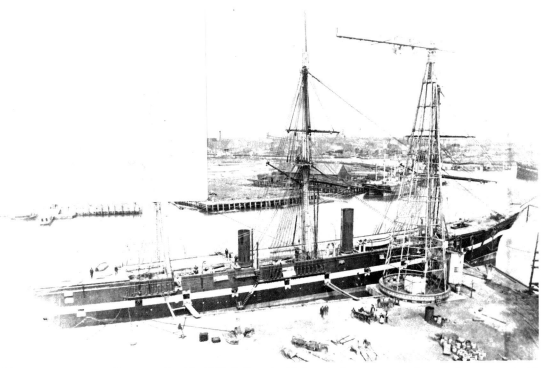

The frigate *Tennessee* at Brooklyn Navy Yard in 1875. Built as the *Madawaska*, her appearance here can be compared with that of *Florida*, her former sister. (U.S. Naval Historical Center)

Another view of the *Tennessee* in dry dock while undergoing conversion to a gun-deck frigate at Brooklyn Navy Yard in 1870. She already has a new bow and two funnels. (Martin Holbrook Collection) (U.S. Naval Historical Center)

Left: The cruiser *Idaho* laid up at Brooklyn Navy Yard after failing her trials in the summer of 1866. Her distinctive two funnels are side-by-side. Her designers used political influence in Congress to force the Navy to buy the ship. (Martin Holbrook Collection) (U.S. Naval Historical Center) *Below*: The fleet lined up in the Hudson River at the funeral of former President Grant in 1885. Left to right are the revenue cutter *Grant*, sloops *Alliance*, *Swatara*, and *Omaha*, and side-wheel frigate *Powhatan*. (Silverstone Collection) (U.S. Naval Historical Center)

BON HOMME RICHARD

Name	Bldr	Laid down	L	Comm
Bon Homme Richard	(Unknown) (Washington)	never	never	never

Tonnage: 3,713 tons D
Dimensions: (U)
Machinery: 2 screws, 2 horizontal direct-acting engines (100″ × 4′)
Armament: (U)

NOTES: Ship never built, engines built and put in storage.

IDAHO

Name	Bldr	Laid down	L	Comm
Idaho	Steers (Morgan)	1863	8 Oct 1864	2 Apr 1866

Tonnage: 3,241 tons D; 2,638 tons B
Dimensions: 298′ (wl) × 44′6″ × 17′
Machinery: 2 screws, 2 engines (type unknown) (30″ × 8′); HP 645 = 8
            knots (removed 1867)
Complement: 400
Armament: 6 32-pdr, 1 30-pdr, 1 12-pdr H

NOTES: Hull designed by Steers; machinery by Dickerson. Failed trials and rejected by Navy. Forced by congressional resolution in 1867, the Navy accepted the ship, which was completed as sail storeship without engines. A fine and very fast sailing ship.
SERVICE RECORD: Rejected by the Navy, 25 May 1866. Converted to full-rigged sailing ship, comm 3 Oct 1867. Storeship for Asiatic Sqn. Dismasted and severely damaged in typhoon off Yokohama, 21 Sep 1869. Hulk sold at Yokohama 1874.

CHATTANOOGA

Name	Bldr	Laid down	L	Comm
Chattanooga	Cramp (Merrick)	1863	13 Oct 1864	16 May 1866

Tonnage: 3,043 tons D
Dimensions: 315′ (dk) × 46′ × 20′6″
Machinery: 1 screw, 2 horizontal back-acting engines (84″ × 3′6″), 8
            boilers; IHP 2,000 = 13.5 knots
Complement: (U)
Armament: 8 8″ SB, 3 60-pdr R

NOTES: Designed by builders. Ship rig, 2 funnels. Failed to meet contract speed.
SERVICE RECORD: Completed at Philadelphia. Decomm 3 Sep 1866. Sunk by floating ice at dock, League Island, Dec 1871.

SCREW SLOOPS

BROOKLYN

Name	Bldr	Laid down	L	Comm
Brooklyn	Westervelt (Fulton)	1857	27 Jul 1858	26 Jan 1859

Tonnage: 2,532 tons D; 2,070 tons B
Dimensions: 233′ (wl) × 43′ × 16′3″
Machinery: 1 screw, 2 horizontal direct-acting cross-head engines (61″ ×
            2′9″), 2 boilers; HP 1,116 = 11.5 knots
Complement: 335
Armament: 1 10″ SB, 20 9″ SB guns. 1862 total: 24 9″ SB, 2 12-pdr H.
            June 63 total: 1 100-pdr R, 22 9″ SB, 1 30-pdr R. 1864
            total: 2 100-pdr R, 2 60-pdr R, 20 9″ SB, 2 12-pdr H.
            1869 total: 2 11″ SB, 18 9″ SB. 1881 total: 1 8″ R, 12 9″ SB

NOTES: Ship rig, Rebuilt 1876–81, spar deck removed, rearmed.
SERVICE RECORD: WGulfBS 1861–64. Passage past New Orleans forts and engagement with CSN vessels, 24 Apr 1862. Bombardment of Grand Gulf, Miss., 26 May 1862. Passage past batteries at Vicksburg, 28 Jun 1862. Attack on Vicksburg, 22 Jul 1862. Bombarded Galveston, Texas, 10 Jan and 24 Feb 1863. Repairing Aug 1863–Apr 1864. WGulfBS 1864. Battle of Mobile Bay, struck 40 times, 5 Aug 1864. Bombardment of Ft. Morgan, Mobile Bay, 9–23 Aug 1864. NAtlBS Oct 1864–Jan 1865. Unsuccessful attack on Ft. Fisher, NC, 24–25 Dec 1864. Second attack on Ft. Fisher, 13–15 Jan 1865. S. American Stn 1865–67. Europe 1871–73. N. Atlantic 1874. S. America 1875 and 1881–84. Damaged in collision with British steamer *Mozart* at Montevideo, 1 May 1882. Asiatic Stn 1886–89. Decomm 14 May 1889. Sold 25 Mar 1891.
Prizes: 29 May 1861: *H. E. Spearing*; 7 Jun: *Pilgrim*; 20 Jun: *Nahum Stetson*; 5 Sep: *Macao*; 19 Feb 1862: str *Magnolia*; 27 May 1863: *Blazer*; 28 May: *Kate*; 30 May: *Victoria* and *Star*.

The screw sloop *Brooklyn* as she appeared early in the 1870s after the addition of a complete spar deck. (Martin Holbrook Collection) (U.S. Naval Historical Center)

The *Brooklyn* after the war. Her funnel can be seen lowered just forward of the mainmast. (National Archives)

LANCASTER

Name	Bldr	Laid down	L	Comm
Lancaster	Philadelphia (Reaney Neafie)	Dec 1857	20 Oct 1858	12 May 1859

Tonnage:	3,250 tons D; 2,362 tons B
Dimensions:	235′8″ (bp) × 46′ × 18′6″
Machinery:	1 screw, 2 direct-acting double piston-rod engines (61″ × 2′9″), 2 boilers; IHP 1,000 = 10 knots; 1879: compound engines, IHP 2,000
Complement:	300
Armament:	2 11″ SB, 2 9″ SB. May 63: add 4 9″ SB, 2 30-pdr SB. 1878 total: 2 100-pdr R, 16 9″ SB.

NOTES: 1879 rebuilt with ram bow and new engines built in 1865.
SERVICE RECORD: Pacific Sqn 1859–66. S. Atlantic Sqn 1870–75, 1885–88, 1895–97. European Sqn 1881–85, 1888–89. Asiatic Sqn 1892–94. Station ship, Key West 1898. Gunnery training ship 1899. Receiving ship Philadelphia 1903–12. Stricken 31 Dec 1915.
Later history: 1 Feb 1913 transferred to U.S. Public Health Service. Quarantine ship, Reedy Island, Del., 1913–20, and New York 1920–30. BU 1933.

HARTFORD

Name	Bldr	Laid down	L	Comm
Hartford	Boston (Loring)	1 Jan 1858	22 Nov 1858	27 May 1859

Tonnage:	2,900 tons D; 1,900 tons B
Dimensions:	225′ (bp) × 44′ × 17′2″
Machinery:	1 screw, 2 horizontal double piston-rod engines (62″ × 2′10″), 2 boilers; IHP 1,024 = 13.5 knots; 1880: horizontal back-acting engines (H. Loring); 1898: compound engines, IHP 2,000
Complement:	310
Armament:	16 9″ guns. Jun 62 total: 20 9″ SB, 2 20-pdr R, 2 12-pdr. Jun 63 total: 24 9″ SB, 1 45-pdr R, 2 30-pdr R. Jun 64 total: 2 100-pdr R, 18 9″ SB, 1 30-pdr R, 3 13-pdr H. 1872 total: 2 11″ SB, 16 9″ SB, 2 20-pdr R.

NOTES: Ship rig. Re-engined 1880 with engines built for *Kewaydin*. Rerigged as bark 1887 for service as training ship. Re-engined again 1898.
SERVICE RECORD: East India Sqn 1859–61. WGulfBS (flag), 1861–65. Passage past New Orleans forts and engagement with CSN vessels, 24 Apr 1862. Made passage past batteries at Vicksburg, 28 Jun 1862. Engagement with CSS *Arkansas* above Vicksburg, 15 Jul 1862. Made passage past Port Hudson, La., 14 Mar, north past Grand Gulf, Miss., 19 Mar, and run south, 31 Mar 1863. Bombardment of Ft. Powell, Mobile Bay, 16–29 Feb 1864. Battle of Mobile Bay, 5 Aug 1864. Bombardment of Ft. Morgan, Mobile Bay, 9–23 Aug 1864. Repairing Dec 1864–Jul 1865.

Asiatic Sqn 1865–68 and 1872–75. Decomm 14 Jan 1887. Apprentice training ship 1887–90. Training ship 1899–1912. Station ship, Charleston, SC, 1912–26. Foundered at her berth at Norfolk NYd, 20 Nov 1956.
Prize: 8 Apr 1863: str *J.D. Clark*.

The screw sloop *Lancaster* dressed overall in 1866. (U.S. Naval Historical Center)

Farragut's future flagship *Hartford* as she appeared in the 1870s, with a complete spar deck. (U.S. Naval Historical Center)

PENSACOLA

Name	Bldr	Laid down	L	Comm
Pensacola	Pensacola (Washington)	Mar 1858	13 Aug 1859	16 Sep 1861

Tonnage:	3,000 tons D; 2,158 tons B
Dimensions:	230'8" (bp) × 44'5" × 18'7"
Machinery:	1 screw, Dickerson condensing engines (58" × 3'); IHP 1,165 = 9.5 knots; 1865: horizontal direct-acting engines (Hazelhurst)
Complement:	269
Armament:	1 11" SB, 18 9" SB guns. Dec 61 total: 1 42-pdr R, 22 9" SB. Jul 63 total: 1 100-pdr R, 1 11" SB, 20 9" SB. 1863: 1 11" SB replaced by 1 30-pdr R. 1868 total: 18 9" SB, 2 60-pdr R.

NOTES: Hull designed by Lenthall and engines by Dickerson. Engines were so unreliable ship was used mainly as a floating battery. Re-engined in 1864–66 with machinery built for *Wanalosett* and given two smoke pipes. Modified to single funnel 1885.

SERVICE RECORD: WGulfBS Jan 1862. Passage past New Orleans forts and engagement with CSN vessels, 24 Apr 1862. Repairing 1864–66. Pacific Sqn 1866–83. European Sqn 1885–88. Pacific 1890–92. Training ship 1898–99. Receiving ship, San Francisco 1901–11. Stricken 23 Dec 1911. Hulk destroyed by burning, May 1912.

The screw sloop *Richmond*, which served throughout the war and was not sold until 1919.

The sloop *Kearsarge* became one of the most famous ships of the Navy by her victory over the *Alabama* in 1864. This picture was probably taken in the 1880s. (Marius Bar)

RICHMOND

Name	Bldr	Laid down	L	Comm
Richmond	Norfolk (Washington)	1858	26 Jan 1860	Oct 1860

Tonnage:	2,700 tons D; 1,929 tons B
Dimensions:	225′ (bp) × 42′6″ × 17′5″
Machinery:	1 screw, 2 direct-acting engines (58″ × 3′); IHP 1,078 = 9.5 knots
Complement:	260
Armament:	14 9″ SB. Feb 62 total: 1 80-pdr R, 20 9″ SB, 1 30-pdr R. Jun 63 total: 1 100-pdr R, 1 30-pdr R, 20 9″ SB, 2 12-pdr SB, 1 24-pdr H. Jun 64 total: 1 100-pdr R, 1 30-pdr R, 18 9″ SB. 1886 total: 12 9″ SB, 1 8″ R, 1 60-pdr BLR, 2 20-pdr BLR.

NOTES: Ship rig. Engines designed by Archbold were not successful, replaced in 1866 by Isherwood engines (60″ × 3′).

SERVICE RECORD: Mediterranean 1860–61. Searched for CSS *Sumter* in Caribbean 1861. GulfBS Sep 1861. Rammed by CSS *Manassas* during engagement near Head of Passes, Miss., 12 Oct 1861. Damaged by gunfire during bombardment of Pensacola, Fla., 22–23 Nov 1861. Hit many times during passage past New Orleans forts and engagement with CSN vessels, 24 Apr 1862. Again hit during passage past batteries at Vicksburg, 28 Jun 1862. Engagement with CSS *Arkansas* above Vicksburg, 15 Jul 1862. Occupation of Baton Rouge, La., 17 Dec 1862. Damaged during attempt to pass Port Hudson, La., 14 Mar 1863. Battle of Mobile Bay, 5 Aug 1864. Bombardment of Ft. Morgan, Mobile Bay, 9–23 Aug 1864. Engagement with CSS *Webb* below New Orleans, 24 Apr 1865.

European Sqn 1869–71. West Indies 1872–73. S. Pacific Sqn 1874–77. Asiatic Fleet (flag) 1879–84. N. Atlantic 1887–89. S. Atlantic 1889–90. Training ship 1890–93. Receiving ship, Philadelphia 1894–1903, and Norfolk 1903–19. Sold 23 Jul 1919 and BU.

MOHICAN CLASS

Name	Bldr	Laid down	L	Comm
Kearsarge	Portsmouth (Woodruff)	May 1861	5 Oct 1861	24 Jan 1862
Mohican	Portsmouth (Woodruff)	Aug 1858	15 Feb 1859	29 Nov 1859

Tonnage:	*Kearsarge*: 1,550 tons D; 1,031 tons B; *Mohican*: 1,461 tons D; 994 tons B
Dimensions:	198′6″ (bp) × 33′10″ × 15′9″
Machinery:	1 screw, 2 horizontal back-acting engines (54″ × 2′6″), 2 boilers; IHP 842 = 11 knots
Complement:	160
Armament:	2 11″ SB, 4 32-pdr/42 guns
Kearsarge:	1864: add 1 30-pdr R, 1 12-pdr SB. 1873 total: 2 11″ SB, 4 9″ SB, 2 20-pdr R
Mohican:	Apr 64 total: 1 100-pdr R, 4 9″ SB, 2 30-pdr R, 2 32-pdr/42, 1 12-pdr H. Nov 64: 2 32-pdr R replaced by 2 9″ SB.

NOTES: Bark rig. *Kearsarge* built under 1861 emergency program. *Kearsarge* re-engined 1887 with engines from *Nantasket*.

SERVICE RECORDS:

Kearsarge—European Sqn 1862–66. Sank CSS *Alabama* in engagement off Cherbourg, 19 Jun 1864. S. Pacific, 1868–70. Asiatic Stn, 1873–77. N. Atlantic Stn 1879–82. Mediterranean 1883–86. West Indies 1888–94. Wrecked on Roncador Reef, Central America, 2 Feb 1894.

Mohican—African Sqn 1860–61. Captured ship *Erie* with 997 slaves off Congo River, 8 Aug 1860. SAtlBS Oct 1861. Damaged during bombardment and occupation of Port Royal, SC, 7 Nov 1861. Capture of Fernandina, Fla., and Brunswick, St. Simons, and Jekyl islands, Ga., 2–12 Mar 1862. Search for CSS *Florida* and *Alabama*, Oct 1862–Apr 1864. NAtlBS Oct 1864–65. Unsuccessful attack on Ft. Fisher, NC, 24–25 Dec 1864. Second attack on Ft. Fisher, 13–15 Jan 1865. SAtlBS Jan–Apr 1865.

One of the 11-inch pivot guns aboard the *Kearsarge* in 1864. (U.S. Naval Historical Center)

Pacific Sqn 1866–72. Cruise to Siberia 1869. Captured Mexican pirate *Forward* off Mexico, 17 Jun 1870. Decomm 25 Jun 1872. Sank at her moorings at Mare Island 1872 and BU.

Prizes: 25 Feb 1862: *Arrow*.

IROQUOIS CLASS

Name	Bldr	Laid down	L	Comm
Iroquois	Brooklyn (Fulton)	Aug 1858	12 Apr 1859	24 Nov 1859
Oneida	Brooklyn (Fulton)	Jun 1861	20 Nov 1861	28 Feb 1862
Wachusett	Boston (Morgan)	Jun 1861	10 Oct 1861	3 Mar 1862

Tonnage:	1,488 tons D; 1,016 tons B (*Iroquois*); 1,032 tons B (*Oneida*)
Dimensions:	198'10" (bp) × 33'10" × 13'
Machinery:	1 screw, 2 horizontal back-acting engines (54" × 2'4"), except *Wachusett*: 2 horizontal steeple engines (50" × 2'6"), 3 boilers (*Iroquois* 2); IHP 1,202 = 11.5 knots
Complement:	123

Armament:

Iroquois:	1862: 2 11" SB, 4 32-pdr/42 SB. Jan 63: add 1 50-pdr R, 1 12-pdr HSB. May 64 total: 1 100-pdr R, 1 60-pdr R, 1 9" SB, 4 32-pdr/42. 1886 total: 2 11" SB, 4 9" SB, 1 60-pdr R.
Oneida:	1862: 2 11" SB, 4 32-pdr/33, 3 30-pdr R, 1 12-pdr H. 1864 total: 2 11" SB, 6 8"/63, 1 30-pdr R, 2 24-pdr H, 1 12-pdr H. 1870 total: 1 11" SB, 1 60-pdr R, 6 32-pdr SB.
Wachusett:	1862: 2 11" SB, 4 32-pdr/27, 2 30-pdr R, 1 20-pdr R, 1 12-pdr R. 1864 total: 3 100-pdr R, 4 32-pdr/42, 2 30-pdr R, 1 12-pdr H. 1878 total: 2 11" SB, 4 8" SB, 1 60-pdr R.

NOTES: Hulls designed by Lenthall. Schooner rig, except *Iroquois*, bark. *Oneida* and *Wachusett* built under 1861 emergency program.

SERVICE RECORDS:

Iroquois—Mediterranean 1860–61. Search for CSS *Sumter* in Caribbean, 1861. WGulfBS 1862. Bombardment of Fts. Jackson and St. Philip below New Orleans, Mississippi River, 18–28 Apr 1862. Occupation of Natchez, 13 May 1862. Bombardment of Grand Gulf, Miss., 9–10 Jun 1862. Passage past batteries at Vicksburg, 28 Jun 1862. Engagement with CSS *Arkansas* above Vicksburg, 15 Jul 1862. NAtlBS 1863–64. Mediterranean 1864. Search for CSS *Shenandoah* 1865. Asiatic Sqn 1867–70 & 1872–74. Decomm 1874. Pacific Stn 1882–92. Decomm 1892. Recomm 1898–99.

Prize: 24 Jul 1863: str *Merrimac*.

Later history: Loaned to Marine Hospital Service, May 1892. Renamed **Ionie**, 30 Nov 1904. Wrecked at Port Townshend, Washington, 26 Aug 1910.

Oneida—WGulfBS 1862. Passage past New Orleans forts and engagement with CSN vessels, 24 Apr 1862. Occupation of Natchez, 13 May 1862. Bombardment of Grand Gulf, Miss., 9–10 Jun 1862. Made passage past batteries at Vicksburg, 28 Jun 1862. Engagement with CSS *Arkansas* above Vicksburg, 15 Jul 1862. Blockade of Mobile, Oct 1863–Aug 1864. Damaged during battle of Mobile Bay, 5 Aug 1864. Asiatic Sqn 1867–70. Sunk in collision when run down by British steamer *City of Bombay* in Yokohama Bay, 24 Jan 1870.

The screw sloop *Wachusett* at Shanghai 1867. Under Commander Napoleon Collins she violated Brazilian neutrality in October 1864 and captured the Confederate cruiser *Florida*. (U.S. Naval Historical Center)

Wachusett—NAtlBS 1862. Supported operations in James River, 1862. Army operations at Gloucester and York, Va., 14–29 Apr and at Yorktown, Va., 4–7 May 1862. Search for CSS *Alabama* and *Florida* in Caribbean 1863. Repairing Jun 1863–Jan 1864. Protected commerce off Brazil 1864. Rammed and captured CSS *Florida* in neutral harbor of Bahia, Brazil, 7 Oct 1864. East Indies 1865–67. Mediterranean 1871–74. Gulf of Mexico 1879. S. Atlantic Stn 1879–80. Pacific Stn 1880–85. Sold 30 Jul 1887 and BU.
Prizes: 18 Jan 1863: str *Virginia*; 25 Mar: str *Dolphin*.

WYOMING CLASS

Name	Bldr	Laid down	L	Comm
Tuscarora	Philadelphia (Merrick)	27 Jun 1861	24 Aug 1861	5 Dec 1861
Wyoming	Philadelphia (Merrick)	Jul 1858	19 Jan 1859	Oct 1859

Tonnage:	1,457 tons D; 977 tons B
Dimensions:	198′6″ (bp) × 32′2″ × 14′10″
Machinery:	1 screw, 2 horizontal back-acting engines (*Wyoming*: direct-acting) (50″ × 2′6″), 3 boilers; IHP 793 = 11 knots
Complement:	198
Armament:	
Tuscarora:	1 11″ SB, 2 32-pdr. Dec 61 total: 2 11″ SB, 4 32-pdr/57, 2 32-pdr/33, 1 30-pdr R. Jul 62 total: 1 100-pdr R, 1 11″ SB, 4 8″/55, 2 30-pdr R. Sep 63: add 2 8″/55. 1872 total: 2 11″ SB, 4 9″ SB.
Wyoming:	2 11″ SB, 4 32-pdr. 1863 total: 2 9″ SB, 4 32-pdr SB. Sep 65 total: 2 11″ SB, 1 60-pdr R, 3 32-pdr/57. 1871 total: 1 11″, 4 9″, 2 20-pdr R.

NOTES: Bark rig. *Tuscarora* built under 1861 emergency program and was rebuilt 1871 with ship rig.

SERVICE RECORDS:

Tuscarora—Search for Confederate raiders in European waters 1862–63. NAtlBS Oct 1863, storeship at Beaufort, NC. Unsuccessful attack on Ft. Fisher, NC, 24–25 Dec 1864. Second attack on Ft. Fisher, 13–15 Jan 1865. S. Pacific Sqn 1866–69. Caribbean 1870. S. Pacific Stn 1872–76. Landed marines at Honolulu to restore order Feb 1874. Decomm 31 May 1880. Sold 20 Nov 1883.

Wyoming—Stationed in California, 1860–62. Search for CSS *Alabama* in East Indies, 1862–64. Engaged batteries at Shimonoseki, Japan, and sank a steamer, 16 Jul 1863. Repairing at Philadelphia Jul 1864–Apr 1865. East Indies Stn and Asiatic Sqn 1865–68. Punitive expedition to Formosa 1867. N. Atlantic Stn 1872–74. Receiving ship Washington 1877–78. European Stn 1878–80. Practice ship, Naval Academy 1882–92. Sold 9 May 1892.

DACOTAH

Name	Bldr	Laid down	L	Comm
Dacotah	Norfolk (Murray)	1858	23 Mar 1859	1 May 1860

Tonnage:	1,369 tons D; 996 tons B
Dimensions:	227′ (oa) 198′5″ (bp) × 32′9″ × 14′8″
Machinery:	1 screw, 2 horizontal cross-head geared engines (63″ × 3′), 2 boilers; IHP 1,000 = 11 knots
Complement:	147
Armament:	2 11″ SB, 4 32-pdr. 1862 total: 1 100-pdr R, 4 32-pdr/41, 1 10″ SB, 2 12-pdr H. 1863: add 1 30-pdr R.

NOTES: Engines removed 1870 and converted to sailing ship. Designed by S.T. Hartt.

SERVICE RECORD: East India Sqn 1860–61. NAtlBS Mar–Sep 1862. Engagement with batteries at Sewells Point, 18–19 May 1862. Search for Confederate raiders in N. Atlantic 1862–63. NAtlBS Jan 1864–Aug 1864. Decomm at Mare Island 26 Jul 1869. Sold 30 May 1873.

NARRAGANSETT CLASS

Name	Bldr	Laid down	L	Comm
Narragansett	Boston (Boston Loco)	Jul 1858	15 Feb 1859	6 Nov 1859
Seminole	Pensacola (Morgan)	Jul 1858	25 Jun 1859	25 Apr 1860

Tonnage:	1,235 tons D; 804 tons B
Dimensions:	208′ (dk) 188′ (wl) × 32′2″ × 11′6″
Machinery:	1 screw, *Narragansett* 2 horizontal direct-acting engines (48″ × 2′4″); *Seminole* 2 horizontal back-acting double piston-rod engines (50″ × 2′6″), 3 boilers; HP 250 = 11 knots
Complement:	120
Armament:	1 11″ SB, 4 32-pdr/42 SB
	Seminole: Jun 63 total: 1 11″ SB, 1 30-pdr R, 6 32-pdr/43, 1 12-pdr R

SERVICE RECORDS:

Narragansett—Pacific coast 1861–65. Caribbean 1869. S. Pacific 1872–75. Decomm 1875. Sold 20 Nov 1883.

Seminole—Brazil Stn 1860–61. AtlBS 1861. Potomac Flotilla 1861. Bombardment at Freestone Point, Va., 25 Sep 1861. SAtlBS Nov 1861–Mar 1862. Occupation of Port Royal, SC, 7 Nov 1861. Capture of Fernandina, Fla., and Brunswick, St. Simons, and Jekyl islands, Ga., 2–12 Mar 1862. Engaged batteries at Sewells Point, Va., 8 May 1862. WGulfBS Jul 1863. Battle of Mobile Bay, 5 Aug 1864. Bombardment of Ft. Morgan, Mobile Bay, 9–23 Aug 1864. Decomm 11 Aug 1865. Sold 20 Jul 1870.

Prizes: 16 Aug 1861: *Albion*; 1 Dec: *Lida*; 11 Jul 1863: str *Charleston*; 11 Sep: *Sir William Peel*; 14 Jan 1865: *Josephine*; 24 May: str *Denbigh*.

Later history: Merchant *Seminole*, rebuilt 1871. SE 1878.

PAWNEE

Name	Bldr	Laid down	L	Comm
Pawnee	Philadelphia (Reaney Neafie)	Oct 1858	8 Oct 1859	11 Jun 1860

Tonnage:	1,533 tons D; 1,289 tons B
Dimensions:	233′ × 47′ × 11′
Machinery:	2 screws, 2 horizontal direct-acting geared engines (65″ × 3′), 3 boilers; IHP 590 = 10 knots
Complement:	151/181
Armament:	8 9″ SB, 2 12-pdr SB. May 63 total: 1 100-pdr R, 8 9″ SB, 1 50-pdr R. Jun 64: add 2 9″ SB. 1865: add 2 9″ SB.

NOTES: Bark rig, small draft with large battery. Engines removed 1870 and converted to storeship.

SERVICE RECORD: Home Sqn off Mexico 1860. Attempted relief of Fort Sumter, Apr 1861. Potomac River 1861. Occupation of Alexandria, Va., 24 May 1861. Engaged batteries at Aquia Creek, Va., 29 May–1

The sloop *Pawnee* as she appeared during the Civil War. The mainmast is forward of the funnel.

The deck of the sloop *Pawnee* showing the starboard battery.

Jun 1861. AtlBS Aug 1861–Jun 1862. Landings at Hatteras Inlet, 28–29 Aug 1861. Engagement with CSN squadron off Port Royal, SC, 5 Nov 1861. Occupation of Port Royal, 7 Nov 1861. Bombardment of forts at St. Helena Sound, SC, 25–28 Nov 1861. Capture of Fernandina, Fla., and Brunswick, St. Simons, and Jekyl islands, Ga., 2–12 Mar 1862. SAtlBS Jan 1863–65. Engaged batteries in Stono River, SC, 16 Jul (damaged) and 25 Dec 1863. Expedition up Stono River, 5 Jul and in Broad River, SC, 27 Nov–30 Dec 1864. Engaged batteries in Togodo Creek, SC, 9 Feb 1865. Expedition to Georgetown, SC, 23 Feb 1865. Decomm 26 Jul 1865. Brazil Stn 1867–69. Converted to storeship 1870. Hospital and receiving ship, Key West, 1871–75 and Port Royal 1875–82. Sold 3 May 1884.

Prizes: 25 May 1861: str *Thomas Collyer*; 9 Sep: *Mary Wood*, *Ocean Wave*, *Harriet P. Ryan*, *Susan Jane*; 3 Mar 1862: str *Darlington*; 9 Jun: *Rowena*.

The screw sloop *Juniata* with funnel down. The screw sloops built in 1859–62 were sturdy units of the fleet that served the Navy for many years. (Martin Holbrook Collection)

The screw sloop *Ossipee*.

OSSIPEE CLASS

Name	Bldr	Laid down	L	Comm
Adirondack	Brooklyn (Novelty)	1861	22 Feb 1862	Jun? 1862
Housatonic	Boston (Globe)	1861	20 Nov 1861	29 Aug 1862
Juniata	Philadelphia (Pusey)	Jun 1861	20 Mar 1862	4 Dec 1862
Ossipee	Portsmouth (Reliance)	6 Jun 1861	16 Nov 1861	6 Nov 1862

Tonnage: 1, 934 tons D; 1,240 tons B
Dimensions: 205′ (bp) × 38′ × 16′7″
Machinery: 1 screw, 2 horizontal direct-acting engines; *Ossipee* 2 horizontal back-acting engines; *Juniata* 2 horizontal double-crosshead back-acting engines (42″ × 2′6″), 2 boilers; IHP 715 = 12 knots
Complement: 160
Armament:
  Adirondack: 2 11″ SB, 2 24-pdr SB, 4 32-pdr/57, 1 12-pdr.
  Housatonic: 1 100-pdr R, 3 30-pdr R, 1 11″ SB, 2 32-pdr/33, 2 24-pdr H, 1 12-pdr H. 1863: add 2 32-pdr SB, 1 12-pdr H.
  Juniata: 1 100-pdr R, 1 11″ SB, 4 30-pdr R, 1 12-pdr, 4 24-pdr H. Jul 64 total: 1 100-pdr R, 2 30-pdr R, 6 8″ SB, 1 12-pdr H. Oct 64: add 2 8″ SB. 1878 total: 1 11″ SB, 6 9″ SB.
  Ossipee: 1 100-pdr R, 1 11″ SB, 3 30-pdr R, 6 32-pdr/57, 1 12-pdr SB, 1 12-pdr R. 1873 total: 1 11″ SB, 6 9″ SB.

NOTES: Hulls designed by Lenthall; machinery by Isherwood.
SERVICE RECORDS:
Adirondack—SAtlBS 1862. Wrecked on Abaco Island, Bahamas, 23 Aug 1862.
  Prize: 23 Jul 1862: *Emma*.
Housatonic—SAtlBS 1862. Engagement with ironclads off Charleston, 31 Jan 1863. Sunk off Charleston by spar torpedo of submarine torpedo boat CSS *H.L. Hunley*, 17 Feb 1864.
  Prize: 19 Apr 1863: *Neptune*.

Juniata—NAtlBS 1863. West Indies 1863. Search for CSS *Tallahassee* off New York Aug 1864. NAtlBS 1864–65. Unsuccessful attack on Ft. Fisher, NC, 24–25 Dec 1864. Second attack on Ft. Fisher, 13–15 Jan 1865. SAtlBS 1865. S. American Stn 1865–67. European Stn 1869–72. Search for survivors of *Polaris* west of Greenland 1873. European Stn 1874–76. Cruise around the world, 1882–85. Decomm 28 Feb 1889. Sold 25 Mar 1891.
  Prizes: 29 Apr 1863: *Harvest*; 28 May: str *Victor*; 12 Jun: *Fashion*; 14 Jun: *Elizabeth*; 2 Jul: *Don Jose*.
Ossipee—NAtlBS 1862–63. WGulfBS May 1863–Jun 1865. Battle of Mobile Bay, 5 Aug 1864. Bombardment of Ft. Morgan, Mobile Bay, 9–23 Aug 1864. N. Pacific 1866–72. N. Atlantic 1873–78. Laid up 1878–83. Asiatic Stn 1884–87. Decomm 12 Nov 1889. Sold 25 Mar 1891.
  Prizes: 30 Jun 1863: *Helena*; 18 Jul: strs *James Battle* and *William Bagley*.

CANANDAIGUA CLASS

Name	Bldr	Laid down	L	Comm
Canandaigua	Boston (Atlantic)	Dec 1861	28 Mar 1862	1 Aug 1862
Shenandoah	Philadelphia (Merrick)	1861	8 Dec 1862	20 Jun 1863

Tonnage: 2,030 tons D; (*Canandaigua*) 1,395 tons B, (*Shenandoah*) 1,378 tons B
Dimensions: 228′ (bp) × 38′9″ × 15′
Machinery: 1 screw, 2 horizontal back-acting condensing engines (42″ × 2′6″), 2 boilers; IHP 1,300 = 12 knots
Complement: 191
Armament:
  Canandaigua: 2 11″ SB, 1 8″ SB, 3 20-pdr R (designed). Aug 62: 2 11″ SB, 1 150-pdr R, 3 20-pdr R, 2 12-pdr R, 2 12-pdr SB. May

The screw sloop *Shenandoah* as she appeared after 1865 with a bowsprit. In 1870 she was given a clipper bow. (U.S. Naval Historical Center)

65 total: 2 11″ SB, 2 9″ SB, 1 60-pdr R, 2 24-pdr, 1 12-pdr R, 1 12-pdr SB. 1878 total: 6 9″ SB, 2 8″ R, 1 60-pdr R.

Shenandoah: 2 11″ SB, 1 150-pdr R, 1 30-pdr R, 2 24-pdr H, 2 12-pdr H. May 65 total: 2 11″ SB, 2 9″ SB, 1 60-pdr R, 2 24-pdr H, 2 12-pdr R.

NOTES: *Shenandoah* modified with clipper bow 1870.

SERVICE RECORDS:

Canandaigua—SAtlBS Aug 1862. Bombarded Charleston forts, 17 Aug 1863. European Stn 1865–69. Renamed **Detroit**, 15 May 1869. Renamed **Canandaigua**, 10 Aug 1869. West Indies and Gulf of Mexico 1872–75. Decomm 8 Nov 1875. BU 1884.

Prizes: 8 May 1863: str *Cherokee* (*Thistle*); 15 May: *Secesh*; 19 Jul: str *Raccoon*.

Shenandoah—Search for Confederate raiders 1863. NAtlBS 1863–64. Unsuccessful attack on Ft. Fisher, NC, 24–25 Dec 1864. Second attack on Ft. Fisher, 13–15 Jan 1865. S. American Sqn 1865–66. Asiatic Sqn 1866–69. European Stn 1870–74. S. Atlantic Sqn 1879–82. S. Pacific Sqn 1884–86. Decomm 23 Oct 1886. Sold 30 Jul 1887.

Prize: 15 Sep 1863: str *Arabian*.

LACKAWANNA CLASS

Name	Bldr	Laid down	L	Comm
Lackawanna	Brooklyn (Allaire)	1862	9 Aug 1862	8 Jan 1863
Ticonderoga	Brooklyn (Allaire)	1862	16 Oct 1862	12 May 1863

Tonnage: 2,526 tons D; 1,533 tons B
Dimensions: 237′ (bp) × 38′2″ × 16′6″
Machinery: 1 screw, 2 horizontal back-acting condensing engines (42″ × 2′6″); IHP 1,300 = 11 knots
Complement: 205
Armament:

Lackawanna: 1 150-pdr R, 2 11″ SB, 4 9″ SB, 1 50-pdr R, 2 24-pdr R, 2 12-pdr H, 2 12-pdr R. 1865: add 1 60-pdr R.

Ticonderoga: 1 150-pdr R, 1 50-pdr R, 6 9″ SB, 2 24-pdr H, 2 12-pdr R, 2 12-pdr SB. Sep 63: 2 9″ SB replaced by 2 11″ SB. Dec 63 total: 1 100-pdr R, 12 9″ SB, 1 30-pdr R, 2 24-pdr H. Apr 64: less 2 9″ SB. May 65 total: 2 11″ SB, 2 9″ SB, 1 60-pdr R, 2 24-pdr H, 2 12-pdr R.

NOTES: Hulls designed by Lenthall; machinery by Isherwood.

SERVICE RECORDS:

Lackawanna—WGulfBS 1863. Battle of Mobile Bay, 5 Aug 1864. Bombardment of Fort Morgan, Mobile Bay, 9–23 Aug 1864. Pacific 1866–71. Far East 1872–75. Decomm 7 Apr 1885. Sold 30 Jul 1887.

Prizes: 14 Jun 1863: str *Neptune*; 15 Jun: str *Planter*.

Ticonderoga—West Indies Sqn Jun–Oct 1863. Search for Confederate raiders in N. Atlantic, 1864. Went aground near Maranham, 25 Aug 1864. NAtlBS 1864–65. Unsuccessful attack on Ft. Fisher, NC, 24–25 Dec 1864. Damaged by explosion of 100-pdr Parrott rifle, 24 Dec 1864. Second attack on Ft. Fisher, 13–15 Jan 1865. SAtlBS Jan–Mar 1865. European Sqn 1866–69. S. Atlantic Sqn 1871–73. N. Atlantic Sqn 1874. Cruise around the world 1877–80. Decomm 10 Sep 1882. Sold 30 Jul 1887.

The screw sloop *Ticonderoga* anchored in the harbor of Venice, Italy, late in the 1860s. The bowsprit was fitted in 1865. (Martin Holbrook Collection) (National Archives)

SACRAMENTO

Name	Bldr	Laid down	L	Comm
Sacramento	Portsmouth (Taunton)	1861	28 Apr 1862	7 Jan 1863

Tonnage:	2,100 tons D; 1,367 tons B
Dimensions:	229′6″ × 38′ × 8′10″
Machinery:	1 screw, 2 horizontal back-acting condensing engines (42″ × 2′6″); 12.5 knots
Complement:	161
Armament:	1 150-pdr R, 2 11″ SB, 1 30-pdr R, 2 24-pdr H, 2 12-pdr R, 2 12-pdr SB. Jun 64 total: 3 100-pdr R, 1 30-pdr R, 6 8″ SB/63. May 65 total: 2 11″ SB, 2 9″ SB, 1 60-pdr R, 2 24-pdr H, 1 12-pdr R, 1 12-pdr SB.

SERVICE RECORD: SAtlBS 1863. European waters 1864–65. Blockaded CSS *Stonewall* at Ferrol, Mar 1865. Far East 1866–67. Went aground at mouth of the Godavari River, state of Madras, India, 19 Jun 1867 and became a total loss.
Prize: 2 May 1863: *Wanderer*.

The screw sloop *Sacramento* at Kingstown, Ireland, in July 1865. (Martin Holbrook Collection) (U.S. Naval Historical Center)

The *Monongahela* was distinguished from other sloops of the period by her large funnel. The bulwarks are lowered to expose the guns.

The sloop *Monongahela* following her conversion to a full-rigged ship. Probably taken during one of her annual training cruises to Europe at the turn of the century. (Marius Bar)

MONONGAHELA

Name	Bldr	Laid down	L	Comm
Monongahela	Philadelphia (Merrick)	Dec 1861	10 Jul 1862	15 Jan 1863

Tonnage:	2,078 tons D; 1,378 tons B
Dimensions:	225' (bp) × 38' × 15'1"
Machinery:	1 screw, 2 horizontal back-acting condensing engines (42" × 2'6"), 3 boilers; IHP 532 = 12 knots
Complement:	176
Armament:	1 200-pdr R, 2 11" SB, 2 24-pdr R, 4 12-pdr R. Dec 63: 1 200-pdr R replaced by 1 150-pdr R, add 5 32-pdr/57. May 65 total: 2 11" SB, 1 60-pdr R, 1 24-pdr, 1 12-pdr R, 1 12-pdr SB. 1878 total: 6 9" SB, 1 60-pdr R.

NOTES: Barkentine rig. Engines removed 1883 and converted to sailing ship, bark rig. Full rigged ship 1890.
SERVICE RECORD: WGulfBS 1863. Went aground and was damaged by gunfire during attempt to pass Port Hudson, La., 14 Mar 1863. Bombardment below Donaldsonville, La., 7 Jul and at Whitehall Pt., La., 10 Jul 1863. Expedition to Brazos Santiago, Rio Grande, Tex., 27 Oct–3 Nov 1863. Damaged by ramming CSS *Tennessee* at Battle of Mobile Bay, 5 Aug 1864. Bombardment of Ft. Morgan, Mobile Bay, 9–23 Aug 1864.

West Indies Sqn 1865–67. Cast aground by tidal wave during earthquake at St. Thomas, 18 Nov 1867; refloated 11 May 1868. S. Atlantic Stn, 1873–76. Far East 1877–79. Converted to supply ship 1883. Storeship at Callao, Peru, 1884–90. Apprentice training ship 1891–1904. Storeship, Guantánamo, 1904–08. Destroyed by fire at Guantánamo, 17 Mar 1908.
Prizes: 5 Nov 1863: *Matamoros, Volante, Dashing Wave, Science.*

CONTOOCOOK CLASS

Name	Bldr	Laid down	L	Comm
Arapaho	(unknown) (Providence)	never	never	never
Contoocook	Portsmouth (Providence)	1863	3 Dec 1864	14 Mar 1868
Keosauqua	(unknown) (Etna)	never	never	never
Manitou	Boston (Woodruff)	1863	25 Aug 1865	27 Feb 1871
Mondamin	(unknown) (Wash IW)	never	never	never
Mosholu	Brooklyn (S. Brooklyn)	Oct 1864	22 Dec 1867	27 Aug 1869
Pushmataha	Philadelphia (Morris Towne)	1863	17 Jul 1868	4 Mar 1870
Tahgayuta	(unknown) (Wash IW)	never	never	never
Wanalosett	(unknown) (Hazelhurst)	never	never	never
Willamette	(unknown) (Poole)	never	never	never

Tonnage:	3,300 tons D; 2,348 tons B
Dimensions:	296'10" (dk) × 41' × 15'6"
Machinery:	1 screw, 2 horizontal back-acting condensing engines (60" × 3'), 4 boilers; IHP 1,220 = 13 knots
Complement:	250
Armament:	Designed 8 9" SB, 1 60-pdr R. 1878 total: 14 9" SB, 2 60-pdr R.
	Contoocook: 8 9" SB, 1 60-pdr R, 4 24-pdr H, 1 12-pdr H, 1 12-pdr HR

NOTES: Smaller versions of *Wampanoag* with engines designed by Isherwood. Built of unseasoned timber and deteriorated quickly. Engines built for *Wanalosett* later used in *Pensacola*. *Worcester* received spar deck 1869.

SERVICE RECORDS:

Arapaho—Canceled 1866.

Contoocook—N. Atlantic Sqn 1868–69. Renamed **Albany**, 15 May 1869. Decomm 7 Jan 1870. Quarantine ship, New York 1870–72. Sold 12 Dec 1872.

Keosauqua—Canceled 1866.

Manitou—Renamed **Worcester**, 15 May 1869. Voyaged to France with war-relief supplies 1871, boiler burst, 8 Mar 1871. N. Atlantic Sqn 1872–75. Receiving ship, Norfolk 1878. Sold 27 Sep 1883 and BU.

Mondamin—Canceled 1866.

Mosholu—Renamed **Severn**, 15 May 1869. N. Atlantic Sqn 1869–71. Decomm 31 Dec 1871. Sold 2 Mar 1877 and BU.

Pushmataha—Renamed **Cambridge**, 15 May 1869. Renamed **Congress**, 10 Aug 1869. S. Atlantic Sqn 1870–71. Mediterranean Sqn 1872–74. Decomm 26 Jul 1876. Sold 20 Sep 1883.

Tahgayuta—Canceled 1866.

Wanalosett—Canceled 1866.

Willamette—Canceled 1866.

ALGOMA CLASS

Name	Bldr	Laid down	L	Comm
Alaska	Boston (bldr)	1867	31 Oct 1868	7 Dec 1869
Algoma	Portsmouth (Boston)	May 1867	18 Aug 1868	1 Dec 1869
Confiance	Boston (bldr)	never	never	never
Detroit	Brooklyn (bldr)	never	never	never
Kenosha	Brooklyn (Norfolk)	27 Jun 1867	8 Aug 1868	20 Jan 1869
Meredosia	(unknown) (Boston)	never	never	never
Omaha	Philadelphia (Brooklyn)	1867	10 Jun 1869	12 Sep 1871
Peacock	Brooklyn (bldr)	never	never	never
Serapis	Boston (bldr)	never	never	never
Taghkanic	(unknown)	never	never	never
Talladega	(unknown)	never	never	never

Tonnage: 2,400 tons D
Dimensions: 250′6″ (bp) × 38′ × 16′6″
Machinery: 1 screw, 2 horizontal back-acting engines (50″ × 3′6″); IHP 800 = 11.5 knots
Complement: 291
Armament:
  Alaska: 1 11″ SB, 6 8″ SB, 1 60-pdr R
  Benicia,
  Omaha,
  Plymouth: 1 11″ SB, 10 9″ SB, 1 60-pdr R, 2 20-pdr R

NOTES: Hulls designed by Lenthall and machinery by Isherwood. *Alaska*, *Algoma*, and *Omaha* ordered in 1867. Bark rig, 2 funnels. Engines of canceled ships used in *Swatara* class.

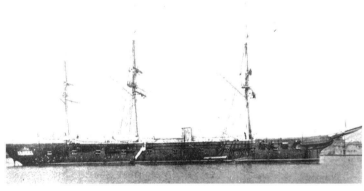

The sloop *Worcester* was launched as the *Manitou*. The spar deck was added in 1869.

The sloop *Congress* of the *Contoocook* class. She was launched as *Pushmataha*, and was in commission only six years. (INRO)

The sloop *Omaha* at Portsmouth Navy Yard in the 1870s.

The sloop *Alaska* during the Korean expedition of 1871. Her funnels are lowered. (U.S. Naval Historical Center)

The sloop *Benicia*, launched as *Algoma*. Like most of the Navy ships built towards the end of the war, she was built of unseasoned wood and lasted a very short time. (Martin Holbrook Collection) (Mariners Museum)

The *Algoma*-class sloop *Plymouth*. This picture was formerly identified as the *Hartford*. (U.S. Naval Historical Center)

SERVICE RECORDS:

Alaska—Asiatic Sqn 1870–73. Korean Expedition, May–Jun 1871. European Sqn 1873–76. Pacific Sqn 1878–82. Decomm 13 Feb 1883. Sold 20 Nov 1883.

Algoma—Renamed **Benicia**, 15 May 1869. Asiatic Sqn 1870–72. Korean Expedition, May–Jun 1871. N. Pacific Sqn 1872–74. Decomm 29 Nov 1875. Sold 3 May 1884.

Confiance—Canceled 1866.

Detroit—Canceled 1866.

Kenosha—European Stn 1869–70. Renamed **Plymouth**, 15 May 1869. Mediterranean 1870–73. Decomm 17 May 1879. BU 1884.

Meredosia—Canceled 1866.

Omaha—Renamed **Astoria**, 15 May 1869. Renamed **Omaha**, 10 Aug 1869. S. & N. Atlantic Sqns 1872–79. Asiatic Sqn 1885–91. Decomm 1891. Sold 17 Apr 1915.

Later history: Transferred to Marine Hospital Service. Quarantine ship, San Francisco. Stricken 1914.

Peacock—Canceled 1866.

Serapis—Canceled 1866.

Taghkanic—Canceled 1866.

Talladega—Canceled 1866.

The sloop *Plymouth* in European waters in the early 1870s. (Marius Bar)

SWATARA CLASS

Name	Bldr	Laid down	L	Comm
Galena	Norfolk (bldr)	1872	13 Mar 1879	26 Aug 1880
Marion	Portsmouth (Boston)	1872	22 Dec 1873	12 Jan 1876
Mohican	Mare Island (bldr)	4 Sep 1872	19 Sep 1883	25 May 1885
Quinnebaug	Philadelphia (Washington)	1872	28 Sep 1875	2 Oct 1878
Swatara	Brooklyn (bldr)	1872	17 Sep 1873	11 May 1874
Vandalia	Boston (bldr)	1872	23 Oct 1874	10 Jan 1876

Tonnage:	1,900 tons D (*Vandalia* 2,033 tons)
Dimensions:	216′ (bp) × 37′ × 16′6″ (*Vandalia* 39′ × 17′3″)
Machinery:	1 screw, compound engines, 10 boilers; IHP 1,200 = 12 knots
Complement:	230
Armament:	1 8″ R, 6 9″ SB, 1 60-pdr R, 2 20-pdr R, except *Marion* 1 11″, 6 9″, 1 60-pdr R, 1 50-pdr R.

NOTES: *Marion*, *Quinnebaug*, *Swatara*, and *Vandalia* had rebuilt engines originally built for *Algoma*-class vessels. They were officially considered as older vessels repaired. Bark rig.

SERVICE RECORDS:

Galena—European Stn 1881–82. S. America 1882–83. Landed troops in Panama 1885. Went aground on Martha's Vineyard while under tow en route for fitting with new boilers, 13 Mar 1891; refloated. Sold 9 May 1892.

Marion—Decomm 11 Dec 1897. California State Militia training ship, 1898–1907. Sold 24 Jul 1907.

Mohican—S. America and S. Pacific 1885–91. Bering Sea 1891–92. School ship 1898. Stn ship, Olongapo, Subic Bay 1905–10. Submarine tender 1910–13 and receiving ship Cavite 1913–1915. Sold 4 Mar 1922.

Quinnebaug—European Stn 1879–89. Decomm 3 Jul 1889. Sold 25 Mar 1891.

Later history: Merchant barge 1892.

Swatara—Decomm 7 Feb 1891. Sold 2 Nov 1896.

Vandalia—European Sqn 1876–79. N. Atlantic Sqn 1879–84. Pacific Sqn 1886–89. Wrecked in hurricane in Apia harbor, Samoa, 16 Mar 1889.

SCREW GUNBOATS

PRINCETON

Name	Bldr	Laid down	L	Comm
Princeton	Boston (Murray)	Jun 1851	29 Oct 1851	18 May 1852

Tonnage:	1,370 tons D; 900 tons B
Dimensions:	184′ (oa) 177′6″ (wl) × 32′6″ × d21′8″
Machinery:	1 screw, 2 direct-acting half-cylinder condensing engines (57½″ × 3′), 3 boilers; HP 195 = 10 knots
Complement:	190
Armament:	4 8″ SB, 6 32-pdr SB

NOTES: Hull designed by Samuel Pook using engines of the gunboat *Princeton* launched in 1843. That vessel was the first screw warship built and the first with machinery (designed by Ericsson) entirely below the waterline. She carried two 12″ guns, one of which, named "Peacemaker," exploded on 29 Feb 1844 killing Secretary of State Abel P. Upshur, Secretary of the Navy Thomas Gilmer, and other personages.

SERVICE RECORD: Eastern Sqn 1853–54 and West Indies 1854–55. Receiving ship, Philadelphia, 1857–66. Sold 9 Oct 1866.

UNADILLA CLASS

Name	Bldr	Laid down	L	Comm
Aroostook	Thompson (Novelty)	1861	Nov 1861	20 Feb 1862
Cayuga	Gildersleeve (Woodruff)	1861	21 Oct 1861	21 Feb 1862
Chippewa	Webb & Bell (Morgan)	1861	14 Sep 1861	18 Dec 1861
Chocura	Curtis & Tilden (Loring)	1861	5 Oct 1861	15 Feb 1862
Huron	Curtis (Loring)	1861	21 Sep 1861	8 Jan 1862
Itasca	Hillman (Morris)	1861	1 Oct 1861	28 Nov 1861
Kanawha	Goodspeed (Pacific)	1861	21 Oct 1861	21 Jan 1862
Katahdin	Larrabee (Morgan)	1861	12 Oct 1861	17 Feb 1862
Kennebec	Lawrence (Novelty)	1861	5 Oct 1861	8 Feb 1862
Kineo	Dyer (Morgan)	29 Jul 1861	9 Oct 1861	8 Feb 1862
Marblehead	Jackman (Highland)	1861	16 Oct 1861	8 Mar 1862
Ottawa	Westervelt (Novelty)	1861	22 Aug 1861	7 Oct 1861
Owasco	Maxson Fish (Novelty)	1861	5 Oct 1861	23 Jan 1862
Pembina	Stack (Novelty)	1861	28 Aug 1861	16 Oct 1861
Penobscot	Carter (Allaire)	1861	19 Nov 1861	16 Jan 1862
Pinola	Abrahams (Reeder)	1861	1861	29 Jan 1862
Sagamore	Sampson (Atlantic)	1861	18 Sep 1861	7 Dec 1861
Sciota	Birely (Morris)	1861	15 Oct 1861	15 Dec 1861
Seneca	Simonson (Novelty)	1861	27 Aug 1861	14 Oct 1861
Tahoma	Thatcher (Reaney)	1861	2 Oct 1861	20 Dec 1861
Unadilla	Englis (Novelty)	3 Aug 1861	17 Aug 1861	30 Sep 1861
Winona	Poillon (Allaire)	1861	14 Sep 1861	11 Dec 1861
Wissahickon	Lynn (Merrick)	1861	2 Oct 1861	25 Nov 1861

The *Aroostook* in Chinese waters around 1867. She has a schooner rig; canvas is erected along the length of the deck. (U.S. Naval Historical Center)

Tonnage:	691 tons D; 507 tons B
Dimensions:	158′4″ (wl) × 28′ × 9′6″
Machinery:	1 screw, 2 horizontal back-acting engines (30″ × 1′6″), 2 boilers; 10 knots
Complement:	114
Armament:	1 11″ SB, 2 24-pdr SB, 1 20-pdr R, except:
Aroostook	Jun 63: 1 24-pdr SB replaced by 1 12-pdr SB. 1864: add 1 12-pdr SB.
Cayuga	Jun 62: add 2 24-pdr SB. Jun 63: add 1 30-pdr R.
Chippewa	Oct 64: add 2 24-pdr SB.
Chocura	Apr 65 total: 1 100-pdr R, 1 30-pdr R, 4 24-pdr SB, 1 20-pdr R.
Huron	Aug 64 total: 1 11″ SB, 1 30-pdr R, 4 24-pdr H.
Itasca	Dec 61 total: 1 10″ SB, 2 32-pdr/27, 1 20-pdr R. Nov 62 total: 1 11″ SB, 2 32-pdr/27, 1 20-pdr R.
Kanawha	Dec 63: add 1 9″ SB until Jun 64.
Katahdin	Oct 62: add 1 20-pdr R.
Kennebec	Mar 65 total: 1 11″ SB, 1 30-pdr R, 1 24-pdr H, 1 12-pdr.
Kineo	Dec 62: add 2 32-pdr/33.
Marblehead	Jun 63: add 2 24-pdr. Jun 64 total: 2 8″/63 SB, 3 30-pdr R, 2 24-pdr.
Ottawa	May 63 total: 1 150-pdr R, 1 30-pdr R, 2 24-pdr H, 1 12-pdr. Aug 64: add 2 24-pdr H.
Seneca	Dec 63: add 2 24-pdr H.
Tahoma	1862 total: 1 10″ SB, 1 20-pdr R, 4 24-pdr H. Jul 63: 1 10″ replaced by 1 150-pdr R.
Unadilla	Oct 62: add 2 24-pdr H, 1 12-pdr SB.
Winona	1863: add 2 32-pdr/33. 1864 total: 1 11″ SB, 1 30-pdr R, 1 12-pdr H, 4 24-pdr H.
Wissahickon	1 11″ SB replaced by 1 150-pdr R.

The screw gunboat *Chocura* probably lying off Charleston in 1862–63. (Dr. Charles L. Peery)

NOTES: Popularly known as "90-day gunboats." Ordered by Navy Department as an emergency measure and built rapidly of unseasoned timber. Two-mast schooner rig. Sailed well but rolled heavily.

SERVICE RECORDS:

Aroostook—NAtlBS Apr–Sep 1862. Engaged batteries at Drewry's Bluff, Va., 15 May 1862. GulfBS Sep 1862–64. Asiatic Sqn 1867–69. Sold at Hong Kong, Oct 1869.

Prizes: 5 Mar 1863: **Josephine*; 9 May: *Sea Lion*; 22 Nov: *Eureka*; 11 Mar 1864: *Mary P. Burton*; 12 Mar: *Marion*; 8 Jul: **Matagorda*.

Later history: FFU.

Cayuga—WGulfBS 1862–65. Passage past New Orleans forts and engagement with CSN vessels, 24 Apr 1862. Bombardment of Baton Rouge, La., and engagement with CSS *Arkansas*, 5 Aug 1862. Occupation of Baton Rouge, 17 Dec 1862. Decomm 31 Jul 1865. Sold 25 Oct 1865.

Prizes: 25 Mar 1862: *Jessie J. Cox*; 3 Apr 1863: *Tampico*; 2 Jul: *Blue Bell*; 10 Aug: *J. T. Davis*; 22 Aug: *Wave*; 7 Oct: **Pushmataha*.

Later history: Merchant *Veteran* 1865. Converted to bark 1869. SE 1885.

Chippewa—Blockade off North Carolina, 1862. Capture of Ft. Macon, NC, 25–26 Apr 1862. Search in N. Atlantic for CSS *Florida*, 1862–

63. SAtlBS 1863–Feb 65. Bombardment of Ft. Wagner, Charleston, 18 Jul 1863. Joint expedition up Ashepoo and S. Edisto Rivers, SC, 25–27 May 1864. Unsuccessful attack on Ft. Fisher, NC, 24–25 Dec 1864. Second attack on Ft. Fisher, 13–15 Jan 1865. Bombardment of Ft. Anderson, 18 Feb, and Fts. Strong and Lee, Cape Fear River, 20–21 Feb 1865. James River, Mar–May 1865. Decomm 24 Jun 1865. Sold 30 Nov 1865.

Prizes: 26 Apr 1862: *Alliance*; 29 Jul: *Napier*.

Later history: FFU.

Chocura—Army operations at Yorktown, Va., 4–7 May 1862. NAtlBS Nov 1862–Aug 1863. WGulfBS Nov 1863–65. Gulf Sqn 1866–67. Decomm 7 Jun 1867. Sold 13 Jul 1867.

Prizes: 19 Nov 1862: **Pearl*; 21 Jan 1863: *Pride*; 3 May 1864: *Frederick the Second* and *Agnes*; 4 May: *Express*; 12 Oct: *Louisa*; 28 Oct: *Cora Smyser*; 24 Nov: **Louisa*; 4 Dec: *Lowood*; 5 Dec: *Julia*; 6 Dec: *Lady Hurley*; 7 Dec: *Alabama*; 22 Jan 1865: **Delfina*.

Later history: FFU.

Huron—SAtlBS 1862. Capture of Fernandina, Fla., and Brunswick, St. Simons, and Jekyl islands, Ga., 2–12 Mar 1862. Bombardment of Ft. McAllister, Ogeechee River, Ga., 29 Jul 1862. Engaged batteries in Stono River, SC, 16 Jul 1863. NAtlBS 1864. Unsuccessful attack

Screw gunboat *Huron* (*Unadilla* class) after the war, flying a huge Italian flag at her main top. (U.S. Naval Historical Center)

on Ft. Fisher, NC, 24–25 Dec 1864. Second attack on Ft. Fisher, 13–15 Jan 1865. Bombardment of Ft. Anderson, 18 Feb and Fts. Strong and Lee, Cape Fear River 20–21 Feb 1865. S. America Stn 1865–68. Decomm 8 Oct 1868. Sold 14 Jun 1869.

Prizes: 19 Apr 1862: *Glide*; 1 May: *Albert*; 26 May: str *Cambria*; 4 Aug: *Aquilla*; 12 Apr 1863: str **Stonewall Jackson*; 16 Dec: str *Chatham*; 2 Jan 1864: **Sylvanus*.

Later history: Merchant *D.H. Bills* 1869. SE 1876.

Itasca—GulfBS 1862. WGulfBS 1862. Severed chain across Mississippi River under heavy fire, 20 Apr 1862. Made passage past New Orleans forts and engagement with CSN vessels, 24 Apr 1862. Damaged during bombardment of Grand Gulf, Miss., 9–10 Jun 1862. Operations below Donaldsonville, La., 4 Oct 1862. Blockade of Galveston, 1863. Battle of Mobile Bay, 5 Aug 1864. Bombardment of Ft. Morgan, Mobile Bay, 9–23 Aug 1864. Sold 30 Nov 1865.

Prizes: 19 Jan 1862: *Lizzie Weston*; 17 Jun 1863: *Miriam*; 22 Jun: *Sea Drift*; 30 Nov 1864: *Carrie Mair*; 8 Dec: **Mary Ann*.

Later history: Merchant *Aurora* 1865. Sold foreign 1867.

Kanawha—GulfBS 1862–65. Sold 13 Jun 1866.

Prizes: 10 Apr 1862: *Charlotte, Cuba, Southern Independence,* and *Victoria*; 20 Apr: *R.C. Files*; 29 Apr: *Annie*; 19 Jun: str *Ann*; 26 Jun: **Monticello*; 17 Nov: **unidentified*; 25 Mar 1863: *Clara*; 1 May: *Dart*; 4 May: *Juniper*; 15 May: *Comet*; 17 May: *Hunter*; 18 May: *Ripple*; 29 Nov: *Wenona (Albert)*; 14 May 1864: *Amanda*; 8 Jul: str **Matagorda*; 8 Jan 1865: *Mary Ellen*.

Later history: Merchant bark *Mariano* 1866. SE 1878.

Katahdin—WGulfBS 1862. Made passage past New Orleans forts and engagement with CSN vessels, 24 Apr 1862. Bombardment of Grand Gulf, Miss., 26 May and 9–10 Jun 1862. Made passage past batteries at Vicksburg, 28 Jun, and at Baton Rouge, La., engagement with CSS *Arkansas*, 5 Aug 1862. Operations below Donaldsonville, La., 4 Oct 1862. Bombardment of Port Hudson, La., 13 Dec 1862. Occupation of Baton Rouge, 17 Dec 1862. Blockade of Galveston, 1863–64. Decomm 14 Jul 1865. Sold 30 Nov 1865.

Prizes: 25 Apr 1862: *John Gilpin*; 10 May 1863: *Hanover*; 13 Jul: *Excelsior*; 31 Oct 1864: *Albert Edward*.

Later history: Merchant *Juno* 1865. Renamed *Katadin?*

Kennebec—WGulfBS 1862. Passage past New Orleans forts and engagement with CSN vessels, 24 Apr 1862. Made passage past batteries at Vicksburg, 28 Jun 1862. Blockade duty, 1862–63. Battle of Mobile Bay, 5 Aug 1864. Blockade duty off Galveston 1864–65. Sold 30 Nov 1865.

Prizes: 31 May 1862: *Ella*; 4 May 1863: *Juniper*; 9 Dec: *Marshall J. Smith*; 31 Dec: str *Grey Jacket*; 8 Jan 1864: str *John Scott*.

Later history: Merchant *Kennebec* 1865. Converted to bark.

Kineo—WGulfBS, 1862. Hit during passage past New Orleans forts and engagement with CSN vessels, 24 Apr 1862. Bombarded Grand Gulf, Miss., 26 May 1862. Bombardment of batteries at Baton Rouge, La., and engagement with CSS *Arkansas*, 5 Aug 1862. Operations below Donaldsonville, La., 4 Oct 1862. Bombardment of Port Hudson, La., 13 Dec 1862. Ran aground during attempt to pass Port Hudson, 14 Mar 1863, towed *Monongahela* off under fire. Bombardment of Donaldsonville, 28 Jun and at Whitehall Pt., La.,

10 Jul 1863. Repairing Aug 1863–64. WGulfBS Mar 1864. Blockade duty off Texas, 1864–65. Decomm 9 May 1865. Sold 9 Oct 1866.

Prize: 22 May 1864: *Stingray*.

Later history: Merchant schooner *Lucy H. Gibson* 1866.

Marblehead—NAtlBS 1862. Army operations at Gloucester and York, Va., 14–29 Apr 1862. SAtlBS Aug 1862. Expedition to Pocotaligo, SC, 21–23 Oct 1862. Engaged batteries in Stono River, SC, 16 Jul 1863. Bombardment of Ft. Wagner, Morris I., Charleston, Aug 1863. Damaged while bombarding batteries in Stono River, 25 Dec 1863. Practice ship, Naval Academy, Jun 1864. N. Atlantic Sqn 1866–68. Decomm 4 Sep and sold 30 Sep 1868.

Prize: 23 Feb 1863: *Glide*.

Later history: Merchant bark *Marblehead* 1868. SE 1876.

Ottawa—SAtlBS 1861–65. Engaged CSN squadron off Port Royal, SC, 5 Nov 1861. Occupation of Port Royal, 7 Nov 1861. Army operations at Port Royal Ferry, 31 Dec 1861–2 Jan 1862. Engagement in Wilmington Narrows, NC, 26–68 Jan 1862. Capture of Fernandina, Fla., and Brunswick, St. Simons, and Jekyl islands, Ga., 2–12 Mar 1862. Operations in St. Johns River, Fla., 16 Apr–3 May 1862. Bombardment of Ft. Wagner, Charleston, 18 Jul–20 Aug 1863. Attack on Jacksonville, Fla., 2–22 Feb 1864. Expedition to Bulls Bay, SC, 12–17 Feb 1865. Decomm 12 Aug 1865. Sold 25 Oct 1865.

Prizes: 6 May 1862: *Gen. C.C. Pinckney*; 21 Jan 1863: *Etiwan*; 11 Jun: str **Havelock*.

Later history: FFU.

Owasco—WGulfBS 1862–65. Passage past New Orleans forts and engagement with CSN vessels, 24 Apr 1862. Capture of Galveston, Tex., 4 Oct 1862. Expedition to Brazos Santiago, Rio Grande, Tex., 27 Oct–3 Nov 1863. Decomm 12 Jul 1865. Sold 25 Oct 1865.

Prizes: 16 Mar 1862: *Eugenia* and *President*; 10 May 1863: **Hanover*; 21 Jun: *Active*; 21 Jul: **Revenge*; 4 Nov: *Dashing Wave, Science, Matamoros,* and *Volante*. 17 Apr 1864: *Lily*; 19 Apr: *Fanny*; 21 Apr: *Laura*.

Later history: Merchant *Lulu* 1865, converted to sail 1869. SE 1885.

Pembina—SAtlBS 1861. Engaged CSN squadron off Port Royal, SC, 5 Nov 1861. Occupation of Port Royal, 7 Nov, and of Beaufort, SC, 9 Nov 1861. Engaged forts in St. Helena Sound, SC, 25–28 Nov and in Wassaw Sound, Ga., 5–6 Dec 1861. Army operations at Port Royal Ferry, 31 Dec 1861–2 Jan 1862. Capture of Fernandina, Fla., and Brunswick, St. Simons, and Jekyl islands, Ga., 2–12 Mar 1862. GulfBS 1863–65. Battle of Mobile Bay, 5 Aug 1864. Decomm 22 Sep 1865. Sold 30 Nov 1865.

Prizes: 6 Jun 1862: *Rowena*; 23 Apr 1863: *Elias Beckwith*; 24 Apr: *Joe Flanner*; 4 Dec 1864: *Geziena Hilligonda*.

Later history: Merchant *Charles E. Gibson* 1865. Converted to schooner 1866. SE 1878.

Penobscot—NAtlBS 1862. Army operations at Gloucester and York, Va., 14–29 Apr 1862. WGulfBS fall 1863. Bombarded batteries at San Bernard, Tex., 11–13 Jan 1863. Decomm 31 Jul 1865. Sold 19 Oct 1869.

Prizes: 8 Jun 1862: **Sereta*; 1 Aug: *Lizzie*; 22 Oct: *Robert Burns*; 2 Nov: **Pathfinder*; 13 Dec: *Golden Eagle*; 12 Jul 1863: **Kate*; 28 Feb

UNARMORED STEAM VESSELS

The first steam warships were driven by paddle wheels, but screw-propelled ships were much more efficient for naval purposes. In particular, the large paddle boxes interfered with the placement of the guns, which were traditionally sited along the ship's broadside. Development of low-pressure and more powerful engines enabled propeller-driven ships to move faster. In addition, the engines could be placed below the waterline for better protection against enemy gunfire.

The Navy built several side-wheel warships, and among the earliest were the frigates *Missouri* and *Mississippi* of 1840. Although the *Missouri* was soon destroyed by fire, succeeding vessels, notably the *Susquehanna* and *Powhatan*, were especially successful and efficient ships. In 1847 the paddle wheeler *Saranac* and propeller *San Jacinto* were built as competitive sisters. In all tests between paddle-wheel and propeller-driven ships, the propeller won, and it soon permanently displaced the earlier system.

In 1854 six large screw frigates were built, the five ships of the *Merrimack* type and the *Niagara*. On her first cruise to Europe, the *Merrimack* created a sensation in naval circles with battery and steaming endurance greater than contemporary European frigates. The *Hartford* class of steam sloops in 1858 again combined superior firepower with high endurance on a smaller hull.

A large number of sturdy steam sloops were built during the war. In addition, smaller warships known as double-enders and 90-day gunboats were produced in large numbers and served throughout the war. Hastily built, they wore out quickly.

A series of new vessels was ordered towards the end of the war that sought to utilize the lessons learned during the war. Unfortunately, most of these were built with unseasoned timber, and the hulls deteriorated very quickly. These included the swift cruisers of the *Ammonoosuc* class, the frigates of the *Java* class, and the sloops of the *Contoocook* and *Algoma* classes. Only a few were actually completed, and all soon disappeared from the Navy list.

Of the cruisers, designed for high speed, the *Wampanoag* attained a sustained speed of 17 knots on her trials, a speed unequalled by steam vessels to that time. Nevertheless, the ships were never put into service and were the subject of some controversy. It was said the engines were too powerful for the frame, and fuel consumption was so great that the space required for coal left no room for sufficient ammunition.

The majority of the ships of these classes were broken up on the stocks, and those that were completed had very short careers.

Most of the ships of the *Swatara* and *Adams* classes were built under the guise of "repairing" older ships, as this was the only way to obtain authorization of funds. Only the frigate *Trenton*, laid down in 1875, was built as a new ship.

SIDE-WHEEL FRIGATES

MISSISSIPPI CLASS

Name	Bldr	Laid down	L	Comm
Mississippi	Philadelphia (Merrick & Towne)	10 Aug 1839	5 May 1841	22 Dec 1841
Missouri	Brooklyn (West Point)	1839	7 Jan 1841	early 1842

Tonnage:	3,200 tons D, 1,732 tons B
Dimensions:	229′ (oa) × 40′ × 21′9″ (66′6″ oa beam)
Machinery:	Side wheels, *Mississippi*: 2 side-lever engines (75″ × 7′), 3 boilers; HP 650 = 11 knots; *Missouri*: 2 inclined direct-acting condensing engines (65.5″ × 10′); HP 515 = 11 knots
Complement:	257
Armament:	2 10″ SB, 8 8″ SB guns
	Mississippi: May 61 total: 1 9″ SB, 10 8″/63, 1 12-pdr; Nov 62 total: 1 10″ SB, 19 8″ SB/63, 1 20-pdr R

NOTES: Wood hull, bark rig. Hulls designed by Lenthall, Hartt & Humphreys; engines by Copeland. Machinery differed to test long- and short-stroke engines. Very successful and good steamers.

SERVICE RECORDS:

Mississippi—Flagship of Commodore Matthew Perry during the Mexican War and the first expedition to Japan in 1853. Far East 1857–60. Blockading operations off Key West, Jun 1861. Passage past

Wissahickon—WGulfBS 1862. Reconnoitered forts in Mississippi River, 28 Mar 1862. Passage past New Orleans forts and engagement with CSN vessels, 24 Apr 1862. Bombardment of Grand Gulf, Miss., 9–10 Jun 1862. Made passage past batteries at Vicksburg, 28 Jun 1862. Engaged CSS *Arkansas* above Vicksburg, 15 Jul 1862. SAtlBS Oct 1862–65. Expedition to Pocotaligo, SC, 21–23 Oct 1862. Engaged batteries at Ft. McAllister, Ogeechee River, Ga, 19 Nov 1862 and 27 Jan–28 Feb 1863. Helped destroy privateer *Rattlesnake* in Ogeechee River, 28 Feb 1863. Bombardment of Ft. Wagner, Charleston, 18 Jul–8 Sep 1863. Expedition in Broad River, SC, 27 Nov–30 Dec 1864 and up Stono and Folly Rivers, SC, 9–14 Feb 1865. Decomm 1 Jul 1865. Sold 25 Oct 1865.

Prizes: 19 Mar 1863: str *Georgiana*; 10 Jun: str *Havelock*.

Later history: Merchant *Adele* 1865. SE 1885.

NIPSIC CLASS

Name	Bldr	Laid down	L	Comm
Kansas	Philadelphia (U)	1863	29 Sep 1863	21 Dec 1863
Maumee	Brooklyn (Stover)	1862	2 Jul 1863	29 Sep 1864
Nipsic	Portsmouth (Woodruff)	24 Dec 1862	15 Jun 1863	2 Sep 1863
Nyack	Brooklyn (S. Brooklyn)	1862	6 Oct 1863	28 Sep 1864
Pequot	Boston (Woodruff)	1862	4 Jun 1863	15 Jan 1864
Saco	Boston (Corliss)	1862	28 Aug 1863	11 Jul 1864
Shawmut	Portsmouth (Corliss)	2 Feb 1863	17 Jun 1863	1 Nov 1864
Yantic	Philadelphia (Merrick)	1862	19 Mar 1864	12 Aug 1864

Tonnage: 836 tons D; 593 tons B
Dimensions: 190' () 179'6" (bp) × 29'8" × 12' 1872: *Yantic* 215' (oa)
Machinery: 1 screw, 2 horizontal back-acting engines (30" × 1'9"); IHP 327 = 11 knots, except *Kansas*, *Yantic*: 2 horizontal direct-acting engines (32" × 1'6"); *Maumee*: 2 horizontal vibrating-lever engines (40" × 1'10"); *Pequot*: 2 segmental cylinder direct-acting engines (30" × 1'9"); *Saco*: 2 horizontal vibrating-lever engines (28" × 2'); 1877: *Yantic*, 2 compound engines, IHP 310 = 11.5 knots

Complement: 154
Armament: 1 150-pdr R, 2 9" SB, 1 30-pdr R, 2 20-pdr R
  Kansas Dec 64: 1 150-pdr R replaced by 1 100-pdr R. Mar 65: 1 100-pdr R replaced by 1 11" SB. Dec 65 total: 2 9" SB, 2 11" SB, 3 12-pdr R, 2 20-pdr SB, 1 30-pdr R. 1870 total: 1 11" SB, 2 9" SB, 1 20-pdr R.
  Maumee Oct 64 total: 1 100-pdr R, 1 30-pdr R, 4 24-pdr H, 1 12-pdr R. Nov 64: add 2 32-pdr/57. Jun 65: 1 100-pdr R replaced by 1 11" SB.
  Nipsic 1863 total: 1 150-pdr R, 1 30-pdr R, 2 9" SB, 2 24-pdr SB, 2 12-pdr SB. Jun 65 total: 1 100-pdr R, 1 30-pdr R, 2 8" SB/63, 2 24-pdr HSB, 2 12-pdr R.
  Nyack Sep 64 total: 1 100-pdr R, 2 9" SB, 1 30-pdr R, 2 24-pdr H, 2 12-pdr H
  Pequot Jan 64 total: 1 150-pdr R, 1 30-pdr R, 6 32-pdr/33, 2 24-pdr H, 2 12-pdr H
  Saco Jul 64 total: 1 100-pdr R, 1 30-pdr R, 6 32-pdr SB, 1 24-pdr H, 1 12-pdr R, 1 12-pdr SB.
  Shawmut Nov 64 total: 1 100-pdr R, 1 30-pdr R, 2 9" SB, 2 24-pdr H, 2 12-pdr H
  Yantic Aug 64 total: 1 100-pdr R, 1 30-pdr R, 2 9" SB, 2 24-pdr H, 2 12-pdr H. Apr 65: 1 100-pdr R replaced by 2 9" SB. 1883 total: 3 8" R, 1 60-pdr R.

NOTES: Built for fast inshore cruising. *Saco* had two funnels. *Nipsic*, *Nyack*, and *Shawmut* had engines designed by Isherwood; *Maumee* and *Saco* by John Ericsson, but those of *Saco* were replaced by Isherwood back-acting engines in 1865 after much engine trouble. *Kansas*'s engines captured as cargo in blockade runner *Princess Royal*. *Yantic* lengthened 1872 and re-engined 1877.

SERVICE RECORDS:

Kansas—NAtlBS 1863–64. Engagement with CSS *Raleigh* off New Inlet, NC, 6–7 May 1864. Unsuccessful attack on Ft. Fisher, NC, 24–25 Dec 1864. Second attack on Ft. Fisher, 13–15 Jan 1865. James River 1865. S. Atlantic Stn, 1865–69. Central American canal survey expeditions 1870–71 and 1873. Decomm 10 Aug 1875. Sold 27 Sep 1883.

Prizes: 15 May 1864: str *Tristram Shandy*; 31 Oct: str *Annie*; 7 Dec: str *Stormy Petrel*.

Maumee—NAtlBS 1864. Unsuccessful attack on Ft. Fisher, NC, 24–25 Dec 1864. Second attack on Ft. Fisher, 13–15 Jan 1865. Bombardment of Fts. Strong and Lee, Cape Fear River, 20–21 Feb 1865. Decomm 17 Jun 1865. Sold 15 Dec 1869.

Nipsic—SAtlBS 1863–65. Expedition to Murrells Inlet, SC, 29 Dec 1863–1 Jan 1864 and to Georgetown, SC, 23 Feb 1865. S. Atlantic Sqn, 1866–73. Decomm 1873 and BU.

Prize: 27 Jun 1864: *Julia*.

Nyack—NAtlBS 1864–65. Unsuccessful attack on Ft. Fisher, NC, 24–25 Dec 1864. Bombardment of Fts. Strong and Lee, Cape Fear River 18–21 Feb 1865. Served off west coast of S. America, 1866–1871. Decomm 15 Mar 1871. Sold 30 Nov 1883.

Pequot—NAtlBS Feb 1864. Operations at Malvern Hill, Va., 14–16 Jul 1864. SAtlBS 1864–65. Unsuccessful attack on Ft. Fisher, NC, 24–25 Dec 1864. Second attack on Ft. Fisher, 13–15 Jan 1865. Bom-

The screw gunboat *Kansas* in the James River 1864. Notice her white-painted funnel and gun on the bow. (National Archives)

Saco, a *Nipsic*-class gunboat, early in the 1870s after modifications with clipper bow and three masts. She was the only ship of the class with two funnels. (U.S. Naval Historical Center)

bardment of Ft. Anderson, Cape Fear River, 17–18 Feb 1865. Decomm 3 Jun 1865. Sold 1869.

Prize: 4 Mar 1864: str *Don*.

Later history: Sold to Haiti 1869, renamed *Terreur*. "Worn out" 1875.

Saco—Search for Confederate raiders in N. Atlantic 1864. Decomm 17 Jan 1865. Caribbean 1866–67. Mediterranean 1870–71. Far East 1871–76. Decomm 13 Jul 1876. Sold 20 Nov 1883.

Shawmut—Towed to New York for installation of engines. NAtlBS 1865. Bombardment of Fts. Strong and Lee, Cape Fear River, 20–21 Feb 1865. Brazil Stn 1865–66. N. Atlantic Sqn 1867 and 1871–77. Decomm 22 Jan 1877. Sold 27 Sep 1883.

Yantic—Search for CSS *Tallahassee* in N. Atlantic, 1864. NAtlBS 1864–65. Unsuccessful attack on Ft. Fisher, NC, 24–25 Dec 1864; 100-pdr gun burst. Second attack on Ft. Fisher, 13–15 Jan 1865. Bombardment of Fts. Strong and Lee, Cape Fear River, 20–21 Feb 1865. Asiatic Stn 1873–77. Caribbean 1881. Training ship, Great Lakes 1898–1929. Designated IX 32, 1921. Foundered at her dock at Detroit, Mich., 22 Oct 1929.

The screw gunboat *Shawmut* of the *Nipsic* class with her funnel lowered.

The screw gunboat *Resaca*. Notice her bark rig, straight stem. (U.S. Naval Historical Center)

RESACA CLASS

Name	Bldr	Laid down	L	Comm
Alert	Washington (Portsmouth)	1865	never	never
Epervier	Portsmouth (Washington)	1865	never	never
Nantasket	Boston (Portsmouth)	1864	15 Aug 1867	22 Oct 1869
Quinnebaug	Brooklyn (Jackson)	Oct 1864	31 Mar 1866	19 Jul 1867
Resaca	Portsmouth (Washington)	1864	18 Nov 1865	1866
Swatara	Philadelphia (Washington)	1864	23 May 1865	15 Nov 1865

Tonnage:	1,129 tons D
Dimensions:	230′ (oa) 216′ (bp) × 31′ × 12′10″ (*Quinnebaug, Swatara,* beam 30′)
Machinery:	1 screw, 2 horizontal back-acting engines (36″ × 3′), IHP 750 = 12 knots. *Quinnebaug*: 2 screws, 2 horizontal direct-acting engines (38″ × 1′9″), 7 knots
Complement:	213
Armament:	1 60-pdr R, 6 32-pdr R, 3 20-pdr R (*Swatara* + others)

NOTES: Isherwood-designed engines except *Quinnebaug*, which had British engines installed for comparison. Built of unseasoned timber that deteriorated rapidly. *Epervier*'s engines exhibited at Centennial Exposition 1876.

SERVICE RECORDS:

Alert—Canceled 1866.

Epervier—Canceled 1866.

Nantasket—N. Atlantic Sqn 1870–72, Santo Domingo. Decomm Jul 1872. Stricken 22 Jul 1875. Sold 1883.

Quinnebaug—S. American Stn 1867–70. Decomm 29 Jul 1870. BU 1871.

Resaca—Pacific Sqn 1866. Alaska 1867–69. Pacific 1869–72. Sold 18 Feb 1873.

Later history: Merchant *Ventura* 1873. Wrecked off Santa Cruz, Cal., 20 Apr 1875.

Swatara—West Indies Sqn 1866. European Sqn 1866–69. N. Atlantic Sqn and Caribbean 1869–71. Decomm 20 Dec 1871. BU 1872 and replaced by a new ship.

A rare picture of the gunboat *Huron*, which was wrecked in 1877 only two years after completion. She is rigged as a schooner. (U.S. Naval Historical Center)

ALERT CLASS

Name	Bldr	Laid down	L	Comm
Alert	Roach (bldr)	1873	18 Sep 1874	1875
Huron	Roach (bldr)	1873	2 Sep 1874	15 Nov 1875
Ranger	Harlan (Roach)	1873	10 May 1876	27 Nov 1876

Tonnage:	1,020 tons D
Dimensions:	199′9″ (oa) 177′4″ (bp) × 32′ × 13′
Machinery:	1 screw, 2 horizontal compound engines, 5 boilers; IHP 560 = 10 knots
Complement:	202
Armament:	1 11″ SB, 2 9″ SB, 1 60-pdr R; *Alert*: also spar torpedo

NOTES: Iron hulls.

SERVICE RECORDS:

Alert—Asiatic Stn 1876–86. In collision with Japanese imperial yacht at Kobe, 18 Apr 1882. Pacific Stn 1887–90. Bering Sea 1891. Asiatic Stn 1891–93. Pacific Sqn 1894–98. Training ship 1901–03. Converted to submarine tender 1911. Pacific fleet 1912–17. Base and repair ship, Bermuda 1918. Pacific 1919–21. Sold 25 Jul 1922.

Huron—Caribbean and Gulf of Mexico 1876–77. Wrecked near Nag's Head, NC, 24 Nov 1877.

Ranger—Asiatic Stn 1877–79. Surveying off Mexico and Pacific coast 1881–89. Bering Sea, fishery protection 1892–94. Central America 1895. Asiatic Stn 1905. Decomm 12 Dec 1908. Training ship,

Massachusetts 1909. Renamed **Rockport**, 30 Oct 1917. Renamed **Nantucket**, 20 Feb 1918. Stricken 30 Jun 1940.

Later history: U.S. Maritime Commission training ship *Bay State*, later *Emery Rice*. BU 1958.

ADAMS CLASS

Name	Bldr	Laid down	L	Comm
Adams	Boston (Atlantic)	Feb 1874	Jul 1876	21 Jul 1876
Enterprise	Portsmouth (Woodruff IW)	1873	13 Jun 1874	16 Mar 1877
Essex	Portsmouth (Atlantic)	1873	26 Oct 1874	3 Oct 1876
Huron	Norfolk (Quintard)	1873	8 Mar 1875	8 Jan 1877
Nipsic	Washington (Wm. Wright)	1873	6 Jun 1878	11 Oct 1879

Tonnage:	1,375 tons D
Dimensions:	185′ (bp) × 35′ × 16′4″
Machinery:	1 screw, 2 vertical compound engines; IHP 800 = 11 knots
Complement:	190
Armament:	1 11″ SB, 4 9″ SB, 1 60-pdr R, except *Nipsic*: 6 9″ SB, 1 8″ R, 1 60-pdr R

NOTES: Bark rigged, wood hulls.

SERVICE RECORDS:

Adams—N. Atlantic Stn 1876–77. S. Atlantic Stn 1877–78. Pacific Stn 1878–89. Bering Sea 1892–94. Training ship 1902–04. Stn ship,

Tutuila, Samoa, 1904–07. Training ship 1907–17. Decomm 5 Aug 1919. Sold 5 Aug 1920.
Later history: Merchant *Stefan Batory* (Polish), 1920.
Enterprise—Surveying Mississippi River 1877 and Amazon River 1878. European Stn 1878–80. Hydrographic survey cruise around the world 1883–86. Training ship 1891–92. Sold 1 Oct 1909.
Essex—N. Atlantic Sqn 1877. Pacific Stn 1881–82. Asiatic Stn 1883–89. Training ship 1893–1903, and on Great Lakes 1904–30. Sold 23 Dec 1930.
Huron—Renamed **Alliance**, 1876. European Stn 1877–79. Search for polar steamer *Jeannette* 1881. N. Atlantic Sqn 1881–86. S. Atlantic Sqn 1886–89. Asiatic Sqn 1890–92. Pacific Stn 1892–94. S. Atlantic Sqn 1894. Training ship 1895–03. Station and store ship, Culebra Island, Puerto Rico, 1904–11. Sold 13 Nov 1911.
Nipsic—West Indies 1879–80. European Stn 1880–83. S. Atlantic Sqn 1883–86. Stn ship, Samoa 1888. Beached and severely damaged during hurricane at Apia, Samoa, 16 Mar 1889. Refloated and rebuilt in Hawaii, 1890. Decomm 2 Oct 1890. Prison ship, Puget Sound, 1892. Sold 13 Feb 1913.
Later history: Merchant barge, 1913.

SIDE-WHEEL GUNBOATS (DOUBLE-ENDERS)

Built for use in narrow and shallow coastal waters, they were designed to be able to proceed forward or backward with a rudder at each end. They were very useful operating in rivers too narrow to permit turning around, but were generally poor sea boats. Hulls were designed by Lenthall and the engines by Isherwood.

MIAMI

Name	Bldr	Laid down	L	Comm
Miami	Philadelphia (Merrick)	1861	16 Nov 1861	29 Jan 1862

Tonnage:	730 tons B
Dimensions:	208'2" (dk) × 33'2" × 8'6"
Machinery:	Side wheels, 1 inclined direct-acting engine (44" × 7'), 2 boilers; 8 knots
Complement:	134
Armament:	1 9" SB, 1 80-pdr R, 4 24-pdr. 1862: add 1 9" SB. Apr 63 total: 6 9" SB, 1 100-pdr R, 1 24-pdr SB.

SERVICE RECORD: GulfBS 1862. Passage past New Orleans forts and engagement with CSN vessels, 24 Apr 1862. Bombardment of Vicksburg, 22–28 Jun 1862. NAtlBS Sep 1862–64. Expedition in Chowan River, NC, 26–30 Jul 1863. Engagements with CSS *Albemarle* at Plymouth, NC, 19 Apr, and in Albemarle Sound, 5 May 1864. James River Sqn 1864–65. Decomm 22 May 1865. Sold 10 Aug 1865.
Later history: Merchant *Miami* 1865. RR 1869.

MARATANZA

Name	Bldr	Laid down	L	Comm
Maratanza	Boston (Loring)	1861	26 Nov 1861	12 Apr 1862

Tonnage:	786 tons B
Dimensions:	209' × 32'11" × 10'
Machinery:	Side wheels, 1 inclined direct-acting engine (44" × 7'), 2 boilers; 10 knots
Complement:	111
Armament:	1 100-pdr R, 1 9" SB, 4 24-pdr H. May 63: add 1 11" SB, 1 9" SB. 1865 total: 1 11" SB, 4 9" SB, 2 24-pdr H.

SERVICE RECORD: James River 1862. Army operations at Gloucester and York, Va., 14–29 Apr 1862. Captured CSS *Teaser* in James River, 4 Jul 1862. Blockade off Wilmington 1862. Engaged blockade runner *Kate* in Cape Fear River, 25 Sep 1862. Second attack on Ft. Fisher, NC, 13–15 Jan 1865. Bombarded Cape Fear River forts, 18–21 Feb 1865. Decomm 21 Jun 1865. Sold 26 Aug 1868.
Prizes: 4 May 1863: *Express*; 7 Dec: *Ceres*; 2 Jun 1864: str *Georgiana McCaw*; 20 Jan 1865: strs *Stag* and *Charlotte*.
Later history: Merchant *Maratanza* 1868. Sold to Haiti as gunboat, renamed *Salnave* 1868. Damaged in action with revolutionaries at Gonaives, 8 Aug 1869. Sunk at Cap Haitien, 13 Nov 1869, repaired, renamed *Union*.

The double-ender *Maratanza* as she appeared during the war. Wind-sails are rigged for ventilation. After the war she served as a gunboat in the Haitian Navy. (U.S. Naval Historical Center)

SEBAGO CLASS

Name	Bldr	Laid down	L	Comm
Mahaska	Portsmouth (Morgan)	1861	10 Dec 1861	5 May 1862
Sebago	Portsmouth (Novelty)	May 1861	30 Nov 1861	26 Mar 1862

Tonnage:	1,070 tons D; *Mahaska* 832 tons B, *Sebago* 852 tons B
Dimensions:	228'2" × 33'10" × 9'3"
Machinery:	Side wheels, 1 inclined direct-acting engine (44" × 7'), 2 boilers; 11 knots
Complement:	148
Armament:	1 9" SB, 1 100-pdr R, 4 24-pdr H
	Mahaska: Nov 62: 2 24-pdr H replaced by 4 9" SB. May 63 total: 6 9" SB, 1 100-pdr R, 2 12-pdr H
	Sebago: 1864 total: 1 100-pdr R, 5 9" SB, 2 24-pdr H, 2 12-pdr H

SERVICE RECORDS:

Mahaska—Chesapeake Bay 1862. Expeditions to West Point, Va., Pamunkey River, 7–9 Jan and in James River, Va., 6–20 Jul 1863. NAtlBS 1863. Bombardment of Ft. Wagner, Charleston, 6 Aug–8 Sep 1863. Assault on Jacksonville, Fla., 2–22 Feb 1864. Expedition to St. Marks, Fla., 23 Feb–27 Mar 1865. Decomm 12 Sep 1868. Sold 20 Nov 1868.

Prizes: 20 Feb 1863: *Gen. Taylor*; 8 Aug: str *Little Magruder*; 17 Feb 1865: *Delia*.

Later history: Merchant *Jeannette* 1868. RR 1869.

Sebago—NAtlBS Apr–Jun 1862. Army operations at Gloucester and York, Va., 14–29 Apr, and at Yorktown, Va., 4–7 May 1862. Expedition up Pamunkey River, Va., 17 May 1862. SAtlBS 1862. Damaged by grounding in Wassaw Sound, 18 Jun 1863. WGulfBS 1864. Battle of Mobile Bay, 5 Aug 1864. Decomm 29 Jul 1865. Sold 19 Jan 1867.

Later history: FFU.

OCTORARA

Name	Bldr	Laid down	L	Comm
Octorara	Brooklyn (Neptune)	1861	7 Dec 1861	28 Feb 1862

Tonnage:	981 tons D; 829 tons B
Dimensions:	193'2" × 34'6" × 4'10"
Machinery:	Side wheels, 1 inclined direct-acting engine (44" × 7'); 11 knots
Complement:	118
Armament:	1 80-pdr R, 1 9" SB, 4 24-pdr. Jul 63 total: 1 100-pdr R, 3 9" SB, 2 32-pdr/33, 4 24-pdr H. Jul 65 total: 2 32-pdr/33, 4 24-pdr.

SERVICE RECORD: NAtlBS 1862. WGulfBS 1862. Helm jammed during passage past batteries at Vicksburg, Miss., 28 Jun 1862. WGulfBS Oct 1863–65. Made reconnaissance into Mobile Bay, 20 Jan 1864. Bombardment of Ft. Powell, Mobile Bay, 16–29 Feb 1864. Damaged during battle of Mobile Bay, 5 Aug 1864. Bombardment of Ft. Morgan, Mobile Bay, 9–23 Aug 1864. Attacked by CSS *St. Patrick* off Mobile Bay, 28 Jan 1865. Capture of Mobile, 10–12 Apr 1865. Decomm 5 Aug 1865. Sold 9 Nov 1866.

Prizes: 24 Jul 1862: str *Tubal Cain*; 5 Nov: *Elias Reed*; 25 Dec: *Mont Blanc*; 10 Jan 1863: *Rising Dawn*; 15 Jan: *Brave*; 13 Mar: *Florence Nightingale*; 16 Mar: *Five Brothers, Rosalie*; 19 Mar: *John Williams*; 20 Apr: *W.Y. Leitch*; 21 Apr: *Handy*; 18 May: str *Eagle*.

Later history: FFU.

PAUL JONES

Name	Bldr	Laid down	L	Comm
Paul Jones	Abrahams (Reaney)	1861	17 Jan 1862	26 Apr 1862

Tonnage:	1,210 tons D; 863 tons B
Dimensions:	216'10" × 35'4" × 8'
Machinery:	Side wheels, 1 inclined direct-acting engine (48" × 7'); 10 knots
Complement:	148
Armament:	1 100-pdr R, 1 11" SB, 2 9" SB, 2 50-pdr R, 2 24-pdr H

SERVICE RECORD: SAtlBS 1862. Bombardment of Ft. McAllister, Ogeechee River, Ga., 29 Jul 1862. Bombardment at St. Johns Bluff, Fla., 17 Sep 1862. Joint expedition to St. Johns Bluff, 1–12 Oct and to Pocotaligo, SC, 21–23 Oct 1862. Bombardment of Ft. Wagner, Charleston, 18–25 Jul 1863. Blockade off Charleston 1863–Aug 1864. EGulfBS Apr 1865. Sold 13 Jul 1867.

Later history: FFU.

The side-wheel gunboat *Paul Jones*.

The double-ender *Genesee* off Baton Rouge, March 1863. (U.S. Naval Historical Center)

PORT ROYAL

Name	Bldr	Laid down	L	Comm
Port Royal	Stack (Novelty)	1861	17 Jan 1862	26 Apr 1862

Tonnage:	1,163 tons D; 805 tons B
Dimensions:	209′ × 35′ × 7′8″
Machinery:	Side wheels, 1 inclined direct-acting engine (48″ × 7′); 9.5 knots
Complement:	131
Armament:	1 100-pdr R, 1 10″ SB, 6 24-pdr H. Apr 63 total: 1 100-pdr R, 1 10″ SB, 2 9″ SB, 2 50-pdr R, 2 24-pdr H, 1 12-pdr SB.

SERVICE RECORD: NAtlBS 1862–63. Engaged batteries at Sewells Point, Va., 8 May and at Drewry's Bluff, Va., 15 May 1862. Bombardment of Ft. Wagner, Charleston, 18 Jul 1863. EGulfBS 1864–65. Bombardment of Ft. Powell, Mobile Bay, 16–29 Feb 1864. Battle of Mobile Bay, 5 Aug 1864. Bombardment of Ft. Morgan, Mobile Bay, 9–23 Aug 1864. Decomm 23 May 1866. Sold 3 Oct 1866.
Prizes: 18 Feb 1863: *Hortense*; 22 May: *Fashion*.
Later history: Merchant *Port Royal* 1866. RR 1886.

CIMARRON

Name	Bldr	Laid down	L	Comm
Cimarron	Mershon (McKnight)	1861	16 Mar 1862	5 Jul 1862

Tonnage:	993 tons D; 860 tons B
Dimensions:	205′ × 35′ × 9′
Machinery:	Side wheels, 1 inclined direct-acting engine, 2 boilers; 10 knots
Complement:	122
Armament:	1 100-pdr R, 1 9″ SB, 6 24-pdr H. 1863: 2 24-pdr H replaced by 2 9″ SB. Jun 64 total: 1 150-pdr R, 3 9″ SB, 4 24-pdr H SB, 4 12-pdr H.

NOTES: Name originally spelled *Cimerone*, changed prior to launch.
SERVICE RECORD: James River Jul–Sep 1862. SAtlBS Sep 1862–65. Bombardment at St. Johns Bluff, Fla., 17 Sep 1862. Bombardment of Ft. Wagner, Charleston, 18 Aug 1863. 100-pdr gun exploded during bombardment near Legareville, SC, 15 Feb 1864. Decomm 17 Aug 1865. Sold 6 Nov 1865.
Prizes: 29 May 1863: *Evening Star*; 13 Sep: str *Jupiter*.
Later history: FFU.

Side-wheel gunboat *Tioga* with her bulwarks down revealing guns forward and aft. This may be *Genesee*, but compare with the previous photo. (William Gladstone Collection)

GENESEE CLASS

Name	Bldr	Laid down	L	Comm
Genesee	Boston (Neptune)	1861	2 Apr 1862	3 Jul 1862
Tioga	Boston (Morgan)	1861	18 Apr 1862	30 Jun 1862

Tonnage:	1,120 tons D; 819 tons B
Dimensions:	209′ × 34′11″ × 10′6″
Machinery:	Side wheels, 1 inclined direct-acting engine (48″ × 7′); 11.5 knots
Complement:	113
Armament:	1 100-pdr R, 1 10″ SB, 6 24-pdr H

Genesee: May 63: 4 24-pdr H replaced by 4 9″ SB. Sep 63 total: 1 100-pdr R, 5 9″ SB, 2 24-pdr H. Dec 63 total: 2 100-pdr R, 1 10″ SB, 4 9″ SB, 2 24-pdr H. Mar 64: less 1 100-pdr R.

Tioga: Jul 63 total: 4 32-pdr/33 replaced 4 24-pdr H. Jun 65 total: 1 10″ SB, 1 60-pdr R, 6 32-pdr/33, 2 24-pdr H, 2 12-pdr R.

SERVICE RECORDS:

Genesee—NAtlBS 1862. Blockade of Wilmington. WGulfBS Feb 1863. Damaged by 10-inch shell during attempt to pass Port Hudson, La., 14 Mar 1863. Blockade off Mobile Sep 1863. Bombardment at Grants Pass, Ala., 13 Sep 1863. Battle of Mobile Bay, 5 Aug 1864. Store ship 1864–65. Decomm 31 Jul 1865. Sold 3 Oct 1867.

Prizes: 12 Sep 1863: str *Fanny*.

Later history: Merchant bark *Hattie C. Besse* 1867. SE 1870.

Tioga—NAtlBS 1862. James River Flotilla. West Indies Sqn Aug 1862. EGulfBS 1863. Decomm 29 Jun 1864–6 Jun 1865. Gulf Sqn 1865–66. Decomm 8 May 1866. Sold 15 Oct 1867.

Prizes: 2 Dec 1862: *Nonsuch*; 20 Jan 1863: str *Pearl*; 14 Feb: *Avon*; 13 Mar: *Florence Nightingale*; 22 Mar: *Brothers*; 22 Mar: str *Granite City*; 23 Apr: *Justina*; 20 Jun: str *Victory*; 27 Jun: *Julia*; 25 Sep: str *Herald*; 20 Mar 1864: *Swallow*.

Later history: FFU.

SONOMA CLASS

Name	Bldr	Laid down	L	Comm
Conemaugh	Portsmouth (Novelty)	1861	1 May 1862	16 Jul 1862
Sonoma	Portsmouth (Novelty)	1861	15 Apr 1862	8 Jul 1862

Tonnage:	1,105 tons D; 955 tons B
Dimensions:	233′9″ × 34′10″ × 8′7″
Machinery:	Side wheels, 1 inclined direct-acting engine (48″ × 7′), 2 boilers; 11 knots
Complement:	165
Armament:	1 100-pdr R, 1 11″ SB, 6 24-pdr H, 1 12-pdr H

Conemaugh: May 63: 4 24-pdr H replaced by 4 9″ SB. Jan 64 total: 6 9″ SB, 1 100-pdr R, 2 24-pdr H, 1 12-pdr.

Sonoma: Oct 63: add 4 9″ SB. Mar 65: add 2 12-pdr R.

NOTES: *Conemaugh* originally spelled *Cinemaugh*; name changed prior to launching. *Sonoma* re-engined 1863.

SERVICE RECORDS:

Conemaugh—SAtlBS Aug 1862–Sep 1863. Expedition to Pocotaligo, SC, 21–23 Oct 1862. WGulfBS Jan–Nov 1864. Battle of Mobile Bay, 5 Aug 1864. SAtlBS 1865. N. Atlantic Sqn 1867. Decomm 27 Jul 1867. Sold 1 Oct 1867.

Prizes: 25 Feb 1863: **Queen of the Wave*; 10 May: **unidentified*; 30 Apr 1864: *Judson*.

Later history: FFU.

Sonoma—West Indies 1862, search for Confederate raiders. SAtlBS Oct 1863. Expedition in Broad River, SC, 27 Nov–30 Dec 1864. Engaged batteries in Togodo Creek, SC, 9 Feb 1865. Expedition to Bulls Bay, SC, 12–17 Feb 1865. Decomm 13 Jun 1865. Sold 1 Oct 1867.

Prizes: 18 Jan 1863: str *Virginia*; 3 Feb: *Springbok*; 15 Mar: *Atlantic*; 14 Apr: *Clyde*; 8 Jul 1864: str *Ida*.

Later history: FFU.

The side-wheel double-ender *Conemaugh* during the war. Notice the large gun forward of the funnel. (U.S. Naval Historical Center)

The gunboat *Agawam* in the James River 1864–65. (Martin Holbrook Collection) (U.S. Naval Historical Center)

SASSACUS CLASS

Name	Bldr	Laid down	L	Comm
Agawam	Lawrence (Portland)	Oct 1862	21 Apr 1863	9 Mar 1864
Algonquin	Brooklyn (Morgan)	1863	21 Dec 1863	never
Ascutney	Jackman (Morgan)	1862	4 Apr 1863	28 Jul 1864
Chenango	Simonson (Morgan)	1862	19 Mar 1863	29 Feb 1864
Chicopee	Curtis (Neptune)	1862	4 Mar 1863	7 May 1864
Eutaw	Abrahams (Vulcan)	1862	Feb 1863	2 Jul 1863
Iosco	Larrabee (Globe)	Sep 1862	20 Mar 1863	26 Apr 1864
Lenapee	Lupton (Wash IW)	1862	28 May 1863	30 Dec 1864
Mackinaw	Brooklyn (Poole)	1862	22 Apr 1863	23 Apr 1864
Massasoit	Curtis & Tilden (Globe)	1862	8 Mar 1863	8 Mar 1864
Mattabesett	Sampson (Allaire)	1862	1863	7 Apr 1864
Mendota	Tucker (S. Brooklyn)	1862	13 Jan 1863	2 May 1864
Metacomet	Stack (S. Brooklyn)	1862	7 Mar 1863	4 Jan 1864
Mingoe	Mershon (Pusey)	1862	6 Aug 1863	29 Jul 1864
Osceola	Curtis & Tilden (Atlantic)	1862	29 May 1863	10 Feb 1864
Otsego	Westervelt (Fulton)	1862	31 Mar 1863	Spring 1864
Pawtucket	Portsmouth (Providence)	3 Nov 1862	19 Mar 1863	26 Aug 1864
Peoria	Brooklyn (Etna)	1862	29 Oct 1863	26 Dec 1866
Pontiac	Hillman (Neafie)	1862	1863	7 Jul 1864
Pontoosuc	Lawrence (Portland)	Oct 1862	May 1863	10 May 1864
Sassacus	Portsmouth (Atlantic)	11 Sep 1862	23 Dec 1862	5 Oct 1863
Shamrock	Brooklyn (Poole)	1862	17 Mar 1863	13 Jun 1864
Tacony	Philadelphia (Morris Towne)	1862	7 May 1863	12 Feb 1864
Tallahoma	Brooklyn (Stover)	1862	28 Nov 1863	27 Dec 1865*
Tallapoosa	Boston (Neptune)	1862	17 Feb 1863	13 Sep 1864 65*
Wateree	Reaney (bldr)	1862	29 Aug 1863	20 Jan 1864
Winooski	Boston (Providence)	1862	30 Jul 1863	27 Jun 1865†
Wyalusing	Cramp (Pusey)	1862	12 May 1863	8 Feb 1864

†completed at Brooklyn
* delivered

Tonnage:	1,173 tons D; 974 tons B
Dimensions:	240' (oa) 205' (pp) × 35' × 9'6"
Machinery:	Side wheels, 1 inclined direct-acting engine (58" × 8'9") (*Algonquin* (48" × 10')), 2 boilers; IHP 665 = 13 knots
Complement:	200
Armament:	2 100-pdr R, 4 9" SB, 2 20-pdr R, except

Algonquin and *Peoria*: none
Agawam 1864 total: 2 100-pdr R, 4 9" SB, 2 24-pdr SB, 1 12-pdr R, 1 12-pdr SB
Chenango, Chicopee, Eutaw, Lenapee, Otsego 1864–65: add 2 24-pdr H
Iosco Mar 64 total: 2 100-pdr R, 4 9" SB, 2 24-pdr R, 2 12-pdr H. Mar 65: 1 100-pdr R replaced by 1 11" SB.
Mackinaw Jan 64: add 2 24-pdr H. May 65 total: 1 15" SB, 6 9" SB, 2 24-pdr, 2 12-pdr.
Massasoit, Mattabesett, Metacomet Mar 64 total: 2 100-pdr R, 4 9" SB, 2 12-pdr R, 2 24-pdr
Mendota Jul 64: 1 20-pdr replaced by 2 24-pdr H
Mingoe Aug 64: add 2 24-pdr, 2 12-pdr R
Osceola Jun 64: add 1 12-pdr SB, 1 12-pdr R, 1 24-pdr, less

2 20-pdr R. Mar 65 total: 2 100-pdr R, 1 11" SB, 1 12-pdr SB, 1 24-pdr.
Pawtucket 1864: add 2 24-pdr H. 1865 total: 1 100-pdr R, 1 11" SB, 2 20-pdr R.
Pontiac Jul 64: add 4 24-pdr H, 2 12-pdr SB, 2 12-pdr R
Pontoosuc 1864: add 2 24-pdr H, 2 12-pdr R. Apr 65 total: 1 100-pdr R, 1 11" SB, 4 9" SB, 2 20-pdr R, 2 24-pdr H, 1 12-pdr.
Sassacus 1864 total: 2 100-pdr R, 4 9" SB, 2 20-pdr R, 2 24-pdr H, 2 12-pdr R. Feb 65: 1 9" SB replaced by 1 100-pdr R.
Shamrock 1864: add 2 24-pdr H, 2 12-pdr R. Dec 64 total: 2 100-pdr R, 6 9" SB, 2 20-pdr R, 2 12-pdr SB.
Tacony Oct 64: 2 11" SB, 3 9" SB, 1 24-pdr H, 2 12-pdr. Sep 65 total: 4 8" SB/63, 2 60-pdr R, 2 24-pdr HSB, 2 12-pdr R, 2 12-pdr SB.
Tallapoosa Dec 64: add 2 24-pdr H; 1875 total: 1 11" BLR, 1 10" R. 1888 total: 1 8" R, 2 60-pdr R.
Wateree Jan 64: add 4 24-pdr H, 4 12-pdr, less 2 20-pdr
Wyalusing 1864 total: 2 100-pdr R, 4 9" SB, 4 24-pdr H, 4 12-pdr H

NOTES: Wooden hulls except *Wateree*, which had an iron hull. Engines designed by Isherwood, except *Algonquin* by Dickerson. *Algonquin* engaged *Winooski* in a celebrated test of machinery in 1866, proving a complete failure. *Tallapoosa* rebuilt as single-ender 1875.

SERVICE RECORDS:

Agawam—NAtlBS 1864–65. Engagement at Howletts Bluff, Trents Reach, Va., 21 Jun 1864. Engaged batteries in Four Mile Creek, Va., Jul–Aug 1864. Decomm 31 Mar 1867. Sold 10 Oct 1867.
Later history: FFU.

Algonquin—Failed trials and never commissioned. Sold 21 Oct 1869.
Later history: Merchant *Algonquin* 1869. Sold foreign 1878.

Ascutney—NAtlBS Jul 1864. Search for CSS *Florida* in N. Atlantic, then blockade off Wilmington, NC. Decomm 22 Sep 1864. Sold 28 Oct 1868.
Later history: FFU.

Chenango—Damaged by explosion of port boiler while leaving New York, 15 Apr 1864. Recomm 1 Feb 1865. SAtlBS 1865. Decomm 1 Jul 1865. Sold 28 Oct 1868.
Prize: 25 Feb 1865: *Elvira*.
Later history: FFU.

Chicopee—NAtlBS Jun 1864–Dec 1865. Expedition to Plymouth, NC, Roanoke River 28 Oct–2 Nov and up Roanoke River to Poplar Point, NC, 9–28 Dec 1864. Decomm 19 Dec 1866. Sold 8 Oct 1867.
Later history: FFU.

Eutaw—NAtlBS 1863. Operations in James River, May 1864. Decomm 8 May 1865. Sold 15 Oct 1867.
Later history: FFU.

Iosco—Protected American shipping in Gulf of St. Lawrence 1864. NAtlBS Oct 1864. Unsuccessful attack on Ft. Fisher, NC, 24–25 Dec 1864. Second attack on Ft. Fisher, 13–15 Jan 1865. Expedition up Roanoke River, NC, 11–16 May 1865. Decomm 28 Jul 1865. Coal hulk New York NYd Feb 1868.
Prizes: 21 Nov 1864: *Sybil*; 23 May 1865: **Sarah M. Newhall*.

The double-ender *Tallapoosa* in wartime gray paint. (Peabody Museum of Salem)

Lenapee—NAtlBS 1865. Bombardment of Ft. Anderson, Cape Fear River, 11–21 Feb 1865. Decomm 17 Oct 1867. Sold 26 Aug 1868.
Later history: FFU.

Mackinaw—NAtlBS 1864, James River. Engagement at Dutch Gap, Va., 13 and 16–18 Aug 1864. Unsuccessful attack on Ft. Fisher, NC, 24–25 Dec 1864. Second attack on Ft. Fisher, 13–15 Jan 1865. Bombardment of Ft. Anderson, Cape Fear River, 11–21 Feb 1865. Decomm May 1865. N. Atlantic Sqn and West Indies 1866–67. Decomm 4 May 1867. Sold 3 Oct 1867.
Prizes: 10 Sep 1864: str *Matagorda*; 3 Dec: *Mary*.
Later history: FFU.

Massasoit—NAtlBS Oct 1864. Engagement at Trents Reach, James River, Va., 24 Jan 1865. Decomm 27 Jun 1865. Sold 15 Oct 1867.
Later history: FFU.

Mattabesett—NAtlBS 1864. Engagement with CSS *Albemarle*, Albemarle Sound, NC, 5 May 1864. Decomm 31 May 1865. Sold 15 Oct 1867.
Prize: 5 May 1864: *Bombshell*.
Later history: FFU.

Mendota—NAtlBS, James River 1864–65. Engaged battery near Four Mile Creek, Va., Jul 1864. Decomm 12 May 1865. Sold 7 Dec 1867.
Later history: FFU.

Metacomet—WGulfBS 1864. Forced steamer *Ivanhoe* ashore, 30 Jun 1864. Battle of Mobile Bay, damaged by CSS *Selma*, 5 Aug 1864.

Bombardment of Ft. Morgan, Mobile Bay, 9–23 Aug 1864. Decomm 18 Aug 1865. Sold 28 Oct 1868.
Prizes: 6 Jun 1864: str *Donegal*; 30 Jun: str **Ivanhoe*; 27 Nov: str *Susanna*; 31 Dec: *Sea Witch*; 6 Jan 1865: *Lilly*.
Later history: FFU.

Mingoe—SAtlBS 1864–65. Expeditions in Broad River, SC, 27 Nov–30 Dec and to Georgetown, SC, 23 Feb 1865. Sold 3 Oct 1867.
Later history: FFU.

Osceola—NAtlBS, James River 1864. Engaged battery near Harrisons Landing, Va., 4 Aug 1864. Unsuccessful attack on Ft. Fisher, NC, 24–25 Dec 1864. Damaged during second attack on Ft. Fisher, 13–15 Jan 1865. Bombardment of Ft. Anderson, Cape Fear River, 11–21 Feb 1865. Decomm 13 May 1865. Sold 1 Oct 1867.
Prizes: 25 Jan 1865: str *Blenheim*.
Later history: Merchant *Eliza* 1868. Converted to schooner. Lost 1868.

Otsego—NAtlBS May 1864. Capture of Plymouth, NC, Roanoke River, 29–31 Oct 1864. Sank in shallow water after hitting two torpedoes (mines) in Roanoke River, 9 Dec 1864.

Pawtucket—NAtlBS Oct 1864–65. Unsuccessful attack on Ft. Fisher, NC, 24–25 Dec 1864. Second attack on Ft. Fisher, 13–15 Jan 1865. Bombardment of Ft. Anderson, Cape Fear River, 11–21 Feb 1865. Decomm 15 Jun 1865. Sold 15 Oct 1867.
Later history: FFU.

Tallapoosa, a double-ender gunboat of the *Sassacus* class, after being rebuilt in 1876. Her newly built-up superstructure aft is quite prominent. (U.S. Naval Historical Center)

The *Wateree* aground at Arica, Peru, 1868, lying 430 yards inland from the usual high-water mark. She was sold where she lay. She was the only ship of the class with an iron hull. (U.S. Naval Historical Center)

Peoria—N. Atlantic 1867, West Indies. Decomm 28 Jul 1867. Sold 26 Aug 1868.
Later history: FFU.

Pontiac—SAtlBS 1864. Damaged during engagement with battery at Sullivan's Island, 7 Nov 1864. Expedition in Broad River, SC, 27 Nov–30 Dec 1864. Decomm 21 Jun 1865. Sold 15 Oct 1867.
Prize: 2 Mar 1865: str *Amazon*.
Later history: FFU.

Pontoosuc—Search for CSS *Tallahassee* in Gulf of St. Lawrence 1864. SAtlBS 1864–65. Unsuccessful attack on Ft. Fisher, NC, 24–25 Dec 1864. Second attack on Ft. Fisher, 13–15 Jan 1865. Bombardment of Ft. Anderson, Cape Fear River, 11–21 Feb 1865. Decomm 5 Jul 1865. Sold 3 Oct 1866.
Later history: FFU.

Sassacus—NAtlBS 1864–65. Damaged in collision with CSS *Albemarle* during engagement in Albemarle Sound, NC, 5 May 1864. Unsuccessful attack on Ft. Fisher, NC, 24–25 Dec 1864. Second attack on Ft. Fisher, 13–15 Jan 1865. Bombardment of Ft. Anderson, Cape Fear River, 11–21 Feb 1865. Decomm 13 May 1865. Sold 15 Aug 1868.
Prizes: 1 Feb 1864: str *Wild Dayrell*; 5 Feb: str *Nutfield*.
Later history: FFU.

Shamrock—NAtlBS 1864–Aug 1865. Capture of Plymouth, NC, Roa-

The double-ender gunboat *Winooski* served only briefly after the war. (Martin Holbrook Collection) (U.S. Naval Historical Center)

noke River, 29–31 Oct 1864. West Indies Sqn Dec 1865. European Sqn 1866–68. Decomm 10 Aug 1868. Sold 1 Sep 1868.
Later history: FFU.
Tacony—NAtlBS 1864. Capture of Plymouth, NC, Roanoke River, 29–31 Oct 1864. Unsuccessful attack on Ft. Fisher, NC, 24–25 Dec 1864. Second attack on Ft. Fisher, 13–15 Jan 1865. Decomm 7 Oct 1867. Sold 26 Aug 1868.
Later history: FFU.
Tallahoma—No service. Sold 29 Aug 1868.
Later history: Merchant *Mary M. Roberts* 1868. SE 1870.
Tallapoosa—Search in N. Atlantic for Confederate raiders, 1864. EGulfBS 1865. Gulf Sqn 1866–67. Training ship, Annapolis 1872. Rebuilt 1876. Sunk in collision with schooner *James S. Lowell* off

Vineyard Haven, Mass., 21 Aug 1884. Raised; recomm, 11 Jan 1886. S. Atlantic Sqn 1886–91. Sold at Montevideo, 3 Mar 1892.
Later history: FFU.
Wateree—Pacific Sqn 1864. Driven ashore during earthquake and tidal wave at Arica, Peru, 13 Aug 1868. Hulk sold ashore 21 Nov 1868.
Winooski—N. Atlantic 1866. Caribbean 1867. Sold 25 Aug 1868.
Later history: FFU.
Wyalusing—NAtlBS 1864. Engagement with CSS *Albemarle*, Albemarle Sound, NC, 5 May 1864. Capture of Plymouth, NC, Roanoke River, 29–31 Oct and up Roanoke River to Poplar Point, NC, 9–28 Dec 1864. Decomm 10 Jun 1865. Sold 15 Oct 1867.
Prize: 9 Jan 1865: *Triumph*.
Later history: FFU.

MOHONGO CLASS

Name	Bldr	Laid down	L	Comm
Ashuelot	McKay (bldr)	1864	12 Jul 1865	4 Apr 1866
Mohongo	Secor (Fulton)	1863	9 Jul 1864	23 May 1865
Monocacy	Denmead (bldr)	1863	14 Dec 1864	early 1866
Muscoota	Continental (Morgan)	1863	1864	5 Jan 1865
Shamokin	Reaney (bldr)	1863	1864	31 Jul 1865*
Suwanee	Reaney (bldr)	1863	13 Mar 1864	23 Jan 1865
Winnipec	Loring (bldr)	1863	20 Aug 1864	1865
				*delivered

Tonnage: 1,370 tons D; 1,030 tons B
Dimensions: 255′ (wl) × 35′ × 9′6″
Machinery: Side wheels, 1 inclined direct-acting engine (58″ × 8′9″), 2 boilers; 15 knots

Complement: 190
Armament: 4 9″ SB, 2 100-pdr R, 2 20-pdr R, 2 24-pdr, except *Ashuelot, Monocacy*:4 8″ SB, 2 60-pdr R, 2 20-pdr R, 2 24-pdr H
              Monocacy 1889: 4 8″, 2 60-pdr BLR

NOTES: Iron hulls, schooner rig. Engines designed by Isherwood.
SERVICE RECORDS:
Ashuelot—Cruise to Europe with USS *Miantonomoh* 1866. Asiatic Stn 1866–83. Wrecked near Swatow, China, 18 Feb 1883.
Mohongo—Pacific Sqn, S. America, 1865–67. Hawaii 1868. Decomm 29 May 1870. Sold 17 Nov 1870.
Later history: Merchant *Mohongo* 1870. SE 1878.
Monocacy—Asiatic Stn 1866–1903. Korean Expedition 1871. Boxer

Side-wheel gunboat *Mohongo*, completed at the end of the war, served for five years in the Pacific Ocean until sold in 1870. (U.S. Naval Historical Center)

Rebellion 1900. Stricken 22 Jun 1903. Sold in Japan, Nov 1903.

Muscoota—Sold 17 Jun 1869.

    Later history: Merchant *Tennessee* 1869. Caught fire and beached near Little River, NC, 29 Jun 1870.

Shamokin—S. Atlantic Stn 1866–68. Decomm 24 Dec 1868. Sold 21 Oct 1869.

    Later history: Merchant *Georgia* 1869. Converted to screw and lengthened 1879. Wrecked in Gulf of Nicoya, Costa Rica, 30 Sep 1878.

Suwanee—Pacific Sqn 1865–68. Wrecked in Queen Charlotte Sound, BC, 9 Jul 1868.

Winnipec—Practice ship, Naval Academy 1866–67. Sold 17 Jun 1869.

    Later history: Merchant *South Carolina* 1869. Converted to screw and lengthened 1879. BU 1891.

The side-wheel gunboat *Monocacy* in China where she served for almost forty years. (U.S. Naval Historical Center)

ACQUIRED VESSELS

The requirements of the Navy's duties during the war were varied and great. Ships of all sizes were needed, larger ones for operations on the high seas and small shallow-draft vessels for inshore and riverine activities.

A number of big and fast vessels were chartered or purchased in the spring of 1861 for use as blockaders and to supplement the regular Navy ships. At a later date some of these were used to protect American commercial vessels on sealanes threatened by Confederate raiders, such as the valuable route from Panama to the East Coast connecting with the Pacific route from California.

Captured blockade runners were taken into service, being very fast and suitable to pursue their former sisters as they attempted to reach or break out of the Confederate ports. After sighting a suspect, a chase would ensue that might last many hours, sometimes resulting in an escape, often in capture or destruction of the vessel.

Medium-size vessels were used as gunboats in the rivers of Virginia and the Carolinas and as close-in blockaders off Wilmington, Charleston, and other Southern ports. New York ferryboats were found to be very useful with their capacity for steaming in either direction and decks already strengthened for carrying heavy loads.

A host of small steamers and tugs were given flower names and were known to some as the "Navy's flower pots."

Most of these vessels were sold after the war. Their unstrengthened hulls and inadequate engines made them ill-suited for regular naval service, and they were disposed of in large batches within a few months after the end of the blockade.

LARGE SIDE-WHEEL COMBATANTS—2ND & 3RD RATE

Name	Bldr	L	Acquired	Comm
Adela	(GB)	(U)	23 May 1863	June 1863

Tonnage: 585 tons B
Dimensions: 211' × 23'6" × 9'3", d12'
Machinery: Side wheels, 2 oscillating engines (52.5" × 4'6"), 4 boilers; 12 knots
Complement: 58/70
Armament: 2 20-pdr R, 4 24-pdr SB

NOTES: Blockade runner, captured by USS *Quaker City* and *Huntsville* in the Bahama Islands, 7 Jul 1862. Brig rig, iron hull. Formerly yacht of the Earl of Eglintoun.
SERVICE RECORD: EGulfBS, Aug 1863–Nov 1864. Engaged batteries at Tampa, Fla., 16 Oct 1863. Potomac Flotilla 1865. Sold 30 Nov 1865. *Prizes:* 12 Oct 1863: sloop *Laura*; 29 Mar 1864: *Maria*; 6 Nov: *Badger*. *Later history:* FFU.

Name	Bldr	L	Acquired	Comm
Advance (ex-*A.D. Vance*, ex-*Lord Clyde*)	Caird (bldr)	3 Jul 1862	Sep 1864	28 Oct 1864

Tonnage: 1,300 tons D, 808 tons B, 700 GRT
Dimensions: 243' () 230' () × 26' × 11'8"
Machinery: Side wheels, 2 side-lever engines (63" × 6'6"); 12 knots
Complement: 98/107
Armament: 1 20-pdr R, 4 24-pdr H

NOTES: Blockade runner *A.D. Vance*, captured by USS *Santiago de Cuba*, 10 Sep 1864. Iron hull. Former Glasgow–Dublin packet steamer.
SERVICE RECORD: NAtlBS 1864–65. Unsuccessful attack on Ft. Fisher, NC, 24–25 Dec 1864. Second attack on Ft. Fisher, 13–15 Jan 1865. Renamed **Frolic**, 2 Jun 1865. European Sqn 1865–69. SAtl Stn 1875–77. Decomm 31 Oct 1877. Sold 1 Oct 1883.

Name	Bldr	L	Acquired	Comm
Alabama	Webb (Novelty)	19 Jan 1850	1 Aug 1861	30 Sep 1861
Florida	Webb (Novelty)	1850	12 Aug 1861	5 Oct 1861

Tonnage: 1,261 tons B
Dimensions: 214'4" × 35'2" × 14'6", d22'
Machinery: Side wheels, 1 side-lever engine (75" × 8'); 13 knots

The Federal fleet off Hampton Roads early in December 1864. One can make out various converted merchant side-wheelers and Navy-built sloops as well as the powerful *New Ironsides* in the distance just to the right of center. (U.S. Naval Historical Center)

Complement: 119/180
Armament: 4 32-pdr/57, 4 32-pdr/42, 1 20-pdr R
Alabama: Dec 62: 1 9″ SB, 2 30-pdr R, 6 32-pdr/57, 1 12-pdr R
Florida: Apr 63: 4 9′ SB, 1 100-pdr R, 1 50-pdr R, 1 12-pdr R

NOTES: Fore-topsail schooner rig. Built for the New York & Savannah Steam Navigation Co.

SERVICE RECORDS:

Alabama—SAtlBS 1861–Jul 63. Capture of Fernandina, Fla., and Brunswick, St. Simons, and Jekyl islands, Ga., 2–12 Mar 1862. NAtlBS May 1864–65. Unsuccessful attack on Ft. Fisher, NC, 24–25 Dec 1864. Second attack on Ft. Fisher, 13–15 Jan 1865. Ordnance and despatch vessel, Hampton Roads, 1865. Decomm 14 Jul 1865. Sold 10 Aug 1865.
Prizes: 25 Nov 1861: *Albion*; 12 Dec: *Admiral*; 20 Jun 1862: *Catalina*; 23 Sep: *Nellie*.

The *Frolic* at Naples, Italy, about 1869. She was originally a Dublin-Glasgow packet before becoming the blockade runner *A.D. Vance*. Commissioned as the USS *Advance*, she was renamed in 1865. (U.S. Naval Historical Center)

Later history: Merchant *Alabama* 1865. Converted to schooner 1872. Destroyed by fire 1878.

Florida—SAtlBS 1861–64. Occupation of Port Royal, SC, 7 Nov 1861. Capture of Fernandina, Fla., and Brunswick, St. Simons, and Jekyl islands, Ga., 2–12 Mar 1862. Gulf of Mexico Mar 1865. W. Indies 1866–67. Decomm 26 Apr 1867. Sold 5 Dec 1868.
Prizes: 19 Jun 1862: *Ventura*; 25 Sep: *Agnes*; 11 Jun 1863: str *Calypso*; 21 Jun: *Hattie*; 10 Feb 1864: str **Emily* and str **Fanny & Jenny*.
Later history: Merchant *Delphine* 1868. Sold to Haitian revolutionaries as gunboat, renamed *Republique* 1869. "Worn out" 1875.

Name	Bldr	Built	Acquired	Comm
Arizona (ex-CSS *Caroline*, ex-*Arizona*)	Harlan (Morgan)	1859	23 Jan 1863	9 Mar 1863

Tonnage: 950 tons B
Dimensions: 201′6″ () 200′ (wl) × 34′ × 8′, d10′
Machinery: Side wheels, 1 vertical-beam condensing engine (44″ × 11′), 1 boiler
Complement: 82/91
Armament: 4 32-pdr/42, 1 30-pdr R, 1 12-pdr R.

NOTES: Blockade runner *Caroline*, captured by USS *Montgomery* off Pensacola, 29 Oct 1862. Iron hull, two-masted schooner.
SERVICE RECORD: WGulfBS 1863–65. Engagement with CSS *Queen of the West* in Berwick Bay, La., 14 Apr 1863. Engagement at Butte-a-la-Rose, La., and capture of Ft. Burton, 20 Apr 1863. Expedition up Red River, 3–13 May 1863. Attack on Sabine Pass, Tex., 8 Sep 1863. Blockade of Texas coast 1863–64. Destroyed by fire 38 miles below New Orleans, 27 Feb 1865.
Prize: 23 Mar 1863: *Aurelia*.

Name	Bldr	Built	Acquired	Comm
Augusta	Webb (Novelty)	1852	1 Aug 1861	28 Sep 1861

Tonnage: 1,310 tons B
Dimensions: 220′8″ × 35′4″ × 14′3″, d21′6″
Machinery: Side wheels, oscillating engine (85″ × 8′), 2 boilers; 11 knots
Complement: 157
Armament: 4 32-pdr/57, 4 32-pdr/42, 1 12-pdr R. Aug 62: add 1 20-pdr R. Feb 63 total: 1 100-pdr R, 2 30-pdr R, 6-8″ SB. June 64 total: 1 100-pdr R, 2 30-pdr R, 4 8″ SB, 2 24-pdr SB.

The *Augusta* sailed between New York and Savannah until being purchased by the Navy in 1861. The side-wheel steamer accompanied the monitor *Mianto-nomoh* on her voyage to Europe in 1865–66, when this picture was taken. In 1877 she foundered in a gale, but all passengers and crew were saved. (INRO)

NOTES: Three-masted schooner rig, wood hull. Built for the New York & Savannah Steam Navigation Co. (Mitchell Line).
SERVICE RECORD: SAtlBS Oct 1861–65. Occupation of Port Royal, SC, 7 Nov 1861. Occupation of Beaufort, SC, 9 Nov 1861. Cruised to Europe with *Miantonomoh* 1866–67. Sold 2 Dec 1868.
Prizes: 6 Dec 1861: *Cheshire*; 31 Dec: *Island Belle*.
Later history: Merchant *Magnolia* 1869. Foundered en route Savannah–New York, 30 Sep 1877.

Name	Bldr	L	Acquired	Comm
Banshee	Jones Quiggin (Laird)	22 Nov 1862	12 Mar 1864	Jun 1864

Tonnage:	533 tons B, 325 GRT
Dimensions:	220′ × 20′4″ × 10′, d12′
Machinery:	Side wheels, 2 oscillating engines (42″ × 3′9″), 2 boilers; 12 knots
Complement:	60/89
Armament:	1 30-pdr R, 1 12-pdr SB

NOTES: Blockade runner, captured on ninth trip by USAT *Fulton* and USS *Grand Gulf* off Wilmington, 21 Nov 1863. Schooner rig, steel hull, two pole masts. First steel vessel to cross the Atlantic. Engines were unreliable.
SERVICE RECORD: NAtlBS 1864–65. Unsuccessful attack on Ft. Fisher, NC, 24–25 Dec 1864. Potomac Flotilla Jan 1865. Sold 30 Nov 1865.
Later history: Merchant *J.L. Smallwood* 1865. British *Irene* 1867. SE 1895.

Name	Bldr	L	Acquired	Comm
Bat	Jones Quiggin (Watt)	21 Jun 1864	Nov 1864	13 Dec 1864

Tonnage:	750 tons B, 505 n/r
Dimensions:	230′ × 26′ × 8′, d12′
Machinery:	Side wheels, 2 oscillating engines (52″ × 4′), 2 boilers; NHP 180 = 16 knots
Complement:	82
Armament:	1 30-pdr R, 2 12-pdr SB

NOTES: Blockade runner, captured on first voyage by USS *Montgomery* off Wilmington, NC, 10 Oct 1864. Iron hull, schooner rig.
SERVICE RECORD: NAtlBS 1865–65. Decomm 17 May 1865. Sold 25 Oct 1865.
Later history: Merchant *Teazer* 1865. British *Miramichi* 1872. BU 1902.

The side-wheel steamer *Bat* after the war as the merchant ship *Teazer*. At the next pier behind is the screw steamer *Fah Kee*, another former Navy ship. (Peabody Museum of Salem)

Name	Bldr	L	Acquired	Comm
Bienville	L & F (Morgan)	1860	14 Aug 1861	23 Oct 1861
De Soto	L & F (Morgan)	25 Jun 1859	21 Aug 1861	1861

Tonnage:	*Bienville*: 1,558 tons B; *De Soto*: 1,675 tons B
Dimensions:	253′3″ × 38′6″ × 16′2″, d26′
Machinery:	Side wheels, 1 vertical-beam engine (68″ × 11′), 2 boilers; HP 400 = 11 knots
Complement:	185
Armament:	*Bienville*: 4 32-pdr/42, 4 32-pdr/57. Jun 63 total: 1 100-pdr R, 1 12-pdr SB, 1 30-pdr R, 8 32-pdr/57. *De Soto*: 8 32-pdr/42, 1 30-pdr R. Dec 62 total: 1 9″ SB, 1 30-pdr R, 6 32-pdr/42, 2 12-pdr SB.

NOTES: Wood hulls. Built for the New York–Mobile service of Livingston Crocheron & Co. *De Soto* reboilered 1864–65.

SERVICE RECORDS:

Bienville—SAtlBS 1861–62. Occupation of Port Royal, SC, 7 Nov. 1861. Occupation of Beaufort, SC, 9 Nov 1861. Capture of Fernandina, Fla., and Brunswick, St. Simons, and Jekyl islands, Ga., 2–12 Mar 1862. WGulfBS 1863–65. Battle of Mobile Bay, 5 Aug 1864. Blockade of Galveston 1865. Decomm 1865. Sold 5 Oct 1867.

Prizes: 11 Dec 1861: *Sarah and Caroline*; 25 Feb 1862: *Arrow*; 26 Feb: *Alert*; 24 May: str *Stettin*; 27 May: str *Patras*; 29 May: *La Criolla*, *Providence*, and *Rebecca*; 27 Jun: *Morning Star*; 21 Aug: *Eliza*; 23 Aug: *Louisa*; 9 Mar 1863: *Lightning*; 7 Feb 1865: *Annie Sophia* and *Pet*.

Later history: Merchant *Bienville* 1867. Destroyed by fire at Watling Island, Bahamas, 15 Aug 1872.

De Soto—WGulfBS, Dec 1861–65. NAtl Sqn, Sep 1865–67. Damaged during an earthquake at St. Thomas, 18 Nov 1867. Decomm 11 Sep and sold 30 Sep 1868.

Prizes: 28 Jan 1862: *Major Barbour*; 8 Feb: *Star* and *Alphonsina*; 29 Jun: *George Washington*; 1 Jul: *William*; 23 Apr 1863: *Bright*; 24 Apr: *Jane Adelie*, *Rapid*, and *General Prim*; 26 Apr: *Clarita*; 14 May: *Sea Bird*; 17 May: str **Cuba*; 19 May: *Mississippian*; 6 Jul: *Lady Maria*; 18 Jul: strs *James Battle* and *William Bagley*; 16 Aug: str *Alice Vivian*; 17 Aug: str *Nita*; 13 Sep: str *Montgomery*; 22 Sep: str *Leviathan*; 5 Feb 1864: str *Cumberland*.

Later history: Merchant *De Soto* 1868. Burned below New Orleans, 7 Dec 1870. (Hulk BU 1880)

The gunboat *De Soto* lying at Ponce, Puerto Rico, 1868. This converted side-wheeler was built for the New York-Mobile run. In October 1865 she rescued the crew of the British gunboat *Bulldog* when that ship was destroyed by rebel gunfire at Cap Haitien, Haiti. (U.S. Naval Historical Center)

Name	Bldr	L	Acquired	Comm
Connecticut (ex-*Mississippi*)	Webb (Morgan)	15 Jan 1861	18 Jul 1861	23 Aug 1861

Tonnage:	1,725 tons, 2,150 n/r
Dimensions:	251'6" × 38'2" × 14', d22'8"
Machinery:	Side wheels, 1 vertical beam engine (80" × 11'); 10 knots
Complement:	166
Armament:	4 32-pdr/42, 1 12-pdr R. Dec 61 total: 10 32-pdr/57, 1 50-pdr R, 1 30-pdr R. Dec 63 total: 1 100-pdr R, 2 30-pdr R, 8 8" SB.

NOTES: Brig rig, two masts. Built for the New York & Savannah Steam Navigation Co., but purchased by the Navy before entering service.

SERVICE RECORD: Transport and supply ship 1861–62. GulfBS 1862–63. Convoy ship off Aspinwall, Panama, 1863. NAtlBS Aug 1863–Jul 1864. Decomm 11 Aug 1865. Sold 21 Sep 1865.

Prizes: 17 Nov 1861: *Adeline*; 17 Jan 1862: *Emma*; 9 Sep: *Rambler*; 30 Oct: *Hermosa*; 22 Sep 1863: str *Juno*; 23 Sep: str **Phantom*; 6 Dec: str *Ceres*; 20 Dec: *Sallie*; 1 Mar 1864: str *Scotia*; 9 May: str *Minnie*; 10 May: str *Greyhound*.

Later history: Merchant *South America*. BU 1879.

The *Connecticut* was purchased for naval service in 1861 prior to completion. As the *South America* she sailed on the New York-Brazil run after the war. (U.S. Naval Historical Center)

Name	Bldr	L	Acquired	Comm
Cornubia (ex-*Lady Davis*, ex-*Cornubia*)	Harvey (U)	27 Feb 1858	Nov 1863	17 Mar 1864

Tonnage:	589 tons B, 411 GRT
Dimensions:	210' () 196' () × 24'6" × 10', d13'3"
Machinery:	Side wheels, 2 oscillating engines (50" × 4'8"), 2 boilers; HP 230 = 13 knots
Complement:	76
Armament:	1 20-pdr R, 2 24-pdr SB. Jul 64: 1 20-pdr R replaced by 1 30-pdr R. Apr 65: add 2 12-pdr R.

NOTES: Blockade runner, captured on 23rd run by USS *Niphon* and *James Adger* off New Inlet, NC, 8 Nov 1863. Iron hull, two masts.
SERVICE RECORD: WGulfBS Jul 1864–May 1865. Blockade of Texas. Decomm 9 Aug 1865. Sold 25 Oct 1865.
Prizes: 21 Apr 1865: *Chaos*; 24 May: str *Denbigh*; 25 May: *Lecompte*.
Later history: Merchant *New England* 1865. Converted to barkentine 1871.

Name	Bldr	Built	Acquired	Comm
Dumbarton (ex-*Thistle*)	Hall (Inglis)	1863	20 Jul 1864	13 Aug 1864

Tonnage:	636 tons B, 471 gross (Br)
Dimensions:	204′ × 29′ × 10′, d11′
Machinery:	Side wheels, 2 oscillating engines (57″ × 5′), 2 boilers; 10 knots
Complement:	96
Armament:	1864: 2 32-pdr/33, 2 12-pdr H. Mar 65: add 1 20-pdr R.

NOTES: Blockade runner *Thistle*(II), captured 4 Jun 1864 by USS *Fort Jackson* off North Carolina coast. Iron hull. Engines unreliable.
SERVICE RECORD: Search for CSS *Tallahassee* 1864. NAtlBS Sep–Dec 1864. James River Feb–Mar 1865. Decomm 27 Mar 1865. Sold 15 Oct 1867.
Later history: Merchant *City of Quebec*, British flag 1867. New engines, rerigged 1868. Sunk in collision with merchant ship *Germany* off Green Island, Saguenay R., 1 May 1870.

Name	Bldr	Built	Acquired	Comm
Emma Henry	Thomson (U)	1864	13 Jan 1865	11 May 1865

Tonnage:	521 tons B
Dimensions:	212′ × 25′2″ × 6′, d10′
Machinery:	Side wheels, 2 oscillating engines (44″ × 4′6″), 2 boilers
Complement:	(U)
Armament:	1 30-pdr R, 2 24-pdr H

NOTES: Blockade runner, captured on second trip by USS *Cherokee*, 8 Dec 1864. Iron hull.
SERVICE RECORD: Search for CCS *Stonewall*, May 1865. Damaged in collision, 22 May 1865. Renamed **Wasp**, 13 Jun 1865. Brazil Sqn and South America 1865–67. Sold at Montevideo, 5 Jan 1876.
Later history: FFU.

Name	Bldr	L	Acquired	Comm
Fort Donelson (ex-*Robert E. Lee*, ex-*Giraffe*)	Thomson (bldr)	16 May 1860	Jan 1864	29 Jun 1864

Tonnage:	642 tons
Dimensions:	283′ (oa) 268′ () × 26′ × 10′, d13′8″
Machinery:	Side wheels, 2 oscillating engines (62″ × 5′6″), 6 boilers; NHP 290 = 11 knots
Complement:	137
Armament:	2 30pdr R, 5 12pdr HR

NOTES: Blockade runner *Robert E. Lee*, captured off Wilmington, NC, on 22nd trip, by USS *Iron Age* and *James Adger* 9 Nov 1863. Iron hull. Built as *Giraffe* for the Glasgow-Belfast Service of the Burns Line.
SERVICE RECORD: NAtlBS 1864, N. Carolina. Second bombardment of Ft. Fisher, NC, 13–15 Jan 65. Decomm 17 Aug 1865. Sold 25 Oct 1865.
Prize: Aug 15 1864: str *Dacotah*.
Later history: Merchant *Isabella* 1865. Sold to Chile 1869 as naval vessel, renamed *Concepcion*.

Name	Bldr	Built	Acquired	Comm
Fort Jackson (ex-*Kentucky*, ex-*Union*)	Simonson (Allaire)	1862	22 Jul 1863	18 Aug 1863

Tonnage:	1,850 tons B, 2,085 n/r
Dimensions:	250′ × 38′6″ × 18′, d27′10″
Machinery:	Side wheels, 1 vertical beam engine (80″ × 12′), 4 boilers; 14 knots
Complement:	194
Armament:	1 100-pdr R, 2 30-pdr R, 8 9″ SB

NOTES: Hermaphrodite brig. Built for Vanderbilt's New York-Aspinwall service but purchased by the Navy on completion.
SERVICE RECORD: NAtlBS Jan 1864. Unsuccessful attack on Ft. Fisher, NC, 24–25 Dec 1864. Second attack on Ft. Fisher, 13–15 Jan 1865. WGulfBS Feb 1865. Decomm 7 Aug 1865. Sold 27 Aug 1865.
Prizes: 3 Jan 1864: str *Bendigo*; 4 Jun: str *Thistle*; 8 Jul: str *Boston*; 21 Oct: str *Wando*; 31 Oct: str *Lady Sterling*.
Later history: Merchant *North America* 1865. BU 1879 at Boston.

The *Fort Jackson* was purchased by the Navy on completion. After the war she sailed between New York and Brazil in service with the former USS *Connecticut*.

Name	Bldr	L	Acquired	Comm
Gettysburg (ex-*Margaret & Jessie*, ex-*Douglas*)	Napier (bldr)	28 May 1858	20 Nov 1863	2 May 1864

Tonnage:	1,100 tons D, 726 tons B
Dimensions:	211′ () 205′ () × 26′3″ × 10′, d13′6″
Machinery:	Side wheels, 2 oscillating engines (54″ × 5′); 15 knots
Complement:	96
Armament:	May 64: 1 30-pdr R, 2 12-pdr R, 4 24-pdr H. Dec 64: 2 12-pdr R replaced by 2 32-pdr/27.

NOTES: Blockade runner *Margaret & Jessie*, captured off Wilmington, NC, by USS *Nansemond*, *Keystone State*, and *Howquah* 5 Nov 1863. Former Isle of Man Packet, world's fastest steamer when built. Iron hull. Two funnels replaced by one 1869.
SERVICE RECORD: NAtlBS 1864. Unsuccessful attack on Ft. Fisher, NC, 24–25 Dec 1864. Second attack on Ft. Fisher, 13–15 Jan 1865. Went aground on Fishers I., NY, while towing monitor *Squando*, 11 Jun 1865. Decomm 23 Jun 1865. Recomm 3 Dec 1866. Caribbean, 1866–67, 1868–69. Mediterranean 1876–79. Sold 8 May 1879 at Genoa.
Prizes: 9 Jul 1864: str *Little Ada*; 24 Aug: str *Lilian*; 4 Dec: str *Armstrong*
Later history: FFU.

Name	Bldr	Built	Acquired	Comm
Hatteras (ex-*St. Mary's*)	Harlan (U)	1861	25 Sep 1861	Oct 1861

Tonnage:	1,126 tons B
Dimensions:	210′ (bp) × 34′ × d18′
Machinery:	Side wheels, 1 condensing beam engine (50″ × 11′), 1 boiler; HP 500
Complement:	110
Armament:	4 32-pdr/27, 1 20-pdr R

NOTES: Iron hull, three-masted schooner.
SERVICE RECORD: SAtlBS 1861. Destroyed 7 schooners and installations during raid on Cedar Keys, Fla., 16 Jan 1862. GulfBS Jan 1862. Engaged CSS *Mobile* off Louisiana, 26 Jan 1862. Sunk in action with CSS *Alabama* off Galveston, 11 Jan 1863.
Prizes: 4 Apr 1862: str *P.C. Wallis* and *Resolution*; 1 May: *Magnolia*; 6 May: str *Fashion*; 11 May str *Governor Mouton*; 17 May: *Poody*; 3 Jul: *Sarah*; 5 Jul: *Elizabeth*; 19 Jul: str *Indian No. 2*; 28 Jul: *Josephine*.

Name	Bldr	Built	Acquired	Comm
James Adger	Webb (Allaire)	1852	26 Jul 1861	20 Sep 1861

Tonnage:	1,152 tons B, 1,085 n/r
Dimensions:	215′ (dk) × 33′6″ × 12′6″, d21′3″
Machinery:	Side wheels, 1 side-lever engine (65″ × 11′), 2 boilers; NHP 240 = 12.5 knots
Complement:	120
Armament:	8 32-pdr/42, 1 20-pdr R. May 63 total: 1 9″ SB, 1 20-pdr R, 6 32-pdr/42, 1 12-pdr H SB.

SERVICE RECORD: SAtlBS 1862. Capture of Fernandina, Fla., and Brunswick, St. Simons, and Jekyl islands, Ga., 2–12 Mar 1862. SAtlBS 1864–65. Caribbean 1866. Decomm 2 May 1866. Sold 9 Oct 1866.
Prizes: 29 May 1862: str *Elizabeth*. 1 Aug 1863: str *Kate*; 8 Nov: str *Cornubia*; 9 Nov: str *Robert E. Lee*; 26 Nov: str *Ella*.
Later history: Merchant *James Adger* 1866. BU 1878.

Name	Bldr	Built	Acquired	Comm
Keystone State	Vaughan & Lynn (Merrick)	1853	19 Apr 1861	19 Jul 1861

Tonnage:	1,364 tons
Dimensions:	219′ × 35′6″ × 14′6″, d21′
Machinery:	Side wheels, 1 side-lever engine (56″ × 8′), 2 boilers; HP 300 = 9.5 knots
Complement:	163
Armament:	4 12-pdr. Jun 63: 1 150-pdr R, 6 8″ SB, 2 32-pdr/57, 2 30-pdr R. Jun 64: 1 50-pdr R, 2 8″ SB, 2 32-pdr/57, 1 30-pdr R.

NOTES: Originally chartered by the Navy, later purchased and commissioned. Built for coastal service of the Ocean Steam Navigation Co.; later chartered by Vanderbilt for service to Nicaragua.
SERVICE RECORD: West Indies 1861. SAtlBS Jan 1862. Capture of Fernandina, Fla., and Brunswick, St. Simons, and Jekyl islands, Ga., 2–12 Mar 1862. NAtlBS Oct 1863. Unsuccessful attack on Ft. Fisher, NC, 24–25 Dec 1864. Bombardment of Masonboro Inlet, NC, 11 Feb 1865. Decomm 25 Mar 1865. Sold 15 Sep 1865.
Prizes: 20 May 1861: *Hiawatha*; 5 Feb 1862: *Mars*; 10 Apr: **Liverpool*; 15 Apr: *Success*; 29 May: str *Elizabeth*; 31 May: *Cora*; 20 Jun: *Sarah*; 22 Aug: *Fanny*; 5 Nov 1863: str *Margaret & Jessie*; 11 Jan 1864: str **Vesta*; 30 May: str *Caledonia*; 5 Jun: str *Siren*; 26 Jul: str *Rouen*; 24 Aug: str *Lilian*; 5 Sep: *Elsie*.
Later history: Merchant *San Francisco* 1865. RR 1879.

Name	Bldr	L	Acquired	Comm
Lady Sterling	Ash (U)	18 Jun 1864	Nov 1864	24 Apr 1865

Tonnage:	835 tons, 906 GRT, 614 n/r
Dimensions:	242′ × 26′6″ × d13′3″
Machinery:	Side wheels, 2 oscillating engines (60″ × 5′), 4 boilers; 13 knots
Armament:	8 guns

NOTES: Blockade runner, captured off Wilmington, NC, by USS *Eolus* and USS *Calypso*, 28 Oct 1864. Iron hull.
SERVICE RECORD: Renamed **Hornet**, 17 Jun 1865. Decomm 15 Dec 1865. Sold 26 Jun 1869.
Later history: Merchant *Hornet* 1869. Cuban filibuster 1869, gun runner to Haiti and Cuba 1871–72. Renamed *Marco Aurelia* (Spanish) 1872. BU c1894.

The gunboat *Hornet* off Wilmington, NC, in 1865. As the blockade-runner *Lady Sterling* she was captured in October 1864. After being sold in 1869 she had a chequered career as gun runner and filibuster to Cuba. (U.S. Naval Historical Center)

Name	Bldr	L	Acquired	Comm
Lilian	Thomson (U)	Mar 1864	6 Sep 1864	6 Oct 1864

Tonnage:	630 tons B, 427 n/r
Dimensions:	225'6" × 26'5" × 8'2", d10'
Machinery:	Side wheels, 2 oscillating engines (50" × 4'4"), 4 boilers; 14 knots
Complement:	63
Armament:	1 30-pdr R, 1 20-pdr R

NOTES: Blockade runner, captured 24 Aug 1864 by USS *Keystone State* and USS *Gettysburg* off Cape Fear. Steel hull, three funnels.
SERVICE RECORD: NAtlBS 1864. Search for CSS *Olustee*, Nov 1864. Unsuccessful attack on Ft. Fisher, NC, 24–25 Dec 1864. Second attack on Ft. Fisher, 13–15 Jan 1865. Decomm 5 Apr 1865. Sold 30 Nov 1865.
Later history: Merchant *Lilian* 1865. Spanish Navy corvette *Victoria de los Tunas*, 1870. Wrecked off Mariel, Cuba, Nov 1870.

Name	Bldr	L	Acquired	Comm
Magnolia	Simonson (Allaire)	22 Aug 1854	9 Apr 1862	22 Jul 1862

Tonnage:	843 tons B, 1,067 n/r
Dimensions:	242'5" × 33'11" × 5', d11'3"
Machinery:	Side wheels, vertical beam engine, 2 boilers; 12 knots
Complement:	95
Armament:	1 20-pdr R, 2 24-pdr. Sep 64: add 2 24-pdr.

NOTES: Blockade runner, captured 19 Feb 1862 by USS *Brooklyn* and *South Carolina* off Pass à l'Outre, La. Schooner rig.
SERVICE RECORD: EGulfBS 1862–65. Repairing Aug 1863–Apr 1864. Expedition to St. Marks, Fla., 23 Feb–27 Mar 1865. Decomm 10 Jun 1865. Sold 12 Jul 1865.
Prizes: 31 Jul 1862: str *Memphis*; 2 Dec: *Flying Cloud*; 27 Dec: *Carmita*; 29 Dec: *Flying Fish*. 10 Sep 1864: str *Matagorda*.
Later history: Merchant *Magnolia* 1865. RR 1866.

The side-wheel gunboat *Magnolia* was a blockader off Charleston. A rare heretofore unpublished picture. (Dr. Charles L. Peery)

Name	Bldr	L	Acquired	Comm
Malvern	Harlan (Morgan)	15 Oct 1860	1863	9 Feb 1864
(ex-*Ella and Annie*, ex-*William G. Hewes*)				

Tonnage:	1,477 tons B, 1,230 n/r
Dimensions:	239′4″ (dk) 234′ (wl) × 33′ × 9′, d18′
Machinery:	Side wheels, 1 vertical beam engine (50″ × 11′), 1 boiler; (HP 500)
Complement:	68
Armament:	4 20-pdr R, 8 12-pdr SB

NOTES: Blockade runner *Ella and Annie*, captured 9 Nov 1863, by USS *Niphon* off New Inlet, NC. Iron hull. Built for Charles Morgan's Southern S.S. Co.
SERVICE RECORD: Provisionally commissioned to search for steamer *Chesapeake* seized by Confederates at sea, 10 Dec 1863. NAtlBS 1864. Unsuccessful attack on Ft. Fisher, NC, 24–25 Dec 1864 (flag of Adm. Porter). Second attack on Ft. Fisher, 13–15 Jan 1865. Bombardment of forts in Cape Fear River, 18–21 Feb 1865. Carried President Lincoln to Richmond, 2 Apr 1865. Decomm 1865. Sold 25 Oct 1865.
Prizes: 20 Jan 1865: strs *Charlotte* and *Stag*.
Later history: Merchant *William G. Hewes* 1865. Wrecked in storm off Colorado Reef, Cuba, 20 Feb 1895.

Name	Bldr	Built	Acquired	Comm
Merrimac	(GB)	(U)	10 Mar 1864	1 May 1864

Tonnage:	684 tons B
Dimensions:	230′ × 30′ × 8′6″, d11′
Machinery:	Side wheels, 2 oscillating engines (U × 9′), 4 boilers; 11.5 knots
Complement:	116
Armament:	2 30-pdr R, 4 24-pdr, 2 12-pdr. Sep 64 total: 1 30-pdr R, 4 24-pdr, 1 12-pdr.

NOTES: Blockade runner, captured 24 Jul 1863 by USS *Iroquois* off Cape Fear, NC. Iron hull.
SERVICE RECORD: EGulfBS 1864–65. Foundered in gale off Florida, 15 Feb 1865.
Prize: 1 Jul 1864: *Henrietta*.

The side-wheel steamer *Merrimac* seen in northeast waters in 1864. She was captured as a blockade runner in July 1863. (U.S. Naval Historical Center)

The *Malvern* seen at Norfolk Navy Yard in 1865 as flagship of the North Atlantic Blockading Squadron. Notice ruined buildings in rear. Built as *William G. Hewes* for Charles Morgan's service between New York and New Orleans where she was taken into service as a blockade runner and captured as *Ella and Annie*. (U.S. Naval Historical Center)

Name	Bldr	L	Acquired	Comm
Quaker City Vaughan & Lynn (Merrick)		2 May 1854	25 Apr 1861	14 Dec 1861

Tonnage:	1,428 tons B
Dimensions:	244′9″ ( ) 227′3″ (bp) × 36′6″ × 13′8″, d20′9″
Machinery:	Side wheels, 1 side-lever engine (85″ × 8′), 4 boilers; 13 knots
Complement:	142
Armament:	2 32-pdr, 2 12-pdr R. Dec 61 total: 8 32-pdr/57, 1 20-pdr R. Aug 63 total: 1 100-pdr R, 1 30-pdr R, 1 20-pdr R, 6 8″ SB. Nov 64: less 2 8″ SB/63.

NOTES: Chartered 25 Apr 1861, purchased 12 Aug 1861. Formerly operated by New York, Havana & Mobile Line.
SERVICE RECORD: NAtlBS 1862. Search for Confederate raiders 1862–63. Went aground on N. Edisto I., SC, 12 Oct 1862. Damaged in engagement with Confederate ironclads off Charleston, 31 Jan 1863. Unsuccessful attack on Ft. Fisher, NC, 24–25 Dec 1864. GulfBS 1865. Decomm 18 May 1865. Sold 20 Jun 1865.
Prizes: 14 May 1861: *North Carolina*; 25 May: *Pioneer* and *Winifred*; 30 May: *Lynchburg*; 4 Jun: *General Green*; 10 Jun: *Amy Warwick*; 26 Jun: *Sally Magee*; 1 Jul: *Sally Mears*; 29 Aug: *Fairwind*; 4 Sep: str *Elsie*; 30 Jun 1862: *Model*; 3 Jul: *Lilla*; 7 Jul: str *Adela*; 24 Jul: *Orion*; 4 Jan 1863: *Mercury*; 9 Mar: str *Douro*; 9 Feb 1864: str *Spunkie*; 4 Sep: str *Elsie*; 12 Mar 1865: *R.H. Vermilyea*; 16 Mar: *Telemaco*; 17 Mar: *George Burkhart*; 24 Mar: str *Cora*.
Later history: Merchant *Quaker City* 1865. The ship of Mark Twain's "Innocents Abroad" 1867. British *Columbia* 1869. Haitian gunboat *Mont Organisé* 1869. Sold Feb 1871, renamed *République*. Foundered at sea off Bermuda after boiler explosion, 25 Feb 1871.

The side-wheeler *Quaker City* as a merchant ship, anchored at Naples in 1867. She later was purchased by the Haitian government for use as a gunboat. (Steamship Historical Society)

Name	Bldr	L	Acquired	Comm
Rhode Island (ex-*Eagle*, ex-*John P. King*)	Westervelt (Allaire)	6 Sep 1860	27 Jun 1861	29 Jul 1861

Tonnage:	1,517 tons B
Dimensions:	236′7″ × 36′9″ × 15′, d18′5″
Machinery:	Side wheels, 1 vertical beam engine (71″ × 12′), 2 boilers; 13 knots
Complement:	257
Armament:	4 32-pdr/42. Dec 61: add 1 30-pdr R, 1 8″/55. Jul 63 total: 1-9″, 1 30-pdr R, 1 12-pdr R, 1 12-pdr SB. Jan 64: add 8 8″/63, 1 50-pdr R. Jan 65: less 1 50-pdr R.

NOTES: After first trial run, almost destroyed by fire at Hudson River pier and scuttled, 18 Dec 1860; salved and completed as *Eagle*. Wood hull.
SERVICE RECORD: Supply ship. Gulf BS 1862. Towing USS *Monitor* south when that ship foundered off Cape Hatteras, 30 Dec 1862. Unsuccessful attack on Ft. Fisher, NC, 24–25 Dec 1864. Second attack on Ft. Fisher, 13–15 Jan 1865. Decomm 1867. Sold 1 Oct 1867.
Prizes: 25 Nov 1861: *Aristides*; 8 Dec: *Phantom*; 26 Dec: *Venus*; 4 Jul 1862: *Richard O'Bryan*; 30 May 1863: str *Margaret & Jessie*; 16 Aug: str *Cronstadt*; 1 Dec: str *Vixen*.
Later history: Merchant *Charleston* 1867. RR 1885.

The large side-wheel steamer *Rhode Island*. She was towing the *Monitor* when that ship foundered off Cape Hatteras, December 31, 1862. (National Archives)

Name	Bldr	L	Acquired	Comm
Santiago de Cuba	Simonson (Neptune)	2 Apr 1861	6 Sep 1861	5 Nov 1861

Tonnage:	1,567 tons B, 1,627 n/r
Dimensions:	238′ (dk) × 38′ × 16′2″, d19′6″
Machinery:	Side wheels, 1 vertical beam engine (66″ × 11′), 2 boilers; 14 knots
Complement:	143/179
Armament:	2 20-pdr R, 8 32-pdr/57. Dec 64 total: 2 20-pdr R, 5 32-pdr/57, 1 30-pdr R.

NOTES: Wood hull, barkentine rig, one funnel, two masts. Built for New York to Cuba service.

SERVICE RECORD: Blockade off Havana 1861. Search for Confederate raiders, 1862–64. Unsuccessful attack on Ft. Fisher, NC, 24–25 Dec 1864. Second attack on Ft. Fisher, 13–15 Jan 1865. Decomm 17 Jun 1865. Sold 21 Sep 1865.

Prizes: 3 Dec 1861: *Victoria*; 8 Feb 1862: **O.K.*; 20 Mar: **unidentified str*; 23 Apr: *W.C. Bee*; 25 Apr: str *Ella Warley*; 26 Apr: *Mersey*; 30 Apr: *Maria*; 27 May: *Lucy C. Holmes*; 3 Aug: str *Columbia*; 27 Aug: *Lavinia*; 25 Dec: *Comet*; 21 Jun 1863: str *Victory*; 25 Jun: str *Britannia*; 15 Jul: str *Lizzie*; 2 Nov: str *Lucy*; 10 Sep 1864: str *A.D. Vance*.

Later history: Merchant *Santiago de Cuba* 1865. Re-engined and converted to screw 1877. Converted to sail 1886, renamed *Marion*. RR 1899.

The *Santiago de Cuba* was built for New York-Cuba service in 1860 and was an active blockader during the war. Three gunports have been cut in the hull forward of the paddle box, and a gun can be seen on the fantail.

Name	Bldr	L	Acquired	Comm
State of Georgia	Vaughan & Lynn (Merrick)	12 Feb 1852	25 Sep 1861	20 Nov 1861

Tonnage:	1,204 tons B
Dimensions:	210' (dk) 200' (bp) × 33' × 14', d21'
Machinery:	Side wheels, 1 side-lever engine (72.5" × 8'), 2 boilers; HP 400
Complement:	113
Armament:	6 8" SB/55, 2 32-pdr/57, 1 30-pdr R. Apr 63 total: 1 100-pdr R, 1 30-pdr R, 6 9" SB.

NOTES: Built for Philadelphia & Savannah S.S. Co.

SERVICE RECORD: NAtlBS 1861–62. Bombardment and capture of Ft. Macon, NC, 25–26 Apr 1862. Damaged in collision with USS *Mystic*, 28 Sep 1862. NAtlBS Nov 1863–Sep 1864. SAtlBS 1865. Decomm 9 Sep 1865. Sold 25 Oct 1865.

Prizes: 22 May 1862: *Constitution*; 28 May: str *Nassau*; 28 Sep: str *Sunbeam*; 24 Feb 1863: str *Annie*; 24 Mar: **Mary Jane*; 25 Mar: *Rising Dawn*; 26 Sep: **unidentified schr.*

Later history: Merchant *Andrew Johnson* 1866. Wrecked in hurricane off Currituck Inlet, NC, 5 Oct 1866.

Name	Bldr	L	Acquired	Comm
Tennessee	Robb (Reeder)	31 Aug 1853	25 Apr 1862	8 May 1862

Tonnage:	1,275 tons B, 852 n/r
Dimensions:	210' (dk) × 33'11" × 12', d19'
Machinery:	Side wheels, 1 vertical beam engine (72" × 9'), 2 boilers
Complement:	217
Armament:	2 32-pdr/33, 1 30-pdr R, 1 12-pdr R

NOTES: One funnel, two masts. Built for James Hooper's West Indies & Venezuela S.S. Co., but later purchased by Charles Morgan for service to Nicaragua. Carried survivors of William Walker's Nicaraguan army from San Juan, then shifted to New York-New Orleans run. Captured at New Orleans, 25 Apr 1862.

SERVICE RECORD: WGulfBS 1682–64. Bombardment at Whitehall Pt., La., 10 Jul 1863. Bombardment of Ft. Morgan, Mobile Bay, 9–23 Aug 1864. Renamed **Mobile**, 1 Sep 1864. Damaged in gale off Rio Grande, late 1864. Sold 30 Mar 1865.

Prizes: 12 Oct 1863: *Friendship* and **Jane*; 5 Oct 1864: *Annie Virdon*; 19 Oct: *Emily & Louisa*.

Later history: Merchant *Republic* 1865. Foundered in hurricane off Savannah, 25 Oct 1865.

Name	Bldr	L	Acquired	Comm
Tristram Shandy	Aitken Mansel (U)	13 Jan 1864	May 1864	12 Aug 1864

Tonnage:	444 tons B, 636 GRT
Dimensions:	222' × 23'6" × 6'4", d9'6"
Machinery:	Side wheels, 2 inclined direct-acting condensing engines (46" × 2'6"), 2 boilers; 12 knots
Complement:	80
Armament:	1 20-pdr R, 2 12-pdr R

NOTES: Blockade runner, captured 15 May 1864 by USS *Kansas* off Wilmington, NC. Iron hull, schooner rig.

SERVICE RECORD: NAtlBS 1864. Destroyed grounded blockade runner off Ft. Fisher, NC, 3 Dec 1864. Unsuccessful attack on Ft. Fisher, NC, 24–25 Dec 1864. Second attack on Ft. Fisher, 13–15 Jan 1865. EGulfBS Feb 1865. Renamed **Boxer**, 21 Jun 1865. Decomm Sep 1865. Sold 1 Sep 1868.

Prizes: 25 Jan 1865: str *Blenheim*.

Later history: Merchant *Fire Fly* 1869. Wrecked off Havana 1874.

Name	Bldr	L	Acquired	Comm
Vanderbilt	Simonson (Allaire)	17 Dec 1855	17 Mar 1862	2 Sep 1862

Tonnage:	3,360 tons B
Dimensions:	340' (oa) 331' (dk) × 47'6" × 21'6", d31'9"
Machinery:	Side wheels, 2 vertical beam engines (80" × 12'), 4 boilers; IHP 2800 = 14 knots
Complement:	209
Armament:	2 100-pdr R, 12 9" SB, 1 12-pdr R. Mar 65 total: 1 100-pdr R, 12 9" SB, 2 30-pdr R.

The side-wheel steamer *Vanderbilt* built by Cornelius Vanderbilt for transatlantic passenger service and given by him to the government. Too large for an Army transport, she was taken by the Navy and converted to a fast cruiser. *Below*: Ships laid up at Philadelphia Navy Yard soon after the end of the war. Three double-enders are nearest the camera at right with a two-stack blockade runner next astern and the large side-wheeler *Vanderbilt* and monitors beyond. (Silverstone Collection) (U.S. Naval Historical Center)

NOTES: Two funnels, two masts, wood hull. Transatlantic passenger ship, maiden voyage 1857 for the Vanderbilt Line. Presented to the government by Commodore Vanderbilt in 1861.

SERVICE RECORD: Search for CSS *Alabama* in N. and S. Atlantic, 1863–64. Flagship of Flying Sqn in West Indies, 1863. Unsuccessful attack on Ft. Fisher, NC, 24–25 Dec 1864. Second attack on Ft. Fisher, 13–15 Jan 1865. Pacific Sqn 1865–67. Decomm 24 May 1867. Sold 1 Apr 1873.

Prizes: 25 Feb 1863: str *Peterhoff*; 16 Apr: str *Gertrude*; 30 Oct: *Saxon*.

Later history: Merchant *Three Brothers*, 1873 and converted to full-rig ship. Anchor Line coal hulk at Gibraltar 1885. BU 1929 in Spain.

Name	Bldr	L	Acquired	Comm
Wando	Kirkpatrick (U)	25 Mar 1864	5 Nov 1864	22 Dec 1864
(ex-*Wando*, ex-*Let Her Rip*)				

Tonnage:	468 tons B
Dimensions:	230′ × 26′ × 7′, d11′5″
Machinery:	Side wheels, 2 oscillating engines (54″ × 4′), 2 boilers
Complement:	86
Armament:	1 30-pdr R, 1 12-pdr R, 1 12-pdr SB

NOTES: Blockade runner *Wando*, captured 21 Oct 1864 by USS *Fort Jackson* off Cape Romain, SC. Iron hull.

SERVICE RECORD: SAtlBS 1865. Blockade of Charleston. Expedition to Bulls Bay, SC, 12–17 Feb 1865. Decomm 10 Aug 1865. Sold 30 Nov 1865.

Later history: Merchant *Wando* 1865. Foundered in gale south of Delaware Lightship, Feb 1872.

LARGE SCREW COMBATANTS — 3RD AND 4TH RATE

Name	Bldr	L	Acquired	Comm
Aries	Laing (Richardson)	12 Feb 1862	20 May 1863	25 Jul 1863

Tonnage:	820 tons B, 611 GRT
Dimensions:	201′ () 198′ () × 27′10″ × 16′, d15.8′
Machinery:	1 screw, 2 vertical inverted direct-acting condensing engines (42″ × 2′), 2 boilers; 12 knots
Complement:	90
Armament:	4 8″/63, 1 30-pdr R, 1 12-pdr R. 1864: add 1 30-pdr R.

NOTES: Blockade runner, captured by USS *Stettin* aground in Bull Bay, SC, 28 Mar 1863. Iron hull.

SERVICE RECORD: NAtlBS Nov 1863–Feb 65. Unsuccessful attack on Ft. Fisher, NC, 24–25 Dec 1864. Second attack on Ft. Fisher, 13–15 Jan 1865. Bombardment of Masonboro Inlet, NC, 11 Feb 1865. EGulfBS 1865. Decomm 14 Jun 1865. Sold 1 Aug 1865.

Prizes: 6 Dec 1863: *Ceres*; 7 Jan 1864: str *Dare*; 11 Jan: *Ranger*.

Later history: Merchant *Aries* 1865. BU 1908.

Name	Bldr	L	Acquired	Comm
Galatea	Van Deusen (Esler)	1863	31 Jul 1863	29 Jan 1864
Glaucus	Van Deusen (Esler)	1863	17 Jul 1863	18 Feb 1864
Neptune	Van Deusen (Esler)	1863	17 Jul 1863	19 Dec 1863
Nereus	Van Deusen (Esler)	21 Mar 1863	5 Oct 1863	19 Apr 1864
Proteus	Van Deusen (Esler?)	1863	30 Sep 1863	10 Mar 1864

Dec 1864. Second attack on Ft. Fisher, 13–15 Jan 1865. Search for CSS *Shenandoah* in Caribbean 1865. Decomm 15 May 1865. Sold 15 Jul 1865.

Later history: Merchant *Somerset* 1865. BU 1887.

Proteus—Blockade duty off Florida 1864–65. Expedition to St. Marks, Fla., Mar 1865. Sold 12 Jul 1865.

Prizes: 9 Jun 1864: *R.S. Hood*; 27 Jun: str *Jupiter*; 6 Sep: *Ann Louisa*. 27 Feb 1865: str *Ruby*.

Later history: Merchant *Carroll* 1865. BU 1894.

Name	Bldr	Built	Acquired	Comm
Grand Gulf (ex-*Onward*)	Poillon (U)	1863	14 Sep 1863	28 Sep 1863

Tonnage:	1,200 tons B
Dimensions:	216′ × 34′6″ × d17′9″
Machinery:	1 screw, 1 vertical direct-acting engine (50″ × 4′6″), 2 boilers; 11 knots
Complement:	201
Armament:	1 100-pdr R, 2 30-pdr R, 3 8″/69, 5 8″/62

NOTES: Acquired new. Wood hull.

SERVICE RECORD: NAtlBS Nov 1863–Jul 1864. WGulfBS Apr 1865. Prison ship, New Orleans, 1865. Decomm 10 Nov and sold 30 Nov 1865.

Prizes: 21 Nov 1863: str *Banshee*. 6 Mar 1864: *Mary Ann*; 6 May: str *Young Republic*.

Later history: Merchant *General Grant* 1865. Burned and sank at wharf at New Orleans, 19 Apr 1869.

Name	Bldr	L	Acquired	Comm
Huntsville	Westervelt (Morgan)	1857	24 Apr 1861	9 May 1861
Montgomery	Westervelt (Morgan)	9 Jan 1858	2 May 1861	27 May 1861

Tonnage:	*Huntsville*: 840 tons B, *Montgomery*: 787 tons B
Dimensions:	*Huntsville*: 196′4″ () 175′ (wl) × 29′8″ × 14′4″. *Montgomery*: 201′6″ () × 28′7″ × 15′6″, d19′
Machinery:	1 screw, 1 inverted vertical direct-acting engine (52″ × 3′6″), 1 boiler; 11 knots
Complement:	143
Armament:	
Huntsville:	1 64-pdr/106, 2 32-pdr/33. Jun 62 total: 1 9″ SB, 1 30-pdr R, 2 32-pdr/57.
Montgomery:	1 8″, 4 32-pdr/33. Jul 62 total: 1 10″/87, 1 30-pdr R, 4 32-pdr/33. Jul 63 total: 1 10″/106, 1 30-pdr R, 4 8″/55.

NOTES: Chartered May 1861, later purchased 18 Aug 1861. Three masts, schooner rig. Operated on New York-Savannah run for American Atlantic Screw S.S. Co.

SERVICE RECORDS:

Huntsville—GulfBS 1861–65. Engaged CSS *Florida* off Mobile Bay, 24 Dec 1861. Refit Apr–Jun 1862. Decomm 19 Aug 1864. Recomm 29 Mar 1865. Transport duties. Decomm 28 Aug 1865. Sold 30 Nov 1865.

Prizes: 13 Aug 1861: *Isabel*; 1 Oct: *Zavala*; 7 Jul 1862: str *Adela*; 16 Jul: *Agnes*; 21 Jul: str *Reliance*; 11 Nov: *Ariel*; 22 Dec: *Courier*; 13

The screw steamer *Proteus*, one of five large sisterships purchased while under construction. This is the first photograph of this class to be found. (Dr. Charles L. Peery)

Tonnage:	1,244 tons
Dimensions:	209′6″ () 203′6″ () × 35′6″ × 14′, d20′8″
Machinery:	1 screw, 2 inverted direct-acting engines (44″ × 3′), 2 boilers; 11 knots
Complement:	164
Armament:	*Glaucus* 1 100-pdr R, 2 30-pdr R, 8 8″/55.
	Galatea, Neptune 1864: 1 100-pdr R, 8 32-pdr/57, 2 30-pdr R. Mar 65: less 2 32-pdr/57.
	Neptune: 1 60-pdr R, 2 30-pdr R, 6 32-pdr/57.
	Nereus, Proteus 1864: 1 100-pdr R, 2 30-pdr R, 6 32-pdr/57, 2 12-pdr R. Dec 1864 total: 1 60-pdr R, 2 30-pdr R, 6 32-pdr/57, 2 12-pdr,
	Proteus Apr 1865: 1 60-pdr R, 1 30-pdr R, 6 32-pdr/57, 1 20-pdr R.

NOTES: Wood hulls, schooner rig. Built for William P. Williams, but purchased prior to completion.

SERVICE RECORDS:

Galatea—West India Sqn, based at Cap Haitien, 1864. Decomm 12 Jul 1865. Sold to Haiti 15 Aug 1865.

Later history: Haitian gunboat *Alexandre Pétion* 1865. Captured by revolutionaries at Cap Haitien 15 Nov 1869. Blew up and sank off Haitian coast, 1893.

Glaucus—NAtlBS 1864–65. Transported Manuel Murillo, President of Colombia, to Cartagena. Severely damaged by fire off Cape Fear while chasing a blockade runner, 28 May 1864. Went aground near Manassas Reef, Bahamas, 30 May 1865. Decomm 6 Jun 1865. Sold 12 Jul 1865.

Later history: Merchant *Worcester* 1865. BU 1884 at Boston.

Neptune—West India Sqn 1864–65. Decomm 31 May 1865. Sold 12 Jul 1865.

Later history: Merchant *Allegany* 1865. Wrecked in fog off Long Island, NY, 5 Dec 1865.

Nereus—NAtlBS 1865. Blockade of Wilmington. Search for CSS *Tallahassee* Sep 1864. Unsuccessful attack on Ft. Fisher, NC, 24–25

Mar 1863: *Surprise*; 6 Apr: *Minnie*; 14 Apr: *Ascension*; 13 May: *A.J. Hodge*; 19 May: str *Union*.

Later history: Merchant *Huntsville* 1865. Destroyed by fire off Little Egg Harbor Light, 19 Dec 1877.

Montgomery—GulfBS 1861. Engaged CSS *Tallahassee* 8 Nov and CSS *Florida* and CSS *Pamlico* off Horn Island Pass, Miss., 4 Dec 1861. EGulfBS Jan 1862. WGulfBS, 1862. NAtlBS 1863. Search for CSS *Tacony* off Nantucket and CSS *Florida* Jun–Jul 1863. Second attack on Ft. Fisher, NC, 13–15 Jan 1865. Bombardment of Masonboro Inlet, NC, 11 Feb 1865. Decomm 20 Jun 1865. Sold 10 Aug 1865. *Prizes*: 29 Aug 1861: *Finland*; 1 Feb 1862: *Isabel*; 5 Apr: **Columbia*; 3 Jun: *Will o'the Wisp*; 8 Oct: str **Blanche*; 29 Oct: str *Caroline*; 20 Nov: *William E. Chester*; 7 Jan 1864: str *Dare*; 13 Jan: str *Bendigo*; 16 Feb: str *Pet*; 10 Oct: str *Bat*.

Later history: Merchant *Montgomery* 1866. Sunk in collision with steamer *Seminole* off Cape Hatteras, 7 Jan 1877.

Name	Bldr	L	Acquired	Comm
Lodona	Samuelson (U)	Jan 1862	20 Sep 1862	5 Jan 1863

Tonnage:	861 tons B, 688 GRT
Dimensions:	210′ × 27′6″ × 11′6″, d16′6″
Machinery:	1 screw, 2 vertical direct-acting engines (34″ × 2′8″), 1 boiler; 7 knots
Complement:	97
Armament:	1 100-pdr R, 1 30-pdr R, 1 9″ SB, 4 24-pdr H

NOTES: Blockade runner, captured 4 Aug 1862 by USS *Unadilla* in Ossabaw Sound, SC. Iron hull, bark rig.

SERVICE RECORD: SAtlBS 1863. Bombardment of Ft. Wagner and Gregg, Charleston, Aug 1863. Decomm 11 May 1865. Sold 20 Jun 1865.

Prizes: 20 Apr 1863: *Minnie*; 15 Nov: *Arctic*; 10 Jul 1864: *Hope*.

Later history: Merchant *Lodona* 1865. Lost 31 May 1879 (cause unknown).

Name	Bldr	L	Acquired	Comm
Memphis	Denny (bldr)	3 Apr 1862	4 Sep 1862	4 Oct 1862

Tonnage:	1,780 tons D, 791 tons B, 1,010 GRT
Dimensions:	227′ × 30′1″ × 15′6″
Machinery:	1 screw, 2 inverted direct-acting engines (46″ × 3′), 2 boilers; 14 knots
Complement:	100
Armament:	4 24-pdr SB, 2 12-pdr R, 1 30-pdr R. Jun 64: add 4 20-pdr R.

NOTES: Blockade runner, captured by USS *Magnolia* off Charleston, 31 Jul 1862. Iron hull, brig rig.

SERVICE RECORD: SAtlBS 1862. Engagement with ironclads off Charleston, 31 Jan 1863. Attacked by torpedo boat *David* in N. Edisto River, 6 Mar 1864, but torpedo did not explode. Decomm 6 May 1867. Sold 8 May 1869.

Prizes: 14 Oct 1862: str *Ouachita*; 4 Jan 1863: *Mercury*; 31 Mar: *Antelope*; 11 Jun: str **Havelock*.

Later history: Merchant *Mississippi* 1869. Destroyed by fire at Seattle, 13 May 1883.

Name	Bldr	L	Acquired	Comm
Peterhoff	Oswald (U)	25 Jul 1861	Feb 1863	Feb 1864

Tonnage:	800 tons B, 819 GRT
Dimensions:	220′ () × 29′ × 17′
Machinery:	1 screw
Complement:	(U)
Armament:	(U)

NOTES: Blockade runner, captured by USS *Vanderbilt* off St. Thomas, 25 Feb 1863. Laid up in New York one year pending decision of prize court. Iron steamer.

SERVICE RECORD: NAtlBS 1864. Sunk in collision with USS *Monticello* off New Inlet, NC, 6 Mar 1864.

Name	Bldr	L	Acquired	Comm
R.R. Cuyler	Sneeden (Allaire)	20 Aug 1859	28 Aug 1861	23 May 1862

Tonnage:	1,202 tons B
Dimensions:	237′ × 33′3″ × d16′
Machinery:	1 screw, 1 vertical direct-acting engine (70″ × 4′), 2 boilers; 14 knots
Complement:	116/154
Armament:	2 32-pdr/57, 6 32-pdr/33. Jul 62 total: 1 30-pdr R, 8 32-pdr/57, 1 12-pdr SB. Jun 63 total: 1 30-pdr, 10 32-pdr/57. Oct 64: add 1 30-pdr R.

NOTES: Chartered May 1861. Wood hull, two funnels. In service between New York, Havana, and New Orleans.

SERVICE RECORD: Blockade off Florida 1861–64. Second attack on Ft. Fisher, NC, 13–15 Jan 1865. Decomm 1 Jul 1865. Sold 15 Aug 1865.

Prizes: 29 Aug 1861: **Finland*; 22 Nov: *A.J. Vein*, str *Anna*, str *Henry Lewis*; 20 Jan 1862: *J.W. Wilder*; 29 Mar: *Grace E. Baker*; 3 May: *Jane*; 27 Aug: *Anna Sophia*; 6 May 1863: str *Eugenie*; 18 May: **Isabel*; 14 Jul: str *Kate Dale*; 4 Dec 1864: str *Armstrong*.

Later history: Merchant *R.R. Cuyler* 1865. Sold to government of Colombia as warship Dec 1866, renamed *El Rayo*. Rejected by new government, remained at Cartagena. Wrecked on reef in storm at Cartagena, 12 Sep 1867.

Name	Bldr	Built	Acquired	Comm
South Carolina	Loring (Bldr)	1860	3 May 1861	22 May 1861

Tonnage:	1,165 tons B, 1,215 n/r
Dimensions:	217′11″ × 33′6″ × 14′6″
Machinery:	1 screw, 1 inverted direct-acting engine (62″ × 3′8″), 1 boiler; 10.5 knots
Complement:	115
Armament:	4 8″/63, 1 32-pdr/42. May 63 total: 2 8″/63, 2 32-pdr/42, 1 30-pdr R, 1 24-pdr H. Jun 63: add 2 8″.

NOTES: Iron hull. Built for service between Boston, Norfolk, Charleston, and Savannah.

SERVICE RECORD: GulfBS 1861–62. SAtlBS Jun 1862–65. Converted to storeship 1865. Decomm 17 Aug 1866. Sold 5 Oct 1866.

Prizes: 4 Jul 1861: *Shark*, *Louisa*, *Dart*, *McCanfield*, *Venus*, *Ann Ryan*; 5 Jul: *Falcon*, *Caroline*; 6 Jul: *George G. Baker*; 7 Jul: *Sam Houston*; 9 Jul:

Tom Hicks; 12 Jul: *T.J. Chambers*; 11 Sep: *Anna Taylor*; 4 Oct: *Isilda* and *Joseph H. Toone*; 16 Oct: *Edward Barnard*; 11 Dec: *Florida*; 19 Feb 1862: str *Magnolia*; 27 Aug: *Patriot*; 29 Mar 1863: *Nellie*; 3 Mar 1864: *Arletta*; 12 Apr: str *Alliance*.

Later history: Merchant *Juniata* 1866. Converted to barge, 1893. Foundered in tow in snowstorm, 17 Feb 1902.

Name	Bldr	L	Acquired	Comm
Varuna	Mallory (U)	Sep 1861	31 Dec 1861	Feb 1862

Tonnage:	1,247 tons B
Dimensions:	218′ × 34′8″
Machinery:	1 screw
Complement:	157
Armament:	6 8″/63, 2 8″/55, 2 30-pdr R

NOTES: Purchased prior to completion.
SERVICE RECORD: WGulfBS 1862. Rammed and sunk by CSS *Governor Moore* and *Stonewall Jackson* during passage past New Orleans forts, 24 Apr 1862.

MEDIUM SIDE-WHEEL COMBATANTS—4TH RATE

Name	Bldr	Built	Acquired	Comm
Britannia	Barclay Curle	1862	29 Sep 1863	16 Sep 1863

Tonnage:	495 tons B, 369 n/r, 594 GRT
Dimensions:	189′ × 26′ × 9′, d11′
Machinery:	Side wheels, 2 vertical steeple condensing engines (45″ × 4′10″), 2 boilers; 12.5 knots
Complement:	75
Armament:	Sep 64: 1 30-pdr R, 2 12-pdr R, 2 24-pdr H. Nov 64 total: 1 30-pdr R, 5 24-pdr H.

NOTES: Blockade runner, captured by USS *Santiago de Cuba* in the Bahamas, 25 Jun 1863. Iron hull.
SERVICE RECORD: NAtlBS Nov 1863–Jan 1865. Engagement with CSS *Raleigh* off New Inlet, NC, 6–7 May 1864. Unsuccessful attack on Ft. Fisher, NC, 24–25 Dec 1864. Second attack on Ft. Fisher, 13–15 Jan 1865. EGulfBS Jan 1865. Expedition to St. Marks, Fla., 23 Feb 1865. Sold 10 Aug 1865.
Later history: Merchant *Britannia* 1865. Sold foreign 1866.

Name	Bldr	Built	Acquired	Comm
Calhoun (ex-*Cuba*)	Sneeden (U)	1851	19 Mar 1862	1862

Tonnage:	508 tons B
Dimensions:	174′4″ × 27′6″ × d11′
Machinery:	Side wheels, 1 vertical beam engine (44″ × 10′)
Complement:	68
Armament:	1 30-pdr R, 2 32-pdr/33

NOTES: Confederate privateer, captured by USS *Samuel Rotan* off Southwest Pass, La., 23 Jan 1862. Wood hull. Originally served out of Charleston, later purchased by Charles Morgan at New Orleans.
SERVICE RECORD: WGulfBS 1862. Engagement off Brashear City, Berwick Bay, La., 1–3 Nov 1862. Engagement and attack at Bayou

Teche, La., 14 Jan 1863. Engagement with CSS *Queen of the West* in Berwick Bay, 14 Apr 1863. Engagement at Butte-a-la-Rose, La., and capture of Ft. Burton, 20 Apr 1863. Bombardment at Grants Pass, Ala., 13 Sep 1863. Bombardment of Ft. Powell, Mobile Bay (flag), 16–29 Feb 1864. Decomm 6 May 1864.
Prizes: 4 May 1862: *Charles Henry*; 5 May: *Rover*; 6 May: str *Lewis Whiteman*; 13 May: *Corypheus*; 14 May: *Venice (Venus)*; 12 Sep 1863: str *Fox*.
Later history: Transferred to U.S. Army, 4 Jun 1864; renamed *General Sedgwick*. Sold 1865. Merchant *Calhoun* 1866. BU 1883.

Name	Bldr	Built	Acquired	Comm
Clyde (ex-*Neptune*)	Napier (U)	1861	25 Jul 1863	29 Jul 1863

Tonnage:	294 tons B
Dimensions:	200′6″ × 18′6″ × d8′
Machinery:	Side wheels, 2 inclined engines (42″ × 3′8″), 2 boilers; 9 knots
Complement:	67
Armament:	2 24-pdr H. Dec 63 total: 2 12-pdr R.

NOTES: Blockade runner *Neptune*, captured by USS *Lackawanna*, 14 Jun 1863. Iron hull. Renamed 11 Aug 1863.
SERVICE RECORD: EGulfBS Sep 1863–65, W. Florida. Decomm 17 Aug 1865. Sold 25 Oct 1865.
Prize: 27 Sep 1863: *Amaranth*.
Later history: Merchant *Indian River* 1865. Went ashore at mouth of Indian River, Fla., 3 Dec 1865.

Name	Bldr	Built	Acquired	Comm
Delaware (ex-*Delaware*, ex-*Virginia Dare*)	Harlan (U)	1861	14 Oct 1861	1861

Tonnage:	357 tons B
Dimensions:	161′ × 27′ × 6′, d8′3″
Machinery:	Side wheels, 1 beam condensing engine (38″ × 10′); 13 knots
Complement:	57/65
Armament:	2 32-pdr/57, 2 32-pdr/27, 1 12-pdr R. Jan 62 total: 1 9″ SB, 1 32-pdr/57, 1 12-pdr R.

NOTES: Iron hull, schooner rig.
SERVICE RECORD: NAtlBS 1861. Landings at Roanoke I., NC, 7–8 Feb 1862. Engagement with enemy vessels, capture of Elizabeth City, NC, and expedition to Edenton, 10–12 Feb 1862. Reconnaissance to Winton, NC, Chowan River, 18–20 Feb 1862. Capture of New Bern, NC, 13–14 Mar 1862. Reconnaissance in Neuse River, NC, 12–16 Dec 1862. Engagements at Dutch Gap, Va., 13 and 18 Aug 1864. Decomm 5 Aug 1865.
Prizes: 10 Feb 1862: *Lynnhaven*; 3 Mar: *Zenith*; 21 Mar: *unidentified str*; 26 Mar: *Albemarle* and *Lion*.
Later history: Revenue Cutter Service, 30 Aug 1865. Renamed *Louis McLane*, 1873. Sold 1903, merchant *Louis Dolive*. RR 1919

An unusual view from above of the USS *Clyde* looking aft. On deck of the former blockade runner can be seen a 12-pounder howitzer (U.S. Naval Historical Center)

Name	Bldr	Built	Acquired	Comm
Eolus	Marvel (Wash.IW)	1864	26 Jul 1864	12 Aug 1864

Tonnage:	368 tons B
Dimensions:	144′ () 140′ () × 25′ × 7′, d10′2″
Machinery:	Side wheels, 1 vertical beam engine (40″ × 8′), NHP 285; 16 mph
Complement:	53
Armament:	1 30-pdr R, 2 24-pdr H

NOTES: Purchased on completion.
SERVICE RECORD: Search for CSS *Tallahassee* 1864. NAtlBS 1864–65. Unsuccessful attack on Ft. Fisher, NC, 24–25 Dec 1864. Second attack on Ft. Fisher, 13–15 Jan 1865. Decomm 24 Jun 1865. Sold 1 Aug 1865.

Prizes: 22 Oct 1864: str *Hope*; 28 Oct: str *Lady Sterling*.
Later history: Merchant *Eolus* 1865. BU 1894

Name	Bldr	L	Comm
Granite City	A. Denny (Tulloch)	11 Nov 1862	16 Apr 1863

Tonnage:	315 tons B, 463 GRT
Dimensions:	160′ × 23′ × 5′6″, d9′2″
Machinery:	Side wheels, 2 inclined engines (38″ × 4′6″), 2 boilers
Complement:	69
Armament:	1863: 1 12-pdr R, 6 24-pdr H. Jan 64: add 1 20-pdr R.

NOTES: Blockade runner *Granite City* captured by USS *Tioga* in Bahama Islands, 22 Mar 1863.
SERVICE RECORD: WGulfBS Aug 1863–64. Attack on Sabine Pass, Tex., 8 Sep 1863. Unsuccessful landing on Matagorda Peninsula, Tex., 31 Dec 1863. Captured with USS *Wave* by Confederate batteries at Calcasieu Pass, La., 28 Apr 1864.
Prizes: 5 Oct 1863; *Concordia*; 27 Oct: *Anita*; 18 Nov: *Teresita* and *Amelia Ann*.
Later history: Ran aground as Confederate blockade runner near Velasco, Texas, 21 Jan 1865.

Name	Bldr	L	Acquired
Harriet Lane (ex-USRC *Harriet Lane*)	Webb (Allaire)	20 Nov 1857	17 Sep 1861

Tonnage:	750 tons, 639 tons B
Dimensions:	180′ (dk), 177′6″ (wl) × 30′ × 5′, d12′6″
Machinery:	Side wheels, inclined direct-acting engine, 2 boilers; 12 knots
Complement:	100
Armament:	2 32-pdr/33. Aug 61 total: 1 8″ SB, 4 32-pdr R. Feb 62 total: 3 9″ SB, 1 30-pdr R, 1 12-pdr R.

NOTES: Two-masted brigantine. Only steam vessel in service in Revenue Cutter Service 1861 and transferred to USN, 30 Mar 1861.
SERVICE RECORD: Served with Navy in Paraguay Expedition 1858–59. Attempted relief of Ft. Sumter, Charleston Harbor; fired first shot by USN ship, 12 Apr 1861. Capture of Hatteras Inlet, ran aground, 28–29 Aug 1861. Engaged batteries at Freestone Pt., Va., 9 Dec 1861. Mortar Flotilla 1862. Bombardment of Fts. Jackson and St. Philip below New Orleans, 18–28 Apr 1862. Passage past New Orleans forts and engagement with CSN vessels, 24 Apr 1862. Occupation of forts at Pensacola, May 1862. Covered operations at Vicksburg, Jun–Jul 1862. Bombardment and capture of Galveston, Tex., 4 Oct 1862. Captured by Confederate vessels during reoccupation of Galveston, 1 Jan 1863.
Prizes: 26 May 1861: *Catherine* and *Iris*; 5 Jun: *Union*; 9 Sep: *Henry C. Brooks*; 23 Feb 1862: *Joanna Ward*.
Later history: Converted to blockade runner, renamed *Lavinia*. Interned at Havana, 1865. Converted to merchant bark, renamed *Elliot Richie*, 1865. Foundered off Pernambuco, 13 May 1884.

The *Eolus* as a merchant vessel after the war. (Steamship Historical Society)

The revenue cutter *Harriet Lane* as a Navy gunboat during the Civil War. She fired the Navy's first shot during the attempt to relieve Fort Sumter in May 1861. (U.S. Naval Historical Center)

The *Harvest Moon* was acquired shortly after being built because of her high speed. Sunk by a mine early in 1865, she is seen here before entering naval service. (Mariners Museum)

Name	Bldr	Built	Acquired	Comm
Harvest Moon	Dyer (U)	1862	16 Nov 1863	12 Feb 1864

Tonnage: 546 tons B
Dimensions: 193′ × 29′ × 8′, d10′
Machinery: Side wheels, 1 vertical beam engine (41″ × 10′); 15 knots/
            mph
Complement: 72
Armament: 1 20-pdr R, 4 24-pdr H, 1 12-pdr H

NOTES: Operated briefly between Maine and Boston.
SERVICE RECORD: SAtlBS 1864–65. Flagship of Admiral Dahlgren off Charleston, 1864–65. Expedition in Broad River, SC, 27 Nov–30 Dec 1864. Expedition to Georgetown, SC, 23 Feb 1865. Sunk by torpedo (mine) in Winyah Bay, SC, 1 Mar 1865.

Name	Bldr	Built	Acquired
Hetzel	(Baltimore)	1845	21 Aug 1861

Tonnage: 301 tons B, 200 tons
Dimensions: 150′ × 22′ × 6′6″, d8′
Machinery: Side wheels, crosshead condensing engine, 1 boiler
Complement: 69
Armament: 1861: 1 9″ SB, 1 80-pdr R. Apr 63 total: 1 9″ SB, 1 32-pdr/
            57. Jul 65 total: 2 12-pdr R, 2 24-pdr.

NOTES: Acquired by U.S. Coast Survey 1849 and transferred to Navy 1861.
SERVICE RECORD: NAtlBS Nov 1861, off N. Carolina. Engagement with CSS *Patrick Henry* near Newport News, 2 Dec 1861. Landings at Roanoke I., NC, 7–8 Feb 1862. Engagement with enemy vessels, capture of Elizabeth City, NC, and expedition to Edenton, 10–12 Feb 1862. Capture of New Bern, NC, 13–14 Mar 1862. Expedition to

Plymouth, NC, 31 Oct–7 Nov 1862. Returned to U.S. Coast Survey, Oct 1865.
Later history: U.S. Coast Survey ship *Hetzel*. Sank at moorings in Edenton Bay, NC, 1873. Refitted and hulked.

The gunboat *Hetzel* was acquired from the Coast Survey in 1861. This drawing was based on a sketch made in March 1862 during the capture of New Bern, NC. (U.S. Naval Historical Center)

Name	Bldr	Built	Acquired	Comm
Isonomia (ex-*Shamrock*)	Stack (Murphy)	1864	16 Jul 1864	16 Aug 1864

Tonnage:	593 tons B, 896 n/r
Dimensions:	215'3" () 212' (dk) × 29'6" × 7'
Machinery:	Side wheels, 1 vertical beam engine (45" × 12'), 1 boiler; 12 knots
Complement:	63
Armament:	1 30-pdr R, 2 24-pdr H

NOTES: Purchased on completion.

The side-wheel steamer *Isonomia* was purchased new in 1864. Notice the walking beam amidships and gun on bow. (Mariners Museum) (Martin Holbrook Collection)

SERVICE RECORD: NAtlBS 1864. Coastal blockade, Florida. Expedition to St. Marks, Fla., 23 Feb–27 Mar 1865. Decomm 28 Jun 1865. Sold 12 Jul 1865.
Prize: 8 May 1865: *George Douthwaite*.
Later history: Merchant *City of Providence* 1865. Sold foreign, 1867.

Name	Bldr	Built	Acquired	Comm
Jacob Bell	Brown & Bell (U)	1842	22 Aug 1861	22 Aug 1861

Tonnage:	229 tons B
Dimensions:	141'3" × 21' × d8'1"
Machinery:	Side wheels
Complement:	49
Armament:	1 8" SB, 1 32-pdr/32. Apr 63: add 1 50-pdr R, 2 12-pdr SB.

SERVICE RECORD: Potomac Flotilla 1861–62. Engaged batteries at Potomac Creek, Va., 23 Aug 1861. Bombardment at Freestone Point, Va., 25 Sep and 9 Dec 1861. Expedition in Rappahannock River,

Tappahannock, Va., 13–15 Apr 1862. NAtlBS 1862. Engaged batteries at Port Royal, Va., 4 Dec 1862. Expeditions to Northern Neck, Va., 12 Jan, in Rappahannock River, 16–19 May and to Northern Neck, 11–21 Jun 1864. Decomm 13 May 1865. Foundered at sea while under tow of USS *Banshee* to New York, 6 Nov 1865.
Prizes: 20 Sep 1862: *Chapel Point*; 4 Nov: *Robert Wilbur*; 23 Aug 1863: *Gold Leaf*.

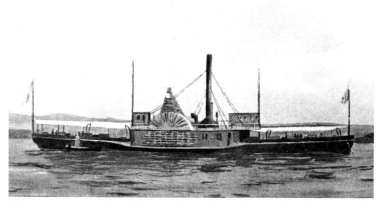

Side-wheel steamer *Jacob Bell*, one of the oldest of the acquired ships, was built in 1842. Nevertheless, she had an active Navy career principally in Virginia coastal waters.

Name	Bldr	L	Acquired	Comm
Mount Washington (ex-*Mount Vernon*)	Birely (Reaney Neafie)	11 Apr 1846	22 Apr 1861	May 1861

Tonnage:	359 tons B
Dimensions:	200' × 24' × 6'6", d9'
Machinery:	Side wheels, 1 LP vertical beam engine (44" × 11'); 12 knots
Complement:	40
Armament:	May 63: 1 32-pdr/47

NOTES: Renamed 4 Nov 1861. Operated on James River until purchased by War Department in 1861, then transferred to Navy.
SERVICE RECORD: Operated in Potomac area 1861. Operations in Nansemond River, Va., 11 Apr–4 May 1863. Disabled by enemy fire at Western Branch, 6 May, and damaged at Hatt's Point, 12 May 1863. Engagement at Dutch Gap, Va., 16–18 Aug 1864. NAtlBS Feb 1865. Sold 21 Jun 1865.
Later history: Merchant *Mount Washington* 1865. BU 1885.

Name	Bldr	Built	Acquired	Comm
Nansemond (ex-*James F. Freeborn*)	L & F (Fletcher)	1862	13 Aug 1863	19 Aug 1863

Tonnage:	335 tons B
Dimensions:	155' (dk) 146' () × 26' × 8'3", d9'6"
Machinery:	Side wheels, 1 vertical beam engine (40" × 9'), 1 boiler; 15 knots
Complement:	55/63
Armament:	Sep 64: 1 30-pdr R, 2 24-pdr

SERVICE RECORD: NAtlBS 1863. Engagement with CSS *Raleigh* off New Inlet, NC, 6–7 May 1864. Unsuccessful attack on Ft. Fisher, NC, 24–25 Dec 1864. Second attack on Ft. Fisher, 13–15 Jan 1865. Decomm 8 Aug 1865.
Prizes: 11 Oct 1863: str *Douro*; 21 Oct: str *Venus*; 5 Nov: str *Margaret & Jessie*.
Later history: To U.S. Revenue Cutter Service, 22 Aug 1865. Renamed *William H. Crawford*, 1884. Sold 24 Apr 1897. Merchant *General J.A. Dumont*, 1900. Burned at Severn Side, Md., 22 Dec 1914.

Name	Bldr	Built	Acquired	Comm
Nita	(Mobile, Ala.)	1856	10 Sep 1863	8 Jan 1864

Tonnage:	210 tons B
Dimensions:	146' × 22'4" × 5', d7'
Machinery:	Side wheels, 1 vertical beam condensing engine (28" × 6'), 1 boiler
Complement:	46
Armament:	1 12-pdr HR, 2 12-pdr HSB, 1 24-pdr HSB. Mar 1864 total: 1 12-pdr HR, 3 24-pdr HSB.

NOTES: Captured 17 Aug 63, by USS *De Soto* en route Havana-Mobile. Wood hull.
SERVICE RECORD: EGulfBS 1864, off west coast of Florida. Decomm 3 May and sold 25 May 1865.
Prizes: 24 Feb 1864: str *Nan Nan*; 11 Apr: *Three Brothers*; 24 Oct: *Unknown*.
Later history: FFU.

Name	Bldr	Built	Acquired	Comm
Philippi	(GB?)	1863	23 Feb 1864	Apr 1864
(ex-*Ella*)				

Tonnage:	311 tons
Dimensions:	140' × 24' × d9'10"
Machinery:	Side wheels
Complement:	41
Armament:	1 20-pdr R, 1 24-pdr H, 2 12-pdr R

NOTES: Blockade runner *Ella*, captured 10 Nov 1863 by USS *Howquah* off Ft. Fisher, NC.
SERVICE RECORD: WGulfBS 1864. Went aground in Mobile Bay near Ft. Morgan, set on fire and sunk by Confederate batteries, 5 Aug 1864.

Name	Bldr	Built	Acquired
Planter	(Charleston, SC)	1860	May 1862

Tonnage:	313 tons B
Dimensions:	147' × 30' × 3'9", d7'10"
Machinery:	Side wheels, 2 HP engines (18" × 6'), 2 boilers
Complement:	(U)
Armament:	1 32-pdr, 1 24-pdr H

NOTES: Delivered to Federal vessels off Charleston by her pilot, slave Robert Smalls, 13 May 1862.
SERVICE RECORD: SAtlBS 1862. Expedition to Pocotaligo, SC, 21–23 Oct 1862. Transferred to War Dept, 10 Sep 1862.
Later history: Merchant *Planter* 1866. Lost off Cape Romain, SC, 1 Jul 1876.

Name	Bldr	Built	Acquired	Comm
Pulaski	Sneeden (Peas)	1854	1858	1858
(ex-*Metacomet*)				

Tonnage:	395 tons B
Dimensions:	169'11" × 26' × d9'
Machinery:	Side wheels, crosshead engine
Complement:	(U)
Armament:	3 12-pdr H

NOTES: Wood steamer. Operated out of Fall River, Mass., until chartered 1858 for Paraguay Expedition; purchased 1859.
SERVICE RECORD: Brazil Station 1859–63. Decomm and sold at Montevideo, 22 Jan 1863.
Later history: Operated in River Plate until 1870.

Name	Bldr	Built	Acquired	Comm
Selma	(Mobile, Ala.)	1856	5 Aug 1864	5 Aug 1864
(ex-CSS *Selma*, ex-*Florida*)				

Tonnage:	320 tons B
Dimensions:	252' × 30' × 6'
Machinery:	Side wheels, 1 inclined direct-acting condensing engine; 9 knots
Complement:	99
Armament:	2 9" R, 1 8" R, 1 6" R

NOTES: Captured in Mobile Bay, 5 Aug 1864.
SERVICE RECORD: Bombardment of Ft. Morgan, Mobile Bay, 9–23 Aug 1864. Decomm 15 Jul 1865 and sold Aug 1865.
Later history: Merchant *Selma* 1865. Foundered off mouth of Brazos River, Tex., 24 Jun 1868.

Name	Bldr	L	Acquired	Comm
Thomas Freeborn	L & F (Allaire)	17 Nov 1860	7 May 1861	May 1861

Tonnage:	345 tons D, 269 tons B
Dimensions:	143'4" ()140' (wl) × 25'6" × 6'6", d8'6"
Machinery:	Side wheels, 1 vertical beam engine (40" × 8')
Complement:	67
Armament:	1 32-pdr/60, 1 32-pdr/27. Apr 63 total: 1 8"/55, 1 32-pdr/27, 1 12-pdr R.

NOTES: Steam tug.
SERVICE RECORD: Potomac Flotilla 1861–65. Engaged batteries at Sewells Pt., 18–19 May and at Aquia Creek, Va., 29 May–1 Jun 1861. Decomm 17 Jun 1865. Sold 20 Jul 1865.
Prizes: 17 Jun 1861: *Bachelor*; 16 Jul: *A.B. Leon*; 2 Aug: *Jane Wright*; 4 Aug: *Pocahontas* and *Mary Grey*. 1 Aug 1862: *Christiana Lee* and str *Mail*; 1 Oct: *Thomas W. Reilly*. 3 Mar 1865: *William Smith*.
Later history: Merchant *Philip*, 1865. RR 1887.

Name	Bldr	Built	Acquired	Comm
Tritonia (ex-*Sarah S.B. Cary*)	(East Haddam, Ct.)	1863	1 Dec 1863	23 Apr 1864

Tonnage:	202 tons B
Dimensions:	178' × 22'4" × d7'6"
Machinery:	Side wheels
Complement:	26
Armament:	2 12-pdr. Dec 64 total: 1 30-pdr R, 1 12-pdr, 1 24-pdr.

SERVICE RECORD: James River Division 1864. WGulfBS Jul 1864. Recovered str *Belfast*, taken by guerrillas, in Tombigbee River, 29 Jan 1866. Sold 5 Oct 1866.
Later history: Merchant *Belle Brown* 1866. Lost 1880.

Name	Bldr	Built	Acquired	Comm
Underwriter	(Brooklyn)	1852	23 Aug 1861	23 Aug 1861

Tonnage:	341 tons B
Dimensions:	185' () 170' () × 23'7" × 8'1"
Machinery:	Side wheels, oscillating engines
Complement:	69
Armament:	1 80-pdr R, 1 8"/63. Oct 61: add 2 12-pdr. Apr 63 total: 2 8"/55, 1 12-pdr R, 1 12-pdr SB.

SERVICE RECORD: Potomac Flotilla 1861. NAtlBS Oct 1861. Landings at Roanoke I., NC, 7–8 Feb 1862. Engagement with enemy vessels, capture of Elizabeth City, NC, and expedition to Edenton, 10–12 Feb 1862. Capture of New Bern, NC, 13–14 Mar 1862. Captured by enemy boat crew while lying at anchor in Neuse River and destroyed by them, 2 Feb 1864.

MEDIUM SCREW COMBATANTS—4TH RATE

Name	Bldr	L	Acquired	Comm
Albatross	Greenman (Corliss)	31 Oct 1858	23 May 1861	25 Jun 1861

Tonnage:	378 tons B, 414 n/r
Dimensions:	158' × 30' × 13', d10'
Machinery:	1 screw, 2 vertical direct-acting engines, 1 boiler; 11 knots
Complement:	68/95
Armament:	4 32-pdr 57, 1 12-pdr R. Jun 63: add 1 30-pdr R.

NOTES: Wood hull, three-masted schooner rig.
SERVICE RECORD: AtlBS 1861. Engaged CSS *Beaufort* at Bodies I., NC, 21 Jul 1861. Occupation of Winyah Bay, SC, 21 May 1862. WGulfBS 1862–Jun 1864. Made passage past Port Hudson, La., 14 Mar and Grand Gulf, Miss., 19 Mar 1863. Severely damaged during action

against Ft. DeRussy, 4 May 1863. WGulfBS 1865. Decomm 11 Aug 1865. Sold 8 Sep 1865.
Prizes: 18 Jul 1861: *Velasco*; 22 Jul: *Enchantress*; 1 Aug: *Elizabeth Ann*; 14 Sep: *Alabama*; 14 Dec: *Jane Campbell*. 16 Jan 1862:* *York*; 20 Jun: *Treaty* and *Louisa*; 2 Jul: *Volante*; 21 Sep: *Two Sisters*.
Later history: Merchant *Albatross* 1865. Converted to sail 1888. SE 1895.

Name	Bldr	Built	Acquired	Comm
Antona	Neilson (U)	1859	28 Mar 1864	19 Mar 1863

Tonnage:	549 tons B, 352 GRT
Dimensions:	166.9' () 157'10" () × 23.1' × 13'
Machinery:	1 screw, 2 vertical engines, 1 boiler; 8 knots
Complement:	56
Armament:	Dec 63: 2 32-pdr/33, 1 20-pdr R, 2 24-pdr. Sep 64 total: 2 32-pdr/33, 2 12-pdr, 2 24-pdr

NOTES: Blockade runner, captured 6 Jan 1863 by USS *Pocahontas* off Mobile. Iron hull. Formally purchased after commissioning.
SERVICE RECORD: WGulfBS 1863–65. Sank USS *Sciota* in collision in Mississippi River, 14 Jul 1863. Sold 30 Nov 1865.
Prizes: 16 Jul 1863: *Cecelia D.*; 6 Aug: *Betsey*; 26 Nov: **Mary Ann*; 20 Dec: *Exchange*. 9 Feb 1865: str **Will o'the Wisp*.
Later history: Merchant *Carlotta* 1865. RR 1874.

Name	Bldr	Built	Acquired	Comm
Augusta Dinsmore	Mallory (U)	1863	17 Jul 1863	1863

Tonnage:	850 tons B, 653 n/r
Dimensions:	169' × 32'6" × 12'6", d9'2"
Machinery:	1 screw, 2 Ericsson engines (40" × 1'10"), 1 boiler; 11 knots
Complement:	70
Armament:	2 12-pdr R. Dec 63 total: 1 20-pdr R, 1 12-pdr R, 2 24-pdr SB.

NOTES: Wood, two-masted schooner.
SERVICE RECORD: SAtlBS 1863–64. Bombardment of Ft. Wagner, Charleston, Jul 1863. WGulfBS 1864, off Texas. Sold 5 Sep 1865.
Prizes: 16 Feb 1864: *Scio*; 10 Sep: *John*.
Later history: Merchant *Gulf City* 1865. Wrecked on Cape Lookout, NC, 11 Jan 1869.

Name	Bldr	L	Acquired	Comm
Calypso	A. Denny (Tulloch)	15 Apr 1855	12 Oct 1863	24 Sep 1863

Tonnage:	630 tons B, 487 n/r
Dimensions:	190.3' () 175'2" () × 26'6" × 12', d14'5"
Machinery:	1 screw, 2 geared steeple engines (44 1/2" × 3'6"), 2 boilers; HP 140 = 12 knots
Complement:	70
Armament:	2 30-pdr R, 4 24-pdr. Nov 63: add 1 30-pdr R. Jul 65 total: 1 30-pdr R, 1 12-pdr R, 4 24-pdr.

NOTES: Blockade runner, captured 11 Jun 1863 by USS *Florida* off Wilmington, NC. Iron hull, three-masted schooner of the Bristol Steam Nav. Co. for the Bristol-Dublin run.

SERVICE RECORD: NAtlBS 1863–65. Blockade off Wilmington, NC. Decomm 15 Aug 1865. Sold 30 Nov 1865.
Prizes: 23 Oct 1863: *Herald*; 28 Oct 1864: str *Lady Sterling*.
Later history: Merchant *Winchester* 1865. BU 1886.

Name	Bldr	L	Acquired	Comm
Cambridge	Curtis, Medford (U)	18 Nov 1859	30 Jul 1861	29 Aug 1861

Tonnage:	858 tons B
Dimensions:	200′ × 32′ × 13′6″
Machinery:	1 screw, 1 vertical direct-acting engine (52″ × 3′2″), 1 boiler; 10.5 knots.
Complement:	96
Armament:	2 8″/55, 1 12-pdr H, 1 6-pdr R. Aug 62 total: 4 8″/63, 1 30-pdr R, 1 24-pdr H. Jul 63 total: 4 8″/63, 4 30-pdr R, 2 24-pdr.

NOTES: 2-mast square-rig.
SERVICE RECORD: NAtlBS 1861–64. SAtlBS 1864–65. Sold 20 Jun 1865.
Prizes: 10 Sep 1861: *Louisa Agnes* and *Revere*, 23 Sep: *Julia*; 6 Nov: **T.W. Riley*. 2 Apr 1862: **Kate*; 27 Jun: str **Modern Greece*; 17 Nov: **J.W. Pindar*; 3 Dec: *Emma Tuttle* and *J.C. Roker*; 23 Jan 1863: *Time*; 6 Feb 1864: str **Dee*.
Later history: Merchant *Minnetonka* 1865. RR; 1878.

Name	Bldr	L	Acquired	Comm
Cherokee (ex-*Thistle*)	Hall (Inglis)	2 Jul 1859	13 Jan 1864	21 Apr 1864

Tonnage:	606 tons B, 386 GRT
Dimensions:	194′6″ × 25′2″ × 11′6″, d12′11″
Machinery:	1 screw, 2 geared beam engines (44″ × 3′6″), 1 boiler; 13 knots
Complement:	92
Armament:	2 20-pdr R, 4 24-pdr SB

NOTES: Blockade runner *Thistle* (I) captured by USS *Canandaigua* off Charleston, 8 May 1863. Iron hull. Former Glasgow-Londonderry packet steamer.
SERVICE RECORD: NAtlBS 1864. Unsuccessful attack on Ft. Fisher, NC, 24–25 Dec 1864. Second attack on Ft. Fisher, 13–15 Jan 1865. EGulfBS Feb 1865. Decomm 23 Jun 1865. Sold 1 Aug 1865.
Prize: 8 Dec 1864: str *Emma Henry*.
Later history: Merchant *Cherokee* 1866. Sold to Chile 1868 as naval vessel, renamed *Ancud*. Sold 1878. Wrecked at Chiloe, SW Chile, 25 Aug 1889.

Name	Bldr	L	Acquired	Comm
Columbia	A. Denny (Tulloch)	19 Jul 1862	4 Nov 1862	Dec 1862

Tonnage:	503 tons B
Dimensions:	168′ × 25′ × d14′
Machinery:	1 screw, 2 inverted engines (36″ × 2′6″)
Complement:	100
Armament:	6 24-pdr SB, 1 30-pdr R

NOTES: Blockade runner, captured by USS *Santiago de Cuba* off Florida, 3 Aug 1862. Iron hull.
SERVICE RECORD: NAtlBS 1862–63. Wrecked off Masonboro Inlet, NC, 14 Jan and burned to prevent capture, 17 Jan 1863.

Name	Bldr	Built	Acquired	Comm
Crusader (ex-*Southern Star*)	(Murfreesboro, NC)	1858	Oct 1858	27 Oct 1858

Tonnage:	545 tons B, 469 n/r
Dimensions:	169′ × 28′ × 12′6″
Machinery:	1 screw, 2 inclined direct-acting engines (23″ × 2′2″), 1 boiler; 8 knots
Complement:	79/92
Armament:	1861: 4 32-pdr/33, 1 12-pdr H. Sep 62: add 2 20-pdr R.

NOTES: Three-masted bark, wood hull. Chartered for Paraguay Expedition 1858–59, purchased 1859.
SERVICE RECORD: Home Sqn 1859–61. Captured slaver *William R. Kibby*, 23 Jul 1860. SAtlBS Jan–Jul 1862. NAtlBS Sep 1862. Chesapeake Bay, 1862–65. Decomm 13 Jun 1865. Sold 20 Jul 1865.
Prizes: 14 May 1861: *Wanderer*; 20 May: *Neptune*; 22 Jun: *President Fillmore*; 20 Feb 1863: *General Taylor*; 22 Feb: *A.P. Upshur*; 9 Mar: **H nry A. Wise*; 14 Mar: **Jemima*; 22 May 1864: *Isaac L. Adkins*; 27 Feb 18 5: *Catherine Coombs*.
Later history: Merchant *Kalorama*, 1865. Wrecked south of San Buenaventura, 25 Feb 1876.

Name	Bldr	Built	Acquired	Comm
Dai Ching	Jewett (McLeod)	1862	21 Apr 1863	11 Jun 1863

Tonnage:	520 tons B
Dimensions:	175′2″ () 170′6″ () × 29′4″ × 9′6″, d11′
Machinery:	1 screw, 2 LP direct-acting engines (32″ × 2′2″), 2 boilers; 6 knots
Complement:	83
Armament:	1 100-pdr R, 4 24-pdr HSB, 2 20-pdr R

NOTES: Ordered for F.T. Ward's Chinese Navy.
SERVICE RECORD: SAtlBS 1863–65. Bombardment of Ft. Wagner, Charleston, 24 Jul–23 Aug 1863. Assault on Jacksonville, Fla., 2–22 Feb 1864. Joint expedition up Ashepoo and S. Edisto Rivers, SC, 25–27 May 1864. Went aground in Combahee River and burned to prevent capture, 26 Jan 1865.
Prizes: 14 Nov 1863: *George Chisholm*; 26 Jan 1865: *Coquette*.

Name	Bldr	Built	Acquired	Comm
Dawn	Sneeden (Delamater)	1857	26 Apr 1861	9 May 1861

Tonnage:	399 tons B
Dimensions:	154′ × 28′10″ × 12′, d9′8″
Machinery:	1 screw, 1 rotary engine (40″ × 2′); 11 knots
Complement:	34/60
Armament:	2 32-pdr/57. 1862: add 1 20-pdr R. May 63 total: 1 100-pdr R, 2 32-pdr/57, 1 30-pdr R, 1 12-pdr.

The *Crusader* was originally chartered for the expedition to Paraguay in 1859. Later that year she was purchased and served in Chesapeake Bay during the war. (U.S. Naval Historical Center)

NOTES: Wood hull. One funnel aft, three masts. New boiler 1862.
SERVICE RECORD: Potomac Flotilla 1861. SAtlBS May 1862–Jul 1863. Engaged batteries at Ft. McAllister, Ogeechee River, Ga., 19 Nov 1862 and 27 Jan–28 Feb 1863. Engaged CSS *Nashville* at Genesis Pt., Ga., 28 Feb 1863. NAtlBS, Jan 1864–65. Decomm 17 Jun 1865. Sold 1 Nov 1865.
Prizes: 24 May 1861: *General Knox* and *Georgiana*; 24 Jul: *Josephus*.
Later history: Merchant *Eutaw* 1865 and rebuilt. Wrecked at Pecks Beach, NJ, 27 Dec 1869.

Name	Bldr	Built	Acquired	Comm
Daylight	Sneeden (Delamater)	1860	10 May 1861	7 Jun 1861

Tonnage:	682 tons B
Dimensions:	170′ × 30′6″ × 13′, d11′
Machinery:	1 screw, 2 rotary engines (44″ × 2′); 5 knots
Complement:	57
Armament:	4 32-pdr/57. May 63 total: 6 32-pdr/57, 1 30-pdr R, 1 12-pdr R.

NOTES: Improved version of *Dawn*, funnel aft.
SERVICE RECORD: Blockade duty 1861–Aug 1863. Damaged during bombardment and capture of Ft. Macon, NC, 25–26 Apr 1862. NAtlBS Sep 1863–Oct 1864. James River 1864–65. Decomm 24 May 1865. Sold 25 Oct 1865.
Prizes: 5 Jul 1861: *John Hamilton*; 25 Aug: *Monticello*; 29 Aug: *Extra*

and *Good Egg*; 26 Apr 1862: *Alliance*; 30 Oct: *Racer*; 4 Nov: **Sophia*; 17 Nov: *unid. brig; 3 Dec: *Brilliant*; 8 Dec: *Coquette*; 26 Dec: *Gondar*; 21 Jan 1863: *unidentified.
Later history: Merchant *Santee* 1865. Converted to barge 1886. RR 1907.

Name	Bldr	Built	Acquired	Comm
Despatch (ex-*City of Boston*)	(Medford, Mass.) (Fulton)	1852	20 Mar 1855	17 Jan 1856

Tonnage:	775 tons D, 558 tons B
Dimensions:	169′6″ () 154 (wl) × 30′6″ × 12′, d13′6″
Machinery:	1 screw, 2 vertical direct-acting engines, 2 boilers
Complement:	95/173
Armament:	Jun 63: 4 32-pdr/57, 1 10″ R, 1 20-pdr R. Nov 63: 1 10″ R replaced by 1 100-pdr R.

NOTES: Reboilered 1857. Rebuilt 1859 at Norfolk NYd as second-class sloop with new engines (Loring), recomm 19 Mar 1860.
SERVICE RECORD: Anti-slavery patrol, 1858. Renamed **Pocahontas**, 27 Jan 1860. Evacuation of Ft. Sumter 1861. Potomac area patrol 1861. SAtlBS Oct 1861–62. Occupation of Port Royal, SC, 7 Nov 1861. Occupation of Tybee Island, Ga., 24 Nov 1861. Engagement at Port Royal, 26 Nov 1861. Capture of Fernandina, Fla., and Brunswick, St. Simons, and Jekyl islands, Ga., 2–12 Mar 1862. WGulfBS Oct 1862.

Damaged in storm Aug 1863. Blockade of Texas 1864–65. Decomm 31 Jul 1865. Sold 30 Nov 1865.
Prizes: 21 May 1861: str *James Guy*; 6 Dec: *Cheshire*; 6 Jan 1863: str *Antona*; 19 Dec 1864: *Morris*.
Later history: Merchant bark *Abby Bacon* 1865. RR 1898.

Name	Bldr	Built	Acquired	Comm
Don	Dudgeon (U)	1863	21 Apr 1864	May 1864

Tonnage: 425 tons D, 390 tons B
Dimensions: 162′ × 23′ × 6′, d12′3″
Machinery: 2 screws, 2 horizontal engines (26″ × 1′9″), 4 boilers; 600 IHP 600 = 14 knots
Complement: 94
Armament: 2 20-pdr R, 6 24-pdr SB

NOTES: Blockade runner, captured by USS *Pequot* off Beaufort, NC, 4 Mar 1864. Iron hull. Mounted experimental 15″ gun, Jan 1866.
SERVICE RECORD: Potomac Flotilla 1864–65. NAtl Sqn 1866–68. Decomm 18 May 1868. Sold 29 Aug 1868.
Later history: Merchant *Don*, 1868. Spanish *Cantabria* 1871. SE 1884.

Name	Bldr	L	Acquired	Comm
Emma	Barclay Curle	24 Nov 1862	30 Sep 1863	4 Nov 1863
Gertrude	Barclay Curle	28 Nov 1862	4 Jun 1863	22 Jul 1863

Tonnage: 350 tons B, 283 GRT
Dimensions: 156′ × 21′ × 9′4″ (*Emma*) 10′6″ (*Gertrude*), d11′
Machinery: 1 screw, 2 oscillating engines (32″ × 3′), 1 boiler; 8 to 12 knots
Complement: 68
Armament: *Emma*: 6 24-pdr H, 2 12-pdr R. Mar 65 total: 4 24-pdr H, 1 20-pdr R, 1 12-pdr R.
              Gertrude: 2 12-pdr R, 6 24-pdr H.

NOTES: Blockade runners. *Emma* captured 24 Jul 1863 by USAT *Arago*; *Gertrude* captured 16 Apr 1863 by USS *Vanderbilt* off Eleuthera. Iron hulls.
SERVICE RECORDS:
Emma—NAtlBS 1863–65. Unsuccessful attack on Ft. Fisher, NC, 24–25 Dec 1864. Second attack on Ft. Fisher, 13–15 Jan 1865. Bombardment of Masonboro Inlet, NC, 11 Feb 1865. Decomm 30 Aug 1865. Sold 1 Nov 1865.
Prize: 3 Dec 1864: str *Ella*.
Later history: FFU.
Gertrude—WGulfBS 1863, off Mobile. Texas May 1864. Decomm 11 Aug 1865. Sold 30 Nov 1865.
Prizes: 16 Aug 1863: str *Warrior*; 16 Jan 1864: *Ellen*; 19 Feb 1865: *Echo*.
Later history: Merchant *Gussie Telfair* 1865. RR 1878.

Name	Bldr	Built	Acquired	Comm
Estrella	(London)	1853	1862	1862

Tonnage: 438 tons B, 566 GRT
Dimensions: 178′ × 26′ × 6′, d8′
Machinery: 1 screw, oscillating engine
Complement: 57
Armament: 1 30-pdr R, 2 32-pdr/33, 2 24-pdr H. Jun 65 total: 1 30-pdr R, 2 12-pdr H.

NOTES: Blockade runner, captured Jul 1862, transferred from Army. Iron hull.
SERVICE RECORD: WGulf BS Nov 1862–67. Engagement off Brashear City, Berwick Bay, La., 1–3 Nov 1862. Engagement at Bayou Teche, La., 14 Jan 1863. Engagement with CSS *Queen of the West* in Berwick Bay, 14 Apr 1863. Engagement at Butte-a-la-Rose, La., and capture of Ft. Burton, 20 Apr 1863. Expedition up Red River, 3–13 May 1863. Battle of Mobile Bay, 5 Aug 1864. Decomm 16 Jul 1867. Sold 9 Oct 1867.
Prizes: Apr 1863: str *Hart*. 6 Apr 1864: *Julia A. Hodges*.
Later history: Merchant *Estrella* 1867. Converted to sidewheels. Lost 1870 (cause unknown).

Name	Bldr	L	Acquired	Comm
Flag (ex-*Phineas Sprague*)	Birely & Lynn (Merrick)	Jun 1857	26 Apr 1861	28 May 1861

Tonnage: 938 tons B, 637 n/r
Dimensions: 195′3″ (bp) 180′ () × 30′10″ × 15′, d10′9″
Machinery: 1 screw, 1 vertical direct-acting engine (48″ × 3′10″), 1 boiler; HP 400 = 12 knots
Complement: 116
Armament: 6 8″/55, 1 6-pdr. Jun 63: 4 8″ SB, 1 10″ SB, 2 30-pdr R.

NOTES: Three masts. Operated between Boston and Philadelphia.
SERVICE RECORD: SAtlBS 1861–65. Occupation of Tybee Island, Ga., 24 Nov 1861. Capture of Fernandina, Fla., and Brunswick, St. Simons, and Jekyl islands, Ga., 2–12 Mar 1862. Decomm 25 Feb 1865. Sold 12 Jul 1865.
Prizes: 6 Oct 1861: *Alert*; 6 Dec: *Cheshire*. 7 Jul 1862: str *Emilie*; 11 Oct: *Elmira Cornelius*; 13 Oct: *David Crockett*; 27 Oct: str *Anglia*. 12 Apr 1863: *Stonewall Jackson*; 8 May: *Amelia*. 12 Jun 1864: *Cyclops*.
Later history: Merchant *Flag* 1865. BU 1876.

Name	Bldr	Built	Acquired	Comm
Flambeau	L & F (Esler)	1861	14 Nov 1861	27 Nov 1861

Tonnage: 791 tons B, 766 n/r
Dimensions: 185′ (dk) 173′6″ () × 30′ × 11′, d18′
Machinery: 1 screw, 1 vertical beam engine, 2 boilers; 12 knots
Complement: 92
Armament: 1 30-pdr R, 1 20-pdr R. Sep 62 total: 2 24-pdr H, 2 30-pdr R, 1 20-pdr R. Feb 65 total: 2 8″/55, 1 30-pdr R. Apr 65: add 2 24-pdr H.

NOTES: Built for China coastal trade. Brigantine rig.
SERVICE RECORD: SAtlBS 1861–65. Decomm 7 Jun 1865. Sold 12 Jul 1865.
Prizes: 26 Apr 1862: *Active*; 20 Jun: *Catalina*. 23 Jun 1863: *Bettie Cratzer*; 28 Nov: *John Gilpin*.
Later history: Merchant *Flambeau* 1865. Stranded and lost off New Inlet Bar, NC, 1 Mar 1867.

Name	Bldr	Built	Acquired	Comm
Governor Buckingham	Mallory (U)	1863	29 Jul 1863	13 Nov 1863

Tonnage:	886 tons B, 1,044 n/r
Dimensions:	177'6″ × 32'2″ × 13'6″, d17'
Machinery:	1 screw, 1 vertical direct-acting engine, 1 boiler; 8 knots
Complement:	112
Armament:	1 100-pdr R, 4 30-pdr R, 1 20-pdr R

NOTES: Hermaphrodite brig.
SERVICE RECORD: NAtlBS 1863–65. Unsuccessful attack on Ft. Fisher, NC, 24–25 Dec 1864. Second attack on Ft. Fisher, 13–15 Jan 1865. Decomm 27 Mar 1865. Sold 12 Jul 1865.
Prizes: 20 Dec 1863: str *Antonica*. 25 Sep 1864: str *Lynx*.
Later history: Merchant *Equator* 1865. Converted to barge 1893.

Name	Bldr	L	Acquired	Comm
Hendrick Hudson (ex-*Florida*)	Whitlock (U)	30 Jul 1859	20 Sep 1862	30 Dec 1862

Tonnage:	460 tons B
Dimensions:	171' (dk) × 29'11″ × d9'6″
Machinery:	1 screw, 1 vertical direct-acting engine (36″ × 3'6″); HP 100 = 11 knots
Complement:	88
Armament:	2 20-pdr R, 4 8″/63

NOTES: Blockade runner *Florida*, captured 6 Apr 1862, by USS *Pursuit* at St. Andrews Bay, Fla. Wood two-masted schooner.
SERVICE RECORD: EGulfBS 1863. Rammed and sank blockade runner *Wild Pigeon* at sea, 21 Mar 1864. Expedition to St. Marks, Fla., 23 Feb–27 Mar 1865. Decomm 8 Aug 1865. Sold 12 Sep 1865.
Prizes: 1 Feb 1863: *Margaret*; 27 Mar: *Pacifique*; 16 Apr: *Theresa*. 21 Mar 1864: *Wild Pigeon*.
Later history: Merchant *Hendrick Hudson* 1865. Wrecked near Havana, 13 Nov 1867.

Name	Bldr	Built	Acquired	Comm
Henry Andrew	(New York)	1847	10 Sep 1861	Oct 1861

Tonnage:	177 tons B
Dimensions:	150' × 26' × d7'6″
Machinery:	1 screw, Swiftsure propeller
Complement:	49
Armament:	2 32-pdr/33, 1 20-pdr R

The gunboat *Hendrick Hudson* with two gunports cut into the hull. She was a former blockade runner captured in 1862. A rare previously unpublished photograph. (Dr. Charles L. Peery)

NOTES: Built as sailing brig and converted to steam 1859.

SERVICE RECORD: SAtlBS 1861. Expedition up Wright's and Mud rivers, SC, Jan–Feb 1862. Engaged enemy in Mosquito Inlet, Fla., 21–22 Mar 1862. Wrecked in storm south of Cape Henry, Va., 24 Aug 1862.

Name	Bldr	Built	Acquired	Comm
Hibiscus	Pook (U)	1864	16 Nov 1864	29 Dec 1864
Spirea	Pook (U)	1864	30 Dec 1864	9 Jan 1865

Tonnage:	406 tons B
Dimensions:	175′ × 30′ × 7′, d10′ (as merchant 1868)
Machinery:	2 screws, 2 Wright's segmental engines, 2 boilers; 9 knots
Complement:	65/86
Armament:	2 30-pdr R, 4 24-pdr H

SERVICE RECORDS:

Hibiscus—EGulfBS 1865. Expedition to St. Marks, Fla., 23 Feb–27 Mar 1865. Decomm 19 Aug 1865. Sold 5 Oct 1866.
  Later history: Merchant *Francis Wright* 1866. Renamed *Hibiscus*, 1870. Lost at sea (cause unknown), 1 May 1873.
Spirea—EGulfBS 1865. Expedition to St. Marks, Fla., 23 Feb–27 Mar 1865. Decomm 23 Aug 1865. Sold 5 Oct 1866.
  Later history: Merchant *Sappho* 1867. Abandoned off Cape Hatteras, 14 Dec 1867.

Name	Bldr	L	Acquired	Comm
Iron Age	Thompson (U)	Nov 1862	28 Apr 1863	25 Jun 1863

Tonnage:	424 tons B
Dimensions:	144′ × 25′ × d12′6″
Machinery:	1 screw
Complement:	107
Armament:	3 30-pdr R, 6 8″ SB

SERVICE RECORD: NAtlBS 1863–64. Went aground in Lockwood's Folly Inlet near Wilmington, NC, 11 Jan 1864 and destroyed to prevent capture.

Prizes: 15 Sep 1863: *unidentified; 21 Oct: str *Venus*; 9 Nov: str *Robert E. Lee*.

Name	Bldr	Built	Acquired	Comm
Isaac Smith	L & F (U)	1861	9 Sep 1861	16 Oct 1861

Tonnage:	453 tons B, 382 n/r
Dimensions:	171′6″ × 31′4″ × 7′, d9′
Machinery:	1 screw, Swiftsure propeller, beam engine
Complement:	96/119
Armament:	1 30-pdr R, 8 8″ SB/63

SERVICE RECORD: SAtlBS 1861–63. Engagement with CSN squadron off Port Royal, SC, 5 Nov 1861. Bombardment and occupation of Port Royal, 7 Nov 1861. Engagement in Wassaw Sound, Ga., 26–28 Jan 1862. Capture of Fernandina, Fla., & Brunswick, St. Simons, and Jekyl islands, Ga., 2–12 Mar 1862. Disabled by Confederate batteries in Stono River, 30 Jan 1863, and surrendered.

Prize: 3 Apr 1862: *British Empire*.

Later history: Renamed CSS *Stono*. Wrecked near Ft. Moultrie, SC, 5 Jun 1863.

Name	Bldr	Built	Acquired	Comm
Iuka (ex-*Commodore*)	Pook (Delamater)	1863	8 Mar 1864	23 May 1864

Tonnage:	944 tons B
Dimensions:	200′ × 31′6″ × 20′
Machinery:	1 screw, 2 horizontal direct-acting engines (40″ × 2′), 1 boiler; 10 knots
Complement:	116
Armament:	Jun 64: 1 100-pdr R, 2 8″/55, 2 30-pdr R, 2 24-pdr. Apr 65 total: 1 100-pdr R, 2 8″/55, 1 30-pdr R, 1 20-pdr R.

NOTES: Wood hull, acquired on completion.

SERVICE RECORD: EGulfBS 1864. Blockade in Gulf of Mexico. Expedition to St. Marks, Fla., 23 Feb–27 Mar 1865. Decomm 22 Jun 1865. Sold 1 Aug 1865.

Prize: 31 Mar 1865: *Comus*.

Later history: Merchant *Andalusia* 1865. Burned and sank off Cape Hatteras, 3 Mar 1867.

Name	Bldr	Built	Acquired	Comm
Louisiana	Harlan (bldr)	1860	10 Jul 1861	Aug 1861

Tonnage:	438 tons D, 295 tons B
Dimensions:	143′2″ × 27′3″ × 8′6″
Machinery:	1 screw, 1 inverted direct-acting condensing engine (32″ × 2′4″), 1 boiler
Complement:	85
Armament:	1 8″ SB, 2 32-pdr/57, 1 32-pdr/33, 1 12-pdr R

NOTES: Three-masted schooner, two funnels, iron hull.

SERVICE RECORD: NAtlBS 1861. Landings at Roanoke I., NC, 7–8 Feb 1862. Engagement with enemy vessels, capture of Elizabeth City, NC, and expedition to Edenton, 10–12 Feb 1862. Reconnaissance to Winton, NC, Chowan River, 18–20 Feb 1862. Capture of New Bern, NC, 13–14 Mar 1862. Expedition to Washington, NC, 21 Mar 1862. Expedition to Pungo River, NC, 16–21 Jun 1864. Used as an explosion ship at Ft. Fisher, NC, 24 Dec 1864, but exploded without effect.

Prizes: 7 Sep 1861: *S.T. Garrison*. 5 Nov 1862: *Alice L. Webb*. 20 May 1863: *R.T. Renshaw*.

Name	Bldr	L	Acquired	Comm
Mercedita	Lupton (Murphy)	20 Apr 1861	31 Jul 1861	3 Dec 1861

Tonnage:	840 tons B, 776 n/r
Dimensions:	195′ (dk) 183′6″ (wl) × 30′3″ × 12′9″, d18′10″
Machinery:	1 screw, 2 inverted direct-acting engines (30″ × 2′8″), 2 boilers; HP 300 = 14 knots

Complement: 121
Armament: 8 32-pdr/57, 1 20-pdr R. May 63 total: 1 100-pdr R, 2 20-pdr R, 4 32-pdr/57, 2 24-pdr.

NOTES: Wood hull. Three-masted schooner rig.
SERVICE RECORD: GulfBS Jan 1862. Engaged batteries at St. Vincent, Fla., 3 Apr 1862. Sank British schr *Ellen* in collision off Nassau, 1 Aug 1862. SAtlBS Sep 1862. Engagement with ironclads off Charleston, 31 Jan 1863, rammed and damaged by CSS *Palmetto State*. West India Sqn Apr 1863, then NAtlBS Jun 1863. WGulfBS Mar 1865. Protection of American interests, Santo Domingo, Aug 1865. Decomm 14 Oct and sold 25 Oct 1865.
Prizes: 24 Jan 1862: **Julia*; 27 Apr: str *Bermuda*; 12 Jul: *Victoria & Ida*. 21 Oct 1863: *William*.
Later history: Merchant *Mercedita* 1865. Converted to barkentine 1879 and to schooner 1886. Mercantile barge 1900, lost 1901.

Name	Bldr	L	Acquired	Comm
Mohawk (ex-*Caledonia*, 14 Jun 59)	Teas (Sutton)	11 Jun 1853	13 Sep 1858	19 Sep 1859

Tonnage: 459 tons B
Dimensions: 162'4" × 24'4" × 14'
Machinery: 1 screw, vertical direct-acting engine (30" × 2'4"); 8 knots
Complement: 65/90
Armament: 1 30-pdr R, 2 32-pdr/33, 4 32-pdr/27

NOTES: Chartered for Paraguay Expedition as *Caledonia*, 1858–59. Purchased and renamed 1859. Three masts, one funnel.
SERVICE RECORD: Captured slaver *Wildfire* in Old Bahama Channel, 26 Apr 1860. EGulfBS May 1861–Apr 1862. Blockade of Pensacola 1862. SAtlBS Jul 1862–63. Guardship, Port Royal 1863–64. Sold 12 Jul 1864.
Prize: 5 Jul 1861: *George B. Sloat*.
Later history: Merchant *Alliance* 1865. Lost by stranding in Hatteras Inlet, NC, 4 Mar 1869.

Name	Bldr	Built	Acquired	Comm
Monticello	Williams (U)	1859	12 May 1861	May 1861

Tonnage: 655 tons B, 525 n/r
Dimensions: 180' × 29' × 12'10", d16'10"
Machinery: 1 screw, 1 vertical direct-acting engine, 1 boiler; HP 220 = 11.5 knots
Complement: 137
Armament: 1 10" SB, 2 32-pdr/33. Sep 61: add 2 32-pdr/42. Aug 62 total: 1 10" SB, 2 30-pdr R, 2 32-pdr/42, 2 32-pdr/33
Dec 62: 1 10" SB replaced by 1 100-pdr R.
Feb 64 total: 1 100-pdr R, 3 30-pdr R, 2 9" SB.

NOTES: Wood hull. Chartered, then purchased 12 Sep 1861.
SERVICE RECORD: NAtlBS, blockade in James River May 1861. Renamed **Star** 3 May 1861. Engaged batteries at Sewells Pt, 18–19 May 1861. Renamed **Monticello**, 23 May 1861. Capture of Hatteras Inlet,

28–29 Aug 1861. Blockade of Wilmington, Mar 1862–64. Sank USS *Peterhoff* in collision, 6 Mar 1864. Unsuccessful attack on Ft. Fisher, NC, 24–25 Dec 1864. Second attack on Ft. Fisher, 13–15 Jan 1865. Decomm 24 Jul 1865. Sold 1 Nov 1865.
Prizes: 21 May 1861: *Tropic Wind*. 11 Oct 1862: *Revere*; 18 Nov: **Ariel* and **Ann Maria*. 30 Mar 1863: *Sue*; 15 Apr: *Odd Fellow*; 27 Apr: **Golden Liner*. 1864: *James Douglas*; 27 Dec: **unidentified str*.
Later history: Merchant *Monticello* 1865. Foundered off Newfoundland, 19 Apr 1872.

Name	Bldr	L	Acquired	Comm
Mount Vernon	Sneeden (U)	10 Jul 1859	23 Apr 1861	May 1861

Tonnage: 625 tons B, 617 n/r
Dimensions: 173'6" × 28'8" × 12', d16'
Machinery: 1 screw, vertical direct-acting engine; HP 220 = 11.5 knots
Complement: 50
Armament: 1 32-pdr/57, 2 32-pdr/33. Apr 63 total: 1 100-pdr R, 2 32-pdr/42, 2 32-pdr/33. Nov 63 total: 1 100-pdr R, 2 20-pdr R, 2 9" SB.

NOTES: Wood hull.
SERVICE RECORD: Blockade off North Carolina. Engagement with CSS *Raleigh* off New Inlet, NC, 6–7 May 1864. Decomm 27 Jun 1865. Sold 12 Jul 1865.
Prizes: May 1861: *East*; 19 Jul: *Wild Pigeon*. 1 Mar 1862: *British Queen*; 2 Apr: **Kate*; 22 May: *Constitution*; 26 Jun: **Emily*; 29 Jul: *Napier*; 4 Nov: **Sophia*; 26 Nov: *Levi Rowe*; 30 Nov: **Emma Tuttle*. 1 Feb 1863: **Industry*; 24 Mar: *Mary Jane*; 25 Mar: *Rising Dawn*; 22 Apr: *St. George*.
Later history: Merchant *Mount Vernon* 1865. Sold foreign, 1869.

Name	Bldr	L	Acquired	Comm
Mystic (ex-*Memphis* (14 Jun 1859), ex-*Mount Savage*)	Cramp (Reaney Neafie)	2 Apr 1853	6 Jun 1859	3 Dec 1858

Tonnage: 452 tons B
Dimensions: 157' × 24'7" × 13'6"
Machinery: 1 screw, 1 vertical direct-acting engine (42" × 4'), 1 boiler; 6 knots
Complement: 65/90
Armament: Oct 61: 4 32-pdr/27, 1 24-pdr. Aug 62: add 1 24-pdr H, 1 20-pdr R.

NOTES: Originally chartered for Paraguay Expedition 13 Sep 1858. Three masts, one funnel.
SERVICE RECORD: Captured slavers *Thomas Achorn*, 27 Jun, and *Triton*, 16 Jul 1860, off Africa. In collision with USS *State of Georgia*, 28 Sep 1862. Potomac Flotilla 1862–65. Expedition to West Point, Va., York R., 5–7 May 1863. Sold 24 Jun 1865.
Prizes: 26 Jun 1862: **Emily*; 29 Jul: *Napier*; 28 Sep: **Sunbeam*. 17 Nov 1863: *Emma D*.
Later history: Merchant *General Custer* 1865. RR 1868.

Name	Bldr	L	Acquired	Comm
Niphon	S. Smith (Atlantic)	Feb 1863	22 Apr 1863	24 Apr 1863

Tonnage:	475 tons B
Dimensions:	157'6" (oa) 153'2" (bp) × 25'6" × 10'6"
Machinery:	1 screw, 2 vertical inverted direct-acting engines (26" × 2'2"), 1 boiler; 10 knots
Complement:	70/100
Armament:	1 20-pdr R, 2 12-pdr R, 4 32-pdr/42. Nov 64: add 2 32-pdr/33.

NOTES: Composite hull, barkentine rig. Built for China coast trade.
SERVICE RECORD: NAtlBS 1863–64. Decomm 1 Dec 1864. Sold 17 Apr 1865.
Prizes: 29 Jul 1863: str *Banshee;* 23 Aug: str **Hebe;* 8 Nov: str *Cornubia;* 9 Nov: str *Ella & Annie.* 25 Sep 1864: str **Lynx;* 29 Sep: str **Night Hawk;* 1 Oct: str **Condor;* 31 Oct: str *Annie.*
Later history: Merchant *Tejuca* 1865. Sold foreign 1867.

Name	Bldr	L	Acquired	Comm
Penguin	Mallory (Delamater)	26 Nov 1859	23 May 1861	25 Jun 1861

Tonnage:	389 tons B, 514 n/r
Dimensions:	155' × 30'5" × 12', d10'8"
Machinery:	1 screw, 1 vibrating-lever engine; 10 knots
Complement:	69
Armament:	1 12-pdr R, 4 32-pdr/57. Apr 63: add 2 20-pdr R.

NOTES: Three-masted schooner.
SERVICE RECORD: NAtlBS Aug 1861. Potomac Flotilla. SAtlBS Oct 1861. Occupation of Port Royal, SC, 7 Nov 1861. Capture of Fernandina, Fla., and Brunswick, St. Simons, and Jekyl islands, Ga., 2–12 Mar 1862. WGulfBS 1863–65. Decomm 24 Aug 1865. Sold 18 Sep 1865.
Prizes: 11 Aug 1861: **Louisa;* 25 Nov: *Albion.* 8 Jul 1864: str **Matagorda.* 21 Jan 1865: str **Granite City.*
Later history: Merchant *Florida* 1865. Converted to schooner, 1884. FFU.

Name	Bldr	Built	Acquired	Comm
Potomska	Capes (Delamater)	1854	25 Sep 1861	20 Dec 1861

Tonnage:	287 tons B
Dimensions:	140' (dk) 134'6" () × 27' × 11', d8'8"
Machinery:	1 screw, 1 vertical direct-acting engine (34" × 2'6"), 1 boiler; 9 knots
Complement:	77/95
Armament:	4 32-pdr/57, 1 20-pdr R.

NOTES: Wooden hull, three-masted schooner.
SERVICE RECORD: SAtlBS 1862–65. Engagement in Wassaw Sound, Ga., 26–28 Jan 1862. Capture of Fernandina, Fla., and Brunswick, St. Simons, and Jekyl islands, Ga., 2–12 Mar 1862. Expedition to Bull Bay, SC, 12–17 Feb 1865. Decomm 16 Jun 1865. Sold 10 Aug 1865.
Prize: 23 Feb 1863: *Belle.*
Later history: Merchant *Potomska* 1865. Wrecked at Saluda, Tex., 15 Jul 1866.

Name	Bldr	Built	Acquired	Comm
Preston (ex-*Annie*)	Dudgeon (U)	1863	31 Oct 1864	6 Feb 1865

Tonnage:	428 tons B
Dimensions:	179' × 23'1" × 10', d13'4"
Machinery:	2 screws, 2 direct-acting engines (26" × 1'8"), IHP 600 = 14 knots
Complement:	(U)
Armament:	1 30-pdr R, 2 24-pdr SB

NOTES: Blockade runner *Annie,* captured off New Inlet, NC, by USS *Wilderness* and *Niphon,* 31 Oct 1864. Iron hull.
SERVICE RECORD: WGulfBS 1865, off Texas. Decomm 8 Aug 1865. Sold 30 Nov 1865.
Later history: Merchant *Rover* 1865. Sold foreign 1868.

Name	Bldr	L	Acquired	Comm
Princess Royal	Tod (bldr)	20 Jun 1861	18 Mar 1863	29 May 1863

Tonnage:	619 tons B, 774 GRT, 973 n/r
Dimensions:	196'9" × 27'3" × 11', d16'
Machinery:	1 screw, 1 horizontal geared engine (49" × 3'3"), 2 boilers; 11 knots
Complement:	90
Armament:	2 30-pdr R, 1 9" SB, 4 24-pdr H

NOTES: Blockade runner, captured by USS *Unadilla* off Charleston, 29 Jan 1863. Built for service in Irish Sea.
SERVICE RECORD: WGulfBS 1863–65. Bombardment of Donaldsonville, La., 28 Jun 1863. Decomm 21 Jul 1865. Sold 17 Aug 1865.
Prizes: 10 Aug 1863: *Atlantic;* 12 Aug: *Flying Scud;* 27 Nov: *Flash;* 19 Dec: *Cora.* 19 Nov 1864: *Neptune;* 6 Dec: **Alabama.* 7 Feb 1865: *Anna Sophia;* 10 Feb: str **Will o'the Wisp;* 24 May: **Le Compt.*
Later history: Merchant *General Sherman* 1865. Foundered off Cape Fear, NC, 10 Jan 1874.

Name	Bldr	Built	Acquired	Comm
Stars and Stripes	Mallory (Delamater)	1861	27 Jul 1861	19 Sep 1861

Tonnage:	407 tons B
Dimensions:	150'6" (dk) 124'3" () × 34'6" × 9', d16'4"
Machinery:	1 screw, 2 vertical direct-acting engines (29" × 2'2"), 1 boiler; 10.5 knots
Complement:	94
Armament:	4 8"/55, 1 20-pdr R, 1 12-pdr

NOTES: Purchased new. Three-masted schooner.
SERVICE RECORD: AtlBS 1861. Landings at Roanoke I., NC, 7–8 Feb 1862. Capture of New Bern, NC, 13–14 Mar 1862. EGulfBS Oct 1862-65. Expedition to St. Marks, Fla., 23 Feb–27 Mar 1865. Decomm 30 Jun 1865. Sold 10 Aug 1865.
Prizes: 15 Dec 1861: **Charity.* 27 Jun 1862: str **Modern Greece;* 24 Aug: *Mary Elizabeth.* 25 Mar 1863: *Pacifique;* 3 Jun: *Florida;* 29 Dec: **Caroline Gertrude.* 18 Jan 1864: str *Laura.*

Later history: Merchant *Stars and Stripes* 1865. Renamed *Metropolis* 1871. Went aground and lost off Currituck Beach, NC, 31 Jan 1878.

Name	Bldr	L	Acquired	Comm
Stettin	Pile (U)	19 Sep 1861	4 Sep 1862	12 Nov 1862

Tonnage:	502 tons B, 480 tons GRT
Dimensions:	171' () 164' () × 28' × 12', d16'6"
Machinery:	1 screw, 2 inverted engines (36" × 2'4"), 2 boilers; 6 knots
Complement:	72
Armament:	1 30-pdr R, 4 24-pdr H

NOTES: Blockade runner, captured off Charleston by USS *Bienville*, 24 May 1862. Iron hull, brig rig.
SERVICE RECORD: SAtlBS 1862–65. Blockade of Charleston. Decomm 6 Apr 1865. Sold 22 Jun 1865.
Prizes: 28 Mar 1863: str *Aries*; 18 Apr: str *St. John's*; 11 Jun: str **Havelock*; 23 Sep: str *Diamond*.
Later history: Merchant *Sheridan*, 1865. Stranded on Bodie Island, 24 Sep 1866.

Name	Bldr	L	Acquired	Comm
Sumter	Hillman (Reaney Neafie)	19 Mar 1853	13 Sep 1858	1859
(ex-*Atlanta* (26 May 1859), ex-*Parker Vein*)				

Tonnage:	460 tons B
Dimensions:	163' × 24'4" × 11'9"
Machinery:	1 screw, 1 vertical back-acting engine (40" × 3'6")
Complement:	64/90
Armament:	4 32-pdr/27, 1 12-pdr R

NOTES: Name also spelled *Sumpter*. Chartered for Paraguay Expedition 1858, purchased 26 May 1859 and renamed.
SERVICE RECORD: Captured slaver brig *Falmouth* off West Africa, 14 Jun 1861. SAtlBS Mar 1862. NAtlBS 1863. Sunk in collision with USAT *General Meigs* off Smith Island, NC, 24 Jun 1863.

Name	Bldr	Built	Acquired	Comm
Trefoil	McKay (U)	1864	4 Feb 1865	1 Mar 1865
Yucca	McKay (U)	1864	25 Feb 1865	3 Apr 1865

Tonnage:	373 tons B
Dimensions:	145'7" × 23'7" × 11'3"
Machinery:	1 screw, 2 engines, 2 boilers
Complement:	44
Armament:	1 30-pdr R, 1 12-pdr SB

NOTES: Wooden hulled steamers acquired new.
SERVICE RECORDS:
Trefoil—WGulfBS 1865, dispatch boat. Decomm 30 Aug 1865. Sold 28 May 1867.
  Later history: Merchant *Gen. H.E. Paine* 1867. Stranded at Grand Haven, Mich., 19 Nov 1879.
Yucca—Gulf Stn 1865–68. Sold 26 Aug 1868.
  Later history: Merchant *Yucca* 1868. Mexican *Union* 1870.

Name	Bldr	Built	Acquired	Comm
Vicksburg	Maxson Fish (U)	1863	20 Oct 1863	2 Dec 1863

Tonnage:	886 tons B, 522 n/r
Dimensions:	185' (oa) 171' () × 33' × 13'8", d17'6"
Machinery:	1 screw, vertical direct-acting condensing engine (36" × 3'), 1 boiler; IHP 200 = 9 knots
Complement:	122
Armament:	1 100-pdr R, 4 30-pdr R, 1 20-pdr R, 1 12-pdr SB

NOTES: Wooden hull, brigantine rig.
SERVICE RECORD: NAtlBS 1864. Blockade of Wilmington 1864. Bombardment of Masonboro Inlet, NC, 11 Feb 1865. Decomm 29 Apr 1865. Sold 12 Jul 1865.
Prize: 30 Apr 1864: *Indian*.
Later history: Merchant *Vicksburg* 1865. RR 1868.

Name	Bldr	Built	Acquired	Comm
Virginia	(Dumbarton, Scotland) (U)	1861	1 Sep 1863	12 Jun 1863
(ex-*Virginia*, ex- *Noe-Daquy*, ex-*Pet*)				

Tonnage:	581 tons B, 442 n/r
Dimensions:	175'6" () 170' () × 26' × 8, d14'
Machinery:	1 screw, 2 vertical direct-acting engines (38" × 2'), 1 boiler
Complement:	61
Armament:	1 30-pdr R, 5 24-pdr H, 1 12-pdr R

NOTES: Blockade runner *Virginia*, captured off Mujeres Island, Mexico, by USS *Wachusett* and USS *Sonoma*, 18 Jan 1863. Iron hull.
SERVICE RECORD: WGulfBS Jun 1863. Blockade of Texas. Expedition to Brazos Santiago, Rio Grande, Tex., 27 Oct–3 Nov 1863. Sold 30 Nov 1865.
Prizes: 6 Oct 1863: *Jenny*; 4 Nov: str *Matamoras*; 5 Nov: *Science, Volante, Dashing Wave*. 15 Feb 1864: *Mary Douglas*; 22 Feb: *Henry Colthirst*; 29 Feb: *Camilla* and **Catherine Holt*; 8 Mar: *Randall*; 10 Mar: *Sylphide*; 11 Apr: **Juanita*; 15 Apr: **Rosina*; 19 Apr: *Alma*; 3 May: **Experiment*; 27 Dec: *Belle*.
Later history: Merchant *Virginia* 1865. Converted to barge 1885.

Name	Bldr	Built	Acquired	Comm
Western World	W. Collyer (Allaire)	1856	21 Sep 1861	3 Jan 1862

Tonnage:	441 tons B
Dimensions:	178' × 34'3" × 8'6"
Machinery:	1 screw, 1 vertical direct-acting engine (34" × 2'10"); 7 knots
Complement:	86
Armament:	1862: 1 30-pdr R, 2 32-pdr/57. Feb 63: add 2 32-pdr/47.

SERVICE RECORD: SAtlBS 1862. Engagement in Wilmington Narrows, NC, 26–28 Jan 1862. NAtlBS Mar 1863. Operated off Virginia coast and Chesapeake Bay. Expedition to White House, Va., Pamunkey River, 23–30 Jun 1863. Potomac Flotilla Feb 1864. NAtlBS Nov 1864–May 1865. Decomm 26 May 1865. Sold 24 Jun 1865.
Prizes: 2 Jul 1862: *Volante*. 24 Dec 1863: *A. Carson* and *Martha Ann*.
Later history: Merchant *Petersburg* 1865. Converted to barge 1880.

Name	Bldr	L	Acquired	Comm
Wyandotte	Birely Lynn (Reaney Neafie)	26 Mar 1853	6 Jun 1859	14 Jun 1859
(ex-*Western Port*–6 Jun 1859)				

Tonnage:	453 tons B
Dimensions:	162′4″ × 24′3″ × 13′6″
Machinery:	1 screw, vertical direct-acting condensing (Beard's) engine (40″ × 3′6″); 7 knots
Complement:	90
Armament:	Dec 61: 4 32-pdr/27, 1 24-pdr H. Dec 62: add 1 20-pdr R, 1 12-pdr R.

NOTES: Chartered for Paraguay Expedition 1858. Purchased 1859 and renamed. Three masts, one funnel.
SERVICE RECORD: Captured bark *William* with 540 slaves off Cuba, 9 May 1860. GulfBS 1861. SAtlBS Jan–May 1862. Potomac Flotilla Sep 1862–65. Guardship, Norfolk 1863–65. Decomm 3 Jun 1865. Sold 12 Jul 1865.
Later history: Merchant *Wyandotte* 1865. Wrecked off Duxbury, Mass., 26 Jan 1866.

Name	Bldr	Built	Acquired	Comm
Young Rover	Curtis, Medford (U)	1860	27 Jul 1861	10 Sep 1861

Tonnage:	418 tons B
Dimensions:	141′ × 28′2″ × 11′, d17′
Machinery:	1 screw, 1 engine (18″ × 2′); HP 75 = 7 knots
Complement:	48
Armament:	1 12-pdr R, 4 32-pdr/42

NOTES: Auxiliary bark.
SERVICE RECORD: AtlBS 1861. NAtlBS 1862. EGulfBS Jun 1862. Blockade off Florida. Guardship, Hampton Roads 1863. Sold 22 Jun 1865.
Later history: Merchant *Young Rover* 1865. Converted to bark 1865. Wrecked near Zanzibar, 29 Jun 1866.

SMALL SIDE-WHEEL COMBATANTS—4TH RATE

Name	Bldr	Built	Acquired	Comm
Ceres	Terry (U)	1856	11 Sep 1861	Sep 1861

Tonnage:	144 tons B
Dimensions:	108′4″ × 22′4″ × 6′3″, d7′7″
Machinery:	Side wheels, 1 beam engine (30″ × 6′8″), 1 boiler; 9 knots
Complement:	45
Armament:	1 30-pdr R, 1 32-pdr/33. Apr 63 total: 2 30-pdr R, 2 24-pdr SB.

SERVICE RECORD: Potomac Flotilla 1861. NAtlBS 1861–65. Landings at Roanoke I., NC, 7–8 Feb 1862. Engagement with enemy vessels, capture of Elizabeth City, NC, and expedition to Edenton, 10–12 Feb 1862. Expedition to Hamilton, NC, Roanoke River, 9 Jul 1862. Engagements with CSS *Albemarle*, at Plymouth, NC, 19 Apr and 5 May

1864. Expedition to Pungo River, NC, 16–21 Jun 1864. Decomm 14 Jul 1865. Sold 25 Oct 1865.
Prizes: 6 Mar 1862: *Actor; 14 May: str *Alice*; 9 Jun: str *Wilson*. 12 May 1864: *Ann C. Davenport*.
Later history: Merchant *Ceres* 1865. RR 1887.

Name	Bldr	Built	Acquired	Comm
Coeur de Lion	(Coxsackie, NY)	1853	Apr 1861	2 Oct 1861
(ex-USLHS *Coeur de Lion*, ex-*Alfred van Santvoord*)				

Tonnage:	110 tons B
Dimensions:	100′ × 20′6″ × 4′6″
Machinery:	Side wheels, 1 HP engine, 1 boiler
Complement:	29
Armament:	1 30-pdr R, 1 12-pdr R, 1 12-pdr H

NOTES: Acquired from Lighthouse Board. Wooden hull.
SERVICE RECORD: Potomac and James River sqns 1861–65. Engaged batteries at Port Royal, Va., 4 Dec 1862. Operations in Nansemond River, Va., 11 Apr–4 May 1863; disabled 18 Apr. Returned to Lighthouse Board 3 Jun 1865.
Prizes: 9 Feb 1863: *Emily Murray*; 11 Jun: *Odd Fellow* and *Sarah Margaret*; 16 Sep: *Robert Knowles*.
Later history: Lighthouse steamer *Coeur de Lion* 1865. Sold 1867, merchant *Alice*. RR 1873.

The small side-wheeler *Coeur de Lion* was acquired from the Lighthouse Board and returned after the war. (Martin Holbrook Collection) (Mariners Museum)

Name	Bldr	Built	Acquired
Commodore	(New Orleans)	1863	31 Jul 1863

Tonnage:	80 tons B
Dimensions:	100′ × 20.4′ × 4.3′
Machinery:	Side wheels
Complement:	56
Armament:	Oct 64: 1 20-pdr R, 2 12-pdr R, 1 24-pdr.

SERVICE RECORD: WGulfBS. Patrolled Lake Pontchartrain 1863–65. Renamed **Fort Gaines**, 1 Sep 1864. Sold 12 Aug 1865.
Prizes: 8 Dec 1864: *Locadie*
Later history: Merchant *Fort Gaines* 1865. RR 1870.

Name	Bldr	Built	Acquired	Comm
Cowslip (ex-Meteor)	(Newburgh, NY)	1863	21 Dec 1863	27 Jan 1864

Tonnage:	220 tons B
Dimensions:	123′ × 24′ × 7′, d8′
Machinery:	Side wheels, 1 beam engine (34″ × 8′), 1 boiler
Complement:	36
Armament:	1 20-pdr R, 2 24-pdr SB

SERVICE RECORD: WGulfBS 1864. Raid into Biloxi Bay, 31 May 1864. Mobile Bay, Aug 1864. Sold 28 Aug 1866.
Prize: 29 May 1864: *Last Push*.
Later history: Merchant *Harry Wright* 1865. Destroyed by fire at New Orleans, La., 27 Jul 1886.

Name	Bldr	Built	Acquired	Comm
Diana	(Brownsville, Pa.)	1858	Nov 1862	1 Jan 1863

Tonnage:	239 tons
Dimensions:	(U)
Machinery:	Side wheels
Armament:	(U)

NOTES: Merchant steamer captured at New Orleans, 27 Apr 1862. Used by Army as transport.
SERVICE RECORD: Engagement off Brashear City, Berwick Bay, La., 1–3 Nov 1862. Engagement at Bayou Teche, La., 14 Jan 1863. Captured by Confederate troops in Grand Lake, La., 28 Mar 1863. Burned by U.S. forces, 12 Apr 1863.

Name	Bldr	Built	Acquired	Comm
Isaac N. Seymour	Terry (U)	1860	26 Oct 1861	Nov 1861

Tonnage:	133 tons B
Dimensions:	100′ × 19′8″ × 6′6″
Machinery:	Side wheels, 1 beam engine; 11 knots
Complement:	30
Armament:	1 30-pdr R, 1 20-pdr R. Jan 62 total: 1 30-pdr R, 1 12-pdr R.

SERVICE RECORD: NAtlBS 1861–65. Engagement with CSS *Patrick Henry* near Newport News, 2 Dec 1861. Landings at Roanoke I., NC, 7–8 Feb 1862. Engagement with enemy vessels, capture of Elizabeth City, NC, and expedition to Edenton, 10–12 Feb 1862. Sank after hitting submerged object in Hatteras Inlet, 20 Feb 1862; raised and repaired. Struck a bank and sank in Neuse River, 24 Aug 1862; again raised and repaired. Expedition to Hamilton, NC, 31 Oct–7 Nov 1862. Reconnaissance in Neuse River, 12–16 Dec 1862. Expedition in James River, 6–20 Jul 1863. Engagement with CSS *Albemarle*, Albemarle Sound, NC, 5 May 1864. Blockade of North Carolina 1864–65. Decomm 16 May 1865.
Later history: To U.S. Lighthouse Board 20 Jun 1865. USLHS *Tulip* 1865. Merchant *Magnolia*, 1882. Sold Canadian, 1888. Burned at Sydney, NS, 15 Jan 1897.

Name	Bldr	Built	Acquired	Comm
John L. Lockwood	(Athens, NY)	1854	1 Sep 1861	21 Sep 1861

Tonnage:	180 tons B
Dimensions:	114′ × 24′ × 6′6″, d7′3″
Machinery:	Side wheels, beam engine (32″ × 7′8″), 1 boiler; 11 knots
Complement:	30
Armament:	1861: 1 80-pdr R, 1 12-pdr R, 1 12-pdr HSB. Apr 63: 1 32-pdr/42, 1 12-pdr R, 1 12-pdr HSB

SERVICE RECORD: NAtlBS 1861–65. Landings at Roanoke I., NC, 7–8 Feb 1862. Engagement with enemy vessels, capture of Elizabeth City, NC, and expedition to Edenton, 10–12 Feb 1862. Capture of New Bern, NC, 13–14 Mar 1862. Expedition to block Chesapeake & Albemarle Canal, 23 Apr 1862. Reconnaissance in Neuse River, NC, 12–16 Dec 1862. Decomm 23 May 1865. Sold 15 Sep 1865.
Prizes: 14 May 1862: str *Alice*. 1 Jan 1865: *Twilight*.
Later history: Merchant *Henry Smith* 1865. War Dept. *Chester A. Arthur* 1876. Merchant *Victor* 1892. BU 1927.

Name	Bldr	Built	Acquired	Comm
Kinsman (ex-Colonel Kinsman, ex-Gray Cloud)	(Elizabeth, Pa.)	1854	1 Jan 1863	Oct 1862

Tonnage:	245 tons
Dimensions:	(U)
Machinery:	Side wheels
Armament:	(U)

NOTES: Steamer commandeered for the Army at New Orleans, May 1862. Transferred to the Navy, 1 Jan 1863.
SERVICE RECORD: Damaged in engagement with CSS *J.A. Cotton* off Brashear City, Berwick Bay, La., 3 Nov 1862. Engagement at Bayou Teche, La., 14 Jan 1863. Struck a snag and sank in Berwick Bay, La., near Brashear City, 23 Feb 1863.
Prizes: 4 Nov 1862: str *A.B. Seger*; 9 Nov: str *Osprey*, and *J.P. Smith*.

Name	Bldr	L	Acquired	Comm
Mercury	W. Collyer (U)	15 Jun 1854	17 Aug 1861	3 Oct 1861

Tonnage:	187 tons B
Dimensions:	128′ × 22′10″ × 5′6″, d8′
Machinery:	Side wheels, 1 engine (36″ × 8′); 1 boiler
Complement:	56
Armament:	1 20-pdr, 1 30-pdr R

SERVICE RECORD: James River 1864. Expedition to Milford Haven, Va., 24 Sep 1864. Army operations in Great Wicomico River, Va., 17 Oct 1864. Sold 29 Aug 1873.
Later history: FFU.

Name	Bldr	Built	Acquired	Comm
Satellite	(New York, NY)	1854	24 Jul 1861	27 Sep 1861

Tonnage:	217 tons B
Dimensions:	120′7″ × 22′9″ × 8′6″
Machinery:	Side wheels
Complement:	43
Armament:	1 8″/55, 1 30-pdr R

SERVICE RECORD: Potomac Flotilla 1861. Expedition in Rappahannock River, Tappahannock, Va., 13–15 Apr 1862. Supported submarine *Alligator*, Jun 1862. With USS *Reliance*, captured by Confederate boarders in Rappahannock River, 23 Aug 1863. Operated briefly with Confederate crew at mouth of Rappahannock River, but destroyed to prevent recapture, 28 Aug 1863.
Prizes: 21 May 1863: *Emily*; 28 May: *Sarah and *Arctic; 17 Aug: *Three Brothers*.

Name	Bldr	L	Acquired	Comm
Shawsheen (ex-*Young America*)	Sneeden Whitlock (U)	8 Aug 1854	23 Sep 1861	1861

Tonnage:	126 tons B
Dimensions:	118′ × 22′6″ × 7′3″
Machinery:	Side wheels
Complement:	40
Armament:	1861: 2 20-pdr R. Apr 63 total: 1 30-pdr R, 1 20-pdr R, 1 12-pdr H R.

SERVICE RECORD: Hampton Roads area 1861, arrived in damaged condition. Engagement with CSS *Patrick Henry* near Newport News, 2 Dec 1861. Landings at Roanoke I., NC, 7–8 Feb 1862. Engagement with enemy vessels, capture of Elizabeth City, NC, and expedition to Edenton, 10–12 Feb 1862. Expedition to block Chesapeake & Albemarle Canal, 23 Apr 1862. Expedition to Hamilton, NC, Roanoke River, 9 Jul 1862. Reconnaissance in Neuse River, NC, 12–16 Dec 1862. James River 1863–64. Disabled by Confederate artillery in James River and blown up to prevent capture, 7 May 1864.
Prizes: 28 Mar 1862: *James Norcon*. 22 Jun 1863: *Henry Clay*; 20 Jul: *Dolphin*, *Elizabeth*, *Helen Jane*, *James Brice*, and *Sally*; 29 Jul: *Telegraph*.

Name	Bldr	Built	Acquired	Comm
Vixen	Brown & Bell (Kemble)	1845	26 Aug 1861	31 Jul 1862

Tonnage:	240 tons B
Dimensions:	118′ (dk) × 22′6″ × 7′10″, d12′
Machinery:	Side wheels, 1 half beam horizontal engine (36″ × 6′), 2 boilers; NHP 50 = 8 knots
Complement:	41
Armament:	Aug 62: 2 20-pdr R. Dec 62 total: 2 32-pdr/27.

NOTES: Acquired from U.S. Coast Survey as reconnaissance vessel. Originally built for Mexican government and seized by U.S. at start of Mexican War; served in USN 1845–55. Two-masted schooner rig. Sister ship *Spitfire* sold by USN 1848.
SERVICE RECORD: Conducted surveys at Port Royal, SC, 1861. Bombardment of forts at St. Helena Sound, SC, 25–28 Nov 1861. SAtlBS 1862. Expedition to Pocotaligo, SC, 21–23 Oct 1862. Returned to

Coast Survey, 8 Nov 1862. Conducted surveys and patrols along coast of Florida 1863–64. Joint expedition up Ashepoo and S. Edisto rivers, SC, 25–27 May 1864.
Later history: Coast Survey *Vixen* 1862.

Name	Bldr	Built	Acquired	Comm
Wilderness (ex-*B.N.Crary (Creary)*)	(Brooklyn)	1864	30 May 1864	20 Jul 1864

Tonnage:	390 tons B
Dimensions:	137′ × 25′ ×6′
Machinery:	Side wheels, beam engine; 13 knots
Complement:	41
Armament:	Oct 1864: 4 24-pdr

NOTES: Wooden hull. Converted to gunboat Oct 1864.
SERVICE RECORD: NAtlBS 1864. Unsuccessful attack on Ft. Fisher, NC, 24–25 Dec 1864. Second attack on Ft. Fisher, 13–15 Jan 1865. Decomm 10 Jun 1865.
Prize: 31 Oct 1864: str *Annie*.
Later history: To U.S. Revenue Cutter Service, 7 Sep 1865. Renamed *John A. Dix* 1873. Sold 18 May 1891. Merchant *Governor John A. Dix* 1891.

Name	Bldr	Built	Acquired	Comm
William G. Putnam	(Brooklyn)	1857	24 Jul 1861	Sep 1861

Tonnage:	149 tons B
Dimensions:	103′6″ × 22′ × 7′6″
Machinery:	Side wheels, single-acting engine (32″ × 6′); 7 knots
Complement:	32/62
Armament:	Oct 61: 4 32-pdr/51, 2 32-pdr/33, 1 24-pdr H. Jun 63 total: 1 20-pdr R, 4 32-pdr/51, 2 32-pdr/33, 1 12-pdr R. Mar 64 total: 1 30-pdr R, 4 32-pdr/51, 2 32-pdr/33, 2 12-pdr R.

NOTES: Wooden tug, sometimes known as **General Putnam**. Reboilered 1863.
SERVICE RECORD: NAtlBS 1861. Landings at Roanoke I., NC, 7–8 Feb 1862. Engagement with enemy vessels, capture of Elizabeth City, NC, and expedition to Edenton, 10–12 Feb 1862. Expedition to block Chesapeake & Albemarle Canal, 23 Apr 1862. Expedition up Pamunkey River, Va., 8–13 Mar 1864. Operated in Virginia waters 1863–64. Decomm 2 Jun 1865.
Prizes: 21 Mar 1862: *Lonely Bell*; 9 Jun: *Scuppernong*.
Later history: To U.S. Lighthouse Board, 2 Jun 1865. USLS *Putnam* 1865. Merchant *Putnam* 1893. RR 1896.

SMALL SIDE-WHEEL COMBATANTS, EX-FERRYBOATS – 4TH RATE

Most were New York and Brooklyn ferryboats, useful in narrow waters because of their ability to move equally in either direction. They also had decks strengthened to carry heavy loads suitable for conversion to gunboats.

Name	Bldr	Built	Acquired	Comm
Clifton	Simonson (Allaire)	1861	2 Dec 1861	1862

Tonnage:	892 tons B
Dimensions:	210′ × 40′ × d13′4″
Machinery:	Side wheels, vertical beam engine (50″ × 10′)
Complement:	121
Armament:	2 9″ SB, 4 32-pdr/57. Jun 62: add 1 9″ SB, 1 30-pdr R. 1863 total: 2 9″ SB, 4 32-pdr SB, 2 30-pdr R.

SERVICE RECORD: WGulfBS 1862–63. Passage past New Orleans forts and engagement with CSN vessels, 24 Apr 1862. Bombardment of Vicksburg, 26–28 Jun 1862. Damaged at Vicksburg, 28 Jun 1862. Bombardment and capture of Galveston, Tex., 4–9 Oct 1862. Bombardment at Lavaca, Tex., 31 Oct–1 Nov 1862. Engagement at Butte-a-la-Rose, La., and capture of Ft. Burton, 20 Apr 1863. Disabled by Confederate batteries and captured at Sabine Pass, Tex., 8 Sep 1863.
Prize: 18 Jul 1863: *H. McGuin*.
Later history: Comm. as CSS *Clifton* (q.v.).

Name	Bldr	Built	Acquired	Comm
Commodore Barney (ex-*Ethan Allen*)	Stack (Novelty)	1859	2 Oct 1861	1861
Commodore Perry	Stack (Novelty)	1859	2 Oct 1861	Oct 1861

Tonnage:	512 tons B
Dimensions:	144′6″ (bp) × 33′ × 9′, d12′
Machinery:	Side wheels, 1 vertical beam engine (38.5″ × 9′); IHP 500 = 11 knots
Complement:	68/108
Armament:	*Barney*: 1862: 3 9″ SB, 1 100-pdr R. Aug 62: add 1 9″ SB, 2 12-pdr H. Sep 63 total: 5 9″ SB, 1 100-pdr R, 1 12-pdr SB.
	Perry: Jan 63: 2 9″ SB, 2 32-pdr/47, 1 12-pdr SBH. Jul 64 total: 1 100-pdr R, 4 9″ SB, 1 12-pdr SB.

SERVICE RECORDS:
Commodore Barney—Damaged in storm off Virginia Oct 1861. NAtlBS 1862–65. Landings at Roanoke I., NC, 7–8 Feb 1862. Reconnaissance to Winton, NC, Chowan River, 18–20 Feb 1862. Capture of New Bern, NC, 13–14 Mar 1862. Operations in Nansemond River, Va., Apr–May 1863. Expeditions to White House, Va., York and Pamunkey rivers, 23–30 Jun, and up James River (damaged by mine explosion, 5 Aug), 4–7 Aug 1863. Expedition up Nansemond River, 13–14 Apr 1864. Sold 20 Jul 1865.
Later history: Merchant *Commodore Barney* 1865. Foundered at wharf at Jacksonville, Fla., 22 Sep 1901.
Commodore Perry—NAtlBS Jan 1862–65. Landings at Roanoke I., NC, 7–8 Feb 1862. Engagement with enemy vessels, capture of Elizabeth City, NC, and expedition to Edenton, 10–12 Feb 1862. Reconnaissance to Winton, NC, Chowan River, 18–20 Feb 1862. Capture of New Bern, NC, 13–14 Mar 1862. Expedition to Hamilton, NC, Roanoke River, 9 Jul 1862. Operations at Franklin, Va., 3 Oct 1862. Expeditions to Plymouth, NC, 31 Oct–7 Nov 1862, in Chowan River, 26–30 Jul 1863, and up Nansemond River, Va., 13–14 Apr 1864. Decomm 26 Jun 1865. Sold 12 Jul 1865.
Prizes: 10 Feb 1862: *Lynnhaven*; 8 Apr: *John* and *Nathaniel Taylor*; 10 Apr: *America*, *Comet*, and *J.J. Crittenden*; 14 May: str *Alice*; 9 Jun: str *Wilson*.
Later history: Merchant *Commodore Perry* 1865. RR 1907.

Name	Bldr	Built	Acquired	Comm
Commodore Hull (ex-*Nuestra Senora de Regla*)	(Brooklyn)	1861	1 Sep 1862	27 Nov 1862

Tonnage:	376 tons B
Dimensions:	141′ × 28′4″ × 9′, d11′
Machinery:	Side wheels, 1 inclined engine (36″ × 9′), 1 boiler; 10 knots
Complement:	68
Armament:	2 30-pdr R, 4 24-pdr SB. Sep 64: 1 30-pdr R replaced by 1 32-pdr R.

The side-wheel steamer *Commodore Perry* was a converted New York ferryboat. (U.S. Naval Historical Center)

NOTES: Built as ferry for Havana Harbor. Seized by U.S. at Port Royal, SC, en route to Cuba, a seizure later ruled illegal.
SERVICE RECORD: NAtlBS 1862–65. Engagement with CSS *Albemarle*, Albemarle Sound, NC, 5 May 1864. Damaged by batteries in Roanoke River during capture of Plymouth, NC, 29–31 Oct 1864. Decomm 8 Jun 1865. Sold 27 Sep 1865.
Later history: Merchant *Waccamaw* 1865. Lost before 1885 (cause unknown).

Name	Bldr	Built	Acquired	Comm
Commodore Jones	(New York?)	1863	12 May 1863	21 May 1863

Tonnage:	542 tons B
Dimensions:	154′ × 32′6″ × d11′8″
Machinery:	Side wheels, 12 knots
Complement:	88/103
Armament:	1 9″ SB, 1 5.1″ R, 4 24-pdr SB. Jul 63 total: 1 9″ SB, 1 50-pdr R, 2 30-pdr R, 4 24-pdr SB.

SERVICE RECORD: NAtlBS 1863–64. Evacuation of West Point, Va., 31 May 1863. Army operations in Mattaponi River, 3–7 Jun and Chickahominy River, 10–13 Jun 1863. Expedition in James River, 6–20 Jul 1863. Sunk by an electric torpedo (mine) in James River, 6, May 1864.

Name	Bldr	Built	Acquired	Comm
Commodore McDonough	(New York?)	1862	5 Aug 1862	24 Nov 1862
Commodore Morris	(New York)	1862	5 Aug 1862	19 Nov 1862

Tonnage:	532 tons B
Dimensions:	154′ × 32′6″ × 8′6″, d12′
Machinery:	Side wheels, 1 inclined engine (38″ × 10′); 8 knots
Complement:	75
Armament:	*McDonough* 1 9″ SB, 1 20-pdr R, 4 24-pdr H. Jun 63 total: 1 9″ SB, 1 100-pdr R, 2 50-pdr R, 2 24-pdr H.
	Morris 1 9″ SB, 1 100-pdr R, 4 24-pdr H. May 63: 2 24-pdr H replaced by 2 30-pdr R.

SERVICE RECORDS:
Commodore McDonough—SAtlBS 1862–65, SC. Engaged batteries in Stono River, 30 Jan and at James I., SC, 17 Apr 1863. Operations in S. Edisto River, 25–27 May 1864. Army operations in Stono and Folly rivers, SC, Feb 1865. Foundered while in tow en route from Port Royal to New York, 23 Aug 1865.
Commodore Morris—NAtlBS 1862–65. Expeditions to West Point, Va., Pamunkey River, 7–9 Jan, to West Point, Va., York River, 5–7 May 1863, and to White House, Va., York and Pamunky rivers, 23–30 Jun 1863. Expedition up Nansemond River, Va., 13–14 Apr 1864. Decomm 24 Jun 1865. Sold 12 Jul 1865.
Prizes: 22 Jan 1863: *John C. Calhoun, Harriet, Music*.
Later history: Merchant *Clinton* 1865. 1917–1920 to U.S. Army as *General John Simpson*. BU 1931.

Name	Bldr	Built	Acquired	Comm
Commodore Read (ex-*Atlantic*)	(Brooklyn)	1857	19 Aug 1863	8 Sep 1863

Commodore Morris, a converted New York ferryboat, saw service in Virginia waters. Notice the eagle on the pilothouse. After the war she returned to New York as a ferryboat until 1931.

Tonnage:	650 tons B
Dimensions:	179′ × 33′6″ × 6′3″, d13′2″
Machinery:	Side wheels, 1 vertical beam engine (45″ × 11′)
Complement:	84
Armament:	2 100-pdr R, 4 24-pdr H. Oct 64 total: 2 100-pdr R, 4 9″ SB.

SERVICE RECORD: Potomac Flotilla 1863–65. Expedition up Rappahannock River, 18–22 Apr 1864. Sold 20 Jul 1865.
Later history: Merchant *State of Maryland*. Wrecked in Chesapeake Bay, 31 Mar 1876.

Name	Bldr	L	Acquired	Comm
Ellen	E. Webb (Novelty)	1 Feb 1853	10 Oct 1861	16 Oct 1861

Tonnage:	341 tons B
Dimensions:	125′6″ × 28′6″ × 8′, d10′6″
Machinery:	Side wheels, 1 Copeland's inclined engine (36″ × 8′); 12 knots
Complement:	50
Armament:	2 32-pdr/33, 2 30-pdr R

SERVICE RECORD: SAtlBS Nov 1861. Army operations at Port Royal Ferry, SC, 31 Dec 1861–2 Jan 1862. Engagement in Wassaw Sound, Ga., 26–28 Jan 1862. Capture of Fernandina, Fla., and Brunswick, St. Simons, and Jekyl islands, Ga., 2–12 Mar 1862. Operations in St.

Johns River, Fla., 16 Apr–3 May 1862. Decomm 30 Oct 1862. Used as carpenter shop at Port Royal. Sold 2 Sep 1865.
Later history: Probably BU 1865.

Name	Bldr	Built	Acquired	Comm
Fort Henry	(New York)	1862	25 Mar 1862	3 Apr 1862

Tonnage:	519 tons B
Dimensions:	150′6″ × 32′ × d11′9″
Machinery:	Side wheels
Complement:	120
Armament:	2 9″ SB, 4 32-pdr/57

SERVICE RECORD: EGulfBS 1862–65, West Florida. Expedition to St. Marks, Fla., Mar 1865. Decomm 8 Jul 1865. Sold 15 Aug 1865.
Prizes: 15 Oct 1862: *G.L. Brockenborough*. 26 Feb 1863: *Anna*; 25 Mar: *Ranger* and *Bangor*; 22 May: *Isabella*; 28 Jun: *Anna Maria*; 3 Jul: *Emma*; 6 Aug: *Southern Star*.
Later history: Merchant *Huntington* 1865. Burned at Hunter's Point, NY, 21 Feb 1868.

Name	Bldr	Built	Acquired	Comm
Hunchback	Simonson (U)	1852	16 Dec 1861	3 Jan 1862

Tonnage:	517 tons B
Dimensions:	179′5″ × 29′3″ × 9′, d11′7″
Machinery:	Side wheels, 1 vertical beam engine (40″ × 8′); 12 knots
Complement:	99
Armament:	3 9″ SB, 1 100-pdr R. Apr 63 total: 4 9″ SB, 1 200-pdr R, 1 12-pdr R, 1 12-pdr H. Mar 65 total: 5 9″ SB, 1 100-pdr R, 1 12-pdr R, 1 12-pdr H.

SERVICE RECORD: NAtlBS 1862. Landings at Roanoke I., NC, 7–8 Feb 1862. Reconnaissance to Winton, NC, Chowan River, 18–20 Feb 1862. Capture of New Bern, NC, 13–14 Mar 1862. Operations at Franklin, Va., 3 Oct 1862. Expedition to Hamilton, NC, 31 Oct–7 Nov 1862. Engagement at Trent's Reach, James River, 24 Jan 1865. Decomm 12 Jun 1865. Sold 12 Jul 1865.
Prizes: 18 May 1862: *G.H. Smoot*; 20 May: *Eugenia*; 21 May: *Winter Shrub*.
Later history: Merchant *General Grant* 1865. BU 1880.

Name	Bldr	L	Acquired	Comm
John P. Jackson	Burtis (Fulton)	2 Aug 1860	6 Nov 1861	14 Feb 1862

Tonnage:	750 tons B
Dimensions:	192′ × 36′6″ × d12′
Machinery:	Side wheels, 1 vertical beam engine (45″ × 11′); 8 knots
Complement:	99
Armament:	Jun 63: 4 32-pdr/57, 1 9″ SB, 1 6″ R. Jul 64: 1 6″ R replaced by 1 100-pdr R.

SERVICE RECORD: WGulfBS, Mortar Flotilla, 1862. Engagement at Pass Christian, Miss., 4 Apr 1862. Passage past New Orleans forts and engagement with CSN vessels, 24 Apr 1862. Disabled by enemy fire at Warrenton, Miss., 25 Jun 1862. Damaged by fire off New Orleans, 8 Oct 1862. Bombardment of Ft. Powell, Mobile Bay, 16–29 Feb 1864. Battle of Mobile Bay, 5 Aug 1864. Decomm 5 Sep and sold 27 Sep 1865.
Prizes: 22 Oct 1862: *Cuba* and *Belle of Mobile*. 12 Jan 1863: *Le Caddie* and *Union*; 4 Apr: str *P.C. Wallis*; 12 Sep: str *Fox*; 21 Oct: *Syrena*. 8 Dec 1864: *Medora*.
Later history: Merchant *J.P. Jackson* 1865. RR 1871.

Name	Bldr	Built	Acquired	Comm
Morse (ex-*Marion*)	Roosevelt (Novelty)	1859	7 Nov 1861	9 Nov 1861

Tonnage:	513 tons B
Dimensions:	142′6″ (bp) × 33′ × 8′6″, d12′4″
Machinery:	Side wheels, 1 vertical beam engine (38″ × 9′); HP 500 = 11 knots
Complement:	78/96
Armament:	2 9″. Feb 63: 2 9″, 2 100-pdr R, 2 24-pdr.

SERVICE RECORD: NAtlBS 1861–64. Landings at Roanoke I., NC, 7–8 Feb 1862. Engagement with enemy vessels, capture of Elizabeth City, NC, and expedition to Edenton, 10–12 Feb 1862. Reconnaissance to Winton, NC, Chowan River, 18–20 Feb 1862. Capture of New Bern, NC, 13–14 Mar 1862. Expeditions to West Point, Va., York River, 5–7 May, to White House, Va., York and Pamunkey rivers, 23–30 Jun 1863, and up Pamunkey River, 8–13 Mar 1864. Rappahannock River, 1865. Decomm 21 May 1865. Sold 20 Jul 1865.
Later history: Merchant *Lincoln* 1865. RR 1885.

Name	Bldr	Built	Acquired	Comm
Shokokon (ex-*Clifton*)	Simonson (Allaire)	1862	3 Apr 1863	18 May 1863

Tonnage:	709 tons B
Dimensions:	185′ (dk) 181′7″ () × 32′ × 8′6″, d13′6″
Machinery:	Side wheels, 1 vertical beam engine (43″ × 10′), 1 boiler; IHP 570 = 10 knots
Complement:	120
Armament:	1 30-pdr R, 4 24-pdr. Mar 64: 1 24-pdr replaced by 1 30-pdr R. Mar 65 total: 2 9″ SB, 2 30-pdr R, 4 24-pdr.

SERVICE RECORD: NAtlBS 1863. Expedition in James River, 6–20 Jul 1863. Blockade off Wilmington 1863. Damaged in hurricane, Aug 1863. Expedition up Pamunkey River, Va., 8–13 Mar 1864. Blockade of Wilmington, Sep 1864. Sold 25 Oct 1865.
Prizes: 18 Aug 1863: str *Hebe*; 23 Aug: **Alexander Cooper*.
Later history: Merchant *Lone Star* 1865. RR 1886.

Name	Bldr	Built	Acquired	Comm
Somerset	(Brooklyn, NY)	1862	4 Mar 1862	3 Apr 1862

Tonnage:	521 tons B
Dimensions:	151′ × 32′4″ × d11′3″
Machinery:	Side wheels, 1 engine (36″ × 9′)
Complement:	110
Armament:	2 9″ SB, 4 32-pdr/57

SERVICE RECORD: EGulfBS 1862–65, Florida coast. Sold 12 July 1865. *Prizes*: 4 May 1862: str *Circassian*: 16 Jun: *Curlew*. 18 Feb 1863: *Hortense*.
Later history: Merchant *Somerset*, 1866. RR 1914.

Name	Bldr	Built	Acquired	Comm
Southfield	Englis (U)	1857	16 Dec 1861	Dec 1861

Tonnage:	751 tons B
Dimensions:	200′ × 34′ × 6′6″, d11′8″
Machinery:	Side wheels, 1 vertical beam engine; 12 knots
Complement:	61
Armament:	1 100-pdr R, 3 9″ SB. Apr 63: add 2 9″ SB.

SERVICE RECORD: NAtlBS 1862–64. Landings at Roanoke I., NC, 7–8 Feb 1862. Capture of New Bern, NC, 13–14 Mar 1862. Damaged while supporting Army troops at Plymouth, NC, 10 Dec 1862. Expedition in Chowan River, SC, 1–2 Mar 1864. Rammed and sunk by CSS *Albemarle* at Plymouth, NC, 19 Apr 1864.

Name	Bldr	Built	Acquired	Comm
Stepping Stones	(New York, NY)	1861	30 Sep 1861	Oct 1862

Tonnage:	226 tons B
Dimensions:	110′ × 24′ × 4′6″, d8′
Machinery:	Side wheels, beam engine (30″ × 6′)
Complement:	21
Armament:	May 63: 1 20-pdr R, 3 12-pdr R, 2 12-pdr SB. Mar 65 total: 3 12-pdr R, 3 12-pdr SB.

SERVICE RECORD: Potomac Flotilla, dispatch boat 1861. Operations in Nansemond River, Va., 11 Apr–4 May 1863. Expedition up Nansemond River, Va., 13–14 Apr 1864. Decomm 23 Jun 1865. Sold 12 Jul 1865.
Prizes: 9 Nov 1864: *Little Elmer* and *Reliance*.
Later history: Merchant *Cambridge* 1865. Converted to barge 1871. FFU.

Name	Bldr	Built	Acquired	Comm
Westfield	Simonson (Morgan)	1861	22 Nov 1861	Jan 1862

Tonnage:	891 tons B
Dimensions:	215′ × 35′ × d13′6″
Machinery:	Side wheels. 1 vertical beam engine (50″ × 10′)
Complement:	116
Armament:	1 100-pdr R, 1 9″ SB, 4 8″/55

SERVICE RECORD: Passage past New Orleans forts and engagement with CSN vessels, 24 Apr 1862. Bombardment of Vicksburg, 26–28 Jun 1862. Bombardment and capture of Galveston, Tex., 4 Oct 1862. Burst gun during bombardment of Lavaca, Tex., 31 Oct–1 Nov 1862. Blown up to prevent capture when Confederates recaptured Galveston, 1 Jan 1863.

Name	Bldr	Built	Acquired	Comm
Whitehall	Burtis (U)	1850	10 Oct 1861	Oct 1861

Tonnage:	326 tons B
Dimensions:	126′ (keel) × 28′2″ × 8′, d10′
Machinery:	Side wheels, inclined engine (36″ × 8′)
Complement:	(U)
Armament:	2 30-pdr R, 2 32-pdr/33

SERVICE RECORD: SAtlBS 1861. Unable to reach station because of poor condition. Engaged CSS *Sea Bird* in Hampton Roads, 29 Dec 1861. Damaged during Battle of Hampton Roads, 8 Mar 1862. Destroyed by fire off Fortress Monroe, 10 Mar 1862.

SMALL STERNWHEEL COMBATANTS — 4TH RATE

Name	Bldr	Built	Acquired
Barataria (ex-CSS *Barataria*)	(New Orleans)	1857	1 Jan 1863

Tonnage:	400 or 52 tons
Dimensions:	125′ × (U) × 3′6″
Machinery:	Stern wheel
Armament:	3 guns

NOTES: Ironclad gunboat, captured at New Orleans, April 1862. One-inch armor plating. Little known about this vessel. Also spelled *Barrataria*.
SERVICE RECORD: WGulfBS 1863. Struck a snag in Lake Maurepas and burned to prevent capture, 7 Apr 1863.

Name	Bldr	Built	Acquired	Comm
Bloomer	(New Albany, Ind.)	1856	1 Jan 1863	24 Jan 1863

Tonnage:	130 or 95 tons
Dimensions:	(U)
Machinery:	Stern wheel, HP engine
Complement:	49
Armament:	Feb 64: 1 32-pdr/57, 1 12-pdr R.

NOTES: Captured by USS *Charlotte* in Choctawatchie River, Fla., 24 Dec 1862.
SERVICE RECORD: EGulfBS 1863–65. Operations in St. Andrews Bay, Fla. 10–18 Dec 1863. Wrecked on coast of Florida, Jun 1865; salved. Sold 22 Sep 1865.
Later history: Merchant *Emma* 1865. Sold foreign 1868.

SMALL SCREW COMBATANTS — 4TH RATE

Name	Bldr	L	Acquired	Comm
Acacia (ex-*Vicksburg*)	(East Boston)	Sep 1863	28 Oct 1863	Dec 1863

Tonnage:	300 tons B
Dimensions:	125′ × 23′2″ × 11′6″
Machinery:	1 screw, 1 condensing engine (36″ × 3′), 1 boiler; 12 knots
Complement:	58
Armament:	2 30-pdr R, 1 12-pdr R, 1 12-pdr SB

NOTES: Schooner rig.
SERVICE RECORD: SAtlBS 1864–65. Decomm 12 May 1865. Sold 20 Jun 1865.
Prize: 23 Dec 1864: str *Julia*.
Later history: Merchant *Wabash* 1865. RR 1881.

Name	Bldr	Built	Acquired	Comm
Anacostia (ex-M.W. Chapin)	(Philadelphia)	1856	17 Oct 1858	28 Jul 1859

Tonnage:	217 tons B, 358 n/r
Dimensions:	129′ × 23′ × 6′, d5′
Machinery:	1 screw, 1 vertical direct-acting engine (24″ × 2′); 7.5 knots
Complement:	67
Armament:	1861: 2 9″ SB. 1864: add 1 30-pdr R, 1 12-pdr SB. Apr 65: 1 50-pdr replaced by 1 30-pdr R.

NOTES: Chartered for Paraguay Expedition 1858–59, purchased 1859 and renamed.
SERVICE RECORD: Potomac Flotilla 1861–65. Engaged batteries at Aquia Creek, Va., 29 May–1 Jun, at Freestone Pt., Va., 9 Dec 1861, and at Cockpit Pt., Va., 1 Jan 1862. Army operations at Gloucester and York, Va., 14–29 Apr 1862. Engaged batteries at Port Royal, Va., 4 Dec 1862. Expedition to Northern Neck, Va., 12 Jan 1865. Decomm 13 Jun 1865. Sold 20 Jul 1865.
Prizes: 20 Apr 1862: str *Eureka*; 6 Jun: *Monitor*; 28 Dec: *Exchange*. 21 May 1863: *Emily*; 2 Jun: *Flying Cloud*. 9 Nov 1864: *Buckskin*.
Later history: Merchant *Alexandria* 1865. Burned at City Point, Va., 22 Mar 1868.

Name	Bldr	Built	Acquired
Curlew	(Williamsburg, NY)	1853	15 Sep 1861

Tonnage:	392 tons B
Dimensions:	126′2″ × 32′8″ × 8′, d12′ 8″
Machinery:	1 screw
Complement:	88
Armament:	6 32-pdr/57, 1 20-pdr R. Feb 63 total: 8 24-pdr H.

SERVICE RECORD: Operations at Port Royal and Beaumont, SC, 5–9 Nov 1861. Transferred to War Dept., 16 Jan 1862.
Later history: Merchant *South Side* 1866. RR 1912.

Name	Bldr	Built	Acquired	Comm
Currituck (ex-Seneca)	(New York, NY)	1843	20 Sep 1861	27 Feb 1862

Tonnage:	193 tons B
Dimensions:	120′ × 23′ × d7′6″
Machinery:	1 screw, 1 direct-acting engine (22″ × 2′)
Complement:	52
Armament:	1 32-pdr/57, 1 20-pdr R. May 64: add 3 32-pdr/57.

NOTES: Wooden hull, schooner rig.
SERVICE RECORD: Towed *Monitor* from New York to Hampton Roads, Mar 1862. Potomac Flotilla 1862–65. Army operations at Yorktown,

Va., 4–7 May 1862. Expedition up Pamunkey River, Va., 17 May 1862. Engaged batteries at Port Royal, Va., 4 Dec 1862. Decomm 7 Aug 1865. Sold 15 Sep 1865.
Prizes: 4 May 1862: *Director*; 5 May: *Water Witch*; 7 May: *American Coaster* and *Planter*. 3 Jan 1863: *Potter*; 13 Jan: *Hampton*; 25 Jan: *Queen of the Fleet*; 14 May: *Ladies Delight*; 21 May: *Emily*; 21 Oct: *Three Brothers*.
Later history: Merchant *Arlington* 1865. Burned at Mobile, Ala., 23 Nov 1870.

Name	Bldr	Built	Acquired	Comm
Dragon	(Buffalo, NY)	1861	Dec 1861	1862

Tonnage:	118 tons B
Dimensions:	92′ × 17′ × d9′6″
Machinery:	1 screw
Complement:	42
Armament:	1 30-pdr R, 1 24-pdr SB

SERVICE RECORD: NAtlBS 1862. Damaged by shell from CSS *Virginia* at battle of Hampton Roads, 8 Mar 1862. James Flotilla 1862. Potomac Flotilla Aug 1862–65. Engaged batteries near Ft. Lowry, Va., 21 Feb 1863. Decomm 13 May 1865. Sold 29 Jul 1865.
Prize: 6 May 1863: *Samuel First*.
Later history: Merchant *Brandt* 1865. RR 1880.

Name	Bldr	Built	Acquired	Comm
E.B. Hale (ex-Edmund B. Hale)	(Sleightsburg, NY)	1861	27 Jul 1861	4 Sep 1861

Tonnage:	220 tons B
Dimensions:	117′ × 28′ × 8′6″
Machinery:	1 screw, 1 vertical engine (26″ × 2′2″); 8 knots
Complement:	50
Armament:	4 32-pdr/42. Feb 63: add 1 20-pdr R. May 63 total: 1 30-pdr R, 4 32-pdr/42.

SERVICE RECORD: Potomac Flotilla 1861. SAtlBS 1862. Army operations at Port Royal Ferry, SC, 31 Dec 1861–2 Jan 1862. Bombardment at St. Johns Bluff, Fla., 17 Sep 1862. Expeditions to St. Johns Bluff, Fla., 1–3 Oct 1862, and up Ashepoo and S. Edisto rivers, SC, 25–27 May 1864. Decomm 11 May 1865. Sold 20 Jun 1865.
Prizes: 9 Oct 1862: str *Governor Milton*; 21 Oct: *Pilot*; 4 Nov: *Wave*.
Later history: Merchant *E.B. Hale*. RR 1867.

Name	Bldr	Built	Acquired
Eureka	(Georgetown, D.C.)	1861	22 Aug 1862

Tonnage:	32 tons
Dimensions:	85′ × 12′8″ × d3′6″
Machinery:	1 screw
Complement:	19
Armament:	2 12-pdr

NOTES: Captured 20 Apr 1862 in Rappahannock River by USS *Anacostia*.

SERVICE RECORD: Potomac Flotilla 1862–65. Expeditions up Nansemond River, Va., 13–14 Apr, and to Northern Neck, Va., 11–21 Jun 1864. Went aground in Nomini Creek, Va., 20 Dec 1864. Sold 15 Sep 1865.

Later history: FFU.

Name	Bldr	Built	Acquired	Comm
Fuchsia (ex-*Kiang Soo*)	Jewett (McLeod)	1862	16 Jun 1863	Aug 1863
Tulip (ex-*Chi Kiang*)	Jewett (McLeod)	1862	16 Jun 1863	1863

Tonnage:	240 tons B
Dimensions:	101'4" () 97'3" () × 21'9" × 8', d11'5"
Machinery:	1 screw, 2 horizontal direct-acting engines (20" × 2')
Complement:	43/57
Armament:	1 20-pdr R, 2 24-pdr H
	Fuchsia: Mar 64: 1 20-pdr R, 4 24-pdr H, 1 12-pdr R.
	Tulip: Sep 64: add 1 12-pdr SB.

NOTES: Lighthouse tenders build for F.T. Ward's Chinese Navy.

SERVICE RECORDS:

Fuchsia—Potomac Flotilla 1863–64. Expeditions in Machodoc Creek, Va., 13 Apr, in Rappahannock River, Va., 16–19 May, and to Northern Neck, Va., 11–21 Jun 1864. Decomm 5 Aug 1865. Sold 23 Sep 1865.

    Prize: 21 Oct 1862: *Three Brothers*.

    Later history: Merchant *Donald* 1865. RR 1889.

Tulip—Potomac Flotilla Aug 1863–64. Expedition to Northern Neck, Va., 12 Jan 1864. Sunk by boiler explosion off Ragged Point, Va., 11 Nov 1864.

The small screw steamer *Fuchsia*, which operated in Virginia waters during the war. *Fuchsia* and *Tulip* and the larger *Dai Ching* were built for Frederick Townsend Ward's "Ever Victorious Army" in China, but after Ward's death they were taken for U.S. Naval service. (U.S. Naval Historical Center)

Name	Bldr	Built	Acquired	Comm
Henry Brinker	(Brooklyn, NY)	1861	29 Oct 1861	15 Dec 1861

Tonnage:	108 tons B
Dimensions:	82' × 26'7" × 7'
Machinery:	1 screw, 2 vertical engines (18" × 1'8"), 1 boiler; 7 knots
Complement:	18
Armament:	1 30-pdr R. Sep 64: add 2 12-pdr.

SERVICE RECORD: NAtlBS Jan 1862–Nov 1863. Engagement with enemy vessels, capture of Elizabeth City, NC, and expedition to Edenton, 10–12 Feb 1862. Landings at Roanoke I., NC, 7–8 Feb 1862. Capture of New Bern, NC, 13–14 Mar 1862. Inactive at Newport News 1864–65. Decomm 29 Jun 1865. Sold 20 Jul 1865.

Later history: FFU.

Name	Bldr	Built	Acquired	Comm
Howquah	(East Boston, Mass)	1863	17 Jun 1863	1 Sep 1863

Tonnage:	397 tons B
Dimensions:	120'7" × 22'10" × 12'
Machinery:	1 screw, 1 vertical engine (36" × 3'); 10 knots
Complement:	55
Armament:	2 30-pdr R, 2 12-pdr R. Apr 64 total: 3 30-pdr R, 1 12-pdr R, 112-pdr HSB.

NOTES: Wooden hull.

SERVICE RECORD: NAtlBS 1863–65. Engagement with CSS *Raleigh* off New Inlet, NC, 6–7 May 1864. Unsuccessful attack on Ft. Fisher, NC, 24–25 Dec 1864. Second attack on Ft. Fisher, 13–15 Jan 1865. Bombardment of Masonboro Inlet, NC, 11 Feb 1865. EGulfBS 1865. Decomm 22 Jun 1865. Sold 10 Aug 1865.

Prizes: 5 Nov 1863: str *Margaret & Jessie*; 10 Nov: str *Ella*. 25 Sep 1864: str *Lynx.

Later history: Merchant *Equator* 1865. RR 1883.

Name	Bldr	L	Acquired	Comm
Little Ada	Simons (U)	23 Dec 1863	18 Aug 1864	5 Oct 1864

Tonnage:	150 tons B, 236 GRT
Dimensions:	112' × 18'6" × 8', d10'
Machinery:	1 screw, 2 direct-acting engines (22" × 1'8"), 1 boiler; IHP 100 = 10 knots.
Complement:	27/53
Armament:	2 20-pdr R

NOTES: Blockade runner, captured by USS *Gettysburg* in South Santee River, 9 Jul 1864. Iron hull.

SERVICE RECORD: NAtlBS 1864–65. Unsuccessful attack on Ft. Fisher, NC, 24–25 Dec 1864. Second attack on Ft. Fisher, 13–15 Jan 1865. Bombardment of Ft. Anderson, Cape Fear River, 18 Feb 1865. Potomac Flotilla 1865. Decomm 24 Jun 1865. Transferred to War Dept. 12 Aug 1865.

Later history: War Dept. *Ada* 1865. Transferred to Coast Survey. Merchant *Peter Smith* 1878. Canadian, renamed *Little Ada* 1909.

Renamed *Buxton* 1921. Renamed *Betty Jane Hearn* 1923. Renamed *Poling Bros. No. 2* 1928. Sunk in ice off Great Captains Island, Conn., 2 Jun 1940.

Name	Bldr	Built	Acquired
Madgie	(Philadelphia)	1858	15 Oct 1861

Tonnage:	220 tons B
Dimensions:	122′6″ × 22′7″ × d8′5″
Machinery:	1 screw, direct-acting engine
Complement:	45
Armament:	1 8″/63, 1 30-pdr R. Mar 62 total: 1 30-pdr R, 1 20-pdr R. May 63: add 2 24-pdr H, 1 12-pdr SB.

NOTES: Wooden hull.
SERVICE RECORD: SAtlBS 1862–63. Bombardment of Ft. McAllister, Ogeechee River, Ga., 29 Jul 1862. Foundered in tow off Frying Pan Shoals, NC, 11 Oct 1863.
Prize: 20 Jun 1862: *Southern Belle*.

Name	Bldr	Built	Acquired
Naugatuck (ex-USRC *E.A. Stevens*, ex-*Naugatuck*)	Dunham (U)	1844	1862

Tonnage:	192 tons B
Dimensions:	110′ () 101′ (bp) × 21′6″ × 6′
Machinery:	2 screws, 2 inclined engines (16″ × 2′), 1 boiler
Complement:	22
Armament:	1 100-pdr R, 2 12-pdr R, 2 12-pdr H. Nov 62 total: 1 6-pdr R, 1 42-pdr R.

NOTES: Loaned to government by John Stevens, taken into Revenue Service and loaned to the Navy. Originally built with single screw, used by Stevens as experimental vessel. Fitted out as twin-screw ironclad to demonstrate plans for "Stevens Battery," including plan of protection in which forward and aft compartments were flooded to submerge the hull partially, increasing draft to 9′10″. As a result of the gun explosion 15 May 1862, protection plan was never tested. Twelve-inch gun was loaded from below by depressing barrel.
SERVICE RECORD: NAtlBS 1862. Engaged batteries at Sewells Point, Va., 8 May 1862, and at Drewry's Bluff, Va., 15 May 1862 (gun exploded). Returned to USRCS.
Later history: USRC *E.A. Stevens* 1862. (q.v.)

Name	Bldr	L	Acquired	Comm
New London	Greenman (Delamater)	5 Oct 1859	26 Aug 1861	29 Oct 1861

Tonnage:	221 tons B
Dimensions:	135′ () 125′ () × 26′ × 9′6″, d7′8″
Machinery:	1 screw, 1 vertical direct-acting engine, 1 boiler; 9.5 knots
Complement:	47
Armament:	1 20-pdr R, 4 32-pdr/57. Apr 62: 1 32-pdr/57 replaced by 1 42-pdr R. Dec 63 total: 1 20-pdr R, 1 8″ SB, 3 32-pdr/57.

NOTES: Wooden hull, three masted schooner rig.

SERVICE RECORD: GulfBS 1861–65. Engagement at Pass Christian, Miss., 25 Mar and 4 Apr 1862. Bombardment below Donaldsonville, La., 7 Jul and at Whitehall Point., La. (disabled), 10 Jul 1863. Decomm 3 Aug 1865. Sold 8 Sep 1865.
Prizes: 21 Nov 1861: *Olive*; 22 Nov: str *Anna*; 28 Nov: *A.J. View* and str *Henry Lewis*; 1 Dec: *Advocate*; 9 Dec: *Delight, Osceola, Express*; 28 Dec: *Gypsy*; 31 Dec: *Capt. Spedden*. 12 Apr 1862: **Zulima*. 2 Apr 1863: *Tampico*; 3 Dec: *Raton Del Nilo*.
Later history: Merchant *Acushnet* 1865. RR 1910.

Name	Bldr	Built	Acquired	Comm
Norwich	(Norwich, Conn.)	1861	26 Sep 1861	28 Dec 1861

Tonnage:	431 tons B, 329 n/r
Dimensions:	132′5″ × 24′6″ × 10′, d16′5″
Machinery:	1 screw, 1 vertical direct-acting engine (34″ × 2′6″), 1 boiler; 6 knots
Complement:	80
Armament:	1862: 1 30-pdr R, 4 8″/55.

NOTES: Wooden hull.
SERVICE RECORD: SAtlBS 1862, blockade of Savannah. Assault on Jacksonville, Fla., 2–22 Feb 1864. Decomm 30 Jun 1865. Sold 10 Aug 1865.
Prizes: 1 Feb 1864: str **Wild Dayrell*; 7 Feb: str **St. Mary's*.
Later history: Merchant *Norwich* 1865. Foundered at sea, 17 Feb 1873.

Name	Bldr	Built	Acquired	Comm
Patroon	(Philadelphia)	1859	28 Oct 1861	18 Mar 1862

Tonnage:	183 tons B
Dimensions:	113′ × 22′5″ × 7′
Machinery:	1 screw
Complement:	49
Armament:	1 20-pdr R, 4 32-pdr/33

NOTES: Wooden hull. Hull in poor condition when purchased.
SERVICE RECORD: SAtlBS 1862. Bombardment at St. Johns Bluff, Fla., 17 Sep 1862. Expedition to Pocotaligo, SC, 21–23 Oct 1862. Decomm 18 Nov 1862. Sold 30 Dec 1862.
Later history: Purchased by War Dept., 8 Dec 1863. Sunk at Brazos, Tex., 10 Nov 1865.

Name	Bldr	Built	Acquired	Comm
R.B. Forbes	Otis Tufts (U)	1845	17 Aug 1861	Aug 1861

Tonnage:	329 tons B
Dimensions:	121′ × 25′6″ × 12′3″
Machinery:	2 screws, 2 inclined condensing engines (36″ × 3′), 1 boiler; 11 knots
Complement:	51
Armament:	2 32-pdr/47. Jan 62: 1 30-pdr R, 1 32-pdr/57.

NOTES: Iron hull wrecking tug. In service before formal acquisition, 20 Sep 1861.

SERVICE RECORD: SAtlBS Oct–Dec 1861. Occupation of Port Royal, SC, 7 Nov 1861. Driven ashore in gale and wrecked south of Currituck Inlet, NC, 25 Feb 1862.

Name	Bldr	Built	Acquired	Comm
Sachem	(New York)	1844	20 Sep 1861	1861

Tonnage:	197 tons B
Dimensions:	121' × 23'6" × d7'6"
Machinery:	1 screw
Complement:	52
Armament:	1 20-pdr R, 4 32-pdr/57

SERVICE RECORD: Survey ship for attack on New Orleans forts, Mar–Apr 1862. Engaged enemy while blockading Aransas Pass, Tex., Jun 1862. Damaged while defending Galveston against enemy attack, 31 Dec 1862. Disabled by enemy batteries during attack on Sabine Pass, Tex., and captured, 8 Sep 1863.

Later history: (see CSN)

Name	Bldr	Built	Acquired
Teaser	(Philadelphia)	1855?	4 Jul 1862
(ex-CSS Teaser, maybe ex-Wide Awake?)			

Tonnage:	64 tons
Dimensions:	80' × 18' × d7'
Machinery:	1 screw, 1 engine (20" × 1'8"), 1 boiler
Complement:	25
Armament:	1862: 1 32-pdr R. Jan 64 total: 1 50-pdr R, 1 24-pdr H. Dec 64: 1 50-pdr R replaced by 1 30-pdr R.

NOTES: Captured in James River by USS Maratanza after being disabled in action, 4 Jul 1862. Wooden-hulled tug.

SERVICE RECORD: Potomac Flotilla Sep 1862. Bombardment of Brandywine Hill, Rappahannock River, Va., 10 Dec 1862. Operations in Nansemond River, Va., 11 Apr–4 May 1863. Expedition in Machodoc Creek, Va., 13 Apr 1864. Decomm 2 Jun 1865. Sold 25 Jun 1865.

Prize: 6 Nov 1862: Grapeshot.

Later history: Merchant York River 1865. RR 1873.

Name	Bldr	Built	Acquired	Comm
Uncas	(New York)	1843	20 Sep 1861	14 Oct 1861

Tonnage:	192 tons B
Dimensions:	118'6" × 23'4" × 7'6"
Machinery:	1 screw, 1 vertical engine; 11.5 knots
Complement:	62/82
Armament:	1 20-pdr R, 2 32-pdr/57. Apr 63: add 2 32-pdr/57.

NOTES: Purchased for Coast Survey. Machinery unreliable.

SERVICE RECORD: WGulfBS Apr 1862. Surveyed Mississippi River for attack on New Orleans, Apr 1862. SAtlBS Apr 1862. Expedition to St.

Johns Bluff, Fla., 1–12 Oct, and to Pocotaligo, SC, 21–23 Oct 1862. Decomm and sold 21 Aug 1863.

Prize: 26 Apr 1862: Belle.

Later history: Merchant Claymont 1863. RR 1886.

Name	Bldr	Built	Acquired	Comm
Valley City	Birely (U)	1859	26 Jul 1861	13 Sep 1861

Tonnage:	190 tons B, 318 n/r
Dimensions:	133' () 127'6" () × 21'10" × 8'4"
Machinery:	1 screw, 1 vertical engine (24" × 2'), 1 boiler; 10 knots
Complement:	48/82
Armament:	4 32-pdr/42. Dec 64: 4 32-pdr/42, 2 20-pdr R, 1 12-pdr.

NOTES: Wooden hull.

SERVICE RECORD: Potomac Flotilla 1861. Bombardment at Freestone Point, Va., 25 Sep 1861. NAtlBS 1862. Landings at Roanoke I., NC, 7–8 Feb 1862. Engagement with enemy vessels, capture of Elizabeth City, NC, and expedition to Edenton, 10–12 Feb 1862. Damaged during capture of New Bern, NC, 13–14 Mar 1862. Expedition to Hamilton, NC, 31 Oct–7 Nov 1862, and in Chowan River, NC, 26–30 Jul 1863. Damaged in collision with transport Vidette, 21 Sep 1863. Expedition to Pungo River, NC, 16–21 Jun 1864. Capture of Plymouth, NC, Roanoke River, 29–31 Oct 1864. Expedition to Poplar Point, NC, 9–28 Dec 1864. Sold 15 Aug 1865.

Prizes: 5 May 1864: M. O'Neill. 10 Jan 1865: str Philadelphia.

Later history: Merchant Valley City, 1865. Foundered off Cape San Blas, Fla., 30 Jan 1882.

Name	Bldr	Built	Acquired	Comm
Victoria	(Philadelphia)	1855	26 Dec 1861	13 Mar 1862

Tonnage:	254 tons B
Dimensions:	119'9" () 113' () × 23' × 12', d9'3"
Machinery:	1 screw, 1 vertical direct-acting engine (28" × 2'6"), 1 boiler; 12 knots
Complement:	44
Armament:	1 30-pdr R, 2 8"/63

NOTES: Wooden hull, in yard for repairs many times because of poor condition of hull.

SERVICE RECORD: NAtlBS 1862–64. Blockade of Wilmington. Damaged in collision with USS Cherokee, summer 1864. Decomm 4 May 1865. Sold 30 Nov 1865.

Prizes: 28 May 1862: str Nassau; 26 Jun: *Emily. 18 Feb 1863: Minna; 21 Mar: str Nicolai I. 2 Jun 1864: str *Georgianna McCaw.

Later history: Merchant Victoria 1866. RR 1871.

Name	Bldr	L	Acquired	Comm
Wamsutta	Capes (Delamater)	13 Aug 1853	20 Sep 1861	14 Mar 1862

Tonnage:	270 tons B
Dimensions:	129'3" × 26'8" × 11', d8'6"
Machinery:	1 screw, 1 vertical engine, 1 boiler; 9 knots

Complement: 57
Armament: 1 20-pdr R, 4 32-pdr/57.

SERVICE RECORD: SAtlBS 1862–65. In collision with steamer *Mayflower*, Nov 1862. Decomm 29 Jun 1865. Sold 20 Jul 1865. *Prizes*: 8 May 1863: *Amelia*. 2 Jun 1864: str **Rose*; 22 Oct: str **Flora*. 4 Feb 1865: **unidentified str.
Later history: Merchant *Wamsutta* 1865. Converted to barge 1879.

Name	Bldr	Built	Acquired	Comm
Whitehead	(New Brunswick, NJ)	1861	17 Oct 1861	19 Nov 1861

Tonnage: 132 tons D
Dimensions: 93' × 19'9" × 8'
Machinery: 1 screw, 2 inclined engines (18" × 1'8"), 1 boiler
Complement: 45
Armament: Jan 62: 1 9" SB. May 63: 1 100-pdr R, 3 24-pdr H.

SERVICE RECORD: NAtlBS 1861–62. Engagement with CSS *Patrick Henry* near Newport News, 2 Dec 1861. Landings at Roanoke I., NC, 7–8 Feb 1862. Engagement with enemy vessels, capture of Elizabeth City, NC, and expedition to Edenton, 10–12 Feb 1862. Reconnaissance to Winton, NC, Chowan River, 18–20 Feb 1862. Expedition to block Chesapeake & Albemarle Canal, 23 Apr 1862. Operations at Franklin, Va., 3 Oct 1862. Expeditions in Chowan River, 26–30 Jul 1863, and 1–2 Mar 1864. Engagement with CSS *Albemarle* at Plymouth, NC, 5 May 1864. Capture of Plymouth, Roanoke River, 29–31 Oct 1864. Decomm 29 Jun 1865. Sold 10 Aug 1865.
Prizes: 10 Apr 1862: *America*, *Comet*, *J.J. Crittenden*; 20 May: *Eugenia*; 22 May: *Ella D.* 28 Jul 1864: str *Arrow*.
Later history: Merchant *Nevada* 1865. Destroyed by fire at New London, Conn., 1 Sep 1872.

SIDE-WHEEL AUXILIARIES—4TH RATE

Name	Bldr	Built	Acquired
Baltimore	(Philadelphia)	1848	22 Apr 1861

Tonnage: 500 tons B
Dimensions: 200' × 26'8" × d10'
Machinery: Side wheels
Complement: 18
Armament: 1 32-pdr/42

NOTES: Captured as Confederate steamer in Potomac River, 21 Apr 1861. Wooden hull.
SERVICE RECORD: Ordnance vessel, Washington NYd. Transported Pres. Lincoln and party to Norfolk, 9 May 1862. Sold 24 Jun 1865.
Later history: Merchant *Baltimore* 1865. Lost 1866. RR 1868.

Name	Bldr	Built	Acquired	Comm
Cactus (ex-*Polar Star*)	(Brooklyn, NY)	1863	9 Dec 1863	4 May 1864

Tonnage: 176 tons B
Dimensions: 110' × 22'6" × 7'
Machinery: Side wheels, 1 LP engine (31" × 7'); 15 knots
Complement: 39
Armament: 1 30-pdr R, 1 12-pdr R, 1 12-pdr SB

SERVICE RECORD: NAtlBS 1864. Supply ship. Decomm 8 Jun 1865.
Later history: To U.S. Lighthouse Board, 20 Jun 1865, sold 1910. Merchant *Prospect* 1910. RR 1921.

Name	Bldr	Built	Acquired
Chatham	(Fayetteville, NC)	1852	22 Jun 1864

Tonnage: 198 tons B
Dimensions: 120' × 26' × 7'7"
Machinery: Side wheels
Complement: 26
Armament: None

NOTES: Confederate vessel, captured in Doboy Sound by USS *Huron*, 16 Dec 1863. Possibly the iron-hulled ship built by Laird in England 1836 and reassembled in Savannah.
SERVICE RECORD: SAtlBS 1864. Transport and store vessel, Port Royal. Decomm Apr 1865. Sold 2 Sep 1865.
Later history: Merchant *Chatham* 1865. RR 1868.

Name	Bldr	Built	Acquired
Darlington	(Charleston, SC)	1849	3 Mar 1862

Tonnage: 298 tons
Dimensions: 132'6" × 30' × d8'4"
Machinery: Side wheels, 1 horizontal crosshead HP engine
Complement: 23
Armament: 2 24-pdr H

NOTES: Captured in Cumberland Sound by USS *Pawnee*, 3 Mar 1862.
SERVICE RECORD: Expedition to St. Johns Bluff, Fla., 1–12 Oct, and to Pocotaligo, SC, 21–23 Oct 1862. Transferred to War Dept., Sep 1862.
Later history: Merchant *Darlington* 1866. BU 1874.

Name	Bldr	Built	Comm
Donegal (ex-*Donegal*, ex-*Austin*)	Harlan (bldr)	1860	3 Sep 1864

Tonnage: 1,150 tons B, 951 n/r
Dimensions: 200' × 36' × 8', d10'6"
Machinery: Side wheels, 1 vertical beam engine (44" × 11'), 1 boiler; 10 knots
Complement: 80/130
Armament: 2 20-pdr R, 2 12-pdr SB

NOTES: Blockade runner, captured off Mobile by USS *Metacomet*, 6 Jun 1864. Iron hull, two masts, one funnel. Built for Charles Morgan's New Orleans-Galveston service.
SERVICE RECORD: Supply ship, SAtlBS 1864. Blockade duty 1865.

Decomm 8 Sep and sold 27 Sep 1865.
Later history: Merchant *Austin* 1865. Struck a wreck in Mississippi River below New Orleans and sank, 6 Jun 1876.

Name	Bldr	Built	Acquired	Comm
Ella	(New York)	1859	30 Jul 1862	10 Aug 1862

Tonnage:	230 tons B
Dimensions:	150′ × 23′ × d8′6″
Machinery:	Side wheels, 1 engine (36″ × 8′); 8 knots
Complement:	39
Armament:	1862: 2 24-pdr H. May 63: 1 12-pdr SBH, 1 12-pdr HR.

SERVICE RECORD: Potomac Flotilla, picket and despatch boat 1862–65. Decomm 4 Aug 1865. Sold 15 Sep 1865.
Later history: Merchant *Ella* 1865. RR 1875.

Name	Bldr	L	Comm
Glasgow (ex-*Eugenie*)	Samuelson (U)	9 Jul 1861	9 Jul 1863

Tonnage:	252 tons B, 428 GRT
Dimensions:	235′ × 24′3″ × 6′9″, d11′9″
Machinery:	Side wheels, 2 oscillating engines (58″ × 4′6″); 13 knots
Complement:	30
Armament:	1 12-pdr H, 1 12-pdr R. Feb 64: None. Dec 65 total: 1 20-pdr R, 1 12-pdr.

NOTES: Blockade runner *Eugenie*, captured by USS *R.R. Cuyler* off Mobile Bay, 6 May 1863. Former South Eastern Railway cross-channel steamer. Renamed 21 Jan 1864.
SERVICE RECORD: WGulfBS, despatch and supply ship. 1863. Sank after hitting a submerged obstruction off Mobile, 8 May 1865; raised 19 Jun. Store ship 1866–68. Decomm 17 Oct 1868. Sold 4 Jun 1869.
Later history: British merchant *Hilda* 1869. BU 1889.

Name	Bldr	L	Acquired	Comm
Honduras	Collyer (Neptune)	22 May 1861	31 Jul 1863	8 Sep 1863

Tonnage:	376 tons B
Dimensions:	150′ × 27′ × 9′, d10′2″
Machinery:	Side wheels, 1 vertical beam engine (38″ × 8′), 1 boiler; 12 knots
Complement:	57
Armament:	1 20-pdr R, 2 24-pdr H, 2 12-pdr R

NOTES: Wood, two masts.
SERVICE RECORD: EGulfBS 1863. Supply ship and despatch boat. Occupation of Tampa, Fla., 4–7 May 1864. Expedition to St. Marks, Fla., 23 Feb–27 Mar 1865. Sold 5 Sep 1865.
Prize: 15 Oct 1863: str *Mail*.
Later history: Merchant *Governor Marvin* 1865. Wrecked off Key West, 1870.

The *Honduras* served as a despatch vessel off the west coast of Florida. (Martin Holbrook Collection) (U.S. Naval Historical Center)

Name	Bldr	Built	Acquired	Comm
Ice Boat (Kensington, Pa)		1837	23 Apr 1861	23 Apr 1861
(Ex-*Philadelphia Ice Boat*)				

Tonnage:	526 tons
Dimensions:	(U)
Machinery:	Side wheels
Complement:	50
Armament:	4 32 pdr

NOTES: Icebreaker. Loaned by City of Philadelphia.
SERVICE RECORD: Served in area of Washington, D.C., and Chesapeake Bay, 1861. Returned to Philadelphia, Nov 1861.

Name	Bldr	Built	Acquired	Comm
King Philip	Robinson (U)	1845	21 Apr 1861	28 Apr 1861
(ex-*Powhatan*)				

Tonnage:	309 tons B
Dimensions:	204′ × 22′11″ × d8′
Machinery:	Side wheels
Complement:	14
Armament:	1 gun

NOTES: Renamed 4 Nov 1861.
SERVICE RECORD: Despatch vessel in Potomac and Rappahannock rivers, 1861–65. Sold 15 Sep 1865.
Later history: FFU.

Name	Bldr	Built	Acquired	Comm
Philadelphia	Reaney Neafie (bldr)	1859	22 Apr 1861	Apr 1861

Tonnage:	504 tons B
Dimensions:	200′ × 30′ × 7′6″, d10′
Machinery:	Side wheels, 1 vertical beam engine (45″ × 11′), 1 boiler; 8 knots
Complement:	24
Armament:	2 12-pdr R

NOTES: Iron hull. Built for service between Norfolk and Baltimore.
SERVICE RECORD: Operated in Potomac area as transport ferry. NAtlBS Oct 1861–62. Capture of New Bern, NC, 13–14 Mar 1862.

SAtlBS Aug 1863–65 (flag). Decomm 31 Aug 1865. Sold 15 Sep 1865.
Later history: Merchant *Philadelphia* 1865. *Ironsides*, 1869. Stranded at Hog Island, Va., 29 Aug 1873.

Name	Bldr	Built	Acquired	Comm
Phlox	(Boston)	1864	2 Aug 1864	14 Sep 1864
(ex-*F.W. Lincoln*)				

Tonnage:	317 tons B
Dimensions:	145′ × 24′ × 6′, d9′
Machinery:	Side wheels, 1 overhead beam engine (28″ × 7′6″), 1 boiler; 12 knots
Complement:	32
Armament:	(U)

NOTES: Wooden hull.
SERVICE RECORD: NAtlBS 1864. Used as despatch vessel. Decomm 28 Jul 1865. Practice ship, Naval Academy. Sold 1894.

Name	Bldr	Built	Acquired
Wyandank	(New York)	1847	12 Sep 1861

Tonnage:	399 tons D
Dimensions:	132′5″ × 31′5″ × d10′10″
Machinery:	Side wheels
Complement:	45
Armament:	1861: 2 12-pdr SB. Jul 65 total: 1 20-pdr R, 1 12-pdr SB.

NOTES: Wooden-hulled ferry. Storeship.
SERVICE RECORD: Potomac Flotilla storeship 1861–65. Floating barracks, Annapolis. BU 1879.
Prizes: 5 Sep 1862: *Rising Sun*; 22 Sep: *Southerner*. 24 Feb 1863: *Thomas C. Worrell*; 28 Feb: *A.W. Thompson* and *Vista*. 14 Mar 1865: *Champanero*.

SCREW AUXILIARIES – 4TH RATE

Name	Bldr	Built	Acquired	Comm
Admiral	Pook (U)	1863	8 Jan 1864	5 Feb 1864

Tonnage:	1,248 tons B
Dimensions:	220′ () 209′ () × 34′6″ × 14′, d10′6″
Machinery:	1 screw, 2 vertical direct-acting engines (36″ × 3′), 1 boiler
Complement:	(U)
Armament:	1 30-pdr R, 1 12-pdr R, 2 24-pdr H

SERVICE RECORD: Storeship, GulfBS 1864–65. Renamed **Fort Morgan**, 1 Sep 1864. Decomm 22 Aug 1865. Sold 5 Sep 1865.
Prizes: 28 May 1864: str *Isabel*; 5 Nov: *John A. Hazard*; 6 Nov: *Lone*.
Later history: Merchant *Cuba* 1865. Reported fitting out as a Fenian privateer 1866. Converted to schooner 1879. RR 1892.

The side-wheel steamer *Philadelphia* served as flagship of the South Atlantic Blockading Squadron. An artist's impression.

Name	Bldr	Built	Acquired	Comm
Arkansas (ex-*Tonawanda*)	Cramp (U)	1863	27 Jun 1863	5 Sep 1863

Tonnage:	752 tons B
Dimensions:	191′ () 176′ () × 30′ × 14′, d19′
Machinery:	1 screw, 1 vertical direct-acting HP or LP engine (40″ × 2′6″); 15 knots
Complement:	88
Armament:	4 32-pdr/33, 1 12-pdr R. Oct 63: add 1 20-pdr R.

NOTES: Transport and tug. Barkentine rig, wooden hull.
SERVICE RECORD: WGulfBS 1863–65. Decomm 30 Jun 1865. Sold 20 Jul 1865.
Prize: 27 Sep 1864: *Watchful*.
Later history: Merchant *Tonawanda* 1865. Wrecked off Grecian Shoals, Fla., 28 Mar 1866.

Name	Bldr	L	Acquired	Comm
Bermuda	Pearse (Fossick)	9 Jul 1861	14 Oct 1862	13 May 1863

Tonnage:	1,238 tons B, 1,003 tons n/r
Dimensions:	211′ × 30′3″ × 16′8″, d21′2″
Machinery:	1 screw, 2 vertical direct-acting engines (45″ × 2′6″), 2 boilers; 11 knots
Complement:	(U)
Armament:	1 9″ SB, 2 30-pdr R

NOTES: Supply ship. Blockade runner, captured off Great Abaco Island by USS *Mercedita*, 27 Apr 1862. Iron hull.
SERVICE RECORD: WGulfBS 1863–65. Sold 21 Sep 1865.
Prizes: 14 Aug 1863: *Carmita*; 15 Aug: *Artist*; 2 Oct: *Florrie*; 14 Nov: *Mary Campbell*. 30 May 1864: *Fortunate*.
Later history: Merchant *General Meade* 1865. Sold foreign 1878.

Name	Bldr	Built	Acquired	Comm
Buckthorn (ex-*Signal*)	(East Haddam, Conn.)	1863	22 Dec 1863	7 Apr 1864

Tonnage:	128 tons B
Dimensions:	87′ × 22′ × d7′7″
Machinery:	1 screw; 8.5 knots
Complement:	22
Armament:	1 30-pdr R, 2 12-pdr SB

SERVICE RECORD: WGulfBS 1864. Tender and despatch vessel. Battle of Mobile Bay, 5 Aug 1864. Laid up 1868. Sold 7 Sep 1869.
Later history: Merchant *Buckthorn* 1869. RR 1900.

Name	Bldr	L	Acquired	Comm
Circassian	Hickson (Elder)	18 Jul 1856	8 Nov 1862	12 Dec 1862

Tonnage:	1,750 tons B, 1,457 n/r, 1,387 GRT
Dimensions:	255′ (Br) 241′ (US) × 39′ × 18′, d23′6″
Machinery:	1 screw, 1 geared beam engine (60″ × 4′); NHP 350 = 12 knots

Complement:	142
Armament:	4 9″ SB, 1 100-pdr R, 1 12-pdr R. Jan 64: add 1 30-pdr R.

NOTES: Blockade runner, captured off Cuba by USS *Somerset*, 4 May 1862. Iron hull, 3 masts, funnel aft of mainmast. Too slow. Built for North Atlantic Steam Nav. Co. (Galway Line) and used as a transport during the Sepoy Mutiny, 1857.
SERVICE RECORD: E&WGulfBS 1863–65, supply ship. Decomm 26 Apr 1865. Sold 22 Jun 1865.
Prizes: 16 Jun 1863: *John Wesley*; 9 Dec: str *Minna*.
Later history: Merchant *Circassian* 1865. Converted to full-rigged ship 1873. Wrecked in gale at Bridgehampton, Long Island, 11 Dec 1876.

Name	Bldr	L	Acquired	Comm
Fahkee	Williams (Pusey)	4 Nov 1862	15 Jul 1863	24 Sep 1863

Tonnage:	660 tons B, 601 n/r
Dimensions:	175′ (dk) 163′ () × 29′6″ × 13′3″, d18′
Machinery:	1 screw, 1 vertical direct-acting engine (36″ × 4′), 1 boiler; 12 knots
Complement:	73
Armament:	2 24-pdr H, 1 10-pdr R. Feb 64: add 2 24-pdr H.

NOTES: Built for China trade. Wooden hulled, hermaphrodite brig, 1 funnel.
SERVICE RECORD: NAtlBS 1863–65, Supply ship. SAtlBS Apr 1865. Decomm 28 Jun 1865. Sold 10 Aug 1865.
Prize: 3 Jan 1864: str *Bendigo*.
Later history: Merchant *Fahkee*. Canadian *Pictou* 1872. Probably burned and sank off Magdalen Island, 18 Nov 1873.

Name	Bldr	Built	Acquired	Comm
Home (ex-*Key West*)	Tucker (McLeod)	1862	14 Aug 1863	21 Aug 1863

Tonnage:	725 tons B, 618 n/r
Dimensions:	168′10″ (dk) × 29′9″ × 13′6″ or 10′
Machinery:	1 screw, 2 horizontal direct-acting engines (32″ × 2′2″), 2 boilers; 6 knots
Complement:	88
Armament:	2 24-pdr H, 1 12-pdr HR

NOTES: Wooden hull.
SERVICE RECORD: SAtlBS 1863. Accommodation ship for monitors, Charleston. Decomm 24 Aug 1865. Sold 16 Sep 1865.
Later history: Merchant *Key West* 1865. Wrecked off Cape Hatteras, NC, 12 Oct 1870.

Name	Bldr	L	Comm
John Hancock	Boston (Washington)	26 Oct 1850	19 Mar 1853

Tonnage:	230 tons B; 1853: 382 tons B
Dimensions:	113′ (bp) × 22′ × 10′6″; 1853: 165′6″ (oa) 151′ (bp) × 22′ × 10′6″

Machinery:	1 screw, 2 oscillating HP engines (20″ × 1.9′), 9 knots; 1853: 2 oscillating LP engines (20″ × 1.9′)
Complement:	20
Armament:	1 6-pdr SB

NOTES: Navy built, designed by Pook with original machinery by Copeland. Rebuilt, re-engined, and lengthened 1853 with bark rig; relaunched 24 Feb 1853.
SERVICE RECORD: N. Pacific Survey Exp 1853–54. Decomm 23 Aug 1856. Receiving ship, San Francisco. Sold 17 Aug 1865.
Later history: Merchant *John Hancock* 1865. Converted to schooner 1869.

Name	Bldr	Built	Acquired	Comm
Kensington	Lynn (Merrick)	1858	27 Jan 1862	15 Feb 1862

Tonnage:	1,052 tons B, 1,003 n/r
Dimensions:	195′ × 31′10″ × 18′
Machinery:	1 screw, 1 vertical direct-acting engine (56″ × 3′8″), 1 boiler; 10 knots
Complement:	72
Armament:	2 32-pdr/42, 1 30-pdr R

NOTES: Wooden hull. Operated between Philadelphia and Boston.
SERVICE RECORD: WGulfBS 1862–63. Supply and water vessel. Bombardment of Sabine Pass, 24–25 Sep 1863. NAtlBS Aug–Nov 1864, supply ship. Decomm 5 May 1865. Sold 12 Jul 1865.
Prizes: 13 Aug 1862: *Troy*; 25 Sep: *Velocity*; 1 Oct: *Adventure*; 6 Oct: *Dart*; Oct: *Conchita*, *Mary Ann, *Eliza*, str *Dan*; 11 Nov: *Course*; 12 Nov: *Maria*.
Later history: Merchant *Kensington* 1865. Sunk in collision with Argentine bark *Templar* off Carolina coast, 27 Jan 1871.

Name	Bldr	Built	Acquired	Comm
Mary Sanford	Mallory (U)	1862	13 Jul 1863	20 Aug 1863

Tonnage:	757 tons B, 442 n/r
Dimensions:	162′ × 31′6″ × 12′6″, d16′9″
Machinery:	1 screw, 2 direct-acting engines (26″ × 2′6″), 1 boiler; 9 knots
Complement:	60
Armament:	2 24-pdr. Mar 64 total: 2 12-pdr R, 3 24-pdr.

NOTES: Wooden hull.
SERVICE RECORD: SAtlBS 1863–65. Transport and freight ship. Expedition to Murrells Inlet, SC, 29 Dec 1863–1 Jan 1864. Blockade of Charleston 1864. Decomm 21 Jun 1865. Sold 13 Jul 1865.
Later history: Merchant *Mary Sanford* 1865. Wrecked off Cape Hatteras, 13 Nov 1871.

Name	Bldr	L	Acquired	Comm
Massachusetts	Loring (bldr)	1860	3 May 1861	24 May 1861

Tonnage:	1,155 tons B
Dimensions:	219′10″ × 33′2″ × 13′8″, d18′

Machinery:	1 screw, 1 vertical direct-acting engine (62″ × 3′8″); HP 600 = 11 knots
Complement:	112
Armament:	1 32-pdr/42, 4 8″/63. Apr 65 total: 1 30-pdr R, 4 8″/63, 2 24-pdr.

NOTES: Iron hull, 1 funnel. Supply ship.
SERVICE RECORD: GulfBS Jun 1861–Jan 1862. Recomm 16 Apr 1862 as transport and supply vessel. SAtlBS 1863. Struck a torpedo (mine) that failed to explode at Charleston, 19 Mar 1865. Decomm 22 Sep 1865. Sold 1 Oct 1867.
Prizes: 9 Jun 1861: *Perthshire*; 17 Jun: *Achilles*; 19 Jun: *Nahum Stetson*; 23 Jun: *Brilliant, Trois Freres, Olive Branch, Fanny, Basile*; 7 Aug: *Charles Henry*. 12 Mar 1864: *Persis*; 30 May: str *Caledonia*.
Later history: Merchant *Crescent City* 1868. Lengthened 1873. RR 1892.

Name	Bldr	Built	Acquired	Comm
New Berne (ex-*United States*)	Poillon (Delamater)	1862	27 Jun 1863	15 Aug 1863

Tonnage:	978 tons B
Dimensions:	202′ (dk) 195′ () × 32′ × 13′6″
Machinery:	1 screw, 2 vertical inverted direct-acting engines (36″ × 3′), 1 boiler; 13 knots
Complement:	92
Armament:	2 24-pdr, 2 12-pdr R. Aug 63 total: 1 30-pdr R, 4 24-pdr, 1 12-pdr R. Jul 64: less 1 30-pdr R.

SERVICE RECORD: NAtlBS 1863, supply ship. Decomm 29 Mar 1868. Transferred to War Dept., 1 Dec 1868.
Prizes: 9 Jun 1864: str *Pevensey; 16 Dec: **G.O. Bigelow*.
Later history: Merchant *New Berne*. SE 1878.

Name	Bldr	L	Acquired	Comm
Queen (ex-*Victory*, ex-*Julie Usher*, ex-*Annie Childs*, ex-*North Carolina*)	Novelty (bldr)	1861	29 Sep 1863	15 Aug 1863

Tonnage:	618 tons B, 554 n/r
Dimensions:	172′ (dk) 168′8″ (wl) × 28′4″ × 9′11″, d13′6″
Machinery:	1 screw, 1 vertical inverted direct-acting engine (40″ × 3′6″); 1 boiler
Complement:	83
Armament:	3 32-pdr/51, 1 12-pdr R. Dec 63 total: 4 32-pdr/51, 1 20-pdr R, 2 12-pdr.

NOTES: Blockade runner *Victory*, captured off Eleuthera Island by USS *Santiago de Cuba*, 21 Jun 1863. Iron hull, two-masted schooner. Operated between New York and Wilmington, NC, seized there in 1861.
SERVICE RECORD: Transport and supply ship. Decomm 21 Jun 1865. Sold 16 Oct 1865.
Prize: 11 Feb 1864: *Louisa*.
Later history: Merchant *Gulf Stream* 1865. Lengthened 1874. Wrecked in gale and fog near Hartford Inlet, NJ, 30 Jan 1903.

Name	Bldr	L	Acquired	Comm
Union	Mallory (Delamater)	9 Aug 1862	1862	20 Jan 1863

Tonnage:	1,114 tons B
Dimensions:	219′6″ (dk) × 34′ × 16′, d23′
Machinery:	1 screw, 2 vertical direct-acting engines (36″ × 3′), 2 boilers; 13.5 knots
Complement:	75
Armament:	1 12-pdr R. Nov 63: 1 20-pdr R.

NOTES: Brigantine rig.
SERVICE RECORD: AtlBS 1861. Damaged in collision with Spanish ship *Ne Plus Ultra* 2 Jul 1861. Potomac Flotilla Aug 1861. Despatch and supply vessel to Gulf of Mexico 1863. Decomm 29 Sep 1865. Sold 25 Oct 1865.
Prizes: 1 Jun 1861: *F.W. Johnson*; 10 Jun: *Hallie Jackson*; 18 Jun: *Amelia*; 28 Jul: *B.F. Martin*. 21 May 1863: *Linnet*; 11 Oct: str *Spaulding*; 14 Jan 1864: str *Mayflower*; 27 Apr: *O.K.*; 10 Jun: *Caroline*.
Later history: Merchant *Missouri* 1865. Burned and sank NE of Abaco Island, Bahamas, 22 Oct 1872.
Note: The steamer *Union*, chartered at Philadelphia in 1861, comm 16 May 1861 and decomm 10 Dec 1861, was apparently a different ship. Described as a "long, low steamer" with a draft of 10′ "when full."

NAVY-BUILT STEAM TUGS

Name	Bldr	L	Comm
Fortune	Tetlow (U)	23 Mar 1865	19 May 1871
Leyden	Tetlow (U)	1865	1865
Mayflower	Tetlow (U)	1865	Feb 1866
Nina	Reany (bldr)	27 May 1865	30 Sep 1865
Palos	Tetlow (U)	1864	11 Jun 1870
Pinta	Reany (bldr)	29 Oct 1864	Oct 1865
Speedwell	Tetlow (U)	1865	13 Nov 1865
Standish	Tetlow (U)	26 Oct 1864	1865
Triana	Perine (U)	29 Apr 1865	25 Oct 1865

Tonnage:	420 tons D; 350 tons B
Dimensions:	137′ (oa) × 26′ × 9′6″
Machinery:	1 screw, vertical compound engines; 10 knots
Complement:	52
Armament:	2 3-pdr

NOTES: *Palos* converted to gunboat for service in China, 1870, and was first U.S. warship to transit the Suez Canal. *Fortune* and *Triana* converted to experimental torpedo boats. Iron hulls.
SERVICE RECORDS:
Fortune—Various duties on East coast 1871–91. Converted to spar torpedo boat 1871. Gunnery training 1899–1901. Submarine tender Mare Island 1903–12. Station ship, Samoa 1915–22. Sold 22 May 1922.
Leyden—Yard tug Boston 1866–79. Portsmouth 1879–97 and Newport 1897. Served off Cuba 1898. Foundered in fog off Block Island, 21 Jan 1903.

The tug *Pinta* in dry dock in 1891. She had been rebuilt for service in Alaska in 1881–83. (U.S. Naval Historical Center)

Mayflower—Survey expedition to Tehuantepec, Mexico, 1870. Despatch boat, Portsmouth 1872. Training ship, Annapolis 1876. Stricken 23 Sep 1892. Sold 27 Dec 1893.
Nina—Yard tug, Washington NYd 1866–71. Yard tug 1883. Submarine tender 1903–10. Missing in gale on voyage from Norfolk to Boston, 6 Feb 1910.
Palos—Yard tug, Boston 1866–69. First U.S. naval vessel to run on oil fuel, May–Jun 1867. Converted to gunboat 1870. First USN ship to transit Suez Canal, Aug 1870. Asiatic Station 1871–93. Fired upon by a Korean fort, 1 Jun 1871. Korean Expedition 1871. Decomm Jul 1892. Sold at Nagasaki, Jan 1893.
Later history: Merchant *Keiko Maru*, 1893.
Pinta—Yard tug Philadelphia. Alaska patrol 1884–97. Training ship 1898–1908. Stricken 2 Jan 1908.
Speedwell—Yard tug Portsmouth 1866–76, and Washington, then Norfolk. Stricken 19 Dec 1890. Sold 1 Aug 1894.
Later history: Merchant barge *Viola W. Tunis*, 1894.
Standish—Yard tug Norfolk 1871–79, then Newport. Practice ship and station tug, Annapolis until 1921. Sold 5 Aug 1921.
Later history: Merchant *Margaret*, 1921.
Triana—Yard tug Washington 1867. Converted to spar torpedo boat 1871. Stricken 13 Apr 1891. Sold 2 May 1891.

Name	Bldr	L	Acquired
Maria	Perine	1864	11 Apr 1865
Pilgrim	Pusey & Jones	1 Nov 1864	2 Mar 1865

NOTES: 170 tons (U) × (U) × 6′; 1 screw, vertical inverted engine; 12 knots. Iron hulls.
SERVICE RECORDS:
Maria—Sunk in collision with monitor *Miantonomoh* off Martha's Vineyard, 4 Jan 1870.
Pilgrim—Stricken 1 Jan 1889. Sold 25 Apr 1891.

Name	Bldr	L
Blue Light	Portsmouth	27 Feb 1864
Port Fire	Portsmouth	8 Mar 1864

NOTES: 103 tons, 1 screw, 1 vertical inverted engine. Powder tugs.
SERVICE RECORDS:
Blue Light—Boston NYd 1864–70. Washington 1871–73. New London 1874–75. Sold 27 Sep 1883.
Port Fire—Sold Jan 1878 and BU.

TUGS AND SERVICE VESSELS

SCREW TUGS

Name	Bldr	Built	Acquired
A.C. Powell	(Syracuse, NY)	1861	3 Oct 1861

Tonnage:	90 tons B
Dimensions:	62′ × 17′ × 6′5″
Machinery:	1 screw, single engine (15″ × 1′3″), 1 boiler; 4.5 knots
Complement:	18
Armament:	1 24-pdr SB

SERVICE RECORD: Potomac Flotilla 1861. James River Flotilla Jul 1862. Renamed **Alert**, Aug 1862. Operations in Nansemond River, Va., 11 Apr–4 May 1863. Burned and sank at Norfolk NYd, 31 May 1863; salved. NAtlBS Oct 1863. James River Flotilla, May 1864. Renamed **Watch**, 2 Feb 1865. Potomac Flotilla, Apr 1865. Decomm 25 May 1865. Sold 5 Jul 1865.
Later history: Merchant *Watch* 1865. RR 1886.

Name	Bldr	Built	Comm
Alpha	(Philadelphia)	1863	3 Jun 1864
(ex-*Fred Wheeler*)			

Tonnage:	55 tons B
Dimensions:	72′ × 16′6″ × 7″
Machinery:	1 screw, 1 vertical HP engine (18″ × 1′6″); 9 knots
Complement:	13
Armament:	spar torpedo

NOTES: Outfitted as spar torpedo boat.

SERVICE RECORD: Designated *Tug No. 1*. Renamed **Alpha**, Dec 1864. James River Flotilla. Sold 23 Sep 1885.
Later history: Merchant *Alpha* 1885. Burned (cause unknown), 5 Jun 1886.

Name	Bldr	Built	Acquired
Althea	(New Brunswick, NJ)	1863	9 Dec 1863
(ex-*Alfred A. Wotkyns*)			

Tonnage:	72 tons B
Dimensions:	70′ × 16′4″ × d7′
Machinery:	1 screw; 9 knots
Complement:	15
Armament:	1 12-pdr SB

NOTES: Converted by Secor & Co. Fitted for torpedoes 1864.
SERVICE RECORD: NAtlBS 1864. James River. WGulfBS 1864. Sunk by torpedo (mine) in Blakely River, Ala., 12 Mar 1865; salved and recomm 7 Nov 1865. Decomm 25 Apr 1866. Sold 8 Dec 1866.
Later history: Merchant *Martin Kalbfleisch* 1867. RR 1896.

Althea, which served as a tug and torpedo boat, is seen here probably shortly after being completed and before entering naval service.

Name	Bldr	Built	Acquired	Comm
Amaranthus	(Wilmington, Del.)	1864	1 Jul 1864	12 Jul 1864

Tonnage:	182 tons B
Dimensions:	117′ × 21′ × d9′
Machinery:	1 screw, 1 vertical engine (30″ × 2′6″), 1 boiler; 9.5 knots
Armament:	3 24-pdr SB

SERVICE RECORD: SAtlBS 1864–65. Storeship and tug. Decomm 19 Aug 1865. Sold 5 Sep 1865.
Later history: Merchant *Christiana* 1865. RR 1900.

Name	Bldr	Built	Acquired	Comm
Anemone (ex-Wicaco)	(Philadelphia)	1864	13 Aug 1864	14 Sep 1864

Tonnage:	156 tons B
Dimensions:	99′ × 20′5″ × 11′
Machinery:	1 screw. 1 vertical LP engine (30″ × 2′2″), 1 boiler; 11 knots
Complement:	30
Armament:	2 24-pdr SB, 2 12-pdr SB

SERVICE RECORD: NAtlBS 1864–65. Unsuccessful attack on Ft. Fisher, NC 24–25 Dec 1864. Sold 25 Oct 1865.
Later history: Merchant *Wicaco* 1865. RR 1896.

Name	Bldr		Built	Acquired	Comm
Arethusa (ex-Wabash)	(Philadelphia)	(Neafie & Levy)	1864	1 Jul 1864	Jul 1864

Tonnage:	195 tons B
Dimensions:	110′ × 22′ × 8′8″
Machinery:	1 screw, 1 direct-acting engine (34″ × 2′6″)
Complement:	32
Armament:	2 12-pdr SB. Dec 64: add 1 20-pdr R.

SERVICE RECORD: SAtlBS 1864. Collier, Port Royal, SC. Sold 3 Jan 1866.
Later history: FFU.

Name	Bldr	L	Acquired	Comm
Aster (ex-Alice)	(Wilmington, Del.)?	25 Jul 1864	12 Aug 1864	1864

Tonnage:	285 tons B
Dimensions:	122′6″ × 23′ × 10′
Machinery:	1 screw, 1 vertical LP engine (40″ × 3′6″), 1 boiler
Complement:	30
Armament:	1 30-pdr R, 2 12-pdr SB

NOTES: Purchased new.
SERVICE RECORD: Ran aground at Ft. Fisher while chasing blockade runner *Annie* and destroyed to prevent capture, 8 Oct 1864.
Prize: 7 Oct 1864: str *Annie*.

Name	Bldr	Built	Acquired	Comm
Azalea	McKay	1864	31 Mar 1864	7 Jun 1864

Tonnage:	176 tons B
Dimensions:	110′ × 21′6″ × 10′
Machinery:	1 screw, 1 vertical engine (30″ × 2′8″); 9 knots
Complement:	42
Armament:	Jun 64: 1 30-pdr R, 1 20-pdr R. Oct 64: 1 30-pdr R, 1 24-pdr SB.

NOTES: Acquired from builder.
SERVICE RECORD: SAtlBS 1864–65. Blockade of Charleston and Savannah. Sold 10 Aug 1865.
Prizes: 8 Jul 1864: *Pocahontas*. 23 May 1865: *Sarah M. Newhall*.
Later history: Merchant *Tecumseh* 1865. RR 1890.

Name	Bldr	Built	Acquired
Belle	(Philadelphia)	1864	2 Jun 1864
Unit (ex-Union)	(Philadelphia)	1862	2 Jun 1864

Tonnage:	56 tons
Dimensions:	62′2″ × 15′2″ × 8′
Machinery:	1 screw, HP engine; 7.5 knots
Complement:	19/24
Armament:	*Belle*: 1 12-pdr R, 1 24-pdr SB

NOTES: *Belle* used as spar torpedo boat.
SERVICE RECORDS:
Belle—NAtlBS. Despatch vessel. Capture of Plymouth, NC, 29–31 Oct 1864. Expedition up Roanoke River to Poplar Pt., NC, 9–28 Dec 1864. Sold 12 Jul 1865.
    Later history: Merchant *Belle* 1865. RR 1891.
Unit—NAtlBS 1864. Hampton Roads. Sold 12 Jul 1865.
    Later history: Merchant *Unit* 1865. RR 1902.

Name	Bldr	Built	Acquired	Comm
Berberry (ex-Columbia)	(Philadelphia)	1864	13 Aug 1864	12 Sep 1864

Tonnage:	160 tons B
Dimensions:	99′6″ × 20′6″ × 8′6″
Machinery:	1 screw, 1 vertical direct-acting condensing engine (30″ × 2′2″), 1 boiler; 5 knots
Complement:	31
Armament:	2 24-pdr SB, 2 12-pdr SB

SERVICE RECORD: NAtlBS 1864–65, off N. Carolina. Sold 12 Jul 1865.
Later history: Merchant *Rescue* 1865. Sold foreign 1902.

Name	Bldr	Built	Acquired
Beta (ex-J.E. Bazeley)	(Gloucester, NJ)	1863	3 Jun 1864

Tonnage:	50 tons
Dimensions:	70′ × 16′ × 7′
Machinery:	1 screw, 1 vertical HP engine (18″ × 1′6″); 10 knots
Complement:	14
Armament:	(U)

NOTES: Also known as *Tug No. 2*.
SERVICE RECORD: James River. New Bern, NC, 1864. Capture of Plymouth, NC, Roanoke River, 29–31 Oct 1864. Sunk by torpedo (mine) in Roanoke River, 10 Dec 1864.

Name	Bldr	Built	Acquired	Comm
Bignonia (ex-Mary Grandy)	(Cleveland)	1863	20 Jul 1864	14 Sep 1864

Tonnage:	321 tons B
Dimensions:	130′10″ × 21′2″ × 10′8″, d12′
Machinery:	1 screw, 1 overhead LP engine (30″ × 2′6″), 1 boiler; 10 knots

Complement: 41/50
Armament: 1 30-pdr R, 2 12-pdr SB

SERVICE RECORD: NAtlBS 1864–65. Sold 12 Jul 1865.
Later history: Merchant *Balize* 1865. Sold foreign 1903.

Name	Bldr	Built	Acquired	Comm
Camelia (ex-*Governor*)	(Buffalo, NY)	1862	17 Sep 1863	28 Nov 1863

Tonnage: 195 tons B
Dimensions: 111′ × 19′10″ × d11′
Machinery: 1 screw, 1 overhead HP engine (30″ × 2′6″), 1 boiler; 10 knots
Complement: 40
Armament: 2 20-pdr R

SERVICE RECORD: SAtlBS 1864–65 off Charleston. Sold 15 Aug 1865.
Later history: Merchant *Camelia*, 1865. RR 1905.

Name	Bldr	Built	Acquired	Comm
Carnation (ex-*Ajax*)	Neafie (U)	1863	17 Aug 1863	20 Oct 1863

Tonnage: 82 tons B
Dimensions: 73′6″ × 17′6″ × 7′6″
Machinery: 1 screw, 1 overhead engine (20″ × 1′8″), 1 boiler; 10 knots
Complement: 19
Armament: 1 20-pdr R, 1 12-pdr R. Feb 65 total: 1 24-pdr SB, 1 12-pdr R.

SERVICE RECORD: SAtlBS 1863–65, South Carolina. Decomm 8 Jul 1865. Sold 10 Aug 1865.
Later history: Merchant *Edward W. Gorgas* 1865. RR 1880.

Name	Bldr	Built	Acquired	Comm
Catalpa (ex-*Conqueror*)	(Brooklyn, NY)	1864	29 Jun 1864	12 Jul 1864

Tonnage: 191 tons B
Dimensions: 105′3″ × 22′2″ × 9′
Machinery: 1 screw, 1 vertical direct-acting condensing engine, (34″ × 2′6″), 1 boiler; 10 knots
Complement: 37
Armament: 2 24-pdr, 1 12-pdr SB. Dec 1864: add 1 12-pdr R.

SERVICE RECORD: SAtlBS 1864. Decomm 1 Sep 1865. Yard tug, New York. Sold 23 Jul 1894.
Later history: Mechant barge *Catalpa* 1895.

Name	Bldr	Built	Acquired	Comm
Clematis (ex-*Maria Love*)	(Cleveland, OH)	1863	30 Jul 1864	14 Sep 1864

Tonnage: 296 tons B
Dimensions: 127′ × 22′ × 10′
Machinery: 1 screw, 1 overhead HP engine (32″ × 2′6″), 1 boiler; 12 knots

Complement: 46
Armament: 1 30-pdr R, 2 12-pdr SB

SERVICE RECORD: James River area 1864–65. Gulf Sqn 1865–66. Decomm 6 Jun 1866. Sold 26 Nov 1866.
Later history: Merchant *Clematis* 1866. Converted to schooner 1879.

Name	Bldr	Built	Acquired	Comm
Clinton (ex-*Lena Clinton*)	(Wilmington, Del.)	1863	14 Jun 1864	1864

Tonnage: 50 tons
Dimensions: 61′ () 58′8″ (bp) × 15′10″ × 7″
Machinery: 1 screw, 1 vertical engine, 1 boiler; 11 knots
Complement: 16

SERVICE RECORD: NAtlBS 1864–65, picket boat in James River and Norfolk NYd. New York NYd 1865–70. Sold 3 Aug 1870.
Later history: Merchant *Mary Lewis* 1870. Renamed *Milburn*, 1909. RR 1933.

Name	Bldr	Built	Acquired	Comm
Clover (ex-*Daisy*)	(Philadelphia)	1863	11 Nov 1863	28 Nov 1863

Tonnage: 129 tons
Dimensions: 92′ × 19′ × 9′
Machinery: 1 screw, 1 vertical condensing engine (26″ × 2′2″); 7 knots
Complement: 19
Armament: 1 12-pdr R, 1 12-pdr SB

SERVICE RECORD: SAtlBS 1864. Beaufort, NC. Decomm 27 Jul 1865. Sold 21 Sep 1865.
Prize: 26 Jan 1865: *Coquette*.
Later history: Merchant *Clover* 1865. Sold foreign 1878.

Name	Bldr	Built	Acquired
Cohasset (ex-*Narragansett*, ex-*E.D. Fogg*)	Neafie (bldr)	1860	13 Sep 1861

Tonnage: 100 tons
Dimensions: 82′ × 18′10″ × 9′
Machinery: 1 screw, 1 inverted vertical HP engine (16″ × 6′); 8 knots
Complement: 12
Armament: 1 20-pdr R, 2 24-pdr H

SERVICE RECORD: AtlBS 1861. Operations in Nansemond River, Va., 11 Apr–4 May 1863. Expedition up James River, 4–7 Aug 1863. Beaufort, NC, 1864. Yard tug Boston NYd, 1865–82 and Newport 1882–92. Sold 9 May 1892.
Later history: FFU.

Name	Bldr	Built	Acquired
Crocus (ex-*Solomon Thomas*)	(Mystic, Conn.)	1863	31 Jul 1863

Tonnage:	122 tons
Dimensions:	79' × 18'6" × 7'6", d9'3"
Machinery:	1 screw, LP engine; 7.5 knots
Armament:	2 guns

SERVICE RECORD: Wrecked on Bodie's Island, NC, 17 Aug 1863.

Name	Bldr	Built	Acquired	Comm
Dandelion (ex-*Antietam*)	Winson	1862	21 Nov 1862	Dec 1862

Tonnage:	111 tons
Dimensions:	90' × 19' × 7'6"
Machinery:	1 screw, 1 direct-acting LP engine (27" × 2'), 1 boiler; 9 knots
Complement:	21
Armament:	2 12-pdr

SERVICE RECORD: SAtlBS 1863–65. Bombardment of Ft. McAllister, Ga., 3 Mar 1863. Bombardment of Ft. Wagner, Charleston, Jul–Aug 1863. Assault on Jacksonville, Fla., 2–22 Feb 1864. Decomm 14 Jul 1865. Sold 15 Aug 1865.
Later history: Merchant *Dandelion* 1865. Sold foreign, 1866.

Name	Bldr	Built	Acquired
Delta (ex-*Linda*)	(Philadelphia)	1863	3 Jun 1864

Tonnage:	44 tons
Dimensions:	66' × 14' × 7'8"
Machinery:	1 screw, 1 engine (16" × 1'4"), 1 boiler; 9 knots
Complement:	4
Armament:	spar torpedo

NOTES: Also known as *Tug No. 4*. Renamed 27 Nov 1864. Converted to torpedo tug.
SERVICE RECORD: James River 1864. North Carolina coast 1865. Sold 5 Sep 1865.
Later history: Merchant *Delta* 1865. RR 1924.

Name	Bldr	Built	Acquired
Emerald (ex-*Fairy*)	Neafie	(U)	3 Aug 1864

Tonnage:	50 tons
Dimensions:	58' × 14' × d6'
Machinery:	1 screw; 12.5 knots

NOTES: Yacht. Not commissioned.
SERVICE RECORD: Ferry at Portsmouth (N.H.) Navy Yard 1864–83. Sold 1883.

Name	Bldr	Built	Acquired
Epsilon (ex-*Harry Bumm*)	(Philadelphia)	1864	3 Jun 1864

Tonnage:	51 tons
Dimensions:	66' × 15' × 7'6"
Machinery:	1 screw, 1 HP direct-acting engine (17" × 1'5"), 1 boiler; 9 knots
Complement:	10
Armament:	none

NOTES: Also known as *Tug No. 5*. Renamed Nov 1864.
SERVICE RECORD: James River, 1864–65. Sold 12 Jul 1865.
Later history: Merchant *Epsilon* 1865. Exploded and sank at New York, 27 May 1872.

Name	Bldr	Built	Acquired
Gamma (ex-*R.F. Loper*)	(Philadelphia)	1863	3 Jun 1864

Tonnage:	36 tons
Dimensions:	65' × 14'3" × d5'4"
Machinery:	1 screw, 1 engine (16" × 1'4"), 1 boiler; 12 knots
Armament:	(U)

NOTES: Also known as *Tug No. 3*.
SERVICE RECORD: James River, picket boat. New Bern, NC, 1865. Sold 25 Oct 1865.
Later history: Merchant *Peter Smith* 1865. Burned at New York, 9 May 1893.

Name	Bldr	Built	Acquired	Comm
Gladiolus (ex-*Sallie Bishop*)	(Philadelphia)	1864	2 Jun 1864	15 Jun 1864

Tonnage:	81 tons B
Dimensions:	88' × 18'6" × 8'
Machinery:	1 screw, 1 vertical LP engine (30" × 2'4"), 1 boiler
Complement:	25
Armament:	2 12-pdr R, 1 24-pdr H

SERVICE RECORD: SAtlBS 1864. Blockade of Charleston. Decomm 30 Aug 1865. Sold 15 Sep 1865.
Prize: 18 Feb 1865: str *Syren*.
Later history: Merchant *Gladiolus* 1865. Lost 1887.

Name	Bldr	Built	Acquired	Comm
Glance (ex-*Glide*)	Reany (bldr)	1863	2 Jun 1864	Jul 1864

Tonnage:	80 tons
Dimensions:	75' × 17' × 8'
Machinery:	1 screw, 1 vertical HP engine (20" × 2'), 1 boiler; 8 knots
Complement:	14
Armament:	none

SERVICE RECORD: Hampton Roads, Va., yard tug 1864–65, and Philadelphia 1865–83. Sold 27 Sep 1883.

Name	Bldr	Built	Acquired
Harcourt	(Buffalo, NY)	1863	14 Jun 1864
(ex-*J.W. Harcourt*)			

Tonnage:	68 tons
Dimensions:	66' × 16'3" × 7'9"
Machinery:	1 screw, 1 HP engine, 1 boiler; 13 knots
Armament:	none

SERVICE RECORD: NAtlBS 1864. James River 1865. Decomm 20 Nov 1865. Sold 16 Apr 1867.
Later history: Merchant *Isaac R. Staples* 1867. Renamed *Gertrude* 1883. RR 1889.

Name	Bldr	Built	Acquired	Comm
Honeysuckle	(Buffalo, NY)	1862	19 Aug 1863	3 Dec 1863
(ex-*William G. Fargo*)				

Tonnage:	241 tons
Dimensions:	123' () 121'6" () × 20'2" × 10'
Machinery:	1 screw, 1 HP overhead engine (30" × 2'6"), 1 boiler; 12 knots
Complement:	39
Armament:	2 20-pdr R

SERVICE RECORD: EGulfBS 1864–65. Despatch and supply vessel 1864. Blockade off Florida 1865. Decomm 30 Jun 1865. Sold 15 Aug 1865.
Prizes: 11 Jan 1864: *Fly*; 20 Mar: *Florida*; 29 Apr: *Miriam*. 17 Jan 1865: *Augusta*; 28 Feb: *Sort*; 3 Mar: *Phantom*.
Later history: Merchant *Honeysuckle* 1865. RR 1900.

Name	Bldr	Built	Acquired
Hoyt	(Philadelphia)	1863	1 Jul 1864
(ex-*Luke Hoyt*)			

Tonnage:	20 tons
Dimensions:	45' × 10'5" × 6'
Machinery:	1 screw, 1 vertical HP engine; 7 knots
Complement:	6
Armament:	1 spar torpedo

NOTES: Spar torpedo boat. Designed as weapon to oppose Confederate rams in Roanoke River, but was never used in combat.
SERVICE RECORD: New Bern, NC, 1864. Sold 10 Aug 1865.
Later history: Merchant *Luke Hoyt* 1865. RR 1914.

Name	Bldr	Built	Acquired	Comm
Hydrangea	(Buffalo, NY)	1862	16 Oct 1863	18 Apr 1864
(ex-*Hippodrome*)				

Tonnage:	215 tons
Dimensions:	120' × 20'3" × d7'
Machinery:	1 screw, 1 overhead LP engine (30" × 2'6"), 1 boiler; 11 knots
Complement:	29
Armament:	1 20-pdr R, 1 12-pdr H

SERVICE RECORD: NAtlBS 1864. SAtlBS 1864. Decomm 1 Sep 1865. Sold 25 Oct 1865.
Later history: Merchant *Norman* 1865. Wrecked off Cape May, NJ, 17 Nov 1886.

Name	Bldr	Built	Acquired
Innis	(Philadelphia)	1863	5 Oct 1863

Tonnage:	112 tons B
Dimensions:	85' × 19'6" × 8'
Machinery:	1 screw, 1 overhead engine, 1 boiler; 12 knots
Armament:	(U)

SERVICE RECORD: NAtlBS 1864. Renamed **Kalmia** 24 Apr 1864. Sold 25 Oct 1865.
Later history: Merchant *Francis B. Thurber* 1865. Renamed *James Hughes* 1898. Destroyed by fire at Bartletts Point, NY, 15 Jun 1905.

Name	Bldr	Built	Acquired
Iris	(Brooklyn, NY)	1863	16 Oct 1863
(ex-*Willet Rowe*)			

Tonnage:	158 tons
Dimensions:	87' × 19' × 9'
Machinery:	1 screw, 1 overhead LP engine (28" × 2'4"), 1 boiler; 12 mph
Complement:	34
Armament:	2 20-pdr R

SERVICE RECORD: SAtlBS 1863. Blockade of Charleston. Expedition to Bull Bay, SC, Feb 1865. Decomm 15 Jul 1865.
Later history: To U.S. Lighthouse Board, 18 Oct 1865.

Name	Bldr	Built	Acquired	Comm
Jasmine	(Brooklyn)	1862	29 May 1863	17 Jun 1863
(ex-*Peter B. Van Hutten*)				

Tonnage:	122 tons
Dimensions:	79' × 18' × 7'6", d9'2"
Machinery:	1 screw, 1 LP engine (26" × 2'2"), 2 boilers
Complement:	19
Armament:	1 20-pdr R, 1 12-pdr H

SERVICE RECORD: WGulfBS 1863. Decomm 12 May 1865.
Prize: 14 Jul 1863: *Relampago*.
Later history: To U.S. Lighthouse Board, 13 Jun 1866. To U.S. Revenue Cutter Service 1873, renamed *William E. Chandler*. Sold 1903.

Name	Bldr	Built	Acquired
Jean Sands	(Brooklyn)	1863	18 Oct 1864

Tonnage:	139 tons
Dimensions:	102′ × 22′8″ × d6′2″
Machinery:	1 screw, vertical inverted engine
Armament:	none

NOTES: Salvage tug.
SERVICE RECORD: Norfolk NYd, tug and salvage vessel 1864–92. Sold 16 May 1892.

Name	Bldr	Built	Acquired	Comm
Jonquil (ex-*J.K. Kirkman*)	(Wilmington, Del.)	1862	21 Oct 1863	28 Oct 1863

Tonnage:	90 tons D
Dimensions:	69′4″ × 17′6″ × 7′
Machinery:	1 screw, 1 vertical condensing engine (20″ × 1′8″); 8 knots
Complement:	15
Armament:	1 12-pdr R, 1 12-pdr SB. Aug 64 total: 2 12-pdr H.

SERVICE RECORD: SAtlBS 1863. Blockade of Charleston. Decomm 2 Aug 1865. Sold 21 Oct 1865.
Later history: Merchant *B. Bramell* 1865. Renamed *Sophie* 1883. RR 1921.

Name	Bldr	Built	Acquired	Comm
Juniper (ex-*Uno*)	(Camden, NJ)	1864	30 May 1864	11 Jul 1864

Tonnage:	116 tons B
Dimensions:	79′6″ × 18′4″ × 9′
Machinery:	1 screw, 1 overhead condensing engine (24″ × 1′8″), 1 boiler; 10 knots
Complement:	26
Armament:	1 20-pdr R, 1 12-pdr R

SERVICE RECORD: Potomac Flotilla 1864–65. Decomm 26 May 1865.
Later history: To U.S. Lighthouse Board, 19 Jun 1865. To U.S. Revenue Cutter Service 1873, renamed *Peter G. Washington*. Sold 1902.

Name	Bldr	Built	Acquired	Comm
Laburnum (ex-*Lion*)	(Philadelphia)	1864	24 Jun 1864	7 Jul 1864

Tonnage:	181 tons B
Dimensions:	110′ × 22′ × 9′
Machinery:	1 screw, vertical direct-acting engine; 10 knots
Complement:	29
Armament:	2 20-pdr R, 2 24-pdr H

SERVICE RECORD: SAtlBS 1864. Blockade of Charleston. Decomm 24 Jan 1866. Sold 16 Mar 1866.
Later history: Merchant *D.P. Ingraham* 1866. Sold foreign 1878.

Name	Bldr	Built	Acquired	Comm
Larkspur (ex-*Pontiac*)	(Wilmington, Del.)	1863	6 Oct 1863	16 Oct 1863

Tonnage:	125 tons B
Dimensions:	90′9″ × 19′2″ × 9′
Machinery:	1 screw, 1 vertical direct-acting engine (26″ × 2′4″); 9 knots
Complement:	26
Armament:	1 12-pdr H, 1 12-pdr R. Feb 65: add 1 24-pdr H.

SERVICE RECORD: SAtlBS 1863–65. Blockade of Charleston. Decomm 8 Jul 1865. Sold 10 Aug 1865.
Later history: Merchant *Larkspur* 1865. Renamed *M. Vandercook* 1885. Renamed *Somerville* 1898. RR 1905.

Name	Bldr	Built	Acquired
Lavender (ex-*May Flower*)	(Philadelphia)	1864	25 May 1864

Tonnage:	173 tons
Dimensions:	112′ × 22′ × d7′6″
Machinery:	1 screw, 1 vertical direct-acting LP engine (30″ × 2′6″); 1 boiler
Complement:	23
Armament:	2 12-pdr R, 2 24-pdr H

SERVICE RECORD: SAtlBS 1864. Wrecked in squall off North Carolina coast, 12 Jun 1864.

Name	Bldr	Built	Acquired
Leslie	(U)	(U)	1861

Tonnage:	100 tons
Dimensions:	(U)
Machinery:	1 screw
Complement:	10
Armament:	2 guns

NOTES: Transferred from War Department.
SERVICE RECORD: Washington NYd 1861. Potomac Flotilla, tender. Returned to War Department, 2 Jun 1865.

Name	Bldr	Built	Acquired	Comm
Lilac	(Philadelphia)	1863	15 Apr 1863	18 Apr 1863

Tonnage:	129 tons B
Dimensions:	92′ () 85′7″ () × 19′1″ × 8′
Machinery:	1 screw, 1 vertical direct-acting condensing engine; 9 knots
Complement:	17
Armament:	1 12-pdr SB, 1 12-pdr R

SERVICE RECORD: NAtlBS 1863. James River, Beaufort, NC, 1864. Decomm 16 Jun and sold 12 Jul 1865.
Prize: 4 Apr 1865: Confederate War Department tug *Seaboard*.
Later history: Merchant *Eutaw* 1865. RR 1888.

Name	Bldr	Built	Acquired
Lupin (ex-*C. Vanderbilt*)	(Philadelphia)	1861	19 Nov 1863

Tonnage:	68 tons	
Dimensions:	69' × 16'2" × d6'6"	
Machinery:	1 screw, 1 HP engine (20" × 1'8"); 1 boiler	
Armament:	(U)	

SERVICE RECORD: Sold 25 Oct 1865.
Later history: Merchant *C. Vanderbilt* 1865. Renamed *Lewis S. Wandell* 1883. Sold foreign 1884.

Name	Bldr	Built	Acquired	Comm
Marigold	(Philadelphia)	1863	13 Jun 1863	13 Jun 1863

Tonnage:	115 tons B
Dimensions:	84'7" × 18'9" × 7'
Machinery:	1 screw, 1 vertical direct-acting condensing engine (26" × 2'2"); 1 boiler
Complement:	17
Armament:	2 12-pdr R

SERVICE RECORD: EGulfBS 1863–65. Sold 6 Oct 1866.
Prizes: 6 Oct 1863: *Last Trial*. 25 Feb 1865: *Salvadora*.
Later history: Merchant *William A. Hennessey* 1866. Destroyed by fire at New York, 30 Nov 1875.

Name	Bldr	Built	Acquired	Comm
Martin (ex-*James McMartin*)	(Albany, NY)	1864	16 Jun 1864	Jun 1864

Tonnage:	25 tons
Dimensions:	45'3" × 11'3" × 5'9"
Machinery:	1 screw, 1 vertical HP engine (13 1/2" × 1'3"); 6 knots
Complement:	9
Armament:	Spar torpedo

NOTES: Iron hull. Spar torpedo boat.
SERVICE RECORD: NAtlBS 1864. North Carolina waters 1864. Capture of Plymouth, NC, 29–31 Oct 1864. Sold 10 Aug 1865.
Later history: Merchant *Martin* 1865. Renamed *John Laughlin Jr.* 1882. RR 1894.

Name	Bldr	Built	Acquired	Comm
Moccasin (ex-*Hero*)	(Philadelphia)	1864	11 Jul 1864	14 Jul 1864

Tonnage:	192 tons B
Dimensions:	104'5" × 22'3" × 9'
Machinery:	1 screw, vertical direct-acting engine (32" × 2'10"), 1 boiler; 10 knots
Complement:	31
Armament:	3 12-pdr R

NOTES: Renamed 25 Jul 1864.
SERVICE RECORD: NAtlBS 1864. Search for CSS *Tallahassee*, Aug 1864. Unsuccessful attack on Ft. Fisher, NC, 24–25 Dec 1864. Potomac Flotilla Mar 1865. Decomm 12 Aug 1865.
Later history: To U.S. Revenue Cutter Service, 18 Sep 1865. Renamed

George M. Bibb 1881. Sold 1891. Merchant *Pentagoet* 1891. Foundered at sea, 27 Nov 1898.

Name	Bldr	Built	Acquired	Comm
Monterey (ex-*Monitor*)	Eden Landing, San Francisco	1862	20 Apr 1863	18 May 1863

Tonnage:	87 tons
Dimensions:	75' × 18' × 7'
Machinery:	1 screw, 1 HP engine

SERVICE RECORD: Mare Island NYd 1863–92. Renamed **Ivy**, 3 Jan 1891. Stricken 7 Oct 1892 and BU.

Name	Bldr	Built	Acquired	Comm
Narcissus (ex-*Mary Cook*)	(East Albany, NY)	Jul 1863	23 Sep 1863	2 Feb 1864

Tonnage:	115 tons B
Dimensions:	81'6" × 18'9" × 6'
Machinery:	1 screw, 1 overhead cylinder engine (20" × 1'10"), 1 boiler; 14 knots
Complement:	19/32
Armament:	1 20-pdr R, 1 12-pdr SB

NOTES: Purchased before completion.
SERVICE RECORD: WGulfBS Feb 1864. Struck a torpedo (mine) and sank off Mobile, 7 Dec 1864; salved and repaired. Wrecked at Egmont. Key, Fla., 4 Jan 1866 (no survivors).
Prize: 24 Aug 1864: *Oregon*.

Name	Bldr	Built	Acquired	Comm
Peony (ex-*Republic*)	(Philadelphia)	1864	7 Dec 1864	Jan 1865

Tonnage:	180 tons
Dimensions:	104'6" × 20'6" × 8'6"
Machinery:	1 screw, 1 vertical direct-acting condensing engine (34" × 2'8"), 1 boiler; 9 knots
Armament:	1 24-pdr SB

SERVICE RECORD: NAtlBS 1865. Second attack on Ft. Fisher, NC, 13–15 Jan 1865. Sold 1 Aug 1865.
Later history: Merchant *Republic* 1865. RR 1894.

Name	Bldr	Built	Acquired	Comm
Periwinkle (ex-*America*)	Neafie (bldr)	1864	9 Dec 1864	Jan 1865

Tonnage:	387 tons B
Dimensions:	140' × 28' × 10'6"
Machinery:	1 screw, 1 vertical condensing engine (40" × 3'), 1 boiler
Complement:	37
Armament:	2 24-pdr

NOTES: Two-masted schooner rig
SERVICE RECORD: Potomac Flotilla Jan–Jun 1865. Decomm 1867. Hall

Scientific Expedition to the Arctic 1871. Renamed **Polaris**, 25 Apr 1871. Reached farthest point north by a vessel, 81°11′N, 1872. Crushed after being caught in ice in Baffin Bay, 24 Oct 1872.

Name	Bldr	Built	Acquired	Comm
Pink (ex-Zouave)	(Newburgh, NY)	1863	14 Dec 1863	6 Feb 1864

Tonnage: 184 tons B
Dimensions: 110′4″ × 24′6″ × d7′
Machinery: 1 screw
Complement: 24
Armament: 1 30-pdr R, 2 12-pdr SB

SERVICE RECORD: NAtlBS 1864. WGulfBS Aug 1864. Ran aground on Dauphin Island and was lost, 22 Sep 1865.

Name	Bldr	Built	Acquired	Comm
Poppy (ex-Addie Douglas)	(Philadelphia)	1862	31 Oct 1863	10 Nov 1863

Tonnage: 93 tons
Dimensions: 88′ × 19′ × 7′3″
Machinery: 1 screw, 1 vertical LP engine (24″ × 2′), 1 boiler; 8 knots
Complement: 20
Armament: 1 12-pdr SB, 1 12-pdr R

SERVICE RECORD: NAtlBS 1863–65. Hampton Roads and James River. Sold 30 Nov 1865.
Later history: Merchant *Isaac M. North* 1865. RR 1893.

Name	Bldr	Built	Acquired	Comm
Primrose (ex-Nellie B. Vaughan)	(Whitehall, NY)	1862	14 Jan 1863	26 Feb 1863

Tonnage: 94 tons
Dimensions: 83′ × 17′6″ × 7′
Machinery: 1 screw, 1 vertical inverted HP engine (20″ × 1′8″)
Complement: 26
Armament: 1 30-pdr R, 1 24-pdr H

SERVICE RECORD: Potomac Flotilla. Operations in Nansemond River, Va., 11 Apr–4 May 1863. Washington NYd 1865–71. Sold 17 Mar 1871.
Prizes: 8 May 1863: *Sarah Lavinia*; 2 Jun: *Flying Cloud* and *Richard Vaux*.

Name	Bldr	L	Acquired	Comm
Reliance	Terry (Cobb & Fields)	4 Jun 1860	7 May 1861	13 May 1861
Resolute	Terry (Cobb & Fields)	4 Jun 1860	7 May 1861	12 May 1861

Tonnage: 90 tons B
Dimensions: 93′ () 88′2″ × 17′ × 8′, d7′5″
Machinery: 1 screw, 2 vertical direct-acting engines (17″ × 1′5″), 1 boiler
Complement: 17
Armament: 1 24-pdr H, 1 12-pdr H

SERVICE RECORDS:
Reliance—Potomac Flotilla 1861. Engaged batteries at Aquia Creek, Va., 29 May–1 Jun 1861. Expedition up Rappahannock River to Tappahannock, Va., 13–15 Apr 1862. Captured with *Satellite* by Confederate boarders in Rappahannock River, 23 Aug 1863. Sunk at Port Royal, 28 Aug 1863.
Prizes: 12 Aug 1862: *Blossom*; 31 Oct: *Pointer*. 20 Mar 1863: *E. Waterman*.
Later history: Raised and sold 1865. Merchant *Reliance* 1865. Lost (cause unknown), 26 Apr 1883.
Resolute—Potomac Flotilla 1861–65. Engaged batteries at Aquia Creek, Va., 29 May–1 Jun 1861. Decomm 26 May 1865. Sold 24 Jun 1865.
Prizes: 28 May 1861: *unknown; 8 Jun: *Somerset; 17 Jul: *Buena Vista*; 18 Jul: *Ocean Wave*; 21 Aug: *Eagle*. 10 Aug 1862: *S.S. Jones*; 8 Nov: *Capitola*.
Later history: Merchant *Resolute* 1865. RR 1899.

Name	Bldr	Built	Acquired	Comm
Rescue	Harlan (bldr)	1861	21 Aug 1861	Sep 1861

Tonnage: 111 tons B
Dimensions: 80′ × 18′ × 8′
Machinery: 1 screw, inverted vertical engine (26″ × 2′); 6 knots
Complement: 20
Armament: 1 20-pdr R, 1 12-pdr R. Oct 64: less 1 12-pdr R.

NOTES: Iron hull. Purchased prior to completion.
SERVICE RECORD: Potomac Flotilla 1861. NAtlBS Nov 1861. Blockade of Charleston Nov 1862–Jun 1864. Potomac Flotilla Sep 1864–65. Washington NYd 1865–89. Sold 24 Mar 1891.
Prizes: 18 Sep 1861: *Harford*; 11 Oct: *Martha Washington*; 6 Nov: *Ada*; 8 Nov: *Urbana*.
Later history: Merchant *Hercules* 1891.

Name	Bldr	Built	Acquired
Rocket (ex-J.D. Billard)	(Mystic, Conn.)	1862	12 Oct 1863

Tonnage: 127 tons
Dimensions: 98′ (oa) 85′8″ (wl) × 18′10″ × 7′
Machinery: 1 screw, 1 vertical inverted HP engine (25″ × 2′); 8.5 knots

NOTES: Reboilered 1884.
SERVICE RECORD: New York NYd, ordnance tug 1863–84. Boston 1884–99. Stricken 27 Oct 1899. Sold 28 Dec 1899.

Name	Bldr	Built	Acquired	Comm
Rose (ex-A.I. Fitch)	(New Brunswick, NJ)	1863	12 Dec 1863	8 Feb 1864

Tonnage: 96 tons
Dimensions: 84′ × 18′2″ × 7′3″
Machinery: 1 screw; 8.5 knots
Complement: 17
Armament: Aug 1864: 1 20-pdr R, 1 12-pdr SB

NOTES: Fitted for spar torpedo 1864.
SERVICE RECORD: Potomac Flotilla 1864. WGulfBS Aug 1864–65. Pensacola NYd 1865–83. Stricken 3 Mar 1883. Sold 20 Sep 1883.

Name	Bldr	Built	Acquired	Comm
Saffron (ex-John T. Jenkins)	(New Brunswick, NJ)	1863	8 Dec 1864	17 Dec 1864

Tonnage:	73 tons
Dimensions:	66′ × 17′1″ × 8′
Machinery:	1 screw, 1 vertical HP engine, 1 boiler
Complement:	16
Armament:	1 gun

NOTES: May also have been known as Theta.
SERVICE RECORD: NAtlBS 1865. Sold 25 Oct 1865.
Later history: Merchant Clifton 1865. Lost (cause unknown), 1885.

Name	Bldr	Built	Acquired
Snowdrop (ex-Albert DeGroot)	(Buffalo, NY)	1863	16 Oct 1863

Tonnage:	125 tons B
Dimensions:	91′ × 17′6″ × 8′
Machinery:	1 screw, 1 overhead cylinder engine (24″ × 2′), 1 boiler; 12 mph
Complement:	14
Armament:	2 guns

SERVICE RECORD: NAtlBS 1864. Hampton Roads area. Norfolk NYd 1865–83. Sold and BU 1884.

Name	Bldr	Built	Acquired
Sorrel (ex-Gen. W.S. Hancock)	(Philadelphia)	1864	1 Aug 1864

Tonnage:	68 tons
Dimensions:	77′ × 16′6″ × 6′6″
Machinery:	1 screw, 1 vertical HP engine (18″ × 1′6″), 1 boiler

SERVICE RECORD: Philadelphia NYd 1864–83. Sold 27 Sep 1883.
Later history: FFU.

Name	Bldr	Built	Acquired	Comm
Sunflower	(East Boston, Mass.)	1863	2 May 1863	29 Apr 1863

Tonnage:	294 tons
Dimensions:	104′5″ × 20′9″ × 12′
Machinery:	1 screw, 1 vertical direct-acting engine (36″ × 3′); 10.5 knots
Complement:	52
Armament:	2 30-pdr R

SERVICE RECORD: EGulfBS May 1863–65. Occupation of Tampa, Fla., 4–7 May 1864. Decomm 3 Jun 1865. Sold 10 Aug 1865.
Prizes: 31 May 1863: Echo; 12 Jun: Pushmataha; 27 Aug: General Worth; 6 Oct: Last Trial; 24 Dec: Hancock. 24 Mar 1864: Josephine; 6 May: Neptune; 6 Dec: Pickwick.

Later history: Merchant Sunflower 1865. Sunk in collision with Juniata in Southwest Pass, La., 29 Jan 1870.

Name	Bldr	Built	Acquired	Comm
Sweet Brier (ex-Dictator)	(Buffalo, NY)	1862	22 Sep 1863	25 Jan 1864

Tonnage:	243 tons
Dimensions:	120′ × 21′3″ × 9′6″
Machinery:	1 screw, 1 vertical direct-acting engine (30″ × 2′6″), 1 boiler; 9 knots
Complement:	37
Armament:	1 12-pdr SB, 1 20-pdr R. Aug 64 total: 1 20-pdr R, 2 24-pdr SB.

SERVICE RECORD: SAtlBS 1864–65. Blockade of Charleston. Decomm 13 Jul 1865. Sold 25 Oct 1865.
Prize: 8 Jul 1864: Pocahontas.
Later history: Merchant Conqueror 1865. RR 1900.

Name	Bldr	L	Acquired
Tigress	(U)	Aug 1861	Aug 1861

Tonnage:	(U)
Dimensions:	(U)
Machinery:	1 screw, 1 HP engine, 1 boiler

SERVICE RECORD: Potomac Flotilla. Sunk in collision with merchant vessel State of Maine off Indian Head, Md., 10 Sep 1861. Wreck raised and sold.

Name	Bldr	Built	Acquired	Comm
Verbena (ex-Ino)	(Brooklyn)	1864	7 Jun 1864	11 Jul 1864

Tonnage:	104 tons B
Dimensions:	78′4″ × 17′6″ × 8′
Machinery:	1 screw, 1 overhead cylinder engine (24″ × 1′8″), 1 boiler; 12 mph
Complement:	20
Armament:	1 20-pdr R, 1 12-pdr SB

SERVICE RECORD: Potomac Flotilla 1864. Decomm 13 Jun 1865. Sold 20 Jul 1865.
Later history: Merchant Game Cock 1865. Renamed Edward G. Burgess 1885. RR 1900.

Name	Bldr	Built	Acquired	Comm
Violet (ex-Martha)	(Brooklyn)	1862	30 Dec 1862	29 Jan 1863

Tonnage:	146 tons B
Dimensions:	85′ × 19′9″ × d11′
Machinery:	1 screw, 1 inverted direct-acting engine (30″ × 2′4″), 1 boiler
Complement:	20
Armament:	1 12-pdr SB, 1 12-pdr R. Feb 64: 2 12-pdr R, 1 24-pdr.

SERVICE RECORD: NAtlBS Feb 1863. Helped capture and refloat

grounded blockade runner *Ceres* at mouth of Cape Fear River, 11 Apr 1863. Ran aground off Cape Fear, NC, while attempting to refloat steamer *Antonica*, 20 Dec 1863; refloated and repaired. Fitted with spar torpedo 1864. Ran aground off Cape Fear River, 7 Aug 1864 and destroyed to prevent capture.

Name	Bldr	Built	Acquired
Young America	(New York)	1857	Apr 1861

Tonnage:	173 tons
Dimensions:	87'1" × 20'2" × 10'6"
Machinery:	1 screw
Complement:	13
Armament:	1 30-pdr R, 1 32-pdr/33, 1 12-pdr R. Apr 63 total: 1 30-pdr R, 1 31-pdr/27. Nov 63 total: 1 30-pdr R, 1 24-pdr H.

NOTES: Confederate tug captured in Hampton Roads by USS *Cumberland*, 24 Apr 1861.
SERVICE RECORD: Potomac Flotilla 1861–62. Decomm 9 Jun 1865. Sold 12 Jul 1865.
Later history: Merchant *Young America* 1865. RR 1901.

Name	Bldr	Built	Acquired	Comm
Zeta (ex-*J.G. Loane*)	(Philadelphia)	1864	3 Jun 1864	8 Jun 1864

Tonnage:	34 tons
Dimensions:	58' × 13' × 7'6"
Machinery:	1 screw, 1 engine (15" × 1'3"), 1 boiler; 8 knots
Complement:	10
Armament:	none

NOTES: Also known as *Tug No. 6*. Renamed Nov 1864.
SERVICE RECORD: Torpedo tug in James River, 1865. Sold 24 Jun 1865.
Later history: Merchant *Zeta* 1865. Renamed *W.H. Mohler* 1892. Burned off Dundalk, Md., 8 Nov 1921.

Name	Bldr	Built	Acquired	Comm
Zouave	(Albany, NY)	1861	20 Dec 1861	1 Feb 1862

Tonnage:	127 tons
Dimensions:	95' × 20'10" × 9'
Machinery:	1 screw, 2 HP direct-acting engines; 10 knots
Complement:	25
Armament:	2 30-pdr R

SERVICE RECORD: NAtlBS 1862. Battle of Hampton Roads, 8 Mar 1862. Operations in Nansemond River, Va., 11 Apr–4 May 1863. Decomm 14 Jun 1865. Sold 12 Jul 1865.
Prize: 18 Jan 1863: *J.C. McCabe*.
Later history: Merchant *Zouave* 1865. Renamed *Three Brothers* 1914. RR 1918.

SIDEWHEEL TUGS

Name	Bldr	Built	Acquired
Columbine (ex-*A.H. Schultz*)	(New York, NY)	1850	12 Dec 1862

Tonnage:	133 tons B
Dimensions:	117' × 20'7" × d6'2"
Machinery:	Side wheels
Complement:	25
Armament:	2 20-pdr R

NOTES: Former identity of this ship questionable.
SERVICE RECORD: SAtlBS 1863–64. Assault on Jacksonville, Fla., 2–22 Feb 1864. EGulfBS 1864–65. Expedition up St. Johns River, 9–12 Mar 1864. Run aground and captured in St. Johns River, 23 May 1864.

Name	Bldr	Built	Acquired
Daffodil (ex-*Jonas Smith*)	Terry (U)	1862	17 Nov 1862

Tonnage:	173 tons B
Dimensions:	110'6" × 22'6" × 5'6"
Machinery:	Side wheels, 1 beam engine (30" × 6'), 1 boiler; 8 knots
Complement:	28/35
Armament:	2 20-pdr R

SERVICE RECORD: SAtlBS 1862. Port Royal, SC, 1862–65. Expedition to Murrells Inlet, SC, 29 Dec 1863–1 Jan 1864, and in Broad River, SC, 27 Nov–30 Dec 1864. Engaged batteries in Togodo Creek, SC, 9 Feb 1865. NAtlSqn 1865. Sold 13 Mar 1867.
Prizes: 13 May 1863: *Wonder*. 12 Mar 1864: str *General Sumter*; 14 Mar: str *Hattie Brock*.
Later history: Merchant *Aaron Wilbur* 1867. U.S. Lighthouse Board 1871, renamed *Arbutus*. Merchant *Cora* 1875. RR 1880.

Name	Bldr	Built	Acquired
Ellis (ex-*CSS Ellis*)	(U)	(U)	19 May 1862

Tonnage:	100 tons
Dimensions:	(U) × (U) × 6'
Machinery:	Side wheels
Complement:	28
Armament:	2 guns

NOTES: Confederate armed tug, captured by the Army at Elizabeth City, NC, 10 Feb 1862.
SERVICE RECORD: NAtlBS 1862. Capture of Fort Macon, NC, 25–26 Apr 1862. Expedition to Swansboro, NC, 15–19 Aug 1862. Ran aground in New River Inlet during attack on Jacksonville, NC, and destroyed to prevent capture, 25 Nov 1862.
Prize: 22 Oct 1862: *Adelaide.

The tug *Geranium* photographed after naval service. (Steamship Historical Society)

Name	Bldr	Built	Acquired	Comm
Geranium (ex-*John A. Dix*)	(Newburgh, NY)	1863	5 Sep 1863	15 Oct 1863

Tonnage:	224 tons B
Dimensions:	128'6″ × 23'3″ × 5', d8'
Machinery:	Side wheels, 1 beam engine (34″ × 8'), 1 boiler
Complement:	39/45
Armament:	1 20-pdr R, 2 12-pdr R. Mar 65 total: 2 20-pdr R, 1 24-pdr H, 1 12-pdr R.

SERVICE RECORD: SAtlBS 1863. Expedition up Stono and Folly rivers, SC, 9–14 Feb 1865. Operations at Bull Bay, SC, February 1865. Decomm 15 Jul 1865.
Later history: To U.S. Lighthouse Board, 18 Oct 1865. Sold 1910.

Name	Bldr	Built	Acquired	Comm
Heliotrope (ex-*Maggie Baker*)	(U)	(U)	16 Dec 1863	24 Apr 1864

Tonnage:	238 tons B
Dimensions:	134' × 24'6″ × 5'
Machinery:	Side wheels, 1 inclined engine (28″ × 4'); 6 knots
Complement:	24/66
Armament:	1 12-pdr H. Apr 65 total: 1 30-pdr R, 2 12-pdr R.

NOTES: Wooden hull.
SERVICE RECORD: NAtlBS 1864, tug and ordnance boat. Expedition up Rappahannock River, 6–8 Mar, and up Mattox Creek, Va., 16–18 Mar 1865.
Later history: To U.S. Lighthouse Board, 17 Jun 1865. Later merchant barge *John Bolgiano*. SE 1893.

Name	Bldr	Built	Acquired	Comm
Hollyhock (ex-*Reliance*)	(U)	(U)	5 Mar 1863	Mar 1863

Tonnage:	352 tons B
Dimensions:	135' × 26'9″ × 7', d11'
Machinery:	Side wheels, 2 engines; 14 knots
Complement:	42
Armament:	1 20-pdr R, 2 12-pdr H

NOTES: Captured by USS *Huntsville* in Bahama Channel, 21 Jul 1862. Renamed Jul 1863.
SERVICE RECORD: Tender and supply ship at New Orleans, 1863–65. Sold 5 Oct 1865.
Later history: Merchant *Hollyhock* 1865. RR 1868.

Name	Bldr	Built	Acquired
Ida	(Gretna, La.)	1860	3 Feb 1863

Tonnage:	104 tons B
Dimensions:	(U)
Machinery:	Side wheels
Armament:	1 gun

SERVICE RECORD: Mortar Flotilla, Mississippi River, 1863. Supported operations in Mobile Bay 1865. Sunk by torpedo (mine) in Blakely River, 13 Apr 1865. Raised and sold, 23 Sep 1865.

Name	Bldr	Built	Acquired	Comm
Island Belle	Terry (U)	1855	4 Sep 1861	Sep 1861

Tonnage:	123 tons B
Dimensions:	100' × 20'4″ × d6'7″
Machinery:	Side wheels
Complement:	24
Armament:	1 32-pdr/27, 1 12-pdr R

NOTES: Tug and despatch boat.
SERVICE RECORD: Potomac Flotilla 1861–62. Tug and dispatch boat. Bombardment at Mathias Point, Va., 12 Oct 1861. Expedition in Rappahannock River, Tappahannock, Va., 13–15 Apr 1862. NAtlBS 1862. Burned to prevent capture after running aground in Appomattox River, 27 Jun 1862.

Name	Bldr	Built	Acquired	Comm
O.M. Pettit	(Williamsburg, NY)	1857	17 Aug 1861	4 Oct 1861

Tonnage:	165 tons B
Dimensions:	106' × 24'4″ × 6'
Machinery:	Side wheels; 8 knots
Complement:	30
Armament:	1 30-pdr R, 1 20-pdr R

SERVICE RECORD: SAtlBS 1862–65. Sold 2 Sep 1865.
Later history: Merchant *Oliver M. Pettit*, 1865. RR 1879.

The tug *Yankee* took part in the relief of Fort Sumter before the Navy acquired her and then served in Virginia throughout the war. (Martin Holbrook Collection) (Mariners Museum)

Name	Bldr	L	Acquired	Comm
Oleander	Terry	10 Jan 1863	28 Mar 1863	Apr 1863

Tonnage:	263 tons B
Dimensions:	144'10" × 22'6" × 6'
Machinery:	Side wheels, 1 vertical beam engine (36" × 7'), 1 boiler; 11 knots
Complement:	35
Armament:	2 20-pdr R

NOTES: Purchased prior to completion.
SERVICE RECORD: SAtlBS 1863–65. Bombardment of New Smyrna, Fla., 28 Jul 1863. Assault on Jacksonville, Fla., 2–22 Feb 1864. Decomm 18 Aug 1865. Sold 5 Sep 1865.
Later history: (probably) merchant *Annie*, 1865. Burned at Point Clear, Ala., 19 Apr 1881.

Name	Bldr	Built	Acquired
Yankee	(New York)	1860	1 Jun 1861

Tonnage:	329 tons B
Dimensions:	146' × 25'7" × d9'7"
Machinery:	Side wheels
Complement:	48
Armament:	2 32-pdr/33. Apr 63 total: 1 50-pdr R, 1-8"/55, -24-pdr H, 1 12-pdr SB.

NOTES: Tug chartered Apr 1861 and acquired.
SERVICE RECORD: Relief of Fort Sumter, April 1861. Potomac Flotilla 1861–65. Engaged batteries at Cockpit Point, Va., 1 Jan 62. NAtlBS 1862. Operations in Nansemond River, Va., 11 Apr–4 May 1863. Decomm 16 May 1865. Sold 15 Sep 1865.
Prizes: 18 Jul 1861: *Favorite*; 16 Aug: *T.W. Riley* and *Jane Wright*; 28 Aug: *Remittance*. 27 Jul 1862: *J.W. Sturges*. 11 Jul 1863: *Cassandra*; 15 Jul: *Nanjemoy*; 1 Aug: *Clara Ann*.
Later history: Merchant *Yankee* 1865. Sold foreign, 1871.

SAILING VESSELS (NAVY-BUILT)

SHIPS OF THE LINE

Name	Bldr	Laid down	L	Comm
Columbus	Washington	Jun 1816	1 Mar 1819	7 Sep 1819

NOTES: 2,480 tons B; 193′3″ × 53′6″ × 16′6″; complement 780; 74 guns; 1850: 12 8″, 68 32-pdr.
SERVICE RECORD: In ordinary from 1848. Burned to prevent capture at Norfolk NYd, 20 Apr 1861.

Name	Bldr	Laid down	L	Comm
Ohio	Brooklyn	Nov 1817	30 May 1820	16 Oct 1838

NOTES: 2,757 tons B; 197′2″ × 53′10″ × 26′6″; complement 840; 74 guns. Aug 63: 1 8″ R, 4 100-pdr R, 12 32-pdr/61.
SERVICE RECORD: Receiving ship Boston 1850–75. Sold 27 Sep 1883.

Name	Bldr	Laid down	L	Comm
Pennsylvania	Philadelphia	1822	18 Jul 1837	1841

NOTES: 3,241 tons B; 210′ × 56′9″ × 36′6″; complement 1,100; 120 guns. 1850: 16 8″, 104 32-pdr. Largest sailing warship built in U.S.
SERVICE RECORD: Receiving ship Norfolk 1842–61. Burned to prevent capture at Norfolk NYd, 20 Apr 1861.

Name	Bldr	Laid down	L	Comm
Alabama	Portsmouth	1 Jun 1819	23 Jan 1864	13 May 1864
Delaware	Norfolk	Aug 1817	21 Oct 1820	Feb 1828
New York	Norfolk	May 1820	never	never
North Carolina	Philadelphia	Jun 1816	7 Sep 1820	27 May 1825
Vermont	Boston	Sep 1818	14 Sep 1848	30 Jan 1862
Virginia	Boston	May 1822	never	never

NOTES: 2,633 tons B; 196′3″ × 54′4″ × 26′2″; complement 820; 74 guns. *Alabama* Jun 64: 4 100-pdr R, 6 9″. Jun 65: add 2 24-pdr. *Delaware* 1850: 12 8″, 72 32-pdr. *North Carolina* Apr 62: 1 30-pdr R, 4

9″ SB. *Vermont* Feb 62: 4 8″/63, 20 32-pdr/57. Apr 63 total: 10 8″/63, 6 32-pdr/57, 2 32-pdr/42.

NOTES: *New Orleans*, 120 guns, laid down 1815 at Sacketts Harbor, NY, on Lake Ontario, remained on the stocks until broken up 1883.
SERVICE RECORDS:
Alabama—Renamed **New Hampshire**, 28 Oct 1863. Completed as a storeship. Depot ship, Port Royal, SC, SAtlBS 1864–65. Receiving ship, Norfolk 1866–76, also Port Royal, Norfolk, and Newport, finally at New London, 1891–92. Training ship New York 1893–20. Renamed **Granite State**, 30 Nov 1904. Burned and sank at pier, 23 May 1921. Sold 19 Aug 1921. Hulk burned and sank under tow in Massachusetts Bay, Jul 1922.
Delaware—In ordinary from 1844. Burned to prevent capture at Norfolk NYd, 20 Apr 1861.
New York—Burned on the stocks to prevent capture at Norfolk NYd, 20 Apr 1861.
North Carolina—Receiving ship New York 1839–66. Sold 1 Oct 1867.
Vermont—Laid down 1818. In ordinary after launching. Completed for use as storeship. Badly damaged in storm while under tow to Port Royal, SC, 24 Feb 1862. Ordnance and depot ship Port Royal 1862–64. Receiving ship New York 1864–1901. Sold 17 Apr 1902.
Virginia—Laid down 1822. Never launched and broken up on stocks 1884.

FRIGATES

Name	Bldr	Laid down	L	Comm
Constitution	Claghorn, Boston	1796	21 Oct 1797	2 Jul 1798
United States	Humphreys, Southwark, Pa.	1796	10 May 1797	11 Jul 1797

NOTES: 1,607 tons; 175′ × 44′2″ × 23′6″; complement 467; 44 guns. *Constitution* Sep 61: 6 32-pdr/42, 10 32-pdr/33.
SERVICE RECORDS:
Constitution—Training ship, Naval Academy 1860–82. Receiving ship,

The ship-of-the-line *Ohio* off Boston Navy Yard in the 1870s while serving as receiving ship. (Silverstone Collection) (U.S. Naval Historical Center)

The *North Carolina*, a ship-of-the-line serving as receiving ship at New York during the 1860s. (Martin Holbrook Collection) (U.S. Naval Historical Center)

Portsmouth, NH, 1884–97, and Boston 1897–1905. Preserved at Boston, Mass.

United States—In ordinary from 1849. Seized by Confederates at Norfolk NYd, 20 Apr 1861. Broken up 1865 after being recovered at Norfolk in 1862.

Name	Bldr	Laid down	L	Comm
Brandywine	Washington	Sep 1821	16 Jun 1825	25 Aug 1825
Columbia	Washington	Nov 1825	9 Mar 1836	6 May 1838
Cumberland	Boston	1825	24 May 1842	20 Nov 1843
Potomac	Washington	9 Aug 1819	22 Mar 1822	15 Jun 1831
Raritan	Philadelphia	Sep 1820	13 Jun 1843	1 Dec 1843
St. Lawrence	Norfolk	1826	25 Mar 1847	4 Sep 1848
Savannah	Brooklyn	Jul 1820	5 May 1842	15 Oct 1843

NOTES: 1,726 tons; 175′ × 45′ × 22′4″; complement 400; 44 guns. *Columbia* 1853: 10 8″, 40 32-pdr. *Cumberland* Mar 62: 22 9″ SB, 1 10″ SB, 1 70-pdr R. *Potomac* May 61: 10 8″/63, 24 32-pdr/57, 16 32-pdr/33, 2 12-pdr SB. Jul 64 total: 4 8″/63, 19 32-pdr/57, 1 32-pdr/33, 10 30-pdr R, 1 20-pdr R. *Raritan* 1848: 8 8″, 42 32-pdr. *St. Lawrence* Jul 61: 10 8″/63, 24 32-pdr/57, 16 32-pdr/33, 2 12-pdr SB. May 63: less 6 32-pdr/33, add 2 50-pdr R. Sep 63 total: 8 9″ SB, 2 32-pdr/57, 2 12-pdr SB. Oct 64: add 1 30-pdr R. *Savannah* Jan 61: 2 10″ SB, 8 8″/63, 14 32-pdr/57. Feb 62 total: 1 10″ SB, 6 8″/63, 12 32-pdr/57. Sep 62 total: 1 11″ SB, 2 9″ SB. Dec 62: add 4 32-pdr/57.

The *Vermont* as receiving ship at New York Navy Yard shortly after the Civil War. Her masts and rigging were later removed, and she was housed over. (Martin Holbrook Collection) (U.S. Naval Historical Center)

The frigate *Cumberland* docked at Portsmouth Navy Yard about 1860. She was sunk by CSS *Virginia* at Hampton Roads on March 8, 1862. (U.S. Naval Historical Center)

SERVICE RECORDS:

Brandywine—Storeship, NAtlBS, Hampton Roads, 1861, later Norfolk. Destroyed by fire at Norfolk, 3 Sep 1864.

Columbia—In ordinary from 1855. Scuttled and burned to prevent capture at Norfolk NYd, 20 Apr 1861.

Cumberland—Razee sloop 1855–56. Towed out of Norfolk NYd Apr 1861. NAtlBS 1861–62. Capture of Hatteras Inlet, 28–29 Aug 1861. Rammed and sunk by CSS *Virginia* in Hampton Roads, Va., 8 Mar 1862.

   Prizes: 23 Apr 1861: *Cambria*; 24 Apr: tug *Young America* and *George M. Smith*; 1 May: *Sarah & Mary*; 2 May: *Carrie*; 3 May: *A.J. Russell*; 4 May: *Elite*; 11 May: *Dorothy Haines*.

Potomac—WGulfBS 1861. Receiving ship Pensacola 1861–67, and Philadelphia 1867–77. Decomm 13 Jan 1877. Sold 24 May 1877.

   Prizes: 24 Dec 1862: str *Bloomer*. 14 Jan 1864: *Champion*.

Raritan—In ordinary from 1852. Scuttled to prevent capture at Norfolk NYd, 20 Apr 1861.

St. Lawrence—AtlBS 1861. Damaged by gunfire of CSS *Virginia* at Hampton Roads, 8 Mar 1862. EGulfBS Mar 1862–May 1863. NAtlBS Aug 1864, Ordnance ship. Barracks ship, Norfolk, 1867–1875. Sold 31 Dec 1875.

   Prizes: 16 Jul 1861: *Herald*; 28 Jul: privateer *Petrel; 6 Nov: *Fanny Lee*.

Savannah—Blockade of Georgia, 1861. Naval Academy practice ship 1862–1870. Sold 27 Sep 1883.

   Prizes: 30 Nov 1861: *E. Waterman*; 6 Dec: *Cheshire*.

Name	Bldr	Laid down	L	Comm
Sabine	Brooklyn	1823	12 Feb 1855	23 Aug 1858
Santee	Portsmouth	1821	16 Feb 1855	9 Jun 1861

NOTES: 1,726 tons; 202′6″ (U) 190′ (pp) × 45′ × 21′6″; 44 guns (lengthened during construction).

Sabine—Aug 61: 2 10″ SB, 10 8″/63, 18 32-pdr/57, 18 32-pdr/33. Sep 61: 2 10″ SB replaced by 2 8″/64. Sep 63 total: 2 100-pdr R, 2 20-pdr R, 10 9″ SB, 18 32-pdr/57, 16 32-pdr/33, 2 12-pdr H. Jul 64 total: 2 100-pdr R, 10 9″ SB, 14 32-pdr/57, 8 32-pdr/33, 2 12-pdr R.

Santee—May 61: 2 64-pdr/106, 10 8″/63, 20 32-pdr/57, 16 32-pdr/33, 2 12-pdr. Oct 62 total: 1 11″ SB, 1 100-pdr R, 10 32-pdr/33.

SERVICE RECORDS:

Sabine—NAtlBS 1861–64. Training ship Norfolk 1864. Receiving ship Portsmouth 1872–76. Laid up 1877. Sold 23 Sep 1883.

Santee—WGulfBS 1861–62. School ship, Naval Academy, Newport, later Annapolis, 1862–1912. Sank at her moorings at Annapolis, 2 Apr 1912. Hulk sold 29 Jul 1912.

   Prizes: 8 Aug 1861: *C.P. Knapp*; 27 Oct: *Delta*; 7 Nov: *Royal Yacht; 30 Dec: *Garonne*.

Name	Bldr	Laid down	L	Comm
Congress	Portsmouth	1839	16 Aug 1841	7 May 1842

NOTES: 1,867 tons; 179′ × 47′8″ × 22′6″; complement 480; 44 guns. Mar 62: 10 8″ SB, 40 32-pdr.

SERVICE RECORD: AtlBS 1861. Damaged by gunfire of CSS *Virginia* in Hampton Roads, Va., and destroyed by fire, 8 Mar 1862.

Name	Bldr	Laid down	L	Comm
Independence	Hartt & Barker, Boston	1813	20 Jun 1814	3 Jul 1815

NOTES: 1,891 tons; 188′ × 51′6″ × 24′; 60 guns. 1854: 10 8″, 46 32-pdr.

SERVICE RECORD: Built as ship-of-the-line, razeed to frigate 1837. Receiving ship, Mare Island 1857–1912. Sold 3 Sep 1913, hulk burned to recover metal fittings, 20 Sep 1915.

SLOOPS

Name	Bldr	Laid down	L	Comm
Falmouth	Boston	5 Dec 1826	3 Nov 1827	20 Jan 1828
John Adams	Norfolk	1829	17 Nov 1830	8 May 1831
St. Louis	Washington	1828	18 Aug 1828	20 Dec 1828
Vandalia	Philadelphia	1828	16 Aug 1828	6 Nov 1828
Vincennes	Brooklyn	1825	27 Apr 1826	3 Sep 1826

NOTES: 703 tons; 127′6″ × 35′11″ × 16′; complement 125; 18 guns
Falmouth Aug 61: 2 32-pdr/33.
John Adams May 62: 2 30-pdr R, 2 8″/55, 4 32-pdr/33. Dec 64: add 2 20-pdr R
St. Louis Oct 61: 4 8″/63, 14 32-pdr/33. Feb 62: 4 8″/55, 12 32-pdr/33, 2 20-pdr R, 1 12-pdr SB.
Vandalia Nov 63: 1 30-pdr R, 4 8″/55, 16 32-pdr/33.
Vincennes May 61: 4 8″/55, 14 32-pdr/33. Nov 61: 4 8″/55, 2 9″ SB.

SERVICE RECORDS:

Falmouth—Stationary storeship Aspinwall, Panama 1860. Sold 7 Nov 1863.

John Adams—Pacific and Far East 1853–62. Training ship, Naval Academy 1862–63. SAtlBS 1863–65. Decomm Sep 1867. Sold 5 Oct 1867.

St. Louis—Home Sqn 1858–61. Patrolled transatlantic area 1862–64. SAtlBS Nov 1864. Decomm 12 May 1865. Receiving ship League Island 1866–94. Training ship 1894. Renamed **Keystone State**, 30 Nov 1904. Stricken 9 Aug 1906. Sold 5 Jun 1907.

   Prize: 5 Sep 1861: *Macao*.

Vandalia—SAtlBS May 1861. Bombardment and occupation of Port Royal, SC, 7 Nov 1861. Receiving ship Portsmouth 1863–70. Broken up 1870–72.

   Prizes: 26 Jun 1861: *Solferino*; 21 Aug: *Henry Middleton*; 6 Oct: *Ariel*; 15 Nov: *Thomas Watson*.

Vincennes—GulfBS 1861. Engagement with CSS *Ivy* at Head of Passes, 9 Oct, and with CSN squadron near Head of Passes, Miss., 12 Oct 1861. Guardship Ship Island, Miss., 1862–65. Decomm 28 Aug 1865. Sold 5 Oct 1867.

   Prizes: 27 Nov 1861: *Empress*. 18 Jul 1863: *H. McGuin*.

Name	Bldr	Laid down	L	Comm
Lexington	Brooklyn	1825	9 Mar 1826	11 Jun 1826
Warren	Boston	1 Jun 1825	29 Nov 1826	22 Feb 1827

NOTES: 691 tons; 127′ × 33′6″ × 16′6″; complement 190; 18 guns.

SERVICE RECORDS:

Lexington—Sold 1860.

Warren—Storeship 1846–1862. Sold at Panama 1 Jan 1863.
  Later history: Used as coal hulk as late as 1874.

Name	Bldr	Laid down	L	Comm
Cyane	Boston	1837	2 Dec 1837	May 1838
Levant	Brooklyn	1837	28 Dec 1837	2 Apr 1838

NOTES: 792 tons; 132′4″ × 36′3″ × 16′6″; complement 190; 22 guns. 4 8″ SB, 14 32-pdr/41. *Cyane* May 65 total, 14 32-pdr, 4 68-pdr, 1 12-pdr H.

SERVICE RECORDS:

Cyane—Pacific Sqn 1858–71. Decomm 20 Sep 1871. Sold 30 Jul 1887.
  Prize: 15 Mar 1863: *J.M. Chapman*.

Levant—Disappeared en route from Hawaii to Panama after 18 Sep 1860.

Name	Bldr	Laid down	L	Comm
Dale	Philadelphia	1839	8 Nov 1839	11 Dec 1840
Decatur	Brooklyn	1838	9 Apr 1839	16 Mar 1840
Marion	Boston	1838	24 Apr 1839	4 Oct 1839
Preble	Portsmouth	Apr 1838	13 Jun 1839	2 Jun 1840

NOTES: 566 tons; 117′7″ × 33′10″ × 15′8″; 150 complement; 16 guns.

Dale—Jul 61: 12 32-pdr/27, 2 32-pdr/33, 1 12-pdr H. Feb 63 total: 2 32-pdr/33, 1 30-pdr R.

Decatur—Apr 63: 4 8″, 4 32-pdr/42. Dec 65 total: 12 32-pdr/27, 4 32-pdr/33.

Marion—Jun 61: 12 32-pdr/27, 2 32-pdr/33, 1 12-pdr H. 1862 total: 10 32-pdr, 1 20-pdr R. Jul 62 total: 4 32-pdr/27, 2 32-pdr/33, 1 20-pdr R, 1 12-pdr H.

Preble—Jan 61: 10 32-pdr/33. Jul 61 total: 2 8″/63, 1 32-pdr/43, 6 32-pdr/33, 1 12-pdr. Jun 64 total: 4 8″/63, 12 32-pdr/33, 2 20-pdr R.

SERVICE RECORDS:

Dale—SAtlBS 1861. Store and guard ship, Port Royal, SC. Storeship, Key West 1863–65. Training ship, Naval Academy 1867. Receiving ship Washington, D.C., 1884. Maryland Naval Militia 1895. Renamed **Oriole**, 30 Nov 1904. Sold 20 Dec 1921.
  Prizes: 12 Oct 1861: *Specie*; 15 Nov: *Mabel*.

Decatur—In ordinary from 1859. Harbor battery, San Francisco 1863. Sold 17 Aug 1865.

Marion—In ordinary from 1860. GulfBS 1861. Practice ship, Naval Academy 1862–70. Decomm and BU 1871.

Preble—Paraguay Expedition 1859. GulfBS 1861–63. Engagement with CSS *Ivy*, 9 Oct, and with CSN squadron, near Head of Passes, Miss., 12 Oct 1861. Guard ship Pensacola 1862–63. Destroyed by accidental fire at Pensacola, Fla., 27 Apr 1863.

An unidentified sloop in dry dock at Boston Navy Yard. From an early daguerrotype, the ship is believed to be possibly either *Decatur, Dale, Marion,* or *Preble*. (Peabody Museum of Salem)

The sloop *Dale* as a training ship during the late nineteenth century. (Martin Holbrook Collection) (National Archives)

Name	Bldr	Laid down	L	Comm
Saratoga	Portsmouth	1841	26 Jul 1842	7 Jan 1843

NOTES: 882 tons; 146'4" × 35'3" × 16'8"; complement 210; 20 guns. Jun 63: 6 8"/55, 12 32-pdr/42, 1 30-pdr R, 2 12-pdr R, 1 12-pdr SB.
SERVICE RECORD: Africa station 1861. Captured slaver *Nightingale* off Kabinda, Angola, 21 Apr 1861. Guard ship off Delaware capes, 1863. SAtlBS Jan 1864. Decomm 28 Apr 1865. Gunnery ship, Annapolis 1875. Training ship 1877–1888. Marine school ship Philadelphia, 1890–1907. Sold 14 Aug 1907.

Name	Bldr	Laid down	L	Comm
Portsmouth	Portsmouth	15 Jun 1843	23 Oct 1843	10 Nov 1844

NOTES: 1,022 tons; 151'10" × 38'1" × 17'6"; complement 200; 20 guns. Sep 61: 16 8"/63, 1 12-pdr. Jul 63 total: 16 8"/63, 2 8"/55, 1 20-pdr R, 1 12-pdr. Jun 64: add 1 100-pdr R.
SERVICE RECORD: Africa Sqn 1859–61. Captured slaver *Virginian* off Congo River 6 Feb 1860. Captured brig *Falmouth* off Porto Praya, 5 Jun 1860. GulfBS 1862. Passage past New Orleans forts and engagement with CSN vessels, 24 Apr 1862. Station ship New Orleans, 1862–65. Training ship 1878–1911. Loaned to Marine Hospital Service 1911–15. Sold 12 Jul 1915.
Prizes: 18 Feb 1862: strs *Labuan* and *Wave*; 20 Feb: *Pioneer*.

The sloop *Saratoga* on a visit to England in 1899. (Imperial War Museum)

The sloop *Portsmouth* at Portsmouth Navy Yard sometime after the war. (U.S. Naval Historical Center)

Name	Bldr	Laid down	L	Comm
Plymouth	Boston	1843	11 Oct 1843	3 Apr 1844

NOTES: 989 tons; 147'6" × 38'1" × 18'; complement 210; 20 guns. 1859: 2 8" SB, 6 32-pdr SB.
SERVICE RECORD: Under repair at Norfolk 1860–61. Seized by Confederates at Norfolk NYd, 20 Apr 1861.

Name	Bldr	Laid down	L	Comm
Germantown	Philadelphia	7 Sep 1843	21 Aug 1846	7 Dec 1846

NOTES: 942 tons; 150' × 36' × 17'3"; complement 210; 20 guns. 1857: 8 8" SB, 12 32-pdr SB.
SERVICE RECORD: In ordinary 1860. Burned to prevent capture at Norfolk NYd, 20 Apr 1861. Hulk raised 22 Apr 1863 and sold.

Name	Bldr	Laid down	L	Comm
Jamestown	Norfolk	1843	16 Sep 1844	15 Jan 1845

NOTES: 985 tons; 163'5" × 36' × 18'; 20 guns. May 61: 6 8"/55, 14 32-pdr/42.
SERVICE RECORD: AtlBS 1861. Pacific Sqn 1862–65. Converted to transport and storeship 1866. N. Pacific Sqn 1867–68. Pacific Sqn

The sloop *Jamestown* at left as a training ship towards the end of the nineteenth century. At right is the *Saratoga* or *Portsmouth*. This picture was previously identified as *Portsmouth* and *Saratoga*. (U.S. Naval Historical Center)

The sloop *Macedonian*, as U.S. Naval Academy practice ship at Newport, Rhode Island, around 1864–1865. (U.S. Naval Historical Center)

1869–71. School ship, Hawaii, 1876–79. Training ship, Atlantic, 1882–88. 1889–92. Transferred to Treasury Dept. 9 Sep 1892. Quarantine ship Hampton Roads 1892–1913. Destroyed by fire at Norfolk, 3 Jan 1913.

Prizes: 5 Aug 1861: *Alvarado; 31 Aug: *Aigburth*; 4 Sep: *Colonel Long; 15 Dec: *Havelock*. May 1 1862: *Intended*.

Name	Bldr	Laid down	L	Comm
St. Mary's	Washington	1843	24 Nov 1844	13 Dec 1844

NOTES: 958 tons; 150′ × 36′6″ × 17′3″; complement 195; 20 guns. Dec 62: 6 8″/55, 16 32-pdr/42.
SERVICE RECORD: Pacific Sqn 1860–66, 1870–72. School ship, New York, 1875–1908. Stricken 14 Jun 1908.

Name	Bldr	Laid down	L	Comm
Macedonian	Norfolk	1832	1 Nov 1836	11 Oct 1837

NOTES:1,341 tons; 164′ × 42′ × 21′8″; complement 380; 20 guns.

1861: 2 10″ SB, 16 8″ SB, 4 32-pdr. Nov 62 total: 1 10″/87, 4 8″/55, 1 12-pdr. May 63 total: 2 100-pdr R, 8 8″/63, 4 32-pdr/42, 2 12-pdr. May 64: 2 12-pdr replaced by 2 9″ SB. Sep 64: 2 100-pdr R, 2 9″ SB, 8 8″/63, 2 32-pdr/42, 4 12-pdr.
SERVICE RECORD: Frigate razeed to sloop 1852–53. Gulf and Caribbean 1861. West India Sqn 1862–63. Practice ship, Naval Academy 1864–70. Decomm 1871. Sold 31 Dec 1875.

Name	Bldr	Laid down	L	Comm
Constellation	Norfolk	1853	28 Aug 1854	28 Jul 1855

NOTES: 1,278 tons; 176′ × 42′ × 19′3″; complement 227; 22 guns. Mar 62: 16 8″/63, 4 32-pdr/57, 1 30-pdr R, 1 20-pdr R, 2 12-pdr SB. 1871 total: 1 100-pdr R, 10 10″. Officially considered to be the frigate built in 1797.
SERVICE RECORD: African Sqn 1859–61. Captured slaver *Triton* off W. coast of Africa, 21 Jun 1861. Mediterranean 1862–64. Receiving ship 1865–1933 at Norfolk, Philadelphia, Annapolis, and Newport. Decomm 4 Feb 1955. Preserved at Baltimore, Md.

BRIGS

Name	Bldr	Laid down	L	Comm
Dolphin	Brooklyn	1836	17 Jun 1836	6 Sep 1836

NOTES: 224 tons; 88′ × 25′ × 13′; complement 80; 10 guns. 1859: 3 11″ SB, 1 9″ SB.
SERVICE RECORD: In ordinary 1861. Burned to prevent capture at Norfolk NYd, 20 Apr 1861.

Name	Bldr	Laid down	L	Comm
Bainbridge	Boston	1842	26 Apr 1842	16 Dec 1842

NOTES: 259 tons; 100′ × 25′ × 13′; 10 guns. Jan 61: 6 32-pdr/27.
SERVICE RECORD: Paraguay Expedition 1859–60. GulfSqn May 1861–Jun 1862. EGulfBS Aug 1862. Damaged in storm at Aspinwall, Panama, 24 Nov 1862. Capsized off Cape Hatteras, 21 Aug 1863.
Prizes: 11 May 1862: *New Castle*; 24 May: str *Swan*; 9 Jun: *Baigorry*.

Name	Bldr	Laid down	L	Comm
Perry	Norfolk	1843	9 May 1843	13 Oct 1843

NOTES: 280 tons; 105′ × 25′6″ × 13′2″; complement 67; 10 guns. Apr 61: 6 32-pdr/27, 1 12-pdr. Apr 62 total: 2 20-pdr R, 6 32-pdr/27, 1 12-pdr.
SERVICE RECORD: AtlBS 1861. Panama May–Nov 1862. NAtlBS Mar–Aug 1863. SAtlBS Nov 1683–May 1865. Decomm 29 Apr 1865. Sold 10 Aug 1865.
Prizes: 31 May 1861: *Hannah M. Johnson*; 3 Jun: privateer *Savannah*; 18 Dec: *Ellen Jane* and *Blooming Youth*. 31 Mar 1863: *Sue*; 2 May: *Alma*.

STORESHIP

Name	Bldr	Laid down	L	Comm
Relief	Philadelphia	1836	14 Sep 1836	1836

NOTES: Ship; 438 tons; 109′ (bp) × 30′ × d12′; complement 51. Jul 62: 1 30-pdr R, 2 32-pdr/33. Oct 64 total: 1 32-pdr/33.
SERVICE RECORD: Expedition to Pocotaligo, SC, 21–23 Oct 1862. Pacific 1864–66. Receiving ship Washington 1871–1877. Sold 27 Sep 1883.

ACQUIRED SAILING VESSELS

MORTAR SCHOONERS

Name	Bldr	Built	Acquired	Comm
Adolph Hugel	(Philadelphia)	1860	21 Sep 1861	13 Jan 1862

NOTES:114′ × 29′6″ × 9′; 269 tons, complement 34. 1 13″ M, 2 32-pdr/57.
SERVICE RECORD: Mortar Flotilla, Mississippi Sqn, 1863. Bombardment of Fts. Jackson and St. Philip below New Orleans, Mississippi River, 18–28 Apr 1862. Bombardment of Vicksburg, 26 Jun–22 Jul 1862. Potomac Flotilla, 1862–65. Decomm 17 Jun 1865. Sold 20 Jul 1865.
Prizes: 24 Feb 1863: *Kate*; 27 Feb: *Chatham*; 17 Sep: *Music*; 1 Dec: *F.U. Johnson*. 26 Oct 1864: *Coquette*; 28 Oct: *James Sandy*; 2 Nov: *Zion*.
Later history: Merchant *Adolph Hugel* 1865. SE 1870.

Name	Bldr	Built	Acquired	Comm
Arletta	(Mystic, Conn.)	1860	7 Dec 1861	30 Jan 1862

NOTES: 103′ × 27′ × 10′6″; 199 tons, complement 21/39. Feb 62: 1 13″ M, 2 32-pdr/57, 2 12-pdr SB. 1863: less 1 13″ M.
SERVICE RECORD: Mortar Flotilla, WGulfBS 1862. Bombardment of Fts. Jackson and St. Philip below New Orleans, 18–28 Apr 1862. Bombardment of Vicksburg, 26 Jun–22 Jul 1862. NAtlBS 1862–65. Ordnance store vessel, Beaufort, NC, 1864. Decomm 28 Sep 1865. Sold 30 Nov 1865.
Later history: Merchant *Arletta* 1865. FFU.

Name	Bldr	Built	Acquired	Comm
C.P. Williams	(Hoboken, NJ)	1851	2 Sep 1861	21 Jan 1862

NOTES: 103′8″ × 28′3″ × 9′; 210 tons, complement 35/48. 1862: 1 13″ M, 2 32-pdr/57, 2 12-pdr SB. May 63: add 1 20-pdr R. Dec 64: add 2 24-pdr SB.

SERVICE RECORD: Mortar Flotilla, Mississippi Sqn, 1862. Bombardment of Fts. Jackson and St. Philip below New Orleans, 18–28 Apr 1862. Bombardment of Vicksburg, 26 Jun–22 Jul 1862. SAtlBS, Nov 1862. Engaged batteries at Ft. McAllister, Ogeechee River, Ga., 19 Nov 1862 and 27 Jan–3 Mar 1863. Engaged batteries in Stono River, SC, 25 Dec 1863. Expedition up Stono and Folly rivers, 9–14 Feb 1865. Decomm 27 Jun 1865. Sold 10 Aug 1865.
Later history: Merchant *Sarah Purves* 1866. SE 1885.

Name	Bldr	Built	Acquired	Comm
Dan Smith	(Fairhaven, Ct)	1859	7 Sep 1861	30 Jan 1862

NOTES: 87′9″ × 25′2″ × 10′; 149 tons, complement 32. Feb 62: 1 13″ M, 2 12-pdr SB.
SERVICE RECORD: Mortar Flotilla, Mississippi Sqn. Bombardment of Fts. Jackson and St. Philip below New Orleans, 18–28 Apr 1862. Bombardment of Vicksburg, 26 Jun–22 Jul 1862. Potomac Flotilla, Oct 1862. SAtlBS Jul 1863. Bombardment of forts in Charleston harbor, 13–15 Aug 1863. Expedition up Stono and Folly rivers, SC, 9–14 Feb 1865. Decomm 28 Jun 1865. Sold 10 Aug 1865.
Prize: 3 Mar 1864: *Sophia.
Later history: Merchant *Volant* 1866. (British) SE 1870.

Name	Bldr	Built	Acquired	Comm
George Mangham	(Philadelphia)	1854	21 Sep 1861	11 Jan 1862

NOTES: 110′ × 28′ × 10′; 274 tons, complement 26. 1862: 1 13″ M, 2 32-pdr/57. Dec 64 total: 6 32-pdr/57, 1 12-pdr R.
SERVICE RECORD: Mortar Flotilla, Mississippi Sqn. Bombardment of Fts. Jackson and St. Philip below New Orleans, 18–28 Apr 1862. Bombardment of Vicksburg, 26 Jun–22 Jul 1862. Potomac Flotilla, Dec 1862–Jul 1863. Anti-raider patrol off Prince Edward Island, Aug–Nov 1863. SAtlBS 1864. Decomm 9 Sep and sold 27 Sep 1865.
Later history: FFU.

An unidentified mortar schooner at New Orleans, 1862. Notice man leaning on the mortar between the masts. (Peabody Museum of Salem)

Name	Bldr	Built	Acquired	Comm
Henry Janes	Bayles, Pt. Jefferson, LI	1854	27 Sep 1861	30 Jan 1862

NOTES: 109′9″ × 29′8″ × 9′; 261 tons, complement 35. Feb 62: 1 13″ M, 2 32-pdr/57. May 64: less 1 13″ M.

SERVICE RECORD: Mortar Flotilla, Mississippi Sqn. Bombardment of Fts. Jackson and St. Philip below New Orleans, 18–28 Apr 1862. Bombardment of Vicksburg, 26 Jun–22 Jul 1862. Engagement with CSS *Arkansas* above Vicksburg, 15 Jul 1862. Bombardment and capture of Galveston, Tex., 4 Oct 1862. Bombardment of Port Hudson, La., 8 May–9 Jul 1863. Bombardment of Ft. Powell, Mobile Bay, 16–29 Feb 1864. NAtlBS Aug 1864. Decomm 12 Jul and sold 20 Jul 1865.

Prizes: Oct 1862: *Eliza*. Jan 1863: *Matilda*.

Later history: FFU.

Name	Bldr	Built	Acquired	Comm
Horace Beals	Roosevelt	1856	19 Sep 1861	5 Feb 1862

NOTES: 121′6″ × 30′8″ × d11′8″; 296 tons, complement 39. 2 32-pdr/33, 1 30-pdr R. Jan 63 total: 1 32-pdr/33. Jan 64 total: 2 32-pdr/33.

SERVICE RECORD: Mortar Flotilla, Mississippi Sqn. Bombardment of

Fts. Jackson and St. Philip below New Orleans, 18–28 Apr 1862. Bombardment of Vicksburg, 26 Jun–22 Jul 1862. Engagement with CSS *Arkansas* above Vicksburg, 15 Jul 1862. Decomm 13 May and sold 30 May 1865.
Later history: Merchant *Horace Beals* 1865. Later Swedish *Britannia*, SE 1885.

Name	Bldr	Built	Acquired	Comm
John Griffith	(New York)	1854	16 Sep 1861	20 Jan 1862

NOTES: 113′8″ × (U); 246 tons, complement 39. Jan 62: 1 13″ M, 2 32-pdr/57; 2 12-pdr H
SERVICE RECORD: Mortar Flotilla, Mississippi Sqn. Bombardment of Fts. Jackson and St. Philip below New Orleans, 18–28 Apr 1862. Bombardment of Vicksburg, 26 Jun–22 Jul 1862. Engagement with CSS *Arkansas* above Vicksburg, 15 Jul 1862. WGulfBS 1862–64. Bombardment of Port Hudson, La., 8 May–9 Jul 1863. Bombardment of Ft. Powell, Mobile Bay, 16–29 Feb 1864. SAtlBS 1864. Decomm 21 Aug and sold 8 Sep 1865.
Later history: FFU.

Name	Bldr	Built	Acquired	Comm
Maria A. Wood	(Philadelphia)	1860	21 Sep 1861	19 Nov 1861

NOTES: 125′ × 29′6″ × 9′; 344 tons, complement 25. Dec 61: 2 32-pdr/57.
SERVICE RECORD: WGulfBS 1861–62. Occupation of Pensacola, 10 May 1862. WGulfBS 1864–65. Decomm 22 Aug 1866. Sold 6 Sep 1866.
Later history: FFU.

Name	Bldr	Built	Acquired	Comm
Maria J. Carlton	Dennison, Saybrook, Ct.	1859	15 Oct 1861	29 Jan 1862

NOTES: 98′ × 27′; 178 tons, complement 28. Feb 62: 1 13″ M, 2 12-pdr R.
SERVICE RECORD: Mortar Flotilla, Mississippi Sqn. Bombardment of Fts. Jackson and St. Philip below New Orleans, 18–19 Apr, and sunk by Confederate gunfire, 19 Apr 1862.

Name	Bldr	Built	Acquired	Comm
Matthew Vassar (ex-*Matthew Vassar Jr.*)	French, Poughkeepsie	1855	9 Sep 1861	25 Jan 1862

NOTES: 93′7″ × 27′2″ × 8′6″; 216 tons, complement 29. Jan 62: 1 13″ M, 2 32-pdr. Feb 62: add 2 12-pdr. May 63 total: 1 30-pdr R, 2 32-pdr/42.
SERVICE RECORD: Mortar Flotilla, Mississippi Sqn. Bombardment of Fts. Jackson and St. Philip below New Orleans, 18–28 Apr 1862. Bombardment of Vicksburg, 26 Jun–22 Jul 1862. NAtlBS 1863–64. EGulfBS Nov 1864–65. Decomm 10 Jul 1865. Sold 10 Aug 1865.
Prizes: 15 May 1862: *New Eagle* and *Sarah*. 11 Jan 1863: *Florida*; 27 Apr: **Golden Liner*. 3 Feb 1865: *John Hale*.
Later history: FFU.

Name	Bldr	Built	Acquired	Comm
Norfolk Packet	Goodspeed	1851	10 Sep 1861	7 Feb 1862

NOTES: 109′6″ × 28′2″ × 11′; 349 tons, complement 51. Feb 62: 1 13″ M, 2 32-pdr/57, 2 12-pdr H. May 63: 2 20-pdr R, 2 32-pdr/57, 1 12-pdr R.
SERVICE RECORD: Mortar Flotilla, Mississippi Sqn. Bombardment of Fts. Jackson and St. Philip below New Orleans, 18–28 Apr 1862. Bombardment of Vicksburg, 26 Jun–22 Jul 1862. SAtlBS Nov 1862–Jun 1865. Bombardment of Ft. McAllister, Ga., 3 Mar 1863. Decomm 12 Jul 1865. Sold 10 Aug 1865.
Prizes: 23 Oct 1863: *Ocean Bird*. 11 Mar 1864: *Linda*; 26 Jun: *Sarah Mary*.
Later history: FFU.

Name	Bldr	Built	Acquired	Comm
Oliver H. Lee	Capes	1851	27 Aug 1861	4 Feb 1862

NOTES: 100′9″ × 28′4″ × 8′; 199 tons; complement 37. Feb 62: 1 13″ M, 2 32-pdr/57, 2 12-pdr SB. Jun 63: less 2 12-pdr SB. Dec 64 total: 4 32-pdr/57, 2 12-pdr R.
SERVICE RECORD: Mortar Flotilla, Mississipi Sqn. Bombardment of Fts. Jackson and St. Philip below New Orleans, 18–28 Apr 1862. Bombardment of Vicksburg, 26 Jun–22 Jul 1862. Engagement with CSS *Arkansas* above Vicksburg, 15 Jul 1862. Bombardment of Port Hudson, La., 8 May–9 Jul 1863. WGulfBS Aug 1863–65. Expeditions up Broad River, SC, 27 Nov–30 Dec 1864 and to St. Marks, Fla., 23 Feb–27 Mar 1865. Decomm 10 Jul 1865. Sold 19 Aug 1865.
Prize: 10 Dec 1864: str *Sorts*.
Later history: Merchant *William S. Doughton* 1865. SE 1895.

Name	Bldr	Built	Acquired	Comm
Orvetta	Carl, Northport, LI	1858	1 Oct 1861	27 Jan 1862

NOTES: 93′ × 27′2″ × 7′; 171 tons, complement 43. Feb 62: 1 13″ M, 2 32-pdr/57. Dec 64 total: 2 32-pdr/33.
SERVICE RECORD: Mortar Flotilla, Mississippi Sqn. Bombardment of Fts. Jackson and St. Philip below New Orleans, 18–28 Apr 1862. Bombardment of Vicksburg, 26 Jun–22 Jul 1862. Engagement with CSS *Arkansas* above Vicksburg, 15 Jul 1862. Bombardment of Port Hudson, La., 8 May–9 Jul 1863. WGulfBS 1863. Bombardment of Ft. Powell, Mobile Bay, 16–29 Feb 1864. Decomm 3 Jul and sold 15 Aug 1865.
Later history: Merchant *Orvetta* 1865. SE 1870.

Name	Bldr	Built	Acquired	Comm
Para	(Wilmington, Del.)	1860	9 Sep 1861	4 Feb 1861

NOTES: 98′ × 24′ × 9′; 190 tons, complement 35. Feb 62: 1 13″ M, 2 32-pdr/57. Mar 64 total: 1 12-pdr R, 2 20-pdr R, 2 32-pdr/57.
SERVICE RECORD: Mortar Flotilla, Mississippi Sqn. Bombardment of Fts. Jackson and St. Philip below New Orleans, 18–28 Apr 1862. Bombardment of Vicksburg, 26 Jun–22 Jul 1862. SAtlBS 1863.

Bombardment of Ft. McAllister, Ga., 3 Mar 1863. Expedition up Stono River, SC, 5 Jul 1864. Decomm 5 Aug and sold 8 Sep 1865.
Prizes: 19 Jun 1863: *Emma.* 21 Feb 1864: str *Hard Times.*
Later history: FFU.

Name	Bldr	Built	Acquired	Comm
Racer	Capes	1852	29 Aug 1861	21 Jan 1862

NOTES: 105′ × 28′10″ × 9′10″; 252 tons; complement 35. Oct 61: 4 32-pdr/57. Jan 62 total: 1 13″ M, 2 32-pdr/57.
SERVICE RECORD: Mortar Flotilla, Mississippi Sqn. Bombardment of Fts. Jackson and St. Philip below New Orleans, 18–28 Apr 1862. Bombardment of Vicksburg, 26 Jun–22 Jul 1862. Potomac Flotilla Sep 1862–63. SAtlBS Sep 1863. Bombardment of Ft. Wagner, Charleston, 13–15 Aug 1863. Expedition up Stono River, SC, 5 Jul 1864. Decomm 2 Sep and sold 27 Sep 1865.
Later history: FFU.

Name	Bldr	Built	Acquired	Comm
Sarah Bruen	(Brookhaven, NY)	1854	3 Sep 1861	3 Feb 1862

NOTES: 105′6″ × 26′7″ × 9′6″; 233 tons; complement 35. Feb 62: 1 13″ M, 2 32-pdr/57. Jul 64: less 1 13″ M.
SERVICE RECORD: Mortar Flotilla, Mississippi Sqn. Bombardment of Fts. Jackson and St. Philip below New Orleans, 18–28 Apr 1862. Bombardment of Vicksburg, 26 Jun–22 Jul 1862. Engagement with CSS *Arkansas* above Vicksburg, 15 Jul 1862. WGulfBS 1862–64. Bombardment of Port Hudson, La., 8 May–9 Jul 1863. Bombardment of Ft. Powell, Mobile Bay, 16–29 Feb 1864. Blockade of Charleston, Jul 1864–65. Decomm 6 Jul and sold 15 Aug 1865.
Later history: Merchant *Sarah Bruen* 1865. Later British *Mollie A. Read.* SE 1885.

Name	Bldr	Built	Acquired	Comm
Sea Foam	(Falmouth, Mass)	1855	14 Sep 1861	27 Jan 1862

NOTES: (Brig) 112′6″ × 26′ × d9′3″; 264 tons, complement 35. Feb 62: 1 13″ M, 2 32-pdr/57. Aug 64 total: 2 32-pdr/33.
SERVICE RECORD: Mortar Flotilla, Mississippi Sqn. Bombardment of Fts. Jackson and St. Philip below New Orleans, 18–28 Apr 1862. Ran aground below New Orleans, Jun 1862. Bombardment of Port Hudson, La., 8 May–9 Jul 1863. WGulfBS 1863. SAtlBS 1864. Storeship, Port Royal, SC, 1864–65. Bombardment of Ft. Powell, Mobile Bay, 16–29 Feb 1864. NAtlBS 1865. Decomm 16 May 1865. Sold 12 Jun 1865.
Prizes: 15 May 1862: *New Eagle* and *Sarah.*
Later history: FFU.

Name	Bldr	L	Acquired	Comm
Sidney C. Jones	Goodspeed	Apr 1856	7 Oct 1861	29 Jan 1862

NOTES: 98′ × 27′ × 7′8″; 245 tons, complement 36. Nov 61: 2 32-pdr/57. Feb 62 total: 1 13″ M, 2 32-pdr/57, 2 12-pdr SB.

SERVICE RECORD: Mortar Flotilla, Mississippi Sqn. Bombardment of Fts. Jackson and St. Philip below New Orleans, 18–28 Apr 1862. Bombardment of Vicksburg, 26 Jun–15 Jul 1862. Engagement with CSS *Arkansas* above Vicksburg, ran aground and was burned to prevent capture, 15 Jul 1862.

Name	Bldr	Built	Acquired	Comm
Sophronia	(New York)	1854	3 Sep 1861	25 Jan 1862

NOTES: 104′6″ × 28′4″ × 8′4″; 217 tons, complement 32. Feb 62: 1 13″ M, 2 32-pdr/57, 2 12-pdr SB.
SERVICE RECORD: Mortar Flotilla, Mississippi Sqn. Bombardment of Fts. Jackson and St. Philip below New Orleans, 18–28 Apr 1862. Bombardment of Vicksburg, 26 Jun–22 Jul 1862. Potomac Flotilla Aug 1862. Decomm 21 Aug 1865. Sold 8 Sep 1865.
Prize: 19 May 1863: *Mignonette.*
Later history: FFU.

Name	Bldr	Built	Acquired	Comm
T.A. Ward	(New York)	1853	9 Oct 1861	17 Jan 1862

NOTES: 114′6″ × 28′2″ × 10′6″; 284 tons; complement 38. Jan 62: 1 13″ M, 2 32-pdr/57. Feb 62: add 2 12-pdr SB. Apr 63 total: 4 32-pdr/57, 1 12-pdr SB.
SERVICE RECORD: Mortar Flotilla, Mississippi Sqn. Bombardment of Fts. Jackson and St. Philip below New Orleans, 18–28 Apr 1862. Bombardment of Vicksburg, 26 Jun–22 Jul 1862. Potomac Flotilla, Aug 1862–63. NAtlBS Jul 1863. SAtlBS Sep 1863. Decomm 22 Jul 1865. Sold 25 Sep 1865.
Prizes: 16 Nov 1862: *G.W. Green.* 17 Oct 1863: **Rover.* 12 Apr 1864: str *Alliance.*
Later history: Merchant *T.A. Ward* 1865. SE 1870.

Name	Bldr	Built	Acquired	Comm
William Bacon	(Brookhaven, NY)	1852	6 Sep 1861	3 Feb 1862

NOTES: 95′ × 26′ × 8′10″; 183 tons, complement 36. Feb 62: 1 13″ M, 2 32-pdr/57, 2 12-pdr SB. May 63 total: 1 30-pdr R, 2 32-pdr/57. Sep 63 total: 4 32-pdr/57.
SERVICE RECORD: Mortar Flotilla, Mississippi Sqn. Bombardment of Fts. Jackson and St. Philip below New Orleans, 18–28 Apr 1862. Potomac Flotilla 1862. NAtlBS Dec 1862. Blockade of Wilmington. Decomm 17 Jun 1865. Sold 20 Jul 1865.
Prizes: 1 Oct 1862: *Ann Squires.* 21 Mar 1863: str *Nicolai I.*
Later history: Merchant *Elizabeth White.* SE 1870.

SHIPS

Name	Bldr	Built	Acquired	Comm
Ben Morgan (ex-Mediator)	(Philadelphia)	1826	27 May 1861	1861

NOTES: 114'6" × 29'6" × d14'3"; 407 tons; complement 35
SERVICE RECORD: Ordnance store ship, Hampton Roads, 1861–65.
Sold 30 Nov 1865.
Later history: FFU.

Name	Bldr	Built	Acquired
Charles Phelps	(Westerly, RI)	1842	24 Jun 1861

NOTES: 110' × 27'4" × 18'; 362 tons; complement 23. Jul 61: 1
32-pdr/33 SB. Feb 64: none. Also reported built 1848 at New London.
SERVICE RECORD: NAtlBS 1861–65, coal supply ship, Hampton Roads.
Sold 25 Oct 1865.
Later history: Merchant *Progress* 1866.

Name	Bldr	Built	Acquired	Comm
Courier	Currier, Newburyport, Mass.	1855	7 Sep 1861	17 Sep 1861

NOTES: 135' × 30' × d15'; 554 tons, complement 82. 2 31-pdr
SERVICE RECORD: Storeship. Wrecked on Abaco Island, Bahamas, 14
Jun 1864.
Prizes: 16 May 1863: *Emeline* and *Angelina*; 17 May: *Maria Bishop*.
Later history: FFU.

Name	Bldr	Built	Acquired	Comm
Fearnot	Jackman	1859	20 Jul 1861	28 Aug 1861

NOTES: 178' × 35' × d23'6"; 1,012 tons; complement 45. Aug 61: 6
32-pdr/33. Sep 63 total: 1 8" SB.
SERVICE RECORD: WGulfBS 1861. Coal and supply ship, Key West.
Decomm 18 Jul 1866. Sold 3 Oct 1866.
Later history: Merchant *Nevada* 1866. SE 1870.

Name	Bldr	Built	Acquired	Comm
Ino	Perrine	1 Apr 1851	30 Aug 1861	23 Sep 1861

NOTES: 160'6" × 34'11" × 18'9"; 895 tons. Sep 61: 6 32-pdr/57, 2
32-pdr/42. Feb 62: add 1 20-pdr R. Mar 63 total: 6 32-pdr/57, 2
100-pdr R, 2 30-pdr R. May 64: add 1 30-pdr R.
SERVICE RECORD: Storeship. Decomm 13 Feb 1866. Sold 19 Mar 1867.
Prize: 23 Aug 1862: *La Manche*.
Later history: Merchant *Ino* 1867. Renamed *Shooting Star III* and *Ellen*.

Name	Bldr	L	Acquired	Comm
Morning Light	Cramp	15 Aug 1853	2 Sep 1861	21 Nov 1861

NOTES: 172' × 34'3" × 19'; 937 tons, complement 120. Nov 61: 8
32-pdr/57.
SERVICE RECORD: WGulfBS 1862. Captured and burned at Sabine
Pass, Tex., 23 Jan 1863.
Prizes: 26 Dec 1861: *Jorgen Lorentzen*. 19 Jun 1862: *Venture*.

Name	Bldr	Built	Acquired	Comm
National Guard	Gildersleeve	1857	6 Jul 1861	23 Dec 1862

NOTES: 160' × 38' × 20'7"; 1,046 tons. Dec 61: 4 32-pdr/33. Jan 64
total: 1 30-pdr R. May 65 total: 1 30-pdr R, 4 32-pdr/57.
SERVICE RECORD: West Indies Sqn, supply ship. 1862–65. Renamed
Guard, 2 Jun 1866. European Sqn supply ship, 1866–69. Darien
Expedition 1870. Decomm 15 Dec 1878. Sold 27 Sep 1883.

Name	Bldr	L	Acquired	Comm
Nightingale	Hanscombe, Portsmouth, NH	16 Jun 1851	6 Jul 1861	18 Aug 1861

NOTES: 177'10" × 36' × d20'; 1,066 tons B, complement 51/186. Aug
61: 4 32-pdr/33. Jun 64: 4 8". A famous clipper ship named after
Jenny Lind. Captured as a slaver near mouth of Congo River by USS
Saratoga, 20 Apr 1861.
SERVICE RECORD: Coal and storeship 1861. EGulfBS 1862. Ordnance
ship, Pensacola 1863–64. Decomm 20 Jun 1864. Sold 11 Feb 1865.
Later history: Merchant *Nightingale* 1865. Foundered in North Atlantic,
27 Apr 1893.

Name	Bldr	L	Acquired	Comm
Onward	Curtis, Medford	3 Jul 1852	9 Sep 1861	11 Jan 1862

NOTES: 167' (bp) × 34'8" × 20'; 874 tons, complement 103. Jan 62: 8
32-pdr/57. Oct 62 total: 1 30-pdr R, 8 32-pdr/57.
SERVICE RECORD: SAtlBS 1862–63. With *Mohican* blockaded Confederate tenders *Agrippina* and *Castor* at Bahia, Brazil, May 1863. Storeship, Callao, Peru, 1866–84. Sold 14 Nov 1884.
Prizes: 26 Apr 1862: *Chase; 1 May: *Sarah. 28 Jan 1863: *Magicienne*.

Name	Bldr	L	Acquired	Comm
Pampero	Mallory	18 Aug 1853	7 Jul 1861	Aug 1861

NOTES: 202'3" × 38'2" × 20'; 1,375 tons, complement 50. Aug 61: 2
32-pdr/33. Aug 63: 4 32-pdr/33, 1 20-pdr R, 1 24-pdr H. Aug 65: 1
24-pdr H replaced by 1 30-pdr R.
SERVICE RECORD: GulfBS 1861. WGulf BS, storeship and collier.
Decomm 20 Jul 1866. Sold 1 Oct 1867.
Later history: FFU.

Name	Bldr	Built	Acquired	Comm
Roman	(New Bedford, Mass.)	1835	18 May 1861	1861

NOTES: Whaler. 112' × 26'3" × 18'; 350 tons, complement 19. Jun 61:
1 32-pdr/33. Feb 64: 1 32-pdr/27.
SERVICE RECORD: NAtlBS 1861, coal and ordnance storeship, Hampton Roads. Sold 30 Nov 1865.
Later history: Merchant *Roman* 1865. Crushed in ice in Bering Strait, 7
Sep 1871.

Name	Bldr	L	Acquired	Comm
Shepherd Knapp	Westervelt	23 Feb 1856	28 Aug 1861	1861

NOTES: 160'10" × 33'8" × 13'; 838 tons, complement 93

SERVICE RECORD: W. Indies 1861–62. Wrecked on reef at Cap Haitien, Haiti, 18 May 1863.
Prize: 4 Sep 1862: *Fannie Laurie*.

Name	Bldr	Built	Acquired	Comm
Supply	Ewell, Medford	1846	8 Dec 1846	19 Dec 1846

NOTES: 547 tons; complement 40. Jul 61: 4 32-pdr/27. Aug 62: add 1 12-pdr R. May 63 total: 4 20-pdr R, 2 24-pdr H.
SERVICE RECORD: Storeship. Paraguay Expedition 1859. Decomm 23 Apr 1879. Sold 3 May 1884.
Prize: 29 Jan 1862: *Stephen Hart*.

Name	Bldr	Built	Acquired	Comm
William Badger	(U)	(U)	18 May 1861	1862

NOTES: 106′ × 26′ × d13′3″; 334 tons. Jun 61: 1 32-pdr/33.
SERVICE RECORD: Stationary supply ship, Hampton Roads, 1862. Supply hulk, Beaufort, NC, 1863–65. Sold 17 Oct 1865.
Later history: FFU.

BARKS

Name	Bldr	Built	Acquired	Comm
A. Houghton	Rideout, Robbinston, Me.	1852	12 Oct 1861	19 Feb 1862

NOTES: 113′4″ × 25′3″ × 12′; 326 tons; complement 27. Mar 62: 2 32-pdr/51. Aug 64 total: 4 32-pdr/42, 2 20-pdr R.
SERVICE RECORD: Mortar Flotilla, ordnance vessel 1862. Storeship, Pensacola, Aug 1862–Mar 1863. Ordnance vessel, Hampton Roads, Apr–Oct 1863. Storeship, Port Royal, SC, Oct 1863–May 1865. Decomm 3 Jun 1865. Sold 10 Aug 1865.
Later history: Merchant bark *A. Houghton* 1865. SE 1870.

Name	Bldr	Built	Acquired	Comm
Amanda	(New York)	1858	6 Aug 1861	1861

NOTES: 117′6″ × 27′9″ × d12′6″; 368 tons; complement 71. Oct 61: 6 32-pdr/42. May 63 total: 6 32-pdr/42, 1 20-pdr R, 1 12-pdr H.
SERVICE RECORD: NAtlBS Nov 1861–62. EGulfBS Jun 1862. Went aground in St. George's Sound, Fla., and was burned to prevent capture, 29 May 1863.
Prizes: 24 May 1862: str *Swan*; 17 Jun: unident. bark.

Name	Bldr	Built	Acquired	Comm
Arthur	(Amesbury, Mass.)	1855	1 Aug 1861	11 Dec 1861

NOTES: 133′ × 31′2″ × 14′1″; 554 tons; complement 31/86
SERVICE RECORD: GulfBS Jan 1862. Blockade off Texas. Guard ship, Pensacola, Oct 1863–Aug 1865. Sold 27 Sep 1865.
Prizes: 25 Jan 1862: *J.J. McNeil*; 9 Jul: *Reindeer*; 10 Jul: *Monte Cristo*

and *Belle Italia*; 12 Aug: *Hannah*, *Elma*, *Breaker*, and str *A. Bee*; 24 Aug: *Water Witch*.
Later history: FFU.

Name	Bldr	Built	Acquired	Comm
Avenger	(U)	(U)	1 Aug 1861	11 Dec 1861

NOTES: 133′ × 31′2″ × 14′1″; 554 tons. Aug 61: 6 32-pdr/42.
SERVICE RECORD: Sold 27 Sep 1865.
Later history: FFU.

Name	Bldr	Built	Acquired	Comm
Braziliera	Abrahams	1856	30 Jul 1861	27 Oct 1861

NOTES: 135′8″ × 28′7″ × 10′; 540 tons. Aug 61: 6 32-pdr/42. Feb 64 total: 6 32-pdr/42, 1 12-pdr SB, 1 24-pdr SB.
SERVICE RECORD: NAtlBS 1862. Damaged in collision with USS *Amanda* in Hampton Roads, 3 Mar 1862. SAtlBS Jun 1862. Engagement with CSS *North Carolina* in Cape Fear River, May 1864. Sold 2 Jun 1865.
Prizes: 28 Jun 1862: *Chance*; 7 Sep: *Defiance*. 13 Oct 1863: *Mary*; 8 Dec: *Antoinette*. 1 Feb 1864: *Buffalo*.
Later history: FFU.

Name	Bldr	L	Acquired	Comm
Ethan Allen	Gardiner	Mar 1859	23 Aug 1861	3 Oct 1861

NOTES: 153′6″ × 35′1″ × 13′; 556 tons, complement 87. Oct 61: 4 32-pdr/51, 2 32-pdr/33. Dec 61: add 1 12-pdr. Apr 63: add 1 20-pdr R.
SERVICE RECORD: GulfBS 1861–63. SAtlBS Nov 1863. Expedition to Murrells Inlet, SC, 29 Dec 1863–1 Jan 1864. Decomm 26 Jun 1865. Sold 20 Jul 1865.
Prizes: 29 Nov 1861: *Fashion*. 21 Jan 1862: *Olive Branch*; 18 Feb: *Atlanta*, *Spitfire*, and *Caroline*. 19 Mar 1863: *Gypsy*.
Later history: FFU.

Name	Bldr	Built	Acquired	Comm
Fernandina (ex-*Florida*)	(Eastport, Me.)	1850	29 Jul 1861	16 Nov 1861

NOTES: 115′ × 29′ × 10′; 297 tons, complement 86. Aug 61: 6 32-pdr/42. Jun 63 total: 6 32-pdr/42, 1 24-pdr H, 1 20-pdr R.
SERVICE RECORD: NAtlBS Dec 1861–Jun 1862. SAtlBS Jun 1862–63. Decomm 29 Apr and sold 2 Jun 1865.
Prizes: 25 Dec 1861: *William H. Northrup*. 2 Apr 1862: *Kate*. 16 Jan 1864: *Annie Thompson*.
Later history: FFU.

Name	Bldr	Built	Acquired	Comm
Fredonia	(Newburyport)	1845	14 Dec 1846	5 Jan 1847

NOTES: 160′ × 32′11″ × d16′6″; 800 tons; complement 37. Dec 65: 4 24-pdr carronades

The bark *Ethan Allen*, seen here at Boston Navy Yard, was an active blockader. *Ohio* is behind at right. (Peabody Museum of Salem)

SERVICE RECORD: Storeship Pacific Sqn, Valparaiso 1853–62, and Callao 1862–68. Lost in earthquake and tidal wave at Arica, Peru, 13 Aug 1868.

Name	Bldr	Built	Acquired	Comm
Gem of the Sea	Chase Davis, Warren, RI	1853	3 Aug 1861	15 Oct 1861

NOTES: 116′ × 26′3″ × d13′4″; 371 tons, complement 65. Aug 61: 6 32-pdr/42. Oct 61 total: 4 32-pdr/42. Jun 63: 4 32-pdr/42, 1 20-pdr R.
SERVICE RECORD: SAtlBS 1861–62. EGulfBS Dec 1862. Decomm 24 Feb 1865. Sold 6 May 1865.
Prizes: 24 Dec 1861: *Prince of Wales. 12 Mar 1862: *Fair Play*; 3 Jun: *Mary Stewart*; 12 Jun: *Seabrook*; 2 Jul: *Volante*; 30 Dec: *Ann. 23 Feb 1863: *Charm*; 10 Mar: *Petee*; 8 Apr: *Maggie Fulton*; 18 Apr: *Inez*; 29 Jul: *George*; 31 Aug: *Richard*; 30 Sep: *Director*; 21 Oct: *Matilda*.
Later history: FFU.

Name	Bldr	Built	Acquired	Comm
Gemsbok	R.E. Jackson, E. Boston	1857	7 Sep 1861	30 Aug 1861

NOTES: 141′7″ × 30′3″ × d17′; 622 tons, complement 103. Sep 61: 4 8″/63, 2 32-pdr/33. Apr 65: add 1 20-pdr R.
SERVICE RECORD: SAtlBS 1861-62. Capture of Ft. Macon, NC, 25–26 Apr 1862. West Indies Sqn, storeship, Feb–Jul 1863. SAtlBS 1865. Sold 12 Jul 1865.
Prizes: 19 Sep 1861: *Harmony*; 22 Sep: *Mary E. Pindar*; 3 Oct: *Beverly*; 18 Oct: *Ariel*. 26 Apr 1862: *Gondar* and *Glenn*.
Later history: Merchant bark *Gemsbok* 1865. SE 1870.

Name	Bldr	Built	Acquired
Ironsides Jr.	(U)	(U)	Aug 1863

NOTES: 200 tons
SERVICE RECORD: Storeship, Port Royal, 1863–64.

Name	Bldr	Built	Acquired	Comm
J.C. Kuhn	Gildersleeve	1859	6 Jul 1861	23 Aug 1861

NOTES: 153′ × 35′ × 13′5″; 888 tons; complement 61. Apr 61: 2 32-pdr/33. Jan 64 total: 6 32-pdr/38
SERVICE RECORD: GulfBS 1861. Supply and coal vessel. Vicksburg, Jun 1862. Storeship, Pensacola 1864. Renamed **Purveyor**, 10 Apr 1866. Sold 7 Jul 1869.
Later history: Merchant *J.C. Kuhn* 1869. Renamed *C.E. Jayne*, later Norwegian *Jason*.

Name	Bldr	Built	Acquired	Comm
James L. Davis	Darling, Pt Jefferson, NY	1857	29 Sep 1861	30 Dec 1861

NOTES: 133′ × 30′7″ × 12′; 461 tons; complement 75. Feb 62: 4 8″/55.
SERVICE RECORD: WGulfBS 1862. EGulfBS 1862. Occupation of Tampa, Fla., 4–7 May 1864. Sold 20 Jun 1865.
Prizes: 10 Mar 1862: *Florida*; 23 Sep: *Isabel*.
Later history: Merchant *Gen. G.G. Meade*. SE 1868.

Name	Bldr	Built	Acquired	Comm
Kingfisher	Fish, Fairhaven, Me.	1857	2 Aug 1861	3 Oct 1861

NOTES: 121′4″ × 28′8″ × 16′6″; 451 tons, complement 97. Oct 61: 4 8″ SB. May 63 total: 4 8″ SB, 1 20-pdr R, 1 12-pdr.
SERVICE RECORD: EGulfBS 1861–62. SAtlBS Dec 1862. Went aground and lost in St. Helena Sound, SC, 28 Mar 1864.
Prizes: 21 Jan 1862: *Olive Branch*; 30 Jan: *Teresita*; 25 Feb: *Lion*.

Name	Bldr	L	Acquired	Comm
Massachusetts	Hall, Boston	23 Jul 1845	1 Aug 1849	1 Aug 1849

NOTES: 178′ or 156′6″ (bp) 161′ × 32′2″ × 15′6″; 750 tons B. 2 9-pdr SB. Jul 63 total: 6 32-pdr/33.
NOTES: Former transatlantic steamer acquired by War Dept. as transport in Mexican War and transferred to Navy. Ericsson lifting screw, 1 inclined direct-acting engine (25″ × 3′), 2 boilers; HP 170 = 8 knots. Machinery removed and converted to sail 1862.
SERVICE RECORD: Pacific Sqn 1849–59. Transferred to War Dept. May 1859, returned Jan 1862. Converted to bark at Mare Island 1862, renamed **Farallones** Jan 1863. Recomm 17 Jun 1863. Storeship, Pacific Sqn, 1863–67. Sold 15 May 1867.
Later history: Merchant *Alaska* 1867. Lost 1881 or earlier off Chile.

Name	Bldr	L	Acquired	Comm
Midnight (ex-*Dawn*)	Collyer	8 Jul 1857	31 Jul 1861	19 Oct 1861

NOTES: 126′ × 27′10″ × 11′; 386 tons, complement 70. Oct 61: 4 32-pdr/42. May 63 total: 1 20-pdr R, 4 32-pdr/42, 2 32-pdr/57. Mar 64 total: 2 32-pdr/57, 4 32-pdr/42, 1 20-pdr R, 1 12-pdr R.
SERVICE RECORD: GulfBS 1861–62 off Texas. SAtlBS Oct 1862–63.

EGulfBS Oct 1864–65. Sold 1 Nov 1865.
Prize: 3 Feb 1864: *Defy*.
Later history: FFU.

Name	Bldr	Built	Acquired	Comm
Pursuit	(Baltimore)	1857	3 Sep 1861	17 Dec 1861

NOTES: 144′ × 34′10″ × d15′; 603 tons; complement 92. Dec 61: 6 32-pdr/57. May 63: add 1 20-pdr R.
SERVICE RECORD: EGulfBS 1862–65. Decomm 5 Jun 1865. Sold 12 Jul 1865.
Prizes: 6 Mar 1862: *Anna Belle*; 4 Apr: **Lafayette*; 6 Apr: str *Florida*; 26 May: *Andromeda*. 23 Jun 1863: *Kate*. 4 Dec 1864: *Peep O'Day*. 16 Mar 1865: *Mary*.
Later history: Merchant *Pursuit* 1865. SE 1870.

Name	Bldr	Built	Comm
Release (ex-*Eringol* or *Elingo*)	Brown & Lovell, Boston	1853	3 Apr 1855

NOTE: 113′9″ × 27′2 × 11′9; 327 tons; complement 85. 1861: 2 32-pdr/27. Feb 63: add 1 30-pdr R, 1 12-pdr R.
SERVICE RECORD: Storeship. Paraguay Expedition 1859. Ordnance storeship, Pensacola, Hampton Roads, Gibraltar, Beaufort, NC, 1861–65. Decomm 6 Oct and sold 25 Oct 1865.

Name	Bldr	Built	Acquired	Comm
Restless	(Madison, Ct.)	1854	26 Aug 1861	24 Dec 1861

NOTE: 108′8″ × 27′8″ × 10′; 265 tons, complement 66. Dec 61: 4 32-pdr/51. Jun 63 total: 1 20-pdr R, 4 32-pdr/51, 2 12-pdr SB.
SERVICE RECORD: SAtlBS Jan 1862–Jan 1863. EGulfBS Jun 1863 off Florida. Operations in St. Andrews Bay, Fla., 10–18 Dec 1863. Sold 21 Sep 1865.
Prizes: 14 Feb 1862: **Edisto*, **Elizabeth*, **Wando*, and **Theodore Stoney*; 27 Mar: **George Washington*, **Mary Louise*, and *Julia Worden*; 29 Mar: *Lydia & Mary*; 2 May: *Flash*; 2 Sep: *John Thompson*; 12 Oct: *Elmira Cornelius*; 24 Oct: str *Scotia*; 31 Oct: *Susan McPherson*. 8 Jul 1863: *Ann*; 19 Aug: *Erniti*. 22 Jan 1864: *William A. Kain*.
Later history: Merchant *Restless* 1865. SE 1870.

Name	Bldr	L	Acquired	Comm
Roebuck	Collyer	6 May 1856	21 Jul 1861	8 Nov 1861

NOTES: 135′ × 27′ × 14′6″; 455 tons, complement 69. Aug 61: 6 32-pdr. Oct 61 total: 4 32-pdr/42. Aug 62: 1 20-pdr R, 4 32-pdr/42.
SERVICE RECORD: SAtlBS 1861–62. EGulfBS Sep 1862–Jul 1864. Decomm 17 Oct 1864. Sold 20 Jul 1865.
Prizes: 27 Dec 1862: *Kate*. 2 May 1863: *Emma Amelia*; 17 Dec: *Ringdove*. 10 Jan 1864: *Maria Louise*; 11 Jan: *Susan*; 14 Jan: **Young Racer*; 18 Jan: *Carolina*; 19 Jan: *Eliza and Mary*; 25 Feb: *Two Brothers*; 27 Feb: **Rebel* and *Nina*; 1 Mar: *Lauretta*; 30 Jun: *Last Resort*; 10 Jul: *Terrapin*.
Later history: Merchant *Roebuck* 1865. SE 1870.

Name	Bldr	L	Acquired	Comm
William G. Anderson	Gardner	1 Sep 1859	23 Aug 1861	2 Oct 1861

NOTES: 149′7″ × 30′1″; 593 tons. Oct 61: 2 32-pdr/33, 4 32-pdr/51, 1 24-pdr H. Jun 63 total: 1 20-pdr R, 2 32-pdr/33, 4 32-pdr/51, 1 12-pdr R.
SERVICE RECORD: WGulfBS 1861. Captured Confederate privateer *Beauregard* in Bahama Channel, 12 Nov 1861. Blockade of Galveston, Jun 1862–65. Decomm 21 Jul 1866. Sold 28 Aug 1866.
Prizes: 12 Nov 1861: *Beauregard*; 11 Jun 1862: *Montebello*; 31 Aug: *Lily*; 4 Sep: *Theresa*; 17 Sep: *Reindeer*. 15 Apr 1863: *Royal Yacht*; 17 Apr: *Nymph*; 25 Aug: *Mack Canfield*; 27 Aug: **America*.
Later history: Merchant *Yokohama* 1866. SE 1870.

BRIGS

Name	Bldr	Built	Acquired	Comm
Bohio	(Williamsburg, NY)	1856	9 Sep 1861	30 Dec 1861

NOTES: 100′ × 24′9″ × d9′4″; 197 tons; complement 34. Jan 62: 2 32-pdr/57. Jul 63 total: 2 32-pdr/57, 2 32-pdr/33, 1 12-pdr R, 1 12-pdr SB.
SERVICE RECORD: WGulfBS Jan 1862–Mar 1864. Converted to coal vessel 1864. Decomm 25 Jul 1865. Sold 27 Sep 1865.
Prizes: 7 Feb 1862: *Eugenie Smith*; 8 Mar: *Henry Travers*; 13 May: **Deer Island*; 21 Jun: *L. Rebecca*; 27 Jun: *Wave*.
Later history: Merchant brig *Bohio* 1865. SE 1870.

Name	Bldr	Built	Acquired	Comm
Valparaiso	(Baltimore)	1836	22 Nov 1861	1861

NOTES: 117′6″ × 27′6″; 402 tons, complement 36. No guns.
SERVICE RECORD: SAtlBS 1861. Storeship, Port Royal, SC. Sold 2 Sep 1865.
Later history: FFU.

SCHOONERS

Name	Bldr	Built	Acquired
Albemarle	(U)	(U)	9 May 1863

NOTES: 85′ × 25′6″ × d7′7″; 200 tons; complement 22
SERVICE RECORD: Captured by USS *Delaware* off Pantego Creek, NC, 26 Mar 1862. Ordnance supply vessel, NAtlBS 1863–65. Sold 19 Oct 1865.

Name	Bldr	Built	Acquired
Dana (ex-U.S. Coast Survey)	(U)	(U)	10 Jun 1861

NOTES: Oct 61: 2 32-pdr/33. Sep 62 total: 2 32-pdr/33, 2 24-pdr SB, 1 12-pdr R.
SERVICE RECORD: Potomac Flotilla, guard ship and coal depot. Stricken Jul 1862.
Prizes: 1861: 1 Sep: *T.J. Evans*, 5 Jul: *Teaser*.

Name	Bldr	Built	Acquired
Eugenie (ex-*Eugenie Smith*)	(Lewiston, Me.)	1844	22 Apr 1862

NOTES: 150 tons; complement 36; 1 gun
SERVICE RECORD: Captured by USS *Bohio* off Mississippi River, 7 Feb 1862. Guard Ship, Key West. Sold Nov 1864.
Prize: 12 Sep 1863: str *Alabama*.
Later history: FFU.

Name	Bldr	Built	Acquired	Comm
G.W. Blunt	(E. Boston, Mass.)	1861	23 Nov 1861	4 Dec 1861

NOTES: 76′6″ × 20′6″ × 9′; 121 tons; complement 16. Jul 63: 2 12-pdr R
SERVICE RECORD: SAtlBS 1862–64. Mail and despatch boat. Salvage ship 1864. Decomm 16 Aug 1865. Sold 20 Oct 1865.
Prize: 19 Apr 1862: *Wave*.
Later history: FFU.

Name	Bldr	Built	Acquired	Comm
Hope	(U)	(U)	29 Nov 1861	14 Dec 1861

NOTES: 85′ × 20′9″ × 9′; 134 tons. Mar 64: 1 20-pdr R
SERVICE RECORD: SAtlBS 1862. Salvage ship 1865. Decomm 6 Sep 1865. Sold 25 Oct 1865.
Prizes: 27 Jan 1863: *Emma Tuttle*; 1 Aug: *Racer*.
Later history: FFU.

Name	Bldr	Built	Acquired	Comm
James S. Chambers	(U)	(U)	4 Sep 1861	16 Dec 1861

NOTES: 124′6″ × 29′3″; 401 tons; complement 62. Jun 62: 4 32-pdr/57. Apr 63: add 1 20-pdr R, 1 12-pdr H
SERVICE RECORD: GulfBS 1862–64. SAtlBS 1865. Expedition to Bull Bay, SC, 12–17 Feb 1865. Decomm 31 Aug and sold 27 Sep 1865.
Prizes: 23 Aug 1862: *Corelia*; 25 Aug: str *Union*. 4 Mar 1863: **Ida* and *Relampago*; 18 Jun: *Rebekah*.
Later history: FFU.

Name	Bldr	Built	Acquired	Comm
Kittatinny (ex-*Stars and Stripes*)	(U)	(U)	21 Sep 1861	9 Dec 1861

NOTES: 129′ × 29′ × d11′6″; 421 tons; complement 66. Dec 61: 4 32-pdr/57. Jul 63 total: 4 32-pdr/57, 1 30-pdr R, 1 12-pdr R.

SERVICE RECORD: GulfBS 1862–63. WGulfBS Sep 1863, Texas. Decomm 14 Sep and sold 27 Sep 1865.
Prizes: 11 May 1862: *Julia*; 26 Sep: *Emma*; 25 Nov: *Matilda*; 26 Nov: *Diana*. 12 Mar 1863: *D. Sargent*; 25 Oct: *Reserve*.
Later history: FFU.

Name	Bldr	Built	Acquired	Comm
Rachel Seaman	(Philadelphia)	1861	21 Sep 1861	16 Nov 1861

NOTES: 115′ × 30′ × d9′; 303 tons; complement 13. Oct 61: 2 32-pdr/57. Feb 64 total: 1 32-pdr/33, 1 12-pdr R. Sep 64 total: 2 12-pdr R.
SERVICE RECORD: GulfBS Nov 1861–May 1864. Blockade of Texas. Bombarded Sabine Pass forts, 25 Sep 1682. Decomm 22 May and sold 30 May 1865.
Prizes: 25 Sep 1862: *Velocity*; 6 Oct 1862: str *Dart*; 11 Nov: *Maria* and *Cora*. 21 Apr 1863: *Nymph*; 13 Apr 1864: *Maria Alfred*.
Later history: FFU.

Name	Bldr	Built	Acquired	Comm
Samuel Rotan	(Tuckahoe, NJ)	1858	21 Sep 1861	12 Nov 1861

NOTES: 110′ × 28′6″ × 9′; 212 tons; complement 29. Oct 61: 2 32-pdr/57. Dec 61: add 1 24-pdr H. Feb 63 total: 1 30-pdr R, 2 32-pdr/57. Dec 63: add 1 24-pdr H. Dec 64 total: 2 30-pdr R, 2 32-pdr/57, 1 24-pdr H.
SERVICE RECORD: GulfBS 1861. EGulfBS 1862. NAtlBS 1863. Decomm 10 Jun 1865. Sold 15 Aug 1865.
Prizes: 23 Jan 1862: str *Calhoun*. 24 Apr 1863: *Martha Ann*; 1 Jul: *Champion*.
Later history: FFU.

Name	Bldr	Built	Acquired
Wanderer	J. Rowland, Setauket, NY	1857	May 1861

NOTES: 106′ × 25′6″ × 9′6″; 300 tons; complement 26. May 63: 1 20-pdr R, 2 24-pdr H. Jan 65 total: 1 20-pdr R. Sometime slaver seized at Key West May 1861.
SERVICE RECORD: EGulf BS 1861–65. Sold 28 Jun 1865.
Prizes: 15 Jul 1861: *Belle*. 25 Mar 1863: *Ranger*; 17 Apr: *Annie B*.
Later history: Merchant *Wanderer*, 1865. Lost off Cape Maisi, Cuba, 21 Jan 1871.

SMALL SCHOONERS AND SLOOPS

Name	Bldr	Built	Acquired
America (ex-*Memphis*, ex-*Camilla*, ex-*America*)	Wm. H. Brown, New York	1851	19 May 1863

NOTES: Yacht; 111′ × 25′ × 12′; 100 tons. Dec 62: 1 12-pdr R, 2 24-pdr SB.
SERVICE RECORD: Found sunk in St. Johns River, Fla., Mar 1862. Raised and refitted. SAtlBS 1862–63. School ship, Naval Academy. Sold 20 Jun 1873.

The yacht *America* at Annapolis around 1870. This famous vessel was found sunk in the St. Johns River, Florida, early in 1862, after she had run the blockade from England. (Martin Holbrook Collection) (U.S. Naval Historical Center)

Prize: 13 Oct 1862: *David Crockett*.
Later history: Reacquired 1 Oct 1921. Scrapped 1945.

Name	Bldr	Built	Acquired
Anna (ex-*La Criolla*)	(U)	1857	11 Mar 1863

NOTES: Schooner; 46′2″ × 14′9″ × 5′; 27 tons; complement 8. Feb 64: 1 12-pdr R. Also spelled *Annie*.
SERVICE RECORD: Captured by USS *Fort Henry* in Suwanee River, 26 Feb 1863. Tender to USS *Dale*, W. coast of Florida. Wrecked by an explosion off Cape Roman, Fla., Jan 1865.

Name	Bldr	Built	Acquired
Ariel	(U)	(U)	24 Jul 1863

NOTES: Schooner; 19 tons; Dec 63: 1 12-pdr SB.
SERVICE RECORD: Captured by USS *Huntsville* in Gulf of Mexico, 11 Nov 1862. EGulfBS 1863–65. Tender. Operation at Bayport, Fla., 10 Jul 1864. Sold 28 Jun 1865.
Prizes: 6 Jan 1863: *Good Luck*; 16 Dec: *Magnolia*. 28 May 1864: *General Finegan*.

Name	Bldr	Built	Acquired	Comm
Beauregard (ex-*Priscilla C. Ferguson*)	(Charleston)	1850	24 Feb 1862	28 Mar 1862

NOTES: Schooner; 101 tons; Apr 62: 1 30-pdr R, 2 12-pdr H SB.
SERVICE RECORD: Captured as privateer by *William G. Anderson* in Bahama Channel, 12 Nov 1861. EGulfBS Apr 1862–Jun 1865.

Engaged batteries at Tampa Bay, Fla., 2–9 Apr 1863. Bombardment of New Smyrna, Fla., 28 Jul 1863. Sold 28 Jun 1865.
Prizes: 20 Jun 1862: *Lucy*. 26 Aug 1863: *Phoebe*, 6 Oct: *Last Trial*; 5 Nov: *Volante*. 15 Jan 1864: *Minnie*; 28 Jan: *Racer*; 11 Mar: *Hannah*, *Linda*; 7 Apr: *Spunky*; 18 Apr: *Oramoneta*; 12 May: *Resolute*.
Later history: FFU.

Name	Bldr	Built	Acquired	Comm
Carmita	(U)	(U)	10 Mar 1863	2 Apr 1863

NOTES: Schooner; 65'2" × 20'2"; 61 tons.
SERVICE RECORD: Captured by USS *Magnolia* off Marquesas Key, 27 Dec 1862. EGulfBS 1863, lighter and storeship. Sold 1866.

Name	Bldr	Built	Acquired
Charlotte	(U)	(U)	6 Nov 1862

NOTES: Schooner. 56' × 17'; 70 tons; complement 14
SERVICE RECORD: Captured as blockade runner by USS *Kanawha* off Mobile, 10 Apr 1862. WGulfBS 1862. Sold 27 Apr 1867.
Prize: 24 Dec 1862: str *Bloomer*.

Name	Bldr	Built	Acquired
Chotank	(Richmond, Me.)	1842	2 Jul 1861
(ex-Savannah)			

NOTES: Schooner; 56' × 17'; 53 tons. Sep 62: 2 9" SB, 1 11" R.
SERVICE RECORD: Captured as privateer *Savannah* by USS *Perry*, 3 Jun 1861. Potomac Flotilla 1862. Laid up 1863–65. Sold 15 Aug 1865.

Name	Bldr	Built	Acquired
Corypheus	(Brookhaven, NY)	1859	12 Jun 1862

NOTES: Schooner; 82 tons; complement 16. Jul 64: 1 30-pdr R, 1 24-pdr H.
SERVICE RECORD: Captured by USS *Calhoun* in Bayou Bonfuca, La., 13 May 1862. WGulfBS 1862–64. Battle of Sabine Pass, 1 Jan 1863. Sold 15 Sep 1865.
Prize: 23 Aug 1862: *Water Witch*.

Name	Bldr	Built	Acquired
Dart	(U)	(U)	4 Jul 1861

NOTES: Schooner; 94 tons.
SERVICE RECORD: Captured by USS *South Carolina* off Galveston, Tex., 4 Jul 1861. BU 21 Oct 1861.
Prizes: 24 Sep 1861: *Cecilia*; Sep: **Reindeer*.

Name	Bldr	Built	Acquired	Comm
Fox	(Baltimore, Md.)	1859	6 May 1863	Jun 1863
(ex-Alabama, ex-Fox)				

NOTES: Schooner; 80 tons. Feb 64: 2 12-pdr R.

SERVICE RECORD: Captured as blockade runner by USS *Susquehanna*, 18 Apr 1863. EGulfBS 1863–65. Sold 28 Jun 1865.
Prizes: 20 Dec 1863: *Edward*; 24 Dec: **Powerful*. 18 Apr 1864: **Good Hope*; 1 May: *Oscar*. 23 Jan 1865: *Fannie McRae*; 2 Mar: **Rob Roy*.

Name	Bldr	Built	Acquired
G.L.Brockenborough	(U)	(U)	15 Nov 1862

NOTES: Sloop.
SERVICE RECORD: Captured by USS *Fort Henry*, scuttled in Apalachicola River, 15 Oct 1862, and raised. EGulfBS 1862. Wrecked in gale in St. George's Sound, Fla., 27 May 1863.

Name	Bldr	Built	Acquired
Granite	(U)	(U)	19 Jan 1862
(ex-U.S. Lighthouse Board)			

NOTES: Sloop; 75 tons; complement 13. Jan 62: 1 32-pdr/57. Aug 64: 1 30-pdr R.
SERVICE RECORD: NAtlBS 1862. Landings at Roanoke I., NC, 7–8 Feb 1862. Returned to U.S. Lighthouse Board, 29 Jun 1865.

Name	Bldr	Built	Acquired
Howell Cobb	(U)	(U)	10 Jun 1861
(ex-U.S. Coast Survey)			

NOTES: Schooner.
SERVICE RECORD: Potomac River, 1861–62. Went aground off Cape Ann, 22 Dec 1861. Returned to U.S. Coast Survey Jul 1862.

Name	Bldr	Built	Acquired
Isilda	(U)	(U)	1 Nov 1861
(ex-Isilda—British)			

NOTES: Schooner; also spelled *Ezilda*.
SERVICE RECORD: Captured as blockade runner by USS *South Carolina* off Timbalier, La., 4 Oct 1861. GulfBS 1862. Sold 1863.
Prize: 5 Jun 1862: str **Havana*.

Name	Bldr	Built	Acquired
Julia	(U)	(U)	15 Feb 1863

NOTES: Sloop; 10 tons; no guns.
SERVICE RECORD: British sloop captured by USS *Sagamore* off Jupiter Inlet, Fla., 8 Jan 1863. SAtlBS 1864. BU at Key West 1865.
Prize: 20 Feb 1863: *Stonewall*.

Name	Bldr	Built	Acquired
J.W. Wilder	(U)	(U)	19 May 1863

NOTES: Schooner.
SERVICE RECORD: Captured by USS *R.R. Cuyler* off Mobile Bay, 20 Jan 1862. WGulfBS 1863, tender. Coal hulk. Sold?

Name	Bldr	Built	Acquired
Lightning	(U)	(U)	9 Mar 1865

NOTES: Schooner.
SERVICE RECORD: Captured at Port Royal, SC, 9 Mar 1865. Sold 5 Aug 1865.

Name	Bldr	Built	Acquired
Percy Drayton (ex-*Hettiwan*)	(U)	(U)	12 Nov 1863

NOTES: Sloop; 20 tons.
SERVICE RECORD: Captured as blockade runner by USS *Ottawa* off Charleston, 21 Jan 1863. SAtlBS, Tender. Sold 2 Sep 1865.

Name	Bldr	Built	Acquired
Renshaw	(U)	1862	28 Oct 1862

NOTES: Schooner; 68′ × 20′ × 6′6″; 80 tons.
SERVICE RECORD: Captured new and unrigged in Tar River, 20 May 1862. Ordnance hulk. NAtlBS. Sold 12 Aug 1865.

Name	Bldr	Built	Acquired	Comm
Rosalie	(U)	(U)	6 May 1863	Jun 1863

NOTES: Sloop; 45′ × 17′ × 3′6″; 28 tons; complement 8. Mar 64: 1 12-pdr SB.
SERVICE RECORD: Captured as blockade runner by USS *Octorara* off Charleston, 16 Mar 1863. Tender, Charlotte, Fla., 1863. Sold 28 Jun 1865.
Prizes: 8 Jul 1863: *Ann*; 26 Jul: *Georgie*; 30 Sep: *Director*. 9 Jun 1864: str *Emma*.

Name	Bldr	Built	Acquired
Sam Houston	(Baltimore)	1859	1861

NOTES: Schooner; 66 tons; complement 15. Jul 63: 1 12-pdr SB.
SERVICE RECORD: Captured by USS *South Carolina* off Galveston, 7 Jul 1861. WGulfBS 1861–65, despatch vessel. Sold 25 Apr 1866.

Name	Bldr	Built	Acquired	Comm
Sea Bird	(U)	(U)	12 Jul 1863	Jul 1863

NOTES: Schooner; 59′8″ × 18′4″ × 7′6″; 58 tons. 1863: 1 12-pdr H R.
SERVICE RECORD: Captured by USS *De Soto* off Pensacola, 14 May 1863. WGulfBS 1863–65. Operation at Bayport, Fla., 10 Jul 1864. Sold 28 Jun 1865.
Prizes: 21 Oct 1864: *Lucy*. 11 Apr 1865: **Annie* and **Florida*.

Name	Bldr	Built	Acquired	Comm
Shark	(Portsmouth, NH)	1860	5 Sep 1863	17 Jan 1865

NOTES: Schooner; 76′ × 22′; 87 tons; complement 24. Feb 65: 2 20-pdr R.

SERVICE RECORD: Captured off Galveston by USS *South Carolina*, 4 Jul 1861. Chartered as despatch boat 1862–64. Renamed **George W. Rodgers**, 17 Jan 1865. SAtlBS 1865. Decomm 16 Aug 1865. Sold 8 Sep 1865.

Name	Bldr	Built	Acquired
Stonewall	(U)	(U)	24 Jul 1863

NOTES: Schooner; 30 tons. Feb 64: 1 12-pdr SB.
SERVICE RECORD: Pilot boat, captured by USS *Tahoma* at Point Rosa, Fla., 24 Feb 1863. Tender, Key West. Sold 28 Jun 1865.
Prize: 24 Mar 1864: *Josephine*.

Name	Bldr	Built	Acquired
Susan A. Howard	(U)	(U)	19 May 1863

NOTES: Schooner; 50′ × 17′4″ × 5′4″
SERVICE RECORD: Ordnance boat, off North Carolina. Sold 15 Sep 1865.

Name	Bldr	Built	Acquired
Thunder (ex-*Annie Dees*)	(U)	(U)	9 Dec 1863

NOTES: Sloop.
SERVICE RECORD: Captured as blockade runner off Charleston by USS *Seneca*, 20 Nov 1862. SAtlBS, 1863, tender. Sold 8 Aug 1865.

Name	Bldr	Built	Acquired	Comm
Two Sisters	(Baltimore)	1856	21 Sep 1862	30 Jan 1863

NOTES: Schooner; 54 tons; complement 15. Dec 63: 1 12-pdr SB. Mar 64: 1 12-pdr R.
SERVICE RECORD: Captured by USS *Albatross* off Rio Grande River, 21 Sep 1862. EGulfBS 1863. Expedition to St. Marks, Fla., 23 Feb–27 Mar 1865. Sold 28 Jun 1865.
Prizes: 1 Feb 1863: *Richards*; 31 Mar: *Agnes*; 16 May: *Oliver S. Breese*; 25 Jun: *Frolic*; 27 Nov: *Maria Alberta*. 13 Jan 1864: *William*.

Name	Bldr	L	Acquired
Velocity	(U)	(U)	30 Sep 1862

NOTES: Schooner; 87 tons
SERVICE RECORD: Blockade runner captured by USS *Kensington* and *Rachel Seaman* at Sabine, Tex., 25 Sep 1862. Recaptured at Sabine Pass, 23 Jan 1863.
Prize: 11 Nov 1862: *Corse*.

Name	Bldr	L	Acquired
Wild Cat	(U)	(U)	1862

NOTES: Schooner; 30 tons.
SERVICE RECORD: Captured 1862. Operated in South Carolina waters 1862–65. Sold 28 Jul 1865.

THE MISSISSIPPI RIVER FLEET

With the secession of the Southern states, it was immediately apparent that whoever controlled the Mississippi River would control the continent. The great river was the north-south highway of the United States, a principal artery of commerce and communication. In addition, the multiplicity of rivers snaking through the region formed a network of waterways into the heart of the South, and these all led to the Mississippi. Control of the river would split the Confederacy, preventing goods and supplies from flowing from the west to the eastern heartland as well as reopening commerce for the Union midwestern states.

In 1861 it was the United States Army that acquired and later built the first armored vessels. These were the "timberclads," three lightly protected river steamers converted at Louisville, Kentucky. The *Conestoga*, *Lexington*, and *Tyler* were soon joined by better protected armored boats built by James B. Eads and several boats converted by him and others.

Although operated by the Army, the Western Gunboat Flotilla steamers were commanded by specially attached Navy officers. It was not until 1 October 1862, following the failure of the first attack on Vicksburg, that most of these Army vessels were transferred to the Navy as commissioned naval vessels.

Another group of ships taken up by the Army were known as Ellet rams, after their progenitor, Colonel Charles Ellet. This officer acquired several river boats and outfitted them as lightly armed rams, which he personally led into battle.

Many flat-bottomed river steamers with their characteristic tall smoke pipes, both side-wheelers and stern-wheelers, were acquired and lightly armored. They were known as tinclads and, uniquely among Civil War naval vessels, bore identifying numbers on their pilothouses.

Larger heavily armored vessels soon appeared on the rivers—*Choctaw*, *Lafayette*, *Eastport*. Powerfully armed ships, their experimental armor included rubber, which was quite useless. Meanwhile the Navy was building monitors designed specially for river operations. The *Ozark*, *Neosho*, and *Osage* and the four vessels of the *Milwaukee* class arrived in time to join in the fighting. The later *Marietta* and *Sandusky* were completed only after the end of combat operations.

To wrest control of the Mississippi, the Federal forces attacked at both its northern and southern ends in a two-pronged drive that aimed to meet midway and split the Confederacy. Farragut's deep-sea Navy gathered strength in the South, finally capturing the major port of New Orleans in May 1862. In the North, supporting the Army, the makeshift armed river steamers setting forth from their base at Cairo, Illinois, joined battle at Fts. Henry and Donelson, Island No. 10, and Memphis, overcoming Confederate defenses and eliminating most of their opponent's river defense fleet.

Several attempts were made to turn the enemy lines at Vicksburg by expeditions up and around the Yazoo River, culminating in success in April 1863. After almost a year of frustrating disappointments, Vicksburg fell on 4 July 1863, finally giving the Union full control of the vital Mississippi along its entire length.

Union gunboats proceeded far up the Cumberland and Tennessee rivers through Kentucky and Tennessee and even into Alabama. In 1864 the river fleet penetrated up the Red River in Louisiana and Arkansas, only to become trapped by the rapidly falling water level of the river. Only by an ingenious arrangement of man-made dams and waterfalls were the heavy ironclads able to escape downriver.

RIVER ARMORED VESSELS

RIVER MONITORS

OZARK

Name	Bldr	Laid down	L	Comm
Ozark	Collier (McCord)	1862	18 Feb 1863	18 Feb 1864

Tonnage:	578 tons B
Dimensions:	180' (oa) × 50' × 5'
Machinery:	2 screws, 4 engines (type unknown) (20" × 2'), 6 boilers; 9 mph
Complement:	120
Armament:	2 11" SB, 1 10" SB, 3 9" SB
Armor:	6" turret, 2.5" sides, 1.25" deck

The river monitor *Ozark* was a unique design with turret forward and casemate aft. Notice gun on the stern.

Monitors laid up at Mound City after the war, about 1868. The stern-wheeler *Neosho* is in center, looking aft. *Yuma*, *Shiloh*, and *Klamath* of the *Casco* class are at left. In the rear at right is one of the *Marietta* class with funnels abreast, and her sister can be seen behind *Neosho*. No photographs exist of the *Marietta*-class ships. (The Public Library of Cincinnati and Hamilton County)

MISSISSIPPI RIVER FLEET 149

The river monitor *Osage* with turret forward and covered stern-wheel aft. (U.S. Naval Historical Center)

NOTES: Combination single turret and 4 guns in casemate. Underpowered.

SERVICE RECORD: Red River Expedition, 12 Mar–16 May 1864. Decomm 24 Jul 1865. Sold 29 Nov 1865.

NEOSHO CLASS

Name	Bldr	Laid down	L	Comm
Neosho	Carondelet (Fulton)	1862	18 Feb 1863	13 May 1863
Osage	Carondelet (Fulton)	1862	13 Jan 1863	10 Jul 1863

Tonnage:	523 tons B
Dimensions:	180′ (oa) × 45′ × 4′6″
Machinery:	Stern wheel, 2 horizontal HP engines, 4 boilers; IHP 400 = 12 mph
Complement:	100
Armament:	2 11″ SB guns 1864: add 1 12-pdr R.
Armor:	6″ turret, 2.5″ sides, 1.25″ deck

NOTES: Single-turret monitors designed by Eads. Wooden hulls, with "turtleback" design and very shallow draft. The only stern-wheel monitors.

SERVICE RECORDS:

Neosho—Red River Expedition, 12 Mar–16 May 1864. Attacked battery near Simmsport, La., 8 Jun 1864. Operations in Cumberland River, Dec 1864. Decomm 23 Jul 1865. Renamed **Vixen**, 15 Jun 1869. Renamed **Osceola**, 10 Aug 1869. Sold 17 Aug 1873.

Osage—Expedition up Black and Ouachita rivers, La., 1–5 Mar 1864. Red River Expedition, 12 Mar–16 May 1864. WGulfBS 1865. Sunk by a torpedo (mine) in Blakely River, Ala., 29 Mar 1865. Raised, and hulk sold 22 Nov 1867.

Later history: Merchant *Osage* 1867. Possibly sunk in Sodo Lake near Shreveport, La., 1870. RR 1870.

MILWAUKEE CLASS

Name	Bldr	Laid down	L	Comm
Chickasaw	Carondelet (Fulton IW)	1862	10 Feb 1864	14 May 1864
Kickapoo	Carondelet (Fulton IW)	1862	12 Mar 1864	8 Jul 1864
Milwaukee	Carondelet (Fulton IW)	27 May 1862	4 Feb 1864	27 Aug 1864
Winnebago	Carondelet (Fulton IW)	1862	4 Jul 1863	27 Apr 1864

Tonnage:	1,300 tons D, 970 tons B
Dimensions:	229′ (oa) × 56′ × 6′
Machinery:	4 screws, 4 horizontal HP engines (type unknown), 7 boilers; 9 knots
Complement:	138
Armament:	4 11″ SB
Armor:	8″ turrets, 1.5″ deck

NOTES: Double-turret monitors designed by Eads with one Ericsson turret and one Eads turret.

SERVICE RECORDS:

Chickasaw—WGulfBS 1864. Battle of Mobile Bay, 5 Aug 1864. Bombardment of Ft. Morgan, Mobile Bay, 9–23 Aug 1864. Decomm 6 Jul 1865. Renamed **Samson**, 15 Jun 1869. Renamed **Chickasaw**, 10 Aug 1869. Sold 12 Sep 1874.

Later history: Merchant *Chickasaw* 1875. Railroad ferry. Converted to side wheels 1881, renamed *Gouldsboro* 1882. BU 1944.

Kickapoo—WGulfBS 1864–65. Decomm 29 Jul 1865. Renamed **Cyclops**, 15 Jun 1869. Renamed **Kewaydin**, 10 Aug 1869. Sold 12 Sep 1874.

Milwaukee—WGulfBS 1864–65. Struck a torpedo (mine) and sank in Blakely River, 18 Mar 1865.

Winnebago—Mississippi Sqn 1864. WGulfBS Jul 1864. Battle of Mobile Bay, 5 Aug 1864, hit 19 times. Bombardment of Ft. Morgan, Mobile Bay, 9–23 Aug 1864. Decomm 27 Sep 1865. Renamed **Tornado**, 15 Jun 1869. Renamed **Winnebago**, 10 Aug 1869. Sold 12 Sep 1874.

The monitor *Milwaukee* with a "torpedo rake" minesweeping device on the bow. A tender is at right. Notice the two turrets and guns on deck. (U.S. Naval Historical Center)

The monitor *Milwaukee* with steam up. Her two turrets, pilothouse, and tall funnel are distinctive of this class. This picture has also been identified as *Kickapoo*. (Martin Holbrook Collection) (Mariners Museum)

MARIETTA CLASS

Name	Bldr	Laid down	L	Comm
Marietta	Tomlinson (bldr)	1862	4 Jan 1865	16 Dec 1865*
Sandusky	Tomlinson (bldr)	1862	20 Jan 1865	26 Dec 1865*
				*completed

Tonnage:	479 tons B
Dimensions:	170′ (oa) × 50′ × 5′
Machinery:	1 screw, 2 HP engines (type unknown), 4 boilers; 9 mph
Complement:	100
Armament:	2-11″SB guns
Armor:	6″ turret, 1.25″ sides

NOTES: Light-draft, single-turret, flat-bottomed river boats. Two funnels abreast. Completed after the end of the war and never commissioned.

SERVICE RECORD:

Marietta—Laid up at Mound City on delivery. Renamed **Circe**, 15 Jun 1869. Renamed **Marietta**, 10 Aug 1869. Sold 12 Apr 1873.

Sandusky—Laid up at Mound City on delivery. Renamed **Minerva**, 15 Jun 1869. Renamed **Sandusky**, 10 Aug 1869. Sold 12 Apr 1873.

RIVER IRONCLADS

CAIRO CLASS

Name	Bldr	Laid down	L	Comm
Cairo	Eads; Mound City (U)	1861	1861	25 Jan 1862
Carondelet	Eads; St. Louis (U)	1861	22 Oct 1861	15 Jan 1862
Cincinnati	Eads; Mound City (U)	1861	1861	16 Jan 1862
Louisville	Eads; St. Louis (U)	1861	1861	16 Jan 1862
Mound City	Eads; Mound City (U)	1861	1861	16 Jan 1862
Pittsburg	Eads; St. Louis (U)	1861	1861	16 Jan 1862
St. Louis	Eads; St. Louis (U)	27 Sep 1861	12 Oct 1861	31 Jan 1862

Tonnage: 512 tons
Dimensions: 175′ (oa) × 51′2″ × 6′
Machinery: Center wheel, 2 horizontal HP engines (22″ × 6′), 5 boilers; 9 mph
Complement: 251
Armament: 3 8″ SB, 4 42-pdr R, 6 32-pdr R, 1 12-pdr R except
  Cairo—As built; also 2 42-pdr R. Apr 62: add 1 42-pdr R. Nov 62 total: 3-8″/63, 3 42-pdr/80, 6 32-pdr/43, 1 30-pdr R, 1 12-pdr SB
  Carondelet—Nov 62: total 4-8″/63, 1-42pdr/80, 6-32pdr/42, 1 50-pdr R, 1 30-pdr R, 1 12-pdr SB. May 63: add 3 9″ SB, less 5 32-pdr/43. Jan 64 total: 2 100-pdr R, 1 50-pdr R, 1 30-pdr R, 3 9 ″SB, 4 8″ SB/63. Dec 64: less 4 8″ SB.
  Cincinnati—Sep 62: 2 42-pdr replaced by 2 30-pdr R. 1865 total: 2 100-pdr R, 3 9″ SB, 2 30-pdr R, 6 24-pdr SB.
  Louisville—Sep 62: 2 42-pdr replaced by 2 30-pdr R. Nov 62: add 3 9″ SB, less 1 8″ SB. 1864 total: 1 100-pdr R, 4 9″ SB, 2 30-pdr R, 6 32-pdr/42.
  Mound City—1863: add 1 30-pdr R, 1 50-pdr R, less 2 42-pdr. Jun 63 total: 3 9″ SB, 3 8″/63, 2 7″/84, 3 32-pdr/42, 2 30-pdr R. 1864 total: 1 100-pdr R, 4 9″ SB, 3 8″ SB, 1 50-pdr R, 3 32-pdr, 1 30-pdr R. 1864: 1 32-pdr replaced by 1 100-pdr R
  Pittsburg—Sep 62 total: 2 30-pdr R, 3 8″ SB, 2 42-pdr R/80, 6 32-pdr/42, 1 12-pdr SB. May 63: 2 32-pdr/42 replaced by 2 9″ SB. Dec 63 total: 1 100-pdr R, 4 9″ SB, 2 8″ SB, 4 32-pdr/42, 2 30-pdr R, 1 12-pdr SB. Sep 64: less 2 32-pdr.
  St. Louis—Oct 62: 2 42-pdr/80 replaced by 2 30-pdr R. Dec 62: add 2 10″ SB. 1863 total: 1 10″ SB, 2 8″/63, 2 9″ SB, 6 32-pdr/42, 2 30-pdr R.
Armor: 2.5″ casemates, 1.25″ pilothouse

NOTES: Designed by Lenthall as modified by Pook and Eads. Known as "Pook Turtles." Had rectangular casemate with sloped armored sides and a paddle wheel amidships near the stern. Built for the Army, all completed within three months. WGF. Transferred to the Navy 1 Oct 1862.

SERVICE RECORDS:

Cairo—WGF. Occupation of Clarksville, Tenn., 19 Feb 1862. Bombardment of Ft. Pillow, Tenn., 13 Apr 1862. Engagement with enemy vessels and batteries at Ft. Pillow, 10 May 1862. Battle of Memphis, 6 Jun 1862. Expedition up Yazoo River, 21 Nov–11 Dec 1862. Struck a torpedo (mine) and sank in Yazoo River, 12 Dec 1862. Wreck raised 1965.

Carondelet—WGF. Capture of Ft. Henry, Tenn., 6 Feb 1862. Attack on Ft. Donelson, Tennessee River, 14 Feb 1862. Siege of Island No. 10, 15 Mar–7 Apr 1862. Bombardment of Ft. Pillow, Tenn., 13 Apr 1862. Engagement with enemy vessels and batteries at Ft. Pillow, 10 May 1862. Battle of Memphis, 6 Jun 1862. Bombardment of St. Charles, Ark., and expedition up White River, 17 Jun 1862. Severely damaged and run around in engagement with CSS *Arkansas* above Vicksburg, 15 Jul 1862. Expedition up Yazoo River, 21 Nov–11 Dec 1862. Expedition to Steele's Bayou, Miss., 14–26 Mar 1863. Ran past batteries at Vicksburg, 16 Apr 1863. Bombardment of Grand Gulf, Miss., 29 Apr 1863. Bombardment of Vicksburg, 18–22 May and 27 May 1863. Red River Expedition, 12 Mar–16 May 1864. Engaged batteries at Bell's Mill, Cumberland River, Tenn., 3–4 Dec 1864. Decomm 20 Jun 1865. Sold 29 Nov 1865.
Later history: Hull became wharfboat at Gallipolis, Ohio. Engines used in towboat *Quaker*.

Cincinnati—WGF. Capture of Ft. Henry, Tenn., 6 Feb 1862. Siege of Island No. 10, 15 Mar–7 Apr 1862. Bombardment of Ft. Pillow, Tenn., 13 Apr 1862. Rammed and sunk during engagement at Ft.

Eads gunboats under construction at St. Louis, 1861. (National Archives)

Eads ironclad gunboat *Louisville* during a calm moment.

The ironclad *Pittsburg*, one of the gunboats built in 1861 by Eads for the Army.

The Eads ironclads *Baron de Kalb*, *Cincinnati*, and *Mound City* anchored off Cairo, Illinois, 1863. Differences in appearance of these sisters can be clearly seen. (U.S. Naval Historical Center) (Silverstone Collection)

Pillow, 10 May 1862. Raised and refitted. Expedition up Yazoo River, 21 Nov–11 Dec 1862. Bombardment of Drumgoulds Bluff, Yazoo River, 28 Dec 1862. Expedition up White River, bombardment and capture of Ft. Hindman, Ark., 10–11 Jan 1863. Expedition to Steele's Bayou, Miss., 14–26 Mar 1863. Sunk by enemy batteries during bombardment of Vicksburg, 27 May 1863. Raised Aug 1863 and refitted. WGulfBS Feb 1865. Took surrender of CSS

Nashville and CSS *Morgan* in Tombigbee River, 10 May 1865. Decomm 4 Aug 1865. Sold 28 Mar 1866.

Later history: Sank at moorings in Cache River, 1866.

Louisville—WGF. Attack on Ft. Donelson, Tennessee River, 14 Feb 1862. Siege of Island No. 10, 15 Mar–7 Apr 1862. Battle of Memphis, 6 Jun 1862. Engagement with CSS *Arkansas* above Vicksburg, 15 Jul 1862. Bombardment of Drumgoulds Bluff, Yazoo

River, 28 Dec 1862. Expedition up White River, capture of Ft. Hindman, Ark., 10–11 Jan 1863. Expedition to Steele's Bayou, Miss., 14–26 Mar 1863. Ran past batteries at Vicksburg, 16 Apr 1863. Bombardment of Grand Gulf, Miss., 29 Apr 1863. Red River Expedition, 12 Mar–16 May 1864. Decomm 21 Jul 1865. Sold 29 Nov 1865.

Mound City—WGF. Action at Columbus, Ky., 23 Feb 1862. Siege of Island No. 10, 15 Mar–7 Apr 1862. Bombardment of Ft. Pillow, Tenn., 13 Apr 1862. Rammed by CSS *General Price* during engagement off Ft. Pillow, 10 May and by CSS *General Van Dorn*, 11 May 1862, and went aground. Expedition up White River, disabled during bombardment of St. Charles, Ark., 17 Jun 1862. Expeditions up Yazoo River, Greenville, Miss., 16–22 Aug 1862, and to Steele's Bayou, Miss., 14–26 Mar 1863. Ran past batteries at Vicksburg, 16 Apr 1863. Bombardment of Grand Gulf, Miss., 29 Apr 1863. Bombardment of Vicksburg, 18–22 May, 27 May and 20 Jun 1863. Red River Expedition, 12 Mar–16 May 1864. Sold 9 Nov 1865. BU 1866.

Prizes: 7 Apr 1862: str *Red Rover*; 14 Jun: str *Clara Dolsen*.

Pittsburg—WGF. Attack on Ft. Donelson, Tennessee River, 14 Feb 1862. Siege of Island No. 10, 15 Mar–7 Apr 1862. Bombardment of Ft. Pillow, Tenn., 13 Apr 1862. Engagement with enemy squadron and batteries at Ft. Pillow, 10 May 1862. Expeditions up Yazoo River, 21 Nov/11 Dec 1862, and to Steele's Bayou, Miss., 14–26 Mar 1863. Ran past batteries at Vicksburg, 16 Apr 1863. Severely

damaged by gunfire at bombardment of Grand Gulf, Miss., 29 Apr 1863. Bombardment of Ft. Beauregard, Harrisonburg, La., 10–11 May, and expedition up Red River, 3–13 May 1863. Red River Expedition, 12 Mar–16 May 1864. Sold 29 Nov 1865. Abandoned Jun 1870.

St. Louis—WGF. Engagement with CSN vessels near Lucas Bend, Mo., Mississippi River, 11 Jan 1862. Bombardment and capture of Ft. Henry, Tenn., 6 Feb 1862. Disabled (hit 59 times) during attack on Ft. Donelson, Tennessee River, 14 Feb 1862. Action at Columbus, Ky., 23 Feb 1862. Siege of Island No. 10, 15 Mar–7 Apr 1862. Bombardment of Ft. Pillow, Tenn., 13 Apr 1862. Engaged enemy vessels and batteries at Ft. Pillow, 10 May 1862. Battle of Memphis, 6 Jun 1862. Expedition up White River, bombardment of St. Charles, Ark., 17 Jun 1862.

Renamed **Baron de Kalb**, 8 Sep 1862. Expedition up Yazoo River, 21 Nov–11 Dec 1862. Bombardment of Drumgoulds Bluff, Yazoo River, 28 Dec 1862. Expedition up White River, capture of Ft. Hindman, Ark., 10–11 Jan 1863. Yazoo Pass expedition, attack on Ft. Pemberton, Tallahatchie River, 11–23 Mar 1863. Bombardment and feigned attack, Haynes' Bluff, Miss., 29 Apr–2 May 1863. Capture of Haynes' Bluff, Yazoo River, 18 May 1863. Destruction of Yazoo City NYd, 20–23 May 1863. Expedition up Yazoo River, 24–31 May 1863. Sunk by a torpedo (mine) one mile below Yazoo City, 13 Jul 1863.

Prizes: 5 Dec 1862: str *Lottie*. 19 May 1863: *Alonzo Child*.

CHILLICOTHE

Name	Bldr	Laid down	L	Comm
Chillicothe	Brown (Junger)	1862	1862	5 Sep 1862

Tonnage:	395 tons D (?), 203 tons B
Dimensions:	162′ × 50′ × 4′ (also given as 159′ × 46.5′ × 6′10″)
Machinery:	Side wheels and 2 screws, 2 engines (type unknown) (20″ × 8′) and (23″ × 4′), 3 boilers; 7 knots
Complement:	(U)
Armament:	2-11″SB. Oct 63: add 1-12pdr SB.
Armor:	2″ sides, 1″ deck, 3″ pilothouse

NOTES: Designed by Samuel Hartt.

SERVICE RECORD: Expedition up White River, capture of Ft. Hindman, Ark., 10–11 Jan 1863. Yazoo Pass expedition, damaged by gunfire (11th and 13th) during attack on Ft. Pemberton, Tallahatchie River, 11–23 Mar 1863. Red River Expedition, 12 Mar–16 May 1864. Sold 29 Nov 1865.

Later history: Destroyed by burning at Cairo, Sep 1872.

The ironclad *Tuscumbia*. The three gunports in the bow are distinctive to this vessel. (U.S. Naval Historical Center) (Martin Holbrook Collection)

The river ironclad *Tuscumbia* with the tinclad *Linden* (no. 10) behind, 1863. In the foreground is a mortar boat. Battle damage to the paddle-wheel box has not yet been repaired. This picture has been misidentified as *Chillicothe*. (U.S. Naval Historical Center)

The ironclad *Benton* off Natchez, Mississippi, in July 1864. The sloping sides of the casemate and her heavy armament made her one of the most powerful ships on the river. (U.S. Naval Historical Center)

INDIANOLA

Name	Bldr	Laid down	L	Comm
Indianola	Brown (Junger)	1862	4 Sep 1862	14 Jan 1863

Tonnage:	442 tons B, 511 tons (U)
Dimensions:	175′ × 52′ × 5″
Machinery:	Side wheels and 2 screws, 4 engines (type unknown) (22″ × 6′6″ and 18″ × 1′8″), 5 boilers; 6 knots
Complement:	144
Armament:	2 11″ SB (for'd), 2 9″ SB (aft) guns
Armor:	3″ casemate, 1″ deck

NOTES: Designed by Joseph Brown for the Army and transferred to the Navy 12 Jan 1863. Reported commissioned 27 Sep 1862 and ready for service, but actually completed later.

SERVICE RECORD: Ran past Vicksburg batteries, 19 Feb 1863. Blockaded mouth of Red River, 19–21 Feb 1863. Rammed by Confederate vessels during engagement near New Carthage, Miss. below Vicksburg, run aground and surrendered, 24 Feb 1863. Destroyed by Confederates to prevent recapture, 4 Mar 1863. Hulk refloated 5 Jan 1865. Sold 19 Nov 1865 and BU.

TUSCUMBIA

Name	Bldr	Laid down	L	Comm
Tuscumbia	(New Albany, Ind.) (McCord)	1862	12 Dec 1862	12 Mar 1863

Tonnage:	575 tons B, 915 tons (U)
Dimensions:	178′ × 75′ × 7′
Machinery:	Side wheels and 1 screw, 4 engines (types unknown) (30″ × 7′ and 20″ × 2′), 6 boilers; 10 mph
Complement:	(U)
Armament:	3 11″ SB (for'd), 2 9″ SB guns (aft)
Armor:	6″ casemates

NOTES: Designed by Joseph Brown as a casemate ironclad; poorly built.

SERVICE RECORD: Recapture of Ft. Heiman in Tennessee River, 12–14 Mar 1863. Ran past batteries at Vicksburg, 16 Apr 1863. Hit 81 times during bombardment of Grand Gulf, Miss., 29 Apr 1863. Bombardment of Vicksburg, 18–22 May 1863. Repairing Aug 1863–May 1864. Decomm Feb 1865. Sold 29 Nov 1865. Abandoned 1867.

CONVERTED RIVER ARMORED VESSELS AND CONVERTED IRONCLADS

Name	Bldr	Built	Acquired	Comm
Benton (ex-*Submarine No. 7*, ex-*Benton*)	Eads; St. Louis (U)	1861	Nov 1861	24 Feb 1862

Tonnage:	633 tons
Dimensions:	202′ × 72′ × 9′
Machinery:	Stern wheel, 2 inclined engines (20″ × 7′); 5.5 knots
Complement:	176
Armament:	2 9″ SB, 7 42-pdr R, 7 32-pdr/43. Aug 62 total: 2 9″/90, 4 42-pdr/80, 8 32-pdr/42, 2 50-pdr R, 1 12-pdr HS. Jan 63: 2 32-pdr replaced by 2 9″ SB. Dec 63 total: 2 100-pdr R, 8 9″, 4 32-pdr/42, 2 50-pdr R
Armor:	2.5″ casemates, 2.5″ pilothouse

NOTES: Converted from a catamaran snagboat to a design by James W. Eads. Had a rectangular wooden casemate with sloping sides. Transferred from War Dept. 1 Oct 1862. The most powerful of the early river ironclads.

SERVICE RECORD: WGF. Flagship, Mississippi Sqn 1862–63. Siege of Island No. 10, 15 Mar–7 Apr 1862. Bombardment of Ft. Pillow, Tenn., 13 Apr 1862. Engagement with squadron and batteries at Ft. Pillow, 10 May 1862. Battle of Memphis, 6 Jun 1862. Engagement with CSS *Arkansas* above Vicksburg, 15 Jul 1862. Expedition up Yazoo River, Greenville, Miss., 16–22 Aug 1862. Expedition in Yazoo River dragging for torpedoes, and bombardments at Haynes Bluff (damaged) and Drumgoulds Bluff, 23–26 Dec 1862. Ran past batteries at Vicksburg, 16 Apr 1863. Bombardment of Grand Gulf, Miss., 29 Apr 1863. Expedition up Red River, 3–13 May 1863. Bombardment of Vicksburg, 18–22 May, 27 May, and 20 Jun 1863. Red River Expedition, 12 Mar–16 May 1864. Expedition up Red River and capture of CSS *Missouri*, 1–6 Jun 1865. Decomm 20 Jul 1865. Sold 29 Nov 1865 and BU.

Prizes: 5 Jun 1862: str *Sovereign*; 18 Aug: *Fairplay*.

Name	Bldr	Built	Acquired	Comm
Essex (ex-*New Era*)	Page & Bacon (Gatz)	1856	1861	15 Oct 1861

Tonnage:	355 tons
Dimensions:	159′ × 47′6″ × 6′. 1862: 198.5′ × 58′ × 6.8′
Machinery:	Center wheel, 2 engines (type unknown) (18″ × 6′), 4 boilers; 5.5 knots
Complement:	134
Armament:	5 9″ SB. Jan 62 total: 1 10″ SB, 3 9″ SB, 1 32-pdr/43, 1 12-pdrBH. Aug 62: add 2 50-pdr R. Jun 63 total: 1 100-pdr R, 4 9″ SB, 1 32-pdr SB, 2 50-pdr R, 4 12-pdr SB. 1864 total: 2 100-pdr R, 6 9″ SB, 1 12-pdr R, 3 12-pdr SB.
Armor:	3″ casemates

NOTES: Converted from a merchant snagboat to a plan by Eads. Originally casemate was timberclad. Armor added, hull lengthened and renamed Dec 1861. Transferred from the Army, 1 Oct 1862.

SERVICE RECORD: WGF. Cumberland River expedition, Nov 1861. Engagement with CSN vessels near Lucas Bend, Mo., Mississippi River, 11 Jan 1862. Boiler burst when struck by shell during attack on Ft. Henry, Tenn., 6 Feb 1862. Attack on CSS *Arkansas* at Vicksburg, 22 Jul, and again at Baton Rouge, La., 5 Aug 1862. Bombardment of Port Hudson, La., 13 Dec 1862. Occupation of Baton Rouge, 17 Dec 1862. Bombardment of Port Hudson, 8 May–9 Jul 1863. Bombardment at Whitehall Point, La., 10 Jul 1863. Red River Expedition, 12 Mar–16 May 1864. Decomm 20 Jul 1865. Sold 29 Nov 1865.

Later history: Merchant *New Era* 1865. Hull burned for scrap Dec 1870.

The ironclad *Essex* was converted from a snagboat by Eads.

Name	Bldr	Built	Acquired	Comm
Eastport	(New Albany, Ind.)	1852	Aug 1862	9 Jan 1863

Tonnage:	570 tons
Dimensions:	280′ × 43′ or 32′ × 6′3″
Machinery:	Side wheels, 2 HP engines (26″ × 9′); 5 boilers
Complement:	(U)
Armament:	6 9″ SB, 2 100-pdr R. Jul 63 total: 4 9″ SB, 2 100-pdr R, 2 50-pdr R.
Armor:	(U)

NOTES: Ironclad ram, captured while conversion incomplete at Cerro Gordo, Tenn., 7 Feb 1862. Completed at Mound City.

SERVICE RECORD: WGF. Damaged by grounding near Vicksburg, 2 Feb 1863. Red River Expedition, 12 Mar–16 May 1864. Capture of Ft. de Russy, Ark., Mar 1864. Damaged by torpedo (mine) explosion below Grand Ecore, La., in Red River, 15 Apr, and destroyed to prevent capture, 26 Apr 1864.

Another view of the *Essex*, a river ironclad, tied up at Baton Rouge. Notice the covered wheel boxes aft. Just astern can be seen the side-wheel frigate *Mississippi*. (Old Court House Museum, Vicksburg)

The ironclad *Eastport*, captured while being converted, was taken to Cairo and completed for the Union Navy. There are two guns forward and three on broadside. (The Public Library of Cincinnati and Hamilton County)

Name	Bldr	Built	Acquired	Comm
Choctaw	(New Albany, Ind.) (U)	1856	27 Sep 1862	23 Mar 1863

Tonnage:	1,004 tons
Dimensions:	260′ × 45′ × 8′
Machinery:	Side wheels, 2 engines (type unknown) (23″ × 8′), 6 boilers; 2 knots (upstream)
Complement:	106
Armament:	1 100-pdr R, 1 9″ SB, 2 30-pdr R. May 63: add 2 24-pdr SB. Sep 63 total: 1 100-pdr R, 2 30-pdr R, 3 9″ SB, 2 12-pdr R
Armor:	1″ + 1″ rubber casemate (forward)

NOTES: Converted from a merchant steamer to plans by William D. Porter. Armor and armament were too heavy for the hull. Rubber armor was useless. Transferred from War Dept. 1 Oct 1862.

SERVICE RECORD: Bombardment and feigned attack (hit 53 times), Haynes' Bluff, Miss., 29 Apr–2 May 1863. Capture of Haynes' Bluff, Yazoo River, 18 May 1863. Destruction of Yazoo City NYd, 20–23 May 1863. Red River Expedition, 12 Mar–16 May 1864. Decomm 22 Jul 1865. Sold 28 Mar 1866.

The ironclad *Choctaw* with a small tug astern. A fine port-side view showing her casemate forward and paddle-wheel boxes aft. (U.S. Naval Historical Center)

Name	Bldr	Built	Acquired	Comm
Lafayette	(Louisville) (U)	1848	14 Sep 1862	27 Feb 1863
(ex-*Fort Henry* (USA), ex-*Aleck Scott*)				

Tonnage:	1,193 tons
Dimensions:	280′ (oa) × 45′ × 8′
Machinery:	Side wheels, 2 engines (type unknown) (26″ × 8′), 6 boilers; 4 knots (upstream)
Complement:	210
Armament:	2 11″ SB, 4 9″ SB, 2 100-pdr R. Apr 63: add 4 24-pdr H. May 63 total: 2 11″SB, 2-9″SB, 2 100-pdr R, 2 24-pdr H, 2 12-pdr H.
Armor:	2.5″ + 2″ rubber casemate

NOTES: Purchased as an Army Quartermaster vessel 1861 and converted by Eads at St. Louis to a design of William D. Porter. Single casemate and ram bow. Rubber armor useless.

SERVICE RECORD: Ran past batteries at Vicksburg, 16 Apr 1863. Bombardment of Grand Gulf, Miss., 21 and 29 Apr 1863. Expedition up Red River, 3–13 May 1863. Red River Expedition, 12 Mar–16 May 1864. Expedition up Red River, capture of CSS *Missouri*, 1–6 Jun 1865. Decomm 23 Jul 1865. Sold 28 Mar 1866 & BU.

An unusual view from the heights of river ironclad *Lafayette* off Vicksburg in 1863. (Martin Holbrook Collection)

TIMBERCLADS

All acquired from War Department. Originally converted at Louisville, Ky. 1861.

Name	Bldr	Built	Acquired	Comm
Conestoga	(Brownsville, Pa.)	1859	3 Jun 1861	1861

Tonnage:	572 tons
Dimensions:	(U)
Machinery:	Side wheels, 2 HP engines (24″ × 7′); 12 mph
Complement:	(U)
Armament:	4 32-pdr/43. Sep 62 total: 1 12-pdr R, 4 32-pdr/43. Jan 64 total: 3 32-pdr/42, 3 30-pdr R, 1 12-pdr SB.

NOTES: Converted side-wheel towboat.

SERVICE RECORD: WGF. Engaged CSS *Jackson* off Lucas Bend, Ky., 10 Sep 1861. Broke up enemy force at Eddyville, Ky., 27 Oct 1861. Capture of Ft. Henry, Tenn., 6 Feb 1862. Expedition to Florence, Ala., Tennessee River, 6–11 Feb 1862. Attack on Ft. Donelson, Tennessee River, 14 Feb 1862. Action at Columbus, Ky., 23 Feb 1862. Expedition up White River, bombardment of St. Charles, Ark., 17 Jun 1862. Expedition to burn Palmyra, Tenn., 3 Apr 1863. Expedition to Trinity, La., Red River, 10 Jul 1863. Expedition up Black and Ouachita rivers, La., 1–5 Mar 1864. Sunk in collision with USS *General Price* below Grand Gulf, Mississippi River, 8 Mar 1864.
Prizes: 16 Sep 1861: strs *V.R. Stephenson* and *Gazelle*. 8 Feb 1862: strs *Muscle* and *Sallie Wood*. 12 Feb 1863: strs *Evansville* and *Rose Hambleton*; 24 Oct: strs *Lillie Martin* and *Sweden*.

The timberclad gunboat *Conestoga*. She was sunk in a collision in March 1864. (The Public Library of Cincinnati and Hamilton County)

Name	Bldr	Built	Acquired	Comm
Lexington	(Belle Vernon, Pa.)	1860	5 Jun 1861	12 Aug 1861

Tonnage:	362 tons D. 448 tons
Dimensions:	177'7" × 36'10" × 6'
Machinery:	Side wheels, 2 HP engines (20" × 6'), 3 boilers; 7 knots
Complement:	(U)
Armament:	2 32-pdr/43, 4 8" SB. Sep 62 total: 4 8" SB, 1 32-pdr/42, 2 30-pdr R, 1 12-pdr H. Feb 64: less 2 8" SB. Sep 64 total: 6 8" SB, 1 32-pdr/42, 2 30-pdr R, 1 12-pdr R.

NOTES: Built by L. M. Speer.
SERVICE RECORD: WGF. Engagements with CSS *Jackson* off Hickman, Ky., 4 Sep and 8 and 10 Oct 1861. Engagement with gunboats at Lucas Bend, Mississippi River, 13 Oct 1861. Supported army at Iron Bank, Ky., 7 Nov 1861. Engaged battery at Columbus, Ky., 7 Jan 1862. Capture of Ft. Henry, Tenn., 6 Feb 1862. Expedition to Florence, Ala., Tennessee River, 6–11 Feb 1862. Engaged battery at Chickasaw, Ala., 12 Mar 1862. Siege of Island No. 10, 15 Mar–7 Apr 1862. Supported Army at Pittsburg Landing (Shiloh), Tenn., 6–7 Apr 1862. Expedition up White River and bombardment of St. Charles, Ark., 17 Jun 1862. Expedition up Yazoo River, 21 Nov–11 Dec 1862. Expedition in Yazoo River dragging for torpedoes, and bombardments at Haynes Bluff and Drumgoulds Bluff, 23–26 Dec 1862.

Expedition up White River, capture of Ft. Hindman, Ark., 10–11 Jan 1863. Defense of Ft. Donelson, Tenn., 3 Feb 1863. Expedition to burn Palmyra, Tenn., 3 Apr 1863. Reconnaissance up White River, Ark., 12–15 Aug 1863. Expedition up Black and Ouachita rivers, La., 1–5 Mar 1864. Red River Expedition, 12 Mar–16 May 1864. Repulsed attack on White River Station, Ark., 22 June 1864. Decomm 2 Jul 1865. Sold 17 Aug 1865.

Name	Bldr	Built	Acquired
Tyler (ex-*A.O. Tyler*)	(Cincinnati)	1857	5 Jun 1861

Tonnage:	420 tons D. 575 tons
Dimensions:	180' × 45'4" × 6'
Machinery:	Side wheels, 2 HP engines (22" × 8'), 4 boilers; 8 knots
Complement:	67
Armament:	6 8"/63, 1 32-pdr/43. Sep 62 total: 6 8"/63, 3 30-pdr R, 1 12-pdr SB. Mar 64: add 4 24-pdr.

NOTES: Sank 17 Jan 1860; salved.
SERVICE RECORD: WGF. Engaged CSS *Jackson* off Hickman, Ky., 4 Sep 1861. Engagement with gunboats at Lucas Bend, Mississippi River, 13 Oct 1861. Supported Army at Iron Bank, Ky., 7 Nov 1861. Engaged battery at Columbus, Ky., 7 Jan 1862. Capture of Ft. Henry, Tenn., 6 Feb 1862. Expedition to Florence, Ala., Tennessee River, 6–11 Feb 1862. Attack on Ft. Donelson, Tennessee River, 14 Feb 1862. Supported Army at Pittsburg Landing (Shiloh), Tenn., 6–7 Apr 1862. Damaged during engagement with CSS *Arkansas* above Vicksburg, 15 Jul 1862. Expedition up Yazoo River, 21 Nov–11 Dec 1862. Expedition up Yazoo River dragging for torpedoes, and bombardments at Haynes Bluff and Drumgoulds Bluff, 23–26 Dec 1862. Bombardment and feigned attack, Haynes Bluff, Miss., 29 Apr–2 May 1863. Engaged battery at Clarendon, Ark., 24 Jun 1864. Sold 17 Aug 1865.
Prizes: 21 Apr 1862: str *Alfred Robb*. 6 Jun 1863: str *Lady Walton*. 25 Feb 1864: str *Gillum*.

The timberclad gunboat *Lexington* was one of the first river ships to be armed. She can be distinguished from *Conestoga* and *Tyler* by the forward position of her funnels. (U.S. Naval Historical Center)

The *Tyler*, a timberclad gunboat, was very active early in the war. She can be distinguished from *Conestoga* by differences in the wheel box. (The Public Library of Cincinnati and Hamilton County)

ELLET RAMS (WAR DEPT.)

River steamers purchased by the Army Quartermaster Department and hurriedly converted into rams by Charles Ellet. Hulls were reinforced and bows filled with timber. They carried little or no armament. The Ellet rams formed an independent command that was never incorporated into the Navy, although it operated under naval orders.

Name	Bldr	Built	Acquired	Comm
Lancaster (ex-Kosciusko, ex-Lancaster No. 3)	(Cincinnati)	1855	Apr 1862	May 1862

Tonnage:	375 or 257 tons
Dimensions:	176′ × 30′ × 5.5′
Machinery:	Side wheels
Complement:	(U)
Armament:	(U)

NOTES: Wooden hull. Converted at Cincinnati.
SERVICE RECORD: WGF. Battle of Memphis, 6 Jun 1862. Damaged in engagement with CSS Arkansas above Vicksburg, 15 Jul 1862. Sunk by Confederate batteries while passing Vicksburg, 25 Mar 1863.

Name	Bldr	Built	Acquired	Comm
Lioness	(Brownsville, Pa.)	1859	22 Apr 1862	May 1862

Tonnage:	198 tons
Dimensions:	(U)
Machinery:	Stern wheel
Complement:	(U)
Armament:	(U)

NOTES: Converted at Pittsburgh.
SERVICE RECORD: WGF. Battle of Memphis, 6 Jun 1862. Expedition up Yazoo River, Greenville, Miss., 16–22 Aug 1862. Expedition in Yazoo River dragging for torpedoes, and bombardment at Haynes Bluff and Drumgoulds Bluff, 23–26 Dec 1862. Yazoo Pass expedition, attack on Ft. Pemberton, Tallahatchie River, 11–23 Mar 1863. Laid up after Jul 1863. Sold 5 Sep 1865.
Later history: Merchant Lioness 1865. RR 1869.

Name	Bldr	Built	Acquired
Mingo	(California, Pa.)	1859	8 Apr 1862

Tonnage:	228 tons
Dimensions:	(U)
Machinery:	Stern wheel; 12 knots
Complement:	(U)
Armament:	none

NOTES: Converted at Pittsburgh.
SERVICE RECORD: WGF. Battle of Memphis, arrived after the action, 6 Jun 1862. Sank accidentally at Cape Girardeau, Mo., Nov 1862.

Name	Bldr	Built	Acquired
Monarch	(Fulton, O.)	1853	23 Apr 1862

Tonnage:	406 tons
Dimensions:	(U)
Machinery:	Side wheels
Complement:	(U)
Armament:	(U)

NOTES: Sank at Louisville 5 Mar 1861; salved. Converted at Madison, Ind.
SERVICE RECORD: WGF. Expedition to Craigheads Point, Miss., 3 Jun 1862. Battle of Memphis, 6 Jun 1862, rammed two Confederate ships. Pursued enemy ships up Yazoo River, 26 Jun 1862. Expedition up White River, bombardment and capture of Ft. Hindman, Ark., 10–11 Jan 1863. Laid up after Jul 1863. Sunk by ice while laid up below St. Louis, Dec 1864 and BU.

Name	Bldr	Built	Acquired
Queen of the West	(Cincinnati)	1854	May 1862

Tonnage:	406 tons
Dimensions:	181′ × 36′ × 6′
Machinery:	Side wheels; 3 boilers
Complement:	120
Armament:	1 30-pdr, 3 12-pdr H

NOTES: Converted at Cincinnati.
SERVICE RECORD: WGF. Rammed at Battle of Memphis and run aground, 6 Jun 1862. Engagement with CSS Arkansas above Vicksburg, 15 and 22 Jul 1862. Expedition up Yazoo River, 21 Nov–11 Dec 1862. Expedition in Yazoo River dragging for torpedoes, and bombardments at Haynes Bluff and Drumgoulds Bluff, 23–26 Dec 1862. Damaged and rammed CSS City of Vicksburg off Vicksburg, 2 Feb 1863. Ran aground while attempting to evade Confederate batteries at Ft. de Russy, La., and captured, 14 Feb 1863.
Prizes: 3 Feb 1863: strs *Berwick Bay, *A.W. Baker, and *Moro; 14 Feb: str Era No. 5.
Later history: Taken into service by Confederate Navy. (q.v.)

Name	Bldr	Built	Acquired
Switzerland	(Cincinnati)	1854	18 May 1862

Tonnage:	413 or 519 tons
Dimensions:	178.4′ × 36.8′ × 8.1′
Machinery:	Side wheels
Complement:	(U)
Armament:	(U)

NOTES: Converted at New Albany, Ind.
SERVICE RECORD: WGF. Battle of Memphis, 6 Jun 1862. Expedition up Yazoo River, Greenville, Miss., 16–22 Aug 1862. Damaged by gunfire while passing batteries at Vicksburg, March 25, 1863. Ran past

The *Switzerland*, an Ellet ram. (The Public Library of Cincinnati and Hamilton County)

batteries at Grand Gulf, Miss., 31 Mar 1863. Expedition up Red River and bombardment of Harrisonburg, La., 3–13 May 1863. Sold 21 Oct 1865.
Later history: Merchant *Switzerland* 1865. RR 1870.

Name	Bldr	Built	Acquired
T.D. Horner	(Brownsville, Pa.)	1859	18 May 1862

Tonnage:	123 tons
Dimensions:	(U)
Machinery:	Stern wheel
Complement:	(U)
Armament:	2 12-pdr R

NOTES: Tug. Never acquired by Navy.
SERVICE RECORD: WGF. Sold 17 Aug 1865.
Later history: Merchant *T.D. Horner* 1865. Damaged beyond repair by hitting a bridge at Louisville, 1 Jan 1868.

Note: There was also a vessel of 175 tons named **Dick Fulton**.

RIVER GUNBOATS & RAMS

Name	Bldr	Built	Comm
Avenger (ex-*Balize*)	(New Albany, Ind.)	1863	29 Feb 1864

Tonnage:	410 or 389 tons
Dimensions:	210' or 181' × 41.5' × 6'
Machinery:	Side wheels, 2 engines (28" × 7'6"), 4 boilers; 11 mph
Complement:	(U)
Armament:	Sep 63: 1 100-pdr R, 4 24-pdr SB, 1 12-pdr R. Dec 64 total: 1 100-pdr R, 5 24-pdr SB, 1 10-pdr R. Apr 65 total: 1 100-pdr R, 11 24-pdr SB, 1 12-pdr R.

NOTES: Built for the War Dept. and transferred on completion.
SERVICE RECORD: Landed party at Bruinsburg, Miss., 22 Nov 1864. Decomm 1 Aug 1865. Sold 29 Nov 1865.
Later history: Merchant *Balize* 1865. RR 1871.

Name	Bldr	Built	Acquired
General Bragg (ex-CSS *General Bragg*, ex-*Mexico*)	Westervelt (Morgan)	1850	9 Jul 1862

Tonnage:	1,043 tons
Dimensions:	208' × 32'8" × 12', d15'
Machinery:	Side wheels, 1 beam LP engine (56" × 10'), 1 boiler; 10 knots
Complement:	(U)
Armament:	1 30-pdr R, 1 32-pdr/42, 1 12-pdr R

NOTES: Confederate cottonclad captured following engagement near Memphis, Tenn., 6 Jun 1862.
SERVICE RECORD: WGF. Patrolled Mississippi from Helena to Yazoo River. Expedition up Yazoo River, Greenville, Miss., 16–22 Aug 1862. Disabled while engaging battery at Tunica Bend, La., 15 Jun 1864. Decomm 24 Jul 1865. Sold 1 Sep 1865.
Later history: Merchant *Mexico* 1865. Sold foreign 1870.

Name	Bldr	Built	Acquired	Comm
General Price (ex-CSS *General Sterling Price*, ex-*Laurent Millaudon*)	(Cincinnati)	1856	Jun 1862	11 Mar 1863

Tonnage:	483 or 633 tons
Dimensions:	182' × 30' × 13'
Machinery:	Side wheels, (24" × 8'), 4 boilers; 12 mph
Complement:	77
Armament:	Mar 63: 4-9" SB. Oct 64 total: 2-9" SB, 1-12-pdr R, 1-12-pdr SB.

NOTES: Former side-wheel towboat converted to ram. Sunk at Battle of Memphis, 6 Jun 1862; captured and salved. Repaired at Cairo, Ill. Also known as **General Sterling Price**.
SERVICE RECORD: WGF. Expedition to Steele's Bayou, Miss., 14–26 Mar 1863. Ran past batteries at Vicksburg, 16 Apr 1863. Expedition

The gunboat *General Bragg* at Cairo or Mound City, Illinois, in 1862, with guns on bow and stern. Two small tugs are fitting out alongside, and the transport *Maria Denning* is at right in the stream. (U.S. Naval Historical Center)

up Red River, 3–13 May, bombardment of Ft. Beauregard, Harrisonburg, La., 10–11 May 1863. Bombardment of Vicksburg, 27 May and 20 Jun 1863. Sank USS *Conestoga* in accidental collision below Grand Gulf, 8 Mar 1864. Red River Expedition, 12 Mar–6 Apr 1864. Decomm 24 Jul 1865. Sold 3 Oct 1865.
Later history: FFU.

Name	Bldr	Built	Comm
Sumter	(Algiers, La.)	1853	1862
(ex-*General Sumter*, ex-*Junius Beebe*)			

Tonnage:	524 tons
Dimensions:	182′ × 28′4″
Machinery:	Side wheels, 1 LP engine
Complement:	(U)
Armament:	(U)

NOTES: Cottonclad captured after Battle of Memphis, 6 Jun 1862.
SERVICE RECORD: Went aground off Bayou Sara, La., Aug 1862 and abandoned.

The gunboat *General Price*, captured at Memphis in June 1862. Notice the guns on the open deck, bow and stern. This picture has been incorrectly identified as the *Sibyl*. (U.S. Naval Historical Center) (Martin Holbrook Collection)

Another view of the *General Price*.

The river ram *Vindicator* tied up at the riverbank. (U.S. Naval Historical Center)

The large tinclad *Black Hawk*, flagship of the Mississippi Squadron during the river campaigns. (Martin Holbrook Collection)

Name	Bldr	Built	Comm
Vindicator	(New Albany, Ind.)	1863	24 May 1864

Tonnage: 750 tons
Dimensions: 210′ × 41.5′ × 9.5′
Machinery: Side wheels, 2 engines (28″ × 7′), 4 boilers; 12 mph
Complement: (U)
Armament: May 64: 1 100-pdr R, 2 24-pdr H, 2 12-pdr R. Dec 64: 1 12-pdr R replaced by 1 30-pdr R.

NOTES: Built for War Dept. and transferred to Navy.
SERVICE RECORD: Expedition up Yazoo River, Nov 1864. Engaged ram CSS *Webb* off mouth of Red River, 23–24 Apr 1865. Decomm Jul 1865. Sold 29 Nov 1865.
Later history: Merchant *New Orleans* 1865. RR 1869.

LARGE TINCLADS

Name	Bldr	Built	Acquired	Comm
Black Hawk (ex-*New Uncle Sam*)	(New Albany, Ind.)	1857	24 Nov 1862	6 Dec 1862

Tonnage: 902 tons
Dimensions: 260′ × 45′6″ × 6′, also given as 285′ × 38′ × 6.5′
Machinery: Side wheels; 2 engines (28″ × 10′), 6 boilers
Complement: 141
Armament: 1862: 2 32-pdr/33, 2 30-pdr R, 1 12-pdr SB, 1 12-pdr R.
              Feb 64 total: 2 30-pdr R, 8 24-pdr SB, 3 12-pdr R.

NOTES: Renamed 13 Dec 1862.
SERVICE RECORD: Mississippi Sqn (flagship). Operations around Vicksburg, Dec 1862. Expedition up White River, capture of Ft. Hindman, Ark., 10–11 Jan 1863. Bombardment and feigned attack, Haynes' Bluff, Miss., 29 Apr–2 May 1863. Siege of Vicksburg, May–Jul 1863. Red River Expedition, 12 Mar–16 May 1864. Destroyed by fire and sank near Cairo, Ill., 22 Apr 1865.
Prizes: 7 Oct 1863: str **Fulton, Argus.*

Name	Bldr	Built	Acquired	Comm
Ouachita (ex-*Louisville*)	(New Albany, Ind.)	1861	29 Sep 1863	18 Jan 1864

Tonnage: 572 tons or 720 tons
Dimensions: 227′6″ × 38′ × 7′
Machinery: Side wheels, 2 engines (26″ × 7′6″), 5 boilers; 8 mph (upstream)
Complement: (U)
Armament: 5 30-pdr R, 18 24-pdr, 15 12-pdr SB, 1 12-pdr.

NOTES: Confederate Army cargo ship *Louisville* captured in Little Red River by USS *Manitou* and *Rattler*, 13 Jul 1863. Converted to gunboat.
SERVICE RECORD: Mississippi Sqn. Expedition up Black and Ouachita rivers, La., 1–5 Mar 1864. Red River Expedition, 12 Mar–16 May 1864. Expedition up Red River, capture of CSS *Missouri*, 1–6 Jun 1865. Decomm 3 Jul 1865. Sold 25 Sep 1865.
Later history: Merchant *Vicksburg* 1865. Destroyed by fire at Cairo, Ill., 6 Jul 1869.

The large tinclad *Ouachita*. There are gunports on both the lower and upper decks as well as two circular pillboxes forward and aft. (U.S. Naval Historical Center) (Martin Holbrook Collection)

TINCLADS

Numbers painted on pilothouse, from 19 Jun 1863.

1 *Rattler, Tempest*	33 *Victory*
2 *Marmora*	34 *Moose*
3 *Romeo*	35 *Reindeer*
4 *Juliet*	36 *Peosta*
5 *Petrel*	37 *Naumkeag*
6 *Cricket*	38 *Exchange*
7 *New Era*	39 *Tensas*
8 *Signal, Grosbeak*	40 *Alexandria*
9 *Forest Rose*	41 *Nyanza*
10 *Linden, Ibex*	42 *Stockdale*
11 *Prairie Bird*	43 *Glide (II)*
12 *Curlew*	44 *Meteor*
13 *Fort Hindman*	45 *Wave*
14 *Kenwood*	46 *Tallahatchie*
15 *Hastings*	47 *Elk*
16 *Little Rebel*	48 *Rodolph*
17 *Fairplay*	49 *Carrabasset*
18 *Brilliant*	50 *Gazelle*
19 *St. Clair*	51 *Fairy*
20 *General Pillow*	52 *Elfin, Oriole*
21 *Alfred Robb*	53 *Naiad*
22 *Springfield*	54 *Nymph*
23 *Silver Lake*	55 *Undine, Kate*
24 *Champion*	56 *Siren*
25 *Covington, Colossus*	57 *Peri*
26 *Queen City, Mist*	58 *Huntress*
27 *Argosy*	59 *Sibyl*
28 *Silver Cloud*	60 *General Sherman Gamage*
29 *Tawah, Collier*	61 *General Thomas*
30 *Fawn*	62 *General Grant*
31 *Paw Paw*	63 *General Burnside*
32 *Key West, Abeona*	

SIDE-WHEELERS

No.	Name	Bldr	Built	Acquired	Comm
32	*Abeona*	(Cincinnati)	1864	21 Dec 1864	10 Apr 1865

Tonnage:	206 tons
Dimensions:	157′ × 31′6″ × d4′6″
Machinery:	Side wheels (14″ × 5′)
Armament:	2 30-pdr R, 2 24-pdr SB, 1 12-pdr R

SERVICE RECORD: Mississippi Sqn, patrol and guard vessel. Decomm 4 Aug 1865. Sold 17 Aug 1865.
Later history: Merchant *Abeona* 1865. Destroyed by fire at Cincinnati, 7 Mar 1872.

No.	Name	Bldr	Built	Comm
40	*Alexandria* (ex-*Yazoo*, ex-CSS *St. Mary*)	(Plaquemine, La.)	1862	Dec 1863

Tonnage:	60 tons
Dimensions:	89′9″ × 15′ × 4′
Machinery:	Side wheels, 1 engine (10″ × 3′6″), 1 boiler; 4 mph
Armament:	1 24-pdr SB, 1 12-pdr

NOTES: Confederate cottonclad steamer *St. Mary* captured at Yazoo City, Miss., 13 Jul 1863.
SERVICE RECORD: Mississippi Sqn, 1863–65. Sold 17 Aug 1865.
Later history: Merchant *Alexandria* 1865. Sank on Amite R, La., 5 Oct 1867.

No.	Name	Bldr	Built	Acquired	Comm
49	*Carrabasset*	(Louisville, Ky.)	1863	23 Jan 1864	12 May 1864

Tonnage:	202 tons
Dimensions:	155′ × 31′7″ × d4′7″
Machinery:	Side wheels

Complement: 45
Armament: 2 32-pdr/42, 4 24-pdr SB

SERVICE RECORD: WGulfBS 1864–65. Expedition in Berwick Bay, La., 21 Mar 1865. Decomm 25 Jul 1865. Sold 12 Aug 1865.
Later history: Merchant *Annie Wagley*. Snagged and lost at Labadieville, La., 1 May 1870.

No.	Name	Bldr	Built	Acquired
25	*Covington* (ex-*Covington No. 2*)	(Cincinnati)	1862	13 Feb 1863

Tonnage: 224 tons
Dimensions: 126' × 37' × d6'6"
Machinery: Side wheels
Complement: 76
Armament: 4 24-pdr SB, 2 30-pdr R, 2 50-pdr R.

NOTES: Converted ferry.
SERVICE RECORD: Tennessee River 1863. Badly damaged by Confederate troops in Red River south of Alexandria, La., abandoned and burned, 5 May 1864.
Prizes 2 Jul 1863: str *Eureka*. 25 Feb 1864: str *Gillum*.

No.	Name	Bldr	Built	Acquired	Comm
47	*Elk* (ex-*Countess*)	(Cincinnati)	1863	8 Dec 1863	6 May 1864

Tonnage: 162 tons
Dimensions: 156' × 29' × d3'10"
Machinery: Side wheels
Complement: 65
Armament: 2 32-pdr/42, 4 24-pdr SB

NOTES: Renamed 26 Jan 1864.
SERVICE RECORD: WGulfBS 1864. Lower Mississippi River 1864–65. Expedition in Lake Pontchartrain, La., 13–15 Oct 1864. Sold 24 Aug 1865.
Prize: 10 Jun 1864: *Yankee Doodle*.
Later history: Merchant *Countess* 1865. Sunk 1868.

No.	Name	Bldr	Built	Acquired
17	*Fairplay*	(New Albany, Ind.)	1859	6 Sep 1862

Tonnage: 162 tons
Dimensions: 138.8' × 27' × 4.9'
Machinery: Side wheels, 2 engines (16" × 5'), 2 boilers; 5 mph
Armament: 2 12-pdr H, 2 12-pdr R SB. May 63 total: 1 32-pdr/33, 2 12-pdr H, 4 12-pdr R. Oct 63 total: 1 30-pdr R, 4 12-pdr R, 2 12-pdr H SB. Mar 64: add 1 30-pdr R.

NOTES: Captured as Confederate transport at Milliken's Bend in Mississippi River, 18 Aug 1862.
SERVICE RECORD: WGF. Defense of Ft. Donelson, Tenn., 3 Feb 1863. Pursuit of Morgan's Raiders up Ohio River, Jul 1863. Engaged battery

The tinclad *Fairplay*, number 17. Notice gunports cut in the armored casemates. (U.S. Naval Historical Center)

at Bell's Mill, Cumberland River, Tenn., 3–4 Dec 1864. Decomm 9 Aug and sold 17 Aug 1865.
Later history: Merchant *Cotile* 1865. BU 1871.

No.	Name	Bldr	Built	Acquired	Comm
50	*Gazelle* (ex-*Emma Brown*)	(Madison, Ind.)	1863	21 Nov 1863	Feb 1864

Tonnage: 117 tons
Dimensions: 135' × 23' × 5'
Machinery: Side wheels, 2 engines (16" × 5'), 2 boilers; 4 mph
Armament: 6 12-pdr R. Sep 64 total: 6 24-pdr R.

SERVICE RECORD: Red River Expedition, 12 Mar–16 May 1864. Decomm 7 Jul 1865. Sold 17 Aug 1865.
Later history: Merchant *Plain City* 1865. BU 1869.

No.	Name	Bldr	Built	Comm
63	*General Burnside*	(Chattanooga)	1864	8 Aug 1864
62	*General Grant*	(Chattanooga)	1864	20 Jul 1864
60	*General Sherman*	(Chattanooga)	1864	27 Jul 1864
61	*General Thomas*	(Chattanooga)	1864	8 Aug 1864

Tonnage: 201 tons (*Grant*: 204; *Sherman*: 187; *Thomas*: 184)
Dimensions: 171' × 26' × 4.8' (*Sherman*: 168'; *Thomas*: 165')
Machinery: Side wheels (16" × 5.5')
Armament: 2 20-pdr R, 3 24-pdr H, except *Grant* 2 30-pdr R, 3 24-pdr H.

NOTES: Built for War Department.
SERVICE RECORDS:
Gen. Burnside—Tennessee River Fleet (flagship) 1864. Supported Army at Decatur, Ala., 12 Dec 1864. Returned to War Department, 1 Jun 1865.

The *General Sherman*, one of four side-wheel steamers built by the Army and converted to tinclads. (U.S. Naval Historical Center)

Gen. Grant—Patrolled upper Tennessee River. Supported Army at Decatur, Ala., 12 Dec 1864. Destruction of Guntersville, Ala., 11–15 Jan 1865. Returned to War Department, 2 Jun 1865.

Gen. Sherman—Mississippi Sqn. Upper Tennessee River. Supported Army at Decatur, Ala., 12 Dec 1864. Returned to War Department, 3 Jun 1865.

Gen. Thomas—Completed Jun 1864. Tennessee River. Engaged enemy force near Whitesburg, Tenn., 28–30 Oct 1864. Supported Army at Decatur, Ala., 22–24 Dec 1864. Returned to War Department, 3 Jun 1865.

Later history: Sold 1866, merchant *Ingomar*. Sank after running onto a sunken barge at Tomlinson's Run, Ohio R., 24 Mar 1868. Raised and sold. Hit a snag and sank above Wheeling, W.Va., 31 Dec 1868.

No.	Name	Bldr	Built	Comm
20	*General Pillow* (ex-CSS *B. M. Moore*)	(U)	(U)	Aug 1862

Tonnage:	38 tons
Dimensions:	81′5″ × 17′1″ × 3′
Machinery:	Side wheels, 2 engines (10″ × 3′6″); 2 boilers
Armament:	2 12-pdr H SB

NOTES: Confederate steamer captured on Hatchee River by USS *Pittsburg*, 9 Jun 1862. Transferred from Army 30 Sep 1862.
SERVICE RECORD: WGF. Mississippi Sqn. Tennessee and Cumberland rivers. Decomm Jul 1865. Sold 26 Nov 1865.
Later history: FFU.

No.	Name	Bldr	Built	Acquired	Comm
8	*Grossbeak* (ex-*Fanny*)	(Cincinnati)	1864	3 Dec 1864	24 Feb 1865

Tonnage:	196 tons
Dimensions:	163′8″ × 28′4″ × d4′6″ (or 179′ × 27′ × 5.5′)
Machinery:	Side wheels (16″ × 5′), 2 boilers
Armament:	2 20-pdr R, 2 30-pdr R, 1 12-pdr SB, 2 24-pdr SB

SERVICE RECORD: Mississippi Sqn. Rescued survivors from burning steamer *Sultana* off Memphis, 27 Apr 1865. Sold 17 Aug 1865.
Later history: Merchant *Mollie Hambleton* 1865. Foundered off Galveston, Tex., 9 Jun 1871.

No.	Name	Bldr	Built	Acquired	Comm
15	*Hastings* (ex-*Emma Duncan*)	(Monongahela, Pa.)	1860	24 Mar 1863	Apr 1863

Tonnage:	293 tons
Dimensions:	173′ × 34′2″ × d5′4″
Machinery:	Side wheels (20″ × 6′), 3 boilers
Armament:	2 30-pdr R, 2 32-pdr/42, 4 24-pdr

NOTES: Renamed 7 Apr 1863.
SERVICE RECORD: Tennessee River 1863–64. Defense of Ft. Pillow, Tenn., 12 Apr 1864. Operations in White River, Jun 1864. Engaged enemy above St. Charles, Ark., 4 Jul 1864. Decomm 7 Jul 1865. Sold 17 Aug 1865.
Later history: Merchant *Dora* 1865. RR 1872.

No.	Name	Bldr	Built	Acquired	Comm
10	*Ibex* (ex-*Ohio Valley*)	(Harmer, OH)	1863	10 Dec 1864	4 Apr 1865

Tonnage:	235 tons
Dimensions:	157′ × 33′ × d4′6″
Machinery:	#Side wheels, 3 boilers
Armament:	2 30-pdr R, 1 12-pdr R, 4 24-pdr H

NOTES: Reported built by Knox, Marietta, Ohio.
SERVICE RECORD: Mississippi Sqn. Decomm 5 Aug and sold 17 Aug 1865.
Later history: Merchant *Harry Dean* 1865. Destroyed by boiler explosion near Gallipolis, Ohio, 3 Jan 1868.

No.	Name	Bldr	Built	Acquired	Comm
13	*James Thompson*	(Jeffersonville)	1 Nov 1862	14 Mar 1863	Apr 1863

Tonnage:	280 tons
Dimensions:	150′ × 37′ × 2′4″
Machinery:	Side wheels, 1 direct-acting engine (16″ × 5′), 2 boilers
Armament:	2 8″/55 SB, 4 8″/63. Jun 64: add 1 100-pdr R. Mar 65 total: 1 100-pdr R, 4 8″/63, 2 8″/55, 1 12-pdr R.

NOTES: Ferry. Built by Howard.
SERVICE RECORD: Mississippi Sqn. Renamed **Manitou**, 2 Jun 1863. Expedition to Trinity, La., Red River, 10 Jul 1863. Expedition up Black, Tensas, and Ouachita rivers, 13–20 Jul, captured CSS *Louisville* at Little Red River, 13 Jul 1863. Renamed **Fort Hindman**, 5 Nov 1863. Expedition up Black and Ouachita rivers, La., 1–5 Mar 1864. Red River Expedition, 12 Mar–16 May 1864. Expedition up Red River, capture of CSS *Missouri*, 1–6 Jun 1865. Decomm 3 Aug and sold 17 Aug 1865.
Prizes: 13 Jul 1863: str *Louisville*; 25 Nov: str *Volunteer*. 27 Jan 1864: str *John L. Roe*.
Later history: Merchant *James Thompson* 1865. RR 1874.

The tinclad *Fort Hindman* had three names during her Navy service, being previously known as *James Thompson* and *Manitou*. She was tinclad number 13. (U.S. Naval Historical Center)

No.	Name	Bldr	Built	Acquired	Comm
41	*Nyanza*	(Belle Vernon, Pa.)	1863	4 Nov 1863	21 Dec 1863

Tonnage:	203 tons
Dimensions:	(U)
Machinery:	#Side wheels
Armament:	Dec 63: 6 24-pdr H. Jun 64: add 2 20-pdr R.

SERVICE RECORD: Mississippi Sqn. Decomm 21 Jul and sold 15 Aug 1865.
Prizes: 15 Mar 1864: *J.W. Wilder*; 13 Apr: *Mandoline*.
Later history: Merchant *Nyanza* 1865. RR 1873.

No.	Name	Bldr	Built	Acquired	Comm
36	*Peosta*	(Cincinnati)	1857	13 Jun 1863	2 Oct 1863

Tonnage:	204 tons
Dimensions:	151′2″ × 34′3″ × 6′
Machinery:	Side wheels, 2 engines (18″ × 5′6″), 2 boilers; 5 mph
Armament:	3 30-pdr R, 3 32-pdr/42, 6 24-pdr H, 2 12-pdr SB

SERVICE RECORD: Mississippi Sqn, Tennessee River. Engaged enemy troops at Paducah, Ky., 25 Mar 1864. Decomm 7 Aug and sold 17 Aug 1865.
Later history: Merchant *Peosta* 1865. Destroyed by fire at Memphis, 25 Dec 1870.

The side-wheel tinclad *Peosta*, number 36. Notice the casemate at the stern. (Mariners Museum) (Martin Holbrook Collection)

No.	Name	Bldr	Built	Acquired	Comm
26	*Queen City*	(Cincinnati)	1863	13 Feb 1863	1 Apr 1863

Tonnage:	210 tons
Dimensions:	(U)
Machinery:	Side wheels
Armament:	2 30-pdr R, 2 32-pdr/42, 4 24-pdr H.

NOTES: Former ferry.
SERVICE RECORD: Mississippi Sqn, Tennessee River. Expedition to Helena, Ark., 13 Oct 1863. Disabled in action with Confederate Army at Clarendon, Ark., and captured 24 Jun 1864; later blown up.

No.	Name	Bldr	Built	Acquired	Comm
22	*Springfield* (ex-*W. A. Healy*)	(Cincinnati)	1862	20 Nov 1862	12 Jan 1863

Tonnage:	146 tons
Dimensions:	134′9″ × 26′11″ × 4′
Machinery:	#Side wheels, 2 engines (10″ × 3′6″), 2 boilers; 5 mph
Armament:	6 24-pdr H

SERVICE RECORD: Mississippi Sqn. Expedition to burn Palmyra, Tenn., 3 Apr 1863. Pursuit of Morgan's Raiders up Ohio River, Jul 1863. Decomm 30 Jun 1865. Sold 17 Aug 1865.
Later history: Merchant *Jennie D.* 1865. RR 1875.

No.	Name	Bldr	Built	Acquired	Comm
29	*Tawah* (ex-*Ebenezer*)	(Brownsville, Pa.)	1859	19 Jun 1863	Oct 1863

Tonnage:	108 tons
Dimensions:	114′ × 33′ × d3′9″
Machinery:	Side wheels
Armament:	4 24-pdr, 2 30-pdr R, 2 24-pdr H, 2 12-pdr

NOTES: Former ferry.
SERVICE RECORD: Mississippi Sqn. Engaged Confederate force on Tennessee River and recaptured USS *Venus*, 2 Nov 1864. Damaged in action with shore batteries at Johnsonville, Tenn., and burned to prevent capture, 4 Nov 1864.

No.	Name	Bldr	Built	Acquired	Comm
39	*Tensas* (ex-CSS *Tom Sugg*)	(Cincinnati)	1860	29 Sep 1863	1 Jan 1864

Tonnage:	62 tons
Dimensions:	91′8″ × 22′5″ × 4′
Machinery:	Side wheels, 2 engines (11″ × 3′), 2 boilers; 4 mph
Armament:	2-24-pdr H

NOTES: Confederate cottonclad *Tom Sugg* captured in Little Red River at Searcy's Landing, Ark., by USS *Cricket*, 14 Aug 1863.
SERVICE RECORD: Mississippi Sqn. Decomm 7 Aug and sold 17 Aug 1865.
Later history: Merchant *Teche* 1865. Wrecked in Bayou Teche, La., 1868.

No.	Name	Bldr	Built	Acquired	Comm
33	*Victory* (ex-*Banker*)	(Cincinnati)	1863	May 1863	8 Jul 1863

Tonnage:	160 tons
Dimensions:	157′ × 30′3″ × 4′2″
Machinery:	#Side wheels, 2 engines (13″ × 4′6″), 2 boilers; 5 mph
Armament:	6 24-pdr H

SERVICE RECORD: Mississippi Sqn. Pursuit of Morgan's Raiders up Ohio River, Jul 1863. Repulsed raid on Paducah, Ky., 4 Nov 1864. Decomm 30 Jun 1865. Sold 17 Aug 1865.
Later history: Merchant *Lizzie Tate* 1865. Snagged and sank near Grand Bayou, La., 8 Feb 1866. Converted to barge 1867.

STERN-WHEELERS

No.	Name	Bldr	Built	Comm
21	*Alfred Robb*	(Pittsburgh)	1860	1 May 1863

Tonnage:	86 tons
Dimensions:	114′9″ × 20′ × 4′6″
Machinery:	Stern wheel, 2 engines (16″ × 5′), 3 boilers; 9.5 knots
Armament:	2 12-pdr R, 2 12-pdr SB

NOTES: Confederate transport captured at Florence, Ala., by USS *Tyler*, 19 Apr 1862. Also known as **Lady Foote**. Converted at Cairo, Ill.
SERVICE RECORD: WGF. Mississippi Sqn. Defense of Ft. Donelson, Tenn., 3 Feb 1863. Expedition to burn Palmyra, Tenn., 3 Apr 1863. Engaged enemy force at Cerro Gordo, Tenn., 19 Jun 1863. Decomm 9 Aug and sold 17 Aug 1865.
Later history: Merchant *Robb* 1865. BU 1873.

No.	Name	Bldr	Built	Acquired	Comm
27	*Argosy*	(Monongahela, Pa.)	1862	24 Mar 1863	29 Mar 1863

Tonnage:	219 tons
Dimensions:	156′4″ × 33′ × 4′6″
Machinery:	Stern wheel, 2 engines (15″ × 5′), 3 boilers; 5 mph
Complement:	71
Armament:	Mar 63: 6 24-pdr, 2 12-pdr R. Jan 64 total: 6 24-pdr, 2 12-pdr SB, 1 12-pdr R. Feb 64 total: 2 32-pdr/42, 4 24-pdr. Jan 65: as Jan 1864.

SERVICE RECORD: Mississippi Sqn. Decomm 11 Aug and sold 17 Aug 1865.
Prize: 12 Dec 1863: str *Ben Franklin*.
Later history: Merchant *Argosy* 1865. Destroyed by fire at Cincinnati, 7 Mar 1872.

No.	Name	Bldr	Built	Acquired
18	*Brilliant*	(Brownsville, Pa.)	1862	13 Aug 1862

Tonnage:	227 tons
Dimensions:	154′8″ × 33′6″ × 5′
Machinery:	Stern wheel, 2 engines (16 3/8″ × 4′6″), 3 boilers; 6 mph
Armament:	2 12-pdr R, 2 12-pdr SB. Dec 64: add 2 24-pdr SB.

NOTES: Purchased by War Department.
SERVICE RECORD: Mississippi Sqn 1862. Defense of Ft. Donelson, Tenn., 3 Feb 1863. Expedition to burn Palmyra, Tenn., 3 Apr 1863. Supported attack on Nashville, 3–16 Dec 1864. Sold 17 Aug 1865.
Later history: Merchant *John S. McCune* 1865. Burned at Prairie Landing, Ark., 6 Dec 1867.

No.	Name	Bldr	Built	Acquired	Comm
24	*Champion* (Cincinnati)	1860	14 Mar 1863	26 Apr 1863
	(ex-*Champion No. 4*)				

Tonnage:	115 tons
Dimensions:	145′8″ × 26′5″ × 3′6″
Machinery:	#Stern wheel, 2 engines (15″ × 6′), 2 boilers; 4 mph
Armament:	2 30-pdr R, 1 24-pdr SB H, 2 12-pdr SB H. Dec 64 total: 2 30-pdr R, 2 24-pdr SB, 4 12-pdr R.

SERVICE RECORD: Mississippi Sqn. Decomm 1 Jul 1865. Sold 29 Nov 1865.
Later history: Merchant *Champion No. 4* 1865. RR 1868.

No.	Name	Bldr	Built	Acquired	Comm
29	*Collier* (Cincinnati)	1864	7 Dec 1864	18 Mar 1865
	(ex-*Allen Collier*)				

Tonnage:	176 tons
Dimensions:	158′ × 30′ × d4′
Machinery:	#Stern wheel
Armament:	2 20-pdr R, 1 12-pdr R, 6 24-pdr H

SERVICE RECORD: Mississippi Sqn. Expedition up Red River, capture of CSS *Missouri*, 1–6 Jun 1865. Decomm 29 Jul 1865. Sold 17 Aug 1865.
Later history: Merchant *Imperial* 1865. RR 1867.

No.	Name	Bldr	Built	Acquired	Comm
25	*Colossus* (Freedom, Pa.)	1863	8 Dec 1864	24 Feb 1865

Tonnage:	183 tons
Dimensions:	155′2″ × 31′9″ × 4′
Machinery:	Stern wheel, 2 engines (13 1/2″ × 4′6″), 2 boilers; 5 mph
Armament:	2 30-pdr R, 4 24-pdr SB, 1 12-pdr SB

SERVICE RECORD: Mississippi Sqn. Decomm 3 Jul 1865. Sold 17 Aug 1865.
Later history: Merchant *Memphis* 1865. Snagged and lost at Pine Bluff, Ark., 17 Dec 1866.

No.	Name	Bldr	Built	Acquired	Comm
6	*Cricket* (Pittsburgh)	1860	18 Nov 1862	19 Jan 1863
	(ex-*Cricket No. 2*)				

Tonnage:	178 tons
Dimensions:	154′1″ × 28′2″ × 4′
Machinery:	Stern wheel, 2 engines (13″ × 4′6″), 2 boilers; 6 knots
Armament:	Jan 63: 6 24-pdr H. Aug 64 total: 2 20-pdr R, 1 12-pdr, 4 24-pdr H.

SERVICE RECORD: Engaged battery above Greenville, Miss., 2 and 4 May 1863. Reconnaissance up White River, Ark., 12–15 Aug 1863. Expedition up Black and Ouachita rivers, La., 1–5 Mar 1864. Red River Expedition, 12 Mar–16 May 1864. Fought off Confederate

The stern-wheel steamer *Cricket*, tinclad number 6, with other river steamers behind. (U.S. Naval Historical Center)

boarders and damaged by artillery, 26 Apr 1864. Decomm 30 Jun 1865. Sold 17 Aug 1865.

Prizes: 14 Aug 1863: strs *Kaskaskia* and *Tom Sugg*.

Later history: Merchant *Cricket No. 2* 1865. BU 1867.

No.	Name	Bldr	Built	Acquired	Comm
12	*Curlew* (ex-*Florence*)	(Elizabeth, Pa.)	1862	17 Dec 1862	16 Feb 1863

Tonnage:	196 tons
Dimensions:	159′ × 32′1″ × 4′
Machinery:	Stern wheel, 2 engines (15 1/2″ × 4′6″), 2 boilers; 4 mph
Armament:	6 32-pdr/57, 1 20-pdr R. Feb 63 total: 8 24-pdr H.

SERVICE RECORD: Expedition up Red, Black, Tensas, and Ouachita rivers, Jul 1863. Engaged battery at Gaines Landing, Ark., 24 May 1864. Decomm 5 Jul 1865. Sold 17 Aug 1865.

Later history: FFU

No.	Name	Bldr	Built	Acquired
52	*Elfin* (ex-*W.C. Mann*)	(Cincinnati)	1863	23 Feb 1864

Tonnage:	192 tons
Dimensions:	155′ × 31′ × d4′4″
Machinery:	Stern wheel
Complement:	50
Armament:	8 24-pdr H

SERVICE RECORD: Mississippi Sqn. After engaging enemy batteries, burned to prevent capture at Johnsonville, Tenn., 4 Nov 1864.

No.	Name	Bldr	Built	Acquired	Comm
38	*Exchange*	(Brownsville, Pa.)	1862	6 Apr 1863	Jun 1863

Tonnage:	211 tons
Dimensions:	155′3″ × 33′5″ × 5′
Machinery:	Stern wheel, 2 engines (16″ × 4′6″), 3 boilers; 6 mph
Complement:	81
Armament:	2 32-pdr/42, 4 24-pdr H

NOTES: Built by Cox & Williams.

SERVICE RECORD: Tennessee River 1863. Expedition up Yazoo River, 2 Feb–22 Apr 1864. Damaged by gunfire of enemy battery at Columbia, Ark., 1 Jun 1864. Decomm 6 Aug and sold 17 Aug 1865.

Later history: Merchant *Tennessee* 1865. Snagged and lost near Decatur, Neb., 25 Apr 1869.

No.	Name	Bldr	Built	Acquired	Comm
51	*Fairy* (ex-*Maria*)	(Cincinnati)	1863	10 Feb 1864	Mar 1864

Tonnage:	173 tons
Dimensions:	157′ × 31′6″ × 5′
Machinery:	Stern wheel, 2 engines (14″ × 5′), 2 boilers; 5.5 mph
Armament:	8 24-pdr H. Jul 64 total: 2 30-pdr R, 6 24-pdr H

SERVICE RECORD: Mississippi Sqn. Tennessee River. Decomm 8 Aug and sold 17 Aug 1865.

Later history: FFU.

No.	Name	Bldr	Built	Acquired	Comm
30	*Fawn* (ex-*Fanny Barker*)	(Cincinnati)	1863	13 May 1863	11 May 1863

Tonnage:	174 tons
Dimensions:	158′8″ × 30′5″ × 3′6″
Machinery:	Stern wheel, 2 engines (12″ × 4′), 2 boilers; 4 mph
Armament:	May 63: 6 24-pdr H. Mar 64: add 1 12-pdr R. Jan 65: add 1 24-pdr H.

NOTES: Renamed 19 Jun 1863.

SERVICE RECORD: Served in White River. Engaged battery at Clarendon, Ark., 24 Jun 1864. Decomm 30 Jun 1865. Sold 17 Aug 1865.

Later history: Merchant *Fanny Barker* 1865. Wrecked near St. Joseph, Missouri, 24 Mar 1873.

Tinclad number 30, the *Fawn*, proceeding downriver. (Mariners Museum) (Martin Holbrook Collection)

No.	Name	Bldr	Built	Acquired	Comm
9	*Forest Rose*	(Freedom, Pa.)	1862	15 Nov 1862	3 Dec 1862

Tonnage:	260 tons
Dimensions:	155′ × 32′3″ × 5′
Machinery:	Stern wheel, 2 engines (16″ × 5′), 3 boilers; 6 mph
Armament:	2 30-pdr R, 4 24-pdr. Aug 63: add 2 32-pdr/42.

SERVICE RECORD: Mississippi Sqn. Bombardment of Drumgoulds Bluff, Yazoo River, 28 Dec 1862. Expedition up White River, capture of Ft. Hindman, Ark., 10–11 Jan 1863. Yazoo Pass expedition, attack on Ft. Pemberton, Tallahatchie River, 11–23 Mar 1863. Capture of

The tinclad *Forest Rose* during the Red River Expedition. This picture has been wrongly identified as the *Signal* (number 8).

Haynes' Bluff, Yazoo River, 18 May 1863. Destruction of Yazoo City NYd, 20–23 May 1863. Expedition up Yazoo River, 24–31 May 1863. Expedition to Trinity, La., Red River, 10 Jul 1863. Red River Expedition, May 5–15, 1864. Decomm 7 Aug and sold 17 Aug 1865.
Prizes: 14 Feb 1863: str *Chippewa Valley*; 13 Jul: str *Elmira*.
Later history: Merchant *Anna White* 1865. Destroyed by ice at St. Louis, Mo., 4 Feb 1868.

No.	Name	Bldr	Built	Acquired	Comm
60	*Gamage* (ex-*Willie Gamage*)	(Cincinnati)	1864	22 Dec 1864	23 Mar 1865

Tonnage:	187 tons
Dimensions:	148'6" × 30'3" × d4'6"
Machinery:	#Stern wheel (14" × 5')
Armament:	6 24-pdr H, 2 20-pdr R, 1 12-pdr R

SERVICE RECORD: Mississippi Sqn. Expedition up Red River, capture of CSS *Missouri*, 1–6 Jun 1865. Decomm 29 Jul 1865. Sold 17 Aug 1865.
Later history: Merchant *Southern Belle* 1865. Burned at Plaquemine, La., 11 Oct 1876.

No.	Name	Bldr	Built	Acquired	Comm
	Glide (I)	(Shousetown, Pa.)	1862	17 Nov 1862	3 Dec 1862

Tonnage:	137 tons
Dimensions:	(U)
Machinery:	Stern wheel
Armament:	6 24-pdr H

SERVICE RECORD: Mississippi Sqn. Bombardment and capture of Ft. Hindman, Ark., expedition up White River, 10–11 Jan 1863. Destroyed by fire while refitting at Cairo, Ill., 7 Feb 1863.

No.	Name	Bldr	Built	Acquired
43	*Glide* (II)	(Murraysville, Va.)	1863	30 Nov 1863

Tonnage:	232 tons
Dimensions:	160.4' × 33' × 5.1'
Machinery:	#Stern wheel
Armament:	2 32-pdr/42, 4 24-pdr H

SERVICE RECORD: WGulfBS 1864. Blockade in Berwick Bay, La., 1864–65. Decomm 1 Aug and sold 12 Aug 1865.
Prize: 3 Mar 1865: *Malta*.
Later history: Merchant *Glide*. Destroyed by boiler explosion 59 miles above New Orleans, 13 Jan 1869.

No.	Name	Bldr	Built	Acquired	Comm
58	*Huntress*	(New Albany, Ind.)	1862	May 1864	10 Jun 1864

Tonnage: 211 tons
Dimensions: 131'8" × 31'3" × 5'
Machinery: Stern wheel, 2 engines (12 1/2" × 4'), 2 boilers; 6 mph
Armament: 2 30-pdr, 4 24-pdr H

SERVICE RECORD: Mississippi Sqn. Patrolled river between Memphis and Columbus, Ky. Decomm 10 Aug and sold 17 Aug 1865.
Later history: Merchant *Huntress* 1865. Snagged and lost near Alexandria, La., 30 Dec 1865.

No.	Name	Bldr	Built	Acquired	Comm
4	*Juliet*	(Brownsville, Pa.)	1862	1 Nov 1862	14 Dec 1862

Tonnage: 157 tons
Dimensions: 155'6" × 30'2" × 5'
Machinery: Stern wheel, 2 engines (13" × 3'6"), 2 boilers
Armament: 6 24-pdr H

SERVICE RECORD: Mississippi Sqn. Expedition in Yazoo River, dragging for torpedoes, 23–26 Dec 1862. Expedition up White River, bombardment and capture of Ft. Hindman, Ark., 10–11 Jan 1863. Red River Expedition, 12 Mar–16 May 1864. Damaged by batteries, 26–27 Apr 1864. Decomm 30 Jun 1865. Sold 17 Aug 1865.
Prizes: 15 Jun 1863: str *Fred Nolte*.
Later history: Merchant *Goldena* 1865. Wrecked in White River Cutoff, Ark., 31 Dec 1865.

No.	Name	Bldr	Built	Acquired	Comm
55	*Kate* (ex-*Kate B. Porter*)	(Belle Vernon, Pa.)	1864	23 Dec 1864	2 Apr 1865

Tonnage: 241 tons
Dimensions: 160' × 31' × 4.1'
Machinery: Stern wheel, 2 engines (15" × 4'6"), 2 boilers
Armament: 2 20-pdr R, 6 24-pdr H, 2 12-pdr H

NOTES: Built by L. M. Spear.
SERVICE RECORD: Mississippi Sqn. Decomm 25 Mar and sold 29 Mar 1866.
Later history: Merchant *James H. Trover* 1866. Stranded 300 miles below Ft. Benton, Montana, 21 Jun 1867.

No.	Name	Bldr	L	Acquired	Comm
14	*Kenwood*	(Cincinnati)	3 Apr 1863	15 Jul 1863	24 May 1863

Tonnage: 232 tons
Dimensions: 154' × 33' × 5'6"
Machinery: Stern wheel, 2 engines (16" × 5'), 3 boilers; 7 mph
Complement: 40
Armament: May 63: 2 32-pdr/42, 4 24-pdr H. Dec 63 total: 2 30-pdr R, 4 24-pdr H, 1 12-pdr. Jun 64: add 2 12-pdr H. Dec 64 total: 2 32-pdr/42, 6 24-pdr SB

NOTES: Built by H. A. Jones.
SERVICE RECORD: Mississippi Sqn. Arkansas River. Expedition to

capture Yazoo City and destroy ships, 13 Jul 1863. Operated off Port Hudson, La., 1863–65. Expedition up Red River, capture of CSS *Missouri*, 1–6 Jun 1865. Decomm 3 Aug and sold 17 Aug 1865.
Prize: 3 Nov 1863: str *Black Hawk*.
Later history: Merchant *Cumberland* 1865. Exploded and sank at Shawneetown, Ill., 14 Aug 1869.

No.	Name	Bldr	Built	Acquired	Comm
32	*Key West* (ex-*Key West No. 3*)	(California, Pa.)	1862	16 Apr 1863	26 May 1863

Tonnage: 207 tons
Dimensions: 156' × 32' × 4.5'
Machinery: Stern wheel
Armament: 6 24-pdr H. Jun 63: add 1 12-pdr R, 2 24-pdr SB.

SERVICE RECORD: Mississippi Sqn, Tennessee River. Expedition to Eastport, Miss., 8–14 Oct 1864. Helped recapture transport *Venus*, 2 Nov, then burned to prevent capture at Johnsonville, Tenn., 4 Nov 1864.

No.	Name	Bldr	Built	Acquired	Comm
10	*Linden*	(Belle Vernon, Pa.)	1860	20 Nov 1862	3 Jan 1863

Tonnage: 177 tons
Dimensions: 154' × 31' × d4'
Machinery: #Stern wheel
Armament: 6 24-pdr H

SERVICE RECORD: Mississippi Sqn. Bombardment and feigned attack, Haynes' Bluff, Miss., 29 Apr–2 May 1863. Capture of Haynes' Bluff, Yazoo River, 18 May 1863. Destruction of Yazoo City NYd, Miss., 20–23 May 1863. Expedition up Yazoo River, 24–31 May 1863. Struck a snag and sank in Arkansas River, 22 Feb 1864.

No.	Name	Bldr	Built	Acquired	Comm
2	*Marmora* (ex-*Marmora No. 2*)	(Monongahela, Pa.)	1862	17 Sep 1862	21 Oct 1862

Tonnage: 207 tons
Dimensions: 155' × 33'5" × 4'6"
Machinery: Stern wheel, 2 engines (15 1/4" × 5'6"), 2 boilers; 6.9 knots
Armament: Oct 62: 2 24-pdr, 2 12-pdr R. Jun 64: add 4 24-pdr. Mar 65 total: 2 12-pdr R, 6 24-pdr.

NOTES: Built by W. Latta.
SERVICE RECORD: Mississippi Sqn. Expedition up Yazoo River, 21 Nov–11 Dec 1862. Expedition in Yazoo River dragging for torpedoes, and bombardment of Haynes' Bluff and Drumgoulds Bluff, 23–26 Dec 1862. Expedition up White River, bombardment and capture of Ft. Hindman, Ark., 10–11 Jan 1863. Yazoo Pass expedition, attack on Ft. Pemberton, Tallahatchie River, 11–23 Mar 1863. Reconnaissance up White and Little Red rivers, Ark., 12–15 Aug 1863. Expedition up Yazoo River, 2 Feb–22 Apr 1864. Decomm 7 Jul 1865. Sold 17 Aug 1865.
Later history: FFU.

The tinclad *Marmora*, with another tinclad behind.

No.	Name	Bldr	Built	Acquired	Comm
10	*Meteor* (ex-*Scioto*)	(Portsmouth, Ohio)	1863	Nov 1863	8 Mar 1864

Tonnage: 221 tons
Dimensions: 156′ × 33′6″ × 4′3″
Machinery: #Stern wheel
Armament: 2 32-pdr/42, 4 24-pdr. Oct 64: 2 30-pdr R, 4 24-pdr.

SERVICE RECORD: WGulfBS 1864. Guard vessel at Head of Passes, Mar 1864–Feb 1865. Operations against Mobile, Mar–Apr 1865. Decomm 12 Sep 1865. Sold 5 Oct 1865.
Later history: Merchant *De Soto* 1865. RR 1869.

No.	Name	Bldr	Built	Acquired	Comm
26	*Mist*	(Allegheny, Pa.)	1864	23 Dec 1864	3 Mar 1865

Tonnage: 232 tons
Dimensions: 157′3″ × 30′4″ × d4′4″
Machinery: Stern wheel, 2 engines (12″ × 5′), 2 boilers; 5.5 knots
Armament: 2 20-pdr R, 4 24-pdr, 1 12-pdr

SERVICE RECORD: Mississippi Sqn. Decomm 4 Aug and sold 17 Aug 1865.
Later history: Merchant *Mist* 1865. RR 1874.

No.	Name	Bldr	Built	Acquired	Comm
34	*Moose* (ex-*Florence Miller No. 2*)	(Cincinnati)	1863	20 May 1863	May 1863

Tonnage: 189 tons
Dimensions: 154′8″ × 32′2″ × 5′
Machinery: Stern wheel, 2 engines (14″ × 4′6″), 2 boilers; 6 knots
Armament: 2 20-pdr, 2 12-pdr, 6 24-pdr

SERVICE RECORD: Mississippi Sqn. Destroyed Confederate guerrilla force at Brandenburg, Ky., on Ohio River, 9–11 Jul 1863. Pursuit of Morgan's raiders up Ohio River, Jul 1863. Defense of Ft. Pillow, Tenn., 12 Apr 1864. Engaged battery at Bell's Mill, Cumberland River, 3–4 Dec 1864. Attacked guerrillas at Centre Furnace, Tenn., 29 Apr 1865. Decomm 12 Apr 1865. Sold 17 Aug 1865.
Later history: Merchant *Little Rock* 1865. Destroyed by fire at Clarendon, Ark., 29 Dec 1867.

No.	Name	Bldr	Built	Acquired	Comm
53	*Naiad* (ex-*Princess*)	(Freedom, Pa.)	1863	3 Mar 1864	3 Apr 1864

Tonnage: 185 tons
Dimensions: 156′10″ × 30′4″ × 4′5″
Machinery: Stern wheel, 2 engines (13″ × 3′6″), 3 boilers; 6 mph
Armament: 8 24-pdr. Dec 64 total: 2 30-pdr R, 6 24-pdr. Jun 65 total: 4 30-pdr R, 6 24-pdr.

SERVICE RECORD: Mississippi Sqn. Damaged engaging battery at Ratliff's Landing, La., 15–16 Jun 1864. Engaged battery near Rowe's Landing, La., 2 Sep 1864. Decomm 30 Jun 1865. Sold 17 Aug 1865.
Later history: Merchant *Princess* 1865. Snagged and lost at Napoleon, Missouri, 1 Jun 1868.

Tinclad number 53, the *Naiad*. Notice the man with telescope forward on the upper deck.

No.	Name	Bldr	Built	Acquired	Comm
37	*Naumkeag*	(Cincinnati)	1863	14 Apr 1863	16 Apr 1863

Tonnage: 148 tons
Dimensions: 154′4″ × 30′5″ × 5′6″
Machinery: Stern wheel, 2 engines (14 1/4″ × 3′6″), 2 boilers; 6 mph
Armament: Apr 63: 2 30-pdr R, 4 24-pdr.

SERVICE RECORD: Mississippi Sqn. Destroyed Confederate guerrilla force at Brandenburg, Ky., on Ohio River, 9–11 Jul 1863. Pursuit of Morgan's Raiders up Ohio River, 19 Jul 1863. Engaged battery at Clarendon, Ark., 24 Jun 1864. Decomm 11 Aug and sold 17 Aug 1865.
Later history: Merchant *Montgomery* 1865. Destroyed by fire at Erie, Ala., 19 Jan 1867.

No.	Name	Bldr	Built	Acquired	Comm
7	*New Era*	(Wellsville, OH)	1862	27 Oct 1862	Dec 1862

Tonnage: 157 tons
Dimensions: 137′1″ × 29′6″ × 4′
Machinery: Stern wheel, 2 engines (14″ × 4′6″), 2 boilers
Armament: 6 24-pdr H

SERVICE RECORD: Mississippi Sqn. Expedition up White River, bombardment and capture of Ft. Hindman, Ark., 10–11 Jan 1863. Defense of Ft. Pillow, Tenn., 12–14 Apr 1864. Decomm 28 Jun 1865. Sold 17 Aug 1865.
Prizes: Feb 1863: *W.A. Knapp, Rowena, White Cloud, Curlew.*

Later history: Merchant *Goldfinch* 1865. Destroyed by fire at Evansville, Ind., 3 Jun 1868.

No.	Name	Bldr	Built	Acquired	Comm
54	*Nymph* (ex-*Cricket No. 3*)	(Cincinnati)	1863	8 Mar 1864	11 Apr 1864

Tonnage: 171 tons
Dimensions: 161′2″ × 30′4″ × 5′
Machinery: Stern wheel, 2 engines (14″ × 4′), 2 boilers; 4 mph
Armament: 8 24-pdr SB, 4 24-pdr

SERVICE RECORD: Mississippi Sqn. Decomm 28 Jun and sold 17 Aug 1865.
Later history: Merchant *Cricket No. 3* 1865. FFU.

No.	Name	Bldr	Built	Acquired	Comm
52	*Oriole* (ex-*Florence Miller No. 3*)	(Cincinnati)	1864	7 Dec 1864	22 Mar 1865

Tonnage: 236 tons
Dimensions: 125′ × 26′5″ × 6′3″ or 160′ × 33.5′ × 5′
Machinery: Stern wheel (14″ × 5′)
Armament: 2 30-pdr R, 1 12-pdr R, 6 24-pdr SB

SERVICE RECORD: Mississippi Sqn. Decomm 4 Aug and sold 17 Aug 1865.
Later history: Merchant *Agnes* 1865. Snagged and sunk at Warrenton, Miss., 3 Mar 1869.

The *Nymph*, tinclad number 54.

No.	Name	Bldr	Built	Acquired	Comm
57	*Peri* (ex-*Reindeer*)	(Cincinnati)	1863	30 Apr 1864	20 Jun 1864

Tonnage: 155 tons
Dimensions: 147′6″ × 28′2″ × 5′6″
Machinery: Stern wheel, 2 engines (13 1/4″ × 4′), 2 boilers; 6 mph
Armament: Jun 64: 1 30-pdr R, 6 24-pdr H. Dec 64: add 1 30-pdr R.

SERVICE RECORD: Sold 17 Aug 1865.
Later history: Merchant *Marietta* 1865. Sunk at Omaha, Neb., 8 Jan 1868.

No.	Name	Bldr	Built	Acquired	Comm
5	*Petrel* (ex-*Duchess*)	(Brownsville, Pa.)	1862	22 Dec 1862	1863

Tonnage: 226 tons
Dimensions: (U)
Machinery: Stern wheel
Armament: 8 24-pdr H

SERVICE RECORD: Mississippi Sqn. Bombardment and feigned attack, Haynes' Bluff, Miss., 29 Apr–2 May 1863. Capture of Haynes' Bluff, Yazoo River, 18 May 1863. Destruction of Yazoo City NYd, 20–23 May 1863. Expeditions up Yazoo River, 24–31 May, to Trinity, La., Red River, 10 Jul, 1863, and up Yazoo River, 2 Feb–22 Apr 1864. Disabled in action and captured in Yazoo River, 22 Apr 1864, then burned.
Prize: 13 Jul 1863: str *Elmira*

No.	Name	Bldr	Built	Acquired	Comm
11	*Prairie Bird* (ex-*Mary Miller*)	(Millersport, OH)	1862	19 Dec 1862	Jan 1863

Tonnage: 171 tons
Dimensions: 159′10″ × 29′3″ × 5′
Machinery: Stern wheel, 2 engines (14″ × 4′), 2 boilers; 6 knots
Armament: 8 24-pdr H

SERVICE RECORD: Mississippi Sqn. Bombardment of Eunice, Miss., 14–15 Jun 1863. Expedition up Yazoo River, 21–22 Apr 1864. Damaged engaging batteries at Gaines Landing, Ark., 11 Aug 1864. Sold 17 Aug 1865.
Prize: 21 Jul 1864: str *Union*.
Later history: FFU.

No.	Name	Bldr	Built	Acquired	Comm
1	*Rattler* (ex-*Florence Miller*)	(Cincinnati)	1862	11 Nov 1862	19 Dec 1862

Tonnage: 165 tons
Dimensions: (U)
Machinery: Stern wheel
Armament: 2 30-pdr R, 4 24-pdr. Dec 63: add 2 24-pdr.

NOTES: Renamed 5 Dec 1862.
SERVICE RECORD: Mississippi Sqn. Expedition up White River, bombardment and capture of Ft. Hindman, Ark., 10–11 Jan 1863. Yazoo Pass expedition, attack on Ft. Pemberton, Tallahatchie River, 11–23 Mar 1863. Raids up Red, Tensas, and Ouachita rivers, Jul 1863. Driven ashore in a gale, struck a snag and sank near Grand Gulf, Miss., 30 Dec 1864.
Prize: 13 Jul 1863: str *Louisville*.

The tinclad *Prairie Bird*, lying off Vicksburg. This picture has been wrongly identified as the *Silver Lake*.

Tinclad number 1, the *Rattler*. She was lost near Grand Gulf, Mississippi, in December 1864. (U.S. Naval Historical Center)

No.	Name	Bldr	Built	Acquired	Comm
35	*Reindeer* (Cincinnati) (ex-*Rachael Miller*)		1863	25 May 1863	25 Jul 1863

Tonnage: 212 tons
Dimensions: 154′ × 32′9″ × 6′
Machinery: Stern wheel, 2 engines (16″ × 5′), 3 boilers; 8 mph
Armament: 6 24-pdr H. Mar 65: 2 30-pdr R, 6 24-pdr H.

NOTES: Placed in service before commissioning.
SERVICE RECORD: Mississippi Sqn. Destroyed Confederate guerrilla force at Brandenburg, Ky., on Ohio River, 9–11 Jul 1863. Pursuit of Morgan's Raiders up Ohio River, 19 Jul 1863. Engaged battery at Bell's Mill, Cumberland River, Tenn., 3–4 Dec 1864. Despatch vessel 1865. Decomm 7 Aug and sold 17 Aug 1865.
Later history: Merchant *Mariner* 1865. Stranded in Missouri River near Decatur, Neb., 9 May 1867.

No.	Name	Bldr	Built	Acquired	Comm
48	*Rodolph*	(Cincinnati)	1863	31 Dec 1863	18 May 1864

Tonnage: 217 tons
Dimensions: (U)
Machinery: #Stern wheel
Complement: 60
Armament: 2 32-pdr/42, 4 24-pdr H. Aug 64: 2 32-pdr replaced by 2 30-pdr R.

SERVICE RECORD: WGulfBS 1864. Operations in Mobile Bay, Aug 1864. Expedition to Bon Secours, Ala., 8–11 Sep 1864. Sunk by torpedo (mine) in Blakely River, 1 Apr 1865.

No.	Name	Bldr	Built	Acquired	Comm
3	*Romeo*	(Brownsville, Pa.)	1862	31 Oct 1862	11 Dec 1862

Tonnage: 175 tons
Dimensions: 154′2″ × 31′2″ × 4′6″
Machinery: Stern wheel, 2 engines (12″ × 4′), 2 boilers
Armament: 6 24-pdr H. Jul 64 total: 8 24-pdr H. Sep 64 total: 6 24-pdr H.

SERVICE RECORD: Mississippi Sqn. Expedition in Yazoo River dragging for torpedoes, 23–26 Dec 1862. Expedition up White River, bombardment and capture of Ft. Hindman, Ark., 10–11 Jan 1863. Yazoo Pass expedition, attack on Ft. Pemberton, Tallahatchie River, 11–23 Mar 1863. Bombardment and feigned attack, Haynes' Bluff, Miss., 29 Apr–2 May 1863. Bombardment of Haynes' Bluff, Yazoo River, 18 May 1863. Expedition up Yazoo River, 2 Feb–22 Apr 1864. Decomm 30 Jun 1865. Sold 17 Aug 1865.
Later history: Merchant *Romeo* 1865. Converted to side-wheeler. RR 1870.

No.	Name	Bldr	Built	Acquired	Comm
19	*St. Clair*	(Belle Vernon, Pa.)	1862	13 Aug 1862	24 Sep 1862

Tonnage: 203 tons
Dimensions: 156′ × 32′ × 2′4″
Machinery: Stern wheel, (15 1/2″ × 5′), 2 boilers
Complement: 66
Armament: 2 12-pdr SB, 2 12-pdr R. May 63 total: 2 24-pdr H, 1 12-pdr R, 2 12-pdr SB. Dec 64 total: 2 50-pdr R, 4 24-pdr H, 2 12-pdr R. Mar 65: 2 50-pdr R replaced by 2 30-pdr R.

SERVICE RECORD: Mississippi Sqn. Defense of Ft. Donelson, Tenn., 3 Feb 1863. Disabled by enemy troops at Palmyra, Tenn., 3 Apr 1863. Sank Army steamer *Hope* in collision in Mississippi River, 16 Feb 1864. Red River Expedition, 12 Mar–16 May 1864. Engaged enemy forces below Alexandria, La., 21 Apr 1864. Decomm 12 Jul 1865. Sold 17 Aug 1865.
Later history: Merchant *St. Clair* 1865. RR 1869.

No.	Name	Bldr	Built	Acquired	Comm
59	*Sibyl* (Cincinnati) (ex-*Hartford*)		1863	27 Apr 1864	16 Jun 1864

Tonnage: 176 tons
Dimensions: 150.5′ × 29.4′ × 5.4′
Machinery: #Stern wheel
Armament: 2 30-pdr R, 2 24-pdr

SERVICE RECORD: Mississippi Sqn, despatch boat. Decomm 31 Jul 1865. Sold 17 Aug 1865.
Later history: Merchant *Comet* 1865. RR 1876.

No.	Name	Bldr	Built	Acquired	Comm
8	*Signal*	(Wheeling, Va.)	1862	22 Sep 1862	Oct 1862

Tonnage: 190 tons
Dimensions: 157′ × 30′ × 1′10″
Machinery: Stern wheel
Armament: Oct 62: 2 30-pdr R, 4 24-pdr H, 1 12-pdr R. May 63 total: 4 24-pdr H, 2 12-pdr R H. Feb 64: add 2 32-pdr/42.

SERVICE RECORD: Mississippi Sqn. Expedition up Yazoo River, 21 Nov–11 Dec 1862. Expedition in Yazoo River dragging for torpedoes, 23–26 Dec 1862. Expedition up White River, bombardment and capture of Ft. Hindman, Ark., 10–11 Jan 1863. Yazoo Pass Expedition, attack on Ft. Pemberton, Tallahatchie River, 11–23 Mar 1863. Bombardment and feigned attack, Haynes' Bluff, Miss., 29 Apr–2 May 1863. Expedition up Yazoo River, 24–31 May 1863. Expedition to capture Yazoo City and destruction of ships, 13 Jul 1863. Disabled in Red River while engaging enemy batteries near Alexandria, La., and run aground, 5 May 1864; set afire to prevent capture.

No.	Name	Bldr	Built	Acquired	Comm
28	*Silver Cloud*	(Brownsville, Pa.)	1862	1 Apr 1863	4 May 1863

Tonnage: 236 tons
Dimensions: 155′1″ × 33′2″ × 6′
Machinery: Stern wheel, 2 engines (16″ × 5′), 3 boilers; 7 mph
Armament: 6 24-pdr H. Sep 64: add 1 24-pdr R.

SERVICE RECORD: Mississippi Sqn. Expedition to Eastport, Miss., May 1863. Defense of Ft. Pillow, 12–14 Apr 1864. Engaged battery at Bell's

Mill, Tenn., Cumberland River, 3–4 Dec 1864. Decomm 13 Jul 1865. Sold 15 Aug 1865.
Later history: Merchant *Silver Cloud* 1865. Converted to side-wheeler. Snagged and lost in Buffalo Bayou, Texas, 2 Oct 1866.

No.	Name	Bldr	Built	Acquired	Comm
23	*Silver Lake* (California, Pa.) (ex-*Silver Lake No. 3*)		1862	15 Nov 1862	24 Dec 1862

Tonnage:	236 tons
Dimensions:	155'1" × 32'2" × 6'
Machinery:	Stern wheel, 2 engines (15" × 5'), 2 boilers; 6 knots
Armament:	6 24-pdr H. May 65 total: 2 20-pdr R, 3 24-pdr H, 3 12-pdr SB. Jul 65: 1 12-pdr SB replaced by 1 24-pdr H.

SERVICE RECORD: Mississippi Sqn. Defense of Ft. Donelson, Tenn., 3 Feb 1863. Bombarded Florence, Ala., 31 Mar and Palmyra, Tenn., 4 Apr 1863. Pursuit of Morgan's Raiders up Ohio River, Jul 1864. Engaged battery at Bell's Mill, Tenn., Cumberland River, 3–4 Dec 1864. Decomm 11 Aug and sold 17 Aug 1865.
Later history: Merchant *Mary Hein* 1865. Converted to side-wheeler. Destroyed by fire in Red River, La., 28 Feb 1866.

No.	Name	Bldr	Built	Acquired	Comm
56	*Siren* (Parkersburg, Va.) (ex-*White Rose*)		1862	11 Mar 1864	30 Aug 1864

Tonnage:	232 tons
Dimensions:	154'7" × 32'3" × 5'
Machinery:	Stern wheel, 2 engines (16 1/2" × 4'), 2 boilers; 7 mph
Armament:	2 30-pdr R, 6 24-pdr H

SERVICE RECORD: Receiving ship, Mound City, Ill. Mar–Aug 1864. Mississippi Sqn. Decomm 12 Aug and sold 17 Aug 1865.
Later history: Merchant *White Rose* 1865. RR 1867.

No.	Name	Bldr	Built	Acquired	Comm
42	*Stockdale* (W. Brownsville, Pa.) (ex-*J.T. Stockdale*)		1863	13 Nov 1863	26 Dec 1863

Tonnage:	188 tons
Dimensions:	(U)
Machinery:	#Stern wheel
Complement:	63
Armament:	2 30-pdr R, 4 24-pdr H

SERVICE RECORD: WGulfBS 1864. Engaged enemy party in Tchefuncta River, 16 May 1864. Battle of Mobile Bay, 5 Aug 1864. Expedition to Bon Secours River, Miss., 8–11 Sep 1864. Decomm and sold 24 Aug 1865.
Prize: 8 Dec 1864: *Medora*.
Later history: Merchant *Caddo* 1865. RR 1871.

No.	Name	Bldr	Built	Acquired	Comm
46	*Tallahatchie* (Cincinnati) (ex-*Cricket No. 4*)		1863	23 Jan 1864	19 Apr 1864

Tonnage:	171 tons
Dimensions:	(U)
Machinery:	#Stern wheel
Complement:	51
Armament:	2 32-pdr, 4 24-pdr

SERVICE RECORD: Mississippi Sqn. Red River Expedition, 12 Mar–16 May 1864. WGulfBS Jun 1864–65. Decomm 21 Jul 1865. Sold 12 Aug 1865.
Later history: Merchant *Coosa* 1865. Destroyed by fire at Licking River, Ky., 7 Sep 1869.

No.	Name	Bldr	Built	Acquired	Comm
1	*Tempest* (Louisville)		1862	30 Dec 1864	26 Apr 1865

Tonnage:	161 tons
Dimensions:	162' × 32.8' × 5.8'
Machinery:	#Stern wheel (17" × 5½')
Armament:	2 30-pdr R, 2 20-pdr R, 2 24-pdr H, 2 12-pdr.

SERVICE RECORD: Mississippi Sqn (flag). Decomm and sold 29 Nov 1865.
Later history: Merchant *Tempest* 1865. Destroyed by fire at Tattoo Landing in Ouachita River, 27 Dec 1869.

No.	Name	Bldr	Built	Acquired	Comm
55	*Undine* (Cincinnati) (ex-*Ben Gaylord*)		1863	7 Mar 1864	Apr 1864

Tonnage:	179 tons
Dimensions:	(U)
Machinery:	Stern wheel, 2 boilers
Armament:	8 24-pdr H

SERVICE RECORD: Mississippi Sqn. Struck a snag and almost sank in Tennessee River off Clifton, Tenn., 25 Jul 1864; raised 31 Jul. Expedition to Eastport, Miss., 8–14 Oct 1864. Disabled during engagement in Tennessee River near Paris Landing, Tenn., and captured, 30 Oct 1864. Burned by Confederates to prevent recapture, 4 Nov 1864.

No.	Name	Bldr	Built	Acquired
45	*Wave* (Monongahela, Pa.) (ex-*Argosy No. 2*)		1863	14 Nov 1863

Tonnage:	229 tons
Dimensions:	154' × 31' × 4.5'
Machinery:	#Stern wheel (15" × 4')
Armament:	6 guns

SERVICE RECORD: WGulfBS 1864. Captured with *Granite City* by Confederate batteries at Calcasieu Pass, La., 6 May 1864.

OTHER TYPES

No.	Name	Bldr	Built	Acquired
16	*Little Rebel* (Belle Vernon, Pa.) (ex-CSS *Little Rebel*, ex-*R. & J. Watson*)		1859	9 Jan 1863

Tonnage: 161 tons
Dimensions: (U) × (U) × 12′
Machinery: 1 screw, 1 engine (18″ × 2′), 2 boilers; 10 knots
Armament: 3-12-pdr R. Mar 63 total: 2-24-pdr H, 2-12-pdr R.

NOTES: Confederate cottonclad ram, captured at Battle of Memphis, 6 Jun 1862. Converted to gunboat at Cairo, Ill.
SERVICE RECORD: WGF. Mississippi Sqn, with Ellet's ram sqn. Expedition up Red River, capture of CSS *Missouri*, 1–6 Jun 1865. Decomm 24 Jul 1865. Sold 29 Nov 1865.
Later history: Merchant *Spy* 1865. RR 1874.

No.	Name	Bldr	Built	Acquired	Comm
31	*Paw Paw* (ex-*Fanny*, ex-*St. Charles*)	(St. Louis)	1862	9 Apr 1863	25 Jul 1863

Tonnage: 175 tons
Dimensions: 120′ × 34′ × 6′
Machinery: Center wheel, 2 engines (20″ × 6′), 2 boilers; 4 mph
Armament: 2 30-pdr R, 6 24-pdr H

NOTES: Renamed 12 May 1863.
SERVICE RECORD: Mississippi Sqn. Struck a snag and sank in Walnut Bend, 6 Aug 1863; salved and repaired. Supported Army on the Tennessee River, Oct–Dec 1863. Engaged enemy troops at Paducah, Ky., 25 Mar 1864. Decomm 1 Jul 1865. Sold 17 Aug 1865. BU 1865.

RIVER SERVICE CRAFT

Name	Bldr	Built	Acquired
Abraham (ex-*Victoria*)	(Elizabeth, Pa.)	1858	30 Sep 1862

Tonnage: 405 tons
Dimensions: 222′ × 32′ × 5′10″
Machinery: Side wheels; 4 boilers
Armament: (U)

NOTES: Storeship. Confederate transport *Victoria*, captured at Memphis, 6 Jun 1862. Renamed 15 Oct 1862.
SERVICE RECORD: Mississippi Sqn, storeship. Blockade of Vicksburg. Wharf and inspection boat, Cairo and Mound City, Ill. Sold 30 Sep 1865.
Later history: Merchant *Lexington* 1865. Rebuilt. Destroyed by fire at Algiers, La., 3 Feb 1869.

Name	Bldr	Built	Acquired
Antelope	(New Albany, Ind.)	1853	1861

Tonnage: 173 tons
Dimensions: 264′ × 34′ × 3′
Machinery: Side wheels
Armament: 2 30-pdr R, 4 24-pdr

SERVICE RECORD: WGulfBS 1862–64. Struck snag and sank in Mississippi River below New Orleans, 23 Sep 1864.

Name	Bldr	Built
Benefit	(Metropolis, Ill.)	1863

Tonnage: 213 tons
Dimensions: (U)
Machinery: Side wheels
Armament: (U)

NOTES: Chartered 1863.
SERVICE RECORD: Red River expedition. 1865 returned to owner.
Later history: Merchant *Benefit*. Burned at Starke Landing, Ala., 6 Apr 1867.

Name	Bldr	Built	Acquired
Clara Dolsen	(Cincinnati)	1861	1862

Tonnage: 939 tons
Dimensions: 268′ × 42′ × d8′9″
Machinery: Side wheels (28″ × 9′); 5 boilers
Armament: 1 32-pdr/33

NOTES: Confederate steamer, captured on White River by USS *Mound City* and tug *Spitfire*, 14 Jun 1862. One of the largest and finest steamers on the river.
SERVICE RECORD: WGF. Mississippi Sqn. Expedition to Henderson, Ky., 19–24 Jul 1862. Receiving ship, Cairo, Ill., 1862–64.
Later history: Returned to owner, May 1864. Merchant *Clara Dolsen*. Destroyed by fire at St. Louis, Mo., 4 Feb 1868.

Name	Bldr	Built	Acquired
General Lyon (ex-CSS *De Soto*)	(New Albany, Ind.)	1860	30 Sep 1862

Tonnage: 390 tons
Dimensions: 180′ × 35′ × 7′
Machinery: Side wheels (23″ × 7′)
Armament: 2 12-pdr R. Feb 64: add 1 32-pdr/42.

NOTES: Confederate gunboat *De Soto* captured at Island No. 10, 7 Apr 1862. Transferred from War Dept. Renamed 24 Oct 1862.
SERVICE RECORD: WGF. Mississippi Sqn. Ordnance, stores, and despatch ship. Decomm 3 Aug and sold 17 Aug 1865.
Later history: Merchant *Alabama* 1865. Destroyed by fire at Grand View, La., 1 Apr 1867.

Name	Bldr	Built	Acquired
Grampus (ex-*Ion*)	(U)	(U)	22 Jul 1863

Tonnage: 230 tons
Dimensions: 180′ × 27′ × d5′
Machinery: Side wheels
Armament: none

SERVICE RECORD: Mississippi Sqn. Receiving ship, Cincinnati, Ohio. Sold 1 Sep 1868.
Later history: FFU.

Name	Bldr	Built	Acquired
Great Western	(Cincinnati)	1857	10 Feb 1862

Tonnage:	429 tons
Dimensions:	178′ × 45′
Machinery:	Side wheels (22 1/2″ × 8′)
Armament:	1 12-pdr, 1 32-pdr/57, 1 6-pdr R

NOTES: Purchased by War Department
SERVICE RECORD: WGF. Western Flotilla. Ordnance boat. Siege of Vicksburg. Receiving ship, Cairo, Ill., Jul 1864, and Mound City, Ill., Mar 1865. Sold 29 Nov 1865.
Later history: FFU.

Name	Bldr	Built	Acquired	Comm
Judge Torrence	(Cincinnati)	1857	10 Feb 1862	25 Dec 1862

Tonnage:	419 tons
Dimensions:	179′1″ × 45′6″ × 9′
Machinery:	Side wheels, 2 engines (20″ × 8′), 3 boilers; 6 knots.
Armament:	2 24-pdr H SB. Oct 64 total: 2 24-pdr H SB, 1 6-pdr R, 1 12-pdr H.

NOTES: Purchased by War Dept. Transferred to Navy, 30 Sep 1862.
SERVICE RECORD: WGF. Mississippi Sqn. Ordnance boat. Decomm 1 Aug and 17 Aug 1865.
Later history: Merchant *Amazon*. Snagged and sank off Napoleon, Ark., 19 Feb 1868.

Kentucky, captured at Memphis, 6 Jun 1862. WGF. No information.

Name	Bldr	Built	Acquired
Lavinia Logan	(Parkersburg, Va.)	1861	31 Aug 1864

Tonnage:	145 tons
Dimensions:	(U)
Machinery:	Stern wheel
Armament:	(U)

NOTES: Purchased by War Dept. as transport and powder boat. Acquired by USN 31 Aug 1864.
SERVICE RECORD: Sunk in Mississippi River, 23 Sep 1864.

Name	Bldr	Built	Acquired
Maria Denning	(Cincinnati)	1858	1861

Tonnage:	870 tons
Dimensions:	275′ × 41′ × 8′
Machinery:	Side wheels (26″ × 9′); 5 boilers
Armament:	(U)

SERVICE RECORD: Receiving ship, Cairo, Nov 1861–Apr 1862. Transferred to War Dept. Dec 1862.

Later history: Stranded in Cumberland River, Mar 1864. Burned at Algiers, La., 11 May 1866.

Name	Bldr	Built	Acquired
New National (ex-*Lewis Whiteman* ?)	(Cincinnati)	1851	6 Jun 1862

Tonnage:	317 tons ?
Dimensions:	178′ × 29′ × 6.5′
Machinery:	Side wheels
Armament:	1 12-pdr R. Dec 63 total: 2 32-pdr/42, 2 12-pdr R.

NOTES: Confederate transport captured at Memphis, 6 Jun 1862. Transferred to Navy 30 Sep 1862. Mail and supply boat. Former identity presumed (details for *Lewis Whiteman*).
SERVICE RECORD: WGF. Mississippi Sqn, mail and supply boat and receiving ship. Returned to owner, 21 Mar 1863 and chartered by Navy. Expedition to capture Yazoo City, 13 Jul 1863. Decomm 12 Apr 1865.
Later history: Merchant *New National* 1865.

Name	Bldr	Built	Acquired	Comm
Red Rover	(Cape Girardeau, Mo.)	1859	30 Sep 1862	10 Jun 1862

Tonnage:	625 tons
Dimensions:	256′ × 40.9′ × 7.5′
Machinery:	Side wheels, 2 engines (28″ × 8′), 5 boilers; 8 knots
Complement:	47 + 30 medical staff
Armament:	1 32-pdr/33

NOTES: Confederate steamer, captured by USS *Mound City* at Island No. 10, 7 Apr 1862. First hospital ship of U.S. Navy.
SERVICE RECORD: WGF. Mississippi Sqn, hospital boat. Damaged by fire off Vicksburg, summer 1862. Decomm 17 Nov and sold 29 Nov 1865.
Later history: FFU.

The *Red Rover*, the Navy's first hospital ship, tied up at a western river anchorage. (U.S. Naval Historical Center)

Name	Bldr	Built
Sallie Wood	(Paducah, Ky.)	1860

Tonnage:	256 tons
Dimensions:	160' × 31'
Machinery:	Stern wheel (14" × 5')
Armament:	(U)

NOTES: Captured by USS *Conestoga* on Tennessee River at Chickasaw, Ala., 8 Feb 1862.
SERVICE RECORD: Transport, Western Flotilla. Damaged by artillery and run aground at Argyle Landing, 30 Jul 1862.

Name	Bldr	Built	Acquired
Samson	(California, Pa.)	1860	30 Sep 1862

Tonnage:	230 tons
Dimensions:	(U)
Machinery:	Stern wheel; 4 boilers
Armament:	(U)

NOTES: Transferred from War Dept. Floating machine shop.
SERVICE RECORD: WGF. Ellet Ram fleet 1862. Mississippi Sqn 1862–65. Sold 17 Aug 1865.
Later history: Merchant *Samson* 1865. BU 1869.

Name	Bldr	Built	Acquired
Sovereign	(Shousetown, Pa.)	1855	9 Jan 1863

Tonnage:	336 tons
Dimensions:	228.6' × 37' × 6.4'
Machinery:	Side wheels (24" × 6'6")
Armament:	(U)

NOTES: Confederate transport, captured near Island No. 37 by *Spitfire*, 5 Jun 1862.
SERVICE RECORD: WGF. Commissary Boat in Yazoo River. Accommodation ship at Cairo, Ill., 1863–65. Sold 29 Nov 1865.
Later history: FFU.

Name	Bldr	Built	Acquired
Volunteer	(Monongahela, Pa.)	1862	29 Feb 1864

Tonnage:	209 tons
Dimensions:	125.1' × 33' × 4.5'
Machinery:	Stern wheel, 2 engines (15" × 5'), 2 boilers; 6 mph
Armament:	1 12-pdr SB

NOTES: Confederate steamer captured off Natchez Island, Mississippi, by USS *Fort Hindman*, 25 Nov 1863.

The stern-wheel steamer *Volunteer*, captured in 1863. (Martin Holbrook Collection)

SERVICE RECORD: Mississippi Sqn. Defense of Ft. Pillow, Tenn., 12 Apr 1864. Decomm Aug 1865. Sold 29 Nov 1865.
Later history: Merchant *Talisman* 1865. Rebuilt 1866. RR 1872.

Name	Bldr	Built	Acquired
William H. Brown	(Monongahela, Pa.)	1860	13 Jun 1861

Tonnage:	200 tons
Dimensions:	230' × 26'
Machinery:	#Stern wheel
Armament:	2 12-pdr

NOTES: Despatch vessel. Transferred from War Dept. 30 Sep 1862. Also known as **Brown**.
SERVICE RECORD: WGF. Mississippi Sqn, despatch vessel and transport. Disabled during engagement with batteries in Red River, 13 Apr 1864. Decomm 12 Aug and sold 17 Aug 1865.
Later history: Merchant *W. H. Brown*, 1865. RR 1875.

TUGS

Name	Bldr	Built	Acquired
Dahlia (ex-*Firefly*)	(St. Louis)	1861	30 Sep 1862

NOTES: 54 tons; 1 screw, 1 single cylinder engine (18" × 1'8"), 1 boiler. 10 mph; no armament. Transferred from War Dept. Renamed 24 Oct 1862.
SERVICE RECORD: WGF. Mississippi Sqn. Sold 17 Aug 1865.
Later history: Merchant *Dahlia* 1865. RR 1872.

Name	Bldr	Built	Acquired
Daisy (ex-*Mulford*, ex-*J.E. Mulford*)	(Chicago)	1854	30 Sep 1862

NOTES: 54 tons; 73'4" × 13'10" × 6'; 1 screw, 1 engine (22" × 1'10"), 1 boiler. 10 mph; no armament; complement 5. Transferred from War Dept. Renamed 24 Oct 1862.
SERVICE RECORD: WGF. Mississippi Sqn. Sold 17 Aug 1865.
Later history: Merchant *Little Queen* 1865. RR 1871.

Name	Bldr	Built	Acquired
Fern (ex-*Intrepid*)	(St. Louis)	1861	30 Sep 1862

NOTES: 45 tons; 62.6' × 14.4' × d6.8'; 1 screw, 1 engine (16" × 1'8"), 1 boiler. 10 knots; 1 12-pdr H. Transferred from War Dept. Renamed 19 Oct 1862.
SERVICE RECORD: WGF. Mississippi Sqn. Expedition up Red River to capture CSS *Missouri*, 1–6 Jun 65. Sold 12 Aug 1865.
Later history: Merchant *Fern* 1865. RR 1877.

Name	Bldr	Built	Acquired
Hyacinth (ex-*Spitfire*)	(St. Louis)	1862	30 Sep 1862

NOTES: 50 tons; (U) × (U) × 6'; 1 screw, 1 engine (18" × 1'8"), 1 boiler. 8 knots; no armament. Transferred from War Dept. Renamed 19 Oct 1862.
SERVICE RECORD: WGF. Mississippi Sqn. Sold 17 Aug 1865.
Prizes: 5 Jun 1862: str *Sovereign*; 14 Jun: str *Clara Dolsen*.
Later history: Merchant *Rolla* 1865. RR 1884.

Name	Bldr	Built	Acquired
Ivy (ex-*Terror*)	(St. Louis)	1861	30 Sep 1862

NOTES: 47 tons; (U) × (U) × 10'; 1 screw, 1 engine (16" × 1'6"), 1 boiler; 10 knots. Transferred from War Dept.
SERVICE RECORD: WGF. Mississippi Sqn 1862. Expedition up White River, capture of Ft. Hindman, Ark., 10–11 Jan 63. Ran past batteries at Vicksburg, 16 Apr 63. Expedition up Red River, 3–13 May 63. Sold 17 Aug 1865.
Later history: Merchant *Ivy* 1865. RR 1874.

Name	Bldr	Built	Acquired
Laurel (ex-*Erebus*)	(St. Louis)	1862	30 Aug 1862

NOTES: 50 tons; 60' × 14'; 1 screw, 1 engine (18" × 1'8"), 1 boiler. 5 knots, no guns. Transferred from War Dept. Renamed 19 Oct 1862.
SERVICE RECORD: WGF. Mississippi Sqn. Expedition up Yazoo River, 21 Nov–11 Dec 62. Decomm 12 Aug and sold 17 Aug 1865.
Later history: Merchant *Laurel* 1865. RR 1903.

Name	Bldr	Built	Acquired
Lily (ex-*Jessie Benton*)	(U)	(U)	5 May 1862

NOTES: 50 tons; 1 screw, no guns. Transferred from War Dept. as *Jessie*. Renamed 19 Oct 1862.
SERVICE RECORD: WGF. Mississippi Sqn. Sank in collision with ironclad USS *Choctaw* in Yazoo River, 28 May 1863.

Name	Bldr	Built	Acquired
Mignonette (ex-*Dauntless*)	(U)	(U)	30 Sep 1862

NOTES: 50 tons; side wheels. Transferred from War Dept. Renamed 19 Oct 1862.
SERVICE RECORD: WGF. Mississippi Sqn. Station tug, Cairo, Ill. 1862–65. Sold 18 Apr 1873.

Name	Bldr	Built	Acquired	Comm
Mistletoe (ex-*Restless*)	(St. Louis)	1861	30 Sep 1862	1 Oct 1862

NOTES: 38 tons; 61.5' × 14.4' × d6.8'; 1 screw. Transferred from War Dept.
SERVICE RECORD: WGF. Cairo, Ill., tug 1862–63. Mississippi Sqn. Sold 20 Nov 1865.
Later history: Merchant *Ella Wood* 1866. RR 1871.

The navy-built tug *Pinta* in Juneau harbor, Alaska, in 1889. (U.S. Naval Historical Center)

Name	Bldr	Built	Acquired
Myrtle (ex-*Resolute*)	(U)	(U)	30 Sep 1862

NOTES: 60 tons; 75′4″ × 16′3″ × 6′; 2 screws, 2 engines (15″ × 1′4″), 2 boilers; 10 knots. Transferred from War Dept. Renamed 15 Oct 1862.
SERVICE RECORD: WGF. Mississippi Sqn. Cairo, Ill. Sold 17 Aug 1865.

Name	Bldr	Built	Acquired
Nettle (ex-*Wonder*)	(U)	(U)	30 Sep 1862

NOTES: 50 tons, side wheels. Transferred from War Dept. Renamed 19 Oct 1862.
SERVICE RECORD: WGF. Mississippi Sqn. Sank in collision with an ironclad warship in Mississippi River, 20 Oct 1865.

Name	Bldr	Built	Acquired	Comm
Pansy (ex-*Sampson*)	(New Haven, Mo.)	1861	30 Sep 1862	30 Sep 1862

NOTES: 46 tons; 1 screw; no armament, Aug 65: 1 12-pdr SB. Transferred from War Dept. Renamed 24 Oct 1862.
SERVICE RECORD: WGF. Mississippi Sqn. Sold 1 Sep 1868.
Later history: FFU.

Name	Bldr	Built	Acquired
Thistle (ex-*Spiteful*)	(U)	(U)	30 Sep 1862

NOTES: 50 tons; side wheels; Sep 63: no armament. Aug 65: 1 12-pdr SB. Transferred from War Dept.
SERVICE RECORD: WGF. Mississippi Sqn. Expedition up White River, capture of Fort Hindman, Ark., 10–11 Jan 63. Expedition to Steele's Bayou, Miss., 14–26 Mar 63. Decomm 12 Aug and sold 17 Aug 1865.
Later history: FFU.

PART II
U.S. Revenue Cutter Service

Overleaf: The Revenue Cutter *Andrew Johnson* was built in Buffalo in 1865 and served until 1897. (Steamship Historical Society Collection)

Right: The small Revenue Cutter *William Pitt Fessenden* in 1871 at Put-In Bay, Lake Erie. (Steamship Historical Society Collection)

UNITED STATES REVENUE CUTTER SERVICE

Established on August 4, 1790, the Revenue Cutter Service had only twenty-eight vessels available at the outbreak of the Civil War. Six had been seized by the rebels and four were on the Pacific coast. Five cutters on the Great Lakes were ordered to the Atlantic, and several ships were loaned from other government agencies, such as the Lighthouse Board and the Coast Survey.

Although the Revenue Marine, as it was known, experimented with steamers in the 1840s, only the *Harriet Lane* remained in service by 1861, together with a number of schooners. She was transferred to the Navy but several other steamers were acquired.

One of those acquired was the *E.A. Stevens* or *Naugatuck*. This curious ship was converted to demonstrate the theories of construction of the never-completed *Stevens Battery*.

In July 1863, the cutter *Caleb Cushing* was seized by rebels at Portland, Maine and destroyed by them when recapture at sea was certain.

In 1863 the six cutters *Mahoning*, *Ashuelot*, *Wayanda*, *Kankakee*, *Kewanee*, and *Pawtuxet* were built. At the end of the war the Navy ships *Delaware*, *Jasmine*, *Juniper*, *Moccasin*, *Nansemond*, and *Wilderness* were among surplus ships transferred for permanent service with the Revenue Marine, while other new construction was already in hand.

STEAMERS

Name	Bldr	L	Comm
Harriet Lane	Webb (Allaire)	30 Nov 1857	4 Feb 1858

NOTES: 639 tons B; 180′ × 30′ × 10′; side wheels, inclined direct-acting engine. Transferred to USN, 10 Sep 1861 (q.v.).

Name
Bibb
Corwin

NOTES: Loaned from Coast Survey (q.v.) 31 May 1861, returned 26 Aug and 17 Sep 1861.

Name	Bldr	L	Acquired
Shubrick	Philadelphia (U)	8 Aug 1857	23 Aug 1861

NOTES: 305 tons; 140′8″ × 29′ × 9′; side wheels, 1 steeple engine. 4 12-pdr, 1 24-pdr, 1 30-pdr R. Acquired from U.S. Lighthouse Board; returned 24 Dec 1866. Sold 1886. Served on Pacific coast.

Name	Bldr	Built	Acquired	Comm
Hercules	(Philadelphia)	1850	10 Aug 1861	11 Sep 1861
Reliance	(Philadelphia)	1850	10 Aug 1861	
Tiger	(Philadelphia)	1850	10 Aug 1861	1861

NOTES: 123 tons; 100′ × 17′6″ × 9′4″; side wheels, 1 direct-acting engine.

SERVICE RECORDS:
Hercules—Sold 18 May 1864. Merchant *Hercules*, RR 1865.
Reliance—Sold Dec 1865. RR 1866.
Tiger—Sold 27 Jul 1865. Sold foreign 1870.

Name	Bldr	Built	Comm
E.A. Stevens	Dunham	1844	12 Mar 1862
(ex-USS *Naugatuck*, ex-*E.A. Stevens*, ex-*Naugatuck*)			

NOTES: 120 tons; 101′ × 21′6″ × 6′; 2 screws. Sold 24 Apr 1890, merchant *Argus* SE 1896.

Name	Bldr	Built	Acquired
Nemaha	(Keyport, NJ)	1854	24 Feb 1862
(ex-*Flora*—13 Jan 64)			

NOTES: 281 tons; side wheels; 1 20-pdr R. Burned at mouth of Wicomico River, 7 Feb 1868.

Name	Bldr	Built	Acquired
Miami	(River Clyde, GB)	1853	28 Jan 1862
(ex-*Lady Le Marchant*—3 Apr 62)			

The revenue cutter *Levi Woodbury*, after 1873 when she was rebuilt as a screw steamer. She was originally built as the side-wheeler *Mahoning*. (U.S. Naval Historical Center)

NOTES: 213 tons; 115′ (length); 1 screw; 2 oscillating engines. 124-pdr, 1 12-pdr. Sold 19 Apr 1871.

Name	Bldr	L
Mahoning	Lynn (U)	29 Jul 1863

NOTES: 375 tons; 130′ × 27′ × 5′4″; side wheels, complement 40. Renamed **Levi Woodbury**, 5 Jun 1873, rebuilt as screw steamer; 330 tons; 146′6″(oa) × 28′6″ × 11′4″. Sold 10 Aug 1915. Merchant *Laksco*. RR 1932.

Name	Bldr	L
Ashuelot	Englis (Novelty)	8 Jul 1863

NOTES: 323 tons; 138′ × 29′ × 6′8″; side wheels, oscillating engines. Sold 20 Jun 1867: Mar 68 to Japan, renamed *Takao*, renamed *Kaiten No. 2*. Destroyed by Imperial ships 1869.

Name	Bldr	L
Wayanda	Fardy (U)	1 Sep 1863

NOTES: 450 tons; 170′ (pp) × 27′ × d11′: Sold 18 Nov 1873. Merchant *Los Angeles*. RR 1896.

Name	Bldr	Built	Acquired
Cuyahoga (ex-General *Santa Anna*—Mexican)	Westervelt (Faron)	1854	Apr 1863

NOTES: 308 tons; 152′ × 27.7′ × 13.1′; 1 screw; oscillating engine. Damaged in collision off Cape Henlopen, 13 Mar 1864. Sold 27 Jul 1867. Japanese *Settsu*, training ship 1872.

Name	Bldr	L
Pawtuxet	Stark, NY	7 Jul 1863

NOTES: 230 tons; 143′ × 26′6″ × 11′6″; 1 screw; oscillating engine. Sold 9 Aug 1867. Merchant *Pawtuxet*. RR.

Name	Bldr	L
Kankakee	Westervelt (Gray)	15 Sep 1863

NOTES: 313 tons; 137′ × 26′6″ × 4′9″; 1 screw; 2 LP oscillating engines (36″ × 3′). 1 30-pdr R, 6 24-pdr H. Sold 28 May 1867. Japanese *Kawachi*, Feb 1869; later BU.

Name	Bldr	L
Kewanee	Robb (U)	23 Sep 1863

NOTES: 236 tons; 141' × 27.2' × 11.2'; 1 screw. Sold 10 Jul 1867. Japanese *Musashi*, 1868. Blew up in Yokohama harbor Apr 1869; salved.

Name	Bldr	L
Commodore Perry	Wright (U)	Oct 1864

NOTES: 403 or 267 tons; 1 screw; 3 guns; complement 37. Sold 3 Oct 1883. Merchant *Periwinkle* 1884. RR 1898.

Name	Bldr	Built	Comm
Lincoln	Fardy (U)	1863	May 1864

NOTES: 546 tons; 165' × 26' ?; oscillating engine. Sold 14 Apr 1874. Merchant *San Luis*; sunk off San Francisco 15 Feb 1887.

Name	Bldr	Built	Acquired
Bronx	(Brooklyn)	1863	1863
(ex-*Addison F. Andrews*)			

NOTES: 220 tons; 119' × 22' × 5'6", d9'; side wheels; beam engine. Foundered after striking rock in Long Island Sound, 4 Apr 1873.

Name	Bldr	Built	Acquired	Comm
William H. Seward	(Wilmington)	1864	Jun 1864	Oct 1864

NOTES: 201 or 254 tons; 140' × (U); side wheels; complement 30. Sold 7 Jun 1906. Merchant barge *Eugenia*.

Name	Bldr	Built	Acquired
Northerner	(Newburgh, NY)	1864	18 Apr 1864

NOTES: 319 tons; 142' × 42' × 9'; side wheels; complement 37. Renamed **Thomas Ewing**, 19 Nov 1874. Sold 5 Jun 1895. Merchant *Clifton*. Wrecked at Beaufort, SC, 18 May 1909.

Name	Bldr	Built
William Pitt Fessenden	Peck & Kirby (Fletcher)	1865
John Sherman	Peck & Kirby (Fletcher)	1865

NOTES: 476 tons; 180' × 29' × d11'; side wheels; vertical beam engine; complement 37.
SERVICE RECORDS:
Fessenden—Sold 29 Mar 1883. (rebuilt)
Sherman—Sold 25 Jun 1872. Converted to schooner. RR 1893.

Name	Bldr	Built
Salmon P. Chase	Murphy	1865

NOTES: 287 tons; 176' × 27' × d11'; side wheels. Sold 15 Jun 1875. Merchant *Admiral*. Sold Foreign 1883.

The Revenue Cutter *Salmon P. Chase* at Oswego, NY. The side-wheeler was sold in 1875. (Silverstone Collection) (U.S. Naval Historical Center)

Name	Bldr	Built	Comm
Hugh McCulloch	Fardy (U)	1865	28 Jul 1865

NOTES: 904 tons; 202' × 32'; side wheels. Sold 20 Mar 1876. Merchant *John H. Starin*. RR 1911.

Name	Bldr	Built
John A. Dix	(Buffalo)	1865

NOTES: (U) tons. Sold 27 Jun 1872.

Name	Bldr	Built	Comm
Andrew Johnson	(Buffalo)(Gray)	1865	Oct 1865

NOTES: 499 tons; 175′ × (U); side wheels; vertical beam engine; 3 guns; complement 37; wooden hull. Sold 2 Jun 1897.

Name	Bldr	Built	Acquired
Uno	(Camden, NJ)	1864	29 Jun 1865
(ex-USLHS, ex-USS *Juniper*, ex-*Uno*)			

NOTES: 111 or 79 tons; 79′6″ × 18′4″ × 9′; 1 screw; overhead engine (24″ × 1′8″); complement 12. Renamed **Peter G. Washington**, 25 Nov 1873. Sold 3 Feb 1906.

Name	Bldr	Built	Acquired
Delaware	Harlan (U)	1861	30 Aug 1865
(ex-USS *Delaware*, ex-*Virginia Dare*)			

NOTES: 357 tons; 161′ × 27′ × 6′; side wheels; 1 beam engine (38″ × 10′); 2 guns; complement 33. Renamed **Louis McLane**, Jun 1873. Sold 23 Oct 1903. Merchant *Louis Dolive*. RR 1919.

Name	Bldr	Built	Acquired
Moccasin	(Philadelphia)	1864	18 Sep 1865
(ex-USS *Moccasin*, ex-*Hero*)			

NOTES: 151 or 192 tons; 104′5″ × 22′3″ × 9′; screw; vertical direct-acting engine (32″ × 2′10″); complement 26. Renamed **George M. Bibb**, 16 Dec 1881. Lengthened at NY (128′), recommissioned 10 Apr 1882. Sold 24 Oct 1891. Merchant *Pentagoet*. Foundered at sea, 27 Nov 1898.

Name	Bldr	Built	Acquired
Nansemond	L & F (U)	1862	22 Aug 1865
(ex-USS *Nansemond*, ex-*James F. Freeborn*)			

NOTES: 325 tons B; 146′ × 26′ × 8′3″; side wheels; vertical beam engine (40″ × 9′). Renamed **William H. Crawford**, 1884(?). Rebuilt 1885 at Columbia IW, Baltimore. Sold 24 Apr 1897. Merchant *General J.A. Dumont*. Burned at Severn Side, Md., 22 Dec 1914.

Name	Bldr	Built	Acquired
Wilderness	(Brooklyn)	1864	7 Sep 1865
(ex-USS *Wilderness*, ex-*B.N. Crary*)			

NOTES: 390 tons; 137′ × 25′ × 6′; side wheels, beam engine; complement 33. Renamed **John A. Dix**, 11 Nov 1873. Sold 18 May 1891. Merchant *Gov. John A. Dix*. RR before 1908.

Name	Bldr	Built	Acquired
Mosswood	(Baltimore)	1863	14 Dec 1866
(ex-U.S. Army ship)			

NOTES: 143 tons; screw; complement 26. Renamed **Hugh McCulloch**, 15 Oct 1877. Sold 20 Feb 1889. Merchant *Jupiter* 1891, Sold Foreign 1892.

Name	Bldr	Built	Acquired
Hannibal Hamlin	(Wilmington, Del.)	1864	12 Dec 1866
(ex-*D. A. Mills*)			

NOTES: 57 or 96 tons; screw; 1 gun; complement 10. Renamed, 11 Jan 1867. Sold 28 Aug 1899.

Name	Bldr	Built	Acquired
James Guthrie	(Baltimore)	1864	29 Aug 1868
(ex-*George J. Loane*)			

NOTES: 113 tons; screw; 1 gun; complement 10. Sold 3 Apr 1882. Merchant *Joseph Cummings*. RR 1894.

Name	Bldr	Built
Schuyler Colfax	Dialogue	1871

NOTES: 486 tons; 179′6″ (oa) × 25′ × 8′4″; side wheels. Station ship Arundel Cove, Md., 1914–24. Sold 16 Jan 1924.

Name	Bldr	Built
U.S. Grant	Pusey & Jones	1871

NOTES: 263 tons; 163′ × 25′; screw; iron; 10 kts. Sold 28 Nov 1906. Merchant *Grant*.

Name	Bldr	Built	Comm
Alexander Hamilton	Bell	1871	Oct 1871
Albert Gallatin	Bell	1871	1871

NOTES: 223 tons; 147′ (oa) 133′ (bp) × 23′ × 9′6″; HP 150; screw; inverted direct-acting engine (34″ × 2′6″), 1 boiler; complement 38. (Fowler propellers, rebuilt 1872–74.)
SERVICE RECORDS:
Hamilton—Sold 6 Mar 1906.
Gallatin—Sunk off Cape Ann, 6 Jan 1892.

Name	Bldr	Built	Acquired
Jasmine	(Brooklyn)	1862	1873
(ex-USLHS, ex-USS *Jasmine*)			

NOTES: 117 or 122 tons; 79′ × 18′ × 7′6″; screw; low-pressure engine ((26″ × 2′2″)); complement 12. Renamed **William E. Chandler**, 18 Dec 1873. Sold 28 Sep 1903.

Name	Bldr	L
Manhattan	Weidner	May 1873

NOTES: 145 (174) tons; 102′ (oa) × 20′6″ × 8′6″; 1 screw; HP 210. Renamed **Arundel** 1 Apr 1918. Sold 28 Apr 1927. Merchant *Express.* SE 1935.

Name	Bldr	L
George S. Boutwell	Bell	29 Oct 1873

NOTES: 326 tons D (152 tons); 138′ (oa) × 23′ × 7′10″; 2 screws; complement 37. Sold 23 Oct 1907. Merchant *E.T. Chamberlin* 1907.

Name	Bldr	L
Oliver Wolcott	Risdon	30 Jul 1873

NOTES: 199 tons; 155′ × (U); 1 screw; wood; complement 35. Sold 19 Feb 1897. Merchant *Wolcott.*

Name	Bldr	Built
Alexander J. Dallas	Fessenden; Portland, Me.	Jul 1874

NOTES: 179 tons; 140′ (oa) 129′6″ (bp) × 21′6″ × 10′6″; 1 screw, 1 inverted LP condensing engine (36″ × 2′6″), 1 boiler; HP 300 = 10 kts; wood. Sold 2 Jul 1908. Merchant *Dallas.*

Name	Bldr	L
Samuel Dexter	Atlantic Wks	18 Jun 1874
Richard Rush	Atlantic Wks	7 Jul 1874

NOTES: 188 tons; 143′6″ (oa) 129′ (wl) × 22′9″ × 9′6″; 1 screw, 1 HP condensing engine (26″ × 3′)(*Dexter*), 1 compound engine (*Rush*), 1 boiler; HP 400.
SERVICE RECORDS:
Dexter—Sold 18 Jul 1908. Merchant *Leroy* 1908. SE 1926.
Rush—Sold 13 Aug 1885 and rebuilt 175 (oa) 163 (wl) × 25 × 14′3″ by Hall Bros, San Francisco. Recommissioned 10 Nov 1885. Sold 22 Jan 1913. Merchant *Rush.*

Name	Bldr	L
John F. Hartley	Risdon	9 Aug 1875

NOTES: 23 tons; 64 × (U); 1 screw. Rebuilt 1895 at Baltimore [48 tons, 88′ (oa) × 17′6″ × 9′3″]. Sank at wharf at San Francisco, 2 Apr 1914; sold 1 Aug 1919. Merchant *Wotoc* 1920.

Name	Bldr	L	Commissioned
Tench Coxe	W.T. Malster, Baltimore	7 Jun 1876	23 Oct 1876

NOTES: 46 tons; screw. Sold 20 Feb 1895. Merchant *Alma.* SE 1908.

Name	Bldr	L
Thomas Corwin	Oregon IW, Portland	1876

NOTES: 213 tons; 145″ (oa) 137′6″ (U) × 24′ × 11′3″; 1 screw; wood; complement 38. Sold 24 Feb 1900. Merchant *Corwin.* RR 1912–17.

Name	Bldr	Built
Salmon P. Chase	T. Brown, Philadelphia	1878

NOTES: 142 or 321 tons; 148′ (oa) × 25′7″ × 11′6″; bark; wood; complement 35. Transferred to U.S. Public Health Service 15 Jun 1912.

Name	Bldr	L
James Guthrie	H.A. Ramsey, Baltimore	13 May 1882

NOTES: 69 or 98 tons; 1 screw; complement 11. Rebuilt 1893–95, Spedden & Co. Sold 24 Feb 1942.

Name	Bldr	L	Comm
Walter Forward	Pusey & Jones	17 Jul 1882	23 Sep 1882

NOTES: 257 tons; 153′6″ (oa) × 25′ × 9′9″, or 163′ (bp) × 27′3‴ × 14′3″; 2 screws. Sold 24 Oct 1912. Merchant *Forward.* SE 1916–20.

Name	Bldr	L
William P. Fessenden	Union DD; Buffalo	26 Apr 1883

NOTES: 330 tons D (452 gr); 191′8″ (oa) 177′ × 28′ × 10′; iron side wheel; IHP 800; vertical beam engines (from old *Fessenden*). Sold Mar 1908. Merchant *Chippewa* 1909. BU 1942.

SMALL SCHOONERS

Name	Length	Bldr	L	Fate
Andrew Jackson	73	Washington	1832	Sold 31 Oct 1865
Washington (brig)	91	(Baltimore)	Aug 1837	Seized by rebels at New Orleans, 31 Jan 1861
Walter B. Forward (Comm: 23 Apr 1842)	90	Easby, Washington		Sold 30 Nov 1865
William J. Duane	102	Tees, Philadelphia	1849	Seized by rebels in Virginia 18 Apr 1861

Name	Length	Bldr	L	Fate
Morris	(U)	Brown, Baltimore	26 Apr 1849	Sold 10 Dec 1868
Joseph Lane	(U)	Graves & Fenbie, Portsmouth, Va.	30 Jul 1849	Sold 20 Jul 1869
(ex-*Campbell*) (11 Mar 1855)				
Robert McClelland	100	Hood, Somerset, Mass	11 Jul 1853	Seized by rebels in Louisiana, 31 Jan 1861; renamed *Pickens*
James C. Dobbin	100	Hood, Somerset, Mass.	13 Jul 1853	Sold 6 Apr 1881
James Campbell	100	Hood, Somerset, Mass.	9 Jul 1853	Sold 8 Jul 1875
Caleb Cushing	100	Hood, Somerset, Mass.	12 Jul 1853	Captured by Confederate privateers & sunk, 29 Jul 1863
William L. Marcy	94	Hood, Bristol, RI	1853	To USCS, 5 Mar 1862
Jefferson Davis	94	Hood, Bristol, RI	Jun 1853	Hospital boat, Washington Terr. 1862
William Aiken	(U)	(U)	1855*	Seized by rebels at Charleston Dec 1860, renamed *Petrel*
(ex-*Eclipse*)				
Henry Dodge	100	Page & Allen	1856	Seized by rebels in Texas, 2 Mar 1861
Lewis Cass	100	Page & Allen	1856	Seized by rebels in Alabama, 30 Jan 1861
Philip Allen	100	Page & Allen	1856	Sold 9 Dec 1865
Isaac Toucey	63	Merry & Gay, Milan, Ohio		Sold 22 Jun 1869
(Comm: Aug 1857)				
John B. Floyd	63	Merry & Gay, Milan, Ohio	1857	Sold 16 May 1864
Jacob Thompson	63	Merry & Gay, Milan, Ohio	1857	Sold 12 Oct 1870
Aaron V. Brown	63	Merry & Gay, Milan, Ohio	1857	Sold 23 Aug 1864
Howell Cobb	63	Merry & Gay, Milan, Ohio	1857	Wrecked off Cape Ann, 27 Dec 1861
Jeremiah S. Black	63	Merry & Gay, Milan, Ohio	1857	Sold 1868
(*Note*: These six 63-footers transferred from Great Lakes via Quebec Dec 1861)				
John Appleton		Page & Allen	1857	To USN 11 Apr 1861
Agassiz			31 May 1861*	Rtnd to USCS, 29 Dec 1865
(ex-USCS)				
Arago			31 May 1861*	Rtnd to USCS, 1861
(ex-USCS)				
Varina			31 May 1861*	Rtnd to USCS 22 Nov 1865
(ex-USCS)				
William H. Crawford	102	Tees, Phila.	31 May 1861*	Sold 21 Jun 1869
(ex-USCS)				
Antietam		Fardy	1 Mar 1864*	Sold Jan 1871
Relief	86	Bierly Hillman	1867	Discarded 1870
Rescue	86	Bierly Hillman	1867	Sold 23 Jun 1874
Reliance	110	Fardy	Jun 1867	Sold 5 Jan 1875
Vigilant	110	Fardy	1867	Discarded 1870
Active	85	Lynn	May 1867	Sold 13 May 1875
Resolute	85	Lynn	Jun 1867	Sold 10 Feb 1872
Petrel		Hathorn	1867	Sold 21 Oct 1873
Racer		Hathorn	1866	Sold 30 Jul 1873
Saville		Richmond, Mystic	1872	Sold 16 Oct 1884
Discover			1871	Sold 19 Mar 1896
Search			1869	Sold 11 Jul 1869
Vanderbilt			1875*	Sold 1 Aug 1891
Alert			1876	Sold 8 Jul 1896

*Acquired

Later history:
   Dobbin: Merchant *John L. Thomas*, 1881.
   Brown: Merchant *A. V. Brown*, 1864.
   Reliance: Merchant *Leo*, 1875. SE 1896.
   Active: Merchant *Addie L. Bird*, 1875.
   Varina: Sunk near Pass à l'Outre, 18 Jan 1870.
   Joseph Lane: Merchant *Pedro Varela*, 1876.
   Rescue: Merchant *Rescue*, 1875.

PART III
U.S. Coast Survey

Overleaf: A fine broadside view of the ironclad *Choctaw* showing the forward armored casemate with gunports and the armored side wheels aft.

Right: The screw sloop *Narragansett* spent the war years on the Pacific coast and is seen here at Mare Island, probably while on surveying service, 1873–75. (U.S. Naval Historical Center)

UNITED STATES COAST SURVEY

STEAMERS

Bibb—Knapp, Pittsburgh; Launched: 10 Apr 1845

409 tons B; 148′ (U) 143′ (bp) × 23′ × 10′; side wheels; side-lever engine; complement 35. Built for Revenue Marine as **Tyler** with Hunter's Wheel propulsion; transferred to USCS 9 Jan 1847 and converted to side wheels. Loaned to Revenue Cutter Service 31 May 1861; returned 1861.

Walker—Tomlinson; Built: 1845

305 tons B, 132 (pp) × 24′6″ × 9′8″; side wheels; 2 horizontal half-beam engines. Built for Revenue Marine, transferred 1852 and rebuilt. Sunk in collision off Absecon, NJ, 21 Jun 1860.

Corwin[†]—Vaughan Lynn (Merrick); Built: 1852

(U) tons; 125′ × 24′ × d10′; side wheels; 1 steeple engine. Served with Revenue Cutter Service 31 May to 17 Sep 1861.
Prizes: 4 May 1862: *Director*; 5 May: *Waterwitch*.

Hetzel[‡] (See p. 84.)
Vixen[‡] (See p. 98.)

SAILING VESSELS

Brig: *Fauntleroy* (78 tons, 1852)
Schooners: *Agassiz,*[†] *Arago,*[†] *Bailey, Bancroft, Bowditch, Caswell, Crawford, Dana*[‡]*, Gerdes, G.M. Bache, Guthrie, Hassler, Howell Cobb,*[‡] *Humboldt, James Hall, John Y. Mason, Joseph Henry, Marcy, Meredith, Peirce, Petrel,** Torrey, Twilight, Varina.*[†]
Tender: *Fire Fly.**

*Seized by Confederates.
[†]Loaned to Revenue Marine.
[‡]Loaned to U.S. Navy.

The Danish casemate frigate *Danmark* seen in 1869 at Copenhagen following the wedding of Crown Prince Frederick to Princess Louise of Sweden. (Martin Holbrook Collection)

PART IV
Confederate States Navy

Overleaf: The cruiser *Rappahannock* detained at Calais, France, in 1864 where she had arrived for repairs after escaping from England. She was built for the Royal Navy in 1855 as HMS *Victor*, one of six wooden gunboats of the *Intrepid* class. (U.S. Naval Historical Center)

Right: A "David"-type torpedo boat afloat off the U.S. Naval Academy, Annapolis, after the war. The funnel is dismounted, and there is no spar on the bow. (U.S. Naval Historical Center)

THE CONFEDERATE STATES NAVY

When South Carolina seceded from the Union on December 20, 1860, followed by the other Southern states, the entity of the Confederate States of America did not automatically come into existence. For a brief period the states were separate and independent, and the ships they seized or armed were not part of a common navy.

Efforts to bring these ships into such a common navy were fraught with difficulties. By judicious strategy the Union had seized points along the long coast, which effectively kept the Southern ships apart. Although finally incorporated into the Confederate States Navy, each state's "navy" fought its own war. Because of the geographical situation, there were no occasions when ships of the different states could join to fight the common foe.

Aside from the few ships it was able to seize in Southern ports, the Confederacy had little hope of building a navy. The industrial revolution had lagged far behind in the South; the few plants capable of making arms, engines, or armor were already in great demand by the military, which, because of the geography of the war, had first priority.

Ingenuity was not to be denied, however, and several memorable naval designs and weapons were produced, some of which have made their mark on history.

Southern engineers devised the casemate ironclad rams—most of similar shape and design—of which the most notable was the *Virginia*, converted from the USS *Merrimack*. Her appearance at Hampton Roads in the midst of the Union fleet caused consternation as she roamed freely among the wooden warships wreaking havoc. It was only the timely arrival of the *Monitor* that stopped her and showed up her defects. But the *Virginia*'s formidable aspect, like that of her near sisters, was belied by defective machinery and jerry-built armor.

Submarines of primitive design were produced, and despite several disasters one of them was the first submarine to sink a warship. Mines (called torpedoes) were used with great success against Union ships.

A most effective weapon against the South was the North's blockade of the major Southern ports. It was absolutely necessary for the South to import manufactured goods, especially war materiel, and in order to pay for these, cotton had to be exported.

A large trade began, with ships running the blockade out of the main Southern ports, such as Wilmington, Charleston, Savannah, Mobile, New Orleans, and Galveston, as well as many other points on the Florida and Texas coasts. The "runners" had only to go to neutral ports where they could leave their cotton and pick up goods destined for the South. Bermuda, Nassau, and Havana became the most widely used exchange points since they required only a comparatively short voyage.

In order to cope with this situation, the Union's navy was required to add many ships to patrol the seas, it being a settled principle of international law that a blockade to be legal had to be effective and actually prevent ships from entering and leaving the blockaded ports.

Some blockade runners were owned by the Confederate Navy, but the majority were private. They were mostly of British registry, many having been specially built for the purpose. These were very fast, low in the water, and cheaply built. Some became very successful making many voyages; others were captured on their first run. A number of these captured ships were taken into the Union Navy to join the blockaders.

The Confederate Navy also took to the high seas in the form of commerce raiders. Ships were outfitted or built in Britain until the British government, severely taken to task by the American ambassador in London, halted the practice. To evade neutrality laws, these ships sailed out as merchant ships and were armed and commissioned at sea. They were quite successful and tied up a substantial number of U.S. warships that were searching for them and guarding American-flag merchant ships. The *Alabama*, *Florida*, and *Shenandoah* are names that became legendary.

Modern and more powerful fighting vessels were also ordered abroad. Small, armored oceangoing turret ships were contracted for in Britain by the industrious Captain James Bulloch, and some other vessels were built in France. Of all these only the *Stonewall* put to sea under the Confederate flag, the others being halted by government decree. They eventually ended up in various foreign navies.

The Mississippi River was the backbone of the Confederacy. It and its major tributaries were highways of commerce and constituted the best line of logistic support for the armies. The Union needed to control these rivers for its own sake and to deny them to the South. Union control of the Mississippi would split the South in two.

On these rivers, the Mississippi, the Ohio, the Cumberland, the Tennessee, and the Red, the South responded to the threat by arming river steamers and building casemate ironclads. But the strength of the Union thrust swept aside these weak forces. Although plans for many vessels were put in hand, most were destroyed or captured incomplete, and only a very few got into action. With the capture of Vicksburg in 1863 the river war moved to lesser streams.

IRONCLADS

SEAGOING ARMORED SHIPS

NORTH CAROLINA CLASS

Name	Bldr	Laid down	L	Comm
Mississippi	Laird	Apr 1862	29 Aug 1863	never
North Carolina	Laird	Apr 1862	4 Jul 1863	never

Tonnage:	2,750 tons D
Dimensions:	224'6″ (bp) × 42'6″ × 17'
Machinery:	1 screw, 1 horizontal direct-acting engine (56″ × 2'9″), 4 boilers; IHP 1,450 = 10 knots
Complement:	153
Armament:	4 9″ R (Royal Navy)
Armor:	turrets 5″ with 10″ faces, sides 3″ to 4.5″

NOTES: Turret ships superior to any Federal warship. Three-masted bark rig, hinged bulwarks, telescopic funnels. These were the famous "Laird Rams" embargoed by the British government and taken over for the Royal Navy. Built under code names *El Monassir* and *El Tousson*, supposedly for the Egyptian government. Seized by the

HMS *Wivern*, intended to become CSS *Mississippi*. She was one of the famous "Laird Rams" taken into the Royal Navy in 1864. The bulwarks are down exposing the two turrets. (Imperial War Museum)

British government Oct 1863 while anchored under guard in the Mersey River and purchased Feb 1864 for the Royal Navy.
Later history:
Mississippi—Completed as HMS *Wivern*, 10 Oct 1865. Coast defense ship at Hong Kong 1880. Floating workshop and depot ship 1904. BU 1922.
North Carolina—Completed as HMS *Scorpion*, 10 Oct 1865. Coast defense ship at Bermuda 1869. Sunk as a target at Bermuda 1901.

SANTA MARIA

Name	Bldr	Laid down	L	Comm
'Santa Maria'	Thomson	1863	23 Feb 1864	never

Tonnage:	4,770 tons D, 3,200 tons B ?
Dimensions:	270'8″ (bp) × 49'6″ × 18'4″
Machinery:	1 screw, horizontal direct-acting engine (77″ × 3'), 4 boilers; IHP 1,000 = 8.5 knots
Complement:	500
Armament:	20 60-pdr R, 8 18-pdr
Armor:	battery and belt 4.5″–3.5″

NOTES: Never named, this vessel was known as *Santa Maria*, *Glasgow*, and *Frigate No. 61*. Iron hull.
Later history: Sold by builders to Denmark Dec 1863, not delivered until Dec 1864 because Denmark was at war with Prussia and Austria. Danish *Danmark*, 1864. BU 1907.

STONEWALL CLASS

Name	Bldr	Laid down	L	Comm
Stonewall (Built under code name *Sphinx*)	Arman (Mazeline)	1863	21 Jun 1864	Jan 1865
(unnamed) (Built under code name *Cheops*)	Arman (Mazeline)	1863	Jun 1864	never

Tonnage:	1,390 tons
Dimensions:	186'9″ (oa) 165'9″ (wl) 157'6″ (bp) × 32'6″ × 14'3″
Machinery:	2 screws, 2 horizontal direct-acting engines, 2 boilers; IHP 1,200 = 10.8 knots
Complement:	135
Armament:	1 11″/300 R, 2 5″/70 R
Armor:	belt 4.5″, c/t 5.5″

NOTES: Ironclad rams built in France under code names, embargoed by French government Feb 1864.
SERVICE RECORD:
Stonewall—Sold to Denmark, renamed *Staerkodder* but refused by Danish government and returned as *Olinde*. Commissioned by CSN at sea. Left Ferrol, Spain, 24 Mar 1865. At Havana at end of the war and turned over to U.S.A.
Later history: Japanese *Kotetsu*, arrived at Yokohama 24 Apr 1868. Transferred to Imperial Government, renamed *Azuma*, 1871. BU 1908.
(unnamed)
Later history: Prussian *Prinz Adalbert*, 29 Oct 1865, rearmed and completed 1866. BU 1878.

The ironclad ram *Stonewall*. The turret aft can be clearly seen. The long ram and large anchor at the bow are prominent.

Another view of the ironclad *Stonewall* at Washington Navy Yard after her capture. The opening in the bow for the 11-inch gun and the ram bow can be clearly seen. (U.S. Naval Historical Center)

A drawing of CSS *Virginia*. No photographs exist of this ship, which was converted from the U.S. frigate *Merrimack*.

CASEMATE IRONCLADS

VIRGINIA

Name	Bldr	L	Acquired	Comm
Virginia (ex-USS *Merrimack*)	Boston	14 Jun 1855	17 Feb 1862	Mar 1862

Tonnage:	3,200 tons B
Dimensions:	263' (bp) × 51'4" × 22'
Machinery:	1 screw, 2 horizontal back-acting engines (72" × 3'), 4 boilers; IHP 1,200 = 9 knots
Complement:	320
Armament:	2 7" R, 6 9" SB, 2 6"/32 R
Armor:	2" + 24" wood

NOTES: U.S. frigate *Merrimack* burned to the waterline at Norfolk Navy Yard to prevent capture 20 Apr 1861; hulk raised and rebuilt as an ironclad ram. Cut down to the waterline and reconstructed with sloping armored sides pierced for guns and a 4-foot ram bow. Designed by Cdr. John M. Brooke.

SERVICE RECORD: Battle of Hampton Roads, 8 Mar 1862. Damaged by gunfire, sank U.S. sloop *Cumberland* by gunfire and ramming, then frigate *Congress* by gunfire. Engaged U.S. ironclad *Monitor*, 9 Mar, in inconclusive battle, the first between powered ironclad vessels. Sortied into Hampton Roads and captured three transports, 11 Apr 1862. Run ashore and burned by crew to prevent capture near Craney Island in James River, 11 May 1862.

ARKANSAS CLASS

Name	Bldr	Laid down	L	Comm
Arkansas	Shirley	Oct 1861	25 Apr 1862	26 May 1862
Tennessee	Shirley	Oct 1861	never	never

Tonnage:	(U)
Dimensions:	165' (bp) × 35' × 11'6"
Machinery:	2 screws, low-pressure engines; IHP 900 = 8 mph
Complement:	200
Armament:	2 9" SB, 2 8"/64, 2 6" R, 2 32-pdr SB
Armor:	18" iron and wood

NOTES: Casemate ironclads with ram bow and sloping sides on long flat hull. Hurriedly built with poor engines.

SERVICE RECORDS:

Arkansas—Taken to Yazoo City for completion when Federal troops occupied Memphis, May 1862. Engaged Federal ironclads in Yazoo River, 15 Jul 1862 and ran past Federal fleet to Vicksburg. Attacked at Vicksburg by ram USS *Queen of the West*, 22 Jul 1862. Attacked by U.S. ironclad *Essex* above Baton Rouge, drifted ashore and burned to prevent capture, 6 Aug 1862.

Tennessee—Burned to prevent capture on the stocks at Memphis, 5 Jun 1862.

CSS *Arkansas*. A drawing of the ironclad that caused havoc near Vicksburg until she was sunk in August 1862.

MANASSAS

Name	Bldr	Built	Acquired	Comm
Manassas (ex-*Enoch Train*)	Curtis, Medford (Loring)	1855	12 Sep 1861	1861

Tonnage:	387 tons B
Dimensions:	143′ × 33′ × 17′ (or 128′ × 26′ × d12′6″ [as merchant])
Machinery:	1 screw, 1 inclined engine (36″ × 2′6″); 4 knots
Complement:	(U)
Armament:	1 64-pdr. Later, 1 32-pdr.
Armor:	1.5″ over 12″ wood

NOTES: Towboat, acquired 1861 and converted at Algiers, La., to an ironclad ram. Commissioned as a privateer, taken over by CSN shortly thereafter. Hull was plated over with a convex shape that caused cannon shot to glance off, projecting only 2′6″ above the water. Purchased by Confederate government Dec 1861.

SERVICE RECORD: Lower Mississippi River. Attacked Federal squadron at Head of Passes, 12 Oct 1861, ramming USS *Richmond*, but damaged during the action. Engaged Federal squadron below New Orleans, 24 Apr 1862, ramming several vessels; run aground and burned in the Mississippi River.

ATLANTA

Name	Bldr	L	Comm
Atlanta (ex-*Fingal*)	Thomson (J & G Thomas)	9 May 1861	Sep 1862

Tonnage:	1,006 tons
Dimensions:	204′ (oa) × 41′ × 15′9″
Machinery:	3 screws, 2 vertical direct-acting engines (39″ × 2′6″), 1 boiler; 8 knots
Complement:	145
Armament:	2 7″ R, 2 6.4″ R, spar torpedo
Armor:	4″ casemate, .5″ deck

NOTES: Converted from iron-hulled blockade runner *Fingal* at Savannah by N. & A. Tift. Cut down to waterline; the armored deck projected 6 feet beyond the hull with a casemate on top.

SERVICE RECORD: Savannah station. Captured in Wassaw Sound, Ga., by U.S. monitors *Nahant* and *Weehawken* after being damaged by gunfire and run aground, 17 Jun 1863. Commissioned in USN, 1864. SAtlBS & NAtlBS 1864–65. Sold 4 May 1869.

Later history: Sold to Haiti, renamed *Triumph*. Disappeared at sea off Cape Hatteras, Dec 1869.

The ironclad ram *Atlanta* serving as a United States ship in the James River 1865. The broadside guns are visible in the casemate. (U.S. Naval Historical Center)

The ironclad *Atlanta* in dry dock after the war at League Island. The armored deck projecting beyond the hull can be clearly seen. (Mariners Museum)

The former U.S. Army steamer *George Page* was active in the rivers of Virginia until sunk in March 1862. (See page 243.)

EASTPORT

Name	Bldr	Built	Acquired	Comm
Eastport	(New Albany, Ind.)	1852	Jan 1862	never

For Details see USS *Eastport*.

NOTES: Converted to ironclad at Cerro Gordo, Tenn. May have been the former *C.E. Hillman*.

SERVICE RECORD: Captured by Union gunboats while undergoing conversion at Cerro Gordo, 7 Feb 1862. Taken to Cairo, Ill., and completed as USS *Eastport*.

ALBEMARLE CLASS

Name	Bldr	Laid down	L	Comm
Albemarle	Elliot	Apr 1863	1 Jul 1863	17 Apr 1864
Neuse	(Whitehall, NC)		Nov 1863	Apr 1864
(unnamed)	Elliot		never	never

Tonnage:	376 tons (*Neuse*)
Dimensions:	139′ (bp) 152′ (oa) × 34′ × 9′
Machinery:	2 screws, 2 horizontal non-condensing engines (18″ × 1′7″), 2 boilers; IHP 400 = 4 knots
Complement:	150
Armament:	2 6.4″/100 R
Armor:	6″

NOTES: Octagonal casemate on a flat hull, designed by Cdr. James W. Cooke.

SERVICE RECORDS:

Albemarle—Damaged at launch and taken to Halifax, NC, for completion. Attacked Union forces at Plymouth, NC, sinking USS *Southfield*, 19 Apr 1864. Attacked Federal squadron below Plymouth, damaged 5 May 1864. Sunk in Roanoke River by spar torpedo boat *Picket Boat No. 1*, 28 Oct 1864. Raised by Union forces and taken to Norfolk NYd, Apr 1865. Sold 15 Oct 1867. BU 1867.

Neuse—North Carolina waters. Ran aground off Kinston, NC, May 1864. Remained there until burned to prevent capture, Mar 1865.

(unnamed)—Destroyed on stocks to prevent capture, Apr 1865.

MISSISSIPPI

Name	Bldr	Laid down	L	Comm
Mississippi	Tift	14 Oct 1861	19 Apr 1862	never

Tonnage:	1,400 tons
Dimensions:	260′ × 58′ × 12′6″
Machinery:	3 screws, 3 engines (36″ × 2′6″); 14 knots
Complement:	(U)
Armament:	2 7″ R, 18 others
Armor:	3.75″

NOTES: Ironclad steamer, never completed. Armament never mounted.

SERVICE RECORD: Burned to prevent capture prior to completion, 25 Apr 1862.

RICHMOND CLASS

Name	Bldr	Laid down	L	Comm
Chicora	Eason	25 Apr 1862	23 Aug 1862	Nov 1862
North Carolina	Berry	1862	1863	Dec 1863
Palmetto State	Cameron	Jan 1862	11 Oct 1862	Sep 1862
Raleigh	Cassidy		1864	30 Apr 1864
Richmond	Norfolk	1862	6 May 1862	Jul 1862
Savannah	Willink	Apr 1862	4 Feb 1863	30 Jun 1863

Tonnage:	(U)
Dimensions:	172′6″ (oa) 150′ (bp) × 34′ × 12′
Machinery:	1 screw; 6 knots
Complement:	180
Armament:	*Chicora* 2 9″ SB, 4 6″ 32-pdr R
	North Carolina 4 guns
	Palmetto State 10 7″ R
	Raleigh 4 6″ R
	Richmond 1 7″ R, 1 10″ SB, 2 6.4″ R, spar torpedo
	Savannah 2 7″ R, 2 6.4″ R
Armor:	4″ + 22″ wood

NOTES: Ironclad rams built to a basic design of John L. Porter. Completion was delayed by shortage of equipment and strikes.

The ironclad *Chicora*. A rare picture taken at Charleston. The casemate extends to the waterline amidships.

Richmond was sometimes referred to as *Virginia II* and *Young Virginia*. *North Carolina* fitted with engine from gunboat *Uncle Ben*; hull was structurally weak.

SERVICE RECORDS:

Chicora—Defense of Charleston. Attacked Federal blockading fleet, 31 Jan 1863. Defense of Charleston forts, 7 Apr 1863. Sunk to prevent capture prior to fall of Charleston, 18 Feb 1865.

North Carolina—Defense of Wilmington, NC. Foundered at Smithville, NC, as result of worm damage, 27 Sep 1864.

Palmetto State—Defense of Charleston. Attacked Federal blockading fleet and rammed USS *Mercedita*, 31 Jan 1863. Defense of Charleston forts, 7 Apr 1863. Sunk to prevent capture prior to fall of Charleston, 18 Feb 1865.

Raleigh—Defense of Wilmington, NC. Engaged Federal blockading vessels off New Inlet, NC, 6 May but went aground and was wrecked on Wilmington Bar the following day, 7 May 1864.

Richmond—Towed to Richmond after launching and completed there. James River. Engagements at Dutch Gap, 13 Aug, Ft. Harrison, 29–31 Sep and Chapin's Bluff, 22 Oct 1864. Attacked while aground at Trent's Reach, 23–24 Jan 1865. Sunk to prevent capture in James River prior to fall of Richmond, 3 Apr 1865.

Savannah—Defense of Savannah. Burned to prevent capture at Savannah, 21 Dec 1864.

LOUISIANA

Name	Bldr	Laid down	L
Louisiana	Murray; N. Orleans	15 Oct 1861	6 Feb 1862

Tonnage:	1,400 tons
Dimensions:	264' × 62' ×
Machinery:	2 screws and 2 paddlewheels
Armament:	2 7″ R, 3 9″, 4 8″, 7 32-pdr R
Armor:	4″

NOTES: Casemate ironclad. Designed with two paddle wheels in a center well one behind the other, and twin rudders. Engines taken from steamer *Ingomar*.

SERVICE RECORD: Towed while incomplete to Ft. St. Philip below New Orleans as a floating battery, 20 Apr 1862. Burned to prevent capture and blew up, 28 Apr 1862.

BRANDYWINE

Name	Bldr	Laid down	L	Comm
(Unnamed) (Details unknown)	Norfolk	1862	17 Apr 1862	never

NOTE: Ironclad floating battery, was to be named *Brandywine*. Towed incomplete to Richmond, May 1862. FFU.

MISSOURI

Name	Bldr	Laid down	L	Comm
Missouri	(Shreveport)	Dec 1862	14 Apr 1863	12 Sep 1863

Tonnage:	(U)
Dimensions:	183′ (oa) × 53′8″ × 8′6″, d10′3″
Machinery:	Center wheel, 2 engines (24″ × 7′6″), 4 boilers
Complement:	(U)
Armament:	1 11″, 1 9″, 2 32-pdr.
Armor:	4 1/2″ rails

NOTES: Two ships planned.
SERVICE RECORD: Served in Red River. Surrendered at Shreveport, 3 Jun 1865. Sold by USN, 29 Nov 1865 at Mound City, Ill.

CHARLESTON

Name	Bldr	Laid down	L	Comm
Charleston	Eason	Dec 1862	late 1863	1864

Tonnage:	(U)
Dimensions:	189′ (oa) 167′ (bp) × 34′ × 14′
Machinery:	6 knots
Complement:	150
Armament:	2 9″ SB, 4 R
Armor:	(U)

NOTES: Ironclad ram. Known as the "Ladies Gunboat."
SERVICE RECORD: Defense of Charleston. Burned to prevent capture at Charleston, 18 Feb 1865.

HUNTSVILLE CLASS

Name	Bldr	Laid down	L
Huntsville	Bassett Selma	1862	7 Feb 1863
Tuscaloosa	Bassett Selma	1862	7 Feb 1863

Tonnage:	(U)
Dimensions:	152′ (oa) × 34′ × 7′
Machinery:	1 screw, high pressure engines; 3 knots
Complement:	(U)
Armament:	3 32-pdr, 1 6.4″ R
Armor:	4″

NOTES: Improved Albemarle type, only partially armored. Engines defective; vessels could not be used.
SERVICE RECORD: Defense of Mobile. Taken to Mobile for completion. Sunk as blockships in Mobile River, 12 Apr 1865.

JACKSON

Name	Bldr	Laid down	L	Comm
Jackson	Columbus	Dec 1862	22 Dec 1864	never

Tonnage:	(U)
Dimensions:	223′6″ (oa) 208′6″ (bp) × 59′ × 8′
Machinery:	2 screws, 2 horizontal direct-acting HP engines (28″ × 2′), 2 boilers
Complement:	(U)
Armament:	4 7″ R, 2 6.4″ R
Armor:	4″ casemate

A rare picture of the never-completed ironclad *Jackson* lying in the Chattahoochee River. (Mariners Museum)

NOTES: Also known as **Muscogee**. Designed with center-wheel machinery, but drew too much water after first launch and was rebuilt early in 1864 as a modified Albemarle type.

SERVICE RECORD: Destroyed by Union cavalry before completion, 17 Apr 1865.

MILLEDGEVILLE CLASS

Name	Bldr	Laid down	L	Comm
Milledgeville	Willink	Feb 1863	Oct 1864	never
(unnamed)	Kenston & Hawks; Savannah		never	never
(unnamed)	(Charleston)		Oct 1864	never
(unnamed)	(Charleston)		never	never

Tonnage:	(U)
Dimensions:	175′ (bp) × 35′3″ × 9′
Machinery:	2 screws
Complement:	(U)
Armament:	6 guns
Armor:	(U)

NOTES: The unnamed vessels may differ in particulars.

SERVICE RECORDS: All destroyed on stocks to prevent capture Dec 1864.

COLUMBIA CLASS

Name	Bldr	L	Comm
Columbia	Jones & Eason; Charleston	10 Mar 1864	1864
Texas	Richmond	Jan 1865	never

Tonnage:	(U)
Dimensions:	*Columbia*: 218′ (oa) 189′ (bp) × 51′4″ × 13′6″
	Texas: 217′ (oa) × 48′6″ × 13′6″
Machinery:	*Columbia*: 1 screw, 2 horizontal direct-acting HP engines (36″ × 2′), 5 boilers
	Texas: 2 screws, 4 horizontal direct-acting condensing engines (26″ × 1′8″)
Complement:	50
Armament:	6 guns
Armor:	6″

NOTES: Similar vessels built to same basic design, with shorter casemate on *Texas*.

SERVICE RECORDS:

Columbia—Defense of Charleston. Ran on a sunken wreck near Ft. Moultrie, 12 Jan 1865. Salvaged by USN and towed to Norfolk, 25 May 1865. Sold by USN 10 Oct 1867.

Texas—Seized incomplete at Richmond by USN, 3 Apr 1865. Sold 15 Oct 1867 and BU.

TENNESSEE II

Name	Bldr	Laid down	L	Comm
Tennessee	Bassett Selma	Oct 1862	Feb 1863	16 Feb 1864

Tonnage:	1,273 tons
Dimensions:	209′ (oa) 189′ (bp) × 48′ × 14′
Machinery:	2 screws and side wheels, 2 HP engines (24″ × 7′), 4 boilers; 6 knots
Complement:	133

The ironclad ram *Tennessee* as a United States ship after her capture at Mobile Bay. (U.S. Naval Historical Center)

| Armament: | 2 7″ R, 4 6.4″ R |
| Armor: | 5″ + 6″ |

NOTES: Modified Columbia type. Engines taken from steamer *Alonzo Child*.

SERVICE RECORD: Defense of Mobile. Battle of Mobile Bay, 5 Aug 1864 (flagship); disabled and captured. Commissioned in USN 19 Aug 1864. Assault on Ft. Morgan, 23 Aug 1864. Decommissioned 19 Aug 1865. Sold 27 Nov 1867 and BU.

FREDERICKSBURG

Name	Bldr	Laid down	L	Comm
Fredericksburg	Richmond	1863	30 Nov 1863	1864

Tonnage:	(U)
Dimensions:	188′ (oa) 170′ (bp) × 40′3″ × 9′6″
Machinery:	2 screws
Complement:	150
Armament:	1 11″ SB, 1 8″ R, 2 6.4″ R
Armor:	(U)

NOTES: Ironclad ram. Did not receive armament until Mar 1864.

SERVICE RECORD: James River flotilla. Action at Trent's Reach, 21 Jun 1864. Blown up to prevent capture in James River following fall of Richmond, 4 Apr 1865.

VIRGINIA II

Name	Bldr	Laid down	L	Comm
Virginia (II)	Richmond	1863	Jun 1864	1864

Tonnage:	(U)
Dimensions:	197′ (oa) 180′ (bp) × 47′6″ × 9′6″
Machinery:	1 screw; 10 knots
Complement:	150
Armament:	1 11″ SB, 1 8″ R, 2 6.4″ R
Armor:	sides 5″, forward 6″

NOTES: Casemate ironclad.

SERVICE RECORD: James River flotilla. Action at Trent's Reach, 21 Jun 1864. Engagements at Dutch Gap, 13 Aug and 22 Oct 1864. Second action at Trent's Reach, 23–24 Jan 1865. Blown up to prevent capture in James River following fall of Richmond, 3 Apr 1865.

NASHVILLE

Name	Bldr	L	Comm
Nashville	(Montgomery, Ala.)	mid-1863	never
(Unnamed)	(Selma, Ala.)	1863	never

Tonnage:	(U)
Dimensions:	271′ × 62′6″ × 10′9″
Machinery:	Side wheels, 2 engines (30″ × 9′)
Complement:	(U)
Armament:	3 7″ R, 1 24-pdr H
Armor:	6″

NOTES: Armor for *Nashville* taken from *Baltic*.

SERVICE RECORDS:

Nashville—Taken to Mobile for completion. Surrendered incomplete in Tombigbee River, 10 May 1865. Sold by USN, 22 Nov 1867 and BU.

(unnamed)—Irreparably damaged when launched and BU Apr 1864.

In addition, the following vessels were under construction during the war. Few details are known:

Wilmington, twin screw vessel building at Wilmington, NC. Destroyed on the stocks Jan 1865.

Unnamed vessel, building at Elizabeth City, NC. No work done.

Unnamed vessel, building at Tarboro, NC. ("Tar River Ironclad") Destroyed on stocks by Union army, Jul–Aug 1863.

Unnamed vessel, building by Eliot at Edwards Ferry, NC. Set adrift at Hamilton, NC, Mar 1865 and sunk by Confederate mine.

Unnamed side-wheel ram building at Oven Bluff, Ala. Destroyed on stocks.

Unnamed screw rams (2) built at Oven Bluff, Ala. Hulls taken to Mobile without armament, armor, or machinery. (These known as "Bigbee boats".)

Unnamed twin-screw side-wheel ram building at Yazoo City, destroyed prior to completion, 21 May 1863.

Unnamed double-ended 4-screw ram building at Richmond.

Unnamed ironclad building at Pensacola, destroyed Mar 1862.

CRUISERS

Name	Bldr	L	Comm
Alabama (ex-*Enrica*)	Laird (bldr)	15 May 1862	24 Aug 1862

Tonnage:	1,050 tons
Dimensions:	220′ (oa) 211′6″ (wl) × 31′9″ × 14′
Machinery:	1 screw, 2 horizontal direct-acting condensing engines (56″ × 2′3″), 4 boilers; IHP 600=13 knots
Complement:	148
Armament:	6 32-pdr/55 SB, 1 110-pdr R (7″), 1 68-pdr SB (8″)

NOTES: Bark-rigged sloop-of-war known as "Hull 290." Made rendezvous with *Agrippina* and *Bahama* and commissioned at sea off the Azores. Took over 60 prizes.

SERVICE RECORD: Cruised in N. Atlantic, captured and sank over 20 ships, 1862. West Indies, sank USS *Hatteras* off Galveston, 11 Jan 1863. Cruised in Indian Ocean and East Indies, 1863. Arrived at Cherbourg, France, 11 Jun 1864. Sunk in action with USS *Kearsarge* off Cherbourg, 19 Jun 1864.

Prizes: 5 Sep 1862: **Ocmulgee*; 7 Sep: **Starlight*; 8 Sep: **Ocean Rover*; 9 Sep: **Alert* and **Weather Gauge*; 13 Sep: **Altamaha*; 14 Sep: **Benjamin Tucker*; 16 Sep: **Courser*; 17 Sep: **Virginia*; 18 Sep: **Elisha Dunbar*; 3 Oct: **Brilliant*; 7 Oct: **Wave Crest* and **Dunkirk*; 9 Oct: *Tonawanda*; 11 Oct: **Manchester*; 15 Oct: **Lamplighter*; 23 Oct: **Lafayette*; 26 Oct: **Crenshaw*; 28 Oct: **Lauraetta*; 29 Oct: *Baron de Custine*; 2 Nov: **Levi*

The Confederate raider *Alabama* as she appeared at Liverpool before starting on her highly successful career. No photographs are known of this famous ship.

Starbuck; 8 Nov: **Thomas B. Wales*; 21 Nov: **Clara L. Sparks*; 30 Nov: **Parker Cook*; 5 Dec: *Nina* and *Union*; 7 Dec: str *Ariel*.
26 Jan 1863: **Golden Rule*; 27 Jan: **Chastelaine*; 3 Feb: **Palmetto*; 21 Feb: **Golden Eagle* and **Olive Jane*; 27 Feb: *Washington*; 1 Mar: *Bethia Thayer*; 2 Mar: **John A. Parks*; 15 Mar: *Punjab*; 23 Mar: *Morning Star* and **Kingfisher*; 25 Mar: *Charles Hill* and **Nora*; 4 Apr: **Louisa Hatch*; 15 Apr: **Kate Cory* and **Lafayette*; 24 Apr: **Nye*; 26 Apr: str **Dorcas Prince*; 3 May: **Sea Lark* and **Union Jack*; 25 May: *Justina* and **Gildersleeve*; 29 May: **Jabez Snow*; 2 Jun: **Amazonian*; 5 Jun: **Talisman*; 20 Jun: *Conrad*; 2 Jul: **Anna F. Schmidt*; 6 Jul: **Express*; 5 Aug: *Sea Bride*; 9 Aug: *Martha Wenzell*; 6 Nov: **Amanda*; 10 Nov: **Winged Racer*; 11 Nov: **Contest*; 18 Nov: **Harriet Spalding*; 24 Dec: *Texas Star*; 26 Dec: **Highlander* and **Sonora*.
14 Jan 1864: **Emma Jane*; 23 Apr: **Rockingham*; 27 Apr: **Tycoon*.

Name	Bldr	L
Alexandra	Miller (Fawcett)	7 Mar 1863

Tonnage: 286 tons B
Dimensions: 230′ × -... or (125′ × 22′ × 9′)
Machinery: 1 screw, 10 knots

Complement: 24
Armament: 4 guns

NOTES: Bark-rigged wooden steamer. Seized by British government Apr 1863 and not released until May 1864. Sailed as merchant *Mary* but detained at Nassau until the end of the war.

Name	Bldr	Built
Chickamauga (ex-*Edith*)	Dudgeon	1863

Tonnage: 585 tons
Dimensions: 175′ × 25′ × d15′, 7′9″
Machinery: 2 screws, 2 engines (34″ × 1′9″), IHP 894 = 13.4 knots
Complement: 120
Armament: 1 84-pdr, 2 32-pdr, 2 24-pdr

NOTES: Former blockade runner *Edith* purchased at Wilmington 1864. Unsuitable as a raider.
SERVICE RECORD: Cruised in North Atlantic, Oct–Nov 1864, taking several prizes. Burned to prevent capture at Fayetteville, NC, 25 Feb 1865.
Prizes: 29 Oct 1864: *Albion Lincoln*; 30 Oct: *M.L. Potter*; 31 Oct: **Emily*

The celebrated raider *Florida* at Brest, France, 1863–64. Notice her distinctive twin funnels and fore-and-aft rig. (U.S. Naval Historical Center)

L. Hall and **Shooting Star*; 1 Nov: **Goodspeed* and **Otter Rock*; 2 Nov: *Speedwell*.

Name	Bldr	L	Comm
Florida (ex-*Oreto*)	Miller (Fawcett)	Jan 1862	17 Aug 1862

Tonnage:	about 700 tons B
Dimensions:	191′ × 27′3″ × 13′
Machinery:	1 screw, 2 horizontal direct-acting engines (42″ × 2′); 9.5 knots (12 under sail)
Complement:	52
Armament:	6 6″ R, 2 7″ R, 1 12-pdr H

NOTES: Sloop rig, 2 funnels, iron hull. Designed after British gunboats. Supposedly built for Italy. Commissioned in the Bahamas. Intended name **Manassas**. Took 33 prizes.

SERVICE RECORD: Commissioned and armed at Green Cay, Bahamas. Made celebrated dash through Federal blockade to Mobile, 4 Sep 1862; sailed 16 Jan 1863. Cruised N. Atlantic, 1863. Laid up at Brest, Aug 1863–Feb 1864. Attacked by USS *Wachusett* while anchored at Bahia, Brazil, 7 Oct 1864, and towed out to sea, a breach of Brazilian neutrality. Sunk in collision with transport *Alliance* at Newport News, Va., 28 Nov 1864.

Prizes: 19 Jan 1863: **Estelle*; 22 Jan: **Corris Ann* and **Windward*; 12 Feb: **Jacob Bell*; 6 Mar: **Star of Peace*; 13 Mar: **Aldebaran*; 28 Mar: *Lapwing*; 30 Mar: **M.J. Colcord*; 17 Apr: **Commonwealth*; 23 Apr: **Henrietta*; 24 Apr: **Oneida*; 6 May: *Clarence*; 13 May: **Crown Point*; 6 Jun: **Southern Cross*; 14 Jun: *Red Gauntlet*; 16 Jun: **B.F. Hoxie*; 27 Jun: *Varnum H. Hill*; 7 Jul: *Sunrise*; 8 Jul: **Wm. B. Nash* and **Rienzi*; 6 Aug: *Francis B. Cutting*; 21 Aug: **Anglo-Saxon*.
29 Mar 1864: **Avon*; 18 May: **George Latimer*; 17 Jun: **W.C. Clark*; 1 Jul: **Harriet Stevens*; 8 Jul: **Golconda*; 9 Jul: **Margaret Y. Davis* and **Greenland*; 10 Jul: **Gen. Berry* and **Zelinda*; str **Electric Spark*; 26 Sep: **Mondamin*.

Name	Bldr	Laid down	L	Comm
Georgia (ex-*Japan*, ex-*Virginian*)	W. Denny	1862	9 Jan 1863	9 Apr 1863

Tonnage:	690 tons, 1,150 tons D, 648 GRT
Dimensions:	212′ × 27′ × 13′9″ or 206.2′ × 27.2′ × 14.7′
Machinery:	1 screw, 2 steeple condensing engines (49″ × 3′9″); IHP 900 = 13 knots
Complement:	75
Armament:	2 100-pdr R, 2 24-pdr SB, 1 32-pdr R

NOTES: Iron hull, single funnel, brig rig. Purchased Mar 1863.

The cruiser *Georgia*; possibly pictured after her naval service. She was captured at sea while operating in commercial service. (P.A. Vicary)

SERVICE RECORD: Met steamer *Alar* off Ushant to take on guns and stores, Apr 1863. Commissioned at sea 9 Apr 1863. Captured 9 prizes in Atlantic, 1863. Arrived at Cherbourg 28 Oct 1863 and decommissioned. Sold 1 Jun 1864 at Liverpool as commercial vessel. Taken at sea by USS *Niagara* off Portugal, 15 Aug 1864, and condemned as a prize.
Prizes: 25 Apr 1863: *Dictator*; 8 Jun: *George Griswold*; 12 Jun: *Good Hope*; 14 Jun: *J.W. Seaver*; 25 Jun: *Constitution*; 28 Jun: *City of Bath*; 16 Jul: *Prince of Wales*; 30 Sep: *John Watts*; 9 Sep: *Bold Hunter*.
Later history: Merchant *Georgia* 1865. Sold Canadian 1870. Stranded off Tenant's Harbor, Me., 14 Jan 1875.

Name	Bldr	L
Georgiana	Lawrie	1 Dec 1862

Tonnage:	519 tons
Dimensions:	205′6″ × 25′3″ × 14′9″
Machinery:	1 screw; IHP 120
Complement:	140
Armament:	(U)

NOTES: Brig rig, iron hull.
SERVICE RECORD: Sailed to Charleston for outfitting as a cruiser. Damaged by gunfire of USS *Wissahickon*, beached and abandoned on fire off Charleston, 19 Mar 1863.

The cruiser *Nashville*, the first Confederate warship to arrive in European waters, entering Southampton harbor on November 21, 1861.

The cruiser *Shenandoah*, hauled out at Melbourne, Australia, in February 1865, with the Confederate flag flying. The funnel can be seen abaft the mainmast, and her rudder and screw are visible. (U.S. Naval Historical Center) (Martin Holbrook Collection)

Name	Bldr	L	Acquired	Comm
Nashville	Collyer (Novelty)	22 Sep 1853	1861	Oct 1861

Tonnage:	1,221 tons
Dimensions:	215′6″ × 34′6″ × d21′9″
Machinery:	Side wheels, 1 side-lever engine (85″ × 8′), 2 boilers.
Armament:	2 12-pdr

NOTES: Brig-rigged passenger steamer, seized at Charleston and fitted as a cruiser 1861.
SERVICE RECORD: Cruised to British waters Nov 1861–Feb 1862, taking two prizes. Escaped from Beaufort, NC, 17 Mar 1862. Sold as a blockade runner 1862, renamed *Thomas L. Wragg*. Commissioned 5 Nov 1862 as privateer **Rattlesnake**. Destroyed in Ogeechee River by USS *Montauk*, 28 Feb 1863.
Prizes: 19 Nov 1861: *Harvey Birch. 26 Feb 1862: *Robert Gilfillan.

Name	Bldr	L	Acquired
Rappahannock (ex-HMS *Victor*)	Mare; Blackwall	24 Nov 1855	Nov 1863

Tonnage:	1,042 tons
Dimensions:	201′ (bp) × 30′3″ × 14′6″
Machinery:	1 screw, 2 reciprocating engines, NHP 350; IHP 1000 = 11 knots
Complement:	100
Armament:	2 9″ R

NOTES: Former British corvette, purchased Nov 1863 in Great Britain as a replacement for *Georgia*. Three-masted schooner rig, 2 funnels. Cover name *Scylla*. Escaped to Calais for repairs, but was detained there by the French government in Feb 1864. Decommissioned in Aug 1864.

The *Sumter*, the first Confederate raider, which took 18 prizes during 1861–62. She was used as the blockade runner *Gibraltar* before dropping out of sight. (Henry E. Huntington Library)

Name	Bldr	L	Comm
Shenandoah (ex-*Sea King*)	Stephen	17 Aug 1863	19 Oct 1864

Tonnage:	1,160 tons, 1,018 GRT
Dimensions:	230' × 32' × 20'6" (220' × 36' × 20')
Machinery:	1 screw, direct-acting engines (33" × 4'), 2 boilers; 9 knots
Complement:	73
Armament:	4 8" SB, 2 32-pdr R, 2 12-pdr SB

NOTES: Composite auxiliary screw steamship, first in the world, designed for transporting troops to East India. Purchased Sep 1864, commissioned at sea. Took 38 prizes mostly after the close of hostilities in the Bering Sea.

SERVICE RECORD: Commissioned off Funchal after meeting steamer *Laurel* and receiving crew, guns, and ammunition, Oct 1864. Captured six prizes in S. Atlantic 1864. Arrived Melbourne 25 Jan 1865. Cruised whaling grounds in Pacific and off Alaska, 1865; took 21 prizes. Learned of war's end in Aug 1865 and surrendered at Liverpool, 6 Nov 1865.

Prizes: 30 Oct 1864: *Alina; 5 Nov: *Charter Oak; 8 Nov: *D. Godfrey; 10 Nov: *Susan; 12 Nov: Kate Prince, Adelaide; 13 Nov: *Lizzie M. Stacey; 4 Dec: *Edward; 29 Dec: *Delphine.

1 Apr 1865: *Edward Cary, *Harvest, *Hector, and *Pearl; 27 May: *Abigail; 22 Jun: *Euphrates, *William Thompson, Milo; 24 Jun: *Jerah Swift and *Sophia Thornton; *Susan Abigail; 23 Jun: *General Williams; 26 Jun: *Catharine, Gen. Pike, *William C. Nye, *Gipsey, *Isabella, and *Nimrod; 28 Jun: *Brunswick, *Congress, *Covington, *Favorite,

*Hillman, *Isaac Howland, James Murray, *Martha, *Nassau, Nile, and *Waverly.

Later history: Sold 1866 to Sultan of Zanzibar, renamed *El Majidi*. Damaged in hurricane off Zanzibar, 15 Apr 1872. (or/and?) Foundered in Indian Ocean en route Zanzibar-Bombay, Sep 1872.

Name	Bldr	L	Comm
Sumter (ex-*Habana*)	Vaughn & Lynn (Merrick?)	12 Dec 1857	Jun 1861

Tonnage:	437 tons
Dimensions:	184' × 30' × 12'
Machinery:	1 screw, 1 vertical direct-acting engine (50" × 2'8"); 10 knots
Complement:	(U)
Armament:	1 8", 4 32-pdr

NOTES: Bark rig. Purchased Apr 1861 and converted to a cruiser at New Orleans. Operated out of New Orleans before the war.

SERVICE RECORD: Cruised West Indies, captured 18 prizes 1861–62. Laid up and disarmed at Gibraltar Jan 1862. Sold Dec 1862.

Prizes: 3 Jul 1861: *Golden Rocket; 4 Jul: Cuba and Machias; 5 Jul: Albert Adams and Ben Dunning; 6 Jul: Lewis Kilham, Naiad, and West Wind; 25 Jul: Abbie Bradford; 27 Jul: Joseph Maxwell; 25 Sep: *Joseph Park; 27 Oct: *Daniel Trowbridge; 25 Nov: Montmorency; 26 Nov: *Arcade; 3 Dec: *Vigilant; 8 Dec: *Ebenezer Dodge. 18 Jan 1862: Investigator and *Neapolitan.

Later history: Blockade runner *Gibraltar* 1863. FFU.

The raider *Tallahassee* in Halifax harbor, August 18, 1864. She was built as an English Channel steamer. Notice the gun aft and the two funnels. (Maritime Museum of the Atlantic, Halifax, NS)

Name	Bldr	Built	Comm
Tallahassee (ex-*Atalanta*)	Dudgeon	1863	Jul 1864

Tonnage:	546 tons D
Dimensions:	250′ × 23′6″ × 13′4″
Machinery:	2 screws, 2 engines (34″ × 1′9″), IHP 1220; 14 knots
Complement:	120
Armament:	1 84-pdr, 2 24-pdr, 2 32-pdr

NOTES: Fast cross-Channel steamer *Atalanta* used as a blockade runner, purchased 1864.
SERVICE RECORD: Sailed from Wilmington, NC, cruised in N. Atlantic Aug 1864. Renamed **Olustee**. Damaged while running Federal blockade, 29 Oct 1864. Disarmed and renamed **Chameleon**, again ran blockade 24 Dec 1864. Unable to return to Confederate port, sailed to Liverpool, Apr 1865, and sold.
Prizes: 11 Aug 1864: **A. Richards*, **Bay State*, **Carrie Estelle*, *Carroll*, **James Funk*, **Sarah A. Boyce*, and **William Bell*; 12 Aug: **Adriatic*, **Atlantic*, *Billow*, *Goodspeed*, **Suliote*, and **Spokane*; 13 Aug: **Lamont Dupont*, **Glenavon*; 14 Aug: **James Littlefield* and *J.H. Hoven*; 15 Aug: **Floral Wreath*, **Etta Caroline*, **Howard*, **Mary A. Howes*, and *Sarah B. Harris*; 16 Aug: **P.C. Alexander*, **Leopard*, **Magnolia*, **Pearl*, **Sarah Louise*; 17 Aug: **Josiah Achom*, *Neva*, and **North America*; 20 Aug: *Rowan*; 23 Aug: *Restless*.
1 Nov 1864: (as *Olustee*) **Empress Theresa*; 3 Nov: **A.J. Bird*, **Arcole*, **E.F. Lewis*, **T.D. Wagner*, and **Vapor*.
Later history: Merchant *Amelia* (British) 1866. Renamed *Haya Maru* (British or German flag) 1867. Struck a rock and sank between Kobe and Yokohama, 17 Jun 1869.

Name	Bldr	L	Comm
Texas (ex-*Pampero*)	Thomson	29 Oct 1863	never

Tonnage:	2,090 tons D, 1,000 tons
Dimensions:	230′ × 32′ × 20′ or 220′6″ × 33′2″ × 19′8″
Machinery:	1 screw; NHP 330 = 13 knots
Armament:	never armed

NOTES: Composite hull, lifting screw, bark rig. Never sailed for CSN. Cover name *Canton*. Seized by British government 10 Dec 1863.
Later history: Sold to Chile 1866. Seized at sea 22 Aug 1866 by Spanish frigate *Gerona* and commissioned in Spanish Navy as *Tornado*. Captured filibuster *Virginius* 1873. Stricken 1896, BU after 1939.

Name	Bldr	L
Ajax	Denny	15 Dec 1864
Hercules	Denny	29 Dec 1864

Tonnage:	515 tons
Dimensions:	176′ × 25′ × 7′6″
Machinery:	2 screws, 2 horizontal back-acting engines (28″ × 1′6″); IHP 525 = 12 knots
Armament:	1 9″ R, 1 8″ R (intended)

NOTES: Completed too late for CSN service. Were to be converted at Wilmington, NC. Brigantine rig.

SERVICE RECORDS:

Ajax—Was to be named **Olustee**. Sailed for Wilmington, NC, 12 Jan 1865, but returned to Britain.

Hercules—Was to be named **Vicksburg**.

   Later history: FFU.

Name	Bldr	Built
Adventure	Denny	1865
Enterprise	Denny	1865

Tonnage:	972 tons, 1,600 tons D
Dimensions:	250′ × 30′ × 12′
Machinery:	2 screws, 2 horizontal direct-acting engines (42″ × 1′9″); IHP 1175 = 14 knots
Armament:	(U)

NOTES: Iron hulls. Bark rig.

The Spanish cruiser *Tornado*, built in Britain as *Pampero*, was intended to become the Confederate cruiser *Texas*. It was this ship that arrested the filibuster *Virginius* in 1873, precipitating the affair that almost led to war between Spain and the United States.

The *Hercules* was built in Britain for Confederate service and completed in 1865, but her later disposition is unknown. She and her sister *Ajax* were to be armed on arrival in America. (Henry E. Huntington Library)

SERVICE RECORDS:

Adventure—Was to be named **Waccamaw**. Cover name *Tientsin*.

Enterprise—Was to be named **Black Warrior**. Cover name *Yangtze*.

Later history:

Adventure: completed as *Amazonas*. Sold to Argentina 1866 as gunboat, renamed *General Brown*. Renamed *Chacabuco* 1884, school ship. Hulked 1893. BU 1910.

Enterprise: completed as *Brasil*. Sold to Brazil 1866 as transport, probably renamed *Leopoldina*. Decomm 1877.

Name	Bldr	L
Louisiana (ex-*Osacca*)	Arman (Mazeline)	May 1864
Mississippi (ex-*Yeddo*)	Arman (Mazeline)	1864
Texas (ex-*San Francisco*)	Jollet (Mazeline)	1864
Georgia (ex-*Shanghai*)	Dubigeon (Mazeline)	1864

Tonnage:	1,827 tons D
Dimensions:	243′ × 35′6″ × 18′ (*Union*) 267′ (oa) 246′8″ (bp) × 36′6″ × 18′ (Prussian ships)
Machinery:	1 screw, single expansion engine, 4 boilers; IHP 1,300 = 13.5 knots.
Complement:	230
Armament:	14 30-pdr R

NOTES: Ordered by Bulloch in Apr 1863, but embargoed by French government Feb 1864. Later sold by builders to Prussian and Peruvian navies.

Later history:

Louisiana—Prussian *Victoria*, May 1864. BU 1892.

Mississippi—Prussian *Augusta*, May 1864. Foundered with all hands in hurricane in Gulf of Aden, 2 Jun 1885.

Texas—Peruvian *Union*. Scuttled to prevent capture by Chilean forces at Callao, Jan 1881.

Georgia—Peruvian *America*. Wrecked in tidal wave at Arica, 13 Aug 1868.

The Peruvian corvette *Union*, built in France for the Confederate Navy. She was launched as *San Francisco* and was to be named *Texas*. (Martin Holbrook Collection) (U.S. Naval Historical Center)

SAILING VESSELS

Name	Bldr	Built	Comm
Clarence (ex-*Coquette*)	(Baltimore)	1857	6 May 1863

Tonnage:	253 tons B
Dimensions:	114′ × 24′ × 11′
Rig:	Brig
Armament:	1 12-pdr H

NOTES: Captured at sea 6 May 1863 by CSS *Florida* en route to Baltimore and armed as a raider.

SERVICE RECORD: Burned at sea 12 Jun 1863, crew transferred to prize *Tacony*.

Prizes: 6 Jun 1863: *Whistling Wind*; 7 Jun: *Alfred H. Partridge*; 9 Jun: *Mary Alvina*; 12 Jun: *Kate Stewart*, *Mary Schindler*, and *Tacony*.

Name	Bldr	Built	Acquired
Tacony	(Newcastle, Del.)	1856	12 Jun 1863

Tonnage:	296 tons B
Dimensions:	(U)
Rig:	Bark
Armament:	1 12-pdr H

NOTES: Captured at sea 12 Jun 1863 by CSS *Clarence*, whose commander transferred his crew to this vessel. Also called *Florida No. 2*.

SERVICE RECORD: Captured 15 vessels while cruising off New England coast. Burned to prevent capture, 25 Jun 1863; crew transferred to prize *Archer*.

Prizes: 12 Jun 1863: *Arabella*; 14 Jun: *Umpire*; 20 Jun: *Isaac Webb* and *L.A. Micawber*; 21 Jun: *Byzantium*, *Goodspeed*; 22 Jun: *Elizabeth Ann*, *Florence*, *Marengo*, *Ripple*, and *Rufus Choate*; 23 Jun: *Ada* and *Wanderer*; 24 Jun: *Archer* and *Shatemac*.

Name	Bldr	Built	Acquired
Tuscaloosa (ex-*Conrad*)	(Philadelphia)	1850	20 Jun 1863

Tonnage:	500 tons
Dimensions:	(U)
Rig:	Bark
Armament:	3 12-pdr

NOTES: American bark *Conrad* captured off Brazil by CSS *Alabama*, 20 Jun 1863 and commissioned at sea as a cruiser.

SERVICE RECORD: Cruised in S. Atlantic 1863, taking several prizes. Seized at Capetown by British authorities 26 Dec 1863 as an uncondemned prize.

Prizes: 31 Jul 1863: *Santee*; 13 Sep: *Living Age*.

GUNBOATS

Name	Bldr	Built	Comm
Chattahoochee	Saffold	1862	Feb 1863
Macon (ex-*Ogeechee*—Jun 1864)	Willink	1863	3 Aug 1864
Peedee	Means	1862	20 Apr 1864

Tonnage:	(U)
Dimensions:	130′ (bp) × 30′ × 7′3″, d10′ or (150′ × 25′ × 8′)
Machinery:	2 screws, 2 horizontal direct-acting LP engines (28″ × 1′8″); 12 knots
Complement:	120
Armament:	4 32-pdr SB, 1 32-pdr R, 1 9″ SB

NOTES: Designed by J.L. Porter, Three-masted schooner rig.

SERVICE RECORDS:

Chattahoochee—Georgia coast. Sunk by boiler explosion at Blountstown, Fla., 27 May 1863. Raised and repaired at Columbus, Ga. Destroyed to prevent capture in Apalachicola River, Fla., Dec 1864.

Macon—Defense of Savannah. Surrendered at Augusta, Ga., May 1865.

Peedee—Destroyed to prevent capture in the Peedee River above Georgetown, SC, 18 Feb 1865.

Name	Bldr	L	Comm
Hampton	Norfolk	1862	
Nansemond	Norfolk	1862	May 1862
Norfolk	Norfolk	never	
Portsmouth	Norfolk	never	

Tonnage:	166 tons
Dimensions:	106′ × 21′ × 5′
Machinery:	2 screws
Armament:	1 9″ SB, 1 32-pdr

NOTES: "Maury gunboats" designed by Capt. Matthew Fontaine Maury. One hundred were planned. Others, building at Pensacola, Edwards Ferry, and Elizabeth City, NC, were destroyed before naming or completion.

SERVICE RECORDS:

Hampton—James River. Action at Trent's Reach, 21 Jun 1864. Action at Dutch Gap, 13 Aug 1864. Action against Ft. Harrison, 29 Sep–1 Oct 1864. Engagement at Chapin's Bluff, 22 Oct 1864. Burned to prevent capture on evacuation of Richmond, 3 Apr 1865.

Nansemond—James River. Action at Trent's Reach, 21 Jun 1864. Action at Dutch Gap, 13 Aug 1864. Action against Ft. Harrison, 29 Sep–1 Oct 1864. Burned to prevent capture on evacuation of Richmond, 3 Apr 1865.

Norfolk—Burned on the ways to prevent capture, 10 May 1862.

Portsmouth—Burned on the ways to prevent capture, 10 May 1862.

Name	Bldr	Built
Gaines	Bassett	1862
Morgan	Bassett	1862

Tonnage:	863 tons
Dimensions:	202′ × 38′ × 7′3″
Machinery:	Side wheels, 2 non-condensing engines (23″ × 7′); 10 knots
Armament:	1 7″ R, 1 6″ R, 2 32-pdr R, 2 32-pdr SB

SERVICE RECORDS:

Gaines—Run aground to prevent capture following Battle of Mobile Bay, 5 Aug 1864.

Morgan—Battle of Mobile Bay, 5 Aug 1864. Damaged in engagement near Blakely, Apr 1865. Surrendered, 4 May 1865. Sold Dec 1865. *Later history*: Merchant *Morgan* 1865. Lost, cause unknown, 10 Oct 1866.

Name	Bldr	L	Comm
Bienville	Hughes	Feb 1862	never
Carondelet	Hughes	Jan 1862	16 Mar 1862

Tonnage:	(U)
Dimensions:	(U)
Machinery:	Side wheels
Armament:	5 42-pdr

SERVICE RECORDS:

Bienville—Destroyed to prevent capture prior to completion in Lake Pontchartrain, 21 Apr 1862.

Carondelet—Engagement at Pass Christian, Miss., 4 Apr 1862. Destroyed to prevent capture in Lake Pontchartrain, 21 Apr 1862.

SPAR TORPEDO BOATS

Name	Bldr	Built
Hornet	Richmond	1864
Scorpion	Richmond	1864
Squib	Richmond	1864
Wasp	Richmond	1864

Tonnage:	(U)
Dimensions:	46′ × 6′3″ × U
Machinery:	1 shaft, condensing engine, 1 boiler
Armament:	1 18′ spar torpedo

NOTES: Wooden hulls built at Richmond late 1864.

SERVICE RECORDS:

Hornet—Sank after collision with flag-of-truce steamer *Allison* in James River, 26 Jan 1865.

Scorpion—Damaged by ammunition explosion near Trent's Reach, Va., 24 Jan 1865. Later captured by Federal forces, or burned in James River, the same day.

Squib—Attacked USS *Minnesota* off Newport News, 7 Apr 1864. FFU.

Wasp—Served in James River 1864–65. FFU.

Name	Bldr	Built
David	(Charleston)	1863

Dimensions:	50′ × 6′ × 5′.
Complement:	4; 1 spar torpedo.

SERVICE RECORD: Attacked USS *New Ironsides* off Charleston, 5 Oct 1863. Attacked USS *Memphis* in North Edisto River, 6 Mar, and USS *Wabash* off Charleston, 18 Apr 1864. FFU.

Name	Bldr	Built
Midge	(Charleston)	1864

Dimensions:	30′ × 12′

NOTES: Similar to *David*.

Later history: Taken to Brooklyn NYd and put on display Jun 1865. Sold 4 May 1877 and BU.

Torpedo boat *Midge* on display at Brooklyn Navy Yard about 1870. Notice the long spar torpedo on the bow and tall smokepipe.

Another view of the torpedo boat *Midge* showing aft quarters and screw. Piles of cannon balls can be seen behind at right.

Name	Bldr	Built
Torch	(Charleston)	1863

Tonnage:	(U)
Dimensions:	(U)
Machinery:	Screw
Armament:	Triple spar-torpedo

NOTES: Ironclad. Not fully completed because of lack of armor.
SERVICE RECORD: Defense of Charleston. Attacked USS *New Ironsides* off Charleston, 10 Aug 1863. Immobilized thereafter.

Several other *David* types were reported built or under construction at various places including Shreveport and Houston. In addition:

Name	Bldr	Built
St. Patrick	(Selma, Ala.)	1864

Dimensions:	30′ × (U)
Complement:	6

NOTES: Built by J.P. Halligan.
SERVICE RECORD: Attacked USS *Octorara* off Mobile, 28 Jan 1865. FFU.

Name	Bldr
No. 1–5, 7–8	(Charleston)

Dimensions:	50′ × 5′6″

NOTES: Screw propulsion. Built at Charleston 1864–65. Captured 1865.

Name	Bldr
No. 6	(Charleston)

Dimensions:	160′ × 11′7″

SUBMARINE TORPEDO BOATS

Name	Bldr	Comm
Pioneer	(New Orleans)	1862

Dimensions: 34′ × 4′ × 4′
Complement: 2

NOTE: Designed by J.R. McClintock.
SERVICE RECORD: Commissioned as privateer 12 Mar 1862. Sunk to prevent capture in Bayou St. John 1862. Now at Louisiana State Museum.

Name	Bldr	Comm
Pioneer II	Park & Lyons, Mobile	1863

Dimensions: 36′ × 3′ × d4′
Complement: 5

NOTE: Designed by J.R. McClintock and H.L. Hunley.
SERVICE RECORD: Swamped while attempting to attack Federal ships off Mobile, 14 Feb 1863.

Name	Bldr	Comm
H.L. Hunley	Park & Lyons, Mobile	spring 1863

Dimensions: 40′ × 3′6″ × d4′
Complement: 9

NOTE: Designed by H.L. Hunley.
SERVICE RECORD: Taken by rail to Charleston Aug 1863. Foundered at her dock 29 Aug 1863. Raised and recommissioned. Again foundered 15 Oct 1863 with all 9 lost; again raised. Sank USS *Housatonic* off Charleston and was lost in the attempt, 17 Feb 1864.

BLOCKADE RUNNERS

General note: These are believed to be Confederate government-owned ships.

Name	Bldr	L
Bat	Jones Quiggin (Watt)	21 Jun 1864
Deer	W.H. Potter & Co.	31 Aug 1864
Owl	Jones Quiggin	21 Jun 1864
Stag	Bowdler Chaffer & Co	1 Aug 1864

Tonnage: 771 tons B
Dimensions: 250′ (oa) 230′ × 26′ × 7′6″
Machinery: Side wheels, 2 vertical oscillating engines (52″ × 4′), 2 boilers; HP 180 = 16 knots

NOTES: Schooner rig, two funnels, steel hull. Government-owned British-register ships.

SERVICE RECORDS:
Bat—Captured by USS *Montgomery* in Cape Fear River on first voyage, 10 Oct 1864. Commissioned as USS *Bat*.
Deer—Captured by USS *Canonicus*, *Catskill*, and *Monadnock* off Charleston, on second voyage, 18 Feb 1865.
  Later history: Merchant *Palmyra* 1865. Sold foreign (Argentina) 1869. FFU.
Owl—Ran blockade several times from Sep 1864 into Wilmington, to May 1865 to Galveston. Sold in Britain 1865.
  Later history: Merchant *Owl* 1865.
Stag—Ran blockade several times. Captured by USS *Monticello* off Wilmington, NC, 20 Jan 1865. Sold 1865.
  Later history: Merchant *Zenobia* 1865. Sold foreign (Argentina) 1867. FFU.

Name	Bldr	L
Curlew	Jones Quiggin (Forrester)	15 Feb 1865
Plover	Jones Quiggin (Forrester)	15 Feb 1865
Snipe	Jones Quiggin (Watt)	15 Feb 1865
Widgeon	Jones Quiggin (Watt)	15 Feb 1865

Tonnage: 645 tons, 409 GRT
Dimensions: 225′ × 24′ × 6′
Machinery: Side wheels, HP 160 = 12 knots

NOTES: Delivered too late for service.

Name	Bldr	L
Albatross	Laird	Mar 1865
Penguin	Laird	Mar 1865

Tonnage: 1,063 tons, 659 GRT
Dimensions: 240′ × 30′ × 10′ or 246′8″ × 30′ × 13′
Machinery: Side wheels, 2 oscillating engines; NHP 260 = 12 knots

Name	Bldr	L
Rosina	Jones Quiggin	15 Oct 1864
Ruby	Jones Quiggin	1865

Tonnage: 1,391 tons, 900 GRT
Dimensions: 270′ (oa) 261′ × 33′ × 9′
Machinery: Side wheels, HP 300 = 14 knots

NOTES: Steel hulls. *Ruby* not launched at the end of the war.
Later history:
Rosina—Sold to Turkey 1865.
Ruby—Sold to Turkey 1865.

Name	Bldr	L
Lark	Laird	Oct 1864
Wren	Laird	Nov 1864

Tonnage: 390 tons GRT
Dimensions: 211′2″ (*Wren*), 210′8″ (*Lark*) × 23′2″ × 6′

Machinery: Side wheels, 2 oscillating engines, 2 boilers; HP 150, 12 knots

NOTES: Steel hull, Two funnels.
Later history:
Lark—Merchant *Port Said* and lengthened 1866. Cut in two parts, 1872, which were renamed *Hankow* and *Lilian*. RR 1890.
Wren—Surrendered at Key West, 21 Jun 1865. Merchant *Tartar* 1865. Sold foreign 1868.

Name	Bldr	L
Condor	Elder	Jul 1864
Falcon	Elder	26 May 1864
Flamingo	Elder	26 May 1864
Ptarmigan	Elder	Jun 1864

Tonnage: 284 tons (446 tons)
Dimensions: 270′ × 24′ × 7′
Machinery: Side wheels; 15 knots
Complement: 50

NOTES: Long, low hulls with straight stem, three tall raked funnels, single mast.
SERVICE RECORDS:
Condor—Went aground at entrance to Wilmington, NC, and wrecked on maiden voyage, 1 Oct 1864. Captained by A.C. Hobart-Hampden, RN, VC. The famous courier and spy Rosa Greenhow was among those lost.
Falcon—Ran blockade several times 1864.
Flamingo—Ran the blockade several times 1864–65. Possibly wrecked off Charleston 1865.
Ptarmigan—Ran blockade several times 1864–65. Possibly renamed **Evelyn**.

Name	Bldr	Built
Arizona	Harlan	1859

For details see USS *Arizona*.

NOTES: Taken for public service at New Orleans 1862.
SERVICE RECORD: Ran blockade several times, renamed **Caroline** Oct 1862. Captured by USS *Montgomery* off Mobile, 29 Oct 1862. Commissioned in USN as *Arizona*.

Name	Bldr	Built
Atlantic	Collyer	1852

Tonnage: 623 tons
Dimensions: 217′ × 27′6″ × d10′6″
Machinery: Side wheels. Vertical beam engines (40″ × 10′).

NOTES: Seized at New Orleans, 14 January 1862. Wooden hull.
SERVICE RECORD: Ran blockade several times under British flag, renamed **Elizabeth** 1863. Ran aground and was burned to prevent capture in Cape Fear River, 24 Sep 1863.

Name	Bldr	Built
Austin	Harlan	1860

For details see USS *Donegal*.

NOTES: Seized at New Orleans, Jan 1862.
SERVICE RECORD: Ran blockade several times. Renamed **Donegal**. Captured by USS *Metacomet* off Mobile Bay, 6 Jun 1864. Commissioned in USN as *Donegal*.

Name	Bldr	Built	Comm
Beauregard (ex-*Priscilla C. Ferguson*)	(Charleston)	1850	14 Oct 1861

For details see USS *Beauregard*.

NOTES: Privateer brig (or schooner).
SERVICE RECORD: Captured by USS *William G. Anderson* in Bahama Channel, 12 Nov 1861, one week after sailing. Comm in USN as *Beauregard*.

Name	Bldr	L
Bahama	Pearse (Fossick)	24 Jan 1862
Bermuda	Pearse	9 Jul 1861

Tonnage: *Bahama*: 888 tons GRT. *Bermuda*: 697 GRT, 1,003 n/r.
Dimensions: *Bahama*: 226′ × 29′2″ × 19′
              Bermuda: 211′ × 30′3″ × 16′
Machinery: 1 screw, 2 vertical condensing direct-acting engines (45″ × 2′6″), 135 HP; 11 knots

NOTES: Near sisters. Iron hull, brig rig. Three masts, 1 funnel.
SERVICE RECORDS:
Bahama—Rendezvous with CSS *Florida* in Bahamas, Apr 1862, with armaments. Rendezvous with *Alabama* Aug 1862 at sea near Madeira, with guns, stores, and crewmembers.
    Later history: Merchant *Bahama* 1864. Sold in Japan and renamed *Meiko Maru* 1864, *Bahama* 1868, *Meiko Maru* 1870; engines removed and renamed *Sumanoura Maru* 1877 (Japanese bark). Sunk in collision with *Yamashiro Maru* 1884.
Bermuda—Blockade runner. Captured by USS *Mercedita* NE of Abaco Island, Bahamas, 27 Apr 1862. Commissioned as USS *Bermuda*.

Name	Bldr	L
Colonel Lamb	Jones Quiggin (Victoria)	1864
Hope	Jones Quiggin	1864

Tonnage: 1,788 tons B, 1,132 GRT
Dimensions: 281′6″ (oa) 279′6″ (bp) × 36′ × 8′9″ (*Lamb*), 281′6″ (bp) × 35′ × 8′ (*Hope*).
Machinery: Side wheels, 2 oscillating engines (72″ × 6′), 4 boilers, NHP 350 = 16 knots

NOTES: Near sisters, steel hulls. *Colonel Lamb* was the largest steel ship built to date.

The *Colonel Lamb* was one of the most famous blockade runners. She survived the war untaken.

SERVICE RECORDS: *Colonel Lamb*—Ran blockade several times.
Later history: Merchant *Colonel Lamb* 1865. Blew up while loading munitions for Brazil at Liverpool 1866.
Hope—Captured by USS *Eolus* in Cape Fear River, 22 Oct 1864.
Later history: Merchant *Savannah* 1865. Sold 1866 to Spanish Navy, as paddle frigate, renamed *Churruca*. Stricken 1880, BU 1885.

Name	Bldr	L
Cornubia	Harvey	27 Feb 1858
For details see USS *Cornubia*.		

NOTES: Cornwall packet steamer.

SERVICE RECORD: Ran blockade 22 times 1861–63. Renamed **Lady Davis**, Jun 1863. Captured by USS *James Adger* and *Niphon* at New Inlet, NC, 8 Nov 1863. Commissioned in USN as *Cornubia*.

Name	Bldr	L
Don	Dudgeon	1863
For details see USS *Don*.		

NOTES: Owned by North Carolina.
SERVICE RECORD: Captured by USS *Pequot* off Wilmington, NC, 4 Mar 1864. Commissioned in USN as *Don*.

A model of the Confederate blockade runner *Hope*. She later became the Spanish frigate *Churruca*. (Liverpool Museum)

Name	Bldr	L
Granite City (ex-USS *Granite City*) For details see USS *Granite City*.	A. Denny	11 Nov 1862

NOTES: Captured at Calcasieu Pass, La., 28 Apr 1864.
SERVICE RECORD: Possibly renamed *Three Marys*. Run ashore off Calcasieu River by USS *Penguin* and destroyed, 21 Jan 1865.

Name	Bldr	L	Acquired
Greyhound	Kirkpatrick (Caird)	19 Oct 1863	1863

Tonnage:	290 tons net; 583 tons n/r
Dimensions:	201.4′ × 22.7′ × 13′
Machinery:	1 screw, 2 oscillating engines

NOTES: Three masts.
SERVICE RECORD: Captured by USS *Connecticut* off Wilmington, NC, 10 May 1864.
Later history: Merchant *Greyhound* 1864. Lost by stranding at Beaver Harbour, NS, 14 Nov 1865.

A ship of this name was reported sunk by a torpedo (mine) near Bermuda Hundred, Va., while serving as floating headquarters of General Ben Butler, but this was undoubtedly a different ship.

Name
Hansa

Tonnage:	257 tons
Dimensions:	(U)
Machinery:	Side wheels; 12 knots

NOTES: Owned by State of North Carolina. Two funnels.
Later history: Lengthened 1864. FFU.

Name	Bldr	L
Harriet Pinckney	Richardson; Middlesboro	Jul 1862

Tonnage:	715 tons GRT
Dimensions:	191.3′ × 28.9′ × d17.6′
Machinery:	1 shaft

NOTES: Brig rig. Iron hull.
Later history: FFU.

Name	Bldr	Built
Juno	G.K. Strothert, Bristol	1853

Tonnage:	298 tons GRT

Dimensions: 163'2" × 19'7" × 11'4"
Machinery: Side wheels, 2 engines; 13.5 knots
Complement: 50

SERVICE RECORD: Ran blockade into Charleston May 1863. Served at Charleston as despatch and picket boat. Sank launch from USS *Wabash* Aug 1863. Returned to blockade running 1863. Captured by USS *Connecticut* off Wilmington, NC, 22 Sep 1864.
Later history: Merchant *Dakotah* 1864. Sold foreign 1867.

Name	Bldr	Built
Laurel	Inglis	1863

Tonnage: 400 tons GRT
Dimensions: 185' × 25'2" × 12'2"
Machinery: Side wheels; HP 140 = 13 knots

NOTES: Former Liverpool packet purchased 1864.
SERVICE RECORD: Armed CSS *Shenandoah* at Funchal, Oct 1864. Ran blockade once then sold 1864.
Later history: Merchant *Confederate States* Dec 1864. Lengthened (207'), converted to screw 1869. Renamed *Walter Stanhope*, later *Niobe*.

Name	Bldr	Built
Lynx	Jones Quiggin	1864

Tonnage: 372 tons GRT
Dimensions: 219' × 21' × d12'
Machinery: Side wheels; HP 150 = 12 knots

NOTES: Two funnels and 2 masts, steel hull.
SERVICE RECORD: Damaged by gunfire of USS *Howquah* and forced aground 6 miles below Ft. Fisher when leaving Wilmington, NC, 25 Sep 1864.

Name	Bldr	L
Magnolia	Simonson (Allaire)	22 Aug 1854
For details see USS *Magnolia*.		

NOTES: Seized at New Orleans, January 1862.
SERVICE RECORD: Captured by USS *Brooklyn* and *South Carolina* off Pass à l'Outre, La., 19 Feb 1862. Commissioned in USN as *Magnolia*.

Name	Bldr	Built
Matagorda (ex-*Alice*)	Harlan	1858

Tonnage: 616 tons, 1,250 GRT
Dimensions: 220' × 30'
Machinery: Side wheels, beam engine (44" × 11')

NOTES: Seized at New Orleans, Jan 1862.
SERVICE RECORD: Ran blockade several times. Captured 75 miles off Cape San Antonio, Cuba, by USS *Magnolia*, 10 Sep 1864.
Later history: Merchant *Matagorda*, 1864. RR 1871.

Name	Bldr	L
Merrimac	(U)	Sep 1862
For details see USS *Merrimac*.		

SERVICE RECORD: Ran blockade several times. Captured by USS *Iroquois* off Cape Fear, 24 Jul 1863. Commissioned in USN as *Merrimac*.

Name	Bldr	Built
Phantom	Fawcett Preston (bldr)	1862

Tonnage: 266 tons, 322 tons gross
Dimensions: 192'9" (bp) × 22' × 8'6"
Machinery: 1 screw; HP 170 = 14 knots
Complement: 33

SERVICE RECORD: Ran blockade 3 times. Wrecked off Cape Fear while being pursued by USS *Connecticut*, 23 Sep 1863.

Name	Bldr	L	Acquired
Robert E. Lee (ex-*Giraffe*)	Thomson	16 May 1860	1862
For details see USS Fort Donelson.			

NOTES: Also known as **R. E. Lee**. Built as an Irish Sea ferry.
SERVICE RECORD: Ran blockade 22 times. Captured by USS *James Adger* and *Iron Age* off Bermuda, 9 Nov 1863. Commissioned in USN as *Fort Donelson*.

Name	Bldr	Built
Theodora (ex-*Gordon*, ex-*Carolina*)	(Greenpoint, NY)	1852

Tonnage: 518 tons B
Dimensions: 175' × (U) × 7'
Machinery: Side wheels, vertical beam engine
Armament: 3 guns

NOTES: Fitted out as privateer *Gordon*, July 1861. Carried Confederate envoys Mason and Slidell to Cuba. (See Trent Affair.)
SERVICE RECORD: Ran blockade many times. Captured by USS *Victoria* and *State of Georgia* off Wilmington, NC, 28 May 1862.

Name	Bldr	Built
Victoria	(Mystic, Ct.)	1859

Tonnage: 487 tons B
Dimensions: (U) × (U) × 8'
Machinery: Side wheels, inclined direct engines

NOTES: Seized at New Orleans January 1862.
SERVICE RECORD: Ran blockade several times 1861–62.
Later history: Merchant *Victoria* 1863. Lost by stranding, Bayou d'Arbonne, La., Jan 1866.

The USS *Fort Donelson* lying off Norfolk, Va., in December 1864. She was a packet on the Glasgow-Belfast service before being purchased for use as the blockade runner *R.E. Lee*.

Name	Bldr	L
William G. Hewes	Harlan (Morgan)	15 Oct 1860
For details see USS *Malvern*.		

Tonnage:	747 tons?

NOTES: Iron hull. Seized at New Orleans, Apr 1861. Name sometimes misspelled "Heines" "Hawes" or "Jewess."
SERVICE RECORD: Ran blockade several times 1861–1863. Renamed **Ella & Annie**, 1863. Captured off New Inlet, NC, by USS *Niphon*, 9 Nov 1863. Commissioned in USN as **Malvern**.

LOUISIANA AREA—MISSISSIPPI RIVER DEFENSE FLEET

Fourteen vessels were purchased at New Orleans and armed by the Confederate War Dept. to defend the Mississippi River. Converted to cottonclad rams, protected by compressed cotton bales, ram of 4″ oak and 1″ iron, they were under command of CSN officers. Former identities of most of these are not known.

Name	Bldr	Built	Comm
Colonel Lovell (ex-*Hercules*)	(Cincinnati)	1845	1861

Tonnage:	521 tons (also 371 tons)
Dimensions:	162′ × 30′10″ × d11′
Machinery:	Side wheels
Armament:	4 8″ guns ?

SERVICE RECORD: Engagement off Ft. Pillow, 10 May 1862. Rammed by USS *Queen of the West* and *Monarch* and sunk off Memphis, 6 Jun 1862.

Name	Bldr	Built	Comm
Defiance	(Cincinnati)	1849	end 1861

Tonnage:	544 tons
Dimensions:	178′ × 29′5″ × d10′11″
Machinery:	Side wheels, HP engines
Armament:	1 32-pdr

SERVICE RECORD: Defense of New Orleans. Burned to prevent capture north of New Orleans, 28 Apr 1862.

Name	Bldr	Built	Comm
General Beauregard (ex-*Ocean*)	(Algiers, La.)	1847	5 Apr 1862

Tonnage:	454 tons
Dimensions:	161.8′ × 30′ × 10′
Machinery:	Side wheels
Armament:	4-8″, 1 42-pdr

NOTES: Converted from towboat at New Orleans.
SERVICE RECORD: Engagement off Ft. Pillow, 10 May 1862. Hit by gunfire, exploded and sank at Battle of Memphis, 6 Jun 1862.

Name	Bldr	Built	Acquired	Comm
General Bragg (ex-*Mexico*)	Westervelt (Morgan)	1850	15 Jan 1862	25 Mar 1862

For details see USS *General Bragg*.

SERVICE RECORD: Damaged by ramming at engagement off Ft. Pillow, 10 May 1862. Captured after running aground at Battle of Memphis, 6 Jun 1862. Commissioned in USN as *General Bragg*. (q.v.)

Name	Acquired	Comm
General Breckinridge	15 Jan 1862	Apr 1862

Tonnage:	(U)
Dimensions:	(U)
Machinery:	Stern wheel
Complement:	35
Armament:	1 24-pdr

SERVICE RECORD: Defense of New Orleans. Burned to prevent capture below New Orleans, 24 Apr 1862.

Name
General Earl Van Dorn

Tonnage:	(U)
Dimensions:	(U)
Machinery:	Side wheels
Armament:	1 32-pdr

SERVICE RECORD: Engagement off Ft. Pillow, 10 May 1862, sank USS *Mound City* by ramming. Engagement of 1 Jun 1862. Only survivor of Confederate force after Battle of Memphis, 6 Jun 1862. Burned to prevent capture at Yazoo City, Miss., 26 Jun 1862.

Name
General Lovell

Tonnage:	(U)
Dimensions:	(U)
Machinery:	Side wheels
Complement:	50
Armament:	1 32-pdr

NOTES: Former Mississippi tug converted to ram.
SERVICE RECORD: Burned to prevent capture below New Orleans, 24 Apr 1862.

Name
General M. Jeff Thompson

Tonnage:	(U)
Dimensions:	(U)
Machinery:	Side wheels
Complement:	(U)
Armament:	(U)

SERVICE RECORD: Engagement off Ft. Pillow, 10 May 1862. Hit by gunfire, ran aground and burned to water's edge, then exploded and sank during Battle of Memphis, 6 Jun 1862.

Name	Bldr	Built	Comm
General Sterling Price (ex-*Laurent Millaudon*)	(Cincinnati, OH)	1856	25 Jan 1862

NOTE: For details see USS *General Price*.
SERVICE RECORD: Damaged by gunfire at engagement off Ft. Pillow, 10 May 1862. Damaged in collision with CSS *General Beauregard* during Battle of Memphis and later sank in shallow water, 6 Jun 1862. Salved and commissioned in USN as *General Price*.

Name	Bldr	Built
General Sumter (ex-*Junius Beebe*)	(Algiers, La.)	1853

NOTES: For details see USS *Sumter*. River towboat converted to cottonclad with 4″ wood and 1″ iron ram. Some sources say *Junius Beebe* became *General Earl van Dorn*.
SERVICE RECORD: Defense of Ft. Pillow, 10 May 1862. Hit by gunfire, ran aground on Arkansas shore during Battle of Memphis, 6 Jun 1862. Refloated and commissioned in USN as *Sumter*.

Name	Bldr	Built
Little Rebel (ex-*R. & J. Watson*)	(Belle Vernon, Pa.)	1859

NOTES: For details see USS *Little Rebel*. Also known as *R.E. & A.N. Watson*.
SERVICE RECORD: Engagement off Ft. Pillow (flag), 10 May 1862. Beached after being damaged at Battle of Memphis, 6 Jun 1862. Commissioned in USN as *Little Rebel*.

Name	Comm
Resolute	31 Mar 1862

Tonnage:	(U)
Dimensions:	(U)
Machinery:	Side wheels
Complement:	40
Armament:	2 32-pdr R, 1 32-pdr SB

SERVICE RECORD: Run ashore by crew and abandoned during engagement at Ft. Jackson, La., 24 Apr, and burned to prevent capture, 26 Apr 1862.

The gunboat *Stonewall Jackson*, one of the Mississippi River Defense Fleet ships that was sunk in the defense of New Orleans.

Name	Comm
Stonewall Jackson	16 Mar 1862

Tonnage:	(U)
Dimensions:	(U)
Machinery:	Side wheels
Complement:	30
Armament:	1 32-pdr or 1 24-pdr SB

SERVICE RECORD: Rammed and sank USS *Varuna* during engagement below New Orleans, then run aground in sinking condition and burned, 24 Apr 1862.

Name	Comm
Warrior	16 Mar 1862

Tonnage:	(U)
Dimensions:	(U)
Machinery:	Side wheels
Complement:	40
Armament:	1 32-pdr

SERVICE RECORD: Damaged by gunfire of USS *Brooklyn*, driven ashore and burned during action below New Orleans, 24 Apr 1862.

GUNBOATS

Name	Bldr	Built	Comm
A.B. Seger	(U)	(U)	1861

Tonnage:	30 tons
Dimensions:	55′ × (U)
Machinery:	Side wheels, 2 locomotive engines
Armament:	2 guns

NOTE: Gunboat and despatch vessel in Berwick Bay.
SERVICE RECORD: Ran aground and was abandoned in Berwick Bay, Atchafalaya River, 1 Nov 1862. Placed in Union service.

Name	Bldr	Built	Comm
Anglo-Norman	(Algiers, La.)	1850	15 Jan 1862

Tonnage:	558 tons
Dimensions:	176′2″ × 29′5″ × 9′
Machinery:	Side wheels
Complement:	35
Armament:	1 32-pdr

NOTES: Towboat seized at New Orleans, Jan 1862.
SERVICE RECORD: Burned at New Orleans, 7 Apr 1862.

Name	Bldr	Built	Comm
Anglo-Saxon	(New York, NY)	1848	15 Jan 1862

Tonnage:	508 tons
Dimensions:	120'3" × 28' × 11'
Machinery:	Side wheels
Armament:	(U)

NOTES: Seized at New Orleans, Jan 1862.
SERVICE RECORD: Defense of New Orleans. Caught fire and drifted downstream in sinking condition at defense of New Orleans forts, 24 Apr 1862. Later U.S. transport.

Name	Bldr	Acquired
Arrow	(U)	Spring 1861

Tonnage:	(U)
Dimensions:	(U)
Machinery:	Screw
Armament:	1 32-pdr

NOTES: Seized 1861 and converted to gunboat.
SERVICE RECORD: Defense of New Orleans. Burned to prevent capture in West Pearl River after capture of New Orleans, 4 Jun 1862.

Name	Bldr	Built
Barataria	(Barataria, La.)	1857

NOTES: For details see USS Barataria. Lytle lists a vessel of this name built at Barataria, La., 1857. Little known about this vessel; believed to have been ironclad.
SERVICE RECORD: Captured at New Orleans by U.S. Army, Apr 1862. Commissioned in USN as Barataria (q.v.).

Name	Bldr	Built
Calhoun	Sneeden	1851

NOTES: For details see USS Calhoun. Built as Cuba, but renamed before completion.
SERVICE RECORD: Commissioned as privateer, captured six prizes, 1861. Attack on Federal sqn at Head of Passes, 12 Oct 1861. Captured by USS Samuel Rotan off South West Pass, La., 23 Jan 1862. Commissioned as USS Calhoun.
Prizes: May 1861: John Adams, Mermaid; 29 May: Panama.

Name	Bldr	Built	Acquired
Diana (ex-USS Diana)	(Brownsville, Pa.)	1858	Apr 1863

Tonnage:	239 tons
Dimensions:	(U)
Machinery:	Side wheels

NOTES: Ironclad, transport, disabled, and captured 28 Mar 1863 at Bayou Teche, La. Previously seized by U.S. 27 Apr 1862.

SERVICE RECORD: Attack on Federal troops at Bayou Teche, La., 11 Apr 1863. Severely damaged by gunfire, and burned to prevent capture at Franklin, La., 12 Apr 1863.

Name	Bldr	Built
Dollie Webb	(Wheeling, Va.)	1859

Tonnage:	139 tons
Dimensions:	125' × 27' × 4.5'
Machinery:	Stern wheel
Armament:	5 guns

NOTES: Probably a converted towboat; little information exists. Reported burned at Algiers, La., 5 May 1861, but this must be an error.

Name	Bldr	Built
General Quitman (ex-Galveston)	Simonson (Allaire)	1857

Tonnage:	945 tons
Dimensions:	230' (wl) × 37' × 6' or 233'3" × 34'3" × 9'
Machinery:	Side wheels, vertical beam engine, 1 boiler
Complement:	90
Armament:	2 32-pdr

NOTES: Converted to cottonclad ram with iron ram. Two masts.
SERVICE RECORD: Defense of New Orleans. Burned to prevent capture below New Orleans, 24 Apr 1862.

Name	Bldr	Built	Acquired
Governor Moore (ex-Charles Morgan)	Westervelt (Morgan)	1854	Jan 1862

Tonnage:	1,215 tons
Dimensions:	220'2" × 34' × 15'6"
Machinery:	Side wheels, 1 vertical beam engine (60" × 11'), 2 boilers
Complement:	93

NOTES: Cottonclad ram. Schooner rig.
SERVICE RECORD: Burned after being severely damaged during Federal attack on the New Orleans forts, 24 Apr 1862.

Name	Bldr	Built
Ivy (ex-V.H. Ivy, ex-El Paraguay, ex-Roger Williams)	Burtis (U)	1845

Tonnage:	447 tons B
Dimensions:	191' × 28' × d9'
Machinery:	Side wheels, 1 vertical beam engine (44" × 11')
Complement:	60
Armament:	1 8" SB, 1 32-pdr R, 2 24-pdr brass H (as privateer)

NOTES: Originally commissioned as privateer 16 May 1861.
SERVICE RECORD: Attack on Federal squadron at Head of Passes, 12 Oct 1861. Destroyed to prevent capture at Liverpool Landing, Yazoo River, May 1863.

The gunboat *Governor Moore*, which was burned during the defense of New Orleans. The bales of cotton around the superstructure were used as protection.

Name	Bldr	Built
J.A. Cotton	(Jeffersonville, Ind.)	1861

Tonnage: 549 tons
Dimensions: 229′ × 36′ × 7′
Machinery: Side wheels
Armament: 1 32-pdr SB, 1 9-pdr R

NOTES: Partially ironclad gunboat. Also spelled **J.A. Cotten**.
SERVICE RECORD: Engagement off Brashear City, Berwick Bay, La., 3 Nov 1862. Second engagement off Brashear City, 13 Jan, and burned to prevent capture, 14 Jan 1863.

Name	Bldr	Built
James L. Day	(New York, NY)	1843

Tonnage: 414 tons
Dimensions: 187′ × 25′6″ × 6′
Machinery: Side wheels
Armament: (U)

NOTES: Mississippi River towboat seized at New Orleans and converted to a gunboat.
SERVICE RECORD: Defense of New Orleans. Engagement at Head of Passes, 12 Oct 1861.

Name	Bldr	Built	Acquired
McRae (ex-*Marquis del Habana* [sic])	(U)	(U)	17 Mar 1861

Tonnage: 680 tons
Dimensions: (U)
Machinery: 1 screw
Armament: 1 9″ SB, 6 32-pdr SB, 1 6-pdr R

NOTES: Former Mexican Navy steamer *Marques de la Habana*, having been seized as a pirate by USS *Saratoga*, 7 Mar 1860: later declared illegal by a U.S. court. Bark rig.
SERVICE RECORD: Defense of New Orleans. Attack on Federal squadron at Head of Passes, 12 Oct 1861. Severely damaged in action below New Orleans, 24 Apr 1862. Sank at her wharf at New Orleans, 27 Apr 1862.

Name	Bldr	Built
Mobile	(Philadelphia)	1860

Tonnage: 283 tons
Dimensions: (U)
Machinery: Side wheels
Armament: 3 32-pdr SB, 1 32-pdr R, 1-8″SB

NOTES: Wooden hull, 3 masts. Identity and chronology of this ship subject to conjecture.
SERVICE RECORD: Ran blockade several times 1861–2. Engaged USS *Hatteras* in Atchafalaya Bay, La., 1 Feb 1862. Burned to prevent capture at Yazoo City, 21 Mar 1863, while undergoing conversion to ironclad.

Name
New Orleans

Tonnage: (U)
Dimensions: (U)
Armament: 17 8″ SB, 1 9″ SB, 2 32-pdr R

NOTES: Floating battery, converted from floating dry dock.
SERVICE RECORD: Defense of Island No. 10, sunk to avoid capture, 7 Apr 1862.

Name	Bldr	Built
Oregon	(New York)	1846

Tonnage: 532 tons
Dimensions: 216′10″ × 26′6″ × 9′6″
Machinery: Side wheels
Armament: 1 8″, 1 32-pdr, 2 H

NOTES: Wooden hull, one mast. Seized in 1861 for blockade running.
SERVICE RECORD: Ran blockade many times in 1861. Engaged USS *New London* at Pass Christian, Miss., 25 Mar 1862. Defense of New Orleans. Destroyed to prevent capture on evacuation of New Orleans, Apr 1862.

The Louisiana gunboat *McRae*. A former Mexican naval vessel seized as a pirate in 1860, she was still at New Orleans in 1861. She was taken into Confederate service and lost in the defense of New Orleans. (U.S. Naval Historical Center)

Name	Bldr	Built	Acquired	Comm
Pamlico	(New York)	1856	10 Jul 1861	2 Sep 1861

Tonnage: 218 tons
Dimensions: (U)
Machinery: Side wheels
Armament: 3 8″ SB, 1 6.4″ R

NOTES: Purchased at New Orleans.
SERVICE RECORD: Defense of New Orleans. Engaged Federal vessels off Horn Island, Miss., 4 Dec 1861. Engaged USS *New London* at Pass Christian, Miss., 25 Mar 1862. Burned to avoid capture in Lake Pontchartrain, 4 Apr 1862.

Name	Bldr	Built	Comm
Tuscarora	(U)	(U)	1861

Tonnage: (U)
Dimensions: (U)
Machinery: Side wheels
Armament: 1 32-pdr R, 1 8″ col.

NOTES: Purchased and converted at New Orleans.
SERVICE RECORD: Attack on Federal sqn at Head of Passes, 12 Oct 1861. Accidentally destroyed by fire near Helena, Ark., 23 Nov 1861.

Name	Bldr	Built	Acquired
Webb (ex-*William H. Webb*)	Webb (Allaire)	1856	17 May 1861

Tonnage: 655 tons B
Dimensions: 206′ () 190′ (dk) 179′7″ (bp) × 32′ × 9′6″
Machinery: Side wheels, 2 vertical overhead beam engines (44″ × 10′), 2 boilers
Armament: 1 130-pdr R, 2 12-pdr H

NOTES: Issued privateer commission but used as a transport. Converted to cottonclad ram, January 1862.
SERVICE RECORD: Engaged USS *Indianola* near New Carthage, Miss., 24 Feb 1863. Ran blockade past Red River, 23 Apr, and past New Orleans, but, pursued by Federal warships, was run ashore and burned to prevent capture south of New Orleans, 24 Apr 1865.

ARMED SAILING VESSELS

Name	Bldr	Built
Corypheus	(Brookhaven, LI)	1859

NOTE: For details see USS *Corypheus*.
SERVICE RECORD: Operated in Lake Pontchartrain and Lake Borgne. Captured in Lake Pontchartrain by USS *Calhoun*, 13 May 1862. Commissioned in USN (q.v.).

Name	Bldr	L	Acquired
Pickens (ex-USRC *Robert McClelland*)	Hood, Somerset, Mass.	11 Jun 1853	18 Feb 1861

Tonnage:	153 tons
Dimensions:	100′ × 23′
Armament:	5 guns

NOTES: U.S. Revenue Cutter seized at New Orleans, 29 Jan 1861. Schooner.
SERVICE RECORD: Engagement at Head of Passes, 12 Oct 1861. FFU.

Name	Bldr	L
Washington	(Baltimore)	1837

Tonnage:	(U)
Dimensions:	91′2″ (bp) × 22′1″
Armament:	1 42-pdr
Complement:	17

NOTES: Brig. U.S. Revenue Cutter seized at New Orleans 1861.

OTHER VESSELS: STEAMERS

Belle Algerine

Screw tug. Defense of New Orleans. Rammed and sunk by CSS *Governor Moore* as a hazard during engagement off Ft. Jackson, 24 Apr 1862. Unfit for service and guns landed.

Boston

Screw tug. Former USN towboat captured at Pass à l'Outre, La., 8 Jun 1863. Reported fitted as privateer, possibly lengthened. May be the ship captured by USS *Fort Jackson* off Bermuda, 8 Jul 1864.

Dan—(Calcasieu, La.); Built: 1858

112 tons, side-wheel steamer.
Captured by a launch from USS *Kensington* in Calcasieu River, Oct 1862. Sunk in Mississippi River while in Union service, Feb 1863.

Darby

Transport. Captured at Bayou Teche, La., 14 Apr 1863.

Empire Parish—(New Albany, Ind.); Built: 1859

279 tons, 170′ × 32′ × d6′2″, side-wheel steamer. Tow and despatch boat. Captured at fall of New Orleans, Apr 1862, and burned there 28 May 1864.

General Quitman—(New Albany, Ind.); Built: 1859

615 tons, 246′ × 36′ × 7′3″, side-wheel steamer (30″ × 10′), 6 boilers. Troop and supply ship on western rivers 1862–65.
Later history: Sold 1865. Merchant *General Quitman*. Snagged and lost at New Texas Landing, La., 22 Oct 1868.

Gossamer—(Pittsburgh); Built: 1863

144 tons, 122.5′ × 23.1′, stern-wheel steamer. Transport in Bayou Teche, 1863. Burned at Franklin, La. Rebuilt after the war. Lost in Red River, 22 Sep 1869.

Hart—(Paducah, Ky.); Built: 1860

175 tons, side-wheel steamer. May be *Ed R. Hart*. Transport in Bayou Teche and Berwick Bay, 1862–63. Sunk to avoid capture at Bayou Teche, La., 14 Apr 1863.

Landis—(Cincinnati); Built: 1853

Ex-*Joseph Landis*. 377 tons, 190′ × 30′ × d9′, side-wheel steamer; 2 engines, 5 boilers; complement 75. Acquired as tender to ironclad *Louisiana*. At defense of New Orleans. Damaged in engagement below New Orleans, 24 Apr 1862. Surrendered off Ft. St. Philip, 28 Apr 1862.
Later history: Used as tug and transport by U.S. Army 1862–65.

Mosher—(Philadelphia); Built: 1857

Ex-*C.A. Mosher*. 45 tons, screw steamer, unarmed. Tug. Sunk by gunfire from USS *Hartford* while towing fireboat during engagement below New Orleans, 24 Apr 1862.

Music—(Jeffersonville, Ind.); Built: 1857

330 tons, 172′ × 29′ × d6′, side wheel; 2 horizontal HP engines (20″ × 8′), 2 6-pdr (as privateer); complement 25/40. Mississippi towboat, commissioned as privateer. Unarmed tender to Fts. Jackson and St. Philip. Active in Atchafalaya and Red rivers 1863. FFU.

Orizaba—Simonson (Allaire); Built: 1858

595 tons, 210′ × 30′ × 6′, side wheel; vertical beam engine, 1 boiler. Seized at Galveston, Tex., Sep 1861. Used as blockade runner, 1862–65.
Later history: Lost by stranding at Liberty, Tex., 15 Jun 1865.

Phoenix

Side-wheel HP tug. Complement 75. Sunk during engagement below New Orleans, 24 Apr 1862.

St. Philip—Simonson (Allaire); L: 17 Jun 1852; Acquired: Apr 1861

Ex-*Star of the West*, ex-*San Juan*. 1,172 tons, 228′4″ × 32′8″ × d24′6″, side wheels; 2 vertical beam engines (66″ × 11′); 2 68-pdr, 4 32-pdr guns. Employed by Federal government to supply Ft. Sumter in Charleston Harbor, Jan 1861. Captured by Confederate steamer *General Rusk* off Texas, 17 Apr 1861. Receiving ship, New Orleans, 1861–62. Scuttled to obstruct channel of the Tallahatchie River, Mar 1863.

The side-wheel steamer *Star of the West* became the Confederate ship *St. Philip* after being captured off Texas in April 1861.

Star—(New Albany, Ind.); Built: 1840

250 tons (420 tons), HP steam tug, unarmed, complement 40. Sunk by Union gunboat during action below New Orleans, 24 Apr 1862.

Tennessee—Robb; Built: 1853

For details see USS *Tennessee*. Seized at New Orleans Jan 1862 for use as blockade runner. Made one voyage. Captured at fall of New Orleans, 25 Apr 1862. Commissioned in USN as *Tennessee* (q.v.).

Texas—(New York); Built: 1852

1,152 tons. Seized at New Orleans, Jan 1862. FIW.

W. Burton—(New Albany, Ind.); Built: 1857

Ex-*William Burton*. 253 tons, 151′ × 25′ × 5′6″, side-wheel steamer; complement 75. Tender to CSS *Louisiana*. Unarmed. Damaged in engagement below New Orleans, 24 Apr 1862. Surrendered to U.S. Navy below New Orleans, 28 Apr 1862.
Later history: Served with U.S. Army.

SAILING VESSELS

Morgan—Builder and launch date unknown

Ex-USRC *Morgan*. Former U.S. Revenue Cutter seized in 1861. FFU.

William B. King—(U); Acquired: 13 Jul 1861.

Schooner. Active service at Berwick, La., 1861.

TEXAS AREA

GUNBOATS

Name	Bldr	L	Comm
Bayou City	(Jeffersonville, Ind.)	Aug 1859	Feb 1862

Tonnage:	(U)
Dimensions:	165′ × 28′ × 5′
Machinery:	Side wheels
Complement:	135
Armament:	1 32-pdr

NOTES: Operated by State of Texas as cottonclad gunboat until taken over by War Dept. Oct 1862.
SERVICE RECORD: Rammed and captured USS *Harriet Lane* at Battle of Galveston, 1 Jan 1863. FFU.

Name	Bldr	Built	Comm
Clifton	Simonson	1861	8 Sep 1863

Ex-USS *Clifton*. For details see USS *Clifton*.

NOTES: Captured at Sabine Pass, Tex., 8 Sep 1863.
SERVICE RECORD: Went aground and was burned to prevent capture off Sabine Pass while running blockade, 21 Mar 1864.

Corpus Christi—No information available. Operated in Texas in 1864.

General Bee

Gunboat at Corpus Christi, 1862.

Name	Bldr	Built	Comm
Harriet Lane	Webb	1857	1863

Ex-USS/USRC *Harriet Lane*. For details see USS *Harriet Lane*.

NOTES: Captured at Galveston, 1 Jan 1863.
SERVICE RECORD: Defense of Texas coast 1863–64. Converted to blockade runner 1864.
Later history: Merchant *Lavinia* 1864. Ran blockade and remained at Havana. Converted to bark and renamed *Elliott Richie* 1867. Foundered off Pernambuco, Brazil, 13 May 1884.

Name	Bldr	Built
Josiah H. Bell (ex-*J.H. Bell*)	(Jeffersonville, Ind.)	1853

Tonnage:	412 tons
Dimensions:	171′ × 30′ × 6.7′
Machinery:	Side wheels
Armament:	1 8″ columbiad, Jun 63: 1 24-pdr, 1 12-pdr H
Complement:	35

NOTES: Cottonclad gunboat.
SERVICE RECORD: Engagement at Sabine Pass, captured USS *Morning Light* and *Velocity*, 20 Jan 1863. Operated off Sabine Pass 1863–65. Scuttled 1865.

Name	Bldr	Built
Mary Hill	(Smithfield, Tex.)	1859

Tonnage:	234 tons
Dimensions:	(U)
Machinery:	Side wheels
Armament:	1 24-pdr, 1 12-pdr

NOTES: Cottonclad gunboat.
SERVICE RECORD: Operated between Matagorda and Galveston.
Later history: Merchant *Mary Hill* 1865. Lost by snagging in Trinity River, Texas, 22 Nov 1865.

Name
Uncle Ben

Armament:	3 12-pdr

NOTES: Cottonclad gunboat.
SERVICE RECORD: Engagement at Sabine Pass, captured USS *Morning Light* and *Velocity*, 20 Jan 1863.

STEAMERS

A. S. Ruthven—(Cincinnati); Built: 1860

144 tons, 127′ × 30′ × 4′8″, side-wheel steamer. Transport, Galveston Bay.

Later history: Merchant *A. S. Ruthven* 1865. Lost 1869.

Dime

Tender and transport, 1863, described as "very small."

Era No. 3—(Freedom, Pa.); Built: 1858

144 tons, 129′ × 28.3′ × d4.3′, stern-wheel steamer. River patrol and transport on Brazos River.
Later history: Merchant *Era No. 3* 1865. RR 1875.

Florilda—(Louisville); Built: 1857.

304 tons, side-wheel steamer. Troop transport. Battle of Sabine Pass, 8 Sep 1863.

General Rusk—Harlan (Morgan); Built: 1857

417 tons, 200′ × 31′ × 5′7″; side-wheel steamer, beam engine (44″ × 11′). Iron hull. Seized at Galveston 1861. Reconnaissance and signal boat. Captured steamer *Star of the West* off Indianola, Tex., 17 Apr 1861. Defense of Buffalo Bayou in San Jacinto River, Dec 1861. Transferred to Army 1862.
Later history: Merchant *Blanche* 1862 as blockade runner. Chased ashore at Marianao, Cuba, by USS *Montgomery*, 7 Oct 1862, and lost during salvage attempt.

Grand Bay—(Mobile, Ala.); Built: 1857

135 tons, 121′ × 26.5′ × 4.5′, stern-wheel steamer. Transport, Sabine River.

Island City—(Brownsville, Pa.); Built: 1856

245 tons, side-wheel steamer. Supply boat, Galveston 1863–65.

Jeff Davis

Transport, 1863.

John F. Carr

Transport and cottonclad gunboat, 1863. Two guns. Battle of Galveston, 1 Jan 1863. Wrecked in Matagorda Bay, Tex., early 1864.

Lone Star—(Louisville, Ky.); Built: 1854

126 tons, 112′ × 26′ × 4.7′, side-wheel steamer. Transport 1863–65.

Lucy Gwin—(Freedom, Pa.); Built: 1859

152 tons, stern-wheel steamer. Transport. Battle of Galveston, 1 Jan 1863. Surrendered at Matagorda, May 1865, but removed to Mexican side of the Rio Grande.

Neptune

Wooden tug, 2 guns. Transport in Galveston Bay. Sank after ramming USS *Harriet Lane* during engagement at Galveston, 1 Jan 1863.

Roebuck—(Brownsville, Pa.); Built: 1857

164 tons, 147′ × 23′ × d5′, side-wheel steamer. Cottonclad transport.

Sun Flower—(Louisville, Ky.); Built: 1857

105 tons, 121′6″ × 25′ × 3′9″, side-wheel steamer. Unarmed cotton-

clad. Transport in Sabine River area.

Later history: Merchant *Sun Flower* 1865. Wrecked in Galveston Harbor, 3 Oct 1867.

SAILING VESSELS

Breaker

Schooner, crew 3. Pilot boat. Chased ashore by USS *Corypheus* at Pass Cavallo, 12 Aug 1862, salved by U.S.

Dodge—Page & Allen, Portsmouth; Built: 1856

ex-USRC *Henry Dodge.* 153 tons; 100'4″ × 23' × 8'; 1 9-pdr; complement 26. Schooner. U.S. Revenue Cutter seized at Galveston, 2 Mar 1861. Defense of Texas coast 1861–63.

Later history: Merchant *Mary Sorly* 1864. Captured as a blockade runner by USS *Sciota* off Galveston, Tex., 4 Apr 1864.

Elma—Acquired: Jul 1862

ex-*Major Minter.* Schooner. Acquired for conversion to patrol ship. Run aground in Nueces Bay and burned, 12 Aug 1862.

Fanny Morgan—Acquired: 22 Oct 1861

Fast sailboat. 8 tons, 26' × 11'. Guard and despatch boat at Galveston.

George Buckhart

Armed schooner. 1 6-pdr gun. Operated in Matagorda Bay area. Captured as blockade runner by USS *Quaker City* off Brazos Santiago, 17 Mar 1865.

Julia A. Hodges

Schooner. 8 tons. Despatch boat. Captured by USS *Estrella* near Indianola, Tex., 6 Apr 1864.

Lecompt

Schooner. Patrol ship, Matagorda Peninsula 1862. Captured by USS *Westfield* and USS *Clifton* in Matagorda Bay, Oct 1862. Recaptured by Confederates at Galveston, 1 Jan 1863. Chased ashore by USS *Cornubia* in Galveston Bay, 24 May 1865.

Royal Yacht—Acquired: Oct 1861

Schooner. 40 tons, (U) × (U) × 6'6″, 1 12-pdr gun, complement 15. Seriously damaged by fire after being attacked off Galveston, 8 Nov 1861. Captured as blockade runner off Galveston by USS *William G. Anderson,* 15 Apr 1863.

Velocity

ex-USS *Velocity.* For details see USS *Velocity.* Schooner. Captured at Sabine Pass, Tex., 23 Jan 1863.

GULF COAST AREA (Alabama, Mississippi, and West Coast of Florida)

GUNBOATS

Name	Bldr	Built
Baltic	(Philadelphia)	1860

Tonnage:	624 tons
Dimensions:	186' × 38' × 6'5″
Machinery:	Side wheels; 5 knots
Complement:	86
Armament:	2 Dahlgren, 2 32-pdr, 2 others

NOTES: River towboat converted to armored ram at Mobile. Unfit for service and dismantled in 1864. Armor used for CSS *Nashville.*

SERVICE RECORD: Operated in Mobile Bay area 1862–65. Captured at Nanna Hubba Bluff in Tombigbee River, Ala., 10 May 1865. Sold by USN 31 Dec 1865.

Name	Bldr	Built	Comm
Danube	Hall Snow, Bath, Me.	1854	1861

Tonnage:	980 tons
Dimensions:	170'4″ × 30'11″ × 16'11″
Armament:	4 42-pdr

NOTES: Full-rigged ship seized 1861 and converted to floating battery.

SERVICE RECORD: Anchored at Apalachee Battery in Mobile Bay, 1864. Sunk as a blockship in Mobile Bay, Nov 1864.

Name	Bldr	Built	Acquired
Gunnison (ex-*A. C. Gunnison*)	(Philadelphia)	1856	25 May 1861

Tonnage:	54 tons
Dimensions:	70' × 15' × d7'
Machinery:	1 screw, 2 engines (16″ × U), HP 80
Complement:	10
Armament:	2 6-pdr (1 spar torpedo added)

SERVICE RECORD: Commissioned as privateer. Despatch and torpedo boat 1862. Surrendered Apr 1865.

Name	Bldr	Comm
Phoenix	(Mobile ?)	1863

Ironclad floating battery. 6 guns.
Sunk as a blockship at Mobile, Aug 1864.

A drawing of the gunboat *Selma* that participated in the defense of Mobile 1861–1864. (U.S. Naval Historical Center)

Name	Bldr	Built	Acquired
Selma (ex-*Florida*) For details, see USS *Selma*.	(Mobile, Ala.)	1856	22 Apr 1861

NOTES: Converted coastal packet steamer. Renamed Jul 1862.
SERVICE RECORD: Engaged USS *Massachussets* off Mobile, 19 Oct 1861. Engaged USS *Montgomery*, 4 Dec 1861. Hit a snag and sank at Mobile, 5 Feb 1863; refloated. Surrendered after Battle of Mobile Bay, 5 Aug 1864. Commissioned in USN as USS *Selma*.

STEAMERS

Alert

1 32-pdr gun, complement 31. Lighthouse tender, seized at Mobile, 18 Jan 1861. Served at Mobile, Ala., 1861–62.

Bradford

Storeship at Pensacola, Fla., 1862.

Crescent—(Mobile, Ala.), 1858

171 tons, side-wheel steamer. Tug at Mobile, Ala., 1861.

Dalman—(Jeffersonville); Built: 1851

ex-*Peter Dalman*. 364 tons, 200′ × 30′ × 6′, side-wheel steamer. Receiving ship, Mobile 1862–65.

Dick Keys—(Cincinnati); Built: 1853; Acquired: 8 May 1861

369 tons, 177′ × 30.5′ × 7.1′, side-wheel steamer. Assisted blockade runners out of Mobile. Transport.

General Sumter—(Palatka, Fla.), 1859

41 tons, side-wheel steamer. Also known as **General Sumpter**. Transport. Captured by USS *Columbine* in Big Lake George, Fla., 23 Mar 1864.

Governor Milton

ex-*G. W. Bird*. 68 tons, 85′ × 20′ × 4′8″, side-wheel steamer. (May be *George M. Bird*, 75 tons, built at Covington, Fla., 1858.) Transport. Captured by a boat from USS *Darlington* above Hawkinsville, Fla., 7 Oct 1862.

Great Republic

Cottonclad steamer. Captured late 1864.

Helen (i)

Steamer, guard boat and transport. Burned to prevent capture at Pensacola, May 1862.

Henry J. King—(New Albany, Ind.); Built: 1856

409 tons, side-wheel steamer. Transport. Operated between Selma and Mobile, Ala., 1864. Captured in Coosa River, Ala., 14 Apr 1865.

Iron King

Coal transport. Operated between Selma and Mobile 1864.

James Battle—(New Albany, Ind.); Built: 1860

407 tons, 225′ × 35′ × 7.5′, side-wheel steamer, HP engines, 5 boilers.

Transport. Captured by USS *De Soto* running blockade 70 miles SE of Mobile, 18 Jul 1863.
Later history: Merchant *James Battle* 1865. RR 1867.

J. H. Jarvis

Little information known. Possibly a new steamer built at Columbus, Ga., 1864.

Marianna

Side-wheel steamer. Towboat and transport.

Neafie—Reaney Neafie; Built: 1856

ex-*Jacob G. Neafie*. 103 tons, #screw steamer; 6 knots; complement 60; iron hull. Transport and tug. Damaged during engagement off Ft. Pickens, Fla., 22 Nov 1861. Captured before 1863.
Later history: U.S. War Dept. 1864. Merchant *Neafie*, 1866. RR 1876.

Nelms

Steamboat at Ft. McRae, Fla., 1861. Remained at Pensacola until Mar 1862. FFU.

Spray

HP steamer. (May be screw steamer, 106 tons, built at Wilmington, Del. 1852.) Operated at St. Marks, Fla., 1863–65.

Swan

487 tons, steamer. Tender at Mobile, Ala., 1861. Captured as blockade runner by USS *Amanda* and *Bainbridge* off Key West, Fla., 24 May 1862.
Later history: Merchant 1863. Foundered en route Key West–New Orleans, 19 Feb 1863.

Time

Steamer. (May be side-wheel steamer built at Elizabeth, Pa., 1860, 263 tons.) Steamer used at Pensacola NYd 1862.

Turel

Transport used at Pensacola, Fla., 1862.

William H. Young—(Brownsville, Pa.), 1860

179 tons, side-wheel steamer. Transport and storeship in Gulf area, 1862–65. Captured by U.S. Army, Jun 1865.

SAILING VESSELS

Helen (ii)

Sloop. Transport, Florida coast. Captured by boat from USS *Sagamore* near Bayport, 2 Apr 1863, and destroyed by fire.

Lewis Cass—Bldr: Page & Allen; L: 1856; Commissioned: 1861

ex-USRC *Lewis Cass*. 153 tons, 100′ × 23′, 1 68-pdr gun, complement 45, schooner U.S. Revenue Cutter seized at Mobile, 30 Jan 1861.

ATLANTIC COAST AREA (Georgia, South Carolina, North Carolina, east coast of Florida)

GUNBOATS

Name	Bldr	Built
Arctic	(Wilmington, NC)	1863

Lightship, converted to ironclad floating battery. Machinery removed late in 1862 for CSS *Richmond*.
SERVICE RECORD: Cape Fear River 1863–64. Sunk as blockship, 24 Dec 1864.

Name
Fanny

Screw steamer; 1 32-pdr, 1 8-pdr R, complement 49. Former U.S. Army vessel, seized at Loggerhead Inlet, NC, 1 Oct 1861.
SERVICE RECORD: Battle of Roanoke Island, 7–8 Feb 1862, and Elizabeth City, NC. Run aground and blown up, 10 Feb 1862.

Name
Ellis

For details see USS *Ellis*.
SERVICE RECORD: Defense of Fts. Hatteras and Clark, 28–29 Aug 1861. Defense of Roanoke Island, 7–8 Feb 1862. Captured during defense of Elizabeth City, NC, 10 Feb 1862. Commissioned as USS *Ellis*.

Name	Bldr	Built
Fisher	(Edwards Ferry, NC)	1865

NOTE: Screw steamer, 66 tons.
SERVICE RECORD: Captured while building, 1865, and taken to Norfolk.
Later history: Merchant *Alexander Oldham* 1865. Lost (U) 1873.

Name	Bldr	Laid down	L	Comm
Georgia	(Savannah)	Mar 1862	May 1862	Jul 1862

Dimensions:	250′ × 60′
Complement:	200
Armament:	4 to 9 guns

NOTE: Ironclad floating battery.
SERVICE RECORD: Defense of Savannah 1863–64. Destroyed to prevent capture at Savannah, 21 Dec 1864.

Name	Bldr	Built
Halifax	(Halifax, NC)	1865

NOTE: Steamer, length 91′.

SERVICE RECORD: Captured on the ways at Halifax, NC, 12 May 1865. Launched and towed to Norfolk, Jun 1865. FFU.

Name	Bldr	Built
Isondiga	(U)	1863

Tonnage: (U)
Dimensions: (U) × (U) × 6′6″
Machinery: Stern wheel; 5 knots
Complement: 60
Armament: 1 9″ shell gun, 1 6.4″ R

NOTES: Wooden gunboat, no masts.
SERVICE RECORD: Defense of Savannah. Burned to prevent capture after fall of Savannah, Jan 1865.

Name	Bldr	Built	Comm
Sampson	(Savannah)	1856	1861

Tonnage: 313 tons
Dimensions: (U)
Machinery: Side wheels
Complement: 49
Armament: 1 32-pdr SB, 1 12-pdr

NOTES: Tugboat. Converted to gunboat.
SERVICE RECORD: Defense of Port Royal, SC, 4–7 Nov 1861. Engagements at Ft. Pulaski, Ga., Dec 1861, and Jan 1862, damaged. Receiving ship, Savannah 1862–63. Damaged during expedition to destroy railway bridge over Savannah River, Dec 1864.
Later history: Merchant *Samson* 1868. Lost (U) 1870.

Name	Bldr	Built	Comm
Savannah (ex-*Everglade*)	Sneden & Whitlock (Morgan)	1856	1861

Tonnage: 406 tons B
Dimensions: 173′ (dk) × 28′8″ × 4′6″, d8′
Machinery: Side wheels, 1 inclined engine, 1 boiler; NHP 90
Armament: 1 32-pdr

NOTES: Purchased by Georgia 1861 and converted to gunboat.
SERVICE RECORD: Defense of Port Royal, SC, 5–6 Nov 1861, damaged. Defense of Ft. Pulaski, SC, 16 Nov 1861, 28 Jan 1862 and 10–11 Apr 1862. Receiving ship, Savannah 1862–63. Renamed **Oconee**, 28 Apr 1863. Sailed as blockade runner, but foundered in a gale at sea, 19 Aug 1863.

Name	Bldr	Built	Comm
Sea Bird	Terry	1854	1861

Tonnage: 202 tons
Dimensions: (U)
Machinery: Side wheels
Complement: 42
Armament: 1 32-pdr SB, 1 30-pdr R

NOTES: Purchased by North Carolina 1861.
SERVICE RECORD: Defense of Roanoke Island, 7–8 Feb 1862. Rammed and sunk by USS *Commodore Perry* at Elizabeth City, NC, 10 Feb 1862.

Name	Bldr	Built	Comm
Stono (ex-USS *Isaac Smith*)	L & F	1861	1863
For details see USS *Isaac Smith*			

NOTES: Captured in Stono River, SC, 30 Jan 1863.
SERVICE RECORD: Wrecked on breakwater near Ft. Moultrie, SC, while attempting to run blockade, 5 Jun 1863.

Name	Bldr	Built
Uncle Ben	(Buffalo, NY)	1856

Tonnage: 155 tons
Dimensions: (U)
Machinery: 1 screw
Armament: 1 gun

NOTES: Lake Erie tug used to reinforce Ft. Sumter, but seized by Confederates at Wilmington, NC, Apr 1861. Engines removed for CSS *North Carolina*, 1862, and converted to schooner. Fitted as privateer **Retribution**.
SERVICE RECORD: Defense of Wilmington, NC.
Prizes (as Retribution): 10 Jan 1863: *J. P. Elliott*; 31 Jan: *Hanover*; 19 Feb: *Emily Fisher*.
Later history: Renamed *Etta*. Lost off Cape Hatteras, 1865.

Name	Bldr	L
Yadkin	(Wilmington, NC)	1863

Tonnage: 300 tons
Dimensions: (U)
Machinery: screw
Armament: 1 or 2 guns

SERVICE RECORD: Operated in North Carolina. Burned to prevent capture on fall of Wilmington, Feb 1865.

STEAMERS

Aid—Builder (Philadelphia); launched: 1852; acquired: 1861.

147 tons, 1 42-pdr, complement 8, screw steamer. Engine removed for ironclad being built at Charleston. Tender, Charleston, SC 1861–62. BU 1862.

Albemarle—Acquired: 1861

Side-wheel steamer.
SERVICE RECORD: Transport and cargo ship in North Carolina 1861. Captured by USS *Delaware* off New Bern, NC, 15 Mar 1862.
Later history: Transport, wrecked in New Bern harbor, 5 Apr 1862.

Amazon—Builder: Harlan; launched: 1856

372 tons B; 157′6″ × 45′ × 5′6″; #side wheels, HP engine (22″ × 6′). Iron hull. Transport, Savannah area. Surrendered to USS *Pontiac*, 2 Mar 1865.
Later history: Merchant *Amazon* 1865. Snagged and sunk in Savannah River, Ga., Feb 1866.

Appomattox—Builder: (Philadelphia); launched: 1850; acquired: 1861.

(ex-*Empire*). 120 tons, 1 32-pdr, side-wheel steamer, tug. Engagement at Roanoke Island, NC, 7–8 Feb 1862. Defense of Elizabeth City, NC, 10 Feb 1862; scuttled to prevent capture later that day.

Beauregard

Side-wheel steamer. Transport, operated at Savannah. Captured at Savannah, Jan 1865.

Berosa

Cargo vessel. Foundered off Florida coast east of St. Mary's River, 8 Apr 1863.

Bombshell

90′ × (U) × 3′5″, 1 20-pdr, 3 H, 2 inclined HP engines (33″ × 10′), complement 37. Erie Canal steamer sunk as U.S. Army transport in Albemarle Sound, NC, 18 Apr 1864 and raised by Confederates. Recaptured by USS *Mattabesett* and USS *Sassacus* during battle in Albemarle Sound, 5 May 1864.

Caswell—Acquired: 1861

Side-wheel steamer. Tender at Wilmington, NC. Burned to avoid capture at Wilmington, Feb 1865.

Catawba

Tender at Charleston, 1861.

Chesterfield—Bldr: (Charleston, SC); L: 1853; Acquired: 1861

204 tons, side-wheel steamer. Transport, South Carolina 1861–65. FFU.

Clarendon—(Portsmouth, Va.), 1860

143 tons, screw steamer, former ferryboat. Despatch vessel and transport, Ft. Fisher, NC, Dec 1864. Captured and burned by U.S. at Fayetteville, NC, 14 Mar 1865.

Colonel Hill

Transport, Cape Hatteras area. Burned by U.S. Army forces near Tarborough, NC, 20 Jul 1863.

Cotton Plant—(Philadelphia, Pa.), 1860

85 tons, 107′ × 18′9″ × 4.5′, screw steamer, iron hull. Operated at Plymouth, NC, with CSS *Albemarle*, Apr–May 1864. Surrendered May 1865 at Halifax, NC.
Later history: Merchant *Cotton Plant* 1865. Barge 1881.

Curlew—Harlan, 1856

350 tons B, 135′ × 23′ × 8′, side-wheel tug, LP engine (29″ × 9′), 1 32-pdr, iron hull. Disabled during attack on Roanoke Island, 7 Feb and destroyed to prevent capture, 8 Feb 1862.

Currituck—(Norfolk, Va.), 1860

44 tons, screw steamer. Despatch vessel and towboat, North Carolina. FFU.

Darlington—(Charleston, SC), 1849

298 tons, side-wheel steamer. Captured by USS *Pawnee* near Fernandina, Fla., 3 Mar 1862.
Later history: Army transport 1862. Merchant *Darlington* 1866. RR 1874.

Dolly

Steamer in Roanoke River; sunk near Edwards Ferry, NC, May 1865.

Egypt Mills—(Poplar Neck, Md.), 1856

70 tons, screw steamer. Transport. Captured in Roanoke River, NC, 22 May 1865.
Later history: Merchant *Alida* 1865. RR 1869.

Equator—(Philadelphia), 1854

64 tons, #screw steamer, torpedo boat. Defense of Cape Fear River area, 1864. Burned to prevent capture at Wilmington, NC, Jan 1865.

Etiwan—(Charleston), 1834

132 tons, side-wheel steamer. Transport and cargo ship, Charleston Harbor. Struck a torpedo (mine) and was run ashore, spring 1863. Sunk by Federal batteries off Ft. Johnson, 7 Jun 1864.
Later history: Salved. Merchant *St. Helena* 1867. RR 1894.

Firefly—Commissioned May 1861

ex-U.S. Coast Survey, seized 29 Dec 1860. Wooden side-wheel steam yacht, 1 gun, complement 15. Tender, Savannah. Burned to prevent capture at Savannah, 21 Dec 1864.

Forrest—Commissioned 1861

(ex-*Edwards*). Steam tug purchased 1861. 1 32-pdr + 1 gun. Disabled during defense of Roanoke Island, 7–8 Feb 1862. Burned to prevent capture at Elizabeth City, NC, 10 Feb 1862.

General Clinch—Bldr: J. Poyas, Charleston; L: 1839; Acquired: Jan 1861

256 tons, 131′ × 24′ × 8′8″, crosshead engine, side-wheel steamer, 2 guns.
SERVICE RECORD: Tender and transport, Charleston Harbor 1861–64. Sank in Charleston Harbor 1864. May have been raised and used as blockade runner. FFU.

General Lee

Side-wheel steamer. Transport at Savannah 1864.

The small steamer *Lady Davis* was an early addition to Southern naval forces, serving at Savannah and Port Royal until her engines were removed in 1862.

Governor Morehead

Stern-wheel steamer. Transport and towboat, Pamlico and Neuse rivers. Destroyed by U.S. Army, Jul 1863.

Huntress—Bldr: (New York); L: 1838; Acquired: Mar 1861

500 tons B, 230' × 24'6" × 6'6", side-wheel steamer, 16 knots, 1 to 3 guns. Fast mail packet purchased by Georgia 1861. Battle of Port Royal, 7 Nov 1861. Transport, Charleston Harbor 1862. Sold 29 Oct 1862.
Later history: Blockade runner *Tropic*. Accidentally burned off Charleston, 18 Jan 1863.

Ida

Side-wheel steamer. (Former U.S. Government vessel.) Transport, despatch boat and towboat in Savannah River, 1862–64. Captured and burned near Argyle Island, 10 Dec 1864.

Indian Chief

Receiving ship, Charleston, 1862–65. Tender for torpedo (mine) operations. Burned on evacuation of Charleston, 18 Feb 1865.

Jeff Davis (i)

Steamer, Savannah area, 1864.

Junaluska—(Philadelphia), 1860

ex-*Younalaska*. 79 tons, screw steamer, 2 guns. Helped capture USS *Fanny* in Loggerhead Inlet, NC, 1 Oct 1861. BU 1862.

Kahukee—Bldr: Harlan (U); L: 1855; Acquired: Jul 1861

150 tons, 85' × 17'6" × 7', screw steamer, vertical HP engine (24" × 1'8"), 9 knots, iron hull. Operated around Hatteras Inlet, NC, 1861.

Kate L. Bruce—Bldr: GB ?; L: (U)

Former schooner, 310 tons. Converted to steamer and armed at Columbus, Ga., 1862. Sunk as blockship in Chattahoochee River, 1864.

Lady Davis—Bldr: (Philadelphia); L: 1858; Acquired: May 1861

ex-*James Gray*. 161 tons, screw steamer, 1 24-pdr, 1 12-pdr R guns, iron hull. Engine removed for CSS *Palmetto State* 1862. Defense of Savannah 1861. Battle of Port Royal, SC, 7 Nov 1861. Used as blockade runner 1862. Captured as hulk at Charleston, Feb 1865.
Prize: 19 May 1861: *A. B. Thompson*.
Later history: U.S. Lighthouse Board 1865.

Leesburg

Transport, Savannah River, 1862–65.

M. E. Dowing

Despatch boat, North Carolina, 1861.

Marion—(Charleston) 1850

258 tons, side-wheel steamer. Transport, Charleston, 1861–63. Sunk accidentally by Confederate mine in Ashley River, 6 Apr 1863.

Moultrie

Steamer. (May be screw steamer *General Moultrie*, 381 tons, built 1856 at New York. Sold foreign 1866.) Charleston station 1862–63. Returned to owner, 24 Aug 1863.

Planter—(Charleston), 1860

For details see USS *Planter*. Despatch boat and transport, Charleston. Spirited out of Charleston Harbor by Robert Smalls, 13 May 1862, and turned over to USS *Onward*. Commissioned as USS *Planter*.

Post Boy

Despatch boat, North Carolina, 1861–62.

Queen Mab

Side-wheel steamer. Transport, Charleston area. Captured, 18 Feb 1865.

Raleigh—(U); Acquired: May 1861

65 tons, screw steamer, 2 6-pdr H, iron hull. Defense of Fts. Hatteras and Clark, NC, 28–29 Aug 1861. Defense of Roanoke Island and Elizabeth City, NC, 7–10 Feb 1862. Tender to CSS *Virginia* at Hampton Roads, Mar 1862. Renamed **Roanoke**, late 1864. Action at Trent's Reach, James River, 21 Jun 1864. Destroyed to prevent capture in James River, 4 Apr 1865.

Rebel

Side-wheel steamer. Transport, North Carolina and Virginia.

Resolute—(Savannah, Ga.), 1858

322 tons, side-wheel steamer, complement 35. Transport and tender to CSS *Savannah*. Defense of Port Royal, SC, Nov 1861. Damaged during engagement in Savannah River, 12 Dec 1864, ran aground and was captured.

Later history: Merchant *Ajax* 1867. RR 1881.

Robert Habersham—(Savannah, Ga.), 1860

173 tons, side-wheel steamer. Transport, Savannah area. Lost with all hands by explosion in Savannah River, 19 Aug 1863.

Skirwan—Captured at Halifax, NC, May 1865

Sumter—(Charleston), Acquired: 1863

Transport and munitions carrier, Stono River and Charleston 1863. Sunk in error by gunfire from Ft. Moultrie, 30 Aug 1863.

Talomico

Side-wheel steamer. 2 guns, complement 20. Transport 1861–63. Sunk accidentally at Savannah, 1863.

Transport—Acquired: 1864

40 tons B, side-wheel steamer, HP engine. Tug. Captured at Charleston, Feb 1865. Transferred to U.S. Army Jul 1865.

Treaty

Tug. Captured by boat from USS *Albatross* in Santee River, 20 Jun 1862.

Waterwitch

ex-USS *Waterwitch*. For details see USS *Waterwitch*. Captured in boarding attack in Ossabaw Sound, Ga., 3 Jun 1864. Remained at White Bluff, Ga., and burned to prevent capture, 19 Dec 1864.

Weldon N. Edwards

Defense of North Carolina 1861. Hulked Aug 1861.

Wilson—(Beaufort, NC); Built: 1856

58 tons, #stern-wheel steamer. Transport. Captured by USS *Commodore Perry*, *Shawsheen* and *Ceres* at Hamilton, NC, on Roanoke River, 9 Jul 1862. Transferred to U.S. Army.

Winslow—Bldr: Terry, New York; L: 1846; Commissioned: 1861

ex-*Joseph E. Coffee*. 207 tons, side-wheel steamer, 1 32-pdr, 1 6-pdr R guns. Also known as **Warren Winslow**. Purchased by North Carolina. Patrolled in Hatteras area 1861. Struck sunken object and was burned to prevent capture in Ocracoke Inlet, NC, 7 Nov 1861, while going to aid of wrecked French corvette *Prony*.

Prizes: Jul 1861: *Mary Alice*, *Priscilla*; 15 Jul: *Transit*; 18 Jul: *Herbert*; 4 Aug: *Itasca*.

SAILING VESSELS

Black Warrior

Schooner. 2 32-pdr guns. Defense of Roanoke Island and Elizabeth City, NC, 7–10 Feb 1862. Burned to prevent capture, 10 Feb 1862.

Gallatin—Bldr: New York NYd; L: 1831; Commissioned: 1861

ex-USRC *Gallatin*. Schooner, 112 tons; 73′4″ (pp) × 20′6″ × d7′4″; 2 12-pdr guns; complement 40. U.S. Revenue Cutter seized in Georgia 1861. Commissioned as privateer 1861. FFU.

Hawley

Schooner. Transport, North Carolina, 1861.

Isabella Ellis

Schooner, 340 tons. Transport, 1861. In Union service 1864.

J. J. Crittenden

Schooner. Captured by USS *Whitehead* off Newbegun Creek, SC, June 1864 and later sunk.

Jeff Davis (ii)

Schooner. Captured off New Bern, NC, June 1864.

M. C. Etheridge—Bldr: (Plymouth, NC); L: 1859

Schooner, 144 tons, 92' × 24' × 7', 2 guns. Storeship, North Carolina. Burned to prevent capture when attacked by USS *Whitehead* in Pasquotank River, 10 Feb 1862.

Manassas—ex-USRC Minot ?

Schooner. Seized as U.S. Revenue Cutter at New Bern, NC, 27 Aug 1861.
SERVICE RECORD: Operated off North Carolina 1861. BU 1862.

Memphis—(New York); Built 1851

ex-*Camilla*, ex-*America*. For details see USS *America*. Blockade runner 1861. Discovered scuttled in St. Johns River, Fla., Mar 1862. Salved and comm. in USN as USS *America*.

Petrel—Bldr: (U); L: (U); Acquired: Dec 1860

ex-USCS, ex-USRC *William Aiken*, ex-*Eclipse*. 82 tons, 1 42-pdr + 1 other gun, complement 38. Seized Dec 1860, comm. as privateer 1861. Sunk by USS *St. Lawrence* off Charleston, 28 Jul 1861.

Renshaw

ex-*R. T. Renshaw*. For details see USS *Renshaw*. Captured by launch from USS *Louisiana* in Tar River, NC, 20 May 1863. See USS *Renshaw*.

VIRGINIA AREA

GUNBOATS

Name
Drewry

Tonnage:	166 tons
Dimensions:	106' × 21' × 5', d8'
Machinery:	(U)
Armament:	1-6.4"R, 1-7"R

SERVICE RECORD: Tender and gunboat, 1863. Action at Trent's Reach, 21 Jun 1864. Destroyed by two hits from artillery fire in Trent's Reach, James River, 24 Jan 1865.

Name	Bldr	Built	Acquired
Jamestown	Webb (Morgan)	1853	Apr 1861
Patrick Henry (ex-*Yorktown*)	Webb (Morgan)	1853	Apr 1861

Tonnage:	1,300 tons
Dimensions:	250' (dk) × 34' × 13', d17'
Machinery:	Side wheels, 2 vertical beam engines (50" × 10'), 2 boilers
Complement:	150 (*Henry*)
Armament:	*Henry*: 1 10" SB, 1 64-pdr, 6 8", 2 32-pdr R

NOTES: Seized by Virginia 1861. Brigantine rig. Built for New York–Richmond run.
SERVICE RECORDS:
Jamestown—Renamed **Thomas Jefferson**, July 1861. Battle of Hampton Roads, 8–9 Mar 1862. Captured three ships at Hampton Roads, 11 Apr 1862. Sunk as a blockship in James River, 15 May 1862.
Patrick Henry—Engaged gunboats above Newport News, 13 Sep and 2 Dec 1861. Damaged at battle of Hampton Roads, 8–9 Mar 1862. Housed the Confederate Naval Academy at Drewry's Bluff, Va., Oct 1863–65. Burned on evacuation of Richmond, 3 Apr 1865.

Name
Satellite (ex-USS *Satellite*)

NOTE: For details see USS *Satellite*.
SERVICE RECORD: Captured by boarders at mouth of Rappahannock River, 23 Aug 1863. Captured 3 schooners in Chesapeake Bay. Stripped and scuttled, 2 Sep 1863.

Name	Bldr	Built
Teaser (ex-*Wide Awake*)	(Philadelphia)	1855?

NOTES: For details see USS *Teaser*. Wooden tug purchased by Virginia 1861. Prior identity conjectural.
SERVICE RECORD: Battle of Hampton Roads, 8–9 Mar 1862. Used as balloon tender and torpedo (mine) layer. Damaged in action with USS *Maratanza* at Haxall's on James River, 4 Jul 1862, and captured. Commissioned as USS *Teaser*.

Name
Torpedo

Tonnage:	150 tons
Dimensions:	70' × 16' × d6'6"
Machinery:	Screw
Armament:	2 20-pdr

SERVICE RECORD: Torpedo boat tender, James River. Burned and sunk to prevent capture at Richmond, Apr 1865. Raised and sent to Norfolk Navy Yard.

STEAMERS

Allison

Transport. Attempt to pass obstructions at Trent's Reach, 23–24 Jan 1865. Sank torpedo boat *Hornet* in collision, 26 Jan 1865. FFU.

Beaufort—Bldr: (Wilmington, Del.); Built: 1854, Comm: 9 Jul 1861

ex-*Caledonia*. 85 tons, 85' × 17'5" × d6'11", 1 vertical direct acting engine (22" × 1'10"), 1 32-pdr R. Battles of Roanoke Island and Elizabeth City, Feb 1862. Tender to CSS *Virginia* at Hampton Roads, 8–9 Mar 1862. James River 1862–65. Action at Trent's Reach, 21 Jun 1864. Captured 3 Apr 1865.
Later history: Merchant *Roanoke* 1865. Barge 1878.

Curtis Peck—Bldr: (New York); Built: 1842; Acquired: 1861

446 tons, side-wheel steamer. Patrol and flag-of-truce boat. Sunk as blockship in James River, Sep 1862.

General Scott

Transport. Burned to prevent capture in York River, May 1862.

George Page—Bldr: Collyer (U); Built: 1853; Acquired: 1861

410 tons, 128' × 26' × 4', d7', side wheels, vertical beam engine, 2 guns. Built as U.S. Army transport, captured in Aquia Creek, Va., May 1861. May have been renamed *City of Richmond*. River defense service. Burned to prevent capture at Quantico, Va., 9 Mar 1862.

Harmony—(Philadelphia), 1859

78 tons, side-wheel steamer, 2 32-pdr R guns. Tug, ordnance transport. Attacked USS *Savannah* off Newport News, 30 Aug 1861. FFU.

John B. White—(Buffalo, NY), 1857

39 tons, screw steamer. Tug. Surrendered near Hampton Roads, 8 May 1862.
Later history: Served with U.S. Army. Sunk by torpedo (mine), 1 Jan 1864.

Logan—Bldr: Harlan (U); Built: 1855; Acquired: 1861

296 tons, 160' × 26' × 7'6", side-wheel steamer (30" × 10'). Burned to prevent capture in Pamunkey River above White House, Va., 1862.

Northampton—(Baltimore, Md.), 1860

405 tons, side-wheel steamer
SERVICE RECORD: Cargo ship, James River, 1861–62. Sunk as a blockship at Drewry's Bluff, Va., Sep 1862.

Powhatan

Tug. Acquired for defense of Roanoke Island 1861.

Rappahannock—Bldr: Burtis (U); Built: 1845; Acquired: 1861

ex-*St. Nicholas*. 413 tons, side-wheel steamer, 1 gun. Merchant passenger steamer seized by passengers in Potomac River, 28 Jun 1861. Operated in the Rappahannock River 1861–62. Burned to prevent capture at Fredericksburg, Apr 1862.

Reliance—Bldr: Terry; Built: 1860; Acquired: 1863

ex-USS *Reliance*. For details see USS *Reliance*. Captured by Confederate boarders in Rappahannock River, 19 Aug 1863. Destroyed to prevent recapture at Port Royal, Va., 28 Aug 1863.

Later history: Apparently salved. Merchant 1865. Lost (U), 26 Apr 1883.

Roanoke (I)

Steamer. Chartered steamer in Nansemond River, Va. 1861 and North Carolina 1862.

Roanoke (II)

See *Raleigh*, p. 241.

Rondout—(Poughkeepsie), 1828

40 tons, side-wheel steamer. Transport. Captured by Potomac Flotilla in Rappahannock River, 20 Apr 1862.

Schultz—(New York), 1850

ex-*A. H. Schultz*. 164 tons, side-wheel steamer.
SERVICE RECORD: Flag-of-truce boat in James River. Blown up by Confederate torpedo (mine), 19 Feb 1865. Also reported as USS *Columbine* (q.v.)

Seaboard—(Philadelphia), 1859

59 tons, side-wheel steamer. Tug operated by CSA Engineer Corps. Captured by USS *Lilac* in James River below Richmond, 4 Apr 1865. Snagged and run aground, May ? 1865.

Shrapnel

Picket boat, James River. Destroyed to prevent capture at Richmond, 3 Apr 1865.

Towns—(Philadelphia), 1855

ex-*W. W. Townes*. 89 tons, side-wheel steamer. Sunk as blockship in Warwick River, Va., Sep 1861.

Young America—(Gloucester, NJ), 1857

For details see USS *Young America*. Captured off Fortress Monroe, Va., by USS *Cumberland*, 24 Apr 1861. Commissioned as USS *Young America*.

SAILING VESSELS

Alena

Sloop seized by USS *Mount Vernon* in Pamunkey River, Jun 1861.

Beauregard

Schooner. Transport. Burned by Union forces off Ragged Island, Va., 4 May 1862.

Duane—Tees, 1849

ex-USRC *William J. Duane*. 153 tons, 102' × 23' × 9'7". Schooner. U.S. Revenue Cutter seized at Norfolk, 18 Apr 1861.

Gallego—(Newburyport, Mass.), 1855

Schooner, 596 tons, 144′ × 30′ × d15′. Cargo and stores ship, James River. Ran aground at Drewry's Bluff, late 1864; raised 18 Jan 1865. FFU.

Germantown—Philadelphia NYd, 1843

For details see USS *Germantown*. USN sloop, sunk at Norfolk NYd and raised by Confederates, Jun 1861. Sunk as blockship in Elizabeth River, 1862.

Plymouth—Boston NYd, 1843

For details see USS *Plymouth*. USN sloop scuttled at Norfolk NYd, Apr 1861. Raised by Confederates. Hulk scuttled to avoid capture at Norfolk, 10 May 1862.

United States—(Philadelphia), 1798

ex-USS *United States*. For details see USS *United States*. USN frigate seized at Norfolk NYd 1861. Receiving ship Norfolk 1861–62. Sometimes called *Confederate States*. Sunk as a blockship in Elizabeth River, Apr 1862. Raised and BU.

INLAND RIVERS

GUNBOATS

Name	Bldr	Built
General Polk (ex-*Ed Howard*)	(New Albany, Ind.)	1852

Tonnage:	390 tons
Dimensions:	280′ × 35′ × 8′
Machinery:	Side wheels
Armament:	2 32-pdr R, 1 32-pdr SB

NOTES: Purchased and converted at New Orleans, 1861.
SERVICE RECORD: Operations off New Madrid, Mo., Dec 1861. Escaped up Yazoo River after fall of Island No. 10. Burned at Liverpool, below Yazoo City, 26 Jun 1862.

Name	Bldr	Built	Acquired
Grand Duke	(Jeffersonville, Ind.)	1859	Feb 1863

Tonnage:	508 tons
Dimensions:	205′ × 35′ × 7′6″
Machinery:	Side wheels (24″ × 7′), 4 boilers
Armament:	(U)

NOTES: Cottonclad gunboat. Built by Howard.
SERVICE RECORD: Attacked by Union vessels on Atchafalaya River, La., 14 Apr 1863. Damaged in action with USS *Albatross* at Ft. de Russy, La., 4 May 1863. Burned by accident at Shreveport, La., 25 Sep 1863.

Name	Bldr	Built	Comm
J.A. Cotton (II) (ex-*Mary T.*)	(Jeffersonville, Ind.)	1861	19 Mar 1863

Tonnage:	372 tons
Dimensions:	185′ × 34′6″ × 4′10″
Machinery:	Side wheels (22″ × 8′)
Armament:	2 24-pdr, 2 12-pdr, 1 H

NOTES: Cottonclad gunboat. Seized in Red River, early 1863. Also known as **Cotton Jr.**
SERVICE RECORD: Engaged USS *Albatross* at Ft. de Russy, La., 4 May 1863. Operated in Red River area 1863–65. Surrendered May 1865. BU at Pittsburgh, hulk crushed by ice Feb 1867.

Name	Bldr	Built	Acquired
Jackson (ex-*Yankee*)	(Cincinnati, OH)	1849	9 May 1861

Tonnage:	297 tons
Dimensions:	(U)
Machinery:	Side wheels
Complement:	75
Armament:	2 32-pdr

NOTES: Purchased at New Orleans, converted and sent up river.
SERVICE RECORD: Engaged Federal gunboats off Hickman, Ky., 4 Sep 1861. Hit by gunfire at Lucas Bend, Mo., 10 Sep 1861. Engagement near Head of Passes, Miss., 12 Oct 1861. Engagement below New Orleans, 24 Apr 1862. Destroyed to prevent capture above New Orleans, Apr 1862.

Name	Bldr	Built	Acquired	Comm
James Johnson	(Jeffersonville, Ind.)	1856	1861	(never)

Tonnage:	526 tons
Dimensions:	(U)
Machinery:	Side wheels
Armament:	(U)

SERVICE RECORD: Destroyed to prevent capture while undergoing conversion at Nashville, Tenn., 23 Feb 1862.

Name	Bldr	Built	Acquired	Comm
James Woods	(Jeffersonville, Ind.)	1860	1861	(never)

Tonnage:	585 tons
Dimensions:	257′ × 37′ × 7′
Machinery:	Side wheels
Armament:	(U)

NOTES: Built by Howard.
SERVICE RECORD: Destroyed to prevent capture while undergoing conversion at Nashville, Tenn., 23 Feb 1862.

Name	Bldr	Built	Comm
Livingston	Hughes, New Orleans	1861	1 Feb 1862

Tonnage: (U)
Dimensions: 180′ × 40′ × 9′
Machinery: Side wheels
Armament: 2 30-pdr R, 4 shell guns or 6 32-pdr R

NOTES: Ferry or towboat converted to a gunboat while under construction. Taken up river for fitting out at Columbus, Ky.
SERVICE RECORD: Defense of Island No. 10, Jan 1862. Burned to prevent capture in Yazoo River, 26 Jun 1862.

Name	Bldr	Built	Acquired
Maurepas (ex-*Grosse Tête*)	(New Albany, Ind.)	1858	1861

Tonnage: 399 tons
Dimensions: 180′ × 34′ × 7′
Machinery: Side wheels
Armament: 7 guns

SERVICE RECORD: Operations at Island No. 10 and New Madrid, Mo., 12 Mar–7 Apr 1862. Sunk to obstruct White River near St. Charles, Ark., 16 Jun 1862.

Name	Bldr	Built	Acquired	Comm
Pontchartrain (ex-*Lizzie Simmons*)	(New Albany, Ind.)	1859	12 Oct 1861	Mar 1862

Tonnage: 454 tons
Dimensions: 204′ × 36′6″ × 10′
Machinery: Side wheels
Armament: 2 32-pdr R & 5 others

NOTES: Purchased at New Orleans. Also known as *Eliza Simmons*.
SERVICE RECORD: Defense of Island No. 10, and New Madrid, Mo., Mar–Apr 1862. Engagement at St. Charles, Ark., 17 Jun 1862. Burned to prevent capture near Little Rock, Ark., 9 Oct 1863.

Name	Bldr	Built	Comm
Queen of the West	(Cincinnati)	1854	Feb 1863

For details see USS *Queen of the West*.

NOTES: Captured off Ft de Russy, La., 14 Feb 1863.
SERVICE RECORD: Engaged USS *Indianola* near New Carthage, Miss., 24 Feb 1863. Caught fire and blew up during engagement in Atchafalaya River, 14 Apr 1863.

Name	Bldr	Built
St. Mary (ex-*Alexandria*)	(Plaquemine, La.)	1862

For details see USS *Alexandria*.

NOTES: Cottonclad gunboat.
SERVICE RECORD: Operated in Yazoo and Tallahatchie rivers, 1863. Captured by joint Army-Navy expedition at Yazoo City, 13 Jul 1863. Commissioned as USS *Alexandria*.

Name	Bldr	Built
Tom Sugg	(Cincinnati)	1860

For details see USS *Tensas*.

NOTES: Cottonclad gunboat.
SERVICE RECORD: Operated in White River. Captured by USS *Cricket* in Little Red River, 14 Aug 1863. Commissioned as USS *Tensas*.

OTHER VESSELS

A. W. Baker—Bldr: (Louisville, Ky.), 1856

112 tons, 95′ × 25′ × d4′6″, side-wheel steamer. Cargo ship. Run ashore by USS *Queen of the West* and burned 15 miles below mouth of Red River, 2 Feb 1863.

Acacia

Steamer. (May be side-wheel steamer *Acacia Cottage*, 109 tons, built at California, Pa., 1857, snagged 25 miles above Helena, Ark., 21 Aug 1862.) Transport. Captured near Memphis, June 1862. Sunk Aug 1862.

Admiral

Side-wheel steamer. Picket boat. Captured at New Madrid, Mo., 7 Apr 1862.

Alamo

Transport. Arkansas River and Matagorda Bay, Texas.

Alfred Robb—Bldr: (Pittsburgh, Pa.), 1860

For details see USS *Alfred Robb*. Transport, Upper Tennessee River. Captured by USS *Tyler* in Tennessee River, 19 Apr 1862. Commissioned as tinclad USS *Alfred Robb*.

Appleton Belle—Bldr: (West Newton, Pa.), 1856

103 tons, stern-wheel steamer. Burned to prevent capture at Paris, Tenn., 7 Feb 1862.

Argo—Bldr: (Freedom, Pa.), 1856

99 tons, 136′ × 21′ × 4′, #stern-wheel steamer, 1 boiler. Burned on Sunflower River, Miss., by USS *Linden*, 25 May 1863.

Argosy

Cargo ship or transport. Burned to prevent capture in Sunflower River, Miss., May 1863.

Argus

Stern-wheel Army transport. Captured and burned in mouth of Red River, La., 7 Oct 1863.

B.M. Moore

For details see USS *General Pillow*. Captured in Hatchee River by *USS Pittsburg*, 9 Jun 1862. Commissioned as USS *General Pillow*.

Beauregard

Transport. Captured at Mound City, 6 Jun 1864.

Ben McCulloch—Bldr: (Cincinnati), 1860

80 tons, 100′ × 22′ × 3.9′, stern-wheel steamer (12″ × 3′6″), 2 boilers. Transport. Escaped up Tallahatchie River after fall of Yazoo City. Burned to avoid capture on Tchula Lake, Jul 1863; or captured as Confederate steamer. Burned at Monroe, La., 26 May 1868.

Berwick Bay—Bldr: (Plaquemine, La.), 1857

64 tons, side-wheel steamer. Transport. Captured and destroyed by Ellet's rams at mouth of Red River, 3 Feb 1863.

Bracelet—Bldr: (Louisville, Ky.), 1857

169 tons, side-wheel steamer. Transport on White and Arkansas rivers 1863. Burned at Little Rock, Ark., 10 Sep 1863.

Charm—Bldr: (Cincinnati), 1860

223 tons, side-wheel steamer. Transport, ammunition and gun carrier. Battle of Belmont, Mo., 7 Nov 1861. Burned in Big Black River, Miss., Jul 1863.

Cheney—Bldr: (Pomeroy, OH), 1859

ex-*B.P. Cheney*. 247 tons, side-wheel steamer. Cottonclad. Burned at Yazoo City, Miss., 14 Jul 1863.

Clara Dolsen—Bldr: (Cincinnati), 1861

For details see USS *Clara Dolsen*. Captured by Union ships in White River, 14 Jun 1862. Commissioned as USS *Clara Dolsen*.

Cotton Plant—Bldr: (Rochester, Pa.), 1859

59 tons, side-wheel steamer. Transport on Tallahatchie and Yazoo rivers. Burned to prevent capture in Tallahatchie River, 23 Jul 1863.

Countess—Bldr: (Cincinnati), 1860

198 tons, 150′ × 30′ × d4′8″, side-wheel steamer. Burned to prevent capture at Alexandria, La., 15 Mar 1864.

De Soto—Bldr: (New Albany, Ind.), 1860

For details see USS *General Lyon*. Surrendered at Island No. 10, 7 Apr 1862. Commissioned as USS *De Soto*; later renamed *General Lyon*.

Dew Drop—Bldr: (Cincinnati), 1858

184 tons, side-wheel steamer. Transport. Burned to prevent capture on Sunflower River, 25 May 1863.

Doubloon—Bldr: (Cincinnati), 1859

293 tons, 165′ × 33′ × 5′, side-wheel steamer. Transport. Scuttled in Red River, May 1864. Raised and repaired.

Later history: Burned at New Orleans, 24 Jun 1867.

Dr. Batey—Bldr: (Louisville, Ky.), 1850

281 tons, 171′ × 28′9″ × d6′, side-wheel steamer, 1 6-pdr gun. Also spelled *Dr. Beatty*. Engaged USS *Indianola* near New Carthage, Miss., 24 Feb 1863. Escaped capture at Harrisonburg, Jul 1863. FFU.

Dunbar—Bldr: (Brownsville, Pa.), 1859

213 tons, side-wheel steamer. Transport. Sunk to prevent capture in Tennessee River during defense of Ft. Henry, Tenn., 6 Feb 1862.
Later history: Raised and used by U.S. Army. Sold 1865, converted to barge.

Edward J. Gay—Bldr: (St. Louis, Mo.); L: 1859; Acquired: 1 Feb 1863

823 tons, 227′ × 39′ × 8.5′, side-wheel steamer. Scuttled and burned to avoid capture in Yalobusha River, 12 Jul 1863.

Elmira—Bldr: (Pittsburgh, Pa.), 1858; Acquired: 1861

139 tons, 125′ × 27′ × 4′6″, stern-wheel steamer. Transport. Captured in Tensas River by USS *Forest Rose* and *Cairo*, 13 Jul 1863. FFU.

Emma Bett—Bldr: (Pittsburgh, Pa.), 1858; Acquired: 1862

79 tons, stern-wheel steamer. Transport. Captured by U.S. and burned in Quirer Bayou, 30 May 1863.

Era No. 5—Bldr: (Pittsburgh, Pa.), 1860

115 tons, stern-wheel steamer. Transport. Captured by USS *Queen of the West* in Red River, 14 Feb 1863. Lost 1863 while serving Army as despatch boat. FFU.

Fairplay—Bldr: (New Albany, Ind.), 1859

For details see USS *Fairplay*. Transport. Captured near Vicksburg by Federal gunboats, 18 Aug 1862. Commissioned as USS *Fairplay*.

Ferd Kennett—Bldr: (St. Louis, Mo.), 1861

591 tons, 238′ × 40.5′ × 6.5′, side-wheel steamer. Transport. Burned and scuttled in Yalobusha River, 17 Jul 1863.

Frolic—Bldr: (Wheeling, Va.), 1860

296 or 393 tons, side-wheel steamer. Operated in Red River above Ft. de Russy, 1863–64. Captured 1864.
Later history: Merchant *Frolic*. RR 1873.

Gordon Grant

Tug. Served in Mississippi River near Columbus, Ky., 1861–62. Went aground and burned by accident above Memphis, 5 Jun 1862.

Grampus—Bldr: (McKeesport, Pa.), L: 1856; Acquired: 1862

ex-*Grampus No. 2*. 252 tons, stern-wheel steamer. Transport. Sunk to prevent capture at Island No. 10, 7 Apr 1862. Probably the same ship that burned and sank, 11 Jan 1863.

Grand Era—Bldr: (Louisville, Ky) 1853

ex-*R.W. McRea*. 323 tons, 171' × 33' × 6.1', side-wheel steamer. Cottonclad tender in Red River 1863. Engaged USS *Indianola* near New Carthage, Miss., 24 Feb 1863. Dismantled 1864; machinery used in ram *Missouri*.

Gray Cloud—Bldr: (Elizabeth, Pa.), 1854

For details see USS *Kinsman*. Former Army steamer sold into merchant service 1859. Operated near Ship Island and Biloxi, 1861–62. Captured before Jul 1862 as *Kinsman*.

H.D. Mears—Bldr: (Wheeling, Va.), 1860

338 tons, 214' × 34' × 5.5', #side-wheel steamer (22″ × 7'), 5 boilers. Scuttled to avoid capture in Sunflower River, 25 Jul 1863.

H.R.W. Hill—Bldr: (New Albany, Ind.), 1852

602 tons, side-wheel steamer (30″ × 10'). Transport. Battle of Belmont, Mo., 7 Nov 1861. Captured after Battle of Memphis, 6 Jun 1862. BU.

Hartford City—Bldr: (McKeesport, Pa.); L: 1856; Acquired: May 1862

150 tons, side-wheel steamer. Transport. Operated around Vicksburg, Miss., 1862–63. Burned to prevent capture in Tallahatchie River, 18 Jul 1863.

Hope—Bldr: (Louisville, Ky.), 1855

193 tons, 128' × 34' × 5', #stern-wheel steamer (14″ × 4'6″). Transport. Operated in Mississippi and Yazoo rivers 1862–63. Burned to prevent capture at Ft. Pemberton, Miss., 25 May 1863.

J.D. Clark

Side wheel. Transport. Captured and scuttled in mouth of Red River, 10 Apr 1863.

J.D. Swain—Bldr: (Jeffersonville, Ind.), 1859

228 tons, 150'6″ × 30' × d6', side-wheel steamer. Also spelled **J.D. Swaim**. Built by Howard. Transport. Sunk in mouth of McCall's River 1862. Raised Apr 1864 and put in Union service.
Later history: Merchant *J.D. Swain* 1865. Stranded in Escambia River, Fla., 1869.

Jeff Davis

Steam gunboat. Captured at Memphis, 6 Jun 1862. Presumed taken into Union service.

John Simonds—Bldr: (Freedom, Pa.), 1852

1,024 tons, 295' × 40.5' × 8', side-wheel steamer (38″ × 10'); 6 boilers. Army support ship. Sunk after capture of Island No. 10, 6 Apr 1862.

John Walsh—Bldr: (Cincinnati), 1858

809 tons, 275' × 38' × d8', side-wheel steamer (24″ × 7'). Transport. Operated in Mississippi and Yazoo rivers 1862–63. Burned to block Yazoo River below Greenwood, Miss., 22 May 1863.

Julius—Bldr: (Paducah, Ky.), 1859

ex-*Julius H. Smith*. 224 tons, stern-wheel steamer. Burned to prevent capture at Florence, Ala., 7 Feb 1862.

Kanawha Valley—Bldr: (Wheeling, Va.), 1860

ex-*Kanawha Valley No. 2* (identity conjectural). 147 tons, #stern-wheel steamer. Hospital boat. Burned at Island No. 10, 6 Apr 1862.

Kaskaskia—Bldr: (Cincinnati), 1859

49 tons, side-wheel steamer. Transport and towboat. Operated in White and Little Red rivers. Captured by USS *Cricket* in Little Red River, 14 Sep 1863.
Later history: U.S. transport 1863. Stranded at Grand Chain, Ill., 20 Feb 1864.

Kentucky

Side-wheel steamer. Transport. Operated at Columbus, Ky., Nov 1861 and Island No. 10, Mar 1862. Captured by Western Gunboat Flotilla at Memphis, 6 Jun 1862.
Later history: Advertised for sale Oct 1862, and probably returned to owners. May be same vessel that was destroyed, perhaps by a boiler explosion, near mouth of Red River, Jun 1865.

Lady Walton—Bldr: (Cincinnati), 1858

150 tons, stern-wheel steamer. Transport. Surrendered at mouth of White River, 6 Jun 1863.
Later history: Merchant 1864. Sunk in collision with steamer *Norman* at Warsaw, Ky., 2 Aug 1864.

Le Grand—Bldr: (New Albany, Ind.), 1856

235 tons, side-wheel steamer (22″ × 7'6″). Transport or storeship.

Linn Boyd—Bldr: (Paducah, Ky.), 1859

227 tons, #side-wheel steamer. Also known as **Lynn Boyd**. Transport. Burned to prevent capture in Tennessee River at mouth of Duck River, 7 Feb 1862.

Louis D'Or—Bldr: (Cincinnati), 1860

343 tons, 180.9' × 32.6' × d7.2', side-wheel steamer (22″ × 5'6″), 3 boilers. Cargo ship. Operated on Mississippi and Red rivers.
Later history: Merchant *Louis D'Or*, 1865. BU 1867.

Louisville—Bldr: (New Albany, Ind.), 1861; Acquired: Feb 1863

For details see USS *Ouachita*. Cargo ship. Captured on Little Red River by USS *Manitou* and *Rattler*, 13 Jul 1863. Commissioned as USS *Ouachita*.

Magenta—Bldr: (New Albany, Ind.), 1861

782 tons, 269' × 39' × 7'9″, side-wheel steamer (30″ × 10'), 8 boilers. Transport. Burned to prevent capture above Yazoo City, Miss., in Yazoo River, 14 Jul 1863.

Magnolia—Bldr: (New Albany, Ind.), 1859

824 tons, 258' × 44' × 7.5', side-wheel steamer (28″ × 7'6″), 5 boilers. Transport. Burned to prevent capture above Yazoo City, Miss., in Yazoo River, 14 Jul 1863.

Mars—Bldr: (Cincinnati), 1856

329 tons, 180' × 34', side-wheel steamer (20" × 7'), 3 boilers. Transport. Captured at Island No. 10, 7 Apr 1862.

Later history: Taken into Union service 1862. Merchant *Mars* 1863. Snagged and sunk at Cogswell Landing, Mo., 8 Jul 1865.

Mary E. Keene—Bldr: (New Albany, Ind.), 1860

659 tons, 238' × 38' × d7'8", side-wheel steamer (20" × 6'), 5 boilers. Transport. Scuttled or burned at Yazoo City, 24 Jul 1863.

Mary Patterson—Bldr: (Grand Glaize, Ark.), 1859

105 tons, #stern-wheel steamer. Transport. Sunk to obstruct White River near St. Charles, Ark., 16 Jun 1862.

May—Cottonclad transport, 1863

Merite

Steamer. Employed as gunboat above New Orleans, Apr 1865.

Mohawk—Bldr: (Elizabeth, Pa.), 1860

100 tons, stern-wheel steamer. Watch boat. Sunk at Island No. 10, 7 Apr 1862.

Moro—Bldr: (Louisville, Ky.), 1858

132 tons, 122' × 24'10" × d4'9", side-wheel steamer. Transport. Almost captured near Vicksburg, Nov 1862. Captured near mouth of Red River by USS *Queen of the West*, 4 Feb 1863, and burned.

Muscle—Bldr: (Allegheny, Pa.), 1856

125 tons, stern-wheel steamer. Also known as *Cerro Gordo*. Transport, Tennessee River. Captured north of Eastport, Miss., 8 Feb 1862. Foundered in Tennessee River while under tow.

Natchez—Bldr: (Cincinnati), 1860

800 tons, 273' × 38' × d8', side-wheel steamer, 6 boilers. Cottonclad. Burned in Yazoo River near Burtonia, Miss., 13 Mar 1863.

Nelson

Mentioned in 1863 in Red River.

New National—Transport

Captured at Memphis, 6 Jun 1862.

Nina Simmes—Bldr: (New Albany, Ind.), 1860

327 tons, 177' × 33' × 6', side-wheel steamer. Transport. Operated near Port Hudson, La., 1861.
Later history: Merchant *Nina Simmes*, 1865. Snagged and lost 60 miles below Bayou Sara, La., 17 Jun 1869.

Ohio Belle—Bldr: (Cincinnati), 1855

406 tons, 185.8' × 39.6' × 7.8', side-wheel steamer. Watch boat. Captured at Island No. 10, 7 Apr 1862.
Later History: Army transport, 1864. Merchant *Alabama Belle*, 1866. BU 1867.

Osceola—Bldr: (Louisville, Ky.), 1858; Acquired: 1861

157 tons, side-wheel steamer. Transport. Operating around Shreveport, La., 1864. FFU.

Pargoud—Bldr: (Jeffersonville, Ind.), 1860

ex-*J. Frank Pargoud*. 522 tons, 219' × 36' × d7', side-wheel steamer (24" × 8'), 5 boilers. Built by Howard. Cargo ship or transport. Burned to prevent capture in Yazoo River, 14 Jul 1863.

Paul Jones—Bldr: (McKeesport, Pa.), 1855

353 tons, 172' × 34' × 6'6", side-wheel steamer (21" × 7'). Transport. Burned with *Charm* in Big Black River, Miss., Jul 1863.

Peytona—Bldr: (New Albany, Ind.), 1859; Acquired: 17 Apr 1862

685 tons, 256' × 37' × 7'6", side-wheel steamer (27½" × 9'), 5 boilers. Tender to CSS *Mississippi* at New Orleans, 1862. Burned and scuttled to avoid capture at Satartia, Miss., in Yazoo River, 14 Jul 1863.

Prince—Bldr: (Cincinnati), 1859

223 tons, side-wheel steamer. Transport. Battle of Belmont, Mo., 7 Nov 1861. Sunk to prevent capture at Island No. 10, 27 Feb 1862. (Also reported snagged and sunk at Hickman, Ky.)

Prince of Wales—Bldr: (Cincinnati), 1860

572 tons, 248' × 40' × 7', side-wheel steamer. Transport. Burned to prevent capture at Yazoo City, 14 Jul 1863.

R.J. Lockland—Bldr: (Cincinnati), 1857

710 tons, 265' × 40' × d7', side-wheel steamer (28" × 8'). Also called *R.J. Lackland*. Transport. Burned to prevent capture in Yazoo River below Ft. Pemberton, Miss., 22 May 1863. (Or sunk below Greenwood, Miss., 14 Jul 1863.)

Red Rover—Bldr: (Cape Girardeau, Mo.), 1859; Acquired: 7 Nov 1861

For details see USS *Red Rover*. Accommodation ship New Orleans, 1861. Defense of Columbus, Ky., 1861. Damaged by gunfire at Island No. 10, 15 Mar 1862. Captured by USS *Mound City* at Island No. 10, 7 Apr 1862. Commissioned as USS *Red Rover*.

Republic—Bldr: (Jeffersonville, Ind.), 1855

689 tons, 249' × 40' × 7.3', side-wheel steamer (24" × 9'). Transport. Burned to prevent capture at Yazoo City while undergoing conversion to a ram, 21 May 1863.

Robert Fulton—Bldr: (California, Pa.), 1860

158 tons, 137' × 29' × 4.3', side-wheel steamer. Transport. Captured by USS *Osage* and burned in Red River, 7 Oct 1863.

St. Francis No. 3—Bldr: (Jeffersonville, Ind.), 1858

219 tons, 160' × 29' × 6', side-wheel steamer. Built by Howard. Transport. Burned at Little Rock, Ark., 10 Sep 1863.

Sallie Wood—Bldr: (Paducah, Ky.), 1860

For details see USS *Sallie Wood*. Transport, Tennessee River. Captured by USS *Conestoga* while laid up at Florence, Ala., 8 Feb 1862.

Sam Kirkman—Bldr: (Paducah, Ky.), 1857

271 tons, 157′ × 36.5′, stern-wheel steamer. Cargo ship. Burned to prevent capture at Florence, Ala., 8 Feb 1862.

Samuel Hill

Transport. Mississippi and Yazoo rivers.

Samuel Orr—Bldr: (New Albany), 1861

ex-*Sam Orr*. 179 tons, 150′ × 29′ × 5′, stern-wheel steamer. Hospital boat, Tennessee River. Burned to prevent capture and blown up at mouth of Duck River, 7 Feb 1862.
Later history: Rebuilt 1865. Towboat *Robert J. Young* 1875.

Scotland—Bldr: (Jeffersonville, Ind.), 1855

567 tons, 230′ × 27′ × d7′, side-wheel steamer (22″ × 8′), 4 boilers. Transport. Burned to prevent capture at Ft. Pemberton, Miss., and to block channel in Yazoo River, Jul 1863.

Sharp—Bldr: (Jeffersonville), 1859

ex-*J.M. Sharp*. 218 tons, 147′ × 29′ × 6.5′, side-wheel steamer. Transport and despatch boat in Tallahatchie River. Burned to prevent capture in Sunflower River, Aug 1863, or in Yalobusha River, Feb 1864.
Later history: Rebuilt 1865 as *J.M. Sharp*. RR 1871.

Slidell—Bldr: (New Orleans), 1862

Gunboat, 8 guns. Destroyed in Tennessee River before 6 Feb 1862.

Sovereign—Bldr: (Shousetown, Pa.), 1855

For details see USS *Sovereign*. Transport. Ran aground and was captured near Island No. 37, 5 Jun 1862. Commissioned as USS *Sovereign*.

Starlight—Bldr: (Jeffersonville), 1858

280 tons, 162′ × 31′ × 6′, side-wheel steamer (20″ × 7′). Transport. Captured in Thompson's Creek north of Port Hudson, 26 May 1863.
Later history: Burned at Algiers, La., 23 Apr 1868.

T.D. Hine—Bldr: (Jeffersonville, Ind.), 1860

ex-*T.D. Hine No. 2*. 205 tons, 147′ × 30′ × 6′, side-wheel steamer. Transport, Mississippi and Red rivers. Captured 1865.
Later history: Merchant *T.D. Hine* 1865. RR 1871.

35th Parallel—Bldr: (Cincinnati), 1859

419 tons, side-wheel steamer. Cottonclad. Burned to prevent capture after running aground in Tallahatchie River, 13 Mar 1863.

Trent

Transport. Mississippi and Red rivers 1862–63.

Twilight—Bldr: (Jeffersonville, Ind.), 1857

392 tons, 215′ × 33′ × 6′, side-wheel steamer. Transport. Ouachita River, 1864–65.
Later history: Merchant *Twilight* 1865. FFU.

Vicksburg—Bldr: (New Albany, Ind.), 1857

625 tons, 244.5′ × 36′ × 7.5′, side-wheel steamer (24″ × 7′), 5 boilers. Also known as *City of Vicksburg*. Rammed and damaged by USS *Queen of the West* at Vicksburg, 2 Feb 1863. Machinery removed, later went adrift and burned, 29 Mar 1863.

Victoria—Bldr: (Elizabeth, Pa.), 1858

For details see USS *Abraham*. Transport. Captured after battle of Memphis, 6 Jun 1862. Commissioned as USS *Abraham*.

Volunteer—Bldr: (Monongahela, Pa.), 1862

For details see USS *Volunteer*. Transport. Captured off Natchez Island, Miss., 25 Nov 1863. Commissioned as USS *Volunteer*.

W.W. Crawford—Bldr: (Cincinnati), 1861

123 tons, side-wheel steamer. Transport. Captured Aug 1863.
Later history: Merchant 1865. RR 1868.

Wade Water Belle

Captured by USS *Conestoga*, prior to Sep 1862.

White Cloud

Transport. Captured near Island No. 10 by USS *New Era*, 13 Feb 1863.

Yazoo—Bldr: (Jeffersonville, Ind.), 1860

371 tons, side-wheel steamer. Transport. Captured and sunk at Island No. 10, 7 Apr 1862.

LIST OF SHIPBUILDERS

Abrahams	John J. Abrahams, Baltimore, MD
Adams	Aquila Adams, Boston, MA
Aitken Mansel	Aitken & Mansel, Greenock, Scotland
Allaire	Allaire Iron Works, New York, NY
Arman	L'Arman Frères, Bordeaux, France
Ash	James Ash, Millwall, London, England
Atlantic	Atlantic Iron Works, Boston, MA
Barclay Curle	Barclay Curle & Co., Whiteinch, Glasgow, Scotland
Bassett Selma	Henry D. Bassett, Selma, AL
Bassett	Bassett & Gates, Mobile, AL
Bell	David Bell, Buffalo, NY
Berry	Berry & Bros., Wilmington, NC
Birely	Jacob Birely, Kensington, Philadelphia, PA
Birely Lynn	Jacob Birely & John W. Lynn, Philadelphia, PA
Boston	Boston Navy Yard, Charlestown, Boston, MA
Boston Loco	Boston Locomotive Works, Boston, MA
Brooklyn	Brooklyn Navy Yard, Brooklyn, NY
Brown	Joseph Brown, Cincinnati, OH
Brown & Bell	Brown & Bell, New York, NY
Burtis	Devine Burtis, Brooklyn, NY
Caird	Caird & Co. Ltd., Greenock, Scotland
Cameron	Cameron & Co., Charleston, SC
Capes	Capes & Allison, Hoboken, NJ
Carondelet	Union Iron Works, Carondelet, MO
Carter	C.P. Carter, Belfast, ME
Cassidy	J.L. Cassidy, Wilmington, NC
City Point	City Point Works, Boston, MA
Cobb	Cobb & Fields, Jersey City, NJ
Collier	Hambleton, Collier, Peoria, IL
Collyer	Thomas Collyer, New York, NY
W. Collyer	William Collyer, Greenpoint, NY
Columbus	Columbus Navy Yard (CSN), Columbus, GA
Colwell	Joseph Colwell, Jersey City, NJ
Coney	James Coney, Boston, MA
Continental	Continental Iron Works, Greenpoint, NY
Corliss	Corliss Steam Engine Co., Providence, RI
Cramp	C.H. & W.H. Cramp, Philadelphia, PA
Curtis	Paul Curtis, Boston, MA
Curtis & Tilden	Curtis & Tilden, Boston, MA
Curtis, Medford	James O. Curtis, Medford, MA
Delamater	C. H. Delamater Iron Works, New York, NY
Denmead	A. & W. Denmead & Son, Baltimore, MD
A. Denny	Archibald Denny, Dumbarton, England
Denny	Wm. Denny & Bros. Ltd., Dumbarton, England
Dialogue	J.H. Dialogue & Son, Camden, NJ
Dolan	Dolan & Farron, Williamsburg, NY
Donahue	Donahue, Ryan & Secor, San Francisco, CA
Dubigeon	Chantiers Dubigeon, Nantes, France
Dudgeon	J. & W. Dudgeon, Millwall, London, England
Dunham	R.H. Dunham & Co., New York NY
Dyer	Joseph W. Dyer, Portland, ME
Eads, Mound City	James B. Eads, Mounds City, IL
Eads, St. Louis	James B. Eads, St. Louis, MO
Eason	James M. Eason, Charleston, SC
Elder	Randolph Elder & Co., Glasgow, Scotland
Elliot	Gilbert Elliot, Edwards Ferry, NC
Ellis	William M. Ellis, Washington, DC
Englis	John Englis, New York, NY
Esler	Henry Esler & Co., New York, NY
Etna	Etna Iron Works, New York, NY
Fardy	J.J. Fardy & Bros., Baltimore, MD
Fletcher	Fletcher Harrison & Co., New York, NY
Fulton	Fulton Iron Works, New York, NY
Fulton IW	Fulton Iron Works, St. Louis, MO
Gardner	C.F. & H.D. Gardner, East Boston, MA
Gatz	Gatz McClune & Co., St. Louis, MO

Gildersleeve	Gildersleeve & Sons (Portland), East Haddam, CT
Globe	Globe Iron Works, Boston, MA
Goodspeed	E.G. & W.H. Goodspeed, East Haddam, CT
Gray	J. & R.I. Gray, New York, NY
Greenman	George Greenman & Co., Mystic, CT
Greenwood	Miles Greenwood, Cincinnati, OH
Hall	Lawrence Hall, Renfrew, Scotland
Hall, Boston	Samuel Hall, Boston, MA
Harlan	Harlan & Hollingsworth Co., Wilmington, DE
Harvey	Harvey & Son, Hayle, England
Hazelhurst	Hazelhurst & Wiegard, Baltimore, MD
Hews	Hews & Philips, Belfast, Ireland
Hickson	Robert Hickson & Co., Belfast, Ireland
Highland	Highland Iron Works, Newburgh, NY
Hillman	Hillman & Streaker, Philadelphia, PA
Hughes	John Hughes & Co., Bayou St. John, LA
Inglis	A. & J. Inglis Ltd., Glasgow, Scotland
Jackman	George W. Jackman, Jr., Newburyport, MA
Jackson	Jackson & Watkins, London, England
Jewett	James C. Jewett & Co., Brooklyn, NY
Jollet	Jollet & Babin, Nantes, France
Jones Quiggin	Jones Quiggin & Co., Liverpool, England
Junger	McCord & Junger, New Albany, IN
Kirkpatrick	Kirkpatrick & McIntyre, Glasgow, Scotland
Laing	Sir James Laing & Sons Ltd., Sunderland, England
Laird	Laird Brothers, Birkenhead, England
Larrabee	Larrabee & Allen, Bath, ME
Lawrence	George W. Lawrence, Thomaston, ME
L & F	Lawrence & Foulkes, Brooklyn, NY
Lawrie	Lawrie & Co., Whiteinch, Glasgow, Scotland
Loring	Harrison Loring, Boston, MA
Lupton	Edward Lupton, Brooklyn, NY
Lynn	John W. Lynn, Philadelphia, PA
Mallory	Charles H. Mallory, Mystic, CT
Mare	Mare & Co., Blackwall, London, England
Mare Island	Mare Island Navy Yard, Vallejo, CA
Marvel	T.S. Marvel, Newburgh, NY
Maxson Fish	Maxson, Fish & Co., Mystic River, CT
Mazeline	Mazeline Engine Works, Le Havre, France
McCord	Charles W. McCord, St. Louis, MO
McKay	Donald McKay, Boston, MA
McKnight	John L. McKnight, Bordentown, NJ
McLeod	Daniel McLeod, Brooklyn, NJ
Means	Gilbert Means, Peedee Navy Yard (CSN), Mars Bluff, SC
Mehaffy	A. Mehaffy & Co., Portsmouth, VA
Merrick & Towne	Merrick & Towne, Philadelphia, PA
Merrick	Merrick & Sons, Philadelphia, PA
Mershon	D.S. Mershon, Jr., Bordentown, NJ
Miller	William C. Miller, Liverpool, England
Moore	Moore & Richardson, Cincinnati, OH
Morgan	Morgan Iron Works, New York, NY
Morris	J.P. Morris & Co., Philadelphia, PA
Morris Towne	Morris Towne & Co., Philadelphia, PA
Murphy	James Murphy, New York, NY
Murray	Murray & Hazelhurst, Baltimore, MD
Mystic	Mystic Iron Works, Mystic, CT
Napier	R. Napier & Sons Ltd., Dalmuir, Glasgow, Scotland
Neafie	Neafie & Levy, Philadelphia, PA
Neilson	Neilson & Co., Glasgow, Scotland
Neptune	Neptune Works, New York, NY
Niles	Niles Tool Works, Niles, OH
Norfolk	Norfolk Navy Yard, Norfolk, VA
Novelty	Novelty Iron Works, New York, NY
Oregon	Oregon Iron Works, Portland, OR
Oswald	T.R. Oswald & Co., Sunderland, England
Pacific	Pacific Iron Works, Bridgeport, CT
Page & Bacon	Page & Bacon, New Albany, IN
Pearse	Pearse & Lockwood, Stockton-on-Tees, England
Peas	Peas & Murphy
Peck	Peck & Kirby, Cleveland, OH
Pensacola	Pensacola Navy Yard, Pensacola, FL
Perine	Perine's Iron Works, Williamsburg, NY
Philadelphia	Philadelphia Navy Yard, Philadelphia, PA
Pile	W. Pile & Co., Sunderland, England
Poillon	C. & R. Poillon, New York, NY
Pook	S.H. Pook, Fairhaven, CT
Pook Mystic	S.H. Pook Iron Works, Mystic, CT
Poole	Poole & Hunt, Baltimore, MD
Portland	Portland Locomotive Works, Portland, ME
Portsmouth	Portsmouth Navy Yard, Kittery, ME
Providence	Providence Steam Engine Works, Providence, RI
Pusey	Pusey & Jones, Wilmington, DE
Quintard	Quintard Iron Works, New York, NY
Reaney Neafie	Reaney & Neafie, Chester, PA
Reaney	Reaney, Son & Archbold, Chester, PA
Reeder	Charles Reeder, Baltimore, MD
Reliance	Reliance Machine Co., Mystic, CT
Richmond	Richmond Navy Yard (CSN), Richmond, VA
Risdon	Risdon Iron Works, San Francisco, CA
Roach	John Roach & Son, Chester, PA
Robb	John A. Robb, Baltimore, MD
Robinson	J.A. & E.T. Robinson, Baltimore, MD
Roosevelt	Roosevelt, Joyce & Co., New York, NY
S. Brooklyn	South Brooklyn Engine Works, Brooklyn, NY
S. Smith	Sylvanus Smith, Boston, MA
Saffold	Saffold Navy Yard (CSN), Saffold, GA
Sampson	A. & G.T. Sampson, Boston, MA
Samuelson	Martin Samuelson & Co., Hull, England
Secor	Zeno Secor & Co., Jersey City, NJ
Shirley	J.T. Shirley, Memphis, TN
Simons	William Simons & Co. Ltd., Renfrew, Scotland
Simonson	Jeremiah Simonson, New York, NY

Sneeden	Samuel Sneeden, New York, NY
Sneeden Whitlock	Sneeden Whitlock & Co., Greenpoint, NY
Snowden & Mason	Snowden & Mason, Pittsburgh, PA
Stack	Thomas Stack, New York, NY
Stack & Joyce	Stack & Joyce, Brooklyn, NY
Stackhouse	Stackhouse & Tomlinson, Pittsburgh, PA
Steers	Henry Steers, Greenpoint, NY
Stephen	A. Stephen & Sons Ltd., Govan, Glasgow, Scotland
Stevens	Robert L. Stevens, Hoboken, NJ
Stillman	Stillman, Allen & Co., New York, NY
Stover	Stover Machine Co., New York, NY
Sutton	James T. Sutton & Co., Philadelphia, PA
Swift	Alexander Swift & Co., Cincinnati, OH
Taunton	Taunton Locomotive Works, Taunton, MA
Teas	Teas & Birely, Philadelphia, PA
Terry	B.C. Terry, Keyport, NJ
Tetlow	James Tetlow, Boston, MA
Thatcher	W. & A. Thatcher, Wilmington, DE
Thompson	Nathaniel W. Thompson, Kennebunk, ME
Thomson	J. & G. Thomson Ltd., Clydebank, Glasgow, Scotland
Tift	N. & A. Tift, Jefferson City, LA
Tod	Tod & McGregor, Glasgow, Scotland
Tomlinson	Tomlinson, Hartapee & Co., Pittsburgh, PA
Tredegar	Tredegar Iron Works, Richmond, VA
Tucker	F.Z. Tucker, Brooklyn, NY
Tufts	Otis Tufts, Boston, MA
Underhill	J.S. Underhill Dry Dock & Iron Works, New York, NY
Union DD	Union Dry Dock, Co., Buffalo, NY
Union IW	Union Iron Works, San Francisco, CA
Van Deusen	J.B. & J.D. Van Deusen, New York, NY
Vaughn & Lynn	Vaughn & Lynn, Philadelphia, PA
Vulcan	Vulcan Iron Works, New York, NY
Wash IW	Washington Iron Works, Newburgh, NY
Washington	Washington Navy Yard, Washington, DC
Watts	Watts & Co.
Webb	William H. Webb, New York, NY
Webb & Bell	Webb & Bell, New York, NY
Webb, E.	Eckford Webb, Greenpoint, NY
Weidner	Charles A. Weidner, Philadelphia, PA
West Point	West Point Foundry, Newburgh, NY
Westervelt	Jacob A. Westervelt, New York, NY
Whitlock	E.S. Whitlock, Greenpoint, NY
Wilcox	Wilcox & Whiting, Camden NJ
Williams	E.F. Williams, Greenpoint, NY
Willink	Henry F. Willink, Savannah, GA
Winson	Winson & Co., Philadelphia, PA
Woodruff	Woodruff & Beach, Hartford, CT
Wright	Wright & Whitaker, Buffalo, NY
Wm. Wright	William Wright & Co., Newburgh, NY

PARTIAL BIBLIOGRAPHY

BOOKS

Bauer, K. Jack. *Ships of the Navy 1775–1969*. Vol. 1, *Combat Vessels*. Troy, NY: Rensselaer Polytechnic Institute, 1969.

Bennett, Frank M. *The Steam Navy of the United States*. Pittsburgh, PA: Warren & Co., 1897.

Bourne, John. *A Treatise on the Screw Propeller*, 1867.

Chapelle, Howard I. *The History of the American Sailing Navy*. New York: Bonanza Books, 1949.

Cooney, David M. *A Chronology of the Navy 1775–1965*. New York: Franklin Watts, Inc., 1965.

Heyl, Erik. *Early American Steamers (1953)*. U.S. Coast Guard, n.d.

Kern, Florence. *The United States Revenue Cutters in the Civil War (1988)*.

Milligan, John D. *Gunboats Down the Mississippi*. Annapolis, MD: U.S. Naval Institute, 1965.

Mitchell, C. Bradford, ed. *Merchant Steam Vessels of the United States, 1790–1868* (The Lytle-Holdcamper List). Staten Island, NY: The Steamship Historical Society of America, Inc., 1975.

Neeser, Robert W. *Statistical & Chronological History of the United States Navy 1775–1907*. New York: Macmillan Co., 1909.

Ridgely-Nevitt, Cedric. *American Steamships on the Atlantic*. Newark, DE: University of Delaware, 1981.

Rush, Richard, ed. *Official Records of the Union and Confederate Navies in the War of the Rebellion*. 30 vols. Washington, D.C.: GPO, 1895–1921.

Scharf, J. Thomas. *History of the Confederate States Navy (1887)*. Columbia, MD: Fairfax Press, reprint 1977.

U.S. Coast Guard. *Record of Movements, Vessels of the U.S. Coast Guard*, 1935.

U.S. Navy. *Civil War Naval Chronology 1861–1865*. Vols. 1-6. Washington, D.C.: Navy Department, 1963.

———. *Dictionary of American Naval Fighting Ships*. Vols. 1-8. Washington, D.C.: Naval Historical Center, Dept. of the Navy, 1959–81.

Ward, J.H. *Steam for the Million*. 1876.

Way, Frederick, Jr. *Way's Packet Directory 1848–1983*. Athens, OH: Ohio University Press, 1983.

Serial Publications

American Neptune

Annual Reports of the Navy Department

Journal of the Franklin Institute (1845–1865)

Merchant Vessels of the United States (various from 1870)

New York Times (1861–1869)

Original American Lloyd's Register, 1860, 1868.

Record, American Bureau of Shipping (various from 1870)

Warship International

UNION SHIPS INDEX

CONFEDERATE SHIPS INDEX

COMPOUND NAME INDEX